THE
ILLUSTRATED ALMANAC
OF
HISTORICAL
FACTS

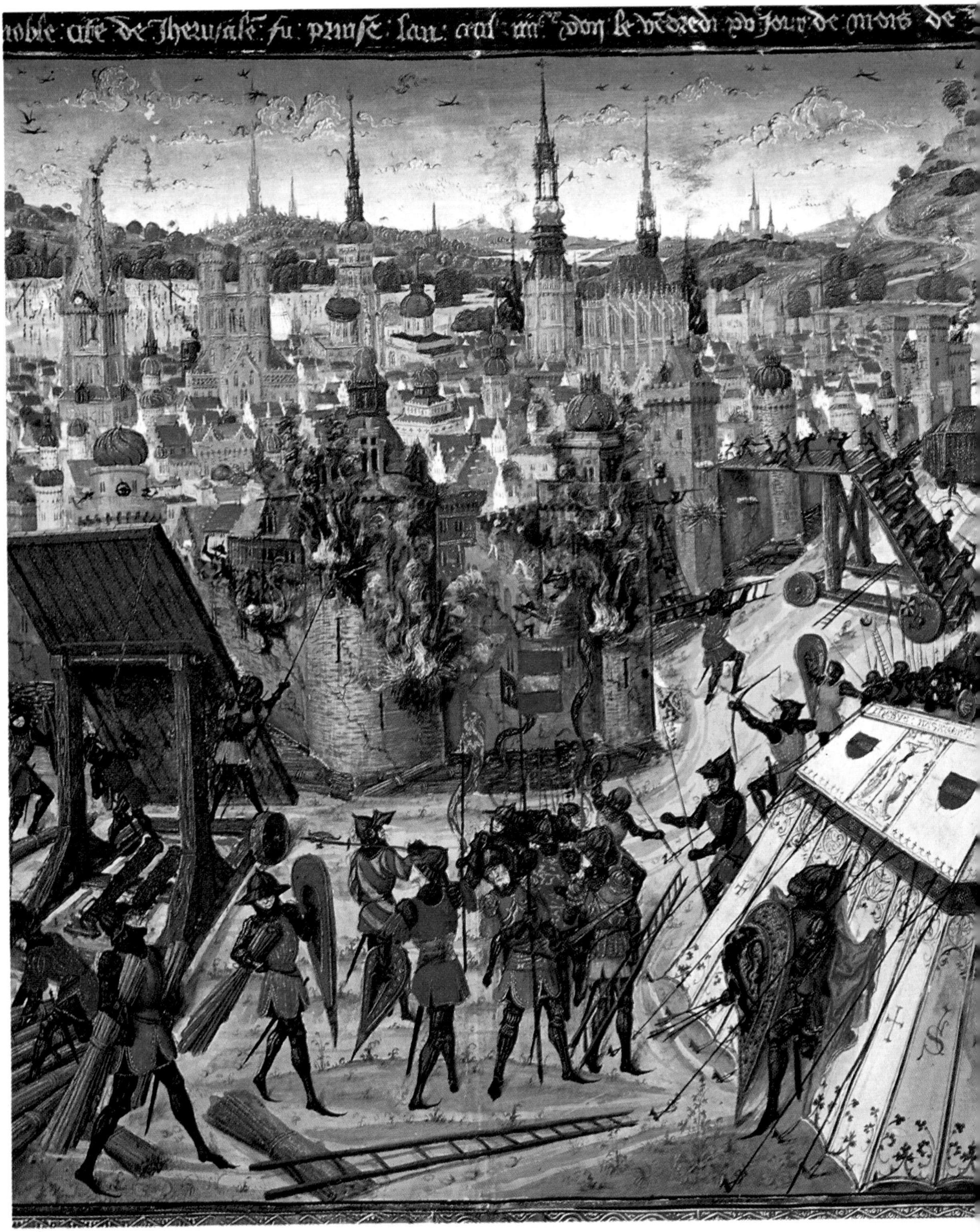

THE
ILLUSTRATED ALMANAC
OF
HISTORICAL FACTS

**From the Dawn of the Christian
Era to the New World Order**

Robert Stewart, Ph.D.

PRENTICE HALL

New York London Toronto Sydney Tokyo Singapore

A Marshall Edition
Conceived, edited and designed by
Marshall Editions
170 Piccadilly, London W1V 9DD

First published in the United States in 1992 by

Prentice Hall General Reference
15 Columbus Circle
New York, New York 10023

Library of Congress Catalog Card Number: 91–66999

ISBN 0–13–276395–8

Editor	Gwen Rigby
Art editor	Ruth Prentice
Assistant editor	Fran Jones
Assistant designer	Alison Shackleton
Editorial assistant	Gina Machin
Copy editor	Lindsay McTeague
Indexer	Hilary Bird
Editorial director	Ruth Binney
Production	Barry Baker
	Janice Storr
	Nikki Ingram

DTP by Ruth Prentice/Alison Shackleton
Originated by CLG, Verona, Italy
Printed and bound in Spain by PIG, Barcelona

10 9 8 7 6 5 4 3 2 1

First Prentice Hall Edition

CONTENTS

INTRODUCTION

"Where Amanda discovered in the world divine intent, benevolent order and rigorous justice, her father had seen only chaos, hazard and malice. Yet they were both examining the same world." The sentences occur in Julian Barnes's novel, *A History of the World in 10½ Chapters*. Why did they see things so differently? The answer is simple. They stood in different places. "Facts," the historian, E. H. Carr, once wrote, "are like sacks. They don't stand up unless you put something in them."

Each of us puts his own experience into them. To the Maya or sub-Saharan African the rise and fall of the Roman empire was neither here nor there. Nor was the rude kingdom of Mercia in the 8th century to the rich and sophisticated merchants of the great Chinese city of Ch'ang-an. We divide history into periods to make some sense of it, and the dividing lines fall where they do according to the angle at which our squint catches the world. We need not apologize for this, as long as we remember that our dividing lines are what they are and nothing more: guides to understanding the history of the world from a European, more specifically, perhaps, from a Mediterranean, vantage-point.

The first entry in this book is the battle of Teutoburger Wald, a portentous occasion on which, for the first time, Roman legions were defeated by a "Barbarian" army. It took place nine years after the birth of Christ. Great charm resides in this coincidence. The end of the ancient world, the first of the five great periods into which modern history, seen from Europe, may be divided, is deeply marked by the twin effects upon Rome of the growth of Christianity from a small breakaway sect of Judaism into a major religion on its own and the explosion into "history" of the "Barbarians."

That first period is followed by the Early Middle Ages: in Europe, the "Dark Ages," but in the eastern Mediterranean, and then spreading westward, the age of Islam and the remarkable expansion of the Arab empire. The High Middle Ages, signaled by the urban revival and intellectual awakening of the 12th century, went on until two nearly coincident events of the mid-15th century—the invention in Europe of movable print and the fall of Constantinople to the Ottoman Turks—ushered in the formative centuries of the Renaissance and the Reformation: the age commonly called Early Modern. Finally comes the Modern Age: the apogee of European civilization, beginning with the Industrial Revolution and the American and French revolutions of the 18th century and continuing until the present day.

Nothing conveys more strongly a sense of history—the continuous study of past events and human affairs—than the great stone dolmens, or burial chambers, erected thousands of years ago by Neolithic peoples. This one, Lanyon Quoit, is in Cornwall, England, but others are found throughout Europe, in north Africa, and as far east as Japan.

THE WANING OF THE ANCIENT WORLD A.D. 1–649

When Trajan conquered Dacia (modern Romania) at the beginning of the 2nd century, the Roman empire was at its greatest territorial extent. It stretched from the Black Sea, along the Danube and Rhine rivers, all the way to Hadrian's Wall in north Britain, and south of the Atlas Mountains. During the last centuries of the Roman empire there was nothing to compare with it: not Confucian China, though it was briefly united under the Han dynasty, nor Hindu India, which experienced its own "Classical Age" under the Guptas; nor central America, where the Maya were building a great culture; nor sub-Saharan Africa. Only Persia, where the Sassanid dynasty that came to power in the early 3rd century recaptured some of the glory that Persia had known in the 5th century B.C. under the Achaemenids, could approach rivalry with Rome.

The Romans were confident that they represented the world's highest "civilization"; beyond the empire's borders everyone was a "Barbarian." Theirs was an urban culture, characterized by great cities such as Antioch and Carthage and Alexandria, and sustained by the agrarian economy of outlying provinces, especially Africa and Anatolia. Slavery lay at its heart, but the empire was non-racial and willing, in 212, to extend Roman citizenship to all free subjects of the empire.

The Romans were not, in fields other than law, architecture and engineering, great creators. They were efficient and thorough governors. The phrase *pax Romana* may cloak the revolts that punctuated the empire's history—especially slave and Jewish revolts—but the idea of *Romanitas* had substance. For Rome's achievement was to build a cosmopolitan culture that absorbed the lands it conquered and brought them within its sophisticated administrative and legal structure.

Yet by the end of the 3rd century the Romans themselves were conscious of incipient decline. The cause, even the nature, of that decline is an abiding question. In the mix were many elements. There was the influence of Christianity, especially in those places, like Africa, where a distinct form of it arose, different from the orthodox faith. Economic pressures associated with a falling population, and the increasing taxation required to sustain a growing army, played a part, as did the sheer burden imposed by the attempt to maintain a unified empire across such a vast extent. The pressures of near-constant warfare with Sassanid Persia and continual defensive action against the "Barbarians" to the north and west added to the empire's difficulties.

Whether the Barbarian "conquest" of the empire in the West was, rather, a gradual process of assimilation and transformation is debatable. The Barbarians who came to rule in Gaul and Spain and Italy itself considered themselves as "Romans," inheritors of the empire, not its destroyers. By the time the last Roman emperor in the West was deposed by the Ostrogoths in 476, the center of the empire had long since shifted to Constantinople. And it was there that the Roman empire—Byzantium—faced the challenge that ended 1,000 years of Greek and Roman hegemony: the rise to dominance in the 7th century of the Arab people, infused with the ardor of a new religion.

The putti treading grapes, top, are part of a mosaic, depicting the vintage, on the vault of the 4th-century church of Santa Constanza in Rome. The combination of Christian and pagan subjects there demonstrates the steady integration of the two strands of Roman life, following Constantine's conversion in 312.

Emperor Justinian, who ruled the empire in the East (527-65), was an Illyrian peasant from present-day Yugoslavia. He was immortalized in this mosaic portrait in the church of San Vitale, Ravenna.

Opposite: The most potent symbols of Roman might are the great buildings, the aqueducts and, above all, the roads, fanning out from the Forum in Rome to all parts of the empire.

THE EARLY MIDDLE AGES 650–1099

Some years ago the French historian, Henri Pirenne, made a famous statement: "Without Mohammed, Charlemagne would have been impossible." The Arab expansion of the 7th and 8th centuries was not the sole determinant of the course of early medieval European history; yet it had an immensely powerful effect.

In 632, when Mohammed made his flight to Medina, the Arabs were unimportant nomads inhabiting the central and northern parts of the Arabian peninsula. By the time that Charlemagne was crowned emperor in the West in 800, the Islamic empire stretched in a vast shallow arc around the whole of the southern Mediterranean from Spain to the Oxus River beyond the Caspian. The Persian empire had vanished, and the Roman empire, or Byzantium, was reduced to a small remnant of its former self. Until the Crusades (beginning at the end of the 11th century), and the Mongol invasions (of the 13th), the Islamic empire was virtually unchallenged.

Europe, largely cut off from the rich trade of the East, fell back on itself and entered the "Dark Ages." The foremost features of the period were the decline of town life and reliance upon a rural, almost subsistence, economy and, despite the rise of the Franks and the short-lived empire of Charlemagne, the political fragmentation of the continent into small rival kingdoms and principalities, too weak, for instance, to offer effective resistance to the Viking founders of a nascent empire in Russia. The introduction of armored horsemen, after the defeat of the Muslims at Poitiers in 732, gave rise, gradually, to the most characteristic institution of medieval western Europe, especially in France and England: the complex, hierarchical system of military organization and land tenure known as feudalism.

Beyond the world of Europe and the Middle East lay Asia, still almost completely unknown in the West. There China was dominant, united under the T'ang and Sung dynasties into a vast empire of perhaps 60 million people and enriched by trade with Japan, Korea and the eastern extremities of the Islamic empire. At the end of the Silk Road, which linked China to Persia, stood Ch'ang-an, the most luxurious and most cosmopolitan city in the world. China at this time was more productive, more inventive and wealthier than Europe.

More remote even than China from the Eurasian "center of the world" were the empires and civilizations that arose in the southern hemisphere, especially in sub-Saharan Africa and South America. In north Africa, Islam eclipsed Christianity; across the desert it made slower progress, but the Arab traders reached deep into west-central Africa and the empire of Ghana waxed on the traffic in gold and slaves. Of the early medieval history of Africa farther to the south, almost nothing is known. Knowledge of the great continents across the Atlantic, whose discovery was not yet even in European men's imaginations, is just as scanty, except for the evidence, chiefly archaeological, of the politically sophisticated and architecturally advanced civilization that was built by the Maya in the Yucatán peninsula and flourished between 300 and 900.

While Europe was sunk in the "Dark Ages," in China under the T'ang dynasty (618-907), sculpture, such as the lively guardian figure, top, flourished. In very different vein is the bas-relief detail of a warrior and his slaughtered foe on a Saxon helmet, found at the ship burial (c. 660) at Sutton Hoo in Suffolk, England.

Charlemagne, whose coronation is commemorated in this 13th-century stained-glass window in Strasbourg cathedral, became the focus for romantic legend and poetry.

THE HIGH MIDDLE AGES 1100–1449

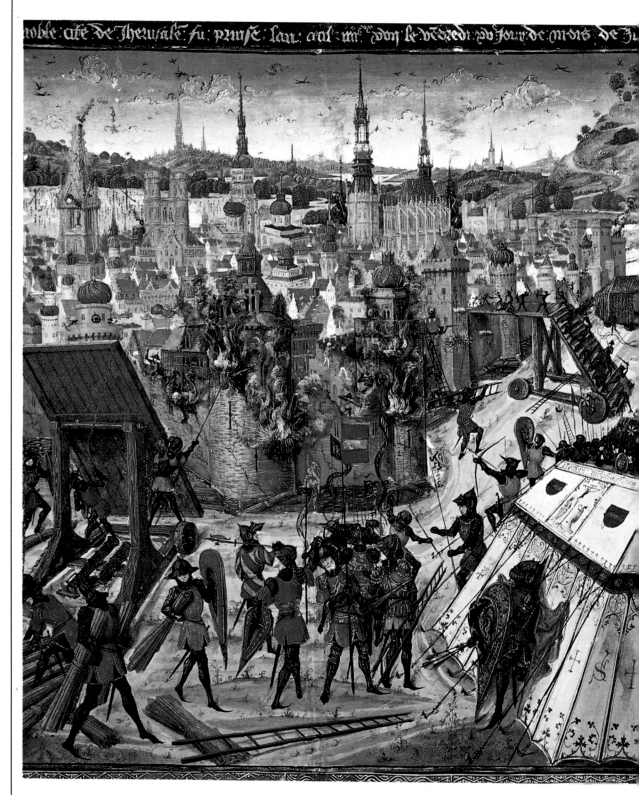

Two dates may be chosen, most arbitrarily, to enclose within them the period that may be called the High Middle Ages. It is a most European term. From an Indian, or Persian, or Bantu perspective there is nothing about the year 1100 that has anything to do with a "middle." Europe and the vast Mongol empire that rose and fell in Asia in the 13th and 14th centuries barely touched one another.

For Europeans two dates—1095 and 1453—stand as beacons lighting the path that their history has taken. Not that either date has a solely European resonance. Each marks an event—the calling of the First Crusade and the fall of Constantinople to the Ottoman Turks—whose effects reverberate in Islamic and Arab history. The invocation to a crusade against the infidel in 1095, for the "recovery" of the Holy Lands, sounded as both the last echo of Roman power and the new note of rising European self-confidence. It signified that Europe's eyes were still focused on the Mediterranean. The fall of Constantinople marked the nadir of the Christian princes' war against expansionist Islam and cut Europe off from the East. But it was also the prelude to a great shift in the European view of the world, a shift away from the Mediterranean toward the Atlantic.

The word "Europe" itself began to come into vogue, as something more than a mere geographical term, at about the turn of the 14th century. For most of the High Middle Ages the phrase it came to supplant, "Christendom," has more authenticity. The Crusades were undertaken on behalf of a society which believed itself to be united in one faith and one Church that distinguished between clergy and laity only by function. The Church was not an element of society; it *was* society. The Holy Roman Empire was a pale shadow of the Roman empire which it pretended to succeed; but its name expressed a reality, the binding together of Europe in one Christendom. By 1500 only a few Jews and slaves were outside its bounds.

The unity of Christendom neither prevented nor concealed rivalries which were important in the shaping of Europe. The most obvious was that between pope and emperor; but the emperor himself was really the king of the Germans with lands stretching to the Netherlands and Spain. Nationhood was an idea for the future, but already, especially in France and England, powerful monarchies were making their presence felt and organizing centralized administrations around their courts. The strict tie between knightly service and land tenure loosened, and an economy founded on feudal dues and obligations gave way to one based on money payments. The decline of feudalism was hastened by the plague; and it was compounded by the growth of towns, with their own governments, under royal charter.

In Italy, where feudalism never took root, the city-states were, by the late 1300s, the characteristic political and social entities. They were to be the nurseries of the explosion of energy called the Renaissance that marked the beginning of modern history. The fall of Constantinople was significant more with reference to the past than the future. Europe, in 1450, stood at the gateway to world dominance.

The climax of the First Crusade was the capture of Jerusalem on July 15, 1099, after a five-week siege, depicted in this late-medieval miniature, opposite. The Crusaders set fire to mosques and synagogues and slaughtered the city's Muslim inhabitants. The hero of the Third Crusade, some 90 years later, was Richard the Lion-Heart, top, whose defeat of Saladin at Arsuf in 1191 broke the long ascendancy of the Muslims in the region.

The period saw the rise of the Mogul empire in India, and the late flowering of its remarkable Persian-inspired painting and architecture.

THE EARLY MODERN ERA 1450–1788

THE EARLY MODERN ERA 1450–1788

In 1683 Vienna was surrounded by a huge Turkish army. Although this print, with its imposed Habsburg crest and adulatory references to Leopold I, implies that it was the Holy Roman Emperor who saved the city, the real victor was John Sobieski, king of Poland. His resounding victory over the Turks marked the end of the Ottoman threat to Christian Europe.

Previous page: The French "Académie des Sciences" had its beginning in 1666 in an informal society organized by Jean-Baptiste Colbert, King Louis XIV's minister. Later it moved to the Louvre, under royal patronage, and at the same time, in 1672, the Paris Observatory was opened, with the Italian astronomer Cassini as director. Testelin's painting captures the splendor of the occasion and gives a fascinating glimpse of the academy's spheres of interest: mathematics and physics, and chemistry and natural history in all its aspects.

Two years after the fall of Constantinople, Gutenberg reinvented for the West the method of movable print that the Chinese had discovered centuries earlier. The rapid dissemination of information and knowledge became possible in Europe. The role that dramatic change played in Europe's advance cannot be precisely calculated; but it was not simply coincidence that from that time Europe began its astonishing progress to unrivaled power and influence around the globe.

In the second half of the 15th century, the frontiers of Europe simultaneously contracted and expanded. They contracted in the east because of Ottoman power and they expanded in the west because of the great Atlantic explorations. The voyages of the great European navigators marked the dawn of a period in world history, of the European overlordship of the world—political, economic and cultural—which has come to an end, perhaps, only in our own century. Before 1453 three societies, Latin Christendom, the Byzantine empire and Islam, had lived in uneasy equilibrium. Turkish conquests had brought an end to Byzantium. Men naturally feared that the same destiny awaited Europe. It was not to be so. The line of Europe was held at the Danube.

China and Japan in the early modern period were stagnant, intellectually unadventurous societies, happy to isolate themselves from the world beyond their borders. They remained so until the late 19th century, when the acquisitive impulses of the Western imperialist powers drew them unwillingly into the orbit of world trade. In the Middle East and north Africa the Ottomans in the 16th century extended their dominion, essentially a form of military feudalism, over almost the whole of the Arab world (only Morocco remained independent). They retained a European foothold in the Balkans. But the heart of their empire, the eastern provinces, was already becoming an economic backwater. The process had begun with the devastation of the land by the Crusaders and the carting off of whole industries to central Asia by the Mongols; it was accelerated by the loss of trade which followed the opening up of the Cape route to the East by Portuguese navigators.

The great age of European overseas discovery coincided with, and was an expression of, that flowering of artistic, scientific and commercial culture that is called the Renaissance. It is a mistake to overstate the secular nature of the Renaissance. But its roots were in pagan classicism—it was, after all, classical values and classical knowledge which were given their "rebirth"—and it led men's minds away from a preoccupation with the world to come.

The central feature of medieval life and thought was the belief that all things, in their true substance, were unchanging. Wars were won and lost, dynasties rose and fell, but men lived under a fixed order which reflected the changeless eternity of God's universe. Medieval life, dominated by the Church, was corporate. It is simplifying matters greatly, but one great contrast between the medieval world and the age of the Renaissance is this: one emphasized the corporate life of men and women, as members of the *respublica Christiana*, who found their rank in the social hierarchy of feudalism at birth and, with rare exceptions, remained in it until death; the other discovered a new delight in men's individuality. Hence arose the term "humanism" to describe the new outlook. Concern for the soul did not, of course, recede into the background; but individual man, with his curiosity about the world around him, was brought forward onto the surface plane.

After 1500 the word "Christendom" loses its richness. (The rise of great national monarchies and the emergence of nation-states meant that Christendom also lost whatever unity it possessed.) Men turned their attention to exploring the world about them. Naturalism in painting found its counterpart in the Scientific Revolution of the 16th and 17th centuries. And that revolution itself broadened into the Enlightenment of the 18th century, that rational inquiry into all forms of knowledge whose roots lay in the humanism of the 16th century. The philosophers Adam Smith and Voltaire were the heirs of Thomas More and Erasmus.

Yet, in the very age of Renaissance and Scientific Revolution, somewhat paradoxically, religion remained the most powerful disruptive force in Europe. From the day that Luther posted his 95 theses at Wittenberg in 1519 up to the Treaty of Westphalia in 1648, Europe was divided into two camps: Protestant reformers and Roman Catholics. Alongside the two main branches of the Protestant world— Lutheranism and Calvinism—sect upon sect sprang up, each secure in the knowledge that it possessed the truth and the key to everlasting salvation. Europe was convulsed by a succession of wars in which religion, dynastic ambitions and national self-assertiveness were inextricably linked.

Habsburg Spain, enriched by the silver which flowed steadily into its coffers from the New World, with a population immune to the Protestant infection (and immunized against it by the Inquisition), had its Golden Age in the 16th century, an age which closed with a revolt in, and the eventual independence of, the Netherlands. Supremacy passed to France in the 17th century, where absolute monarchy reached its apogee in the reign of the "Sun King," Louis XIV, resplendent in his lavish, ostentatious court at the Palace of Versailles. Louis's wars drained France's resources while gaining little for his kingdom. The stage was set for Great Britain's entry into history as a world power.

Five contenders—Spain, Portugal, France, the Netherlands, England—entered the race for colonial supremacy that began when Columbus landed in the New World in 1492. Men thought the prize lay in the East. It turned out to lie across the Atlantic. From the long series of wars in the 18th century, wars which had overseas trade and Anglo–French rivalry at their center, it was Great Britain that, despite the loss of the American colonies in 1783, emerged the victor.

Under Suleiman I, the Magnificent, pictured here after his conquest of Belgrade in 1521, the Ottoman empire reached the height of its power, both militarily and culturally, for the sultan was a generous patron of the arts. The greatest Turkish architect, Sinan, designed most of Suleiman's buildings, the finest of which is the mosque in Constantinople (Istanbul) that bears his name.

THE MODERN WORLD 1789–1990

The French Revolution broke out a quarter of a century after James Watt built his improved steam engine. The repercussions of both events have shaped the modern world. No part of the world has escaped their influence. Nationalism and the appeal to democratic "rights," which were the chief legacies of revolutionary France, have everywhere lodged themselves in modern consciousness. The history of the Balkans in the years leading up to World War I is one example of the consequences. But the infection (if that word may be used neutrally) spread eventually to every corner of the world—to Latin America, Asia and Africa.

The French Revolution occurred just at the time that the Industrial Revolution achieved lift-off in Great Britain. By the middle of the 19th century the industrial transformation of society was well under way in Belgium, Germany, France and the United States. Industrialization brought an increased standard of living to the factory owners. In its wake came also a new range of social problems, principally associated with conditions of work in mines and factories and with the quality of life in the new urban landscape which it created.

The wealth that the middle class accumulated gave it a leverage to press for a share in political power; the workers' wretched lives (though historians are unable to agree on whether workers' standard of living in Great Britain rose or fell in the first half of the 19th century) demanded the attention of legislatures. The clamor for democracy and social justice grew insistent. And the institutions of democracy, along with the labor skills required by the advance of technology, required the education of the mass of the people. It is not merely coincidence that the 1832 Reform Act in Great Britain, which enfranchised prosperous householders, was followed in 1833 by the first effective act to regulate employment in the textile mills and by the first parliamentary grant of money to primary schools.

Modern imperialism—a matter of investment as much as of conquest and settlement—was the offspring of industrialization. The search for markets, both for goods and investment capital, and the need for raw materials drove businessmen and governments to seek control over any part of the world which promised to yield profits. Imperialism was one aspect of a much more profound product of industrialization: the population explosion. That explosion began in Europe because that is where industrialization began. In 1750 Europe's population (including European Russia) was about 144 million; in the following century it nearly doubled and by 1950 it was nearing 600 million.

The expansion would have been even greater had Europeans not migrated in record numbers to all parts of the world, but especially to North and South America. Between 1840 and 1930 more than 50 million Europeans uprooted themselves to start new lives overseas. It was an epic migration, probably the largest and undoubtedly the most significant in human history. Europeans took their values and their technology overseas. And even where they did not themselves go,

The dominant figure of the early years of the modern period was Napoleon Bonaparte. This painting by Baron Gros presents a romantic image of the young commander on the bridge at Arcole where, in 1896, he defeated the Austrians. His brilliant successes in the Italian campaign of 1896-97 made him the idol of the French people, and set him firmly on the path toward his eventual coronation as emperor in 1804.

THE MODERN WORLD 1789–1990

their ideas did. No other non-European country in the past 100 years has been so thoroughly westernized as Japan. During the period of that migration the Caucasian proportion of the world's population increased. In 1800 Caucasians comprised about 22 percent of the total; the proportion had risen to 35 percent by 1930. On the other hand, Europe's share of the total has declined in the 20th century, while Asia has come to include half of the world's people and one country, China, one-fifth of it.

Industrialization, by giving the West a great material advantage over the rest of the world, added urgency to nationalist and democratic ambitions. Never before in the history of the world was the gap between rich and poor so wide nor, owing to the speed and range of modern communication systems, so visible. In 1980, in the United States, there was one doctor for every 520 people; in Ethiopia there was one for every 58,000. The gap has continued to widen, partly because, while population growth in the rich countries in the late 20th century slowed down—some Western countries have enjoyed periods of zero, or even negative, growth— in the poorest countries it has been proceeding at unprecedented rates. The pressure of population on essentially agricultural countries has been severe, and without improved yields from cereal crops would have been catastrophic. India, for example, despite doubling its rice crop between 1945 and 1970, has struggled to keep pace with an additional million mouths a month to feed.

By the mid-20th century the United States was absorbing nearly half of the world's energy resources. The rise to world-power status of the United States at the turn of the 20th century heralded the decline of European influence. Two world wars hastened it on. The European country with the most to lose was Great Britain. In the 19th century it was proud to believe that it ruled over a *pax Britannica* and it did rule the largest empire in modern times. It had also taken the lead in laying the foundations of liberal democracy and the welfare state. It entered World War I a creditor nation and came out of it a debtor nation. The war, by dislocating and embittering societies, checked the "march of democracy" and laid the ground for the triumph of totalitarianism in Russia and Germany.

Against the liberal-democratic tradition of the Atlantic nations was pitted the messianic message of revolutionary Marxism. Marxism was only one of a number of revolutionary creeds that arose in the 19th century. It overthrew the Christian basis of traditional Western political thought. Following in the path of the philosophers of the 18th century Enlightenment, and the worship of the goddess Reason by the French Revolutionary, Jacques Hébert, it brought heaven down to earth. Man's goal was not salvation, but the classless society.

The first volume of *Das Kapital* appeared in 1867, the same year that manhood suffrage came to Great Britain. Marxism (except in Germany, where it gained widespread currency early) did not come to exert its powerful influence until after the Bolshevik *coup* of 1917.

Karl Marx was the prophet of socialism; most modern socialist thinking stems from his economic and political philosophy. The 20th-century phenomenon of Communism was founded on his belief that it was only through revolution that the workers would succeed in overthrowing the "bourgeoisie" who had exploited them. In the classless society that would follow, the state would become an instrument of economic and social cooperation.

The Great Exhibition, held in Hyde Park, London, in 1851, was housed in a revolutionary structure of glass and iron, designed by Joseph Paxton, which became known as the Crystal Palace. The first international showcase for goods and manufacturing achievement, with almost 14,000 exhibitors, half of whom were from abroad—this lithograph shows the foreign department—it was visited by more than six million people in the five and a half months it was open.

THE MODERN WORLD 1789–1990

The two great world wars in the first half of this century brought sickening destruction and loss of life. This moving painting by Georges Leroux entitled "L'enfer"—Hell—expresses the horror of the appalling conditions on the western front during World War I, where men had to endure days and months of bombardment by heavy guns, while at the same time almost drowning in the mud of Flanders.

The anticolonial movements that dominated Africa and African politics after 1945 succumbed to it; only North America remained largely proof against its utopian seduction. The spread of Communism added an ideological element to the rivalry between the United States and the Soviet Union, a rivalry which, thanks to the manufacture of nuclear weapons, held the attention of an anxious world throughout the years of the Cold War.

The 20th century has been a century of warfare, a new, or at any rate extreme, kind of warfare that has involved whole nations. War has been caused by whole peoples and suffered by whole peoples. Here, too, the French Revolution was something of a turning point. Total war has its origins in the *levée en masse* of 1793, with its aspiration to create a truly national people's army, and in the prosecuting of war, not simply for dynastic ends or the glory and status of kings and emperors, but for the advance of the French nation—*la grande nation*—and the ideas that it was supposed to represent.

War in the 20th century has not been more terrible in its human consequences than before. The Mongol conquest of China in the 13th

century is estimated to have been achieved at the cost of 30 million lives. But war, persecution and torture in this century have drawn a shadow across the modern Western mind which, since the 18th century, had been trained to believe in human progress. No previous age constructed such elaborate means to secure peace and promote international cooperation. The League of Nations and the United Nations are the outstanding examples.

Whether differences of nationality and belief will one day be accommodated within a peaceful world order is not a historical question. Drawing out the major events in history discloses an inescapable fact. War and religion have been the chief preoccupations of humans, at least in their public behavior, throughout recorded time. Often they have been found in each other's clasp. Since the 7th century one of the commanding themes of world history has been the conflict between the Christian West and the Islamic Middle East. Where once the underlying issue was the control of the world's vital trade routes, it is now control of the world's precious oil supplies. History may never repeat itself. Nor does it ever really change.

In October 1945, immediately after the end of World War II, the United Nations came into being. Its stated aims are to maintain peace and security in the world; to promote friendly relations between states; and, through cooperation, to attempt to solve the world's economic, social, cultural and humanitarian problems. The assembly, which meets in New York, is often regarded merely as a talking shop, but the United Nations has played an active and valuable role in peacekeeping, in dealing with the problems of refugees, and in imposing sanctions against nations that transgress, for example Iraq in 1990.

A.D. 9

Roman Legions Routed at Teutoburger Wald

Arminius leads the Germans to a victory that startles the empire

In the Gallic Wars of the mid-1st century B.C., Julius Caesar had established the Rhine and the Danube rivers as the northeastern frontier of the Roman empire. Beyond that boundary lay the marshes, mountains and forests inhabited by semi-nomadic Germanic tribes, who resented paying heavy tribute in gold to Rome and posed a persistent threat to the Romans.

These tribes had little military organization and few swords. Yet when Augustus tried to extend Roman control by creating a buffer zone between the Rhine and the Elbe in the early years of the 1st century A.D. he met fierce resistance.

In the summer of the year 9, Publius Varus, the governor of Gaul, received news of a rising led by Arminius (or Hermann), a German of equestrian rank who had been granted Roman citizenship. Varus dispatched three legions of some 20,000 men to the Teutoburg forest, just southwest of modern Bielefeld, to quell the rebellion, but they were utterly destroyed. The "Barbarians" had inflicted their first defeat on the Romans and the Rhine remained forever the northeastern limit of Latin rule.

c.A.D. 30

Jesus Christ Crucified

Pontius Pilate executes Jesus on the Cross for blasphemy

Jesus had been preaching and performing miracles for three years, chiefly in Galilee, and had collected a small band of disciples around him, when, *c.* 30, he made his triumphant entry into Jerusalem for the Passover. A few days after his arrival Jesus threw the money-changers out of the Temple, so he appeared as not only a messianic preacher but also a political radical. These events so excited the multitude that the Jewish authorities decided to act against him; they persuaded one of his disciples, Judas Iscariot, to betray him.

After having supper with his disciples for the last time, Jesus spent the night praying in the garden of Gethsemane, where he was arrested. He was then tried for the capital crime of blasphemy before the Jewish court, the Sanhedrin, and convicted on the evidence of having called himself the Messiah and the Son of God.

Pontius Pilate, the Roman procurator of Judea, had to decide whether to carry out the sentence. He sought to save Jesus, but later yielded to the multitude and crucified him, between two thieves, on a hill outside Jerusalem. The place of Christ's Crucifixion is known as Calvary.

Europe's history has been shaped largely by the Christian Church, itself epitomized by Cimabue's moving image of Christ on the Cross (1290-95).

A.D. 33

Paul of Tarsus "Converted" on the Road to Damascus

The first great evangel of Christ's teachings takes up his mission

St. Paul, whose Jewish name was Saul, was a tentmaker from Tarsus, in Asia Minor, the son of a Roman citizen and a Pharisee of the tribe of Benjamin. He was educated in Jerusalem, whose chief rabbi sent him to Damascus to help suppress Christianity there. On the road to Damascus Paul was temporarily blinded by a vision and heard the voice of Jesus ask, "Saul, Saul, why persecutest thou me?" He was led into the city and, after recovering his sight, he consented to be baptized a Christian by Ananias.

Paul then spent 13 years meditating in the deserts of eastern Palestine before beginning a life of itinerant Christian preaching *c*. 47. By emphasizing the divinity of Christ, Paul's teaching forced an irreparable breach between Judaism and Christianity and established the Pauline foundations of the Christian Church.

A.D. 43

The Romans Conquer Britain

Emperor Claudius adds a province to the Roman empire

In August 43, four Roman legions and auxiliary forces totaling more than 40,000 men, under the command of Aulus Plautius, landed on the Kent coast. Emperor Claudius needed a military conquest to strengthen his position in Rome, and he may have heard rumors of mineral wealth, especially tin, in the remote island of Britain.

The legions advanced to the Medway River, where they met slight resistance, and on to the Thames. Plautius then sent a message to Claudius, who arrived with an elephant corps on September 5 and two days later routed the British charioteers at a site somewhere between London (Londinium) and Colchester (Camulodunum). About 4,700 Britons were slain and another 8,000 taken captive.

A fortnight later Claudius left for Rome, where he was awarded the name "Britannicus"; Plautius took command of the new province. When Maiden Castle, the fortified earthwork in Dorset, succumbed to the brilliant young general Vespasian in 44, British resistance crumbled. A year later a fortified road, today known as the Fosse Way, was built from Exeter to Lincoln—the first frontier of Roman Britain.

A.D. 1–A.D. 68

ROMAN EMPIRE

● **A.D. 1-15 Migration of the Belgae**
Belgae people of northeast Gaul settled in southeast Britain in 1st century; brought skills in minting coins and using potter's wheel; traded with Gaul and partly Romanized Britain before Claudius's invasion.

● *c*. **A.D. 65 St. Mark's Gospel**
First Gospel written, attributed to St. Mark; with Paul's epistles forms earliest record of the life and teachings of Jesus; a source for the Gospels of St. Matthew and St. Luke.

● **A.D. 68 Death of Nero**
Dispute over succession among four rivals to the Roman throne caused by Augustus's failure to establish rules of succession; Vespasian emerged from bloody civil war as emperor in 69 and began system in which each emperor "adopted" his successor; brought greater stability to the Roman empire.

A.D. 61

Boudicca's Revolt Fails

The queen of the Iceni leads a rebellion against the Romans

Of the numerous early revolts by the Britons against Roman rule, the one that came nearest to success was led by Queen Boudicca, widow of Prasutagus, the Roman client-king of the East Anglian tribe, the Iceni. Angered by the loss of land to Roman soldiers (especially the depredations after King Prasutagus's death) and the heavy tribute imposed on them, the Iceni rose in rebellion toward the end of 60. They had already rebelled 13 years earlier when the Romans deprived them of the right to bear arms.

Fierce fighting lasted for several months. But after taking London and St. Albans (Verulamium), burning them and massacring their inhabitants while the main army of the Roman governor, Seutonius Paulinus, was in Wales fighting the Druids, the Iceni disintegrated into separate plundering bands.

The final battle took place in the south Midlands, when 17,000 Roman soldiers easily overcame a vastly larger, but untrained, rebel horde. About 80,000 British men, women and children were slain. Boudicca escaped to the woods where she is believed to have committed suicide by taking poison.

c. A.D. 83

Agricola Defeats Calgacus at Mons Graupius

North Britain is brought under Roman rule

Julius Agricola arrived in Britain as governor of the new Roman province c. 77. His mission was to secure the final conquest of the whole island. In a series of campaigns his infantry and armored cavalry put down revolts in north Wales and conquered the Scottish lowlands. A string of Roman forts was erected along the Forth-Clyde line.

The last great battle took place c. 83, at an unknown site called Mons Graupius, perhaps not far from the Moray Firth. There Agricola faced the Caledonian warrior-chief, Calgacus. An initial exchange of missiles was followed by the irresistible advance of the Roman army—about 8,000 infantry and 3,000 cavalry—until the Caledonian lines were broken and put to flight. The Caledonians lost about 10,000 men, the Romans fewer than 400.

Yet that crushing victory was not followed up, largely because trouble on the Danube frontier necessitated the transfer of Roman troops there. The Roman conquest of north Britain was, as a result, never consolidated. Within a generation the Roman garrisons had retreated to the Tyne-Solway isthmus, where Hadrian's Wall was to be built.

c. 105

Paper Invented in China

Ts'ai Lun produces the world's first lightweight writing material

Little is known about the invention of paper except that it is believed first to have been made by a Chinese man named Ts'ai Lun in the early years of the 2nd century. Before then, writing had been done on papyrus or parchment, heavy materials which made communication laborious and expensive. Ts'ai Lun's paper was made of bark and hemp, which produced thin, lightweight sheets capable of easy transport; it was, therefore, of the greatest significance in the development of commerce and the extension of central political authority. The invention spread to Japan in the 7th century and central Asia in the 8th century. But it did not reach Europe until the mid-12th century, when it was carried into Umayyad Spain by the Moors.

WAR-PAINTED BRITONS

The ancient Britons went into battle against the Romans wearing little clothing, if any. But they painted themselves in bright colors, probably as a means of tribal identification. It has been traditionally believed that the gaudy blue they most frequently used was produced by a dye from the woad plant. Research into the ion content of Lindow Man, a peat-preserved body discovered in Cheshire in 1984, suggests, however, that the coloring came from copper-rich earth steeped in hot water. The use of mineral pigments for coloring was known to Europeans at least 30,000 years ago—as the cave paintings at Lascaux, in southwest France, attest. And the unearthed bodies of nomads buried in the icy Altai region of central USSR 2,500 years ago still bear elaborate tattooing.

c. 105

Trajan Conquers Dacia

The Roman empire reaches its greatest territorial extent

The reign of Trajan, the first non-Italian Roman emperor (he was born in Spain), was marked by a vigorous and successful policy of foreign expansion. In two campaigns, conducted in 102 and 105, he subdued Dacia, the region that is modern Romania, and he followed that conquest with victories in the east against the Parthians, bringing Armenia and upper Mesopotamia within the empire.

By the time of Trajan's death in 117, Roman authority reached across the whole of north Africa to the Persian Gulf in the south, through Asia Minor to the northern shore of the Black Sea, and through all of Europe west of the Danube and the Rhine, north to Britain. Together with his program of public works, these conquests earned Trajan a reputation as one of the greatest Roman emperors, and his victory over the Daci was commemorated by the magnificent carved column, known as Trajan's Column, still standing in Rome.

Defeated Dacians fall beneath the onslaught of shield-bearing Roman soldiers in this detail from the continuous bas-relief on Trajan's 125-ft.-high marble Column.

122

Hadrian's Wall Seals off Northern Britain

The Romans build a massive bulwark against invasion by the Picts

By the early years of the 2nd century the northern frontier of Britain was settled along the Tyne-Solway isthmus. The Roman army had fallen back to this position soon after Agricola's defeat of the Caledonians at Mons Graupius *c.* 83. Along the 73-mile-long line, Emperor Hadrian began to build a wall in 122 as a defense against the Picts.

The wall was made of turf and stone and was fortified by blockhouses or milecastles every Roman mile (1,620 yd.), and 17 larger stone forts, one every 3–7 miles. The wall was about 6 feet high, rising to 14 feet in places in the east, and reached a thickness of 8 feet. It was protected to the north by a ditch 27 feet wide and 9 feet deep, while to the south was a *vallum*, a 20-foot-wide ditch that ran between turf walls 10 feet high and served as a road.

About 20 years after it was completed in 126, the wall was abandoned as the last line of defense, when it became Roman policy to attempt the reoccupation of southern Scotland and to build a new bulwark, the Antonine wall, on the Forth-Clyde line. When that project was abandoned *c.* 163, Hadrian's Wall once more became the northern frontier, and it remained so until Roman Britain came to an end in 410.

The formidable bulwark of Hadrian's Wall made full use of natural defenses, such as Walltown Crags in Northumberland, and the wide view they afforded over enemy territory.

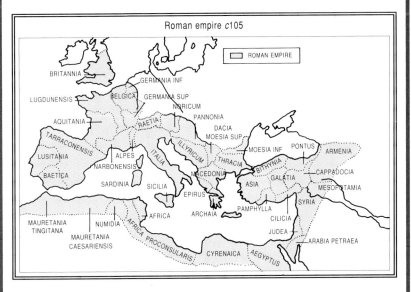

Roman empire c105

BRITANNIA
GERMANIA INF
LUGDUNENSIS
BELGICA   GERMANIA SUP
NORICUM
AQUITANIA   RAETIA   PANNONIA
DACIA
TARRACONENSIS   MOESIA SUP
ILLYRICUM   MOESIA INF   PONTUS   ARMENIA
LUSITANIA   ALPES   ITALIA   THRACIA   BITHYNIA
NARBONENSIS   MACEDONIA   CAPPADOCIA
BAETICA   ASIA   GALATIA   MESOPOTAMIA
SARDINIA   SICILIA   EPIRUS   SYRIA
ARCHAIA   PAMPHYLLA   CILICIA
MAURETANIA   NUMIDIA   AFRICA   JUDEA
TINGITANA   MAURETANIA   ARABIA PETRAEA
CAESARIENSIS   AFRICA PROCONSULARIS   CYRENAICA   AEGYPTUS

ROMAN EMPIRE

132

Bar Kokba Leads Last Great Jewish Revolt

The suppression of the Jews leads to the second diaspora

When the Roman empire was at its peak, the Jews fought a long and ultimately losing battle to resist Roman authority and maintain Judea as a national homeland. A great rising in Jerusalem, begun in 66 by extremists known as Zealots, was put down, after much bloodshed, by Titus, son of Emperor Vespasian, and the Temple was burned to the ground. During the four years of atrocious violence, the Jews had resorted to cannibalism in their struggle to survive.

In 132, Simon Bar Kokba, who may have called himself a Messiah, led the last important Jewish revolt, but after initial success against the Roman army, he and his followers were defeated by Julius Severus. Bar Kokba was killed at Bether, near Caesarea. The Romans made Jerusalem an Italian colony and allowed Jews entry only once a year.

So began the second diaspora, or dispersion, of the Jews throughout the empire (the first was the Babylonian captivity of the 6th century B.C.), and the history of the Jews until the creation of modern Israel in 1948 became the story of those scattered communities.

c. 150

Ptolemy Completes the "Almagest"

A Greco-Egyptian establishes a long-lasting cosmology

Ptolemy of Alexandria, the last of the great ancient mathematicians and astronomers, summed up Greek science in his massive, 13-volume *Almagest*. He discovered the eccentricity of the moon's orbit and made other independent astronomical observations, but his place in history rests on his magisterial statement of classical geocentric cosmology. Despite the heliocentric beliefs of Aristarchus of Samos and Herakleides, for the next 14 centuries Ptolemy's theory held sway.

The earth was the stationary center of the universe. Around it, in concentric, nesting spheres, moved the sun, moon and planets. Their motion, which created the "harmony of the spheres," was circular because only the perfect circle was the fitting path for a celestial body. The irregularities in the planetary orbits were explained by "wheels within wheels," which allowed the planets to make only circular motions.

Ptolemy is shown discoursing with the German astronomer Regiomontanus (1436-76) on the frontispiece of a book on the Ptolemaic system. This theory persisted until it was exploded by Copernicus in the 16th century.

220

Revolts Bring Down the Han Dynasty

China's great "Imperial Age" comes to a close

During the four centuries of its power the Han dynasty created a vast central state that rivaled the Roman empire in size. Its neighbors lacked the technology to make the bronze locks the crossbow required, and its warriors' skill with that weapon extended the dynasty's control into Indochina (modern Vietnam, Laos and Cambodia) in the south and Korea in the north. It also drove the forerunners of the Huns, the Hsiung-nu, north of the Gobi desert.

Military success was followed by commercial expansion: caravans along the Silk Road traded as far afield as the eastern edges of the Greek world. Han pottery and the bronze horses found in tombs at Wu-wei, as well as the use of brush and ink on paper, are evidence of a brilliant culture; new methods of irrigation and the invention of water-clocks and sundials show great scientific advance.

The attempt to relieve pressure on the frontiers by bringing tribes within the Great Wall and using them for defense, combined with the oppression of the peasantry by the landlords and the mandarin bureaucracy, led to a series of internal disorders. These destroyed the dynasty and left China with no central authority for 350 years.

c. 224

Sassanids Conquer Persia

Ardashir captures Ctesiphon and overthrows the Parthians

Ardashir (or Artaxerxes) laid the foundations of a great Middle Eastern empire when, *c.* 224, he defeated the Parthians, killed their last ruler, and captured their capital, Ctesiphon, on the Tigris River. The Sassanid empire, which took its name from an ancestor of Ardashir named Sassan, stretched, at its peak, from Mesopotamia to the Indus valley and as far north as the Aral Sea. Persia was thus reunited after a period of decline under the Seleucids and the Parthians.

Ardashir made monotheistic Zoroastrianism the state religion, endowing the priests with great power and proclaiming the king to be vice-regent on earth of the great creator, Ahura Mazda. Persecution of Christians led to a series of wars with Byzantium, from which the Sassanids emerged the more powerful. And, with Rome in decline, the Sassanids restored the Persian empire to the height it had enjoyed under the Achaemenids.

Sassanid empire, greatest extent

Han dynasty tombs at Wu-wei yielded impressive finds when they were excavated in 1969. Among these was the lively 10-in.-high bronze "Flying Horse," whose hoof rests on the back of a swallow.

251

Visigoths Overrun Dacia

The "Barbarian" threat to the Roman empire appears in the Balkans

In the 3rd century, Rome faced a double challenge: from the vigorous Sassanid empire of Persia to the east and from the "Barbarians" to the north. Fighting on two fronts was a heavy burden. Beyond the northern frontier three tribes posed a powerful threat. On the Rhine border lived the Franks and the Alamanni; on the Danube lived the Goths. At any one time these tribes between them could muster probably no more than 25,000 warriors, but Rome's difficulties enabled even that small a force to breach the empire's defenses.

In 251 the Visigoths crossed the Danube and settled in Dacia (modern Romania); five years later the Franks crossed the Rhine. The Alamanni followed and penetrated as far as Milan. In 270 Rome abandoned Dacia and began to fortify itself. By the end of the century the Goths were raiding Asia and Greece from the sea. Europe was on the verge of entering world history.

276

Mani Executed by the Persians

A great religious teacher is martyred for heresy

In the middle of the 3rd century, a Persian preacher named Mani (known in the Latin West as Manichaeus) announced himself as the prophet of a new religion. At the heart of his religion, called Manichaeism, was an emphasis upon the cosmic struggle between good and evil. Spirit was good; matter was evil. Hence the way to truth and salvation was by mortifying the flesh and abjuring the world. Mani rejected the Old Testament and called himself the paraclete ("holy spirit") promised by Christ. Manichaeism drew on many sources, but it was in essence a Christian heresy.

Exiled by the Sassanid rulers of Persia to India *c.* 240, Mani was recalled on the accession of Sharpur I in 242. In an empire in which Zoroastrianism was the state religion and its main rival, Christianity, systematically persecuted, Sharpur was remarkable for his religious tolerance. He gave Mani freedom to wander the empire and make converts. Sharpur died in 272 and with him his policy. Mani's followers were persecuted, and in 276 he was himself flayed alive, perhaps on a cross.

The martyrdom nurtured the spread of his ideas. Manichaeism grew throughout Asia and the Roman empire, surviving in the latter until the 6th century. In nascent Europe it sustained itself much longer, in the somewhat modified shape of the medieval heresy adhered to by the Cathars and Albigenses.

285

Diocletian Divides the Roman Empire

Autocratic rule accompanies the reorganization of the empire

When Diocletian was elected emperor in 284, he set about remodeling the administrative structure of the Roman empire in order to preserve it. In 285 he made Maximian co-emperor, with authority over the lands west of a line running from the Danube to Dalmatia. In 293, each of the two emperors was given an assistant caesar, or coadjutor, so establishing the Tetrarchy.

This devolution of authority coincided with the growth of autocratic power. The Roman senate had declined into a mere formality; the office of senator conferred only social dignity. Administrative reform brought with it a recovery of military strength (aided by introducing conscription) and renewed political stability. But the cost was high. Doubling the army's size meant increased taxes, which, together with the attempt to freeze prices and wages by an edict in 301, produced an ever-growing, more expensive, bureaucracy.

Diocletian's reforms bolstered the empire for the time, but in them can be seen the seeds of the next century's decline.

Diocletian's reforms included the reintroduction of silver and gold coins of specific design, such as this gold aureus bearing his portrait. He also minted a new bronze coin and small denomination coins to make everyday transactions easier.

313

Edict of Milan Promulgated

Constantine makes Christianity lawful throughout the Roman empire

Persecution of the Christians by Rome, which began in earnest under Nero (r54-68) and fluctuated in its ferocity thereafter, was formally ended by Constantine, who earned himself the sobriquet, "the 13th apostle." Constantine made an abrupt turnabout. In 303 he launched the last great persecution against Church officials and Christian books and buildings. Then in 312, on the eve of the battle at Milvian Bridge against Maxentius, a rival for the imperial title in the West, he is reported to have seen a vision of a flaming cross in the sky. Although still a sun-worshipper, he at once ordered his soldiers to put a Christian cross on their shields and won the battle.

A year later, by the Edict of Milan, he and the emperor in the East, Licinius, granted toleration to Christians throughout the empire. Property was restored to them and bishops were given a share of civil administration. As long as they acknowledged the rule of the emperor, Christians were permitted freedom of worship and the right to make converts. In just three centuries, a small, breakaway sect of Judaism had risen to become identified with the empire.

c. **320**

Gupta Dynasty Founded in the Ganges Valley

A brilliant age of Indian arts and sciences is ushered in

India's so-called "Classical Age" began with Chandragupta I, whose reign, beginning *c.* 320, founded a Hindu dynasty that lasted until the mid-6th century. Chandragupta made his capital in Patna, and he and his successors extended Gupta rule over the northern half of India.

General prosperity is suggested by the large number of Gupta gold coins unearthed by archaeologists. The period was distinguished by great stone temples decorated with finely carved symbols, and by literary splendors, especially the poems and dramas of Kalidasa and the *Kama Sutra*. In the 5th century, Indian mathematicians invented the decimal system.

Politically, this classical age was marked by the consolidation of a mature caste system. But the Gupta period was a brief interlude between the five centuries of confusion which it ended and the political disunity to which its demise gave rise.

A profusion of carvings and statues with symbolical meaning adorns the buildings of the Gupta period. This classical and sophisticated figure from Sarnath in Uttar Pradesh dates from the 5th century.

325

First Ecumenical Council Meets at Nicaea

The Eastern and Western Churches unite against the Arian heresy

In the early 4th century, the civil and religious peace of the Roman empire in the East was threatened by the preachings of an itinerant priest from Alexandria named Arius. He taught that Christ, though part-divine, was neither equal to nor eternal with God the Father. To combat this heresy, Constantine called a council of bishops from both East and West—the first ecumenical council in the history of the Church—at which the chief opponent of Arius was Athanasius, later recognized as one of the Four Doctors, or Fathers, of the Eastern Church.

The Council made belief in the co-substance of God the Father and God the Son a test of Christian faith, the first such universal statement of Christian doctrine. Arius and two bishops who refused to accept the dogma were banished to Illyricum, more or less the region covered today by Yugoslavia and the Balkan states.

The Nicene Creed ("I believe in one God, the Father Almighty, maker of heaven and earth...") was formulated not at Nicaea but at the ecumenical Council of Constantinople in 381. After that date, Arianism rapidly expired in the East, though it lived on among Barbarians in the West until the 7th century.

325

King Erzana of Axum Invades Kush

The Meroitic civilization of the Middle Nile is obliterated

The kingdom of Kush, which arose in present-day Sudan during the 7th century B.C., was the first iron-working civilization in Africa. It had resources of iron ore and wood fuel, which Egypt lacked, and it learned techniques of iron-smelting from its Assyrian enemies. The iron hoe and the iron spear enabled the Meroitic people of Kush—their name comes from the capital, Meroë, situated on the Nile—to provide for themselves and to grow rich by exporting slaves, ivory, ebony and, possibly, gold to Egypt and countries bordering the Red Sea and the Indian Ocean.

Kushite culture was derived from the Egyptian; but it was an independent civilization, which developed its own deities and rituals and invented its own alphabetic script. By A.D. 100, however, Kush was being challenged by a rival trading empire, Axum, in present-day Ethiopia.

Axum's rulers were converted to Christianity in the mid-4th century, at just about the time that King Erzana's armies made their last, decisive invasion of Kush, burning Meroë, scattering its inhabitants and turning a 1,000-year-old civilization to dust.

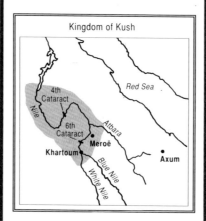

Kingdom of Kush

330

Constantinople Made Capital of the Roman Empire

A new Christian center is founded on the site of ancient Byzantium

When the emperor in the East, Licinius, died in 325, Constantine became sole ruler of the Roman empire. In 330 he moved his capital from Rome to the East and ordered a new city, named Constantinople after him, to be built on the site of the ancient Greek colony of Byzantium, which lay at the gateway to the Black Sea.

Despite the Milan Decree of 313, which made Christianity lawful within the empire, Constantine did not publicly announce his own adherence to the faith until 324, and his decision to found a new city as a center of Christian worship was, he said, made "at God's command."

But Constantine continued to have his court at Nicomedia, on the opposite side of the Bosporus, and it was another 50 years before the new city became the permanent imperial residence. Nevertheless, for the next 11 centuries, until it fell to the Ottoman Turks in 1453, Constantinople was the principal Christian city in the world.

c. **350**

Pallava Dynasty Established in Southern India

Kanchipuram is made the capital

At the time that Gupta rule in northern India was approaching its peak, southern India, too, was being united by the Pallavas, a ruling dynasty that made its capital at Kanchipuram, near the east coast. The Pallavas retained control of the south for 500 years.

Southern India benefited from the Pallavas' attachment to the priestly caste of Brahmins, whose religion was evolving into Hinduism, and who placed great importance upon education and intellectual achievement.

The most lasting legacy of Pallavan rule was the art and architecture that flourished under it, which is known as Dravidian after the general name for the 20 or more languages spoken in southern India. Most notable is the monumental temple complex, built in the mid-7th century at Mamallapuram, which is popularly called the "Seven Pagodas."

The ornateness and antiquity of the temples is strikingly conveyed in this photograph, taken in the 1860s.

INDIA

● *c.* **200 Hindu resurgence in India**
Expulsion of the central-Asian Kushans marked by spread of Sanskrit; the great Sanskrit epics, the *Mahabharata* and the *Ramayana*, together with the Hindu code, the *Laws of Manu*, probably written in 3rd century; thus foundations laid for classical age of the Gupta era.

AFRICA

● *c.* **200-300 Use of iron**
Known in the Nile valley since about 500 B.C., had spread to the sub-Saharan central plateau north and south of the Zambezi; by 800 almost all of Africa had made the transition from late Stone Age to Iron Age and from hunting and gathering to settled farming; in same period occurred great expansion and spread of Bantu-language people from Nigeria-Cameroons region over most of sub-Saharan Africa.

● *c.* **300 Alchemy**
Perhaps practiced in ancient China and Egypt centuries before, developed in Alexandria in 4th century by Zosimos; in addition to attempting to convert base metals into silver and gold, the art of distillation developed.

PACIFIC OCEAN

● **400 Polynesian expansion**
Migration eastward from Tonga and Samoa began; settlers carried crops and livestock in canoes to islands as far east as Easter Island; settlements flourished and social structures were built over next few centuries.

378

Visigoths Win Battle of Adrianople

A victory over the Roman empire opens up Thrace to the "Barbarians"

Rome faced a mounting crisis in the last quarter of the 4th century: the second phase of the *Völkerwanderung*, or "wandering of the nations," began. The first decisive movement was made by the Goths who lived beyond the Danube, a people already becoming Christianized, though their faith took the heretical Arian form. In 370 the Huns, from Asia, overran their lands, and the Visigoths, perhaps 40,000 of them, sought refuge within the empire.

In 376 Emperor Valens allowed them to settle south of the Danube. He intended to disarm them and, as had happened before, absorb them into the imperial way of life. The Barbarians have often been said to have helped to destroy the empire, yet they most often entered it, not as enemies, but as *foederati* (allies) promised land and subsidies to defend the empire against other Germanic tribes. Once they enlisted in the army—*barbarus* became a word for "soldier"—they had a legal claim to remain. But in 378 the Visigoths rose against their masters, and their cavalry won a crushing victory at the Battle of Adrianople, during which the emperor was killed.

The battle marked a turning point: the Teutonic advance now became irresistible. Using Germans to defend the empire against Germans was proving to be an outworn policy. The Barbarian tribes were poised, if not quite to destroy the empire in the West, at any rate to inherit it.

c. 390

Jerome Prepares the "Vulgate"

A Father of the Church provides the standard edition of the Bible

The oldest extant version of the complete Bible was made in the last decade of the 4th century by Jerome, a scholar, who abandoned pagan studies *c.* 375 after experiencing a vision of Christ. He fled to the desert to live as a hermit and study the Scriptures. Three years later he returned to civilization and was ordained at Antioch in 379.

By 382 he was in Rome, acting as secretary to Pope Damasus I, who enjoined him to prepare a new version of the Bible. The existing text was a Latin translation from the Greek. In Jerome's version, which came to be called the "Vulgate," or "common," edition, the Old Testament was prepared from original Hebrew texts. The Gospels are essentially a revision of the Latin texts, but whether Jerome altered the remainder of the New Testament is doubtful.

The Vulgate won great popularity in the West early on, although the Church did not make it the official Bible until the Council of Trent in 1545. Many of the first translations of the Bible into European languages (though not the Authorized Version prepared for James I of England in 1611) were taken from the Vulgate.

410

Visigoths Sack Rome

Alaric carries the offensive to the heart of Italy

When Emperor Theodosius died in 395, the Visigoths, who had settled south of the Danube and entered the imperial service, rebelled and chose Alaric, one of their own commanders, as their leader. Under Alaric they ravaged the whole of Thrace, Macedonia and Greece before being defeated by the Vandal Roman general, Stilicho, in 397. Constantinople and the Eastern empire, for the moment at least, were thus made secure.

Alaric then turned north to invade Italy in 401, withdrawing after indecisive warfare only to return to the attack in 408. A successful siege of Rome in 409 enabled him to impose a puppet emperor on the senate. Negotiations with Emperor Honorius, who was holding out at Ravenna, were fruitless, and in 410 Alaric sacked the Eternal City, before setting out on an assault on Sicily and Africa. But a storm destroyed most of his fleet, and Alaric died on the return journey.

Under Alaric's successor, Ataulf, the Visigoths left Italy in 412 and crossed the Alps into southern Gaul and northern Spain, where Honorius made peace with them and allowed them to settle.

St. Jerome (c. 347-420?) spent the last 34 years of his life in Bethlehem, where from 391-406 he worked on his translation of the Old Testament. In 1514 Albrecht Dürer made this fine engraving of the old man in his study, attended by his symbolic lion. On the wall hangs the cardinal's hat awarded to him by Pope Damasus, although Jerome was never actually a cardinal.

410

Last Roman Troops Leave Britain

The faltering Roman empire abandons its northwestern outpost

In 367 Roman Britain was faced with a three-pronged Barbarian attack: while Picts from the north broke through Hadrian's Wall, Saxons from the east and Irish from the west launched raids on the island's coasts. Emperor Valentinian sent his general, Theodosius, to restore order, and the Barbarians proved to be no match for him.

But as the empire's difficulties mounted in the last quarter of the century, Britain became less important to Rome. The first withdrawal of troops from Britain—to defend Italy against the Visigoths—took place about 400. A few years later imperial coinage ceased to be imported into Britain, and in 409 the Britons expelled all the Roman officials and decided to abandon Roman rule completely. In 410 the last Roman troops left the island.

All this was accomplished without a revolution because Rome was ready to abandon Britain just at the time that the Romano-British landowners were tiring of paying heavy taxation to support the vast imperial administration and of sacrificing agricultural laborers as conscripts to the Roman army. So when General Constantine, appointed emperor by the Roman troops in Britain, did not return after crossing with his men to defend Gaul in 408, the landowners suggested no successor, nor was one appointed. Britain was now cut off from the continent of Europe for the first time in 400 years, and remained so until the arrival of the Saxons in the 440s.

The splendid mosaic floors are the most notable feature of Fishbourne Palace, near Chichester in Sussex. One of the major Roman relics in Britain, it was built in the 2nd century for the British-born viceroy, Cogidubnus.

c. 412

St. Augustine Publishes "The City of God"

A mighty defense of Christianity is erected against paganism

Augustine, born in Africa, was baptized a Christian at Milan in 387 and spent the remainder of his life at Hippo, now Annaba in Algeria, first as a hermit, then as a bishop. Christian evangelicalism had had a triumphant 3rd century: the Gospels had been carried as far as Ethiopia. But the Church was in danger from the Arian heresy, which was the faith of the Gothic peoples of Italy, Gaul and Spain, and from other heresies as well. Moreover, some men blamed the Church for the difficulties facing the empire

The sack of Rome in 410 was a grave shock. In response to it, St. Augustine wrote the greatest book of early Christianity, *The City of God*, with the subtitle, *Against the Pagans*. The events of 410, he wrote, were God's punishment of sinful man. There were two cities, the earthly city of man's lower nature and the heavenly city of God. The heavenly city was attainable by anyone who followed the Church's teachings. St. Augustine believed that the Church was a new factor in history, transforming it and opening up a new destiny for man.

The state, too, had a place in the divine scheme of things, and Christian government was divinely ordained. Its purpose, like that of the Church, was to fight for good against evil. Here were ideas pregnant with the future of European Christendom.

429

Vandals Establish a Kingdom in North Africa

The granary of the Western empire passes out of Roman control

The Rhine frontier of the Roman empire was breached in 406, when vast hordes of Vandals poured into the western part of Gaul known as Aquitania, followed four years later by the Visigoths. Whether, like the Goths on the Danube 30 years earlier, the Vandals were pushed by invading Huns, is not known. Overpopulation and land hunger may be sufficient to explain the migration.

The Vandals swept southward, pillaging and looting as they went, across the Pyrenees into Spain, whither they had been invited by the rebel Roman general, Gerontius. To meet this fresh challenge, Emperor Honorius enlisted the aid of the Visigoths, granting them peaceful settlement in Aquitania in return for helping him to oust the Vandals from Spain.

The Visigothic raids on Spain that followed contributed, perhaps, to the Vandals' decision to cross the Mediterranean and conquer north Africa. This was a mortal blow to the Roman economy, for Africa was the chief supplier of grain. By 439 the Vandals had taken Carthage, from which naval base they were to set forth and sack Rome in 455, the action which, more than any other, has given the word "vandalism" to the English language.

432

St. Patrick Arrives in Ireland

The conversion of the Celtic island to Christianity begins

The Church of Gaul consecrated Patrick, a Roman citizen born in Britain, a bishop in 432 and sent him to Ireland. He had been taken to Ireland as a slave *c.* 405, but had escaped 10 years later. Now his mission was to convert the pagan island to Christianity. The Roman Church had not previously sent missionaries beyond the boundaries of the empire—Barbarians were assumed to lie beyond the will of God. Patrick was the first to quote the Gospels as truth for *all* men.

His first converts were made at Tara, the court of the most powerful kings of Erin, but his work finally centered on northeastern Ulster. Details of his mission are little known beyond that a local prince gave him land to build a church at Armagh, which was destined to become the metropolis of Irish Christianity and of which Patrick became the first bishop. Three other bishops were also appointed: for northern Leinster, southern Leinster and Meath.

When Patrick died in 461 the foundations of Christianity were well laid among the people, though no king had yet been converted. Ireland was thus opened to Latin civilization and began to turn itself into a land of learning and Christian culture.

c. 449

Hengist and Horsa Land in Kent

Germanic invaders settle in numbers in Britain

In the course of the 5th and 6th centuries Britain became split into small kingdoms, Celtic to the north and west, Saxon to the east. The name "Saxon" describes a variety of Germanic tribes who arrived in the mid-5th century—Angles, Saxons, Jutes, probably Frisians and Franks—none of whom kept a distinct identity for long.

Bede, in his *History* written 200 years later, dated the Saxon invasions from the landing of Hengist and Horsa on the Kent coast in 449, and although there were earlier small "Saxon" settlements, such as Muckling on the Thames Estuary, occupation in numbers dates from the mid-century. Kent and East Anglia were the first regions to be densely settled. According to tradition, impossible to verify, Horsa was killed in a battle against the British king, Vortigern, in 455. In turn, Vortigern and the Britons are said to have been defeated by Hengist at a place called Crecgan Ford in 457 and to have fled to London. What is certain is that the Saxons had established a kingdom in Kent, with its frontier at the Medway, by 500.

Saxon expansion to the north and west was a gradual process. By the end of the 6th century the whole of the eastern seaboard and most of present-day England south of the river Trent were Saxon, but Scotland, Wales, northwestern England and Cornwall remained British or Celtic.

SHIPS OF THE DESERT

The introduction of the camel to Egypt by the Persians *c.* 200 eventually wrought an economic and social revolution in Africa. By the end of the Roman era the camel had moved beyond Egypt, and its suitability as a pack animal broke down the ancient natural barrier that the Sahara had imposed between northern and sub-Saharan tribes. It transformed certain Berber tribes from sedentary agriculturalists to nomadic pastoralists and thus brought them into contact with Islam and turned them into a warrior tribe. It also enabled the great sub-Saharan empires from Kanem to Ghana to amass wealth by exporting gold and slaves across the desert to Mediterranean ports and thence to Byzantium and the Arab empire.

451

Huns Invade Gaul

Attila is repulsed after failing to advance to Rome

The Huns, a nomadic people of obscure Asiatic origin, entered the history of the Roman empire in 376, when they forced the Visigoths to cross the Danube. The Huns, as true nomads, knew no civilization and had no agriculture. They were a wagon-people of horse-archers, and as soldiers they were mere plunderers.

For half a century they raided the Eastern empire (Emperor Theodosius was forced to pay tribute to them) without inflicting lasting damage upon it. About 447, under their most famous leader, Attila, the "Scourge of God," who had his palace in Hungary and controlled most of what is now European Russia, Germany and Poland, they turned their attention to the West, to Visigothic Gaul.

In 451 Attila's huge army (though almost certainly smaller than contemporary estimates of 500,000) rampaged through Gaul, burning and pillaging, until it encountered the army of the Roman general Aetius on Mauriac plain in northeastern France, near present-day Châlons-sur-Marne. There Attila suffered a catastrophic defeat. Perhaps one-third of his men were slain. Whatever the number, the Huns retreated and Latin Christendom was preserved.

A year later Attila led his forces into Italy but withdrew before he reached Rome. He died in his bed in 453, and with him, divided among his sons, died his empire. Within two or three generations the Huns had vanished.

Apart from the Huns, fighting men abounded in Europe. Best equipped was the Roman in his iron-banded leather cuirass and kilt, greaves and sandals. The Gaul, protected by a surcoat, carries a bow, while the Vandal, a raider, is mounted and lightly armed.

451

The Church Defines Christ's Nature at Chalcedon

Condemnation of Monophysitism fails to ward off schism in the Church

The heresy of Monophysitism erupted in the Eastern empire in the first half of the 5th century, chiefly as the result of the teaching of a fervent believer in the doctrine that Christ had only one nature. His name was Eutyches, and in its early phase Monophysitism went by the name of Eutychism. The doctrinal quarrel arose because Nestorius, who was appointed patriarch of Constantinople in 428, held that Christ had two separate natures, human and divine. Eutyches held that Christ's humanity was subsumed in his divinity.

This dispute was the central business of the Council of Chalcedon, called by Macian, emperor in the East, in 451. The council declared that Christ had two distinct natures which resided in one person, and that definition was intended to be the test of orthodoxy in both parts of the empire. But a mere conciliar decree was insufficient to end Monophysitism; Basiliscus, the usurper of the imperial title in the East, declared the council's decisions invalid in 476.

An attempt to end the schism between East and West was made in 519, when Emperor Justin I upheld the Council of Chalcedon. But his successors, from Justinian onward, took a more lenient view of the Monophysites and vacillated between tolerating and suppressing them. So, by the end of the 6th century, the Western Church was almost irreparably alienated from the Eastern.

476

The Western Empire Collapses

The last emperor is deposed by invading Ostrogoths

When the Western empire defeated Attila and the Huns in 451, it was already on its last legs. Gaul was coming under the control of the Barbarian Franks, who were building a kingdom there; Spain was in the hands of the Visigoths; and north Africa of the Vandals.

The formal end came in 476 when Odoacer, the commander of the Ostrogothic mercenaries in the Roman army, led his troops in revolt. Odoacer defeated an imperial army commanded by General Orestes, captured Ravenna and deposed the last emperor in the West, the boy-emperor Romulus, nicknamed Augustulus ("little emperor"). The emperor in the East, Zeno, recognizing a *coup* that he was powerless to reverse, bestowed on Odoacer the Roman title of patrician.

Thus the old policy of entrusting the defense of the empire to *foederati*, the Barbarians who for two centuries had filled the ranks of the army, bore its final fruit. Italy, like all the other former provinces of the Western empire, became a Barbarian kingdom, and those Italians who retained a notion of *Romanitas* now looked to the emperor at Constantinople.

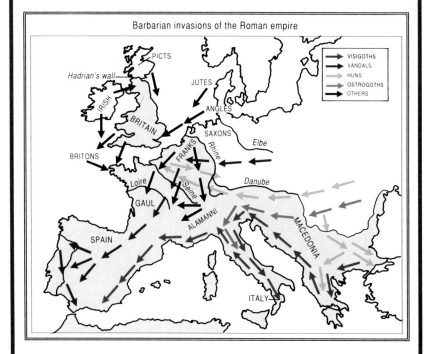

Barbarian invasions of the Roman empire

497

Ostrogoth Kingdom of Italy Recognized

Theodoric gains Byzantium's acceptance of his rule

After the retreat of the Huns, the Ostrogoths (eastern Goths) moved out from their base on the Black Sea to threaten the Eastern empire. After storming through Macedonia and Thessaly, they launched an attack on Constantinople in 487, where their king, Theodoric, was bought off by Emperor Zeno and persuaded to advance on Italy instead and to overthrow Odoacer. Once more the Eastern empire had averted the fate that befell the empire in the West.

Theodoric won a succession of victories in Italy, culminating in the capture of the Visigothic capital, Ravenna, after a three-year siege, in 493. Odoacer surrendered and shortly afterward he was murdered by Theodoric, whose kingdom in Italy was formally recognized by Zeno's successor, Anastasius I, in 497.

Theodoric ruled Italy well for 33 years. He improved harbors and roads and maintained public buildings. Although his army remained Gothic, he appointed Romans to civilian posts, retained Roman laws and institutions, and was always at pains to stress the need for religious tolerance and for Goths and Romans to live amicably together.

497

King of the Franks Baptized

Clovis lays the foundations of European Christendom

The origins of modern France lie in the second half of the 5th century, when Clovis, king of the Salian, or western, Franks, won a victory over the Roman general Syagrius at Soissons and thus secured Frankish rule over western Gaul. Meanwhile, the eastern Franks were subduing the Alamanni, and when Clovis was elected their king also, the Merovingian dynasty of which he was the true founder (although his father, Childeric, was the actual founder) came into possession of almost all of present-day France. The only exceptions were Burgundy and the two southern provinces of Provence and Languedoc.

In 493 Clovis married Clotilda, the Christian Princess of Burgundy, and four years later, after a battlefield conversion reminiscent of Constantine's, he was himself baptized. Clovis was the first of the Gothic kings to adopt the true Roman faith rather than the heretical Arian form of Christianity. His conversion brought the support of the Church and won him friends in the Romano-Gallic world.

Before he died in 511, Clovis had subdued the Burgundians and moved the Merovingian capital from Tournai to Paris. His kingdom was divided on his death among his three sons, who ruled what came to be called Austrasia (in the extreme north and east), Neustria (in the west, centered on Paris) and Burgundy (in the southeast). Even so, medieval France, the heart of European Christendom, was already in embryo.

A French woodcut (1516) shows Clovis's battlefield conversion and later baptism by the Bishop of Reims.

> **THE "MAN-PRICE"**
> Nearly every Barbarian society was ordered in strictly defined ranks, from an aristocracy at the top to slaves or semi-free serfs at the bottom, and every free man had a legal price in accordance with his status. The Franks and Saxons called this the *wergild*, or "man-price." A free Frank was worth 200 *solidi*, a free Anglo-Saxon, or *ceorl*, 200 shillings. The greatest aristocrat might be worth six times as much. If a man were murdered, his *wergild* was paid to his bereaved kin by the murderer and his kin. It became, too, the fine for offenses such as adultery, and a man's oath in court was valued according to his *wergild*. Noblemen were able to clear themselves of some criminal charges simply because of the "worth" of their testimony.

c. 500

Saxons Defeated at Mons Badonicus

Britons record a rare victory over the Germans

Knowledge of a British victory over the Saxons at a place called Mons Badonicus comes from the chronicle written by a monk, Gildas, in the mid-6th century. He did not place the battle (it may have been at Badbury Rings in Dorset), but he presented it as a rare event and an important turning point in the Saxon settlement of Britain, one that gave the British a respite and slowed down the Germanic advance.

Probably some such battle did occur; archaeological evidence points, at any rate, to a disruption of German settlement at about this time. But the scale of fighting in general, after the first Saxon landings, was almost certainly neither as fierce nor as destructive as Gildas painted it.

For one thing, no Saxon war band appears to have been larger than a few hundred men. And swords were precious possessions, owned only by the rich and powerful; other, lesser warriors had to be content with spears.

It is uncertain whether military conquest was the chief method of Saxon settlement, or whether it proceeded as well by mass migrations and small infiltrations of kinship groups, at some places dislodging indigenous inhabitants and at others coming to live peacefully among them. Many more were dislodged than were assimilated into the new culture, however, and few elements of Roman life survived. This was, above all, because the towns and roads built by the Romans held little significance for a new population entirely unused to urban life.

THE DECLINE OF THE ROMAN EMPIRE

The wall painting from the Villa Boscoreale at Pompeii, above left, shows a house with several stories and an ornate front door, while in the background are, unmistakably, pillared official buildings. The ordered, urban society reflected in this sophisticated painting makes a striking contrast with the much later, but almost crude, 4th-century Christian painting in the Catacombs of Rome of Samson slaying the Philistines with the jawbone of an ass.

This fine glass wine jug, dating probably from the late 1st century, was found at Reims in France, an indication of how the Romans' civilized lifestyle was adopted throughout the empire. It was a way of life that continued to depend largely on slaves, who were regarded as property, as the inscription on this 4th-century bronze slave-tag makes clear: "Hold me, lest I flee, and return me to my master Viventius on the estate of Callistus."

How deeply the ways of Western society are rooted in the culture of Rome is almost comically brought home by the instant recognition afforded by the scene in a Roman butcher's shop carved on this stone panel. Even his block and cleaver would not seem out of place today.

The victory of Augustus (he was then still simply Octavius) over Antony and Cleopatra at Actium in 31 B.C. ended a period of civil wars and brought Augustus to supreme power in the Roman empire. Although he continued to respect the forms of the republic, and of civilian rule, in fact he presided over a military autocracy. There followed the greatest period in the history of the empire, two and a half centuries of administrative stability, peace and prosperity. Those were the great years of the *pax Romana*. After Trajan's victories in the east early in the 2nd century, the empire was at its greatest territorial extent.

Within little more than a century of Trajan's conquest of Dacia *c.* 105, the Goths were knocking at the gate. Natural frontiers gave way to stone walls—built along the Rhine and the Danube, even in the north of Britain, and in Syria and Egypt—to keep out invaders. It was a cosmopolitan empire in which a single currency prevailed and few barriers impeded the free flow of trade.

By the end of the 3rd century the administration of so vast an empire exceeded the powers of a single man. Diocletian divided the empire and by 330, when a new capital was established at Constantinople, its center of gravity was shifting to the eastern Mediterranean. By then the empire had already adopted Christianity as its official religion, and during the next century the Christian Church made a great advance, erecting hundreds of new places of worship and organizing its administration into dioceses. Christianity did not destroy, nor even help to destroy, the Roman empire; but it transformed it, diluting its pagan strength and undermining the traditional Roman emphasis upon public virtue and the affairs of this world with a teaching that emphasized the cultivation of private virtues and the seeking of salvation after death.

The "fall" of the Roman empire was, in fact, a long process of fragmentation, a crisis that lasted from the last quarter of the 4th century until the deposition of the last Roman emperor in the West in 476.

It was a tale partly of economic decline, marked by persistent high inflation, and high taxes to pay for the military defense of the empire. The "Barbarian" invaders, who came gradually to win more of the empire during the 5th century, believed themselves to be the Romans' successors. For two centuries many of the Barbarians had been taken into the Roman army as *foederati*, or allies, usually to defend the empire against other alien peoples. Most of them were Christians, or were soon to be converted, although commonly to the Arian heresy denounced by the Council of Nicaea in 325.

But, however they thought of themselves, they were a Germanic people, not molded by Greek culture, and agricultural, not urban. The Frankish kingdom established by Clovis in the 6th century was not a continuation of Rome, but a break from it. The true bearers of the classical heritage in the centuries that followed, of the Latinity of Rome with its ideal of universality, were, paradoxically, to be the scholar-clerics of the Christian Church.

527

Justinian Becomes Byzantine Emperor

Administrative reform is crowned by the "Corpus Juris Civilis"

As the West entered the so-called "Dark Ages," a sun rose in the East. In 527 the first great ruler of the Byzantine empire, Justinian, came to the throne. Constantinople was then the largest and richest city in civilization, a great trading center, with a flourishing silk industry. It had six arcaded forums and scores of palaces and domed churches surrounded by 12 miles of land and sea walls. And during Justinian's reign the stupendous Hagia Sophia (532-37) was added to the city's splendors, a magnificent symbol of the Eastern Church's claim to be the head of universal Christendom.

It was Justinian's ambition to reunite East and West and restore the universal empire to its former glory; that was never accomplished. Justinian's enduring achievement, along with the Hagia Sophia, was the great codification of Roman law, the *Corpus Juris Civilis* (issued in 534), which he directed the Roman jurist Tribonian to prepare. It gave legal unity to his centralized state and it bequeathed the principles of Roman law to succeeding European generations, who rediscovered them in the 12th century.

St. Scholastica, founder of the Benedictine order of nuns, was St. Benedict's twin sister. When she died, he is reported to have sent her soul to heaven, as this charming 15th-century illustrated manuscript depicts.

529

First Benedictine Monastery Founded at Monte Cassino

An Italian hermit establishes the model of Western monasticism

An epoch in the history of the Christian Church, and therefore of European civilization, began when St. Benedict founded a monastery at Monte Cassino, in southern Italy. Monasticism itself was not new; it dated from St. Anthony's retirement to the Egyptian desert to live the life of an ascetic *c.* 270. It spread to Syria and the Levant, then to southern Gaul, where monks followed the example set by St. Anthony and devoted themselves to seclusion, fasting and other forms of self-mortification.

The rule introduced by Benedict was less severe. The Benedictines, known from their habit as the "black monks," lived apart from the world, but in a community in which an individual's responsibility to his fellows was given as high an importance as the salvation of his own soul. Austerity gave way to moderation. Manual labor was combined with worship. Western monasticism, therefore, became outward-looking, whereas in the Roman empire monasteries had been retreats from the world. Benedictines led the mission to convert pagan Europe to Christianity.

The monastery building at Monte Cassino itself was sacked by the Lombards in 581—the first of many such acts which culminated in its total devastation in 1944 during the fighting between Nazi Germany and the Allies. Each time it has been painstakingly rebuilt.

554

Ostrogoths Driven from Rome

Justinian's struggle to recover the West reaches its pinnacle

Justinian's great object, the reunification of the Roman empire, was rewarded with limited success. The long wars, which for much of his reign he fought against Sassanid Persia, and the tribute he had to pay to the Persian king, Chosroes I, dissipated his resources. The wars secured Byzantium's southeastern flank, however, and enabled Justinian to send the most brilliant of his generals on missions to recover the West from the Barbarians.

Belisarius recaptured Africa from the Vandals in 533, and that tribe vanished from history, leaving no monuments behind it. Naples and Rome fell to him in 536, Milan and Ravenna in 540. A stalemate lasted for the next 14 years, until another general, Narses, drove the Ostrogoths from Rome and restored imperial authority over all of Italy. For a few years, too, Córdoba was again brought within the empire.

The achievement was great—the Mediterranean was once more a "Roman lake"—but it was short-lived. By the end of the 6th century everything that Justinian had regained was lost by Byzantium, never to be recovered.

St. Columba's monastery was destroyed in Norse raids in the 8th–10th centuries. The present cathedral is largely 15th century, as are the carved Celtic crosses of St. John (seen here) and St. Martin.

563

Columba Founds Monastery at Iona

An Irish missionary spreads the Gospel in Scotland

When Columba, one of the great saints of the 6th century, sailed for Scotland, he was following in the train of Christian "Scots" from Ireland who had already settled among communities of Picts and founded the kingdom of Dalriada in what is now Argyllshire.

Columba was by then already a notable man, a prince in the O'Donnell clan of Donegal and the founder of monastery schools in Derry, Durrow and Kells. He was an ascetic, scholarly man, and his mission to Scotland may have been simply the result of his desire to live a secluded, monastic life.

The king of the Picts gave him, and the few companions who arrived with him in 563, the island of Iona on which to found a monastery. From there they traveled in the Highlands, spreading the Gospel. So successful were they that, before Columba died in 597, the whole of northern Scotland was brought within the Christian fold, and the Columban Church had become strong enough to carry the Christian faith into England.

531–c. 547

PERSIA

● **531 Accession of Chosroes I**
Reign of the greatest Sassanid monarch saw protracted Persian–Byzantine wars and the last great period of the Persian empire. Chosroes extended Persian rule east to the Indus by capturing Bactria (560); conquered the Abyssinians of southern Arabia (576); gained part of Armenia and Caucasia from Byzantium.

BRITAIN

● **c. 547 Kingdom of Bernicia**
Founded by King Ida, with its center at the coastal fortress of Bambrugh in northeast England; with the kingdom of Deira, one of the first two Anglian kingdoms north of the Humber, spread over the lands between the Forth, the Solway and the Tees; more powerful than Deira and by the 7th century united with it to form kingdom of Northumbria.

568

Lombards Invade Italy

Germanic warriors extinguish imperial power in the peninsula

The last Barbarian invasion of Italy took place in 568. The Lombards, a German people from the lower Elbe, whom Justinian I had allowed to settle in Pannonia and Noricum (present-day Hungary and eastern Austria), burst across the Alps, capturing Milan in 569. After a siege of Pavia, which lasted for three years, they established a kingdom in the north, with Pavia as the capital.

So ravaged had Italy been by the wars in which Justinian's generals had ousted the Ostrogoths just a decade earlier that the Lombard leader, Alboin, had little difficulty in extending his control over all of northern and central Italy. His advance was also made easier by local resentment of imperial taxes and by the presence of a "fifth column" of underpaid German mercenaries.

Rome remained a papal domain, the center of what was to become known from the 8th century as the Papal States. Ravenna and much of the east coast remained in Byzantine hands. But Justinian's grand scheme of a reunited Roman empire was dealt its deathblow, though not until around 680 did Byzantium, forced to turn in on itself by the advance of the Arabs, formally recognize the kingdom of the Lombards.

581

Sui Dynasty Reunites China

Yang Chien builds an empire from the Great Wall to Annam

The demise of the later Han dynasty in 220 had ushered in 350 years of disunity in China known as the "Era of the Warring States." That era came to an end in 581, when the first emperor of the Sui dynasty, Yang Chien, usurped the throne and, with the aid of nomadic horse-mounted warriors, extended his rule throughout China, from the Great Wall in the north to Annam (present-day Vietnam) in the south. Yang Chien was succeeded by his son, Yang Kuang, who came to the throne by murdering his father.

Under these two emperors, the Great Wall was refortified and, more important, a grand system of canals was built to link the Yangtze valley to the Yellow River in the north and to Hangchow in the south. This tremendous engineering feat employed millions of laborers, many of whom were conscripted (as they were for the vast irrigation works that were also laid down in these years), and was the cause of recurrent peasant revolts. But it unified the country as mere military conquest could not have done and prepared the way for the major shift in population from the Yellow River valley to the Yangtze, the heartland of the T'ang dynasty, which followed in 618.

This Sui dynasty figurine shows a girl playing the short lute from Asia. A popular instrument in China, it often figured in poetry and literature.

590

Gregory the Great Elected Pope

A Benedictine monk lays the foundations of medieval papal power

Gregory I, a Benedictine, was the first monk to become pope. He was elected to the office at a time when Rome was cut off from the exarch of Ravenna, Byzantium's representative in the West, by the Lombard conquest of Italy. In theory, the pope was subject to the temporal authority of the emperor, but when the Lombards attacked Rome in 592, the empire did nothing to assist in its defense, which was organized by Gregory. He also negotiated the peace.

Gregory held to his belief that pope and emperor were both God's vice-regents on earth, the one supreme in spiritual matters, the other in temporal matters. Yet by governing Rome in the absence of any civilian authority, he laid the foundations of the medieval papacy's temporal power, though its formal beginning dates only from the establishment of the Papal States by Pepin's "donation" of Ravenna "to St. Peter" in 756.

In a final break with the classical past, Gregory also fully accepted the permanent existence of Barbarian Europe and made it his mission to rid it of paganism and Arianism. He did not speak Greek and seems not to have felt the need to. He directed his view toward Europe rather than Constantinople, and so ensured that European Christianity would be tied to Rome, not to the East.

S. GREGORIVS I. MAGNVS PONT. LXV.
ANNO DOMINI DXC.

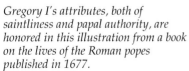

Gregory I's attributes, both of saintliness and papal authority, are honored in this illustration from a book on the lives of the Roman popes published in 1677.

597

Augustine Begins Christian Mission in England

The first Archbishop of Canterbury is consecrated

In 596 Pope Gregory the Great commissioned Augustine, a Benedictine monk, to undertake the conversion of "the land of Angles" to Christianity. Augustine and 40 fellow missionaries landed in Kent the next year and were warmly welcomed by Ethelbert, king of Kent, who, with the aristocracy, embraced Christianity at once.

Ethelbert, the first Anglo-Saxon king to be converted to the Roman faith, resolved to make Canterbury, his capital, into a great Christian center. A church and monastery were built on the site of the present cathedral, and Augustine was appointed Archbishop of Canterbury, an office he filled until his death in 604. Bishoprics were also founded at Rochester and London.

There were now two Christian Churches in England. The older Celtic Church—more severe in its monastic rule than the moderate Benedictine Church of Rome, keeping a different date for Easter, and conferring greater power on abbots than on bishops—resisted Augustine's mission. Paganism was also slow to be eradicated.

Edwin, king of Northumbria, was converted by Paulinus in 627; the first West Saxon bishopric was founded at Dorchester in 635; and Sussex was converted by Wilfrid in 681. But when Bede died in 735, parts of the country were still untouched by Christianity.

615

Sassanids Sack Jerusalem

The relic of the True Cross is carried off to Ctesiphon

The Roman empire's failure to recover the West in the 6th century, and the virtual abandonment of that great project after Justinian's death in 565, left it an Eastern power. Greek replaced Latin as the official language, and the Eastern Church diverged more and more from Rome.

Byzantium's great enemy, before the rise of Islam in the mid-7th century, was Sassanid Persia, a highly centralized, prosperous state with a magnificent capital at Ctesiphon, on the Tigris River. In the first quarter of the 7th century the 1,000-year struggle between the Greeks and the Persians came to its climax in the last "world war" of antiquity.

In 615 the armies of the Persian king, Chosroes II, overran the Levant and plundered the cities of Syria, carrying off with them to Ctesiphon Jerusalem's most priceless treasure, the relic of the True Cross. A year later they conquered Egypt. By 620 the Sassanid empire stretched from Cyrenaica to Afghanistan. The glorious days of Darius seemed to have returned.

But Persia's latter heyday was short-lived. So was the Byzantine revival. Emperor Heraclius swept through Assyria and Mesopotamia from 622 to 628, provoking a Persian mutiny which led to the murder of Chosroes in 628. He captured the True Cross, taking it to Hagia Sophia in Constantinople, and finally crushed Persia at Nineveh. In 651 the last of the Sassanid kings was murdered. But Hellenism had also had its last hour in the Levant. The heirs to the region were the Muslim Arabs.

618

T'ang Dynasty Founded in China

Li Yuan overthrows the Sui

In 615 the last Sui emperor of China suffered a military defeat at the hands of Li Yuan, supported by Turkish allies, and three years later he was assassinated. The T'ang dynasty ruled China for the next 300 years, making its capital at Ch'ang-an, the luxurious, cosmopolitan city at the end of the Silk Road in the western province of Shensi.

The T'ang reaped the benefit of the canal network and the administrative order created by the Sui. For 150 years the arts and sciences flourished in a liberal culture that permitted the practice of every religion—Buddhism, Zoroastrianism and Christianity—which foreign merchant-traders brought with them. Sculpture, especially of horses, and literature flourished.

Horses, such as this caparisoned mount with his armored rider, were a favorite subject of sculptors during the period of T'ang rule.

In the first half of the 8th century China came to exercise sway over Korea, Manchuria, Mongolia and Tibet. But defeat by the Arabs in western Turkestan (751), followed by a long and costly peasant revolt (755-63), marked the beginning of its decline.

In the 9th century both printing and gunpowder were developed, though by then central rule from Ch'ang-an had virtually collapsed, especially in the south. The dynasty held on until 907, when its demise ushered in half a century of disorder until the advent of the Sung dynasty in 960.

622

Mohammed Makes His Flight to Medina

The Muslim era begins

Mohammed spent his first 40 years as a successful trader in Mecca and was a member of that city's leading tribe, the Quraysh. In 610, while he was sleeping in a cave north of the city, the archangel Gabriel appeared to him in a vision. Mohammed awoke with the conviction that it was his duty to preach the existence of one God, called Allah, to the Arab people, whose polytheistic religion was marked by the existence of many local cults.

For the remainder of his life Mohammed wrote down in short verses the divine illuminations he received from Allah. They were collected after his death into the Koran, which became by far the most important element of Arabic culture, not only because of its divine truth but because it crystallized the Arabic language. Mecca, for centuries a place of pilgrimage because of the Ka'aba, a shrine containing a sacred black meteoric stone which Islam was to absorb into its worship, was unreceptive to the new religion, and the Quraysh persecuted Mohammed and his followers.

In 622, preceded by about 200 disciples who prepared the way, Mohammed made his *hegira*, or "flight," to Yathrib, 280 miles to the northeast. There the new religion made rapid headway. The city changed its name to Medina, which means "city of the prophet," and the Islamic calendar took the year 622 as its starting point.

The plan of the holy city of Mecca, on glazed tiles with a decorative border, shows the great mosque whose courtyard encloses the huge black Ka'aba and the sacred well, Zamzam.

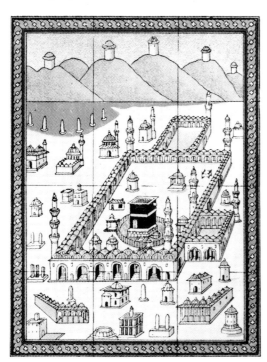

637

Arab Armies Overrun Persia

Ctesiphon falls and Islam begins to build an empire

The unification of the tribes of Arabia after Mohammed's flight to Medina was extremely rapid. In 633, the year following the prophet's death, Arab armies, ardent in the Islamic faith, set out on a trail of conquest that was to alter the course of history and redraw the map of the Mediterranean and Middle Eastern worlds. Byzantine Syria was invaded in 633, and Emperor Heraclius, astonished by the sudden emergence of a new challenge, sent an army to defend Damascus. That army was defeated at the Battle of Ajnadayn, in southern Palestine, in 634. Damascus fell to the Arabs in 636, Jerusalem in 638.

This was a great turning point in history: the Arabs had torn from the empire those eastern provinces from which for centuries it had drawn economic and technical sustenance. It was the end of a 1,000-year-old world. Europe was thrown back upon itself, to enter the "Dark Ages."

Islamic armies had, meanwhile, advanced into Mesopotomia to attack a Persian state already tottering from its defeats a few years earlier at the hands of Byzantium. Outnumbered and outarmed, for they had no siege equipment, the undisciplined Arab tribesmen, mounted on camels and horses, used their only method of warfare—repeated javelin assaults to break the enemy's formations, followed by hand-to-hand combat—to capture the capital, Ctesiphon, in 637. Five years later an Arab victory at Nehawand, in the Zagros mountains of modern Iran, brought Sassanid rule to an end.

661

Umayyad Caliphate Founded

A coup establishes the governor of Syria as head of the Arab world

Mohammed was succeeded in 632 as head of the Muslim community by Abu Bakr, one of the band of the prophet's close disciples and the father of his young wife, Aisha. He was called *Khalifat rasul-Allah*, "successor to the apostle of God"; hence the term "caliph" for the ruler of Islam. Abu Bakr was succeeded on his death in 634 by Omar, who led the Arabs to victory in Syria and Persia. But when Omar was assassinated in 644, having nominated no successor, a council went beyond Mohammed's immediate family and selected Othman as the new caliph.

Othman was a member of the wealthy Umayyad family of Mecca and his election opened up a rift in the Muslim community, or *umma*. Othman was killed in a revolt in 656, and the succession was disputed between Mu-Awiyah, the Umayyad governor of Syria, and Ali, a son-in-law of the prophet. For a few years there were two rival caliphs, until, after indecisive fighting between the two camps, Ali was assassinated in 661, and his son, after a brief attempt to maintain himself as caliph at Kufa, yielded to Mu-Awiyah.

Thus was founded the Umayyad caliphate, an aristocratic dynasty, ruling from Damascus, which lasted until 750. But there were many who did not accept the Umayyad right to the office and who continued to assert the claim of Ali's descendants as the true caliphs. They became known as the *shi'a*, or "partisans" of Ali, while their opponents were called the *sunnis*, the people of the *sunna*, or "the custom."

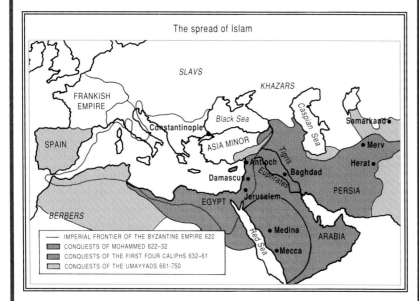

The spread of Islam

SLAVS
KHAZARS
FRANKISH EMPIRE
Black Sea
Constantinople
Caspian Sea
Samarkand
SPAIN
ASIA MINOR
Merv
Antioch
Tigris
Baghdad
Herat
Damascus
Euphrates
Jerusalem
PERSIA
EGYPT
BERBERS
Red Sea
Medina
ARABIA
Mecca

IMPERIAL FRONTIER OF THE BYZANTINE EMPIRE 622
CONQUESTS OF MOHAMMED 622–32
CONQUESTS OF THE FIRST FOUR CALIPHS 632–61
CONQUESTS OF THE UMAYYADS 661-750

664

Synod of Whitby Secures Roman Faith in Britain

Celtic Christians accept the authority of the pope

While the Roman Church was establishing itself in southern England in the 7th century, the older Celtic Church, begun in Ireland and taken to Scotland by Columba, was working itself into Northumbria. In 663 Oswry, the king of Northumbria, summoned the leaders of both Churches to Streoneshalh (Whitby) to resolve their differences.

The synod took place in 664. The main question was the dating of Easter, though behind it lay the larger issue of the administrative role of bishops and hence of the overall authority of the Archbishop of Canterbury. In the Celtic Church bishops were assigned a curative function only; administration was the office of the abbots. But at Whitby victory went to the Roman Church, whose chief advocate at the synod was Wilfrid, abbot of Ripon in Yorkshire.

Wilfrid maintained that it was folly to resist the authority of St. Peter, to whom the keys of heaven had been granted, in favor of St. Columba and so remain outside the universal body of European Christendom. His argument won over King Oswry and brought the whole of the English Church (apart from a small number of dissidents who returned unreformed to Iona and Ireland) over to Rome. The monks of Iona were persuaded by King Egbert to accept the Roman Easter in 716, and the Welsh Church submitted to the authority of Rome in 768.

678

Muslim Blockade of Constantinople Defeated

Armed truce ushers in temporary peace between Byzantium and the Arabs

Early Arab successes against the Byzantine empire in Syria and the Persian empire in Mesopotamia were followed in 643 by the capture of Alexandria and the ending of Greek rule in Egypt. Within little more than a decade, the Arabs had also forced Byzantium out of north Africa, Cyprus and Armenia. With the Bulgars pressing from the other direction, the Eastern empire appeared to be doomed.

In 673 the Arabs launched an assault on Constantinople, a difficult military target since its great walls were impregnable by all but the heaviest of siege weapons and the imperial navy could prevent a sea landing. For five years the Arabs kept up a blockade of the city without being able to storm it. "Greek fire"—the secret weapon of the imperial fleet, which was a combination of petroleum, sulfur and pitch, shot from copper tubes—drove them back. The Arab advance, which had seemed irresistible over the previous 40 years, had suffered a temporary check.

710

Nara Period Opens in Japan

Buddhism and Chinese cultural forms take hold in Japan

The brilliant achievements of the T'ang dynasty in China, with its empire stretching from the Yellow Sea to the Caspian, gave rise to a desire in Japan to copy all things Chinese. During the 7th century Buddhism was widely adopted, though it lived alongside, rather than supplanted, the ancient religion of Shintoism. And the defeat of the Soga clan in 645 by Fujiwara Kamatari, which began the long period of Fujiwara power behind the throne, led to a systematic replication, which was not entirely successful, of the Confucian administrative system of China.

By the "Taika Reforms" of 646, central control of rice growing, central taxation, and a network of imperial officials throughout the land were established. Then, in 706, by imperial decree, a new city was ordered to be built at Nara to rival the Chinese metropolis of Ch'ang-an. It became the first permanent capital of Japan in 710 and remained the imperial court until 794. In that short period of time it witnessed a great architectural flowering, especially of Buddhist temples, of which the most outstanding was Todai-ji, with a 52-foot-high sculpture of Buddha that remains one of the largest bronze figures in the world.

The largest wooden building in Japan, the present temple of Todai-ji dates from 1709.

711

Berbers Cross the Strait of Gibraltar

Muslims overthrow the Visigothic kingdom in Spain

In its beginnings the Islamic state was an Arab confederation. The Koran sanctioned the conversion of non-Arabs to Islam, but these converts were classified as clients, or *mawali*, of their conquering masters. Such were the Berbers of north Africa, whom it took the Arabs a century to subdue. In the end, however, the process was more complete than anything the Phoenicians or Romans had achieved—partly because of the cultural similarities between two warlike, nomadic peoples and partly because of the unifying power of Islam.

By 700 the great Arab-Berber cities of Kairouan in Tunisia and Fez in Morocco had been founded. But since there were only a few hundred thousand Arabs, they were a minority in the lands they had conquered and they needed extra manpower for their armies. So they recruited *mawali*, among them the Berbers, who were eager for the booty of war to which they would be entitled.

In 711 the Berbers, led by Tariq, a former slave, landed at Gibraltar (Jebel Tariq, or "rock of Tariq") with 7,000 men and defeated Roderic, the Visigoth king of Spain. Oppressed sections of the population, especially the Jews, welcomed the Moors as liberators, and by 714 the whole of Spain and Portugal, except for the small northeastern kingdom of Asturias, was in the hands of the Arabs.

716

Ethelbald Becomes King of Mercia

The first true overlord makes his appearance in England

The Anglo-Saxon word for a king who had superiority over other kings was *bretwalda*. Such kings, Ethelbert of Kent, for example, first appeared during the 6th century, but they were essentially warrior-chieftains of mobile tribal confederations. The first English kingdom to attempt what the Franks were achieving in Merovingian Gaul, the imposition of a continuous overlordship, not simply roving military expeditions, was Mercia.

Mercia was landlocked and rich in resources of lead, salt, wool and hides. It needed access to continental trade and it needed to protect its resources; therefore, it needed continuity of control. From the reign of Ethelbald onward, Mercian rulers began to organize a labor force and to tie an army to the land in a way never before attempted in Saxon England. Even Church lands were made subject to common duties such as bridge building and military service. In this way the Mercians acquired a distinct sense of territory, of a realm.

Anglo-Saxon kingdoms

716

Byzantium Recognizes Bulgarian Independence

The first Slav kingdom arises in the Balkans

The Slavic peoples first made their appearance about 2000 B.C. in the east Carpathian mountains, whence they spread slowly eastward into what became Russia. From the beginning of the 5th century A.D. they began to migrate into the Balkans, where they settled as an agricultural people. Between them and the Aegean lived the Bulgars, a non-Slavic people descended from tribes left behind by the Huns.

During the 7th century the Bulgars were gradually assimilated, by marriage and cultural influences, into the Slavic community, and the Bulgarian empire, or Great Moravia, established by Khan Asparukh in 681 may be considered the first Slavic state. Its independence was recognized by Byzantium in 716. It remained an alien power with no cultural ties with the Greek world until 865, when the Prince of Bulgaria was baptized into the Christian faith, a momentous occasion which began the process of bringing the Slavs within the orbit of European Christendom and detaching them from Asia.

718

Muslim Siege of Constantinople Fails

Arab expansion is halted at the Bosporus

In 717, Leo III, a provincial official who had successfully resisted Arab assaults on Anatolia, became emperor in Constantinople. He was the first of the Isaurian dynasty and the ruler who, by pushing back Arab frontiers, began the "Isaurian recovery" of the empire's fortunes.

Throughout the winter of 717-18 the Arabs laid siege, for the second time, to Constantinople. They were again driven back, and a permanent line was drawn against Muslim advance to the north until the fall of the city to the Ottoman Turks in 1453. But failure did not stop the Arabs from returning, time and time again, to the attack, and the persistent challenge wrought a profound change in the structure of the empire.

The Persian system of mounted horsemen—cataphracts, the Greeks called them—had already been adopted; now, also in the Persian manner, the empire was organized increasingly on military lines. The military and civil power were united and then sustained by territorial, hereditary landlords with horsemen in their service. Byzantium, like Gaul under the Arab threat a few years later, developed an embryonic form of feudalism.

Persian horsemen were renowned for their skill in the saddle, whether in war or the hunt, as depicted on this 8th-century silver dish.

730

Imperial Edict Bans Worship of Images

Iconoclasm widens the gulf between East and West

The depiction of saints, the Virgin Mary, even of Christ himself, as a means of encouraging devotion became prominent in the Eastern Church in the 6th century. But the practice gradually aroused opposition among some Christians, who believed that man-made icons came to be worshipped for themselves. In the early 8th century the iconoclasts argued that victories by the Arabs over the empire were God's punishment of the Greeks for their idolatry.

Iconoclasm suggested an Asiatic denial of Hellenic humanism, for Islam prohibited the representation of the human figure. In 730 Emperor Leo III published an edict which banned the use of images in public worship on the ground that material forms could not express spiritual realities. The edict was confirmed by the emperor, Constantine V, and a council of bishops in 754.

Iconoclasm tended to pit the bishops against the monks and to exalt Constantinople's central authority: icons depicting local saints were replaced by more universal symbols, especially the Cross. But its greatest effect was to drive deeper the wedge between East and West. The emperor's claim to legislate in spiritual matters was an affront to the papacy, which denounced the iconoclast synod of 754. In the East the public worship of icons, never as popular in the West, was restored in 843 on the first Sunday in Lent, a day ever since celebrated as a feast of the Orthodox Church.

732

Charles Martel Defeats the Muslims at Poitiers

Islam fails to make inroads into northern Europe

In 720, only six years after they had conquered Spain, the Arabs crossed the Pyrenees, took Narbonne and sacked the monasteries of southern Gaul. Their progress took them as far as the banks of the Loire, 1,000 miles from Gibraltar, and they were only halted at the Battle of Poitiers by Charles Martel (or Charles the Hammer), the "mayor of the palace" in Frankish Austrasia and the grandfather of Charlemagne.

The Arab assault on northern Europe was repulsed, never to be taken up again. Charles Martel's victory also marked his ascendancy over the duke of Aquitaine and began his reconquest of the south of Gaul for the Merovingians and their successors, the Carolingians, the dynasty which took his name.

Poitiers was a turning point in other ways, too. Charles Martel, like Emperor Leo III, understood that only the Persian system of raising great warrior-horsemen could hold off mobile invaders like the Arabs. To maintain such horsemen, the prototypes of the knightly class, was expensive, and Charles confiscated a great deal of Church property and endowed his horsed warriors with land so they could afford it. For this he may be regarded as the founder of that system of tying land ownership to the fulfilment of military obligations which in time became known as feudalism.

THE STIRRUP REVOLUTION

The adoption of stirrups, lances and body armor enabled mounted knights to become the shock troops of their age, capable of mounting a rapid and ferocious attack on the enemy.

The simple device of the stirrup, probably invented in China in the 4th century, was introduced into western Europe *c.* 700 and at once gave rise to the supremacy of the mounted knight in warfare and hence in society. By giving him a firm foothold, the stirrup enabled a horseman to fight at a gallop without restraint. He could wield his sword without fear of being unseated by an air shot and could put the full weight of himself (heavily armored) and his mount behind his charges. Consequently the 8th-century Frankish cavalry was a far superior force to the Persian and Byzantine cavalries of the previous century. Mounted knights were too expensive ever to be more than a small element of a feudal host, but their strength and mobility made them the decisive factor in most battles.

750

Abbasids Assume Rule of Arab World

A cannibal banquet celebrates the triumph of Abu-al-Abbas

From its inception in 661 the *sunni* Umayyad caliphate, though it ruled with some success, faced great difficulties. Chief among these were the continuing opposition of the *shi'ites*; feuding among Arab tribes which eroded the régime's military strength; and local resentments of central authority. The caliphs had also to contend with an aggrieved *mawali* class (non-Arab converts to Islam), who looked enviously upon the privileges granted to Arabs, and the financial crisis that mounted as more and more people were converted to Islam, for believers were not taxed. In these circumstances, the *shi'ites* made headway, above all in the east.

The Abbasid movement, which took its name from al-Abbas, one of Mohammed's uncles, raised its black banners of revolt in eastern Persia in the 720s. The rebel movement spread westward, and in 749 a new caliph, Abu-al-Abbas, was proclaimed at Kufa, in Iraq. His name meant "shedder of blood." In 750 he murdered the last Umayyad caliph, Marwan II. The males of the defeated dynasty were invited to a banquet, murdered, and served up to their hosts.

So began the Abbasid caliphate which, in recognition of its support in the east, moved the Arab capital from Damascus to Baghdad, where it ruled until its demise in 1258.

756

Umayyads Take Power in Spain

Spain passes out of Baghdad's control

In 755 an Umayyad prince, Abdul Rahman, who had managed to escape the massacre of his family in Damascus in 750, arrived in Spain. Within a year he had established himself at Córdoba as ruler of the province, protected by an imperial guard of Berbers and European slaves. Though he called himself *emir*, or governor, and the caliphate of Córdoba was not proclaimed until the 10th century, Spain was, from his accession, practically independent of Baghdad.

Under the Umayyads, Spain was for four centuries the most civilized, prosperous, and artistically creative part of Europe. Córdoba alone, by the 10th century, had 70 libraries, 700 mosques and 900 public baths. The caliphate was also notably tolerant; Jews and Christians were not persecuted and they formed thriving urban communities.

One of the finest surviving examples of Arab architecture is the mosque, now a cathedral, at Córdoba.

785

Charlemagne Conquers Saxony

Thousands of Saxons are deported to make way for Frankish colonists

Pepin the Short, the founder of the Carolingian dynasty, died in 768, leaving his kingdom to be divided between his two sons, Carloman and Charles. When Carloman died three years later, Charles, known to history as Charlemagne, or Charles the Great, was recognized as sole king of the Franks.

At once he began to build an empire, crossing the Alps in 773 and proclaiming himself king of the Lombards. His great ambition was to unite all Gaul under his rule and, in the process, to convert to Christianity the Saxons, a warlike people still attached to their ancient gods, and the Avars, who had settled on the middle Danube. Year after year, Charlemagne raided Saxon lands, and year after year his garrisons were overwhelmed as soon as he departed. In retaliation, he resorted to the decapitation of the Saxon chieftains and the deportation of thousands of their tribesmen to the west to make room for the Frankish colonization of eastern Gaul.

By 785 the Saxons had been subdued. In 788 Charlemagne seized Bavaria, and by 796 he had driven the Avars almost into extinction. When the 9th century opened, he ruled a realm which stretched from the Elbe to the Pyrenees and from the North Sea to central Italy, larger than anything in the West since the decline of Rome.

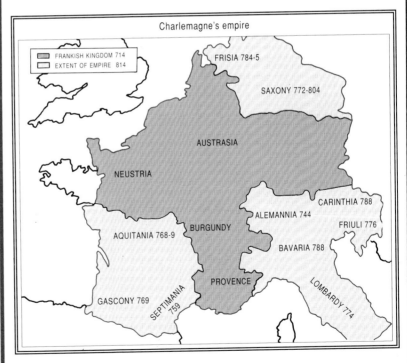

Charlemagne's empire

FRANKISH KINGDOM 714
EXTENT OF EMPIRE 814

FRISIA 784-5
SAXONY 772-804
AUSTRASIA
NEUSTRIA
CARINTHIA 788
ALEMANNIA 744
FRIULI 776
AQUITANIA 768-9
BURGUNDY
BAVARIA 788
GASCONY 769
SEPTIMANIA 759
PROVENCE
LOMBARDY 774

793

Vikings Sack the Monastery of Lindisfarne

Two centuries of Norse raids on Christian Europe begin

England suffered the first recorded Viking raid on Europe in 793, when Norsemen from Scandinavia beached their longships on Holy Island, off the coast of Northumbria. They sacked the monastery of Lindisfarne, founded in 615 by St. Aidan, a missionary from the Hebridean island of Iona, stocked their ships with cattle, carried off precious metals and departed. The burned-out monastery recovered and survived until 875. Bede's monastery at Jarrow was attacked in 794, Iona in 795.

The Vikings remained raiders of the east coast of England until 851, when they wintered on the Isle of Thanet in Kent, by which time they had also penetrated deep into Gaul. Seville was stormed in 844 and Pisa in 859. One of their leaders, Rurik, took Novgorod *c.* 862 and founded Kievan Rus. As pirate-traders they plundered everywhere they went, collecting furs, timber and slaves (chiefly Slavs, hence the word "slave") to be delivered by Jews to Byzantium and the Arab empire in exchange for gold.

Until the Christianization of Scandinavia in the 11th century and the rise of strong European states, rulers such as Charles the Bald of France and Alfred the Great of England contained the Norsemen by the payment of tribute and recognition of their principalities. Nevertheless, they profited from the Arabian gold—"unhappy gold," as it was called—for its price was eunuch-slaves.

794

Heian Period Opens in Japan

The powerful Fujiwara clan gains ascendancy over the imperial court

The Heian era of Japanese history ran from 794, when the capital was moved from Nara to Heian-kyo (later Kyoto), until 1185. The real rulers of Japan in this period were not the emperors but the Fujiwara family, who infiltrated the imperial court by marriage and intrigue and governed first as regents (*sessho*) and then, if an emperor did not abdicate on reaching his maturity, as civil dictators (*kampaku*).

This system began in 857, when Fujiwara Yoshifusa became grand minister and made his grandson child-emperor with himself as regent, although the the Fujiwara had come to exercise effective power long before then.

The Heian period was one of increased isolation: Chinese and Korean influences receded as contacts with neighboring countries diminished. New phonetic characters were introduced to supplement the Chinese script, and an indigenous, delicate style of painting emerged, most notably in the scrolled illustrations to the *Tale of the Genjii*. And a distinctly Japanese architecture, less ornate than the Chinese, reached its peak in the conversion (*c.* 1050) of the Phoenix Hall, a nobleman's palace near the capital, into a temple.

Carved from wood, with the arms made separately, this 40-in.-high statue of "The Immovable King of Light" dates from the 1100s, the late Heian period. The god's fierce expression shows his intolerance of evil, which he uses his sword to punish, at the same time cutting through the world's wickedness to reveal its ultimate reality.

c. 800

Ghana rises to Prominence

An African empire prospers on the trans-Saharan trading route

Of the black kingdoms that emerged in Sudanese, or sub-Saharan, Africa before 1000 there is little record beyond what is contained in the writings of Arab traders and travelers. The greatest of these kingdoms, surpassing Kanem, which lay northeast of Lake Chad, was almost certainly Ghana, with its center 500 miles northwest of the modern boundary.

By 800 Ghana was the most powerful empire in west Africa. Its prosperity derived from trade in slaves, salt and gold, which were carried across the desert on camels. The trade was a monopoly of the king, or *ghana* ("warlord"), who was also called *kaya maghan* ("master of the gold").

Although for three centuries after the Muslim conquest of the north the Sudanese empires were left alone, Ghana's wealth made it famous and eventually attracted invaders. Raids by the Almoravid Berbers in the 11th century fatally weakened the empire, and *c.* 1230 a people from Takrur, in modern Senegal, seized the capital and destroyed the kingdom.

800

Charlemagne Crowned Roman Emperor

Pope Leo III anoints the king of the Franks

Charlemagne went to Rome in 800 to help Pope Leo III, who was under a cloud because of his alleged adultery and perjury, put down a revolt. His position secured, Leo anointed Charlemagne (apparently much to his surprise) on Christmas Day at St. Peter's and crowned him as "Carolus Augustus, Emperor of the Romans." The pope then knelt and paid him homage, as the bishops of Rome had formerly done to the emperors at Constantinople.

The Islamic world welcomed the elevation of the king of the Franks as a blow to Byzantium. Harun al-Rashid, the caliph of Baghdad, even sent gifts to the opulent court at Aachen, which Charlemagne had made a brilliant intellectual and Christian center under the English cleric and scholar, Alcuin.

The re-creation of the Roman Empire in the West was, however, more symbolic than real, for Charlemagne's empire was later divided among his grandsons. But the coronation, which took place when the controversy over iconoclasm was still in men's minds, emphasized the division between Rome and Constantinople, since there were now rival emperors. It marked a decisive rejection of the East by the papacy, which began to stress its political as well as ecclesiastical authority, and it gave an impetus to the nascent idea of a separate European identity.

In 812, two years before the death of Charlemagne, Byzantium reluctantly recognized the title, and Charlemagne, in return, renounced his claims to Istria, Venice and Dalmatia.

Ancient Ghanaian metal-working skills were not lost, as this later Ashante ceremonial helmet of antelope skin, decorated with gold, shows.

756–c. 796

CHINA

● **756 Rebellion in Ch'ang-an**
Uprising in the Chinese city, the capital of the T'ang dynasty, at the end of the Silk Road; most cosmopolitan city in the world and probably the most luxurious; in 754 had opened a National Academy of Letters nine centuries before any similar institution in Europe; disruption began its terminal decline.

GAUL

● **756 Donation of Pepin**
Grant of Ravenna to the papacy by the Frankish king after he defeated the Lombards (756) in return for Pope Stephen's anointing Pepin king at St. Denis in 751; origin of the Papal States and of the temporal authority of the pope, with lands to rule like any other secular ruler.

● ***c.* 771 Battle of Roncesvalles**
Engagement in Charlemagne's war with the Muslims in Spain; count Roland was killed during the action and the incident was celebrated in the epic *chanson de geste*, the *Song of Roland*, in which the virtues of Christian knighthood are extolled.

ENGLAND

● ***c.* 796 Offa's Dyke**
Massive entrenchment against the Welsh, built by Offa, King of Mercia, completed *c.* 796; ran from the Dee Estuary to the Wye River along the border of Mercia; testament to the power of 8th-century Mercia ●

THE SPREAD OF ISLAM

The Alhambra at Granada in Spain is one of the few medieval Islamic palaces to have survived. Its simple exterior is offset by the dazzlingly ornate decoration of the interior, especially the Hall of the Two Sisters.

Ever since the rapid expansion of Islam in the generation after Mohammed's flight to Medina in 622, there has been a strong and persistent impulse to create a united Arab/Islamic world. Its most recent expression was the short-lived (1958-61) union of Egypt and Syria in the United Arab Republic. From the beginning the Islamic world was torn by dissensions, yet from the 7th century up to the beginning of the 20th, the Arab story has been one of empire.

The term "Arab" was first used only for the nomadic inhabitants of the central and northern desert of present-day Saudi Arabia. Gradually, after the 6th century, the word came to include all those people brought under the sway of the caliph—the successor to the prophet—from the borders of Turkey and Armenia to the far reaches of north Africa. The earliest Arab empire was built by the Umayyad caliphs, who ruled from Damascus in Syria from 644 until 750. It was they who built navies to rival the seapower of Byzantium, and, after conquering Egypt and the Berbers of north Africa (who then conquered Spain), founded great cities such as Fez in Morocco and Kairouan in Tunisia. They thus laid the foundations of the Arab Mediterranean empire. Apart from Spain, the only European land brought under Arab sway was Sicily, in the late 9th century.

The Arabs did little more than collect taxes from the peoples they overran. They scarcely attempted to convert non-Arabs to Islam—indeed, in the early days it was considered impossible for a non-Arab to be a Muslim. But both their language and their religion came gradually to be adopted by large numbers of their subjects. And Islam was carried by the Umayyads as far as Samarkand and the Punjab.

The successors to the Umayyads, the Abbasid dynasty, which ruled from Baghdad (with a brief interruption in the mid-9th century) from 750 to 1258, presided over the most brilliant era in Arab history. By the 11th century Arabic was the vernacular from Persia to Spain. Before then the great works of Greek scholarship had been translated into Arabic, and Arabic art, architecture and learning had made the culture of Spain the most sophisticated as well as the richest in the Western world. But the Abassid empire was never a unified administrative whole. Independent caliphates arose, most powerfully in Spain and Egypt. The Crusades, too, weakened the dynasty, in decline long before Baghdad fell to the Mongols in 1258 and the Mamluks of Turkish descent asserted their rule over Egypt and Syria in 1260.

The Abassids were the last Arab rulers of an Islamic empire. In time imperial sway passed to the Seljuk, and then the Ottoman, Turks, who conquered Syria, Egypt and Arabia, extended their dominion over Mesopotamia and the Balkans and finally destroyed the Byzantine empire. Under the Ottomans the offices of sultan and caliph were merged. Muslims divide the world into two categories the "domain of Islam" (*dar al-Islam*) and the "domain of war" (*dar al-harb*), and the Ottoman empire was regarded by its non-Turkish subjects as the true *dar al-Islam*. Yet it was not until the 18th century, when the era of Ottoman expansion had passed, that the sultans called themselves caliphs.

The 16th-century miniature, top, shows the first court of the Topkapi Palace in Constantinople, which contained a mint, an arsenal, barracks for the palace guards and the church of St. Irene. The lower painting depicts Mohammed at the Battle of Uhud. His men could find no water, so the prophet held out his hand, and water flowed from his fingers.

c. 820

Al-Khwarizmi Gives Algebra to the World

A mathematician epitomizes the Arabic scientific achievement

During the Dark Ages, Islamic civilization kept ancient science alive; the Arabs were not so much creative inventors, but rather preservers and developers. Their scientific culture, which was at its height in the 9th and 10th centuries, passed on to the West the Indian decimal system and the Arabic numerals still in use today. From them, too, came the notion of zero (from the Arabic *sifr*, Latinized as *ziphirum*, whence "cypher" and "zero"), without which modern mathematics is impossible.

The greatest Arabic mathematician was Al-Khwarizmi of Baghdad, whose astronomical tables were a genuine advance on Greek cosmology. And his treatises on Hindu mathematics gave algebra to the West, although the credit for its invention belongs to the Indians Arya-Bhata and Brahmagupta.

FROM TOWN TO COUNTRY
Roman civilization was quintessentially urban, its empire a confederation of planned cities linked by roads. For food it depended on Africa and, in the East, Anatolia. At one blow the Arabs, by imposing themselves between Europe and the East in the 7th century, ended that civilization. There is meaning to the phrase "Dark Ages." Europe became a rural backwater, a primitive agricultural society. The towns and roads built by the Romans fell into disuse and crumbled into ruins. Gold, silks and spices disappeared from Europe, as did the Syrian traders who had brought them there. Commerce gave way to the rural self-sufficiency that was to be the economic support of feudalism.

843

Treaty of Verdun Breaks up Carolingian Empire

The Frankish kingdom is divided into east and west

Charlemagne's empire, already weakened by economic decline, was divided by his son and successor, Louis the Pious, who made his eldest son, Lothar, co-emperor in 817 and allotted frontier kingdoms to two younger sons, Pepin and Louis the German.

In 823 Louis's second wife bore him a fourth son, known to history as Charles the Bald, and her determination to secure him a part of the imperial inheritance led to a generation of civil wars. They came to an end at the Battle of Fontenoy in 841, with the victory over Lothar of Charles and Louis the German, who had leagued themselves by the Strasburg Oaths (significantly, sworn in French and German, not in Latin).

By the Treaty of Verdun in 843 the Carolingian empire was divided into three parts: Lothar, with the title of emperor, was given a long central territory running from the North Sea to Rome, called Lotharingia; Charles was granted the lands to the west; Louis those to the east. The arrangement did not survive Lothar's death in 969, after which date his domain was absorbed, partly by what was to become France and Germany and partly by the kingdom of Burgundy in the south.

868

China Makes the First Printed Book

The "Diamond Sutra" inaugurates a communications revolution

Nearly six hundred years before Gutenberg "invented" movable type in Germany, China under the T'ang dynasty produced the world's first printed book, the *Diamond Sutra*. It was made from wood blocks and contained both script and illustrations. Movable type, engraved on clay blocks, appeared in China in the 11th century.

The spread of books that followed had little impact on the mass of the population, who remained largely illiterate until the late 20th century. But printing greatly facilitated the consolidation of central authority by the mandarin bureaucracy, and, especially under the Sung dynasty which succeeded the T'ang, gave impetus to commercial expansion by the circulation of paper money (introduced in China *c.* 650) and credit notes.

In the same era, China invented gunpowder and the mariner's compass; these, with printing, were the three inventions which, according to Francis Bacon, "changed the whole face and state of things throughout the world." For centuries, however, the Chinese used gunpowder only for firework displays and the compass not at all.

869

Slave Revolt Rocks Islam

A rising of Zanj slaves in Iraq spreads to Persia

The Roman empire exploited slaves for heavy manual labor; the Islamic empire used them chiefly as domestic servants and soldiers. But there were exceptions. In the middle of the 9th century thousands of Zanj, or Negro, slaves were imported from east Africa to reclaim the marshes of southern Iraq for cultivation and to extract salt for sale. They rose in revolt in 869, and black troops of the Abbasid caliphate, sent to quell the disturbances, joined the revolt in numbers.

Racial conflicts were at work in the Islamic empire. So were religious and political ones. Only a few years earlier a peasant rising, led by Babak, who preached the breakup of the great estates and a landowning peasantry, had won a series of remarkable victories over the imperial army before being subdued.

The Zanj rebellion was initially even more successful. It spread into southern Persia; the town of Basra was taken and Baghdad itself threatened. Not until 14 years had passed were the Zanj overcome and their leader, Ali, executed.

At the very time that the *shi'a* Ismaili movement (the forerunner of the Fatimids) was gaining converts with a radical message appealing to women and to the materially dispossessed, the Zanj revolt, though ultimately defeated, was a sign of the strains that were undermining, and were eventually to destroy, the unity of the Arab empire.

c. 875

Vikings Discover Iceland

An accidental landing is followed by rapid settlement

The origins of the discovery and settlement of Iceland are obscure. Irish monks almost certainly visited it before the 9th century, but they did not remain there long. It was sometime between *c.* 850 and *c.* 875 that Viking seamen, probably sailing from northwest Scotland, landed accidentally on its shores and began the permanent settlement of the empty and inhospitable island.

Immigrants arrived in great numbers from Norway, where Harold Fairhair, usually considered to be Norway's first king, had asserted his rule over the western part of the country. Whether because his defeated rivals and their followers sought refuge from the domination of their new overlord, or because Harold promoted overseas exploration, his reign (872- *c.* 933) was notable for the rapid settlement of Iceland.

Viking colonization of remote islands, such as the Orkneys, the Shetlands and the Faroes, was a frequent and somewhat eccentric activity. Nowhere was it as successful as in Iceland. By 930, the year in which the general assembly, called the Althing, first met, there were perhaps 10,000 Icelanders established as farmers and fishermen. Christianity was introduced *c.* 1000 by Olaf I of Norway, but it was many years before paganism was eradicated.

A typical long ship had a high stern, a high prow adorned with an animal carving, and striped square sails; it carried a crew of around 90 men.

878

Alfred Recognizes the Danelaw

A treaty acknowledges Danish rule in northern England

The extensive Danish, or Viking, settlement of England began in 865, when the greatest host that any European ruler had had to face for several centuries invaded England. The Danes settled in Northumbria, East Anglia and eastern Mercia. As a result, they lost their great advantage of mobility and, being outnumbered by the English, were defeated by the West Saxon forces of Alfred the Great at the Battle of Edington in 878, so preserving Wessex for the English.

A treaty divided England into two parts: what became known as the Danelaw (because Danish law prevailed there) ran east of the ancient Roman road, called Watling Street, from Durham through the east Midlands to London; the English retained control of the west and south. Alfred's successors reconquered most of the Danelaw, but renewed Danish attacks in the 10th century forced King Ethelred to levy a tax, called the Danegeld, to pay off the enemy in tribute.

The Danelaw

CHIEF DANISH TOWNS

● York
● Lincoln
Derby ● ● Nottingham
Leicester ● ● Stamford

888

Chola Dynasty Replaces Pallavas in Southern India

An ancient Tamil power re-emerges on the Coromandel coast

The Chola line, an ancient Tamil dynasty from India's southeastern coast, had lain in obscurity for centuries when it rose again late in the 9th century to overthrow the Pallavas, who had created a united kingdom in the south. Continuity was thus preserved in the south, while the north, after the high achievements of the Gupta era, fragmented into small states and was subject to Muslim raids from central Asia.

The peak of Chola rule came in the reigns of Rajaraja I (*r*985-1014) and Rajendra I (*r*1014-42), when Ceylon was added to the empire, Bengal invaded and for a while occupied, and a naval expedition sent to colonize (unsuccessfully) Malaya, Burma and Sumatra. In the political stability and economic prosperity that the Cholas brought to the Coromandel coast, Hinduism blossomed. The great temple, the Brahadeswara, a masterpiece of the Dravidian style, was built at the capital, Tanjore (now Thandjavur), in the 11th century.

Strange sculptured columns in the form of warriors stand guard near one of the pyramids at Tula which is crowned with a temple to the hero-god Quetzalcoatl.

c. 900

Toltecs Gain Ascendancy in Mexico

The fall of Teotihuacán paves the way for the "master-builders"

The successors to the Mayans as the dominant culture in central America were the Toltecs, a warrior aristocracy from highland Mexico. Little is known of their early history, but they came to dominate the valley of Mexico after the decline of Teotihuacán *c.* 900. By 1000 they had expanded southward and overwhelmed the Mayan culture of the Yucatan peninsula.

The Toltecs' name, which in Nahuatl means "master-builders," derives from their sophisticated understanding of smelting metal and building in stone. The latter is evident from archaeological remains in their chief city, Tollan (now Tula), where the ceremonial quarter included pyramids and a court in which the sacred ball game, tlatchli, was played.

The Toltecs were polytheistic sun-worshippers, whose rites included human sacrifice. Nomadic tribes from the northern extremity of the valley of Mexico, who were known collectively as the Chichimec people, destroyed Tollan in the 13th century, ending Toltec ascendancy and opening the way for the rise to supremacy of the Aztecs.

910

Burgundian Abbey Founded at Cluny

A new era of reform begins in the Roman Church

The reform movement that began to invigorate the Roman Church in the 10th century had its roots in the renewal of monasticism and the founding of new monastic houses in northern Europe. Of these, the most illustrious was founded by Berno at Cluny in Burgundy, in 910, with a great abbey church surpassed in the West only by St. Peter's in Rome. The monastery was, from its origins, free of lay supervision (unlike many houses founded by local magnates) and, after 1016, was free from control by bishops also.

The Cluniac monks followed a modified Benedictine rule, but whereas each Benedictine monastery was a single entity, the new order was a highly disciplined organization. The 1,000 houses that were founded in the two centuries after 900 were all obedient to the rule of the abbot at Cluny, where future monks were trained before entering their own monasteries. Many of them later became bishops and carried Benedictine ideals into the Church.

More important, by staunchly supporting the popes in their struggles with secular rulers in the great "investiture controversy" of the 11th century, the monks helped the papacy to extend its influence from its narrow Italian base. They also provided the impetus for that reform and standardization of ecclesiastical discipline which, commencing with Pope Leo IX (r1049–54), brought a spiritual renewal and a greater homogeneity to the Roman Church.

The abbey church at Cluny, once the largest in the world, was destroyed during the French Revolution.

955

Otto I Checks Magyars at Lechfeld

German arms contain the Magyars within Hungary

The Magyars were a Finno-Turkic tribe of nomads who, in the mid-5th century, began to migrate from the Urals to the northern Caucasus. There they remained until the 9th century, when they were pushed westward into modern Romania by the Pechengs, a tribe of mounted warriors from the Mongolian steppes. By 900 the Magyars had been driven by the Bulgars to settle in the middle Danube basin (modern Hungary), where, by their destructive incursions, they presented a threat to the eastern Franks, or Germans.

In 955 the king of the Germans was Otto I, a man of great ambition. By bringing Lotharingia, the central Carolingian kingdom, within his control, and subduing rebellions in his own kingdom by appealing to east-Frankish unity against the raiding Magyars, he brought an end to the anarchy that had prevailed in central Europe since the Treaty of Verdun (843) and laid the foundations of modern Germany. The victory over the Magyars at Lechfeld in 955 crowned this achievement, and earned Otto the title of "the Great." It also restricted—permanently as it later turned out—the Magyars to Hungary.

960

Sung Dynasty Brings Peace to China

Confucianism triumphs over Buddhism and Taoism

The "Period of the Five Dynasties" in China, the name given to the years of confusion after the fall of the T'ang dynasty in 907, came to an end when the congeries of rival states was brought together under Emperor Chao K'uang-yin, the founder of the Sung dynasty. A general during the brief later Chou dynasty, he usurped the throne in 960 and by the time of his death in 979 had reunited China from the Great Wall to Hainan Island. In doing so he greatly diminished the power of local warlords by bringing their armies under centralized control, a reorganization which laid the basis for 300 years of Sung rule.

The Sung era was notable for completing the Confucian hold on government that had begun with the introduction of competitive examinations for the civil service under the T'ang. It was also famous for the excellence of its ceramics, which restored pottery making to the heights achieved in the Han period, and its landscape painting, which the Chinese believe has not since been surpassed. The period saw, too, a great expansion in the cultivation of tea and rice to feed a rapidly growing population.

In 1126 the Jurchen (later known as the Manchu) gained control of the Yellow River valley, and the Sung retreated to central and south China, which they ruled from Hangchow until the Mongol conquest of 1279.

962

Otto the Great Crowned Emperor

A historic ceremony in Rome gives birth to the Holy Roman Empire

Although Charlemagne's coronation in 800 may be said to have contained the seed of later developments, his empire was so short-lived that it is customary to date the institution of the Holy Roman Empire to the coronation of Otto the Great by Pope John XII in 962. The name itself was not used until the 12th century.

Otto, who had been the German king since 936, had added Lombardy to his realm in 951 and, just before his coronation, had helped the pope to defeat an attempt by Berengar to seize, not for the first time, the throne of Italy. The imperial title was his reward. An enduring link was thus forged between Italy and Germany. During the existence of the Holy Roman Empire, the title remained a monopoly of successive German dynasties.

THE "GERMAN" PLOW

Europe's rising population in the 10th century was supported by an expansion of agriculture. This was largely the result of the replacement of the old Middle Eastern scratch plow (a sharp spike drawn by two oxen back and forth across a square plot, suitable only for light soils) by the bigger "German" plow, able to work the heavy soil of northern Europe. It consisted of a plowshare to dig into the earth and a moldboard to turn the sod sideways and form ridges and furrows for drainage. Set on wheels and drawn by a team of oxen, it was too expensive for individual small farmers and it worked best on long strips of land. It thus contributed to the rise of medieval northern Europe's characteristic strip-farming based on communal ownership of land and equipment.

969

Fatimids Found an Independent Caliphate in Egypt

A shi'ite breakaway delivers a blow to Arab unity

In the 10th century, the Abbasid caliphate at Baghdad suffered the first crumblings of its Arab empire at the hands of a *shi'ite* faction known as the Fatimids. Their origin lay in the mid-9th century, when a reform movement of Ismailis (named after Ismail, a descendant of the prophet Mohammed) traveled throughout the empire preaching the return of Ismail's son, also Mohammed, as the true Messiah, or *mahdi*, and calling for greater social and economic equality.

The Ismailis gained the adherence of oppressed groups in the empire. In 901 they also won over the emir of Yemen and in 908 they installed their own Imam Ubaydallah in Tunisia as an independent caliph of a rival dynasty to the Abbasids. That dynasty became known as the Fatimids, after the prophet's daughter, Fatima.

The Fatimids conquered Egypt in 969 and set up an independent caliphate in Cairo in 973. There they built the mosque of al-Azhar and established it as a great institution of learning. Cairo transformed itself from an outpost of Islam into one of its intellectual and spiritual centers. The Cairo caliphate, which expanded into Sicily, Syria and western Arabia in the 11th century, came to outshine Baghdad, but Norman and Crusader depredations in the 12th century hastened its decline. The last Fatimid caliph died in 1171.

980

Vladimir Takes Power in Kievan Rus

A Viking warlord brings Russia within the Greek Church

By the start of the 10th century two Norse, or Varangian, principalities had been established in the Slavic lands of western Eurasia: one in Novgorod (founded by Rurik in 862) and one in Kiev (perhaps founded earlier). Russian history is traditionally regarded as beginning with their foundation. Straddling the great river route from the Baltic to the Black Sea and thence to Byzantium, the states grew rich on the trade in slaves, fur and timber.

In 980, after a series of dynastic quarrels, they were united under Prince Vladimir, a Viking warlord who still adhered to paganism, although there had been a Christian church in Kiev since 882. Cut off from Islam by the central Asian empire of the Khazars, Russia was poised between East and West when, in a decision of profound significance for the future of Russia and Europe, Vladimir was baptized into the Greek Orthodox Church c. 986. A metropolitan see, subordinate to Constantinople, was soon established in Kiev.

Vladimir, grand duke of Kiev, is portrayed splendidly robed and with a saintly halo on this ancient banner.

987

Hugh Capet Becomes King of France

Modern France has its origins in a fragile monarchy centered on Paris

While England and Germany were taking the first steps toward some kind of national unity in the 10th century, France had disintegrated after the great days of the Carolingian empire into a number of duchies, none of which was able to assert superiority over the others. The throne, dwindled to a titular office, passed to and fro between Carolingians and descendants of Robert the Strong, count of Anjou.

When the last Carolingian died in 987, the duke of Paris, Hugh Capet, was elected king, though the dukes of Normandy and Burgundy and the counts of Flanders and Champagne were richer, with vaster holdings of land, than he. In theory they became his vassals. But Hugh's writ did not run beyond his own small domain, a strip of land running from Compiègne to Orléans and including Paris, nor did he attempt to extend his authority.

Little is known of Hugh beyond that he retained the support of the Church and maintained his dignity in relations with pope and emperor. His achievement was to pass on his domain and crown to his son unopposed, so making the Capetian monarchy hereditary and giving France an advantage over Germany, where the crown remained elective. In short, he established the French monarchy, with its capital at Paris. The Capetians ruled France, in an unbroken succession of 14 kings, up to 1328.

1001

Stephen of Hungary Crowned

The "apostle of Hungary" receives his crown from the pope

Between Kievan Rus and the emerging Ottonian kingdom of Germany stood forests and grasslands, peopled by nomads who were of various Slavic and Asiatic provenances. The region lay for centuries scarcely touched by urban growth and uncivilized by politics, law or the Church. Perhaps because of pressure from Germans to the west and Vikings to the north, the tribes who roamed these lands east of the Elbe began to form communities; by 1000 the Magyars of Hungary, the Bohemians and the Poles had each become united under a single ruler.

Christianity also made headway, first in Bohemia, whose first king, St. Wenceslaus (r 907-29), was reared in the faith. The rulers of Poland and Hungary followed where King Wenceslaus led. Boleslav the Mighty, duke of Poland, (r 992-1025) established the Polish national church and, with the aid of Emperor Otto III, succeeded in freeing it from German supervision. In 1000 Gneizno became the first capital and was made a metropolitan see. Just before his death in 1025, Boleslav was crowned the first king of Poland, the most powerful kingdom in eastern Europe, with Russia as a vassal state.

Hungary received recognition in 1001, when Stephen, the duke of Hungary, was sent a crown by Pope Sylvester II, an act symbolic of the birth of national states in eastern Europe.

1010

Holy Sepulcher Destroyed

Fatimids pull down the Church of the Holy Sepulcher in Jerusalem

Islam was, from its origins, a faith which laid great stress on the toleration of other religions by its adherents. Throughout the Arab empire the "people of the book," the Jews and Christians, or *dhimmis*, whose early prophets were also those of Islam, were, on the whole, well treated. Though they were not equal with Muslims before the law (they had to pay taxes from which the Muslims were exempt), they did enjoy religious freedom.

The Fatimid caliph at Cairo, Hakim (r 996-1021), broke with this tradition. He initiated a campaign of persecution against both Jews and Christians throughout his north African empire and those other parts of the Arab world— Palestine and parts of Syria and western Arabia—gained by the great general, Jauhr, in the years after the Fatimid conquest of Egypt. Hakim hindered Christians from making pilgrimages to Jerusalem, which had been under Muslim control since 637, and in 1010 destroyed the Church of the Holy Sepulcher itself, an outrage which helped to swell the anti-Islamic sentiment that was to lead to the Crusades.

1014

Danes Defeated at Clontarf

Brian Boru extinguishes the Viking threat to Ireland

Danish power in Ireland reached its zenith in the middle of the 10th century, when the counties of Dublin, Wicklow, Meath and Munster all lay under the Norse yoke, ruled by kings of the line of Ivar. It began to decline when Brian Boru and Malachy overthrew Ivar's forces in Tipperary in 968. Brian ruled as king of Munster from 976, while in the north Malachy, after defeating the Danes at Tara in 980, emerged supreme.

In 998 the two leaders divided Ireland between them, but jealousies soon broke the pact, and in 1002 Brian challenged Malachy to a battle at Tara. Malachy was unable to rally the northern princes and Brian, without a struggle, became high king of all Ireland. He was now able to fulfill his last task: to expel the Danes from Ireland.

This he accomplished on Good Friday, 1014, at the Battle of Clontarf, on the high ground outside Dublin. In the course of the battle, although he was then aged nearly 75 and too old to fight, Brian was slain in his tent. He had ended the Viking presence in Ireland, rebuilt churches and founded others, restored learning, and given Munster a predominance that might, in time, have led to a real monarchy in Ireland.

1014

Basil II Annexes Bulgaria

The "slayer of Bulgars" ends a Balkan challenge to the empire

The recovery of Byzantium under the Isaurian emperors began with the pushing back of Arab frontiers in the 8th century. It continued with the recapture of Cyprus, Crete and Antioch in the 10th century, and reached its culmination in the 11th with the annexation of Bulgaria. In 865 Boris I, the ruler of Bulgaria, had accepted Christianity, and Constantinople had recognized the independence of the Bulgarian Church.

Boris's son, Simeon I (*r*893-927), took the title of tsar. But in the years after his death, Bulgaria was weakened by the growth of a religious sect called the Bogomils, who preached a modified Manichaean heresy and combined it with a strongly anti-Slav, anti-Byzantine nationalism.

These internal dissensions encouraged the empire to strike at the Bulgars, and in 1014 they were overwhelmed by the armies of Emperor Basil II, who gained thereby the name Bulgaroktonos, "slayer of Bulgars." After his victory, Basil blinded 15,000 Bulgar prisoners and sent them home *pour encourager les autres*. Within a few years Bulgaria was made a Byzantine province, although it was never fully absorbed, and a second Bulgarian empire rose under Ivan I in 1186. The annexation of Bulgaria and of Armenia in the middle of the century were the last conquests of the Byzantine empire.

Cnut and his wife, Aelgyfu, appear in the "Liber Vitae" of Hyde Abbey, Winchester (1031), bestowing a cross on the abbey's altar.

1016

Cnut Becomes King of England

The Danish king receives homage from the Saxon kingdoms

A second spasm of Viking raids on England, conducted by the Danes in the late 10th century, ended with the enthronement of Cnut, the pagan Danish king, as king of all England in 1016. War between the English and the Danes was in progress when the English king, Ethelred the Unready, died in April 1016.

His son and successor, Edmund Ironside, concluded a truce with Cnut, and they divided the kingdom between them. Edmund, however, died a few months later, in November, and the Danish king was accepted as sole ruler by all the English kingdoms. Cnut thus became the first king to hold sway over the whole of England, which for a short time became a part of the Scandinavian empire.

Cnut was soon converted to Christianity (he made a pilgrimage to Rome in 1027), and he ruled England well, notably in the codifying of the law, which he prepared with Wulfstan, the Archbishop of Canterbury. After his death in 1035 the English throne became a matter of contest among Cnut's successors on the Danish throne, Ethelred's descendants, and the Normans, who emerged the victors in 1066.

991–1042

ENGLAND

● **991 Battle of Maldon**
Fought between the Viking, Olaf Tryggvasson, later king of Norway, and Brihtnoth, *ealdorman* (royal military officer) of Essex; Brihtnoth refused to buy peace with gold and was killed in action; defeat was followed by the first payment of the Danegeld by Ethelred II.

● **1042 Accession of Edward the Confessor**
Last Saxon king of England, ruled until 1066; under Norman protection from 1013 to 1042, he promoted Normans in Church and state and granted English property to Norman monasteries; thus paved the way for the invasion of 1066.

GERMANY

● **1024 Salian Dynasty**
Founded by Conrad II, who succeeded Henry II as German king and Holy Roman Emperor (1027). At a time of high papal authority, Conrad took imperial power to its height; ruled Germany, Burgundy and Italy and saw himself as the ruler of the city of Rome.

1018

Council of Pavia Imposes Church Discipline

Benedict VIII enforces celibacy on the clergy

For the Roman Church during the dark years through which Europe passed in the 9th and 10th centuries, lay control of the Church was a disaster. Learning and culture were the preserve of the clergy, as they were not in the East, while benefices were at the disposal of illiterate local magnates. So the demand for spiritual and moral reform of the Church, which arose from both monks and secular clergy in the 11th century, became entangled in temporal politics, leading eventually to the great "investiture contest" waged between pope and emperor.

One of the first successes of the reform movement came at Pavia in 1018. Celibacy had long been a characteristic form of Christian asceticism and in the West had been habitual among the parish clergy since the 3rd century. It remained voluntary, but the papacy grew increasingly opposed to clerical marriage, which fell into disrepute, and by the early Middle Ages the chief laxities were concubinage and violations of the vow of chastity. To put an end to this situation, Benedict summoned a council in Pavia in 1018 and decreed that the clergy of the Roman Church must be both celibate and chaste.

1031

Caliphate of Córdoba Collapses

Muslim Spain fragments into small, independent states

The *sunni* Muslim leaders of Spain realized their ambitions in 929 when, in the face of the Fatimid threat across the Mediterranean, they recognized the Umayyad emir Abd ar-Rahman as caliph in his own right, thus establishing the independent caliphate of Córdoba. At its height the caliphate threatened the Christian kingdoms in the north, Asturias, Navarre and Castile (so named because of the number of castles that Alfonso II built there in the late 9th century to defend his realm against Muslim incursions).

But unity among the old semi-autonomous regions was difficult to maintain, and civil wars from the beginning of the 11th century dismembered the caliphate. Córdoba was sacked, and many of its finest buildings were destroyed in 1013. In 1031 the caliphate was dissolved, and Muslim Spain fragmented into about 30 small states, each controlled by a *taifa*, or local ruler. The way was thus opened up for the Christian reconquest of the peninsula.

1054

Church Schism Sealed by Leo IX

Eastern churches in Italy are closed for "unorthodox" practices

In 1054, the last year of Pope Leo IX's short pontificate (he was elected only in 1049), the schism between the Roman and Eastern Churches, which had been growing apart from each other for centuries, became formal. Leo was the first great reforming pope, working with Hildebrand (later Pope Gregory VII) to root out corruption among the Roman clergy and establish a more uniform ritual and ecclesiastical discipline throughout the West.

In 1054 Leo closed Eastern churches in southern Italy to worship on the ground that they indulged in "unorthodox practices." The rites of the two branches of the Church had long since taken divergent paths (the Eastern Church used unleavened bread at the Eucharist, for example), and the veneration of the Virgin Mary in the East had kept alive the iconoclastic quarrel that had erupted in the 8th century.

Behind those quarrels, however, lay the deeper antagonism fed by the papacy's increasing temporal power and its unwillingness to submit to the authority of the emperor or the patriarch in Constantinople. The patriarch, Michael Cerularis, attacked Pope Leo in 1053, and a year later Leo retaliated by excommunicating him and all of those in his communion. The Eastern churches were thus banned in Italy.

CHESS

Chess came to Europe from the Arabs in the 10th century and underwent some modifications, if not in the rules, then in the pieces. Since Islam allowed no representation of the female in art, the Muslim version of the game had no queen, which was introduced in Europe to replace the grand vizier. The European bishop took the place of the Muslim elephant. The Asian tradition of making pieces of elaborately carved ivory and precious stones was continued, and the board itself was often of crystal or precious metals. Strangely, the game—along with the keeping of ferrets and hawks, dice-playing and leaping and singing—was banned at some Oxford colleges in the 13th century as "noxious, inordinate and unhonest."

1054

Almoravids Invade Morocco

The Berbers establish an empire in the Maghrib

For three centuries after the Arab conquest of north Africa the Berbers of the western Sahara remained quiescent, trading peaceably with their neighbors. Their adoption of Islam was slow but profound, and by the 11th century had progressed so far that a tribal confederation, called the Sanhaja Tuareg, was ready for the puritanical message of the *shi'ite* revivalist Ibn Yasin. Ibn Yasin arrived among the Sanhaja Tuareg before the middle of the century and set up an island retreat, or *ribat* (hence Almoravid, from *al-murabitun*, "people of the *ribat*"), where he trained his disciples to spread the gospel of social equality.

Inflamed by his message, the Berbers conquered and pillaged to north and south. In 1054 they invaded Morocco, where they established a new city, Marrakesh, as their capital in 1062. By 1069 they had overrun the whole of Morocco and within a few years had wrested the entire Maghrib (supra-Saharan Morocco, Tunisia and Algeria) from Fatimid control. Their empire lasted until 1147, when the head of the Almohads, a rival tribe which rose to prominence in reaction to Almoravid rule, was installed in Marrakesh as the lord of all Morocco, with the title of caliph.

1066

Normans Win Battle of Hastings

King Harold falls to William the Conqueror

Three weeks after defeating Harald Haardraade, the Norwegian king, at Stamford Bridge in Yorkshire, King Harold of England sent his forces, exhausted after a 250-mile march south, into battle against the invading Normans led by Duke William. The Normans, or Norsemen, who had settled in northwestern France in the 10th century and adopted Christianity, had long coveted England. They were the preeminent European warriors of the late 11th century, having introduced the use of couched lances and adapted the stirrup and saddle to make their mounted knights into superb instruments of war.

At the Battle of Hastings, near the south coast of England, the heavily armored Norman cavalry defeated an English army which fought on foot. King Harold was killed in the battle, and while the Saxon thanes quarreled over the succession, William advanced to capture Dover, Canterbury and Winchester, where the royal treasure was kept. After the surrender of Winchester, the thanes and Church leaders met William at Little Berkhampstead and swore fealty to him. He was crowned William I of England at Westminster Abbey on Christmas Day, 1066.

King Harold is usually thought to be the man pulling an arrow from his eye, but he is more likely to be the one slain by a sword, for when the Bayeux tapestry was made, the dead were always shown prostrate.

THE BYZANTINE EMPIRE

The glass mosaics at Ravenna are the finest expression of Byzantine art in the West. The shimmering mosaic of the Three Kings is one of the scenes from the New Testament, dating from the time of the Ostrogoth king, Theodoric (493-526), that cover the walls of the church of Sant'Apollinare. Byzantine craftsmen perfected a method of glazing over the top of gold leaf and setting the tesserae at a sharp angle to catch the maximum amount of light.

The Roman empire in the East became known as the Byzantine empire after the ancient Thracian town of Byzantium. On its site the emperor Constantine founded his capital and began to build a new city in 330. The imperial split into East and West was made permanent in 395, when Theodosius died. Honorius became emperor in the West and Arcadius in the East. The Western empire was overrun by the Barbarians, but in the East the Visigoths and Ostrogoths were repelled and the empire endured until 1453.

That empire was a brilliant mixture of Greek and Roman traditions, married to the Christian religion. Every emperor was crowned by the patriarch of Constantinople. He was both secular autocrat and God's representative on earth, and the empire, despite the ultimate failure of Justinian to recover the West in the 6th century, never abandoned its theoretical claim to universal jurisdiction. The emperor had never to contend with a supreme ecclesiastical power like the papacy in the West. The long conflict between Church and state, which played so crucial a role in developing the institutions of western Europe, had no parallel in the East. The imperial court at Constantinople remained the fountainhead of all power.

The Orthodox religion of the East increasingly diverged from the Roman faith, just as Greek became the official language of the empire, thus marking it off from the Latin West. The divergence expressed itself in relatively small ways (the Orthodox Church allowed priests to

Justinian's vast church of Hagia Sophia in Constantinople, started in 532 and completed just five years later, is one of Christianity's great monuments. It was converted to a mosque after the capture of the city by the Ottoman Turks in 1453.

marry) and also in large ones (the Monophysite controversy and the dispute over iconoclasm, which finally divided the Church for good in the 11th century). It had great consequences for eastern Europe, which was Christianized from Constantinople, not Rome.

The Middle East and north Africa were wrested from the empire in the 7th century by the Persians and the Muslim Arabs and were never regained. Thereafter the core of Byzantium was the Balkan peninsula and Asia Minor (present-day Turkey). The years from the mid-9th to the mid-11th centuries saw a revival—the borders of Islam were pushed back to the Euphrates, and Cyprus and Crete were retaken. Constantinople grew wealthy as the natural junction of the world's great trading routes, and art and learning flourished. Extensive redecoration of churches, begun in the late 9th century, produced the brilliantly colored flowering of Byzantine mosaic art during the Comnenian dynasty (1081-1185).

But the end was near. The victory of the Seljuk Turks over the empire at Manzikert in 1071 entailed the loss of Asia Minor. In the Balkans the Serbs and Bulgars regained their independence. Then followed a great blow to the empire's pride. In 1204 Crusaders attacked Constantinople and established Latin kingdoms on the eastern shore of the Mediterranean. By the 14th century the empire was little more than Constantinople itself. With the fall of the city in 1453, it came to its formal end.

During the reign of Constantine, above, Christianity was tolerated in the empire, but it was only in 380 under Theodosius I, whose portrait, top, appears in his missal, that it became the state religion.

69

1069

Northern Revolt Crushed in England

William the Conqueror consolidates his rule

The Norman hold on England was tested in 1069 when a northern uprising developed into a general war. Trouble began when Robert of Comines, a Norman placed by William the Conqueror as earl over Northumbria beyond the Tees, was burned to death in Durham. His death was a signal for Yorkshire to rise in revolt. In preparation for such an event, William had built a network of castles in the north and Midlands; York castle itself fell to the insurgents, assisted by reinforcements from Denmark, and that success incited the English of Mercia and west Wessex to rebel.

William persuaded the Danes to retire by offering them a bribe and then, in the winter of 1069-70, set about the devastation of the most fertile and most populous parts of Yorkshire. Livestock was slaughtered; food stores were burned; farm implements were destroyed. Norman troops then crossed the Pennines and laid waste much of northwestern Mercia. Oddly, the two leaders of the revolt, Cospatric, the former earl of Northumberland, and Waltheof of Huntingdon were left in power, the former beyond the Tees, the latter in the east midlands.

Earl Morcar made a last stand at Ely, assisted by Danes (until William bought them off) and Hereward the Wake. Danish persistence might have brought the rebels victory; as it was, William swiftly broke their resistance, blocked escape routes with ships, and forced the surrender of all but a few of the rebels (Hereward escaped). The last great national rising against the Norman invaders was over.

1071

Byzantine Army Routed at Manzikert

The Seljuks capture the emperor and gain control of Asia Minor

In 1071 a new enemy from the east struck Constantinople a lethal blow. The Seljuk Turks, *sunni* Muslims since the 8th century and recruited as mercenaries by the Abbasids, had crossed the Oxus into Khorasan in 1034, attacked the outlying Byzantine province of Armenia in 1049 and captured Baghdad in 1055. Their ascendancy in Syria was crowned by the capture of Jerusalem from the Fatimid caliphate in 1070.

Thus began that gradual Turkish infiltration and transformation of the Islamic empire which, though Seljuk power itself waned in less than a century, was to reach its apogee under the Ottomans.

In 1071 the Byzantine emperor, Romanus Diogenes, marched against the Seljuk sultan, Alp Arslan, and in the Armenian town of Manzikert, Byzantium suffered one of the worst defeats in its history. The Seljuks then overran Asia Minor, an occupation with profound historical consequences.

By reducing Byzantium to a small area around Constantinople, the Seljuk occupation signaled the fact that real power within Christendom now lay in the West. (The Normans had already seized Apulia in 1042 and by 1071 expelled the Greeks from Bari, their last foothold in Italy.) And by giving Islam a domain in the old Roman empire—the sultanate established in Asia Minor was known as the sultanate of Rum, or Rome—it contributed to the crusading fever now mounting in the West.

1075

Papacy Bans Lay Investiture

The election of bishops by temporal rulers is outlawed

A ban issued by Pope Gregory VII in 1075 on the nomination, or investiture, of bishops and abbots in the Roman Church by secular landlords and rulers, or lay patrons, brought the "investiture contest" to a head. The double claim of the papacy, that in all spiritual matters the clergy was superior to the laity and that in temporal affairs the papacy was a monarchy, were novel.

In the days of Western empire there had been no suggestion that the clergy was not answerable to lay magistrates, even in matters spiritual. Nor was the Roman Church originally a monarchy: the bishop of Rome was one among many, and Rome was no greater a see than others such as Antioch, Alexandria and Hippo. But the Muslims had swept them away and, though the primacy of the Eastern emperor was officially acknowledged, Rome had grown in self-esteem.

Gregory's ban, which came in the midst of a flurry of reform in the Church against corruption and the taint of worldly ties, sought to secure for the clergy, under the authority of the papacy, control of an independent, monarchical Church. This ambition was a challenge to the Eastern emperor, who continued to follow the old system and was denounced by Rome as a schismatic. More important, it was a challenge to the European kings, who believed that they had inherited the authority of the vanished Roman emperors.

1077

Henry IV Humbled at Canossa

The Holy Roman Emperor gives in to Pope Gregory VII

Gregory VII's ban on the lay investiture of abbots and bishops aroused great opposition in Germany. Here the Carolingian tradition of royal control of the Church persisted, and the pope had made enemies by excommunicating a number of Emperor Henry IV's officers for obtaining their positions by simony, or purchase.

Gregory summoned Henry to appear before him in Rome to answer charges of misconduct. Henry's reply was to convene, in 1076, a synod of the German clergy, which "deposed" the pope. The pope then excommunicated Henry and released the subjects of the Holy Roman Empire from obedience to him, with the result that the German princes declared that they would desert him unless he obtained absolution.

Henry crossed the Alps in January 1077 and (according to tradition) waited for three days in the snow-covered courtyard of Gregory's castle in Canossa, in northern Italy, for an audience with the pope. He pleaded for forgiveness and was absolved. The papacy seemed to have triumphed over the empire.

But Gregory had overreached himself in claiming for the papacy (explicitly in the *Dictatus Papae* of 1075) the right to remove rulers whom it deemed unworthy. In 1080, when Henry was fighting for his throne against the rebel duke of Swabia, Gregory again excommunicated him. Henry carried the war into Italy, occupying Rome in 1084, driving Gregory into exile (where he soon died) and installing Clement VII as antipope.

Henry's humiliation in Canossa soon passed into legend, which later artists embroidered to include his wife and child as well as a triumphant pope.

1084

Carthusian Order Founded at the Grande Chartreuse

St. Bruno founds an eremetical monasticism

In 1084 a German scholar, Bruno, retired with six companions to the Alps of southeastern France, near Grenoble. There he founded a new monastic order, known as the Carthusians after the monastery he built there, La Grande Chartreuse. Amid the reforming, outward-looking monasticisim of the early Middle Ages, dominated by the rule of St. Benedict and active in the ferment that later produced the Crusades, the austerely ascetic, eremetical rule established by Bruno was an anomaly.

The Carthusian life was almost entirely meditative. Each monk lived alone, in a private cell with a garden, and, except for communal worship three times a day, was rarely in contact with his fellow monks. It remained a very small order.

HERESY

Christian heresies may always have been intellectual in origin and in their outward expression. But they were usually manifestations of social or national dissent also, and authorities were right to take them seriously. Conquered societies often adopted heresies as a mark of their separate identity or as a way of refusing to be absorbed into an imperial culture. The Barbarians, for instance, all adopted the heretical Arian form of Christianity. So, too, in the Arab empire, the defeated Persians adopted the heretical *shi'a*, not the orthodox *sunni*, form of Islam. Even within an apparently single culture the same forces were sometimes at work. Albigensianism flourished in Provence, of all the Gallic provinces the most proud of its own language and the most determined to resist absorption by the French monarchy.

1085

Alfonso VI Captures Toledo

The reconquest of Spain from the Muslims begins

When Ferdinand the Great died in 1065, he bequeathed his Christian kingdom of Castile and León to his two sons; Sancho was given Castile, and Alfonso was given León. War between the brothers ended with Sancho's death in 1072, and Alfonso inherited Castile.

As Alfonso VI of the reunited kingdom, he embarked on a campaign of conquest. He seized Rioja and the Basque provinces in 1072 and in 1077 assumed the title "Emperor of all Spain." He then turned his attention to Muslim Toledo, a vassal state which paid him tribute, and, after a long siege, captured it in 1085. This was a conquest of great significance, restoring to Christian Spain an important historical and cultural center that had been in Muslim hands since the 8th century.

Although the Almoravids responded to Muslim appeals for aid and inflicted a series of defeats on Alfonso after 1086, Toledo was never retaken. The year 1085 is, therefore, accounted the start of the *reconquista*—the Christian reconquest—of Muslim Spain.

1086

Domesday Book Compiled

The Normans undertake the first "census" in England

In 1085 William the Conqueror appointed investigators to carry out a great national survey of the property of England so that he could gather the greatest possible income from the land tax. The commissioners visited the whole country, except for London and those areas of the north (Durham, Northumberland, Cumberland, Westmorland, and parts of Lancashire) the Normans had not yet conquered.

The commissioners recorded every landholding from the greatest estate down to the poorest hide (60-120 acres, the smallest division of land owned by freeholders), together with the names of its past and present owners. They also recorded the extent and value of the land and livestock and any additional assets such as mills or ponds. Much of the information in the Domesday Book came also from pre-conquest taxation lists and court records.

The book was compiled in 1086 in two volumes, Little Domesday (covering Norfolk, Suffolk and Essex) and Great Domesday (covering the rest of the country). The name may derive from the *Domus Dei* in Winchester Cathedral, where the books were first deposited, or it may be merely a corruption of "Doomsday," meaning the Day of Judgment.

The Domesday Book provides, too, a pictorial record of everyday life in 1086. Here peasants till a field with a "German" plow, while behind them another man broadcasts seed from a pouch slung at his side.

1094

Valencia Falls to El Cid

The banished Castilian hero becomes the ruler of the kingdom

The legendary El Cid (from the Spanish Arabic *as-sid*, or "lord") was a Castilian whose real name was Rodrigo Diaz de Vivar. He was the greatest military leader of 11th-century Spain, an age when the Christian population was beginning to push forward its frontiers. A shortage of manpower encouraged the relaxation of social bonds, and military heroes could be made almost overnight.

El Cid made his name first in the service of Sancho, who from 1065 until 1072 disputed the control of Castile and León with his brother, Alfonso VI. He was banished from Castile in 1081 for having led an unauthorized raid on Alfonso's client Muslim state, Toledo, and entered the service of the Muslim rulers of Saragossa. By winning victory after victory, against both Christian and Muslim opponents, he gained a reputation as the general who never lost a battle.

Alfonso's attempts at reconciliation, after the conquest of Toledo in 1085 was followed by Almoravid invasions, failed. El Cid followed his own star. In 1094 he conquered Valencia and ruled it as his independent kingdom (though in the name of Alfonso) until his death in 1099. But El Cid's achievement was transient. The Almoravids recovered Valencia in 1102 and retained it until 1238.

1095

Council of Clermont Calls for a Crusade

Pope Urban II sanctions a "holy war" to recover Jerusalem

When Byzantium found itself hemmed in by the Seljuk Turks, Emperor Alexius appealed to the West for aid. He found a ready ear in Pope Urban II, who seized the opportunity to score a triumph over the East by asserting papal protectorship over the Holy Lands. Urban summoned a council in Clermont in France, at which he exhorted the knights of Europe to rescue Asia Minor from the Turks and to recover Jerusalem for Christendom.

Itinerant preachers, such as Peter the Hermit and Walter the Penniless, spread the call throughout Europe with such resounding success that the First Crusade, which no king came forward to lead, was called the "People's Crusade." Allied to the religious motive was the opportunity for the nobility of an expanding feudal Europe to vent its aggression (the Normans coveted both Syria and Palestine) and for Italian ports, especially Venice, to extend their commercial markets.

The first excursions were marred by the slaughter of Jews in towns along the Rhine and Danube and by the massacre of the motley "People's Crusaders," who crossed the Bosporus before the arrival of the massed Frankish armies at Constantinople in 1097. Those armies captured Nicaea, defeated the Turkish army at Dorylaeum, and then moved south to take Antioch and Jerusalem. By 1100 there were Crusader states at Jerusalem, Antioch, Tripoli and Edessa, each ruled by a Christian prince, and the Crusaders returned home to Europe.

Brilliant and fearless, El Cid became a fabled figure and he is often portrayed as a romantic hero.

1098

Cistercian Order Founded

An austere, reforming monasticism is established

The Cistercian order dates from 1098 when Robert, the abbot of the Cluniac house in Molesme, some 75 miles southeast of Paris, left with a few followers to found a new order in Cîteaux (Cistercium in Latin), near Dijon. They gave up the black habit of the Cluniacs and became known as the "white monks." Their objects were to re-establish a strict daily discipline more severe than the Benedictine rule—they ate only once a day, abjuring fish, meat and animal fats, and left their churches unadorned —and to find, in their organization, a middle way between the highly centralized Cluniac order and the isolation of the independent Benedictine houses.

The order made rapid progress, especially under St. Stephen Harding, the second abbot, and St. Bernard, who founded a house in Clairvaux in 1115 and is often called the order's "second founder." By 1200 there were more than 500 Cistercian abbeys joined in a loose federation. Each abbey was visited by the abbot of a "mother house" once a year and each year the abbots convened in Cîteaux.

Farming was the monks' chief activity. By hiring lay brothers to live with them and assist in their manual labor—sending out colonies to found new houses and clear wasteland, plant grains and raise cattle—the Cistercians took the lead in the great monastic contribution to the spread of agriculture in feudal Europe during the 12th and 13th centuries.

1122

Concordat of Worms Agreed by Papacy and Empire

A truce is declared in the "investiture contest"

The quarrel between pope and emperor, which Gregory VII had begun with his ban in 1075 on the lay investiture of officers of the Church, was given a respite in 1122 when Emperor Henry V and Pope Calixtus II met in Worms in Germany. At issue was the conflict of authority between the two heads of Christendom, both of whom were considered the divinely appointed vice-regents of God on earth.

In Worms the two sides agreed that within the Holy Roman Empire (Germany, Burgundy and Italy) bishops and abbots should be freely elected by the Church, but that in Germany the elections should be made in the emperor's presence. The emperor would no longer invest bishops with the ring and staff, which were the spiritual symbols of their office, but he would continue to invest them with the scepter, which represented their estates and lay rights—in Germany before consecration, in Burgundy and Italy after it.

The concordat cooled, but did not end, the investiture controversy, especially not in France and England. Similar agreements had been reached there in 1106-07, but relations with the papacy remained highly sensitive as the central monarchies developed in power and authority.

1123

First Ecumenical Council Held in the West

Decrees are issued in the name of the pope

The ninth ecumenical council of the Church, called by Pope Calixtus II in 1123, chiefly to confirm the Concordat of Worms agreed between him and the emperor in the previous year, was the first to be held in the West. It met in the Lateran Palace in Rome, which was the pope's residence until the 14th century, and was the first of seven such councils held between then and 1312.

All the bishops of the Western Church were summoned to attend these councils, and their frequency is a mark of the papacy's resolve to impose its authority on the Church. Celibacy declined greatly in the 13th century; the practice of individual confession, encouraged from Rome, greatly increased; and the doctrine of transubstantiation was enforced. The councils reflected also the great intellectual and, indeed, architectural renaissance of the Church. The 12th and 13th centuries were the great age of Gothic architecture, when cathedral after cathedral arose, above all in England and northern France.

Pope Innocent III (*r*1198-1216) and his successors maintained Gregory VII's claim to papal monarchy and, especially through the growth of the Curia (the papal bureaucracy), played an active role in international politics and diplomacy. The Vatican frequently acted as a final court of appeal in disputes and at times appeared to be run not as much by clerics as by lawyers and imperial administrators.

MEDIEVAL TABLE MANNERS

At an English feudal lord's table the food was sumptuous, the utensils primitive. Spoons and drinking cups were earthenware or wooden until the introduction of pewter in the 15th century; forks were unknown until they were borrowed from Italy in Elizabethan times and were not standard until about 1750; and knives were brought individually to the table and kept in a sheath attached to the diner's belt. Food was served and eaten on trenchers, originally thick slices of bread which gave way to wooden plates; by the 16th century these were made of pewter or silver. Wine was drunk from a common cup or "mazer" (a shallow bowl usually made of maple wood), passed from person to person. The lord sat at the middle of the long trestle table and to his left was placed the salt bowl. Important guests sat to his right, "above the salt," lesser ranks to his left, "below the salt"; hence the phrase "worth his salt."

1135

Death of Henry I Plunges England into Civil War

Stephen and Matilda battle for the succession to the throne

Henry I's only legitimate male heir, Prince William, was drowned in the wreck of the White Ship in the English Channel in 1120. His daughter, Matilda, was thus left as the sole direct representative of the line of Norman kings, and on several occasions Henry's barons (including his nephew Stephen) swore on oath to support her when he died. On his death in 1135, however, they broke their oath and supported Stephen, who arrived from Normandy to lay claim to the throne.

Stephen's reign was, from the start, beset by baronial rivalries and feudal wars, as some of the barons drifted back to Matilda. Stephen was defeated by Matilda, who was backed by her half-brother, the earl of Gloucester, and imprisoned in 1141. Matilda then reigned until Stephen, released in exchange for the captured Gloucester, regained the throne in 1142. Stephen lost further ground among the nobility and clergy when Normandy was conquered in 1144 by Geoffrey of Anjou, Matilda's husband.

In 1148 the barons refused to accept Stephen's son Eustace as heir to the throne. When Eustace died in 1153, Stephen finally yielded and in the Treaty of Winchester recognized as his heir Geoffrey and Matilda's son, Henry of Anjou, who in 1154 became Henry II of England, the first Angevin king. Normandy and England were thus reunited.

1145

Second Crusade Preached by Bernard of Clairvaux

The fall of Edessa to the Turks provokes a second "holy war"

Alarm spread through Europe in 1144 when the news reached it that the Muslims had recaptured Edessa, the northern outpost of Christian lands taken during the First Crusade. Bernard of Clairvaux was charged by Pope Eugenius II to preach a new crusade, and his eloquent prophecy of a terrible Day of Judgment awaiting Christians who failed to take up the Cross gained royal leadership for the Second Crusade.

Led though it was by Emperor Conrad III and Louis VII of France, it was a complete failure. The two armies, having again massacred Jews on their progress through eastern Europe, arrived separately in Constantinople and pillaged Byzantium before proceeding to Asia Minor. When they converged in 1148, their ranks were already severely depleted by encounters with the Turks.

A joint siege of Damascus failed, partly because of lack of cooperation between the two armies, partly because the Christian princes, having learned to live alongside their Muslim neighbors, had not trembled at the fall of Edessa and did not lend their support. Conrad returned home in 1148, Louis a year later, having accomplished nothing.

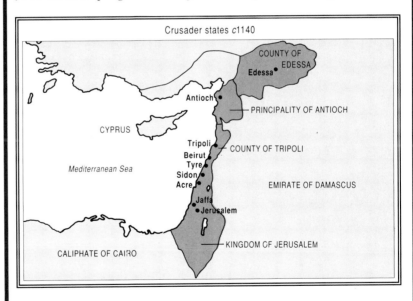

Crusader states c1140

COUNTY OF EDESSA
Edessa
Antioch
PRINCIPALITY OF ANTIOCH
CYPRUS
Tripoli
COUNTY OF TRIPOLI
Beirut
Tyre
Sidon
Acre
EMIRATE OF DAMASCUS
Mediterranean Sea
Jaffa
Jerusalem
KINGDOM OF JERUSALEM
CALIPHATE OF CAIRO

1147

Alfonso Henriques Drives the Moors from Lisbon

The national independence of Portugal is secured

When Alfonso Henriques became count of Portugal in 1128, his domain stretched south only as far as Coimbra; the mass of present-day Portugal had been in Muslim control since the 8th century. His ambition was to recover the whole of the country. In 1139 he began to call himself king, and in 1143 his cousin, Alfonso VII of Castile, recognized his autonomy. A body of English Crusaders was pressed into his service on its way to the Holy Land, and with their assistance Alfonso captured the great town of Lisbon from the Moors in 1147. Its mosque was rebuilt as a cathedral and the Moorish *alcazar* became a royal palace. The kingdom of Portugal was thus firmly established on the Tagus, although Lisbon did not become the capital until 1256, and the Algarve was not finally recovered from the Moors until 1270.

Born in the castle of Guimarães c. 1109, Alfonso Henriques was initially little more than a rebel leader, but by the time he died in 1185, he had created a stable hereditary monarchy.

1166

Trial by Jury Takes Root in England

The Assize of Clarendon signals a reform of criminal justice

Henry II is remembered as one of the great architects of the English system of justice, above all for extending the power of the king's courts, in both civil and criminal actions, at the expense of private feudal courts. His first notable achievement in law reform was the Assize of Clarendon of 1166, a set of instructions given to royal judges appointed to tour the country and see that the "king's peace" was upheld.

This practice of sending out royal justices on circuit—"justices in eyre" as they became known—instead of relying on local justices and sheriffs, quickly became regular procedure. The Assize of Clarendon empowered the judges to have all suspected criminals presented to them by juries of 12 worthy men from each hundred—a subdivision of a county or shire. No baronial or other privilege conferred exemption from this duty.

Juries of presentment were not new; linking them closely to central, royal government was. So was the power given to juries in the wake of the Assize of Clarendon to pronounce judgment in disputes arising from dispossession of land, inheritance of land, or the right to present a parson to a church living. This was the origin of trial by jury, which became standard after the Lateran Council of 1215 banished trial by ordeal.

By the end of Henry's reign in 1189, not only were the itinerant justices a normal feature of English life but a permanent session of the king's court, the forerunner of the Court of Common Pleas, was in existence at Westminster.

1167

Italian Cities Form the Lombard League

Merchants resist Frederick Barbarossa

At the imperial diet of 1157 in Besançon, the papal legate presented a document which seemed to imply that the pope considered the empire to be a papal fief. The reply of Emperor Frederick I, known as Barbarossa because of his red beard, was to invade Italy, seize Milan and claim for himself, as king of the Lombards, the authority to appoint an imperial governor to every Italian city. In 1166 he also seized Rome and nominated an antipope against Alexander III.

His action took place at a time when the Italian cities, growing prosperous on long-distance trade, were developing the forms of communal government that were to turn them into city-states. The Lombard League was formed by 16 such cities in 1167 to counter Frederick's initiative and to pit their civic militias against the weight of the imperial armies. In 1176 the League inflicted a heavy defeat on Frederick at Legnano, and the emperor was forced to accept the quasi-autonomy of the Italian cities ratified in the Peace of Constance (1183).

The League, renewed in 1198, 1208 and 1226, successfully maintained itself against Emperor Frederick II and, having served its purpose, disintegrated after his death in 1250.

1169

The Normans Arrive in Ireland

Henry II lays claim to English overlordship of the island

In 1166 Dermot MacMurrough, king of Leinster, was driven out of Ireland by the high king, Rory O'Connor. Dermot arrived in Bristol and appealed for help to Henry II, who licensed his subjects to go to Dermot's aid. A number of Welsh magnates responded, including the earl of Pembroke, nicknamed "Strongbow." They overran Leinster in 1169-70 and captured Dublin.

Strongbow put himself in line for the Leinster crown by marrying Dermot's daughter, but before Dermot's death in 1171, King Henry, alarmed at the prospect of his tenants-in-chief winning kingdoms of their own, ordered the conquerors home. Strongbow surrendered his newly won lands to Henry, who himself crossed with a knightly force to Waterford in 1171.

Henry seized the coastal towns, including Dublin, and gave the rest of Leinster to Strongbow as a feudal tenure. He stayed in Ireland for six months, during which time the kings and chiefs of the southern half of the country swore homage to him. Leinster, Meath, eastern Munster and Ulster passed into English control.

1170

Thomas à Becket Murdered in Canterbury Cathedral

Four knights assassinate the primate of England

Henry II's assertion of royal authority over the Church in the Constitutions of Clarendon (1164) brought him into fierce conflict with Thomas à Becket, previously chancellor of England and Archbishop of Canterbury since 1162. Becket refused to accept the Constitutions, among whose provisions were that no clergy should communicate with Rome without royal permission nor any appeals be made to the papal court before being heard in England.

After appearing at the Council of Northampton to answer charges of financial impropriety while chancellor, Becket fled to France. There he remained until 1170 when, meeting Henry in Normandy and agreeing to be reconciled, he returned to Canterbury. On Christmas Day he excommunicated his foes (that is, clerical supporters of the Crown) from the pulpit, driving Henry to curse "idle cowards who stand by while this miserable priest insults me."

Four knights took the king at his word and plotted to arrest Becket and deliver him to Henry. They arrived at Canterbury on December 29 and made known their purpose. Becket took refuge in the cathedral and was murdered on the steps of the high altar; three years later he was canonized.

Henry and Becket appear together in one of the great 13th-century stained glass windows in Canterbury Cathedral depicting miracles ascribed to the martyr.

1152–1170

HOLY ROMAN EMPIRE

• 1152 Accession of Frederick Barbarossa
Frederick crowned successor to Conrad III in Aix-la-Chapelle; ushered in era of Hohenstaufen imperial expansion and rivalry with papacy. Frederick gained homage of Burgundy by marriage (1156), of Poland by war (1157); conquered Milan (1158); entered Rome (1167), enthroned antipope Paschal III, but was forced to return to Germany when army destroyed by plague.

ENGLAND

• 1166 Assize of Novel Disseisin
Jury of 12 men of the neighborhood to judge disputed dispossession of land; empaneled by sheriff acting on royal writ; jury decided whether a man had been wrongfully dispossessed of land by another; if so, land returned.

• c.1170 Assize of Mort d'Ancestor
Jury of 12 men of the neighborhood to judge disputed inheritance; empaneled by sheriff acting on royal writ; jury decided whether a man died with lawful title to possession of land and, if so, which of the disputing parties was the lawful heir.

1185

Kamakura Period Opens in Japan

Power passes to the military as the shoguns enter history

Toward the end of the 12th century the Japanese imperial family began to recover ground against the Fujiwara, only to find itself engulfed in a struggle for power between two great military families, the Taira and the Minamoto. The rise to prominence of these families rested on their tenure of tax-exempt estates and their private armies, which had grown mighty under the patronage of quarreling factions within the Fujiwara clan.

Taira influence was the first to preponderate at court, but the Taira were ousted by the Minamoto in 1185 in a great sea battle in the Straits of Shimonoseki. Under the Minamoto leader Yoritomo, whom the emperor entitled Sei-i tai-shogun, or "great general," in 1192, a system of national military government, called the *bakufu* ("camp office"), was established in the coastal town of Kamakura, south of Tokyo. The emperor remained the theoretical ruler in Kyoto, but in fact became a puppet of Japan's first shogunate.

After Yoritomo's death in 1199, power passed to his widow's family, the Hojo, under whom the Mongol invasions sent by Kublai Khan in 1274 and 1281 were repulsed. The second incursion was foiled by a typhoon, which wrecked the Mongol armada and was given the name *kamikaze*, or "Divine Wind." The Kamakura period ended with the rise of the Ashikaga shogunate in 1339.

Yoritomo's portrait, painted on silk, shows an aloof, powerful man; an able administrator, he gave Japan a lasting system of firm central government.

1187

Saladin Captures Jerusalem

The hero of the Muslim reconquest of the Levant provokes the Third Crusade

During the 40 years after the Second Crusade a Muslim revival took place under the lead of the heroic Saladin, a Kurdish officer who became vizier of Egypt in 1169 and proclaimed himself sultan in 1174. Saladin subdued Mesopotamia and received the homage of the Seljuk rulers of Asia Minor before devoting the rest of his life to a *jihad*, or holy war, against the Christians. In 1187 Crusader strongholds fell to him one after the other—Acre, Jaffa, Beirut—until at last he took Jerusalem itself (allowing the Christians, in the chivalric manner for which he was famous, safe passage to the nearest Christian place).

Pope Gregory VIII's call for a new crusade to oust the Muslims was supported by Emperor Frederick Barbarossa, Richard I of England and Philip II of France. Frederick was drowned before the Third Crusade reached the Holy Land, and Philip returned to France after the recapture of Acre, leaving Richard to battle on alone.

Richard's defeat of Saladin at Arsuf earned him the name "the Lion-heart"; but after a further brilliant victory at Jaffa, his forces were steadily reduced by plague, famine and desertions, and the campaign ended in stalemate. In 1192 Richard made a truce with Saladin, by which the Christians kept the coastal towns they had captured and, provided they were unarmed, were given access to the Holy Sepulcher in Jerusalem.

1190

Order of the Teutonic Knights Founded

A Christian aristocracy is established on the Baltic

During the siege of Acre in the Third Crusade (1190–91), the Order of the Knights of the Hospital of St. Mary of the Teutons in Jerusalem was founded by German merchants to care for Christian pilgrims to the Holy Land. From the beginning the order adopted a military role and admitted knights to its vows; by 1198 it was known as the Teutonic Knights. The order fought in Palestine in the early 13th century, but under Grand Master Hermann von Salza (r1210-39) it transferred its operations to eastern Europe when opportunities in the Levant ran out.

The knights settled on the lower Vistula in the service of the Polish duke, Conrad of Mazovia, and, in 1233, with an army of central German volunteers, set out to conquer and Christianize the pagan population of the Baltic lands later known as Prussia. During the next 50 years that native population was virtually wiped out and replaced by a knightly aristocracy, whose state, called the Ordenstaat, was confirmed in its integrity by pope and emperor. So the *junker* ("young lord") class that was to play so large a role in Germany's future was born.

The Teutonic Knights extended agriculture and expanded the already lucrative Prussian grain trade. By 1308, when they established a capital in Marienburg, they ruled over a vast feudal kingdom that included Prussia and the eastern Baltic, Pomerania and lands in central and south Germany.

1204

Constantinople Falls to the Crusaders

The emperor flees as a Latin empire and patriarchy are established

The Fourth Crusade, called by Pope Innocent III to promote the cause of the papacy, turned out instead to be an almost exclusively commercial adventure. The band of French and Flemish Crusaders, who set out in 1199 under Boniface, marquis of Montferrat, hired ships from Venice at considerable cost and, when they were unable to raise the money, paid Venice by conquering Zara, the Christian port on the Dalmatian coast.

They were then diverted from the papal intention of an assault on Saladin's Egypt by the Byzantine prince, Alexius, who offered them money and supplies if they would restore his deposed father to the imperial throne. In this they were greatly aided by the Venetians, who wished to install a pliant emperor to give them a commercial monopoly in the East. The Crusaders sailed to Byzantium and in 1204 sacked Constantinople.

That Christian assault on the world's greatest Christian city was a dreadful moment in the history of Byzantium, one from which it never really recovered. Manuscripts were burned, paintings stolen and bronze sculptures melted down or carried off (including the four horses which until 1981 stood on the gallery above the entrance to St. Mark's Basilica in Venice). The emperor and patriarch fled, to be replaced by the Latin empire of Constantinople. But the real victor was Venice, which retained its Eastern possessions, above all Crete, and so founded a commercial empire more durable than the Latin empire, which, feeble from the start, tottered on until 1261.

Venetian involvement in the sack of Constantinople was commemorated in 1579/80 by Tintoretto's painting of the assault made for the Doge's palace.

1204

Philip Augustus Captures Château-Gaillard

The seizure of Richard I's castle leads to England's loss of Normandy

Philip II, known as Philip Augustus, came to the French throne in 1180, when the Anglo-Norman empire was at its height. He seized the opportunity presented by King Richard I's absence on the Third Crusade to occupy large portions of the English domain in France. Richard recovered some of it in two years of warfare, which ended in the treaty of Loviers (1196). To regain the rest he built Château-Gaillard, an imposing fortress on the border of Normandy.

But Richard was killed in 1199, and the following year the barons of Brittany and Maine rose in revolt against his successor, King John. John withdrew to England and refused to attend Philip's court to answer charges connected with his marriage to Isabella, daughter of the count of Angoulême. Philip declared that John had forfeited his French lands and launched a campaign to enforce the judgment.

In 1204, after an eight-month siege, Château-Gaillard surrendered to Philip's forces. Normandy, Anjou, Maine and Brittany passed to the French Crown, and John was left with only Gascony and the Channel Islands.

Angevin lands in France

1206

Muslim Kingdom Established at Delhi

Islam finds a permanent home in India

Islam first came to India in the 8th century, when Arab traders were followed by armies and Muslims settled peaceably in the Sind. The first wave of destructive and conquering invasions took place in the late 12th century, when an Islamic dynasty of Turks moved into northern India from Ghazni in central Afghanistan. Led by their brilliant general, Mohammed Ghuri, who commanded an armored cavalry of Turks, Afghans and Persians, they defeated a Hindu coalition of Rajput chiefs at Tarain in 1192 and then took Delhi and the surrounding territory of the Ganges valley.

The first ruler of Muslim India was Qutb-ud-Din Aybak, one of Mohammed Ghuri's slaves—it was common for slaves to rise to political eminence in Turkish culture—who was chiefly responsible for extending Turkish control over Benares, Gujarat and the whole of the north. His reward was to be named sultan of Delhi in 1206.

The sultanate survived until Delhi was sacked by Timur in 1398; local rulers lasted until the Mongol conquest of 1526. It was not a unified empire, for Hindu kingdoms retained their identity by paying tribute to the sultan. But it was the first permanent Islamic presence that was not absorbed into the Indian way of life. By bringing India into intimate contact with Islamic, especially Persian, influences, it ended a long period of Indian isolation and spawned a fresh flowering of music, painting and religious poetry.

1208

Innocent III Launches Albigensian Crusade

The papacy makes war on heresy

In the latter years of the 11th century there appeared in the south of France a heretical sect of Christians called the Albigensians, after the town of Albi. Their central belief, derived from Manichaeism, was in the absolute divide between the pure world of the spirit, which God had created (hence the name Cathari, from the Greek word for "pure," for similar heretics in other parts of Europe), and the corrupt world of matter, which was Satan's creation. They lived as extreme ascetics; baptism was rejected along with the other sacraments that involved contact with the physical world.

The heresy spread among the towns of southern France, which were not absorbed into the French kingdom and whose inhabitants spoke their own Provençal language. Albigensian missionaries won converts by the contrast which their lives displayed with the laxity of the Roman clergy and they found a powerful protector in Raymond, count of Toulouse.

When attempts to convert the Albigensians failed, Pope Innocent III induced the barons of northern France to wage a "holy war" against them. It began with the massacre of 15,000 in Béziers in 1209 and the surrender of Carcassonne and Narbonne shortly afterward and continued until 1229, by which time it had become a war to incorporate Provence into France. That objective was accomplished by the Treaty of Paris of 1229.

1212

Children's Crusade Sets Out for the Holy Land

The adventure ends at the Mediterranean

Thousands of young boys and girls left France and Germany in 1212 on a mission to rescue Christendom. Their inspiration came from a French shepherd boy aged about 12, named Stephen, who believed that Christ had visited him and told him to preach a crusade. A few weeks later a German boy, Nicholas, took up the same theme.

The French children gathered in Vendôme, the German in Cologne. Each leader attracted perhaps 20,000 followers; neither crusade got farther than the Mediterranean. The French journey ended in Marseilles. The Germans made it to Rome, where Pope Innocent III gave them an audience and bade them return home. Some died on the journey there and back, and a few were sold into slavery to Alexandria and Cairo. Most simply stayed in the south of France and in Italy.

ESCAPING SERFDOM

By 1200 about half of the English peasantry were wage-earners, half serfs, or villeins, who could gain their freedom in a number of ways. It could simply be bought, though few peasants could afford the price. It could be granted by a charter from the lord (usually when the peasant was no longer of use). It could be gained by running away to a chartered borough in which every inhabitant was a freeman and remaining there for a year and day, after which time a villein could not be compelled to return to his manor (though he could be reclaimed if ever he left the borough). Or it could be gained when a lord decided to turn a village into a borough, thus making all the inhabitants of the village freemen.

1213

Mongols Storm the Great Wall of China

Genghis's tribe breaks out of its homeland

Mongolia in the 12th century was disputed between two tribes, the Tatars and the Mongols. The Mongols gained ascendancy by 1206, when their leader, Genghis, was acknowledged as head, or *khan*, of all the Mongolian tribes. Genghis was one of the greatest nomadic warriors in history, unlike most of them less interested in booty, or even in settlement, than in a mission to conquer the world.

After reorganizing his warriors and issuing a code of conduct, he led them across the Great Wall of China in 1213. By 1215 he had conquered vast tracts of the Ch'in empire, including the capital in Yenching, though he did not overthrow the dynasty. In 1218 he turned to the west, overrunning Turkestan, sacking great cities like Samarkand and Bokhara and conducting a devastating raid on Persia, before turning in a great sweeping arc through the Caucasus into southern Russia.

At his death in 1223 he had become the greatest conqueror the world had ever seen, and the foundations had been laid of the vast Mongol empire, stretching over China, India, the Near East and parts of Europe, that his successors were to build with astonishing speed in less than half a century.

Mongol warriors were trained and kept ready for war by constant hunting and by a vast annual round-up of game.

1215

King John Seals Magna Carta

English barons extract privileges from the Crown at Runnymede

The extension of royal control under Henry II nurtured baronial resistance to the Crown, since the ancient right of the magnates to be consulted in matters affecting the *communitas regni*, the community of the realm, was gradually eroded, without the provision of any constitutional means for the redress of grievances. In the reign of King John a crisis of confidence, inspired in great measure by the loss of Normandy in 1204 and the failure to recover it at the Battle of Bouvines in 1214, emboldened many barons, who had been heavily taxed to pay for the king's continental disasters, openly to rebel.

John was forced to deal with them at Runnymede and to accept their conditions in the great charter of liberties, Magna Carta. The charter concerned itself with the feudal privileges of the wealthy knightly class; it was later misinterpretations which made it appear as a great national charter of the English people. It lacked sanctions, and the performance of its terms relied on the king's will. Even so, it carried great constitutional implications— that royal government must rest on consent (not in itself a novel idea) and that kings, far from exercising arbitrary power, could be constrained by law.

1223

Papacy Approves Franciscan Order

An Italian merchant's son dedicates himself to a life of poverty

In 1209 Francis of Assisi, the son of a rich Umbrian merchant, was attending mass when the message of the Gospels persuaded him to take up a life of lay preaching. He cast aside worldly ambitions, embraced poverty, and began to wander among the sick and needy, bringing them spiritual comfort and what material benefit he was able to offer. He collected a group of friars around him, but established no formal organization. His movement, however, with its emphasis upon humility and poverty, posed a threat to the Church.

The papacy, in its increasingly bureaucratic and secular role as a temporal power among European princes, saw the need to prevent Francis's evangelical and mendicant movement from dividing the Church. Pope Innocent III bade them elect a superior, through whom the fraternity of friars should owe obedience to the Holy See. Francis himself abandoned active leadership of the order in 1221 at a meeting of friars in the little chapel of Porziuncola, near Assisi. A year later, while praying on the Monte della Verna, he received the stigmata during a vision (the first such occurrence recorded and the only one celebrated in the Roman liturgy).

In 1223 Pope Honorius III bestowed official recognition upon the order of "Friars Minor," and though older monastic orders, fearing the Franciscans' freedom to preach without local episcopal sanction, opposed them, the order flourished. To this day it remains the greatest order in the field of missionary work among the poor.

1232

Gregory IX Establishes the Inquisition

Dominican Friars are dispatched to France to root out heresy

The Roman ecclesiastical court known as the Inquisition was first established by Pope Gregory IX in Toulouse in 1232. Its aim was to root out the last traces of Albigensianism after the incorporation of the heretics' Provençal homeland into the French kingdom in 1229. It was staffed largely by Dominicans (a new monastic order founded by St. Dominic in Languedoc in 1216) and was known as the Dominican Inquisition, or Holy Office.

Inquisitors, arriving in a district, gave suspected heretics a month to confess and recant; those who did not were tortured into confession or brought to secret trial, where they were not told the names of their accusers. Burning at the stake was rare, the usual punishments being fines and imprisonment. Albigensian armed resistance was finally broken when their last stronghold, the castle in Montségur, fell to French knights in 1244.

It took until the beginning of the 14th century, however, for the inquisitors to root out the heresy. By then a fortified cathedral in Albi and a university in Toulouse had risen as architectural symbols both of Christian orthodoxy and of French authority in the region.

Giotto's fresco in the upper church at Assisi shows St. Francis preaching to the birds—an endearing image of the man who regarded all God's creatures as his fellows and called the sun brother.

c. 1240

Khanate of the Golden Horde Founded

*Batu builds a Mongol empire
in Russia*

The Mongol cavalry, greatly strengthened by the addition of Turkic peoples, swept into Russia in 1236 and established itself in tents on the lower Volga. Kiev was razed in 1240 and the era of Kievan Rus brought to an end by the subsequent conquest of almost the whole of Russia.

In 1256 Batu, the grandson of Genghis, was made khan of the region, which became known as the empire of the Golden Horde. The Russian principalities, which retained their own rulers and maintained control of their internal administration, became tributary states of the khanate, which itself was subordinate to Karakorum, the central Mongolian city founded as his capital by Genghis c. 1220. The Golden Horde lasted until it was weakened by civil war in the late 14th century; in 1419 it was divided into three independent khanates, Crimea, Astrakhan and Kazan, which continued a precarious existence until their demise at the beginning of the 16th century.

c. 1241

Hanseatic League Formed

*German towns band together for
commercial security*

The German penetration in the 11th century of the Slavic lands on the Baltic, which the Teutonic Knights came to dominate in the early 13th century, gave Germanic people control of the rich Baltic trade that flowed from Scandinavia east to Novgorod, west to London and south to the Mediterranean.

The origins of the Hanseatic League (a *hansa* was a merchant company) are murky, but the firmest association between those towns that acted as middlemen in this great northern trade was formed c. 1241, when Lübeck and Hamburg signed a treaty of mutual protection. Their purpose, in an era when there was no strong central German government, was to provide for the safety of their traders, to extend trading rights and, where possible, to gain a monopoly of those rights. More and more towns joined the league, which by 1300 had nearly 100 members. It retained its ascendancy until the 15th century and was only formally dissolved in 1669.

1258

Mongols Take Baghdad

*A grandson of Genghis overthrows
the Abbasids*

The Abbasid dynasty, which had overthrown the Umayyads in 750, came to its end in 1258, when the Mongols, under Hulagu, a grandson of Genghis, rampaged through Persia and captured Baghdad. The last Abbasid caliph, Mustasim, was murdered—according to tradition, rolled in a carpet and stomped upon, because the Mongols were superstitious about shedding his blood. Mesopotamia was brought within the Mongol empire and cut off from the Islamic world of the eastern Mediterranean.

By the mid-13th century, the Abbasid caliphate had long been in decline. The rot set in with the rise of independent Islamic caliphates throughout the Arab empire in the 9th and 10th centuries and continued under the invasions of the Seljuk Turks and the Crusaders. The significance of the Mongol invasion was thus more economic than political. The magnificent public works and the irrigation system the Persians had built were destroyed, and Mesopotamia remained an economic backwater until its revival in the 20th century.

*Economic power
shifted gradually
during the Middle
Ages from the
Mediterranean to
northern Europe.
By 1487, when this
miniature appeared in
the Hamburg city
records, ships crowded
the port and merchants
were men of wealth
and importance.*

EUROPEAN FEUDALISM

Courtly love was part of the medieval knightly code of chivalry, whose chief virtues were piety, honor, valor, courtesy, chastity and loyalty. In peacetime these ideals found their expression largely in the tournament, and this Flemish painted wooden shield of parade shows a knight kneeling before a lady with the weapons of tournament—poleaxe, helmet and gauntlets—lying on the ground in front of him. The inscription reads "You or Death."

The social and economic system which characterized most European societies in the Middle Ages goes by the name of feudalism. The system was not unique to western Europe. Indeed its essence, the granting of land in return for military service, has appeared all over the world in many different kinds of society— Japan under the shogunates in the 19th century, for example.

The center of the feudal system in medieval Europe was the king, and a medieval king was, above everything else, a warrior. From the 9th to the 14th centuries—the heyday of feudalism—the most important element in making war was the armored and mounted knight. To maintain a retinue of knights was, however, very expensive. In return for providing the king with warriors, tenants-in-chief were granted large holdings of land. A grant of land was known as a "feud" or a "fief": hence the term "feudalism." The tenants-in-chief (commonly called barons in England) received their lands directly from the king and, in turn, leased parts of their estates to the knights, who in their turn gave leases to yeomen. That, at any rate, was the theory. There were places where feudalism scarcely gained a hold, and where men held land with no obligation to anyone else: such unfettered ownership of land, known as an *allod*, was, for instance, prevalent in the south of France and in Spain.

Feudalism, by its very nature, gave rise to a hierarchy of rank, to a predominantly static social structure in which every man knew his place, according to whom it was that he owed service and from whom it was that he received his land. In order to preserve existing relationships in perpetuity, rights of succession to land were strictly controlled by various laws, or customs, of entail. The most rigid control was provided by the custom of primogeniture, by which all the property of a deceased landholder must pass intact to his eldest son.

Every man was the vassal, or servant, of his lord. He swore homage to him, and in return the lord promised to give him protection and to see that he received justice. In theory, then, feudalism was the expression of a society in which every man was bound to every other by mutual ties of loyalty and service. In fact, feudal society was marked by a vast gulf between the very few, very rich, great landholders and the mass of the poor who worked for the profit of the nobility. (The nobility included bishops, for the Church was one of the greatest of medieval landowners.) At the bottom of the social pyramid were the agricultural laborers, or peasants, and beneath them, the villeins, or serfs.

Until the rise of powerful monarchies with central bureaucracies, it was the lord of the manor who was the real ruler of society. The peasant worked the land for him and owed him a number of feudal dues (more and more commuted to money payments as time went by); justice was dispensed in the manorial courts. Customs varied, but it was usual for a peasant to have a small plot, or to share a communal plot, on which to grow food for himself and his family and to be entitled to gather firewood from forest land for the hearth-fire.

While the knights were jousting and proving themselves before the ladies, as in this delightful late 15th-century French miniature, above, the peasants were, at best, allowed to watch; mostly they toiled in the fields. In the illustration for July in the manuscript known as the "Très Riches Heures du duc de Berry," made in 1485-89, they are shown reaping grain with sickles and shearing sheep with spring shears.

By 1399, when Henry IV was crowned king of England, the heyday of feudalism had passed. With the rise of strong, centralized monarchies in England, France and Spain, the basic relationship of society changed from that of vassal and lord to monarch and subject. And the local manorial system was gradually eroded by the growing ease of communications and the growth of towns, with a wealthy and influential merchant class.

1260

Kublai Khan Establishes Yuan Dynasty in China

The Mongol empire reaches its greatest extent

From the beginning of the 10th century Chinese dynasties were vulnerable to "Barbarian" pressure from the north. For 200 years they bought off the Tatar kingdom of Liao, which controlled Mongolia and Manchuria, but northern China fell in 1125 to the Jurchen tribe, which set up the Ch'in dynasty. The ruling Sung dynasty was forced to retreat to Hangchow, from where it continued to rule the south.

At the beginning of the 13th century Genghis began an attack on the Sung, and his conquest was completed by his grandson, Kublai, who in 1260 became khan of the Mongol empire. In the same year he founded the Yuan dynasty in China, though it was not until 1279 that his troops finally subdued the Sung. With all China under its rule, the Mongol empire was at its territorial peak, but Kublai's campaigns against Japan and Indonesia failed.

Kublai made Peking (modern Beijing) into a magnificent capital and modernized the 1,100-mile canal that joined it to Hangchow. Reluctantly, he came to accept Confucianism in the civil service; indeed, since the Mongols were a tiny population in the vast land of China, they absorbed Chinese influences, rather than imposed Mongol ones. After Kublai, Mongol China can be thought of as being Chinese, not Mongol.

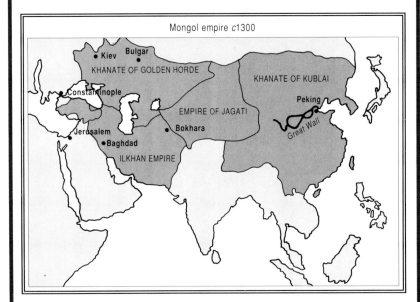

Mongol empire c1300

1260

Mamluks Defeat the Mongols at Goliath Springs

Mongol conquests end as Mamluks take power in Syria and Egypt

The Mamluks were slaves, of Turkish descent, who, from the 10th century, were brought from the steppe lands north of the Caspian to Cairo to serve in the armies of the caliphate. After being trained as soldiers, they entered the army and from their garrisons ruled over the local populations in the name of the caliph. They were granted land and grew in power until they were able to challenge their masters.

In 1250 Egypt came under the rule of a Mamluk dynasty when Aybak married the mother of the last Ayyubid sultan (whom she had murdered). Ten years later the Mamluks recorded an even greater triumph by bringing the era of Mongol conquests to an end. The Mongols had taken Baghdad in 1258 and ended the Abbasid caliphate. The following year they invaded Syria and forced the Muslims of Damascus to surrender. That was their last great victory.

A Mamluk force fell upon the Mongols at Goliath Springs, just outside Nazareth, in 1260, killed their general and won a decisive victory, shattering the belief in Mongol invincibility. The victory raised Baybars to the sultanate in Cairo, the capital of the Mamluk empire in Egypt and Syria, which lasted until it was overthrown by the Ottomans in 1517.

1265

Henry III Meets England's First Parliament

Simon de Montfort wins a historic victory for the baronial opposition

Henry III's ambitious attempt to conquer Sicily, begun in 1254, left the Crown bankrupt and forced him, four years later, to accept the Provisions of Oxford, which imposed a permanent baronial council on the king. Henry at once, however, began to recoup royal power, and the great barons, led by Simon de Montfort, renewed their opposition and defeated the king's forces in battle in Lewes in 1264.

To draw up a peace, Henry met the barons at Westminster Hall in London in March 1265, just as King John had met them at Runnymede in 1215. The difference was that Simon, to bolster his power, invited two knights from each shire and two burgesses from each of the nation's important towns to join the assembly.

The peace won at Westminster by Henry's submission—he promised to rule according to the Provisions of Oxford—was short-lived. War broke out again and Simon himself was slain in the Battle of Evesham in August. But the foundations of parliament, as the national assembly consisting of king, lords and commons, had been laid. In 1275 Henry's successor, Edward I, summoned his first parliament, and the evolution of England's most enduring institution of government began.

1271

Marco Polo Travels to the Far East

A Venetian merchant enters the service of Kublai

The Mongol empire vanished as swiftly as it arose, making no enduring impact on Christendom or Islam. But it did serve to bring the Far East into commercial contact with the Mediterranean world. In 1271 Marco Polo, a Venetian merchant, set out overland with his father and uncle for Kublai's court in Peking (modern Beijing). He was following in the footsteps of Christian missionaries to "Cathay" and of his father, who had already made a trading expedition to the Far East in 1266.

They arrived in 1275, and Marco became a favorite of the khan, who employed him over the next 16 years or so, largely as a commercial factor. His presence in China was not remarkable; other Italian merchants also voyaged to the Far East. The Franciscans, for example, founded a factory, or trading post, in Zaiton, a port facing Taiwan which was one of the busiest in the world at the time.

Marco Polo's fame rests on the account that he published of his travels in *Il Milione* (written in the two years after he was taken captive in 1296 by the Genoese in a war against Venice). It is a detailed account of the manners, governments and economies of the places that he visited, not simply China. For centuries it was almost the only source of information about paper currency, coal, asbestos and other wonders available to the West.

In the Catalan Atlas, made in 1375 for Charles V of France, Marco Polo and his brothers are pictured setting out from Bokhara for Peking. Marco's tales of new worlds stimulated immense interest in Europe in exploration and map making.

1282

"Sicilian Vespers" Break Out in Palermo

The French in Sicily are massacred in a rebellion against Charles of Anjou

The long battle for supremacy waged between the papacy and the Hohenstaufen imperial house began with Frederick Barbarossa's incursions into Italy. It reached its peak under Frederick II, who made Italy and Sicily the heart of his empire, and ended in 1266, when Charles of Anjou allied himself with the papacy and defeated Manfred, the last Hohenstaufen ruler of Sicily, at Benevenuto.

Charles was crowned king of Naples and Sicily by Pope Clement IV and the Sicilians were forced to accept the replacement of one set of foreign rulers by another. Charles's oppressive rule was made worse by the heavy taxation he levied to pay for extensive foreign wars—of no concern to the Sicilians—waged to extend the Angevin empire into the Balkans and the eastern Mediterranean.

In 1282 the Sicilians (perhaps encouraged and subsidized by Constantinople) rose in revolt, massacred hundreds of French officials and drove Charles from the island. The revolt began in Palermo at vespers on Easter Monday. The Sicilians were assisted by Peter III of Aragon, to whom the throne of Sicily was then given, thus extending Catalan influence in the Mediterranean region.

1282

Edward I Subdues Wales

The end of Welsh independence ushers in an era of castle building

Edward I's ambition to bring all of Britain under the English Crown began in Wales, where in two devastating campaigns, of 1276-77 and 1282, the principality was overwhelmed by English arms. The Welsh prince, Llewellyn ap Gruffydd, who had pushed back the English advance under King Henry III and forged a new political unity in Wales, was forced to sue for peace and sign the Treaty of Conway in 1277.

Its terms were so humiliating—Llewellyn had to swear homage to Edward, relinquish the territory that Edward had gained, and pay debts to the English Crown—that in 1282 he rose with his brother, David, in rebellion. Eight months later Llewellyn was killed, near Builth, and the revolt was over.

Edward I made his own son prince of Wales and by the Statute of Rhuddlan (1284) settled the English criminal law upon Wales (the civil law remained Welsh). He also extended the English shire-system of government to most of the land, although some lordships in the marches, or border territory, in Brecon were not absorbed.

The conquest proved final, not least because in the next 25 years, in the greatest feat of royal building in English history, Edward placed a ring of seven massive stone castles around the northwestern coast of Wales, from Flint to Aberystwyth; an eighth was located inland, in Builth.

Caernarfon, built 1283-1330, is the largest and most noble of Edward's castles. Its massive stone walls and many-angled towers resemble the 5th-century Roman walls surrounding Constantinople.

1290

Ottoman Principality Founded in Bythnia

The roots of a future Turkish empire are put down in Asia Minor

The Turkish domination of the Islamic world by the Seljuks, interrupted by the Mongol conquests, was resumed in the 14th century by a new dynasty, the Ottoman Turks, who were the last of the Turkic peoples to settle in the Near East. In the political disorder created by the devastation of the Arab heartlands by the Mongols, border chieftains, or *ghazi*, achieved considerable autonomy. One of these was Osman, who in 1290 proclaimed the independence from the Seljuk sultanate of Rum of his small kingdom in Bythnia, on the Sea of Marmora. This was the origin of the mighty Ottoman empire that was to follow.

Osman (the Ottomans were also known as the Osmanli Turks) offered mercenaries plunder and land, and his kingdom was reinforced by a stream of land-hungry refugees from Mongol rule. He quickly absorbed the petty Christian states that were his immediate neighbors and in doing so gave to the title *ghazi* a new meaning—"warrior of the faith." By the time of his death in 1326 his son Orkhan, who succeeded him, had taken Bursa from Byzantium. Orkhan was the first Ottoman to take the title of sultan.

1295

Edward I Summons the "Model Parliament"

The assembly of king, Lords and Commons takes shape

Edward I's expensive campaigns against Wales and Scotland required revenue that could be raised only by imposing heavy taxation. To gain consent for that taxation he had to resort to frequent meetings of parliament. The composition of the parliaments varied, as did their business, much of which was merely judicial, but the writ that went out in 1295, summoning representatives from the shires and the towns to meet with the king and the great barons, became the model for the future.

The "Model Parliament" of 1295 did not give the Commons—the representatives of the towns and shires—power: they were required to accept the decisions by the king and the barons, or Lords, and carry them back to the country. But the frequency with which Edward called parliament helped to turn an event (such as Simon de Montfort's parliament of 1265) into an accepted institution.

It also made that institution the place where two great principles of the English constitution, which had been evolving since Anglo-Saxon days, should be worked out by the whole community of the realm. Those principles were that the redress of grievances should precede the supply of money to the Crown and that "extraordinary" taxation, money raised beyond the ordinary feudal payments due to the king as tenant-in-chief, needed national consent.

1275–1296

ENGLAND

• **1275 Statute of Westminster**
Great remedial piece of legislation, amending and confirming the law over a wide area; assented to by Lords (spiritual and temporal) and Commons (knights and burgesses). Together with many other statutes of reign of Edward I, notably Winchester (1285)—which compelled every man between 15 and 60 to possess arms for the defense of the realm and maintenance of the peace—Westminster II (1285) and Quia Emptores (1290) increased the status of monarch and parliament. Effect of statutes was to speed transformation of law of England from basis in custom to basis in statute.

PAPACY

• **1296 Bull "Clericis Laicos"**
Issued by Pope Boniface VIII; made it an excommunicatory sin for any layman to tax the clergy and for any clergyman to pay lay taxes. Resisted by Philip IV of France and Edward I of England; Edward withdrew protection of the clergy by royal courts; clergy evaded the bull by making gifts of money to the Crown.

1309

Papacy Enters its "Babylonian Captivity"

French popes make Avignon their headquarters

The persistent quarrel between secular rulers and the papacy erupted in 1301, when a French bishop was tried for the slander of King Philip IV in a royal court and Pope Boniface VIII insisted he be tried by a papal court. Boniface was asserting supremacy in both spiritual and temporal matters (at a jubilee in 1300 he had two swords carried before him as symbols of his double authority). The French episcopacy was tepid in its support, while Philip rallied the French people, including numbers of the clergy, to his national cause.

When Boniface was imprisoned and brought to trial before a general council in 1303, no one rose to defend him, not simply because of his political arrogance but also because of his unspirituality and lukewarm interest in clerical reform. The quarrel was awkward for the papacy, which needed French support in its struggle against the Guelphs in Italy. Pope Clement IV, elected in 1305, therefore absolved the French monarchy of any wrong against Boniface and moved his headquarters to Avignon in 1309. So began the "Babylonian Captivity" of the papacy, which lasted until 1377.

To the English and Germans the papacy now appeared to be a tool of the French Crown. At the same time, the splendid papal palace that was built in Avignon and the luxury of the life there, combined with increasing instances of simony and pluralism (the holding of more than one Church living at a time), drew the fire of reformers and fed a swelling tide of popular anti-papalism and anti-clericalism.

1314

Robert Bruce Routs Edward II at Bannockburn

Scotland secures its independence from England

After conquering Wales, Edward I turned his attention to Scotland and was at first successful. In 1296 he defeated the Scots at Berwick, deposed their king, John Baliol, and removed the coronation stone from Scone to Westminster. Over the following 10 years Edward got the better of William Wallace (who was executed in 1305) and, without gaining a decisive victory, brought much of Scotland under his sword. When he died in 1307, his successor, Edward II, continued the campaign.

By then Scotland had found a new military hero in Robert Bruce, who was crowned Robert I in 1306. He regained most of the territory won by Edward I until, in 1314, Stirling Castle, overlooking Bannockburn Plain, was the last stronghold in English hands.

There, on Midsummer Day, 1314, a vast English army of perhaps 20,000 men arrived to do battle. The next morning they were routed by the Scots. Edward escaped to Dunbar and sailed back to England, but the earl of Hereford and 1,500 men were captured, while retreating, at Bothwell Castle.

The Scots regained Berwick two years later and the winning of Scotland's independence was complete. But it was not formally acknowledged until Edward III signed the Treaty of Northampton (1327), in which the validity of Robert's title to the Scottish throne was accepted.

Legend has it that Robert I, whose seal shows a truly regal figure, learned the kingly virtues of hope and fortitude by watching a spider persevere in spinning her web.

1324

Mansa Musa Makes a Pilgrimage to Mecca

The emperor of Mali astonishes the world with his great wealth

After the demise of Ghana, the next great empire to arise in West Africa was Mali, the emergence of which dates from a great battle at Kirina *c.* 1240. There Sundiata Keita, the warrior-chief of the Mandinka tribe, who had a small kingdom, Kangaba, on the banks of the upper Niger, defeated Sumanguru, head of a rival tribe of would-be empire-builders from Takrur.

The Mandinka rulers adopted Islam, though there is no evidence that it penetrated deeply into the tribal culture, and during the next century they came to dominate West African trade. The Mandinka were also among the earliest Africans to cultivate the soil, planting rice and other produce on the banks of the Gambia. Agricultural and commercial prosperity enabled Kangaba to grow into the Mali empire. By the time the greatest of Mali kings, Mansa Musa, came to the throne in 1312, it stretched from the Atlantic to the borders of modern Nigeria and from the Sahara to the edge of the tropical forest belt.

When Mansa Musa made his pilgrimage to Mecca in 1324, he carried so much gold with him that the metal was debased in Cairo. His wealth and the size of his retinue astonished the East—so much so that Mali and the "Lord of the Negroes" appear in the first European map of West Africa (1375). From Arabia Mansa Musa brought back architects who introduced bricks to sub-Saharan building and Muslim scholars who made Timbuktu and Jenne on the Niger, in present-day Mali, into great centers of law and theology.

Mansa Musa's wealth and generosity were recalled many years after his visit to Cairo and, orb and scepter in hand, he dominates the first, Catalan, map of West Africa.

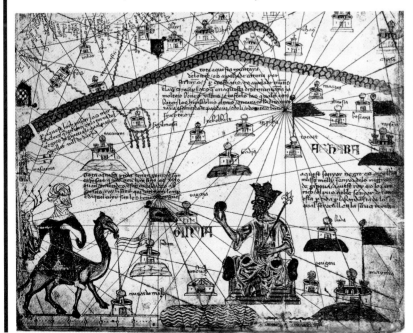

c. 1325

Aztecs Make Tenochtitlán their Capital

A new empire arises in Central America

After the fall of the Toltecs in the late 12th century no power arose in Central America until the Aztecs, a nomadic tribe, entered the vacuum from the north in the early 13th century. They founded their capital in Tenochtitlán about 1325, and by 1428, when their greatest ruler, Itzcoatl, was on the throne, they had conquered the neighboring city-states, whose culture they had slowly absorbed.

For the rest of the century they extended their empire until it stretched from the Pacific to the Gulf of Mexico and reached into Guatemala. It was not a unified empire: within it the landlocked states of Tlaxaca and Teotitlán remained independent. It was ruled by an elected priest-king, chosen from the royal family by the aristocracy, and supported by tribute exacted from defeated tribes in the form of gold, cotton, incense and food.

Tenochtitlán was a magnificent city, rivaling Constantinople, and it exhibited the great skills in engineering and building (especially temples and pyramids) that the Aztecs had absorbed from the Toltecs and other predecessors.

The center of Aztec culture was its blood-religion: a human sacrifice was offered up to the sun god once a day (20,000 were said to have been offered at the dedication of the great pyramid in Tenochtitlán). Conquest supplied the victims. The Aztec empire could not survive except by war, and when the Spanish arrived in 1519 many tribes welcomed them as deliverers from Aztec tyranny.

THE BLACK DEATH

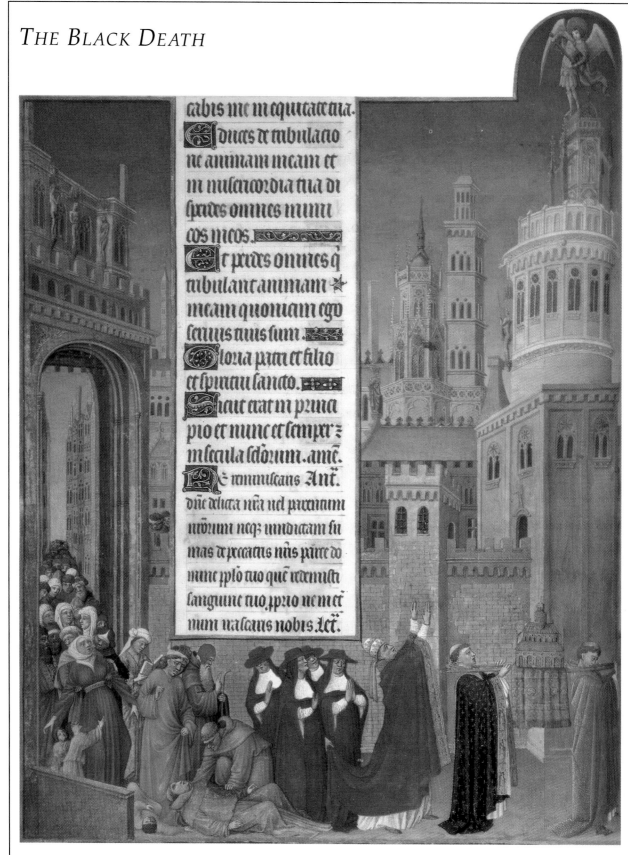

The first outbreak of the plague that swept across Europe from Asia was recorded at Constantinople in 1334. From there the deadly visitation was spread westward by Genoese traders in 1347-49. The toll of lives that it claimed was dreadful, even to a population in which infant mortality was commonplace and adult life-expectancy about half the biblical threescore years and ten.

Recent suggestions that the infection was anthrax remain unproven; the traditional account is that the disease was bubonic plague, carried by the black rat, *Rattus rattus*. It was a virulent disease. Infection was severely painful—the chief symptoms were high fever, delirium, vomiting, swollen lymph glands and suppurating lesions—and almost always fatal. But the "sweating sickness," as it was known, was mercifully swift in its action. Victims succumbed within two or three days of being infected.

Accurate estimates of the death-toll are difficult to make. Europe's economy had been suffering a long decline from the beginning of the century—colder winters and shorter summers, crop failures and famine were already causing·a fall in population, which, had it been healthier, might have had a higher resistance to the disease. As it was, probably somewhere between one-quarter and one-third of Europe's people were carried off in just two years. A few places, notably Bohemia, seem for some reason to have escaped. Elsewhere the devastation was fairly evenly spread, though monastic communities and towns, in whose closely packed and unsanitary strèets and dwellings rats abounded, suffered more grievously than the less densely populated countryside. Lesser outbreaks occurred with persistent regularity for another 150 years.

The chief economic consequences of the Black Death were a shortage of labor and surplus work—on abandoned farmlands, in urban trades, in the Church and in armies. (The largest force sent by England to the continent during the Hundred Years' War was assembled in 1347, a year before the onset of the plague there.) Wages rose and prices fell. Social mobility produced social tensions. Both free and bonded laborers looked forward to material improvement in their lives, and when they found their advance thwarted by wage limitations—such as those imposed by the Statute of Laborers in England in 1351—and by the closing of ranks against social upstarts by town guilds, frustration issued in revolt. The Jacquerie in France (1358) and the Peasants' Revolt in England (1381) are the most famous of the wave of protests that swept over Europe.

Open rebellion everywhere was quashed. But the effects of the Black Death in breaking down barriers of status contributed to the waning of the ordered, static social economy of feudalism and the emergence in the 15th century, throughout northern Europe, of a money economy with increased credit facilities and early forms of capitalism. In the growing towns of the Low Countries and England, resources previously thinly spread were opened to merchant adventurers and bankers, who seized the opportunity to amass capital.

The constant fear of sudden death generated by the plague created an almost morbid fascination with it in the medieval mind, and artists produced paintings depicting every aspect of the subject. Here, Sammael, the Angel of Death, with his scythe, triumphantly cuts down the exalted and humble, devout and sinful, without regard for their status.

Opposite: The famous medieval manuscript, the "Très Riches Heures du duc de Berry," shows Pope Gregory the Great in 590, leading a procession around Rome in an appeal to Heaven to rid the city of plague. But even his benign influence, and the fact that an angel on the top of Hadrian's mausoleum—henceforth known as Sant'Angelo—is sheathing a bloody sword to signify that God's wrath has been appeased, seem to have afforded Gregory's followers no protection.

1327

Edward II Driven from the English Throne

Opponents murder the king at Berkeley Castle

Edward II's reign was bedeviled from the start by his reliance on a foreign favorite, the Frenchman Piers Gaveston, whose influence at court was resented by the barons. Neither Edward's acceptance of the Ordinances of 1311, establishing a council of magnates, led by the earl of Lancaster, to rule the country, nor the execution of Gaveston in 1312, were able to reconcile the baronage to his rule.

Opposition again grew strong after 1322, when Edward, having defeated Lancaster at the Battle of Boroughbridge near York and executed him, persuaded parliament to repeal the Ordinances of 1311 and put himself in the hands of a new favorite, Hugh le Despenser. Edward's wife, Isabella, placed herself at the head of the opposition. She went to France with her lover, Edward Mortimer, and returned in 1326 with an army, which toppled Hugh le Despenser.

In 1327 parliament deposed Edward on the justification that he was incompetent to rule and had placed government in the hands of others, unmindful of the interests of the state. The deposition was an illegal act. Since the high court of parliament was, in fact, king-in-parliament, there was no constitutional means for getting rid of a monarch. Nevertheless, the deed was associated with parliament, which thereby gained in status, as did the idea of the supremacy of the law. Edward was imprisoned in Berkeley Castle and murdered.

1346

Spoils of Crécy Fall to Edward III

English longbows prove superior to the French crossbows

The Hundred Years' War between France and England was fought chiefly to deliver English feudal possessions in France from vassalage to the French Crown and to advance Edward III's claim to that crown. (His mother, Isabella, was the daughter of Philip the Fair.) English dislike of France's alliance with Scotland and French dislike of England's commercial ties with Flanders were in the background.

The war, which lasted intermittently from 1337 to 1453, began well for England. A naval victory at Sluys (1340) was followed by victory at Crécy (1346) and the capture of Calais (1347). At Crécy, 30 miles south of Boulogne, a 40,000-strong French army, one of the largest ever raised in France, faced an English army one-third the size. The English won a handsome victory, not because they used cannon for the first time on a battlefield, but because the novel combination of longbowmen and foot soldiers proved superior to the traditional crossbow and cavalry charge.

Against the longbow, with its rapid rate of fire and 280-yd. range, the chain-armor of the French knights and the Genoese mercenaries, who wielded crossbows, was a flimsy protection. In the single day of fighting, France lost some 10,000 men and England gained a new hero of chivalry—the king's heir, Edward, who bore the brunt of French fire. He became known as the Black Prince from the color of his armor.

The victory gained Edward III no real advantage, but it ensured that he would continue the war.

1356

Charles IV Issues the Golden Bull

Electoral princes of Germany are granted local autonomy

Germany's long history, after the demise of the Hohenstaufen line in 1250, as a country broken into numerous princely states owes much to the Golden Bull issued by Emperor Charles IV in 1356. (Edicts, or bulls, were customarily affixed with a golden seal.) Its immediate purpose was to establish the method of election of the Holy Roman Emperor.

The electors were declared to be the archbishops of Mainz, Trier and Cologne and the count Palatine of the Rhine, the duke of Saxony, the margrave of Brandenburg and the king of Bohemia. Its consequence was to give *de facto* recognition to the wide authority which the electors and lesser princes wielded in their territories.

The bull stated that electoral estates were indivisible and inheritable only by an eldest son and that electors had royal rights to mine salt and metal, to mint coinage, and to tax Jews. It also stated that no subject of an elector could appeal to a court outside his realm, and that conspiracy against an elector was *lèse majesté*. In short, the electors were little less than kings.

The rights conferred on the electors were gradually adopted by other German princes and they provided the constitutional basis for the steady growth of local states against the emperor, whose office became increasingly titular. By making no mention of the papacy, the bull implicitly denied the pope's right to influence or confirm elections to the imperial throne.

1356

John II Captured at Poitiers

The Black Prince leads England to a famous victory over the French

In 1354 papal mediators in the war between France and England suggested a peace plan: Edward III of England should renounce his claim to the French throne and in return be made sovereign ruler of those French lands—Anjou, Aquitaine, Maine, Touraine, Poitou and Calais—which he held as a vassal of the French king. The breakdown of negotiations resulted in the renewal of war and the resounding English victory at Poitiers.

Once more, as at Crécy, English tactics and the longbow won the day against superior French numbers. John II of France was captured and taken to London, where he was held for ransom. The ransom price was fixed at 3 million gold *ecus* by the Treaty of Brétigny (1360), in which Edward III renounced his claim to the French throne in return for sovereign control of an enlarged Aquitaine (to be ruled by the Black Prince), Poitou and Calais. The French failure to honor these conditions led to a renewal of the Hundred Years' War in 1368.

A French book of "Chronicles" c. 1415, shows the two armies at Poitiers in close combat. In reality, the mounted French knights became stuck in the mud and were picked off by the English archers.

1358

Jacquerie Ruthlessly Suppressed

Thousands of rebel French peasants are massacred

The collapse of French royal authority after the defeat at Poitiers and the capture of John II was followed by a great peasant uprising, known as the Jacquerie (from the traditional name, "Jacques Bonhomme," for a French peasant). Peasant resistance to the payment of feudal dues and tithes to the clergy, which had been growing since the outbreak of sporadic revolts earlier in the century, was fed by the financial demands of the Hundred Years' War.

The immediate provocation for the uprising of 1358 was the battening of troops, English and French, on the Ile de France. Parisian artisans and merchants, led by Etienne Marcel, joined the revolt, which spread southeastward from Paris. Many nobles were murdered and perhaps 200 castles burned to the ground before the aristocracy rallied around the dauphin, Charles. The massacre of 20,000 rebels and the execution of Marcel brought the rising to an end after just six weeks.

TOURNAMENTS
The most colorful aspect of feudal chivalry was the tournament. The first tournaments, full mock-battles between knightly hosts, were discouraged by the Church (which refused to bury knights slain at them), but as time passed they evolved into entertainments at which knights squared off two-by-two to show their prowess and win the admiration of the ladies, who were sometimes offered as prizes. These festive occasions, called Round Tables, lasted for days and included lavish feasting and drinking and all manner of sports and games. Only gentlemen could take part, but the common people were welcome as spectators.

1368

"Red Turbans" Drive Mongols from Peking

Chu Yuan-chang establishes the Ming dynasty

By the end of the 13th century all of China had been overwhelmed by the Mongols, but the regime never won acceptance by the Chinese. As the 14th century ran its course, China was subjected to a wave of rural rebellions fomented chiefly by inflationary prices and high taxation, combined with the breakdown of flood control in the Yellow River valley.

The insurrections were often the work of nationalist secret societies. One of these, the "Red Turbans," also known as the "White Lotus," became powerful in the heartland of the Yangtze valley by attracting adherents to the peasant cause from among the gentry and the official class. Its leader was a Buddhist monk, Chu Yuan-chang, who seized Nanking in 1359, established control over the south and then expelled the Mongol Yuan dynasty from Peking (Beijing) in 1368. He became the first Ming emperor, with the name Hung-wu.

By 1382 he had conquered Sichuan and Yunnan, thus bringing all of China under his rule. The Ming dynasty, which ruled China in a conservative manner and kept it in isolation (subjects were forbidden to travel abroad and ships to sail beyond coastal waters), lasted until 1644.

1379

Timur Conquers Persia

The ruler of Samarkand extends his dominion over the Near East

The last great Mongol conqueror was Timur Lang (Timur the Lame), or Tamerlane, who aspired to rival the exploits of the great khan, Genghis (from whom he claimed to be descended). From his base in Samarkand, in present-day Turkestan, which he ruled from 1369, Timur swept southward, conquering Persia in 1379, and advancing across the Euphrates to the Black Sea in 1392. Finally he ravaged India and brought the Delhi sultanate to an end by the sack of the capital in 1398.

In his cruelty he was matchless: 75,000 Indians are believed to have been slaughtered in the defense of Delhi and a pyramid built with their skulls. In his irreligion he was exceptional for his era: he treated fellow Muslims as harshly as other believers, and Asiatic Christianity was almost eradicated by him.

Timur left little in the way of achievement behind him, although an accidental consequence of his brief empire was that by winning a great victory over the Ottoman Turks of Anatolia at Angora (Ankara) in 1402, he delayed the Ottoman assault on Byzantium, whose life was thus prolonged. On his death in 1405 his lands were divided among his sons and his empire withered away.

Despite Timur's reputation for savagery, he encouraged the arts, music and literature, and himself inspired Christopher Marlowe's "Tamberlaine the Great" (c. 1597), a play of violence and passion, written in language of great poetic beauty.

1380

Moscow Defeats the Tatars at Kulikovo

A new center of Russia emerges on the Moskva

Muscovy, one of the tributary states of the Golden Horde, had its true founder in the grand duke of Moscow, Ivan I Kalita (r1328-40). He won from the khan the right to collect the tribute himself (hence the nickname Kalita, or "money-bags") and, in return for paying it to the khan, the right also to absolute rule over his subjects, a function unknown by grand dukes of the Kievan era and one in which may be seen the roots of later tsarist autocracy.

By diplomacy and political maneuvering, Muscovy grew in strength, and in Dmitri Donskoi (r1359-89) it found the first ruler willing to engage the Tatars (as the Mongols of the Golden Horde are usually called) on the battlefield. He had already successfully resisted encroachments by the emerging power of Lithuania to the west when, in 1380, he defeated the Tatars at the Battle of Kulikovo, a plain on the banks of the Don. That victory ensured that Moscow, fortunate in its position at the junction of the great east–west and north–south trading routes, should be the beneficiary of the Golden Horde's decline in the 15th century.

1381

Peasants Revolt in Southern England

Wat Tyler and his followers demand just government from Richard II

Henry II's legal reforms, by making justice available to all free men in the royal courts, gave enhanced status to free tenants of the great landowners. At the same time, they increased, if only by distinction, the dependency of the villeins, or serfs, bound by money rents and labor services to their lords. The villeins did not share in the wage increases that followed the depopulation by plague in the mid-14th century. Nor did the landed class grant villeins freedom of action in the favorable labor market, and in an age of declining prices, they kept money rents high.

Discontent reached a peak in 1380, when a series of harsh taxes culminated in the imposition of a poll tax of one shilling a head. The attempt to force the payment out of evaders produced the revolt of 1381, which began in Essex and spread through Kent and East Anglia. Led by Wat Tyler and an excommunicated priest, John Ball, the rebels stormed London, where William Walworth, the mayor, and King Richard II parleyed with them, though not before Tyler was killed by Walworth in a scuffle.

The peasants withdrew from the capital when Richard disingenuously promised to grant their remarkably articulate demands—the abolition of serfdom, the commutation of personal services into rents, and the abolition of the poll tax and the Statute of Laborers (1351), which attempted to freeze wages. Rural insurrection in the counties was not finally subdued until the end of the year.

The magnificent sable-trimmed crown of Kazan is a gauge of the wealth of the khanates of the Golden Horde.

Under John I, Portugal entered upon its heroic age in European history.

1385

Portugal Defeats Castile at Aljubarrota

Nun 'Alvares Pereira secures Portuguese independence

Portugal's independence, which Spain and the papacy had recognized in the 12th century, was threatened in the late 14th century, when John of Castile proclaimed himself king of Portugal on Ferdinand's death in 1383. John (who had married the daughter and heir of the Portuguese king, Ferdinand I) gathered support among the Portuguese nobility. But opposition from the peasantry and the urban merchant class elevated the grand master of the Knights of Aviz, also called John, into the popular candidate for the throne. John of Aviz was also backed by John of Gaunt, duke of Lancaster.

At the Battle of Aljubarrota in 1385 English archers played a decisive role in the national victory won by Nun 'Alvares Pereira, John of Aviz's counselor and general, over the Castilians. In 1386 a treaty of friendship was signed with England—the Treaty of Windsor—and thus was founded the longest alliance between two powers in European history, for it is still unbroken.

1386

Lithuania United by Marriage to Poland

A vast kingdom emerges as a rival to Muscovy

One of the greatest of medieval European states was the duchy of Lithuania; it rose to power as the result of the people's need to unite against the Teutonic Knights to the west. They were also encouraged by the opportunity to expand east provided by Tatar disruption in Russia. Under grand duke Olgierd (r1341-77), Lithuania reached the Black Sea and included present-day Belorussia and most of the Ukraine.

In 1386 a personal union was formed between Lithuania and Poland, which also feared German domination, when Olgierd's son, Jagiello, married Hedwig of Poland. Jagiello became king of Poland as Ladislaus II, while his cousin, Witold, ruled Lithuania. The marriage brought Lithuania within the orbit of Roman Catholicism, creating a gulf between it and the Orthodox Russian states.

After a great Polish-Lithuanian victory over the Teutonic Knights in Grünwald (modern Tannenberg) in 1410, Lithuania was the greatest state in eastern Europe. But friction with the Poles, combined with the continuing need to defend itself against the Teutons, distracted Lithuania's attention from the east, where Moscow grew so powerful that by a treaty of 1494 Lithuania conceded Ivan III's right to call himself tsar of "all Russia."

1389

Turks Win Battle of Kossovo

The Ottomans burst into the Balkans

A milestone in the advance of the Ottoman Turks from their base in northwest Anatolia was reached at Kossovo Field in Serbia. There, in 1389, Sultan Murad I defeated a force of Serbians, Bulgarians, Bosnians and Montenegrins and so broke the power of Serbia and Bulgaria. The Ottoman Turks, benefiting from the civil wars that racked the Byzantine empire in the mid-14th century, had already taken Nicaea and Nicomedia in 1345. In 1354 they captured Gallipoli; the conquest of Thrace followed. A European future beckoned and in 1365 a new Turkish capital was established in Adrianople (Edirne).

The Ottoman state had by then grown from its origins as a marcher region ruled by *ghazi*, or border chieftains, into an organized military enterprise, backed by an efficient Muslim bureaucracy. The victory at Kossovo brought Serbia under Ottoman control; Bulgaria was added four years later.

The local rulers were allowed considerable autonomy as long as they furnished the Ottomans with soldiers and tribute, but Ottoman authority in Europe now stretched from the Danube to the Aegean and the Gulf of Corinth. Constantinople was isolated behind its forbidding walls, and its puppet emperor looked in vain to the West for relief.

1399

Richard II of England Deposed

Henry Bolingbroke seizes the English throne

After eight years on the throne, Richard II reached his majority (the age of 18) in 1385. He at once resolved to rid himself of the shackles of the parliamentary council, led by John of Gaunt, which had governed during his minority, and, indeed, of parliament itself. His attempt to rule by royal prerogative made his reign one long struggle against the great magnates. In 1386 the "Wonderful Parliament" appointed a commission to control the king, and Richard's reply, to muster an army in his defense, led him to defeat at Radcot Bridge in 1387.

Several of Richard's friends and councilors were found guilty of treason by the "Merciless Parliament" of 1388 and executed. The king promised to be more conciliatory in the future, but in 1397 his restraint broke. He demanded oaths of loyalty from Lords and Commons, extracted forced loans and issued charters placing subjects' land at his mercy. His great blunder was to exile John of Gaunt's son, Henry Bolingbroke, in 1398 and, on Gaunt's death in 1399, to sequester his estates. Richard then left to conduct a campaign against the Irish.

Henry returned from France, raised an army with the support of the powerful Percy and Neville families, persuaded parliament to renounce fealty to Richard, and placed the crown on his own head. Richard was imprisoned in Pontefract Castle, where in 1400 he died, by starvation or by smothering at the hands of his jailers.

ALEHOUSES

Drinking establishments in the Middle Ages fell into three classes: the inns in towns and on main highways, frequented by the rich; the taverns which sold wine and were respectable; and the alehouses. Most brewers and ale-sellers were women: in the small English town of Wallingford, for example, 56 of the 60 brewers in the early 13th century were women. Alehouses were not numerous until the 14th century, before which time ale was simply fetched in jugs from the brewer or hawked at fairs and on market stalls. By the late 14th century, the quality of the ale was much improved by the replacement of spices by hops, and the gradual reduction in price, set against rising wages, had brought it within the budget of the common man.

1408

Fall of Aberystwyth Ends Welsh Revolt

Owain Glyndwr's dream of an independent Wales vanishes

The Anglo-Norman conquest of Wales in the 13th century introduced feudal social relations into a tribal culture based on ties of kinship. To this dislocation were added the ravages of the plague in the mid-14th century. Out of this social discontent was brewed the national revolt led by Owain Glyndwr at the start of the 15th century.

Glyndwr was one of the greatest of Welsh lords, trained in the law in England and for a time a soldier in the English army. He returned to Wales in 1400, proclaimed himself prince of Wales, and gained the alliance of the Percys in England, who had broken with Henry Bolingbroke and were contesting his right to the English throne.

In 1404 Glyndwr captured the strategic castles of Aberystwyth and Harlech, and in 1405 he summoned a Welsh parliament. That was the peak of his achievement. With the English recapture of Aberystwyth in 1408 and Harlech in 1409 the revolt ended.

The devastation of land and the destruction of town property impoverished the Welsh economy. And the English parliament for the first time placed legal disabilities upon Welshness. Welshmen were banned from acquiring land in the boroughs or holding municipal office; from carrying arms or fortifying their houses; and from assembling without permission.

1414

Council of Constance Heals Papal Schism

Martin V is elected pope as the conciliar movement fails to win reforms

The Great Schism in the Church began in 1378, when the college of cardinals, having elected Urban VI as pope, found him wanting and declared the election void. A second college, consisting only of French cardinals, then elected Clement VII in his place. Urban refused to acknowledge his deposition and continued in office in Rome, while Clement established himself in Avignon. For the next 30 years there were always two popes, one in Italy, one in France, and the emerging nation-states of Europe allied themselves with one or the other for reasons of secular rivalry.

The scandal gave rise to the conciliar movement, with reformers, especially the French, seeking to deliver the papacy from its embarrassment by making popes subject to the decisions of general councils of the Church. The schism was ended at the Council of Constance, which lasted from 1414 to 1418 and in 1415 elected Martin V as sole pope. Once he was elected, the reform movement lost impetus, and within a few years it was made a heresy to appeal from the pope to a general council. The schism, however, had greatly raised the pretensions of national churches, and the papacy steadily became a more narrowly Italian office.

The seal of Owain Glyndwr, dating from 1404, shows him holding the orb and scepter, but uncrowned. The rampant lions are the ancient arms of Gwynedd in North Wales.

1376–1407

ENGLAND

● **1376 "Good Parliament"**
Criticized royal administration for corruption and military failure; elected Peter de la Mare, first Speaker of the House of Commons, to treat with the king; used impeachment process (accusation by the Commons, trial by Lords) for the first time.

● **1387 Questions to Judges**
Royal judges, in answer to questions put by Richard II, entirely upheld all royal prerogatives—taxation without parliamentary consent, unfettered choice of officials, necessity of royal assent to impeachment proceedings; reforms of 1386 parliament thus made illegal; stiffened opposition to Richard.

● **1388 "Merciless Parliament"**
Five royal officials accused by a group of great nobles of treason for exercising undue influence over Richard II; appeal heard in the Lords; officials found guilty and three executed. The "Appellants" appointed a ruling council, dismissed by Richard in 1389.

FRANCE

● **1407 Murder of Louis, duke of Orléans**
Arranged by John the Fearless, duke of Burgundy; 15 years of civil war followed between Burgundians and Armagnacs (so called after Louis's son, the count of Armagnac). Both sides wooed English support; by Treaty of Troyes (1420), Philip, duke of Burgundy, made co-regent of France with Henry V of England. When Charles VII came to the throne in 1422, was not accepted in the north and became known as the *"roi de Bourges,"* where he held his court for 15 years.

1415

John Hus Burned at the Stake

A Bohemian priest dies for alleged heresy

During the years of the Great Schism the Church faced a new threat: an assault on its doctrines and authority from England and Bohemia. In England, John Wycliffe, an Oxford don who was England's first important heretic, preached against transubstantiation (the belief that at the mass the bread and wine are changed by consecration into the body and blood of Christ), thus robbing the Eucharist and the priesthood of much of their significance. He also translated the Bible into the vernacular (implying that believers could have direct access to God without middlemen-priests) and advocated that the Church should abandon its wealth in land.

Wycliffe's views may have influenced the anti-clericalism that accompanied the Peasants' Revolt of 1381. At any rate, he was condemned by the English Church in 1382 and restricted to his living in Lutterworth in Leicestershire, where he died in 1384. During the 15th century, his followers, the Lollards, continued where he had led.

That Wycliffe's contemporary, the Bohemian theologian, John Hus, was a heretic is debatable. He accepted transubstantiation and upheld the sacraments, while attacking sloth and corruption in the Church. Like Wycliffe, he stressed the importance of the Bible, but without questioning the role of the bishops. Summoned to the Council of Constance in 1415, however, he would not condemn, though he rejected, Wycliffe's views, and was himself condemned and burned at the stake.

The nobility of Bohemia and Moravia supported Hus against the Church, and in this national and doctrinal opposition to Rome lay the seeds of the Reformation.

1415

English Archers Triumph at Agincourt

England wins its last great victory in the Hundred Years' War

At Agincourt in 1415, on a field turned into a muddy marsh by heavy rains, an army of 4,000 English foot soldiers and longbowmen under Henry V exploited its mobility to defeat a cumbersome French cavalry force 10 times larger. The French lost 7,000 lives, the English only 100.

Henry V invaded Normandy again in 1417 with the objective of making a permanent occupation of northern France. By the Treaty of Troyes in 1420 he agreed to marry the daughter of Charles VI and was made heir to the French throne. Henry died in 1422, and his year old son, Henry VI, was proclaimed king of France by the English when Charles died later in the same year. The French, however, recognized the dauphin as King Charles VII.

In a French manuscript of the period French archers are incorrectly shown using longbows at Agincourt.

1429

Siege of Orléans Raised

Joan of Arc turns the tide of the war in France's favor

After Henry VI of England became king of France in 1422, the regency that ruled in his name, backed by the duke of Burgundy against central and southern France (which recognized Charles VII), extended English control southward. They added Maine to Normandy and in 1428 laid siege to Orléans.

Joan of Arc, a peasant girl, heard "voices" telling her to bring aid to Charles, who lent her troops; inspired more by her spirit than her military prowess, they raised the siege in 1429. Joan's later fame, resting on her death at the stake for witchery in 1431, is greater than her contemporary reputation, but she persuaded Charles to be crowned at Rheims in 1429.

In the drawn-out fighting that brought the Hundred Years' War to an end, England never regained the initiative. By 1453, English possessions were reduced to Calais and the Channel Islands.

1438

Habsburgs Inherit Imperial Title

Albert II becomes the Holy Roman Emperor

The Habsburgs, the ruling house of Austria from 1282 to 1918, were the most powerful family in European history. They came inauspiciously to the command of the Holy Roman Empire. When Emperor Sigismund died in 1437 he left no male heir. His daughter, however, was married to Albert of Habsburg, the near-penniless duke of Austria, who was elected without opposition as Albert II, king of the Germans, and, therefore, Holy Roman Emperor. In 1438 he also succeeded to the thrones of Bohemia and Hungary, both left vacant by Sigismund's death.

Albert's short reign was undistinguished. He was unable to put down Hussite revolts in Bohemia (where he inherited the Czechs' hatred of Sigismund for burning Hus at the stake) and he was killed in a campaign against the Ottoman Turks in 1439. A century was to pass before the Habsburgs established their dominance in central and eastern Europe, but the imperial title was to remain in the family's hands, in a succession broken only by the interregnum of 1740-42, until the dissolution of the Holy Roman Empire in 1806.

c. 1438

Pachacuti Inca Comes to the Throne

A powerful empire is built in Peru

The greatest of all empires in pre-Columbian America had its origins in a valley high in the Peruvian Andes. Here the Incas settled and established a capital in Cuzco *c.* 1300 under the semi-legendary leader, Manco Capac. Expansion did not really begin until the mid-15th century, when the first great Inca conqueror, Pachacuti, became king.

The subjugation of the Chimu people brought the northern coast of Peru under Inca control by 1475 (and with it the road network and the metal and textile skills of the Chimu). By 1500 the Inca empire stretched for some 2,000 miles from Quito to the Maule River in Chile.

Inca kings used a standing army and an aristocratic bureaucracy to maintain absolute rule over both their own people and conquered tribes. Those tribes' existing agriculture supported the empire, and their conscripted laborers built a vast complex of mountain tunnels and coastal roads for trade (borne on llamas and human backs) and the verbal transmission of royal instructions by human convoys. (The Incas had no form of writing, and information was recorded in *quipu*, a system of color-coded knotted cords.)

The Incas, like the Aztecs, were not great creators; they were "barbarians" who inherited the arts and skills of the higher cultures they absorbed. Like the Aztecs, too, they were sun-worshippers. And, as with their northern contemporaries, their oppressive rule commanded so little loyalty that their empire disintegrated at the first Spanish challenge.

LEPROSY

Leprosy, though at no time did it infect more than one in 20 of the English population, was a dreaded disease from the 10th to the 14th centuries. Lepers were segregated in lazar houses (after Lazarus, the beggar "full of sores," in the Gospels) and given land so that they might be self-sufficient. If a place could not be found in a lazar house, a leper was given a hermit's hut, a begging bowl and a distinctive hooded cloak (women wore veils). He was required to carry a rattle to warn of his approach and was forbidden to touch anything. A special Church office was instituted, in which a priest threw earth on the leper's feet and sent him away with the words: "Be thou dead to the world, but alive unto God." Thanks in part to the Black Death, leprosy was virtually wiped out in Europe by 1400.

Dürer's engraving of the Habsburg escutcheon in the time of Emperor Maximilian I (1493-1519) shows the arms of Austria and Burgundy (Mary of Burgundy was Maximilian's first wife) surmounted by the crown of the Holy Roman Empire. As more lands were added over the centuries, so the Habsburg arms changed.

1453

Constantinople Falls to the Ottomans

European trading routes to the East are cut off

The seizure of Constantinople by the Ottoman sultan, Mohammed II, in 1453 was a great feat of arms and a greater turning point in history. When the attempt to use a gigantic cannon (it was moved by 100 oxen and could fire only seven times a day) to breach the city's walls failed, the Turkish army carried 70 ships overland to bypass the imperial fleet guarding the Golden Horn.

Constantinople fell after a two-month siege and Mohammed, on entering the city, marched straight to the great domed church of Hagia Sophia, and turned it into a mosque. Europe shuddered at the end of 1,000 years of Christian history.

The Ottoman presence in the Balkans was now secure, since Constantinople was the only base from which a rearguard action might have been launched. The Roman Empire was finally destroyed, and its greatest city, a cultural, administrative and commercial hub at the principal point of intersection between Europe and Asia, passed into Muslim hands.

Revived by the Muslims after its long decline, it served as the capital of an empire that stretched to Syria and Egypt, though Cairo remained nominally Mamluk until 1517. Cut off from traditional overland trading routes to the East, Europe was thrown back on the Atlantic. The great age of European overseas exploration was at hand.

1455

Wars of the Roses Begin

The houses of York and Lancaster struggle for mastery in England

The "Wars of the Roses" was a phrase invented in the 19th century by Sir Walter Scott for the dynastic and political struggle, marked by occasional battles in the field, between the houses of Lancaster and York, both descended from Edward III, for the English throne. They lasted from the time of the Battle of St. Albans in 1455 to the accession of Henry Tudor in 1485. The nobility, able to release its energies in English quarrels after the end of the Hundred Years' War, ranged itself about equally in support of the rival houses.

First blood went to the Yorkists, when Richard, duke of York, was made regent on the insanity of his cousin, the Lancastrian Henry VI. Richard was exiled from the court when Henry regained his mind, and he was killed at the Battle of Wakefield (1460). But the Yorkists seem to have triumphed when Richard's son, Edward IV, usurped the throne in 1461 after victory at Towton in Yorkshire, the largest battle of the wars, with 50,000 in the field.

Henry VI, feebler than ever, regained the throne in 1470, but his imprisonment in the Tower of London in 1471 was followed by the death of his son, Edward, the great Lancastrian hope, during a crushing Yorkist victory at the Battle of Tewkesbury (1471). Henry was murdered a few days later. Three Yorkist kings—Edward IV, Edward V and Richard II—then held the crown, until it was picked up on Bosworth Field by Henry Tudor in 1485.

MAGICAL CURES

The orthodox Christian view that illness was a divine infliction and must therefore be cured by supernatural remedies meant that, alongside herbal treatments and leechings, magical cures had a high place in medieval medicine. The sign of the Cross kept evil spirits and vampires at bay, and soil from a churchyard, a relic of the Cross, or a piece of bone from the corpse of a martyr or saint were all efficient in warding off sickness. Christians who wished to safeguard themselves against calamity or disease wore verses from the Bible on their person, often on a scroll of parchment hung around the neck—an *agnus dei*. Insomnia was thought to be curable by placing a Bible on the forehead of the sufferer.

c. 1455

Mazarin Bible Published at Mainz

Gutenberg's printing machine produces its first masterpiece

Although printing was known in China in the 9th century, the discovery did not reach Europe, where it was reinvented in the 15th century. In 1454 Pope Nicholas V announced an indulgence, a remission of spiritual penalties for sin, on a piece of paper printed with movable type—the earliest European printing to which a definite date can be assigned.

The European discovery of printing is attributed to Johann Gutenberg of Germany, although there are other candidates. His machine used movable type, cast in molds, which was hand-set and printed on handmade paper or vellum. The first important book printed by his press was the Mazarin Bible, so named because a copy was found in the library of Cardinal Mazarin of France in the 17th century. It was several years in the making, but was completed at the latest by 1455. It is also called the Mainz Bible (Gutenberg was born in Mainz and worked there after 1437), the Gutenberg Bible and the 42-line Bible (after the length of its two columns per folio). The typeface is a Gothic script, with hand-painted colored initials and other illuminations.

Presses were established in Cologne in 1464, Rome in 1467 and Paris in 1470. The new technology facilitated the spread of classical learning during the Renaissance, and by making vernacular translations of the Bible widely available (the Mazarin Bible was in Latin) it helped to win popular support for the Protestant Reformation.

1469

Aragon and Castile United by the Marriage of Ferdinand and Isabella

Christian Spain is brought under one crown

The Iberian peninsula in the 15th century, a barren land with a much smaller population than that of France, divided by great natural barriers, comprised Portugal, Castile, Aragon and the remaining Moorish lands around Granada. While Islam was advancing in eastern Europe, the Christian kingdoms of Iberia were gaining at its expense. In 1462 Castile conquered Gibraltar and other Moorish lands and acquired the right to an annual tribute from the Moors.

Castile was a feudal power with little sea-borne trade. It coveted union with one of its neighbors, either independent Portugal to the west, a great trading state on the verge of an Atlantic explosion, or Aragon to the east, a Mediterranean power in possession of Sardinia, Sicily and the Balearic islands. The marriage of Ferdinand of Aragon to Isabella of Castile in 1469 united the two countries, a union formalized when Isabella succeeded in 1474 and Ferdinand became king of Aragon in 1479.

Full constitutional union was not achieved—each kingdom retained its own *cortés* and its own laws—but Ferdinand and Isabella built up a centralized monarchy that gradually extended its sway over other institutions.

Ferdinand and Isabella, known as the "Catholic kings," are portrayed looking much alike in a carved wood panel, dating from the 1490s, in the Royal Chapel at Granada. Under their vigorous rule Spain was united and the New World discovered.

PRE-COLUMBIAN AMERICA

What, based on the Mesopotamian experience, we call "civilization"—the organization of life around settled agricultural communities with enough mastery of the rudiments of existence to allow for leisure and some specialization of labor—came later to the Americas than to Asia and Europe. The first civilizations in the western hemisphere arose in Meso-America, south of the Rio Grande in Mexico, in the centuries just before the Christian era. A little later, beginning *c*. 300, Colombia and Peru spawned the South American civilizations that began with the Mochica people of the Moche River valley (in northern Peru) and reached their height in the brilliant Inca era of the late 15th century.

Of the Meso-American cultures, four are marked out by their achievements above the rest: the Olmec, Maya, Toltec and Aztec civilizations. All of them were dependent on the cultivation of corn and all of them developed complex rituals for the worship of a pantheon of gods. The Olmecs, who inhabited the fertile lowlands of Mexico's gulf coast, introduced hieroglyphics and the calendar to America and built vast ceremonial sites for the worship of their gods. A neighboring people built the first great American city, some time in the first four centuries A.D., at Teotihuacán. It was both a religious and commercial center and at its peak, before its mysterious destruction in the 7th century, it contained perhaps 200,000 people.

The Olmec culture lasted until after 1000, but long before then it was overshadowed by that of the Maya. Their early empire (*c*. 300-650) extended over the Yucatán peninsula and Guatemala; thereafter they were restricted to Yucatán. Although they had no metal tools, the Maya raised monumental buildings—temples, pyramids, courts (including those for their ball games)—to compare with those of ancient Egypt and practiced an ornate style of polychromatic pottery. They were the only American people to develop their own ideographic writing. Their building works required an advanced grasp of mathematics, and by their astronomical observations they arrived at notions of chronology which suggest a deeper understanding of historical time than had been reached in Europe, perhaps even an understanding that time had no beginning.

Maya civilization gradually declined after *c*. 900, when the second great Mexican warrior-culture, that of the Toltecs, was making its appearance in central Mexico. The Toltecs made Tollan (probably on the site of modern Tula) their capital and by the 11th century were making conquering raids into Yucatán. Polytheists in religion, like all the pre-Columbian Americans, they worshiped the sun god above all other gods and sacrificed human beings to him. They were the first metal-working people of America, and their advance in technology laid the basis for the great culture of the Aztecs, another warrior-tribe, who descended upon the Yucatán valley *c*. 1350 and overcame the Toltecs. The Aztecs absorbed and built on the skills of the defeated Toltecs, becoming efficient engineers and architects and developing the arts of music, sculpture, weaving and picture-writing.

The Maya Tro-Cortesianus Codex, top, is one of only three not destroyed by the Spanish. The codices were made from the bark of the wild fig tree, pounded paper-thin.

The stone carving shows a Maya rain priest with a headdress in the form of a rain serpent topped by a jaguar mask. He tears his tongue with a spiked cord—an offering of pain to the god.

The Aztec's royal aviaries were full of brilliantly plumaged birds, whose feathers were fashioned into headdresses and shields, such as the one above, few of which have survived.

The most complete urban remains from pre-Columbian times are those of the Inca fortress-city of Machu Picchu. Perched on ledges and terraces high in the Andes, it covers an area of 5 sq mls.

The Aztec capital, Tenochtitlán, was built on a group of islands in Lake Texcoco and was connected to the land by a number of giant stone causeways. The Aztecs carried their wars of conquest as far south as Panama. They were not colonizers, but empire-builders, who rarely settled where they conquered. They were content simply to collect tribute from the people they subjugated. At the beginning of the 16th century, their empire, like that of the Inca empire of Peru, was at its peak and even expanding. Like the Inca empire, it was also at its end, doomed to be swept away by the superior technology and the military might of the Europeans.

This little gold figure of a young Inca girl has a removable head, so it may have been used as a vial to hold precious oil or perfume.

1472

Ivan the Great Takes Title of Tsar

Moscow asserts its supremacy over Novgorod as the capital of Russia

In 1472 the grand duke of Moscow, Ivan the Great (as he came to be called) married Sophia, niece of the last Byzantine emperor, and, with a view to making Moscow the new Constantinople, announced himself to be "tsar of all Russia." Byzantine ceremonies were adopted in Moscow, and to the Muscovite tradition of autocracy was added the religious splendor of the Eastern emperors, who had been supreme in both church and state. That inheritance from Byzantium was to be the foundation of tsarist rule in Russia.

Ivan conquered the old rival center of Novgorod in 1478, destroyed its republican institutions and, by bringing its merchants to Moscow and sending Muscovite traders to Novgorod, brought its northern commercial network within Moscow's sphere. In 1480 he ended Moscow's tributary yoke to the Mongols. By the end of his reign in 1505 he had welded the several Russian principalities into a unit under his rule, forestalling rebellions by removing local notables to Moscow and replacing them by loyal officials of his own. He had also regained some of the western Russian lands from Poland-Lithuania, thus ushering in a century of Russian expansionism.

The strong Byzantine influence on the architecture, manners and dress in Ivan's Muscovy is evident in this contemporary illustration.

1480

Inquisition Established in Spain

Pope Sixtus IV yields to the Spanish Crown

Spain was the most tolerant part of medieval Europe, where Jew, Christian and Muslim lived at peace with one another. But in the 15th century antagonisms grew to the point at which Pope Sixtus IV bowed to pressure from Ferdinand and Isabella and from Dominican monks and agreed to the establishment of the Spanish Inquisition. Its original object was to rid Spain of Jews, as much in pursuit of racial purity as of Christian exclusivity; it extended its activities far wider, however, and became the instrument of enforcing Christian orthodoxy and political loyalty.

The cruelty of the Inquisition, compared to the standards of contemporary tribunals active in other countries, has been overstated, though it was indeed liberal in its use of the death penalty. Its great importance lay in strengthening royal authority and forging national unity. It took no account of rank, feudal privileges, or ancient divisions between Aragonese and Castilian, and so made all men equal before the law, and it was entirely under the thumb of the monarchy, managed, not by the papacy, but by the *suprema*, a royal council.

With the Church, the Inquisition worked to raise moral and intellectual standards among the clergy. The consequent relative absence of ecclesiastical abuses in Spain helps to explain why the Reformation gained little sympathy there; so does the Inquisition's mere existence as a chief weapon of the Counter-Reformation.

1484

Innocent VIII Publishes the "Witch Bull"

The papacy directs Dominican inquisitors to extirpate sorcery

Persecution of witches was well under way before Pope Innocent VIII issued the bull *Summis Desiderantes Affectibus* in 1484, calling upon two Dominican inquisitors to rid Germany of them. The inquisitors, in their turn, published the *Malleus Maleficarum*, or "Hammer of Witches," two years later. Together the bull and the *Malleus*, by their wide circulation, turned local persecutions into a general crusade and provided the papal and intellectual foundations of the craze that was to engulf western Europe (but not the countries under the Orthodox Church) in the 16th and 17th centuries.

At this time—the very age of Renaissance humanism and scientific revolution in which Europe was supposedly emerging from the mists of medieval irrationality and superstition—the belief that witches flew in their thousands to secret Sabbats to plot the overthrow of Christian society reached deep into all classes. The witch replaced the Jew as the chief object of hatred.

Persecution was often more social than religious in its impulses: mountain communities, difficult to absorb into settled agrarian and urban cultures, were from the beginning prominent targets. At the peak of the witch craze in the mid-17th century, the Spanish Inquisition was burning to death as many as 100 victims a day. The total of deaths during the craze, which had come to an end by 1700, is guesswork, but it certainly ran into hundreds of thousands.

1485

Henry Tudor Wins the Crown on Bosworth Field

The Plantagenet line dies with Richard III

Edward IV died in 1483, leaving the English throne to his 12-year-old son, Edward. The late king's brother, however, seized the crown as Richard III and imprisoned Edward and his sibling, Richard, in the Tower of London. There they died in circumstances still obscure, although the evidence suggests that King Richard had them murdered.

Richard was soon challenged by the Welsh head of the house of Lancaster, Henry Tudor, who returned from refuge in France in 1485. The armies of the antagonists met at the Battle of Bosworth Field, but the nobility was wary of taking sides, so the battle was a small one. The issue was decided by the desertion of the men of the earl of Northumberland and of Lord Stanley to Henry. Richard, the last Plantagenet king, died in the fray and, according to legend, Sir William Stanley removed the crown from the dead king's head and placed it on Henry's.

1492

Moors Driven from Spain

All of Spain falls under the rule of the Crown

When the Moorish kingdom of Granada, on Spain's southern coast, refused to pay tribute to the Spanish monarchy and seized a Spanish border fortress, it provoked a 10-year conflict which came to an end with Granada's defeat in 1492. The last Muslim kingdom in western Europe disappeared, and all of Spain passed under the rule of Ferdinand and Isabella.

A liberal peace treaty granted the Moors freedom to exercise their religion, but the treaty was abrogated after a Moorish rebellion of 1501, which served to justify an edict of the Spanish Crown that all Muslims in Spain must choose between Christian baptism and exile. Most chose the former (while inwardly retaining their faith) and became known as Moriscos. They joined the Marranos, Jews who had made the same choice under a similar edict of 1492, as the chief victims of persecution by the Inquisition.

By his marriage to Edward IV's daughter, Elizabeth, Henry VII united the houses of York and Lancaster and founded the Tudor royal line. This, coupled with his firm, just rule, political ability and promotion of trade and exploration, restored England after the chaos of civil war.

1492

Columbus Discovers America

The age of transatlantic European exploration begins

Christopher Columbus, an Italian seaman, arrived in Portugal after being shipwrecked in 1476 and remained there, taking a variety of maritime jobs. Portugal led the world in overseas navigation, but in 1484 King John II turned down Columbus's request for support for a voyage to find a western route to the East. So Columbus went to Spain and put his suggestion to Ferdinand and Isabella. They took six years to decide to outfit Columbus, in 1492, with three ships, during which time, in 1488, the Portuguese navigator Bartholomew Diaz rounded the Cape of Good Hope. Columbus was promised the governorship of any lands he discovered and a share of any profits they might bring in.

That first voyage brought Columbus to the Bahamas, where he disembarked, naming the island San Salvador. He also sighted Haiti and Cuba. He believed that he was at the tip of the Japanese archipelago, though on three return voyages, between 1493 and 1502, he found nothing remotely resembling reports of India or Cathay. Columbus died in 1506, neglected and embittered by Spain's failure to honor its agreement of governorships and wealth, and still believing that he had found the route to Asia.

1494

Treaty of Tordesillas Divides the New World

New discoveries are divided up between Spain and Portugal

On his first return voyage from America in 1493, Columbus was forced by bad weather to take refuge in the harbor in Lisbon. John II heard him explain that he had reached the Far East and, though his description of the natives and his geographical reasoning were unconvincing, the Portuguese king decided to lay claim to the discoveries. To counter his claim, the Spanish monarchy appealed to the only acknowledged international authority, the papacy.

Pope Alexander VI was Spanish. He issued two bulls: the first gave the new lands to Spain; the second drew an imaginary line from pole to pole 100 leagues west of the Portuguese-discovered Azores and Cape Verde islands and declared all sea and lands west of it a Spanish sphere of influence, what lay east of it a Portuguese sphere.

The Spanish, still believing Columbus's interpretation of his discoveries, were happy with the arrangement and in Tordesillas a treaty was signed by the two countries accepting the pope's arbitration. Portugal had secured a diplomatic triumph, since their sphere contained the true route to the East, but the future in the New World lay, however obliquely hinted at the time, with Spain.

By moving the demarcation line 370 leagues west, the treaty did, however, allow Pedro Cabral to claim Brazil for Portugal in 1500. The northern powers—England, Holland and France—never considered themselves to be bound by the treaty.

1494

Charles VIII of France Invades Italy

The seizure of Naples initiates 50 years of Habsburg–Valois wars

Italy during the early Renaissance, culturally and economically rich and fragmented into rival city-states, was the arena for a prolonged series of wars known as the Habsburg–Valois wars. They began in 1494, when, without a battle, Charles VIII of France marched through Milan, Florence and Rome. Early in 1495 he seized Naples. The Valois monarch thus broke the precarious peace that had existed since the Treaty of Lodi (1454) and awakened slumbering rivalries, dynastic and territorial, among the major players in European politics: the Holy Roman Empire, Spain, Burgundy, and the papacy.

Pope Alexander VI, Emperor Maximilian I and Ferdinand II of Spain joined forces in the Holy League of Venice in 1495 and ousted Charles from Italy. Charles's successor, Louis XII, returned to the attack in 1499. His capture of Milan was recognized by the emperor in the Treaty of Blois (1504), but the agreement to partition Naples with Ferdinand (the Spanish house of Aragon already possessed Sicily) foundered on a boundary dispute, and military victories in 1503 left Ferdinand in control of Naples.

France, having conquered Venice in 1509, was invaded in 1511 by a renewed alliance of the other powers in a second Holy League and compelled to abandon Italy. The first phase of the wars ended in 1515, when France defeated Maximilian at the Battle of Marignano, thus gaining possession of Milan and ousting the empire from Italy.

1494

Medici Expelled from Florence

Savonarola assumes moral leadership of the city-state

During the 15th and 16th centuries Florence flourished as the leading banking and artistic city in Europe. For most of that period its affairs were controlled by the Medici family of merchant-bankers, whose first great representative, Cosimo, drove out the rival Albizzi family in 1434. Cosimo and his successor, Lorenzo the Magnificent, retained republican forms of government while in reality ruling Florence as autocrats. They brought the city-state stability and prosperity. But they made enemies. In 1494, two years after Lorenzo's death, the democratic party took the opportunity offered by Charles's invasion to expel the Medici.

The real victor was Girolamo Savonarola, the Dominican prior of St. Mark's convent. For years he had been preaching asceticism and delivering scathing judgments against both the Medici and the corrupt Borgia pope, Alexander VI, whom he declared an imposter. Without office, he acted for the next four years as the moral guardian of Florence. During a carnival in 1497, Florentine citizens, at Savonarola's instigation, threw paintings and other worldly vanities into public bonfires.

In the same year, Savonarola was excommunicated for refusing to stop preaching against the pope; still he refused, and the pope threatened to place Florence itself under interdict. In 1498 a riot broke out at one of Savonarola's public ceremonies. He was arrested and, after allegedly confessing to being a false prophet, was convicted of heresy and schism and hanged and burned in the city's public square. By 1512 Florence was once again in Medici hands.

1495

Poynings' Laws Subject Ireland to English Rule

The Irish parliament at Drogheda hands over sovereignty to London

After the conquest of Ireland under Henry II, English authority there gradually waned until it came to be exercised only in a small area around Dublin known as "the pale." Henry VII's accession revived English interest in Ireland, largely because the defeated Yorkists used Ireland to hatch plots against the Tudor occupancy of the English throne, first through Lambert Simnel and then through Perkin Warbeck.

Large sections of the Anglo-Irish nobility, who had virtually taken control of Ireland and made Dublin their capital, supported the two pretenders to serve their own cause of Irish "home rule." Neither pretender came near to success, but to stifle the recurring threat, Henry sent Edward Poynings to Ireland to subject it to the sovereignty of England.

The "Poynings' Parliament" met at Drogheda in 1494 (Ireland had its own parliament from the late 13th century) and passed the famous statutes known as "Poynings' Laws" in 1495. They made the summoning of the Irish parliament, and its legislation, subject to English approval and acts of the English parliament valid in Ireland; they also forbade the holding of artillery by anyone but the king's deputy. The result—in what was in fact, though not formally, an act of union—was to emasculate the Irish parliament and to destroy Ireland as a Yorkist citadel.

The unknown artist who painted the burning of Savonarola in the Piazza Signoria gives, incidentally, an intriguing glimpse of Florence at that time—its aspect and its people.

1497

Perkin Warbeck Surrenders to Henry VII

An ill-managed rebellion comes to a tame end

Perkin Warbeck was a young Flemish boatman who arrived in Ireland in 1491 in the service of a silk merchant. He was persuaded by Anglo-Irish Yorkists to assume the identity of Richard, duke of York, one of the princes murdered in the Tower of London, and lay claim to Henry VII's crown. Perkin had the backing of Emperor Maximilian I, Charles VIII of France, Margaret of Burgundy and James IV of Scotland.

But by the time he landed in Dover in August 1494, Henry had struck terror into English Yorkists by the execution of several of their leaders. Perkin, therefore, found little support in England. He returned to Ireland, where his cause was defeated by Edward Poynings, and he was then taken up by James IV of Scotland. Two Scottish raids on England, in 1496 and 1497, were easily deflected, and Warbeck's last adventure, a landing in Cornwall in September 1497, when he proclaimed himself Richard IV, was a fiasco.

Warbeck's international allies had faded away and his few supporters were no match for Henry VII's troops. He surrendered (after briefly taking sanctuary in Beaulieu Abbey) and was imprisoned. After two failed escape attempts, he was executed in 1499. With him died the last Yorkist challenge for the English crown.

1497

Cabot Lands on Newfoundland

Rich cod banks are discovered on the North American coast

European Atlantic explorations of the 15th and early 16th centuries were all attempts to find a route to the fabled riches of China and the East. The first important northern expeditions were led by John Cabot, an Italian navigator and spice merchant in the Levant who entered the service of Henry VII of England. In 1496 Henry commissioned him to discover new lands. Cabot and some Bristol merchants provided the capital for the voyage and in return were promised a monopoly of trade.

On his second voyage in 1497, Cabot landed somewhere on the coast of Labrador, Newfoundland or Cape Breton Island. This first recorded landfall on the continent since the Norse voyages of Leif Ericsson *c.* 1000 is sometimes called the "intellectual" discovery of North America.

Cabot himself believed he had landed in Asia. He planted the English standard and, although no permanent settlement was made there until 1605, his discovery was the basis of the English claim to North America and to the rich cod fisheries off Newfoundland.

Navigation aids in use by early explorers are shown in this German manual of 1558.

1498

Vasco da Gama Reaches Calicut

The Portuguese navigator is the first European to reach India by sea

Christopher Columbus's return from the New World in 1493, with the report that he had reached eastern Asia, threatened to undo nearly a century of Portuguese exploration. So in 1497 the Portuguese government sent Vasco da Gama on a trading mission to India with a fleet of four sailing ships. The voyage was remarkable as a feat of seamanship: Vasco sailed far out across the Atlantic to reach the belts of trade winds and so avoid being trapped in the Doldrums, a bold course to follow in the days when astronomical navigation was in its infancy.

At a stop for water in Malindi, on the east African coast, he picked up a Muslim navigator, Ibn Majid, who helped him steer a route across the Indian Ocean to Calicut, a spice port on the Malabar coast. There he encountered opposition from established Arab merchants, who pressed the local Hindu ruler to refuse him facilities or goods. But Vasco managed to purchase a cargo of pepper and cinnamon and returned to Lisbon (having lost one-third of his crew from scurvy) two years almost to the day after setting out.

A European had reached India by a sea route for the first time, and the West's long history of commercial and political involvement in the subcontinent had begun.

Da Gama's fleet had two three-masted sailing ships, a 50-ton caravel and a large storeship. After a voyage lasting more than four months, da Gama had rounded the Cape of Good Hope, and on November 25 reached Mossel Bay, where he erected a stone marker pillar which can still be seen. The South African province of Natal received its name from da Gama as he sailed by on Christmas Day.

SPICE TRADE

The European search for spices from the East was driven not simply by a taste for fine cuisine but also by necessity. Until at least 1700, Europe's farms suffered from a shortage of winter feed for cattle, large numbers of which were therefore slaughtered in the autumn and pickled or salted. Salt, cheaper than spices, came chiefly from Portugal, but in insufficient quantity, and much of it went for pickling fish, especially Baltic herring. Hence the need for preservative spices: pepper from India and the East Indies, cinnamon from Ceylon (Sri Lanka), nutmeg and mace from the Celebes (Sulawesi), and ginger from China and the Malabar coast.

1487–1610

EUROPE'S SEARCH FOR THE EAST

● **Principal Voyages**

Southeast Route
1487-88 Diaz *(P)* to Cape Agulhas
1497-99 Vasco da Gama *(P)* to India
1500 Cabral *(P)* to India
1509 Sequeira *(P)* to Malacca
1512-13 Abreu *(P)* to the Moluccas

Southwest Route
1492-93 Columbus *(S)* to Bahamas
1493-94 Columbus *(S)* to Cuba
1498 Columbus *(S)* to Venezuela
1499 Vespucci and Ojeda *(S)* to the Amazon
1501 Vespucci and Coelho *(P)* to Uruguay
1502-04 Columbus *(S)* to Panama
1515 Solis *(P)* to the River Plate
1519-22 Magellan and El Cano *(P)* around the world

Northwest Route
1497 Cabot *(E)* to Newfoundland
1500 Corte-Réal *(P)* to Greenland and Newfoundland
1524 Verrazano *(F)* to New England
1526 Verrazano *(F)* to West Indies
1534-35 Cartier *(F)* to the St. Lawrence River
1576 Frobisher *(E)* to Baffin Island
1587 Davis *(E)* to Davis Strait
1610 Hudson *(E)* to Hudson Bay

Northeast Route
1553 Willoughby and Chancellor *(E)* to Archangel
1594 Barents *(H)* to Novaya Zemlaya

E=England *F*=France *H*=Holland *P*=Portugal *S*=Spain

THE RENAISSANCE

The huge bronze doors to the east portal of the Baptistery in Florence, completed in 1452, were named the Gates of Paradise by their maker, Lorenzo Ghiberti. In the 10 square panels—this one shows Jacob and Esau—Ghiberti's handling of the relief, from almost flat to rounded, and his naturalistic figures reveal the influence of humanist thinking, with its return to classical ideals of beauty.

This portrait of the great Dutch humanist and scholar Erasmus was painted in 1523 by Hans Holbein.

The rebirth, or *renaissance*, of classical learning, which began in Italy in the 15th century, led, ultimately, to so fundamental a reshaping of the European world that it has become habitual to mark it as the beginning of modern history. The Renaissance is best known for the flowering of the arts, above all for the burst of creativity in painting, sculpture and architecture in the Italian city-states of Rome, Florence, Venice and Siena. It is impossible to define the Renaissance, however, other than to say that it included whatever happened in western Europe between, roughly, 1450 and 1600.

What were the outstanding developments of those years? There were the great maritime explorations that brought Europe and the New World into contact; the accumulation of capital (partly through the great price rise of the early 16th century) which enabled lavish sums to be expended on buildings and paintings; the proliferation of capitalist forms of business organization (especially in the new printing industry) and banking; the emergence of the great credit houses of the Low Countries. There was the concentration of power in central monarchies in France, England, Portugal and Spain, and the extinction of the threat from the Ottoman empire. All these changes contributed to a new spirit of confidence and optimism in a Europe that was emerging from the closed world of feudal Christendom.

Ghirlandaio's altarpiece (1485) for the Sassetti Chapel in Sta Trinità, Florence, was commissioned by a Medici banker, Francesco Sassetti. The subject is religious—the Adoration of the Shepherds—but the setting, with a sarcophagus instead of a manger and a Roman triumphal arch, shows the artist's interest in classical antiquity. At the same time, the procession in the background is made up of closely observed Florentine citizens.

The most complete return to classical ideals in architecture was made by Andrea Palladio, who set out in his villas and palaces to reproduce those of ancient Rome. He later adapted his characteristic arch and column motifs to create classical facades on churches of great simplicity and beauty such as San Giorgio Maggiore in Venice (1556-1610).

Both the rise of powerful national monarchies and the inheritance of pagan traditions from the classical world worked to undermine the universal authority of the Church and papacy. The scholarship of humanists questioned long-accepted dogmas of the Church. But the Renaissance remained, as the Reformation proved, an intensely Christian age. Art had long been almost exclusively in the service of the Church; but Renaissance artists also served secular masters like the Medici bankers of Florence and Lodovico Sforza, the ruler of Milan. And although biblical subjects continued to dominate painting and sculpture, the figure was treated by artists with a fresh realism, with an individualism that reflected the new interest in things worldly and mirrored the artist's own rise in status from an anonymous craftsman to a valued member of society. Leonardo's *Mona Lisa*, in its attempts to portray sensuality and tenderness, even to make of its subject a psychological study, is entirely humanist in intention and effect.

The spirit of the Renaissance may be caught in the writings of Niccolo Machiavelli, the first great political theorist of the modern world. They have no reference to Christian virtues, nor to the sacerdotal nature of kingly rule. In place of the ruler as the divine representative of God in things temporal is placed the secular ruler who needs to understand only how to win and maintain power. *The Prince* (1532) was a primer to guide him. The spirit is caught even better, perhaps, in the great churches and cathedrals of the Renaissance. The prevailing style of Renaissance churches, like St. Peter's in Rome (rebuilt in 1506), was not elongate in the medieval tradition of the Romanesque and the Gothic, but circular. In Gothic churches the eye is led by vaulting arches and long naves upward to heaven and forward to the altar. The mind is led to a transcendental goal. To appreciate the beauty of a circular church you need to stand in the center, underneath the dome. So humans become the center of their world.

c. 1501

Spanish Take African Slaves to the Caribbean

The extermination of Hispaniola natives creates a demand for labor

Initial doubts about the value of Portuguese exploration of Africa's west coast under Henry the Navigator, son of John I, were stilled in 1441, when a caravel returned to Lisbon with gold and a handful of Negro slaves. During the next five years 1,000 slaves were imported, and in 1448 Portugal established its first African trading station on Arguin Island, just off the coast of Mauritania. Pope Nicholas V sanctioned war on the Moors and the conversion of pagans, in bulls which implicitly legitimized the slave trade.

Slaves were of little economic value to Portugal, though in the 16th century about 10,000 a year were imported as agricultural laborers by Spain. Spain's colonization of Hispaniola after Columbus's discovery of the New World in 1492, however, brought the native Arawak Indians near to extermination and created the need for fresh labor in the Caribbean.

The first slaves were supplied to the Spanish in Hispaniola *c.* 1501 and the trade grew so rapidly that by 1513 the Spanish Crown was making a handsome profit from the sale of licenses to import Africans. For the next 300 years the maritime European powers competed in the lucrative slave market and carried to the New World, at a conservative estimate, 15 million slaves.

Slaves were regarded merely as a commodity, to be crammed into every available space, as these plans for their transport in the holds of a "tumbeiro," or coffin ship, demonstrate.

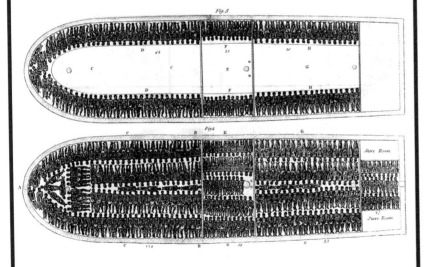

1510

Alfonse de Albuquerque Seizes Goa

Portugal establishes a trading headquarters on India's west coast

When Vasco da Gama returned from Calicut in 1499, the Portuguese monarchy already had a plan to establish factories, or trading stations, in India and to send annual fleets there under royal charter. Establishing a commercial empire in the East meant war with the Arabs who controlled the spice trade, and in 1503 Vasco, with a fleet of 14 ships, bombarded Calicut and won the first naval victory over the Arabs. It also meant converting dependence on the goodwill of local rajas for the tenure of factories and the right to trade into an independent presence, backed by a permanent Indian Ocean fleet with a secure naval base.

Acquiring this was the work of Portugal's most able naval commander, Alfonse de Albuquerque, who went to India in 1503 and chose as his target Goa, a rich city with a good harbor and a thriving ship-building industry. Albuquerque's capture of Goa in 1510 gave Portugal the first permanent European settlement in India. He also captured the Muslim island of Hormuz at the mouth of the Persian Gulf, which, with Goa, gave Portugal control of the western end of Arab trading routes.

By taking Malacca in 1511 he also gained control of the eastern routes across the Bay of Bengal. China now lay open to Portugal, and in 1514 Portuguese traders put into Canton, the first recorded European visit to China since the start of the Ming dynasty in 1368.

1516

Mamluks Defeated at Marj Dabiq

The Ottoman empire incorporates Syria and Egypt

In the opening years of the 16th century a fanatical *shi'a* sect from the southern shores of the Caspian Sea won a series of great military victories. By 1508 its leader, Ismail Safavai, had brought most of Iran and Iraq under his control. The *shi'a* revival threatened the unity of the Ottoman empire, especially in Anatolia, where the might of the whole Turkish army was needed to put down a Safavid-inspired rebellion. It also provoked Sultan Selim to renew the Ottoman campaign of conquest.

A direct assault on Safavid power in 1514 failed to dislodge Ismail from Persia, but a Turkish victory at Tchaldiran brought upper Mesopotamia and Kurdistan into the Ottoman empire. Ismail now looked to an alliance with the Mamluk sultanate of Egypt and Syria; to prevent it, Selim advanced into Syria and, in 1516, at the great battle of Marj Dabiq, north of Aleppo, Turkish janissaries, or infantrymen, and artillery overwhelmed the Mamluk army. In 1517 Cairo, too, fell. The last Mamluk sultan, Tuman Bey, was executed and Egypt and Syria were absorbed into the Ottoman empire.

As a class the Mamluks were not destroyed. They kept their lands (some local rulers even retained private armies) and during the Ottoman decline of the 18th century, recaptured some power and influence. They were eventually extinguished by Napoleon's invasion of Egypt in 1798.

Bloodthirsty conquest and the spread of Ottoman power marked the reign of Sultan Selim I, pictured here in a 16th-century miniature. But, as often seems the case with such tyrants, he was also a reformer and a poet.

1517

Luther Publishes Ninety-five Theses at Wittenberg

The papacy is challenged to reform itself

Martin Luther, an Augustinian friar and lecturer at the university at Wittenberg, had for 10 years been wrestling with the question of salvation when a Dominican monk, Johann Tetzel, arrived in Saxony to sell indulgences. These bits of paper, promising remission of sins, were being peddled on behalf of the pope, who needed money for the rebuilding of St. Peter's in Rome, and of the archbishop of Mainz, who was deep in debt.

Luther challenged the place of indulgences in the Church in a series of 95 theses, or propositions, which he posted on the door of the church at Wittenberg. This was a traditional medieval method of starting a debate, in itself unprovocative. Nor were the theses themselves revolutionary. But they contained the revolutionary implication, which subsequent events were to bring out, that belief in God alone, according to Scripture, was sufficient for salvation, and that no man, therefore, had need of either a hierarchy of bishops or the accumulated doctrines and customs of the Church to gain it. The pope's authority was thus implicitly challenged.

Luther was attacked by Johann von Eck, a German theologian, who went to Rome and in 1520 returned with a papal bull, *Exsurge domine*, condemning him. Luther burned the bull, together with volumes of canon law, in front of a public gathering and was excommunicated in January 1521, by which time German opinion was polarizing into support for Luther and backing for Rome. The Reformation had been set in motion.

1519

Charles V Becomes Holy Roman Emperor

The Fuggers secure the imperial title for the Habsburg king

When the Habsburg king of Spain, Charles V, was elected Holy Roman Emperor in 1519 he ruled a vast empire. He had inherited from his mother the Spanish crown, Sicily and Spanish lands in the New World; from his father, the Netherlands; and from his grandfather, Austria and the Tyrol. The imperial title added the disunited principalities of Germany. This was the greatest dynastic accumulation in European history and it made the Habsburgs preeminent in Europe throughout the whole of the 16th century.

The election of Charles as emperor, rather than the Valois king of France, was secured only by bribes. They were paid to the electors, who feared that German interests would be neglected if the empire were simply made a part of the Habsburg dominions, with money supplied by the great Fugger banking house.

Charles wished to rule as a great medieval emperor, personally visiting his various lands and uniting all of Christendom under him. His greatest asset was Spanish wealth, fed throughout his reign (which lasted until 1558) by silver from America. The task he faced was daunting: Protestantism in Germany had to be quelled, nationalism in the Netherlands contained, the Valois challenge broken and the Turkish advance in the east brought to a halt.

The Reformation proved to be unstoppable. Though Charles himself was largely successful on the other fronts, by the end of the century Habsburg Spain was in decline, its resources were overstretched, and France and the Netherlands were in the ascendant.

1521

Charles V Takes Milan

The Habsburg–Valois rivalry is renewed in Italy

The election of Charles V as Holy Roman Emperor in 1519 raised the stakes in the Habsburg–Valois rivalry. Since Charles was also king of Spain, France felt more threatened than before. Francis I declared war but was defeated at Milan in 1521 by an alliance of empire, papacy and Henry VIII of England. As a result, he lost the rule of Milan which had been granted to him by the Franco-Spanish Treaty of Noyon in 1516. Continuing military success by Charles's armies led to the Treaty of Madrid (1526) and the Treaty of Cambrai (1529), by which Francis agreed to abandon claims to Naples, Milan, Genoa and Asti.

The death without heirs of Francesco Sforza, ruler of Milan, in 1535 encouraged Francis to break the terms of those treaties. In alliance with the Ottoman Turks and the Protestant princes of Germany, he invaded Savoy and captured Turin in 1536. Charles's invasion of Provence was repelled, and in 1538 Pope Paul III negotiated a truce between the two kings. It lasted only until 1542, when Francis struck out in every direction, with the aid of the Turks and also of Denmark and Sweden.

The middle phase of the wars between the Habsburgs and the Valois ended with the Treaty of Crépy of 1544, by which Francis lost Artois and Flanders, again renounced claims on Italy and agreed to help Charles V against the Turks. He also agreed, by organizing a Church council of reform, to try to bring Lutherans back within the fold, against the Protestant princes of Germany.

Luther's uncompromising nature is captured in this portrait by Hans Holbein, who also made woodcuts to illustrate Luther's Bible.

1521

Luther Outlawed at Diet of Worms

Luther is driven into opposition and the Reformation begins

Between his condemnation in 1520 and his excommunication in January 1521, Martin Luther published pamphlet after pamphlet on the state of the Church.

In *The Babylonian Captivity of the Church* he restated his central tenet: that men were justified in the eyes of God by faith alone, without any need of intercession by priests. In the *Address to the Christian Nobility of the German Nation* he brought nationalism into the religious dispute by appealing to the German princes, over the head of the papacy, to put their own churches in order. In other tracts he rejected transubstantiation in favor of the doctrine of the "real presence" of Christ in the sacrament.

The newly elected Habsburg emperor, Charles V, faced a crisis. He supported ecclesiastical reform, but he was a staunch defender of the Roman faith, and he knew that the empire's fortunes were allied to those of the papacy. Fearing that the Lutheran religious movement might turn into a rebellion against the empire, he summoned Luther to explain his views at an imperial diet at Worms. Luther refused to recant his opinions, and Charles placed him under a ban, making him an outlaw in Germany. But the ban proved impossible to enforce, and Luther continued his campaign without hindrance.

1521

Cortes Overcomes the Aztecs

Horses and guns enable a handful of men to overcome Montezuma

Hernan Cortes, a minor Spanish nobleman, had voyaged to Hispaniola in 1504 and had fought in the expedition, under Diego Velazquez, that took Cuba for Spain in 1513. In 1519 he was sent by Velazquez to explore the Central American mainland. He took with him 600 soldiers, horses and muskets. On landing he destroyed his fleet of 11 ships to make return impossible. He was elected captain-general by his men and made his headquarters in Vera Cruz.

Cortes now considered himself released from Velazquez's command and responsible only to the Spanish Crown. He gained allies from the tribes of Tlaxaca (an independent province encircled by the Aztec empire) and marched on the Aztec capital, Tenochtitlán. Emperor Montezuma mistook him for a manifestation of the sun god, Quetzalcoatl, and tried to buy him off with gold. Cortes imprisoned Montezuma but retained him as a puppet emperor, and began a mission to convert the Aztecs to Christianity.

Velazquez sent an army against Cortes under the command of Panfilo de Narvaez, whom Cortes left Tenochtitlán to encounter. He defeated Narvaez and returned to the capital to learn that the Aztecs had risen against the Spanish and killed Montezuma. He retreated from the city but recaptured it after a three-month siege in 1521. In 1522 Cortes began the process of rebuilding war-torn Tenochtitlán into a new capital, renamed Mexico City, but Charles V refused to nominate him governor of New Spain officially.

1521

Magellan's Expedition Sails Around the World

A century of Iberian navigation has its crowning achievement

The famous Portuguese navigator, Ferdinand Magellan, knew the latitude of the Spice Islands, or Moluccas, in Indonesia but not their longitude. He believed them (wrongly) to lie within the Spanish sphere of influence established by the papacy in 1494. He also believed (rightly) that they could be reached by a western voyage around the southern tip of South America and that most of the continent lay within the Spanish sphere. Reasoning that the Portuguese would not, therefore, be interested in such a voyage, he applied to the Spanish monarchy for backing.

In September 1519, Magellan set out from Seville's port, Sanlucár de Barrameda, with five ships, bound apparently for the Moluccas in defiance both of the papacy and of Portugal, which had already reached the islands by an easterly route. The voyage was traumatic: shipwreck and mutiny off Patagonia; a terrifying 38-day passage through the strait that now bears Magellan's name; a long Pacific crossing which reduced the sailors to a diet of rats and leather; and, finally, a landing on the Philippines, where Magellan and 40 of his men were killed in a local war.

Sebastian del Cano took over command of the voyage, reached the Moluccas and returned home via the Indian Ocean and the Cape of Good Hope. The world had been circumnavigated for the first time, in an expedition lasting three years. In 1529, by the Treaty of Saragossa, Charles V yielded all claims on the Moluccas to Portugal in exchange for 350,000 ducats.

SCURVY

Sailors on long voyages of exploration were subject to scurvy, a debilitating disease marked by swollen gums, wasted muscle and lethargy. The Chinese understood the relationship between dietary deficiency and beriberi, caused by the lack of Vitamin B, and had for centuries carried fresh ginger on ships. By 1600 the West was learning the importance of fresh greens and citrus fruits containing Vitamin C in a sea diet, knowledge probably brought back from the East by Dutch traders. The first ship sent out by the British East India Company in 1601 carried lemons and oranges against scurvy. In the 18th century British sailors were given lime juice with their daily ration of rum, which accounts for the name "limeys" given to them. This diluted rum was first issued by Admiral Vernon, who was called "Old Grog": hence the words "grog" for the drink and "groggy" for being drunk.

1525

Peasants' War Put Down in Germany

Martin Luther allies himself with the rich and powerful

Rising prices and a series of bad harvests in early 16th-century Europe led landowners to put the squeeze on the peasantry by raising rents, enclosing common lands and increasing feudal dues. In Germany the peasants, inspired with a vision of social justice partly drawn from Lutheran theology, rose in revolt. The uprising began in the Black Forest and spread north along the Rhine and south along the Danube into Austria.

The peasants were encouraged by the Anabaptist leader, Thomas Munzer, but opposed by Luther, who believed civil government to be divinely instituted and rebellion disobedience to God. His tract, *Against the Thieving and Murdering Horde of Peasants*, called for the princes to be merciless in putting down the uprising. So they were. The rebels were slaughtered by the thousand, most notably in Frankenhausen in Saxony in May 1525, when the war came to an end.

Luther lost much popular support for his religious movement by turning his back on the common people, support which drifted toward the more extreme form of Protestantism, Anabaptism. But he had gained the backing of the German princes and ensured that the Reformation would be as much a national movement as a religious one.

1526

Mogul Dynasty Founded in India

Babur's invasion culminates in the Battle of Panipat

Few young men in history have made so early an impact as Babur, founder of the Mogul dynasty in north India. In 1494, at the age of 12, he inherited the rule of the kingdom of Fergana (in modern Uzbekistan) and took Samarkand by arms from his cousin two years later. He could hold on to neither Samarkand nor his inheritance in Fergana, however, and driven by a fierce sense of destiny and a supreme confidence in his right to empire—he was descended from Timur and Genghis—he drove south, taking Kabul in 1504.

In 1526, invited by the ruler of the Punjab to invade India and overthrow the Delhi sultan, Ibrahim Lodi, he led 12,000 armored horsemen across the Punjab plain and won a great victory at Panipat. The sultan was killed in the battle and Babur proceeded in triumph to Delhi. When he died in 1530 he had extended his rule over most of north India, from Kabul to the borders of Bengal. Thus was founded the Mogul dynasty which lasted until 1857.

Babur's Mogul empire was a precarious thing, based on the loose loyalty of his followers rather than on any administrative structure. It was also somewhat misnamed (Mogul was the Persian for Mongol), since Babur was a Turk, who always thought of himself as Turco-Persian in culture, and his followers were a mixture of Turks, Timurids (from Persia), Uzbegs, Afghans and Mongols.

The founder of the Mogul dynasty, Babur, flanked by his ancestor Timur (left) and his son Hamuyan, are depicted in this jewel-like miniature. Mogul painting, which developed from the work of Persian artists invited to his court by Hamuyan in 1549, reached its peak in the mid-1600s.

1529

Ottomans Lay Siege to Vienna

Suleiman the Magnificent leads the Turks to the height of their power

Suleiman the Magnificent became sultan of the Ottoman empire in 1520. He celebrated his accession by invading the Hungarian empire and capturing Belgrade, a critical fortress town at the confluence of the Danube and its associated river systems. The way to Buda now lay open, but Suleiman did not press his advantage until 1526, when he once again invaded Hungary.

At the great Battle of Mohács the heavy cavalry of the Hungarian nobility was no match for the huge Turkish army, whose combination of artillery fire and lightning attacks by janissaries, or infantrymen, proved decisive. Buda fell a few weeks later, and central Hungary lay wide open to Ottoman plundering.

The death of the Hungarian king at Mohács led to a contest for the succession between Archduke Ferdinand of Austria, brother of Emperor Charles V, and the Hungarian magnate John Zapolya. Zapolya was elected to the throne by the Hungarian aristocracy but driven from Buda by the Habsburg forces of Ferdinand. He then appealed for help to Suleiman, who, happy to have a puppet king in Hungary, came to his aid and reinstated him in Buda.

In 1529 the Ottomans laid siege to Ferdinand's capital of Vienna. The assault failed, the task of compressing the march to Vienna and a long siege of the city into a single season proving too great even for the mighty Ottoman army. But most of Hungary now lay in effect under the rule of the Turks, who settled in Buda on the left bank of the Danube. The Ottoman empire had penetrated deeper into Europe than ever before.

1529

Henry VIII Sues to Divorce Catherine of Aragon

The Tudor king's quarrel with Rome sets off the English Reformation

Henry VIII's "great matter"—his wish to be rid of his first wife, Catherine of Aragon—came to a head in 1527, when the king first began to voice qualms about the validity of his marriage in 1509 to the widow of his brother, Arthur. He began to argue that the papal dispensation gained at the time could not overrule scriptural objections to the marriage. The true reasons were the disruption of the Anglo-Spanish alliance in 1525 and Henry's wish to cement good relations with France, Catherine's failure to bear him a male heir (Mary I was her daughter), and the king's appetite for Anne Boleyn.

Negotiations with the papacy were conducted by Cardinal Wolsey, and in 1529 the pope agreed that the divorce issue be tried at a special court in England. That hearing reached no conclusion, and the pope's envoy, Cardinal Campeggio, adjourned the hearing to Rome. Papal refusal to grant the divorce then led Henry into a remarkable assertion of lay and national authority against Rome. He married Anne Boleyn in 1533 and induced parliament to sanction the divorce and to declare him, in the Act of Supremacy of 1534, Head of the English Church.

No ecclesiastical or doctrinal dispute set off the Reformation in England. Henry was still what the papacy had named him, "Defender of the Faith." But a national and constitutional revolution (for it was parliament that had brought the new Church of England into being) paved the way for the Puritan reformation of the next century.

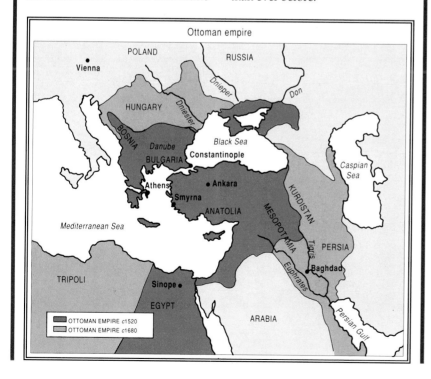

Ottoman empire

OTTOMAN EMPIRE c1520
OTTOMAN EMPIRE c1680

1530

Confession of Augsburg Fails to Bring Peace

Charles V attempts to end the empire's religious divisions

Although the Turkish siege of Vienna was repelled in 1529, the Ottoman presence in Hungary posed a continuing threat to the Holy Roman Empire. Charles V needed a united front against the Muslim threat, and at the diet of Augsburg in 1530 he was eager to end the religious divisions that had arisen in Germany and to make peace between the Protestant princes and the Roman Church. At his request the Protestant princes prepared a statement of their position, the Augsburg Confession, drawn up chiefly by the Lutheran theologian Philip Melanchthon (Luther was still outlawed and banned from the diet).

Its purpose was reconciliation; it stressed points of similarity between Protestant and Roman Catholic and, while affirming justification by faith alone, omitted reference to the priesthood of all believers. But the reply of the Roman theologians, the *Confutatio*, stressed points of contention. The Protestant princes withdrew from the diet, and the rump confirmed the Edict of Worms and threatened military action if the reformers did not return to the fold by April 1531. Protestantism remained condemned, its adherents virtually outlawed.

The result was to invigorate Protestant organization. In February 1531, eight princes and 11 cities formulated the League of Schmalkalden (after a town on the Hesse-Saxony border) for mutual defense if any of them were attacked for their religion. For the first time, a section of the empire had declared open resistance to the emperor and his diets.

1532

Portugal Colonizes Brazil

A permanent settlement is founded at São Vicente

Six years after the signing of the Treaty of Tordesillas in 1494, the Portuguese navigator Pedro Alvares Cabral, en route to India, landed accidentally on the South American coast and claimed Brazil for Portugal. The economic value of the heavily forested land was not at first appreciated, and the first permanent settlement, at São Vicente, on the island of São Paulo, was founded only in 1532. In 1549 Tomé de Sousa became Brazil's first captain-general, in Bahia.

Some early traders exported the red dyewood (pau-brasil) that gave the country its name. But it was not until mid-century that sugarcane was introduced from Madeira and the carving-out of plantations in the jungle began. Brazil was the first colony in the New World to be put to agricultural use, and by 1600 it was producing half of the world's sugar supply. (Gold mining did not begin before the early 18th century, and coffee became a major crop only in the 19th.)

The wealth that the sugar trade offered attracted more Portuguese settlers to Brazil than to the rest of Portugal's colonies put together: by 1550 some 20,000 had already established themselves. Brazil also became the most voracious consumer of slaves from West Africa, importing 3½–4 million of them between 1530 and the ending of the trade in 1870.

An engraving in de Hooghe's "Les Indes Orientales" shows every stage of sugar production in Brazil in the late 1600s carried out by slaves, from cutting the cane to cooking and refining the sugar juice.

1533

Pizarro Conquers Peru

The fall of Cuzco completes the destruction of the Inca empire

The Inca empire was discovered by the Spaniards in 1530 after eight years of exploration, and its conquest was organized by a syndicate at whose head was an obscure adventurer, Francisco Pizarro. Pizarro arrived on the Peruvian coast in 1532 with forces smaller even than those of Cortes, but by befriending the usurper on the Inca throne, Atahualpa, he was able to capture and execute him. The capital, Cuzco, fell to Pizarro in 1533, and the high degree of organization in the Inca empire—the slave economy and network of roads—made conquest simple.

Pizarro was a brutal man, but the severity of Inca rule cast him in the role of deliverer. He was appointed governor of Peru by Spain, but a series of civil wars among the conquerors, in which Pizarro died in 1541, raged for 20 years.

Local native rulers sought to gain advantage from these quarrels, but only in Chile were they able to resist Spanish arms. By 1550 most of Central America, the Caribbean and the west coast of South America were part of Spain's New World empire.

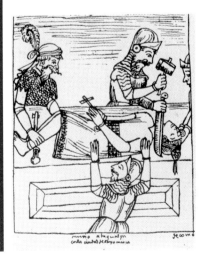

1536

Act of Union Joins England and Wales

Welsh representatives are admitted to the English parliament

Since the accession of Henry VII in 1485 Wales had been governed by England as a dependent territory, with no voice in its own affairs. Two acts of the English parliament, passed in 1536 and 1543, changed the relationship and brought the two countries into union, the prelude to the long course of the centralization of English rule in London, to run throughout the British Isles.

The new Tudor monarchy, in an age of rising nation-states in Europe, wanted to be rid of local differences and feudal privileges in the pursuit of administrative uniformity. Henry VIII also wanted to extend his religious reformation to Wales and to secure his western flank against the foreign invasion which religious change might provoke.

By the complementary acts of 1536 and 1543 the centuries-long struggle between the English Crown and the Welsh marcher lords was brought to a close. The English system of land tenure was introduced into Wales; English common law was extended to Wales; the Welsh shires were empowered to elect justices of the peace; and each Welsh shire and borough was to send a representative to the Westminster parliament. One unintended long-term consequence of the acts was to deal a blow to the Welsh language: all legal proceedings were henceforth to be conducted in English.

The gruesome execution of Atahualpa by Pizarro's men is one of many drawings of Inca life and customs and the Spanish conquest by Felipe Guaman Poma in the only extant codex from 16th-century Peru.

1536–1546

GERMANY

● **1536 Anabaptists Executed**
John of Leyden, the Dutch Anabaptist, who had established theocratic rule at Münster in 1534, executed there with leading followers; had offended more by advocating communism and polygamy than by doctrinal opposition to infant baptism; massacre of Anabaptists followed.

● **1546 Schmalkaldic War**
Charles V, in formal alliance with the papacy, began war to crush Lutheranism in rebel German princedoms; supported by troops from Italy and the Netherlands. Won decisive victory at Mühlberg in Saxony, 1547, but armed victory did not stamp out reformed religion in northern Germany.

ENGLAND

● **1536 Pilgrimage of Grace**
Rising of Roman Catholics in northern counties against Henry VIII's dissolution of the monasteries; demanded removal of Thomas Cromwell as Henry's chief minister, an end to the dissolutions and the restoration of papal authority. Many leaders executed after second rising in 1537; dissolution of monasteries completed by 1540.

1536

Calvin Publishes the "Institutes of the Christian Religion"

Extreme Protestantism is given its most influential statement

John Calvin, 26 years younger than Luther, was the moving spirit of the second generation of Protestant reformers. His brand of Protestantism was destined to spread most widely throughout the world, especially to Scotland and the Netherlands and from there to North America. The statement of his beliefs, the *Institutes of the Christian Religion,* was published in 1536.

Luther directed attention to human salvation and the means of achieving it. Calvin agreed with Luther's idea of justification by faith alone and with the priesthood of all believers. But he directed attention to God, the purpose of life was to know God, and the primary importance of his incarnation as Christ lay less in redemption, more in the evidence which it provided of his existence.

At the core of Calvin's teaching, separating Calvinism from Lutheranism, was the doctrine of predestination. Omnipotent and omniscient, God had from the beginning decreed some people to be saved (the elect) and some to be damned (the reprobates) and as the means for executing that implacable decree had instituted the infusion of grace, through faith in Christ, in the elect. Good works afforded no redemption (nor did they for Luther), but they might be a sign of election. Hence the strong impetus that Calvin gave to strict Puritan morality, and also, perhaps, by the emphasis on hard work and material success, to the rise of capitalism.

1540

Ignatius Loyola Founds Jesuit Order

The papacy gives its approval to a new religious house

One of the most potent weapons in the Counter-Reformation was the Society of Jesus. The new religious order was founded by the Spaniard, Ignatius of Loyola, and six disciples in 1534 and recognized by the papacy in 1540. Ignatius had been set on a course of religious mission by reading devotional works while convalescing from wounds received during the French siege of Pamplona in 1521. Following this, he wrote *Spiritual Exercises,* a severe guide to purging the soul of sins, which became the Jesuit handbook.

The Jesuit order, headed by a "general" who resided in Rome, was rigidly hierarchical and totally subordinate to the papacy. Entry was difficult, and utter obedience to superiors and unstinting service wherever called were demanded of those who gained it. Ignatius's chief object was missionary work beyond Europe, and, although this began early (one of his disciples, Xavier, went to the Portuguese East Indies in 1541), the Jesuits were pressed into the service of the papacy in its struggle against the Protestant reformers.

Secular rulers were wary of an order so tied to the papacy: the Jesuits were effectively resisted in France and Spain (Charles V refused them entry to the Netherlands), and their greatest success was achieved in Italy, Portugal and Germany. By the time of Ignatius's death in 1556, the order had 1,000 members.

Hernando de Soto had been with Pizarro in Peru and was governor of Cuba when he embarked on his quest for the riches of North America.

1541

Hernando de Soto Discovers the Mississippi

A Spanish search for treasure ends in failure

In 1539 or '40 Hernando de Soto, the Spanish conquistador, landed on the Florida coast with 600 men and 200 horses. He had been given the right to conquer North America by Emperor Charles V.

De Soto was less concerned with conquest than with finding silver and gold. In the search, he spent two years traveling halfway across the continent, battling with Indians and, in 1541, crossing the Mississippi (the exact point is disputed). De Soto and his men were the first Europeans to set eyes on the mighty river. They continued their quest for gold up the Arkansas River into Oklahoma before turning back to the Mississippi. De Soto died on its banks in 1541.

The river was not seen again by Europeans until the French explorers Jacques Marquette and Louis Joliet reached it via the Wisconsin River in 1673. They paddled their canoes down the west bank of the Mississippi as far as the Arkansas, then back up the east bank, exploring the Illinois River and eventually reaching Lake Michigan via the Chicago River.

1541

Calvin Establishes Puritan Theocracy in Geneva

The French theologian begins a reformation of manners

In 1541 Calvin, at the invitation of the city's Protestant leaders, established a new form of civil government in Geneva that subordinated the state to the Church. Its purposes were to make Protestantism prevail by giving it a clear, defined shape and to enforce a reformation of manners.

There were four orders of office: doctors (to define doctrine and instruct in it), pastors (to preach the Gospel), lay elders (to administer the Church) and deacons (to oversee charitable works). A consistory (court) of pastors and elders was to enjoin moral and ecclesiastical discipline. Nowhere else did Protestantism have as systematic and severe an organization of religion and daily life.

"FISH DAYS"

The ban on meat eating on Fridays and Lenten days had more to it than a penitential purpose. Tudor England, for example, was becoming a maritime power and it was essential to maintain a thriving fishing industry (fishermen sailed west as far as Newfoundland for cod and east for herring) to supply the navy with seaworthy recruits and to swell its forces in time of war. The eating of fish also had the merit of reducing the consumption of mutton and beef, for Tudor monarchs were always concerned about the rising unemployment that accompanied the enclosure of arable land and its conversion to pasture. So "fish days" were severely upheld by the law and offenders against them punished, often by being consigned for several days to the pillory.

1543

Vesalius Publishes "De Humani Corporis Fabrica"

A Flemish pioneer produces the first standard work of modern anatomy

The reintroduction of classical texts to the West during the Renaissance brought the anatomical knowledge of the ancients, especially of the "father of medicine," Galen, to attention. The chief fruit of this scientific revival was *De Humani Corporis Fabrica* ("Of the Fabric of the Human Body"), published in 1543 by Andreas Vesalius, the Flemish professor of anatomy at the university of Padua. The introduction of printing made accurate reproductions of Vesalius's drawings—in their naturalism a break with medieval tradition—widely available, and the book became the standard anatomical work.

Vesalius's methods were far more important than his results: he himself carried out dissections, on human cadavers as well as on animals, and he invented new instruments for the purpose. He contested Galen's idea that blood passed from the right to the left ventricle of the heart through the thick wall called the septum, but he retained the view, which arose from dissecting animals that had bled to death and was to be exploded a century later by William Harvey, that the arteries conveyed air.

Vesalius's achievement in laying the groundwork of modern anatomy might have been greater had he not, at the age of 31, left Padua because of the storm of criticism raised by human dissections. Abandoning research, he accepted the post of physician to Emperor Charles V.

The detailed and elegant drawings for Vesalius's "Fabrica"—this one is of a man's musculature—were made in Venice, probably in the artist Titian's studio. Vesalius himself took them, with the text, to Basel in Switzerland, where the book was printed in 1543.

THE REFORMATION

Luther stressed the spiritual, inward nature of Christianity, symbolized by the administration of the sacrament. This composite picture shows him, with Hus, at the court of his protector, John Frederick of Saxony.

Another crucial tenet of Luther's doctrine was to make the word of God accessible to ordinary people. He achieved this by his translation of the Bible into German and by his constant writing and preaching. This picture of Luther in the pulpit of St. Marien's church in Wittenberg, painted by Lucas Cranach in 1547, today hangs in the church.

The Reformation that began, as it turned out, when Martin Luther nailed his 95 theses to the door of Wittenberg cathedral in 1517, was both a spiritual and a political crisis. The very attack on the papacy and the Roman faith had both religious and economic origins. The clergy was widely regarded as both immoral and corrupt: absenteeism and pluralism (the holding of more than one church office) were perhaps the most frequent charges brought against parish priests. The Church was also deeply involved in worldly affairs, in law, finance and government.

One of the reasons why Luther brought down a storm on the Church, where Wycliffe and Hus before him had not, is that Germany was ripe for revolt. German agriculture in the early 16th century was in a recession marked by sharply falling prices. Both the lesser nobility and the peasantry were feeling the pinch. In their discontent they found an enemy in the large landowners; they reserved their deepest animosity for the rich and powerful ecclesiastical landlords. Many of the great German princes, too, for different reasons were ready to listen to Luther. They wanted their independence from the meddlings of pope and emperor. They wanted an end to the payments in taxes and dispensations that annually went to the Vatican.

The lavish expenditure of three successive popes, Innocent VIII, Julius II and Leo X, had plunged the papacy into severe debt. To help relieve the debt burden Leo had recourse to the sale of indulgences, pieces of paper whose purchase was said to shorten a soul's time in purgatory. In 1517 indulgences went on sale in Luther's diocese of Magdeburg. Luther decided to attack the practice. His decision began the Reformation.

At the heart of Luther's doctrine, as it evolved over the next decade, were two propositions: "justification by faith alone" and "the priesthood of all believers." It was Luther's contention that good works, such as the purchase of indulgences, were, like the mere observance of Church rituals, of no assistance in gaining a person eternal

salvation. The only path to salvation was faith in the redemptive power of Jesus Christ. Hence, the vast hierarchy of archbishops and bishops was also unnecessary. Every believer was his own priest, with direct access to God through his own faithful mind and heart. Hence, more dramatically, the very authority of the papacy, though Luther in the beginning intended no such thing, was brought into question.

Luther's arguments made an implicitly democratic appeal. Every man could make up his own mind by reading the Bible and believing in the name of Jesus. And thanks to Gutenberg's printing machine, and the translation of the Bible into the vernacular, more and more people were reading the Scriptures for themselves.

Luther's preaching won converts across Germany. The empire and papacy felt compelled to quell the rising agitation by striking directly at Luther himself. Men with a quarrel against the papacy and the empire were drawn to his support, not just the German princes and electors, but, for example, the leaders of the Netherlands, eager to be rid of the Spanish yoke. Luther's lead gave rise to a second generation of Protestant leaders, above all, John Calvin and Huldreich Zwingli. By the mid-16th century Europe was divided into two camps, Roman Catholic and Protestant, and a century of religious conflict lay ahead.

The corruption of Pope Leo X first drove Luther to rebel; others followed suit. The satirical painting, bottom, shows Henry VIII bestowing his throne and his title as Head of the Church on his heir, in disregard of a moribund pope.

1543

Copernicus's Heliocentric Theory Published

A Polish astronomer lays the foundations of modern cosmology

Nicholas Copernicus spent most of his adult life as a canon at Frauenberg cathedral. At university, however, he had studied astronomy and he never ceased to be, in his own words, a "mathematician of the skies." The phrase was accurate: he did not make observations himself but relied on the data of others. He accepted the Ptolemaic notion that celestial bodies must move in circles (and so retained epicycles in his system), but he knew that in Ptolemy's model they did not move at a uniform velocity. To eliminate this defect Copernicus arrived at his heliocentric model: the earth moved around the sun and the appearance to the contrary was caused by the earth's rotation on its own axis.

Copernicus did not publish his epoch-making conclusion (a rediscovery of Greek heliocentricity), which was the first step on the road to Kepler's and Newton's planetary laws, because he feared ridicule from his inability to prove it beyond question. It was not fear of the Church that made him timid. *On the Revolutions of the Heavenly Spheres* was published in 1543, a few weeks after his death, but it was not placed on the Church's Index of Forbidden Books for another 90 years, in the year of Galileo's trial.

On the Copernican map of the heavens, the earth, planets and zodiac are all still shown wheeling around the sun in perfect circles.

1545

Council of Trent Starts Counter-Reformation

Pope Paul III calls a crisis meeting of Roman Catholic leaders

The movement of Roman Catholic reform and revival, which has come to be known as the Counter-Reformation, was taking place even while Charles V was making the avoidance of schism his great object. The movement achieved its first great official success at the Council of Trent, called by Pope Paul III in 1545. That council went beyond mere reform. Putting hopes of reconciliation aside, it gave new doctrinal clarity to the Roman faith and threw into relief the outstanding points of difference that existed between Protestantism and Catholicism.

Justification by faith alone was condemned, while transubstantiation, the equal authority of Church doctrines with Scripture, and people's freedom to accept or reject God's grace were affirmed. No concessions were made to Protestant objections to practices such as the worship of saints, clerical celibacy and indulgences.

The Council lasted until 1563 and its decrees were confirmed by Pope Pius IV in 1564. Papal supremacy was strengthened and the division between Protestantism and Roman Catholicism defined. And the Roman Church, though reduced in its territorial sway as the idea of universal Christendom united in one faith vanished, emerged armed with strength and purpose to enter a new period in its history.

1547

Ivan IV Crowned Tsar

Moscow's supremacy in Russia is given ceremonial confirmation

Ivan III had called himself tsar. But Ivan IV, in 1547, was the first grand duke of Moscow officially to be crowned as "ruler, tsar and grand duke," a great title implying inheritance of imperial sway from fallen Constantinople and dominion over Poland and Lithuania. Less contentiously, Ivan's coronation marked the fact that in his predecessor's reign the last of the independent Russian states, Pskov, had been incorporated within the grand duchy of Muscovy.

The first official tsar is known to the West as Ivan the Terrible (although his nickname, *grozny*, is better translated as "stern"). Egomaniacal, given to outbursts of violence, excessively cruel—all these things he was, especially as he grew older. But in the middle years of his reign (1533-84) he fully justified the title of tsar.

He conquered the Tatar khanate of Kazan in 1553 and Astrakhan in 1556, thus uniting the region surrounding the Volga, from the Urals to the Caspian, with Moscow and opening up a vast market for trade. And although he gained nothing from a long war (1558-83) against Poland-Lithuania for control of Livonia, it was during his reign that Russia began its historic expansion into Siberia.

1555

Latimer and Ridley Burned at the Stake

"Bloody Mary" persecutes English Protestants

Mary I of England succeeded to the throne in July 1553, determined to marry Philip, heir to the throne of Roman Catholic Spain, and to restore papal supremacy in England. Both objects were achieved in 1554. Papal courts and papal laws against heresy were reintroduced, and for the rest of Mary's reign the Protestants were persecuted.

In 1554 Mary had arrested and imprisoned in the Tower of London Thomas Cranmer, archbishop of London; Hugh Latimer, the most famous Protestant preacher in the land; and Nicholas Ridley, bishop of London. In the autumn of 1555 they were tried and condemned for heresy in Oxford. Latimer and Ridley were forthwith burned at the stake. Cranmer was returned to prison in the hope that he might there recant.

After a few months' torment he did, but when brought to St. Mary's Church to make a public confession, he refused to do so. He was burned at the stake in March 1556. The three "Oxford martyrs" were the most prominent of the nearly 300 Protestants whom Mary put to death during her five-year reign.

The exact spot of Latimer's and Ridley's burning, so vividly depicted in Fox's "Book of Martyrs," is today marked by a brick cross set into Broad Street, Oxford.

1555

Peace of Augsburg Tempers Religious Divisions

The idea of the nation-state is advanced by the settlement

The Treaty of Augsburg, which was made at the imperial diet there in 1555, brought an end to the religious wars that had raged in Reformation Germany. It had two main provisions: that princes should be free to choose either Lutheranism or the Roman Catholic faith for their principalities (while granting dissenters the right to leave); and that both faiths should be practiced without disability in free and imperial, that is, independent cities.

Together with the decrees of the Council of Trent (1545-63) the treaty sealed the schism in the Church. And just as the council strengthened the papacy at the empire's expense, so the treaty dealt a deathblow to the already fading vision of a universal empire and greatly enhanced the pretensions of the emerging national monarchies of Europe.

1558

Calais Captured by France

England loses its last foothold on the continent

Mary I's marriage to Philip of Spain, who inherited the Spanish crown as Philip II in 1556, drew England into the Habsburg orbit. One of Philip's objects in marrying Mary was to encircle France, and in 1557 he gained his end when England joined in his war against France. For England the chief result of this war was the loss of Calais, a military base on the continent and a prosperous town that was the center of England's lucrative export trade in wool. The town, which had been an English possession since 1347, was captured by the French, under François de Lorraine, duke of Guise, in 1558. England thus lost its last foothold on the continent of Europe.

1559

Elizabeth I Defines the Church of England

Protestantism is given a wide meaning in a broad settlement

The persecutions of Mary I—Bloody Mary—and the loss of Calais enabled Elizabeth I to start her reign amid an upsurge of "patriotic Protestantism." Elizabeth at once set about the task of undoing Mary's Roman restoration. By act of parliament the monarch was again made head of the Church, under the new title of "supreme governor," and Cranmer's Book of Common Prayer was restored, in a slightly amended version, as the liturgy of the Church.

About 300 Roman clergy who refused to accept the new order were deprived of their livings, but generally the settlement, which Elizabeth's long reign did much to make permanent, was broad enough to satisfy divergent views within Protestantism. The contentious issue of the content of the mass, for example, was left unresolved, since the new Book of Common Prayer included both words implying a "real presence" from the 1549 edition and others from the 1552 edition implying a mere symbolic presence.

And extreme Calvinists, who disliked the Church's retention of the bishops and the sacraments, were somewhat placated by Article 17 of the Thirty-Nine Articles of the Church of 1563, which upheld predestination. (Sworn adherence to the Articles was required of those seeking ordination.) Even so, the avoidance of a direct attack on Roman practices in the Elizabethan settlement was to drive many extreme Protestants, or Puritans, toward secession.

Religious settlement of Europe 1555

SCOTLAND
RUSSIA
IRELAND
ENGLAND
POLAND–LITHUANIA
FRANCE
HOLY ROMAN EMPIRE
Geneva
PORTUGAL
ITALY
SPAIN
OTTOMAN
EMPIRE

☐ ROMAN AND ORTHODOX
▨ PROTESTANT
▨ MIXED

1562

Wars of Religion Start in France

The Huguenots are drawn into a war of the Crown and the nobility

For nearly 40 years France was absorbed in a series of petty and inconclusive wars, fought between noble factions for control of the throne and bringing in their train the long struggle of the French Protestants, or Huguenots, for religious and civil liberty.

The trouble started in 1559 with the death of Henry II, which left the crown in the hands of his widow, Catherine de' Medici, and their weak sons, Francis II, Charles IX and Henry III. The provincial nobility, resentful of central authority, saw its opportunity to make gains in a country rendered unstable by the economic costs of the long Habsburg–Valois wars and the growing strength of the Calvinist church.

Intermittent fighting, prolonged by the intervention of Spain and Rome on the side of the Roman Catholic monarchy, and England, Holland and some German princes on the Huguenot side, broke out in 1562. It was at its bloodiest in the so-called Third War (1568-70), which ended in substantial Huguenot gains; by the Treaty of Saint-Germain (1570) they were given the right to fortify four citadels (*places de sûreté*).

Reverses over the next three decades were made good in 1598, when the wars came to an end, and Henry IV granted the Huguenots almost full toleration in the Edict of Nantes.

1567

Netherlands Revolt Against Spain

William the Silent initiates an 80-year struggle for independence

The 17 provinces that made up the duchy of Burgundy were, in the mid-16th century, the most commercially advanced and prosperous in Europe. They were also part of the Habsburg empire ruled by Philip II of Spain. Soon after his accession in 1559, Philip made clear his intention to bring them together in a centralized union obedient to his rule. He also meant to introduce the Inquisition into an essentially Calvinist population.

The result was a revolt of the northern provinces—the Netherlands—led by the prince of Orange, William the Silent. It began in Brabant and Flanders in 1562. Its demands were greater autonomy and the removal of Spanish officials. By 1574 the rebels had succeeded in expelling the Spanish garrisons.

At its peak, the rebellion united all of the Low countries in the Pacification of Ghent (1576). But Alessandro Farnese, the governor of the Netherlands, recovered the southern provinces (modern Belgium and Luxembourg) for Spain, and in 1581 only the seven northern provinces, who had formed the Union of Utrecht two years earlier, declared their independence.

Fighting continued at intervals until the truce of 1609 and was resumed at the onset of the Thirty Years' War in 1618. The United Provinces (as the Netherlands were then called) finally won independence at the end of the war by the Treaty of Münster, signed in 1648.

1576–1618

THE NETHERLANDS

● **1576 Antwerp Massacre**
Spanish troops killed 6,000 people and burned 800 houses; known as the "Spanish Fury"; led to Low Country citizens of all religious persuasions leaguing together in the Pacification of Ghent. The north and south then drifted apart; in 1579 the south formed the Union of Arras (confirming Philip II as sovereign), the north, the Union of Utrecht. The latter effectively marked the foundation of the Dutch republic (the United Provinces), whose states-general formally deposed Philip II by the Act of Abjuration (1581).

● **1609 Truce**
Twelve-year ceasefire agreed between Spain and the United Provinces; opposed by Maurice of Nassau (captain-general and stadtholder), but successfully negotiated by Johan van Oldenbarnevelt, leader of the states-general. War began again in 1621 when neither side would renew the truce.

● **1618 Synod of Dordt**
International Calvinist synod, dominated by extremists; denounced Arminianism, the religious *via media* descended from Erasmus, which preached the universality of grace, free will and toleration of dissent; imprisoned the leading Dutch Arminian, Hugo Grotius, for life (escaped, 1621) and absurdly sentenced Oldenbarnevelt to death for treason. Effected a political revolution in Holland and, together with the advance of the Counter-Reformation, widened the ideological rift in Europe on the eve of the Thirty Years' War.

1569

William Cecil Defeats the Northern Earls

A rebellion of the English nobility fails

The appearance of Mary, Queen of Scots, in England in 1568 stimulated opposition to the rule of Elizabeth I among Roman Catholics. They supported Mary's claim to the throne against Elizabeth, who was in their eyes illegitimate. Other malcontents, too, were willing for their own purposes to ally themselves with the Roman Catholic cause. Chief among these were three great northern families, the Percys, the Nevilles and the Dacres, who resented the encroaching centralization of the Tudor monarchy.

In the remote and poor northern extremity of the kingdom, where Protestantism had made little headway, they therefore championed Mary, plotting with the earl of Leicester and the duke of Norfolk to overthrow Elizabeth's secretary, William Cecil. But when Norfolk was imprisoned in 1569 he revealed the plot. Thomas Percy, earl of Northumberland, and Charles Neville, earl of Westmorland, ignored a summons to the court to answer for their behavior and were declared outlaws.

They rallied supporters, occupied Durham and celebrated a Roman mass in the city's cathedral. But the revolt, a much smaller affair than the Pilgrimage of Grace, was, in fact, restricted to the three great families and was easily put down by royal troops. About 400 rebels were executed, including Northumberland; Westmorland lived out his life in exile in Flanders. Cecil kept his position as first minister, and the Protestant Tudor monarchy was securely established.

1571

Christian Powers Overcome the Turks at Lepanto

The Holy League gains a victory over the Ottoman navy

The fall of Constantinople to the Ottoman Turks in 1453 was followed by two centuries of naval warfare and Turkish expansion westward. The Ionian Islands, for example, were taken by the Turks in 1479, and Cyprus was constantly under threat. In 1570 it was known that the Ottomans were planning an assault on the fortressed island and a Holy League was formed by Spain to defend it.

A year later Ottoman forces seized Cyprus, and the fleet of the Holy League, led by 200 galleys, put out from Messina in Sicily, under the command of the most illustrious admiral in the West, Don John of Austria.

In the Gulf of Patras, off the Greek town of Lepanto, he engaged the Turkish fleet and inflicted a heavy defeat on it. It was a famous battle, the first naval defeat of the Turks by the Christian powers. The West lost 7,000 men, but the Turks had twice as many killed or captured and their fleet was virtually destroyed.

Yet the victory was not followed up and its consequences were nil (unless it be said that an Ottoman victory would have led to Turkish authority over the whole of the Mediterranean). Cyprus was not recovered, Turkish possessions in Europe were unaltered, and the Mediterranean remained under Ottoman control in the east and Italian (particularly Venetian) domination in the west.

In four hours of fighting, Don John's fleet captured or sank around 117 Turkish ships and freed some 10,000 Christian galley slaves.

1572

Huguenots Slain in Massacre of St. Bartholomew's Day

French persecution of Protestants reaches its peak

The Treaty of St. Germain in 1570, which secured French Protestants certain rights, was accompanied by the eclipse of the Roman Catholic Guise party at the royal court and the ascendancy of the Huguenots, led by the comte de Coligny, in the counsels of the 22-year-old king, Charles IX. The Guise faction took alarm at the prospect that Charles might be led into an alliance with England and Holland to make war against Spanish rule in the Netherlands.

Catherine de' Medici, the queen mother, therefore organized a plot to assassinate Coligny. He was shot, but not killed. Undeterred, Catherine persuaded the king to eliminate all the Huguenot leaders then assembled in Paris for the wedding of her daughter, Margaret de Valois, to the Protestant leader, Henry of Navarre. Coligny was stabbed in his bed and thrown from his window at 2 a.m. on August 24, 1572—St. Bartholomew's Day.

Lesser Huguenot leaders were also murdered, and the assassinations inflamed the Parisian Roman Catholics. Over the next two days about 3,000 Protestants were slain. Henry of Navarre saved himself by announcing his conversion to Rome. But passions flowed into the provinces and by the end of the autumn another 10,000 Protestants had lost their lives.

1580

Portugal and Spain United

Philip II adds the Portuguese empire to his own

King Sebastian of Portugal was killed in battle in 1578, leaving the throne to the aged Cardinal Henry, just at the time that the Spanish Crown was bankrupt. Next in line to the throne was Philip II of Spain, who cast a covetous eye on the wealth of the vast Portuguese overseas empire. At once he began to woo the Portuguese nobility and clergy, so successfully that Cardinal Henry nominated him as his successor.

Philip inherited the throne when Henry died in 1580. Securing it was a more difficult matter. The common people, in whose memory the victory over Castile at Aljubarotta in 1385 was a potent event, were hostile to Philip's accession. Philip had, in preparation, outfitted a fleet in Gibraltar and placed 27,000 troops under the command of the veteran duke of Alba on the Portuguese frontier. Alba preceded Philip into Portugal, ensuring that the king's progress was unimpeded. In Thomar, in January 1581, Philip summoned the *cortés*, which swore him allegiance; he then made his way to his coronation in Lisbon.

Philip had gained an immensely valuable prize. In return he promised to uphold the liberties of the Portuguese people, to nominate no Spaniards to Portuguese offices, and to reserve their overseas commerce to the Portuguese. He honored his part of the bargain until his death in 1598. The union endured until 1640.

The massacre of St. Bartholomew's Day sparked off a renewal of the Wars of Religion. The horrors of the orgy of killing are dramatically recorded in François Dubois's contemporary painting.

1584

Boris Godunov Becomes Sole Ruler of Russia

The "Time of Troubles" begins

On the death of Ivan the Terrible in 1584, the Russian throne passed to the weak Fydor I. Real power fell into the hands of Ivan's favorite, the Tatar Boris Godunov. Seven years later the murder of Fydor's half-brother, Dmitri (in which Boris almost certainly was implicated), left no heir to the throne. The ancient Rurik dynasty therefore came to an end when Fydor died in 1591 and Boris was proclaimed as tsar.

Throughout his years of power Boris did much to extend serfdom and chain the peasants to the will of their landlords. Even so, he incurred the hostility of the noble class of boyars, who opposed him as a usurper and upstart and looked, in the "Time of Troubles" (as the era came to be called), for a reaction against absolutism and a restoration of the political power they had previously enjoyed.

As for the peasants, they saw in the appearance of a false Dmitri, a pretender to the throne, a savior to deliver them from bondage and famine (1602-04). A national revolt, strongest in the south, rallied to the pretender and joined his march on Moscow, so when Boris died in 1605, Dmitri succeeded in getting himself elected tsar.

There followed eight years of civil war. Sweden and Poland intervened, and the boyars, hoping to use foreign rule to prosper their own fortunes, elected the heir to the Polish crown, Vladislav, as tsar. That was the signal for a new revolt. Led by the patriarch, a great people's army relieved Moscow of the foreigner and drove out the Poles. A national assembly then elected a new tsar, the great-nephew of Ivan IV, Mikhail, and the Romanov dynasty, which lasted until 1918, was founded.

The legend to this bird's-eye view of Moscow at around Boris's time describes the city as having wooden buildings, many squares and wide meadows irrigated from the river.

1585

Raleigh Colonizes Roanoke Island

The first English attempt to settle in the New World ends in disaster

In 1583 Sir Humphrey Gilbert, who had claimed Newfoundland for Elizabeth I, was lost on the voyage home. His patent to North America above Florida was then given to Walter Raleigh, to whom, in 1584, English navigators brought back excellent reports of a little island off the southerly coast. Roanoke Island, off North Carolina, had the advantage of being far enough north to escape Spanish attention, and Raleigh decided to finance a colonizing expedition—the first attempt at an English settlement in the New World.

Raleigh's first expedition, led by Sir Richard Grenville, landed on the island in 1585, found the pioneering life unpalatable, and returned home within a year. For the second expedition of 1587, a group of 117 men, women and children was more carefully chosen. Once they were established, the commander, John White, returned to England for supplies.

When he again crossed the Atlantic in 1591, he found the island completely uninhabited. He also found the letters CROATOAN carved on a tree, giving rise to two theories, neither proven: that the colonists had removed themselves to Croatoan Island, 30 miles to the north, or that they had joined the tribe of Croatoan, or Hatteras, Indians. The failure of the venture demonstrated that overseas colonization was beyond the means of private purses and required the full backing of government.

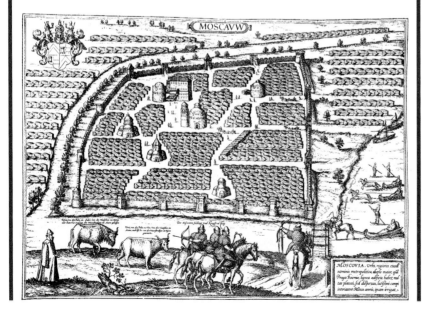

1587

Mary, Queen of Scots, Beheaded

Elizabeth I eliminates a rival to the throne

The marriage in 1563 of Mary, Queen of Scots, to the Roman Catholic Henry Stuart, Lord Darnley, alienated the Protestant nobility of Scotland. It also alarmed Elizabeth I of England, since Henry's descent from Margaret Tudor strengthened Mary's claim to the English throne. The murder of Darnley in February 1567 by Mary's favorite, the earl of Bothwell (in which Mary's complicity is unproven), and her subsequent marriage to Bothwell, raised a revolt in Scotland.

In 1568 Mary was forced to abandon her Scottish crown and take refuge in England. Her presence there was an embarrassment and a threat to her cousin Elizabeth, who could not take her side by making war on the Protestant Scottish rebels. Mary was held captive in Fotheringay Castle, Northamptonshire, under the eye of the earl of Shrewsbury.

A papal bull of 1570, which excommunicated Elizabeth and called upon the Catholic monarchies of Spain and France to overthrow her, made Mary the center of a number of plots (although fewer than were alleged) against Elizabeth. Mary was gulled into implicating herself in the last of them, the Babington plot of 1586, by Sir Francis Walsingham, and with that evidence Walsingham persuaded Elizabeth to try Mary for treason. She was convicted by a royal commission and, after Elizabeth had dithered for four months, executed at Fotheringay in 1587.

1588

Spanish Armada Driven onto the Rocks

England's victory deals a blow to Spanish power

The Spanish fleet that set sail for England in May 1588, under the command of Medina Sidonia, was truly an armada: 24 galleons, 40 merchantmen converted for war and 25 supply vessels. Its purpose was to overthrow Elizabeth and place the Catholic Philip II of Spain on the English throne.

Against it, waiting in Plymouth harbor, was Admiral Charles Howard of Effingham's fleet of 21 front-line ships, with 14,000 sailors to Spain's 30,000. The modern English fleet consisted no longer of bulky, castle-like sea fortresses but of streamlined galleons. Capturing ships was giving way to outmaneuvering and sinking them.

After a week's progress up the English Channel, the Armada reached Calais unharmed in late July. There it waited for transports carrying invasion soldiers from the duke of Parma's forces in the Netherlands, which failed to arrive. Effingham sent seven fireships into the harbor at night, scattering the Armada. Its formation broken, the Armada set out northward into the open sea. The decision was fatal. A combination of English attacks and stormy weather, which drove the Spanish onto the rocks off the northwest tip of Scotland, brought England a crushing victory. Just over half the fleet and one-third of its men made it back to Spain.

Within a few years the Armada was stronger than ever. But the prestige of Europe's greatest power (already on the wane financially) had been dealt an irreparable blow by a small Protestant nation.

The sumptuous "Armada" portrait of Elizabeth I epitomizes the self-confidence and splendor of the age.

1598

Henry IV Issues Edict of Nantes

French Huguenots are granted religious freedom and civil rights

Henry IV of France, a leader of the Protestant Huguenots, having saved his own life during the St. Bartholomew massacre of 1572 by announcing his conversion to Roman Catholicism, spent four years in the Louvre as a virtual prisoner of the court. On his release in 1576 he returned to Protestantism. But four years after ascending to the French throne in 1589, he once again publicly embraced Rome, to the delight of the Paris mob. "Paris," he said privately, "is well worth a mass."

The Huguenots' reward was the Edict of Nantes, by which the Wars of Religion were finally brought to an end. Protestants were given full liberty of conscience and private worship, together with freedom of worship in those towns, about 200, where they had previously enjoyed it. The right was extended to new towns and to the estates of Protestant nobles. They were also secured in their fortified towns, or *places de sûreté*, and permitted to hold public office. The edict, a milestone in the growth of religious tolerance in Europe, remained in force until it was revoked by Louis XIV in 1685.

1600

Edo Period Opens in Japan

A centralized feudal government is established by the shoguns

The Portuguese traders and Jesuit missionaries who infiltrated Japan in the latter part of the 16th century brought with them one of the latest developments of European technology, the musket. This helped to bring to an end the long period of wars among the nobility and to establish the supremacy of one clan, the Tokugawa family, based in Edo (modern Tokyo).

On the death of Hideyoshi, the great warrior-ruler of the country, in 1596, the headship of the family passed to his five-year-old son; power passed to his council of guardians. At the Battle of Sekugahara in 1600, fought between the two rival combinations of territorial lords on the council, the Tokugawa Ieyasu emerged the victor and the supreme power in Japan. Though his ascendancy was not complete until a victory over Hideyoshi's son, Hideyori, in 1616, the earlier battle marks the beginning of the period known in Japanese history both as the Edo era and as the "great peace."

The Tokugawa shogunate pushed the emperor further away from real power and authority, though its government, a military dictatorship known as the *bakufu* ("government of the camp"), ruled in the emperor's name. The Tokugawa shoguns, who by the mid-17th century owned one-quarter of Japan's rice fields, presided over a highly centralized form of feudalism, in which society was strictly stratified from the great vassal chieftains, the samurai, down to the humblest peasants. The great peace, a remarkable achievement of political and social stability, endured until the Meiji restoration in 1868.

The processions of feudal lords, who had to spend alternate years in Edo, started as armed marches, but later became occasions for the display of wealth and for self-indulgence.

1603

Scottish and English Crowns United

James VI of Scotland becomes James I of England

Elizabeth I died on March 24, 1603, without an heir, having indicated her wish that James VI of Scotland, the son of Mary, Queen of Scots, should succeed her. Within eight hours of her death the Scottish king was proclaimed James I of England, its first Stuart ruler.

James was, perhaps, the most learned king ever to sit on the English throne. He had published an attack on witchcraft, the *Demonology*, in 1597 and a treatise on kingship, *The Trew Law of Free Monarchies*, in 1598. His month-long progress from the north to London was attended by joyful celebrations. He described his new kingdom as a "promised land" where he sat "amongst grave, learned and reverend men, not as before, elsewhere, a king without state, without honor, without order."

James began well by making peace with Spain. But he inherited a large debt from Elizabeth and to overcome it he needed to work in harmony with parliament, a sturdier and prouder institution in England than anywhere else in early 17th-century Europe. James, however, openly avowed his attachment to the prevailing orthodoxy of the "divine right of kings"; nor did he disguise his distaste for extreme Puritans in religion. His first parliament, in 1604, brought him into conflict with the House of Commons over the Church, the revenue and the privileges of the House. The enduring 17th-century quarrel between the Stuart kings and the people of England was foreshadowed.

1605

Gunpowder Plot Foiled in England

Guy Fawkes is executed for attempting to blow up parliament

One of James I's first acts as king of England was to confirm the penal statutes against Roman Catholics. They remained barred from holding public office, and the penalty for the high treason of avowing allegiance to the pope remained death. A tiny group of Catholics, led by Robert Catesby, therefore plotted to blow up the Houses of Parliament at the opening in 1605, killing the king and his ministers. They then planned to place the infant Prince Charles on the throne, with the aim of returning England to the Roman faith.

One of the plotters, Thomas Percy, rented a cellar under the House of Lords and placed coal and firewood in it; guarding the cellar was a man named John Johnson. But the plotters warned the few Catholic peers to stay away from the opening, and one of them, Lord Mounteagle, passed the warning note to the Privy Council.

On the night of November 5, Johnson opened the door to Percy's cellar. He was at once arrested, and the stock of combustibles, to which a fuse was attached, discovered. Johnson, an explosives expert brought over from Flanders by the conspirators, disclosed that his real name was Guido (Guy) Fawkes.

Catesby and his band fled to the north but were found at Holbeach House in Staffordshire, where Catesby and three others were killed. Fawkes stood trial with seven more plotters, all of whom were convicted of treason and sentenced to be hanged, drawn and quartered. So the plot failed, and the result was to deal an enduring blow to the cause of tolerance for Roman Catholics.

1605

French Settlers Found Port Royal

The first permanent European colony in Canada takes root

French exploration of Canada began in the 1530s, when Jacques Cartier made his voyages of discovery up the St. Lawrence River. But Cartier had been searching for a northwest passage to the East, and the region remained untouched until 1605.

In that year his great successor, Samuel de Champlain, and François Grave founded a *habitation* on the north shore of the Annapolis Basin in modern Nova Scotia. It consisted of a few wooden buildings around a courtyard, in which was planted a garden, the first European experimental seedplot in North America. A theater was established and a play produced.

The hopes for a prosperous colony having been disappointed, in 1607 the site was abandoned. But it was resettled by one of the original colonists in 1610. The first permanent settlement north of the Spanish town of St. Augustine in Florida (founded in 1565), Port Royal (now Annapolis Royal) developed by mid-century into the administrative and military center of French Acadia.

TEA DRINKING
Tea first appeared in the West *c.* 1610, brought from Japan to Portugal and Holland; the first public tea sale in England was in 1657. Merchants claimed it could cure migraine, paralysis, colic, epilepsy—indeed, almost every known ailment. After the English, the most avid consumers of tea were the Russians, although its great popularity among them was delayed until the 19th century. The Russian samovar, a charcoal-burning metal urn with a teapot on top, was the counterpart to the English kettle, the most important household item.

1608

Virginia Company Builds Jamestown

England establishes its first colony in North America

The success of the Muscovy and the Levant companies in opening up profitable trade with Russia and the Near East inspired two groups of English capitalists to form joint-stock companies for the exploration and settlement of Virginia. So the Atlantic seaboard of North America was called in honor of the virgin queen, Elizabeth. Northern Virginia, renamed New England in 1620, fell to the Bristol Company; the London Company gained rights by royal charter to present-day Virginia, Maryland and the Carolinas.

In 1608 the London Company founded the first English colony in the New World at Jamestown (a nearby malarial site had been abandoned a year earlier). Strange food and inadequate shelter (log cabins were a later Swedish development) left the colony with only 53 survivors of the original 144 settlers after the first winter. But Captain John Smith placated the Indians and learned how to plant corn.

More important, John Rolfe, later the husband of the Indian princess Pocahontas, in 1612 brought tobacco seed from the West Indies. The London Company had hoped to find gold and a passage to the Pacific. In tobacco they found something just as valuable; some 2,500lb. were sent to England in 1616; 50,000lb. in 1618. Capital and labor were drawn to the colony by this exotic source of wealth.

Democracy was born in America in 1619 with the election of the first Virginia assembly of burgesses. By 1625 Virginia was a flourishing commonwealth, and the plantation economy of the South had put down strong roots.

1608

The Telescope Invented

A Dutch invention is improved by Galileo

At the annual Frankfurt fair in 1608 an exhibitor offered for sale a telescope, with both a convex and a concave lens, which could magnify objects seven times. A month later, the Dutch spectacles-maker Hans Lippershey was granted a license to manufacture the instrument by the Netherlands states-general. Within a year, primitive telescopes had reached France and Italy.

In Venice Galileo Galilei heard of the invention, and in August 1609, he exhibited his own "spyglass" to the Venetian senate, whose members looked through it from the tower of St. Mark's. That instrument magnified nine times. Galileo sold it to the senate on the ground that it would be invaluable in war: the enemy's ships could be sighted two hours before the naked eye could see them.

Galileo then attended to his real work, improving the telescope so that it could be usefully trained on the moon and stars. In 1610 he published *Siderius Nuncius* ("Messenger from the Stars"), in which he announced that he had made a telescope so powerful that it could magnify a thousand times. With it he had seen a myriad of stars previously unknown. The Milky Way had dissolved into discrete clusters of stars. And four "new planets" (in fact, moons of Jupiter) had swum into his ken. Astronomy had taken its greatest step forward since the days of Copernicus.

Galileo's exploration of the skies with his astronomical telescope finally exposed the errors of the Ptolemaic system. And by his methodical examination of the laws of physics Galileo opened the way for modern experimental science. This portrait was painted by Ottanio Leoni.

1618

Thirty Years' War Begins

The Defenestration of Prague sparks off a European conflict

In May 1618, Protestant members of the Bohemian diet, or assembly, threw two royal officers and a secretary from a window of Prague castle and declared Ferdinand II deposed. None of the victims was killed, but the incident, known as the Defenestration of Prague, incited a general revolt in Bohemia against Austria. The revolt spread and soon brought all the European powers into a general war, fought mostly on German soil.

Territorial ambitions, dynastic issues and religious differences all played their part in the war, which ranged the Protestant princes of Germany and their chiefly Protestant allies (Holland, England, Denmark, Sweden and Catholic France) against Catholic Spain and the Habsburg Holy Roman Empire. Initial imperial success in Bohemia and the Palatinate, capped by victory at Stadtlohn (1623), brought Denmark into the field in 1625.

By 1627, after crushing victories over the Danish by the imperial armies under Tilly and Wallenstein, Ferdinand (elected emperor in 1620) seemed ready to impose Habsburg rule on a unified German state. But then, in 1630, Sweden entered the lists, and fortunes fluctuated until the Battle of Lützen (1632) inflicted a grievous blow to the Protestant cause.

1619

Kepler Announces his Third Law

A German astronomer describes the motion of the planets

Tycho Brahe, the tireless Danish recorder of celestial observations, took on Johannes Kepler as an assistant at his Prague observatory in 1600. The German's poor sight made him an indifferent observer, but he was an imaginative theorist and an excellent mathematician.

It was Kepler's belief, as it had been the Greeks', that all nature could be explained in simple mathematical laws. His life's work was to find a true mathematical expression of the motions of the planets and to rid astronomy of the cumbersome "wheels within wheels" of the Ptolemaic system.

In 1609, after a decade devoted to the study of Mars, Kepler published his first two laws. These stated, first, that Mars followed an elliptical orbit with the sun at one focus and, second, that an imaginary line joining Mars to the sun swept out equal areas in equal lengths of time. In 1619 Kepler announced that these laws applied to all the planets. And he added a third: that the square of the time taken by a planet to complete its orbit was proportional to the cube of its mean distance from the sun.

Kepler had reduced the chaos of Brahe's data to order. The Greek insistence, not abandoned by Copernicus, that all planetary motion must be circular was overthrown. Kepler's laws broke with ancient authority, giving him, rather than Copernicus, a fair claim to be regarded as the first truly modern astronomer. The old earth-centered system, with its Ptolemaic epicycles, was not yet generally rejected. But Kepler's elegant, heliocentric model had rung its knell.

"Mayflower" leaving Dartmouth harbor in September 1620.

1620

The "Mayflower" Lands at Plymouth Rock

The Pilgrim Fathers found a Puritan commonwealth in Massachusetts

In 1604 James I of England vowed to "harry Puritans out of the land." A small group of East Anglian separatists sought refuge from persecution in Leyden in 1609 and, 10 years later, with a grant from the London Virginia Company, set sail in the *Mayflower* for America.

They landed at Plymouth Rock, on November 11, 1620. Before landing, they signed the Mayflower Compact, by which they agreed to be governed by the will of the majority. It stands alongside the meeting of the Virginia Assembly in 1619 as a foundation stone of American democracy.

The small band of shopkeepers and farmers learned from Indians how to plant corn and catch fish. Despite a hard first winter, not one of the survivors returned to Europe when the *Mayflower* set sail in the spring. The next autumn they celebrated Thanksgiving, a meal of venison and turkey shared with the Wampanoag Indians.

In 1630 the Massachusetts Bay Company sent a fleet of 17 ships with 1,000 settlers to New England. Boston was founded and a representative government, with voting rights for members of the Puritan Church only, was formed. By virtue of the company's charter neither king nor parliament had any say in its workings. The seeds of independence had been sown.

1624

New Netherland Founded by the Dutch

The Dutch West Indies Company plants a colony on the Hudson

No other European nation was so enterprising in developing overseas commerce in the 17th century as the Dutch. The Dutch East Indies Company expelled the Portuguese from most of their Far East trading stations and built a rich empire there for themselves.

In the search for a northwest passage to that empire, Henry Hudson sailed in 1609 up the river that now bears his name into the rich fur-trading country of the Iroquois Indians. Hudson's employers, the East Indies Company, were not impressed. But in 1624 the new Dutch West Indies Company established New Netherland as a trading post at the mouth of the river; New Amsterdam was built as a fort on Manhattan Island in 1626. It became the center of the fur trade and a base for Dutch ships trading in Virginia tobacco.

Settlement was slow, despite grants of land to anyone bringing out 50 tenant families at his own expense, and the colony was mismanaged by a succession of corrupt and tyrannical Dutch governors. The last of them, Peter Stuyvesant, had so little support, both from Holland and from his fellow colonists, that when a small English fleet appeared in 1664 he surrendered without a fight. New Amsterdam passed into English hands, and its name changed to New York.

1628

Harvey Discovers the Circulation of Blood

The English "father of medicine" uncovers the heart's function

In 1602 a young English student, William Harvey, went to study medicine in Padua. There he met the great anatomist Vesalius and learned the most up-to-date methods and knowledge connected with physiology. On his return to England he devoted himself to studying the working of the heart.

He experimented with live animals because he believed that the erroneous notion that the arteries carried air arose from the practice of examining arteries drained of blood. He noticed that arteries dilated simultaneously with the contractions of the heart, and concluded that either the arteries must suck blood from the heart or the heart must pump it into them. He punctured arteries and found that they continued to receive blood; therefore, they had no power of suction. The heart was a muscle that acted as a pump.

Harvey went on to show that blood flows without cease in one direction, from the heart and back again, but he could not trace the path because he worked without a microscope. (The capillaries that pass blood from arteries to veins were discovered by Malpighi in 1661.) Harvey's work inspired the study of physiology, because the behavior of blood, which is so closely related to bodily functions, was the key to understanding.

1628

Petition of Right Presented to Charles I

The English parliament demands royal assent to basic liberties

The running quarrel between the Stuart monarchy and parliament flared up in 1626, when parliament refused to vote taxes for English forces in the Thirty Years' War. Charles I's reply was to raise a forced loan and to imprison 76 defaulters. King's Bench upheld his right to imprison them without showing just cause. The Puritan party in parliament was also disturbed by Charles's Anglo-Catholic leanings.

In 1628 parliament presented the king with the Petition of Right. It contained four chief demands: that taxation should not be levied without parliament's consent; that no one should be imprisoned without fair trial; that troops should not be billeted on private households; and that martial law be abolished. Both Houses voted for the petition, and Charles was forced to give his assent to it.

A truce between parliament and monarch lasted for a year, until Charles asked for an adjournment of parliament and members of the House of Commons held down the Speaker in his chair, preventing him from following the king's command until four resolutions were passed condemning, most importantly, non-parliamentary taxation and imprisonment without cause. Charles's response was to dissolve parliament and to rule personally. The "Eleven Years' Tyranny" followed. Parliament was not summoned again until 1640, by which time the dispute had become so wide as to threaten civil war.

TOBACCO

Tobacco, taken to England from Virginia, was an expensive luxury. The Earl of Bedford, a heavy smoker, paid 2s 6d a pound for it in the latter part of the 17th century. Pipes were relatively cheap—a gross cost £1 4s in 1695. To protect American planters, growing tobacco in England was prohibited, and troops were employed to destroy crops. During the 1660s, tobacco was frequently used to ward off the plague, and Eton schoolboys were beaten for not taking it. From the beginning it was considered rude to smoke in front of ladies, and pre-Regency Bath gained a reputation for tawdriness partly because this social convention was regularly breached there.

1632

Imperial Armies Defeated at Battle of Lützen

Gustavus Adolphus is mortally wounded

Backed by French money, Sweden entered the Thirty Years' War in 1630 and swiftly overran Pomerania, Mecklenburg and other small north German provinces. The Protestant cause then suffered a major setback: in 1631 the imperial armies under Tilly captured and sacked Magdeburg, on the Elbe. That defeat, followed by Tilly's advance into Saxony, brought Sweden and the German Protestant princes of Brandenburg and Saxony into an alliance.

The fruit of that alliance was the wide sweep which the Swedish king and commander, Gustavus Adolphus, made into southwest Germany. The great imperial commander, Wallenstein, drove him back, however, and in 1632 the two armies clashed at Lützen in Saxony. There the empire suffered a defeat.

But the anti-imperial cause also suffered a grievous blow: Gustav, one of the great commanders in history, renowned for his courageous leadership, technical foresight and tactical brilliance, fell in the battle.

The Austro-Spanish army's victory at Nordlingen 18 months later persuaded the German princes to make peace. The Peace of Prague (1635) ended the fighting insofar as it was a German civil war, and it might have brought the Thirty Years' War to a close. But the international powers, especially France, had ambitions unfulfilled, and the war continued for another 13 years.

Gustavus's seal proclaims him "By the grace of God, king of the Swedes, Goths and Vandals, crown prince of Finland, duke of Estonia and Karelia."

1633

Galileo Recants

The Inquisition compels the Italian astronomer to renounce Copernicus

Ever since his publication of *Siderius Nuncio* in 1610 Galileo, a pious Roman Catholic, had been taken up and protected by the Jesuits. But the Church harbored enemies of Copernicanism, which seemed to contradict scriptural implications that the earth was the center of God's creation.

Their opportunity came in 1632, when Galileo (with the Church's encouragement) published *A Dialogue on the Two Chief Systems of the World*. In it he surveyed the points at issue between the Ptolemaic and Copernican astronomies and came down on the side of a sun-centered system. The Holy Office, or Inquisition, confiscated the book and summoned Galileo to appear in Rome before a special commission of investigation.

In 1633, after a five-day trial during which he was threatened with torture if he did not retract his adherence to the "opinion of Copernicus," Galileo recanted the views stated in his publication. "I am here to obey and I have not held this opinion." That he added *e pur si muove* ("and yet it [the earth] moves") is undoubtedly apocryphal. Everyone knew that he was lying. But the lie relieved the Church of the embarrassment of sentencing him to torture. The *Dialogue* was banned and Galileo sentenced to imprisonment at the Holy Office's pleasure.

But the imprisonment was not enforced, beyond a brief confinement in the archbishop's palace in Siena. Galileo lived out his life in Florence and in 1636 published his most important work, on dynamics, the *Dialogues Concerning Two New Sciences*.

THE SCIENTIFIC REVOLUTION

The rapid expansion of scientific knowledge and the refinement of scientific method in Europe during the 16th and 17th centuries—for simplicity's sake, from the publication of Nicholas Copernicus's *On the Revolutions of the Heavenly Spheres* in 1543 to Isaac Newton's *Principia Mathematica* of 1687—goes by the name of the "Scientific Revolution." It included many elements: the investigation of the human body by anatomists like William Harvey, the development of analytical geometry by René Descartes, the rediscovery of atomic theory by Pierre Gassendi. But its central preoccupation, dating from Copernicus's overthrow of the earth-centered universe in favor of a sun-centered one, was cosmology, or astronomy. Its achievement was to describe the laws governing the behavior of the celestial bodies in mathematical language. Its method was essentially inductive.

Inductive reasoning, arguing from the particular to the general, requires the slow accumulation of observations, followed by the formulation of general statements. It was given its first formal expression as the logic of scientific discovery in Francis Bacon's *Novum Organum* of 1620. None of this was unknown to the Greeks. Aristarchus had proposed a heliocentric universe; Aristotle, unlike Plato, had founded his vast corpus of scientific publication on observation; and mathematics had been used to express physical relationships by Pythagoras. The Greeks laid the foundations. The early moderns, in a bold expression of the spirit of inquiry that characterized the Renaissance, built the first comprehensive, self-consistent, model of the physical universe.

The construction of that model was made possible by the painstaking charting of the planets' orbits. The explanation of their motion lay in the concept of gravity. Much of the work was done by men who were essentially accumulators of data, not theorists. By far the most important was Tycho Brahe, the Danish astronomer whose detailed maps of the heavens provided the material for Johannes Kepler, the German cosmologist who discovered that the planets moved, not in circles, but in ellipses. Seven years after Brahe's death in 1601, astronomy entered a new age with the invention of the telescope.

The Scientific Revolution set new, rigorous standards of scientific proof. The 17th-century French mathematician and philosopher, Blaise Pascal, argued that no hypothesis could be regarded as true unless its denial involved a logical contradiction. Logical rigor of that severity would have stopped the revolution in its tracks. Pascal had no reverence for the ancients, but he was forced by his own argument to reject the heliocentric system. The Scientific Revolution proceeded because Pascal's unqualified skepticism was bypassed by men eager to take a stab at explaining how things worked. In his great treatise of 1687, Newton stated that "the whole burden of [natural] philosophy" was "from the phenomena of motions to investigate the forces of nature, and then from these forces to demonstrate the other phenomena." In short, observe, then theorize, then predict. That method remains the foundation of modern science.

Isaac Newton, mathematician, physicist and astronomer, made his most significant discoveries when he was only 23. He later became professor of mathematics at Cambridge and president of the Royal Society. This portrait was painted by Antonio Verrio between 1680 and 1690.

The study of anatomy by the dissection of human cadavers, introduced by Vesalius at Padua (c. 1537), soon spread to other centers of learning. This manuscript illustration, dated 1581, shows the famous English surgeon, John Banister, instructing his students in anatomy.

Like many early scientists, Galileo's interests were wide ranging, and it was he who first suggested the idea of pendulums for clocks. The model, far left, shows his escapement, which was designed in 1641.

The microscope, left, was thought to have belonged to Robert Hooke, who used one to study plant tissue. He also discovered the law of elasticity, named for him, which states that a solid body, such as metal, stretches in proportion to the force applied to it.

141

1640

Portugal Casts off Spanish Yoke

*Philip IV is forced to accept
Portuguese independence*

After the death of Philip II in 1598, Spain increasingly ignored the guarantees that had accompanied the union of Spain and Portugal in 1580. The count of Olivares, the energetic and absolutist minister of Philip IV, working through the Portuguese-born Miguel Vasconcelos, filled Portuguese offices with Castilians. At the same time he aroused anger by his failure to defend Portugal's overseas empire against the Dutch.

In 1636 he extended a Castilian property tax to Portugal. The ensuing rebellion was easily crushed, and in 1640 Olivares was emboldened to proclaim the abolition of the Portuguese *cortés*, or national assembly, and the virtual merging of the Portuguese and Castilian armies. Within only three hours, a national revolt broke out.

Portugal's greatest noble, the duke of Braganza, declared himself King John IV of an independent Portugal. Spain's ability to suppress the revolt was seriously hampered by simultaneous anti-Castilian revolts in Catalonia and Andalusia. But Spain refused to accept Portuguese independence and persuaded the pope to withhold his recognition.

In 1648 Portugal was excluded from the peace negotiations in Westphalia that concluded the Thirty Years' War. Don Juan almost captured Lisbon for Spain in 1663. But the war of liberation finally ended in Portuguese victory at the Battle of Montesclaros in 1665, and Portugal's independence was formally acknowledged by Spain three years later.

Affairs between king and parliament reached the nadir when it tried to wrest command of the army from Charles, who countered by demanding the arrest of five parliamentarians.

1640

Charles I Recalls Parliament

*Poverty compels the Stuart king to
treat with his subjects*

After 11 years of personal rule, Charles I was forced to summon parliament in 1640. He needed revenue from taxes to put down a Scottish rebellion against the imposition of an Anglican episcopy and ritual on the essentially Presbyterian nation. The "Short Parliament" of 1640 lasted only three weeks, dissolved by Charles when it refused to grant funds until its grievances were redressed.

Only months later, after a Scottish invasion of England, Charles had to summon a new parliament, famous as the "Long Parliament" because it remained in existence until 1660. Those in opposition to the king quickly gained ascendancy and in a series of measures in 1641 effected a constitutional revolution.

It was made unlawful for more than three years to elapse without the calling of parliament and for parliament to be dissolved without its own consent; the royal prerogative courts of Star Chamber and High Commisssion were abolished; extra-parliamentary taxation was effectively banned. In addition, parliament impeached and imprisoned the king's two chief ministers, the earl of Strafford (executed in 1641) and Archbishop Laud (in 1645).

In all those measures the "Long Parliament" was nearly unanimous. It had deprived the Crown of all the prerogative powers enjoyed by Tudor monarchs, but the members believed (or professed to) that they were simply restoring ancient liberties. However, two new issues, the Church and the control of the army, arose to divide them into root-and-branch reformers (parliamentarians) and moderates (royalists).

1642

Civil War Begins in England

Charles I raises his standard in Nottingham

In October 1641, rebellion against English rule broke out in Ireland. Behind it lay, somewhat paradoxically, resentment at Charles I's efforts to impose on Ireland an aristocracy of English planters and fear of the Puritan Long Parliament's ambition to outlaw popery and convert Ireland to some form of Protestant faith. But the great effect of the rebellion was to drive deeper the wedge between Charles and parliament.

Parliament had already seen its attempts to reform the English Church blocked by a royalist House of Lords. It distrusted Charles's willingness to uphold its constitutional reforms, so it was unwilling to vote supplies to raise an army to put down the Irish revolt unless control of the army was placed in its own hands. This was the central clause of the Nineteen Propositions addressed to Charles in 1642.

To grasp at the sword itself was an audacious assault on the king's ancient prerogative. It drove moderates to the king's side and gave him a party in the House of Commons. The opposition was thereby rendered more homogeneously Presbyterian in religion and radical in matters constitutional. The king and his opponents were now so divided that the issue could be resolved only by war.

1644

Manchu Rule Begins in China

Fu-lin deposes the "rebel emperor" and founds the Ch'in dynasty

When a peasant revolt in 1640 threatened to place a usurper on the throne of China, an imperial general sought military assistance from north of the Great Wall. Led by Fu-lin the Manchu tribe (known as the Jurchen until after their conquest of China) obliged. Once before, in the 12th century, it had invaded China, only to be expelled by the Mongols in the 13th. It had then slowly changed from a nomadic to an agrarian way of life.

Finding themselves in China once more, the Manchu claimed a right to rule by virtue of their relation to the 13th-century Ch'in dynasty, and in 1664 they assumed power. The conquest cost 25 million lives. But it was made easier by the fact that the Manchu had copied Confucian administrative methods in their own capital of Mukden; they therefore asked little change of the Chinese bureaucrats pressed into their service beyond the adoption of the pigtail. By the reign of K'ang-hsi (1662-1722) the conquest was complete.

K'ang-hsi rebuilt Peking (Beijing), which had been destroyed in the fighting, extended his rule to Formosa, occupied Tibet, and reduced the Mongols to servility. That last achievement was something of a watershed, for it marked the beginning of a final chapter in oriental history. The long nomadic traditions of central Asia began permanently to fade and to give way to settled, agricultural cultures. The Manchu, or Ch'in, dynasty itself lasted until 1912.

A contemporary pamphlet shows the royal standard being raised in Nottingham on August 22, 1642—the start of the English Civil War.

1637–1648

ENGLAND

• **1637 Ship Money**
Tax traditionally levied on coastal areas for support of navy; in 1635 extended inland by Charles I (hence exemplary of his unparliamentary "tyranny"); made *cause célèbre* in 1637 by John Hampden of Buckinghamshire, who refused to pay it; judges of the Court of Exchequer came down by seven votes to five on the king's side.

• **1642 Nineteen Propositions**
Last parliamentary manifesto before the outbreak of civil war; undertook to supply Charles I with revenue in return for severe curtailment of the royal prerogative; asserted parliament's right to approve ministers of the Crown and to exercise more control over the army; demanded reformation of Church and alliance wih United Provinces. Rejected by the king in moderate answer upholding "mixed government," which won waverers to the royalist cause.

• **1648 Second Civil War**
Charles surrendered to Scots Presbyterians (1646); failed to agree on establishment of Presbyterian Church in England and was returned to parliament (1647); negotiations failed and Charles escaped to Isle of Wight and made treaty with Scots, promising trial period for Presbyterianism. Scots invaded England in 1648, but Second Civil War ended with their rout by Cromwell's army at Preston.

1645

New Model Army Triumphs at Naseby

*The English parliamentarians find a
new leader in Oliver Cromwell*

Until 1644 the royalist cavalry,
under the command of the dashing
Prince Rupert of the Rhine,
remained undefeated in the English
Civil War. The tide began to turn
that year at the Battle of Marston
Moor, where Rupert was beaten by
a Scottish force under David Leslie
and Oliver Cromwell's "Ironside"
cavalry from the eastern counties.
"Ironsides" was Rupert's epithet of
praise after the battle.

Many of the Ironsides were distinguished by Puritan zeal, an
unshakeable belief, which they
shared with Cromwell, that God
was on their side against the Anglican royalists. When the parliamentary forces were regrouped under
General Fairfax—nationally organized and regularly paid—the core
of the "New Model Army" was
Cromwell's Eastern Association of
well-drilled, highly motivated
horsemen.

At Naseby, near Northampton,
in June 1645, the New Model Army
faced its first great test. It outnumbered the royalist forces by two to
one and it inflicted on them the
decisive defeat of the war. King
Charles retreated from the field at
the height of the action, and the
royalist cavalry was put to flight.
From that defeat royalist fortunes
never recovered.

The New Model Army had
shown itself to be the most powerful force, military and political, in
the land. It was the instrument by
which Cromwell was to rise to
supreme power.

1648

Treaty of Westphalia Ends Thirty Years' War

*The peace lays the foundation of the
modern European state system*

The Treaty of Westphalia, signed
in 1648, which brought the Thirty
Years' War to a close, did not end
the long Franco–Spanish rivalry for
mastery in Europe. It was, however, a landmark in European history, for it marked the failure of the
Habsburg empire to impose either
absolutism or Roman Catholicism
on a united Germany.

In settling the national boundaries of the European states—in a
pattern that was to last virtually
unchanged until the 19th century—
the treaty also gave recognition to
the growing strength of national
states. The notion of national
sovereignty triumphed over the
waning influence and authority of
both empire and papacy (the pope
denounced the treaty in 1651).

Within the empire, 334 states
and free cities were recognized as
sovereign members of the diet, free
to deal with their own affairs.
Sweden obtained west Pomerania;
Brandenburg gained east Pomerania; France gained Alsace; and the
independence of the Netherlands
and the Swiss confederation was
explicitly recognized.

The treaty's settlement of the
religious issue was momentous.
Calvinist rulers were given the
rights granted to Protestants by the
Peace of Augsburg (1555). And by
granting some measure of protection to Christian minorities, the
treaty took a step toward religious
tolerance and the separation of
Church and state. Although most of
these things would have come to
pass without the Thirty Years' War,
the treaty served to enshrine them.

Central Europe 1648

1648

The Fronde Rages in France

Opposition to Mazarin's rule erupts into violence

When Louis XIV came to the throne in 1653 he was only five years old. Power rested with Cardinal Mazarin, the dominant member of the council of regency. Mazarin's ascendancy alienated a section of the nobility, at a time when the bankruptcy of the Crown made it necessary to find devious means of raising revenue—manipulation of the *rentes* (investments in the town government of Paris) and the sale of offices. The pockets and the pride of the financial and official classes suffered.

In 1648 France was still at war with Spain (and remained so after the Treaty of Westphalia). To raise money, Mazarin issued a *lit de justice* to the Paris *parlement*, a device which compelled it to carry out royal commands without discussion. The *parlement* rebelled, and Mazarin ordered the arrest of three members. When one of them escaped and was seized in full view of the Paris mob, a riot broke out. So the Fronde (named after the French word for a sling) began.

The rebellion never developed into a full-scale anti-absolutist revolution. Though fighting went on for five years, the *frondeurs* were, for the most part, noblemen eager to settle private quarrels and Parisians of the merchant and professional classes eager to gain control of the city's administration. When the army, under the prince of Condé, captured Paris in 1652, the Fronde collapsed. Absolute monarchy survived intact, and the young Louis learned valuable lessons: to stifle the Paris *parlement*, to turn the nobles into court dandies, and to make his home, not at mob-infested Paris, but at Versailles.

1649

Charles I Executed in Whitehall

Cromwell becomes the ruler of republican England

The Long Parliament, purged of all its moderate members by Colonel Thomas Pride, was by 1649 a rump of fewer than 60 members. It was no more than the tool of Oliver Cromwell and the army. Its decision to try Charles I for treason was nevertheless a momentous one. Kings had been deposed before or murdered in secrecy. Yet in the mid-17th century, age of the "divine right of kings," of kings as the anointed vice-regents of God on earth, a national assembly took the unprecedented step of bringing a monarch to justice in the full light of day.

The court that tried Charles was illegal: parliament was, by the constitution, king-in-parliament, and the king could not try himself. The proceedings made a mockery of justice. The purpose of the special court established by parliament was not to try Charles but to find him guilty. Charles's refusal to plead was taken as proof of guilt.

On January 30 he was taken to a scaffold erected outside the Banqueting Hall in Whitehall, London, and beheaded.

Among his last words, delivered to those within earshot of the scaffold, was an unrepentant defense of monarchical government: "For the people... I must tell you that their liberty and freedom consist in having of government those laws by which their life and their goods may be most their own. It is not for having a share in government. Sirs, that is nothing pertaining to them. A subject and a sovereign are clean different things."

For the next 11 years, under the rule of Oliver Cromwell, England enjoyed the only republican period in its history.

Soon after Charles's execution, this crude woodcut, showing a remarkably bloodless decapitation, appeared in a widely distributed tract informing people of the event.

1651

English Navigation Acts Come into Force

The economic basis of the British empire is laid down

The English colonial empire was in its infancy when the Long Parliament laid down the ground rules for its economic development. In 1651 it passed the first Navigation Act, followed by a second act in 1660. The acts were drawn up and enforced according to the prevailing European economic orthodoxy, known as mercantilism.

That was a doctrine which believed that power rested on wealth, and that a country's wealth was measured by the quantity of gold bullion in its possession. Since wealth came from trade, all trade had to be tightly controlled by government. Profits gained by individuals were incidental to the chief purpose of augmenting the national wealth and power.

Spain, in its "golden age" of the 16th century, had given the monarchy control of all silver and gold entering the country from the New World. France in the 17th century, under Colbert, devised a strict mercantilist policy. The English acts provided that imports from, and exports to, overseas colonies should be carried only in English-built and English-owned ships (a provision directed chiefly against Dutch shipping). Certain items of colonial produce, chiefly sugar and tobacco, could be shipped only to England or to English colonies.

An additional element, that the mother country should export manufactured goods and the colonies only raw materials, eventually so hampered the development of New England industry that it fed the American colonists' demand for independence.

1653

Protectorate Established in England

Lord Protector Cromwell introduces the rule of the major-generals

After the execution of Charles I in 1649 the new republican "Commonwealth" of England was ruled by the Long Parliament, a Presbyterian assembly known as the "Rump" Parliament after it was reduced to one-third of its original size by Pride's Purge (1648). Executive authority was vested in a Council of State.

The Commonwealth lasted until 1653, when Cromwell answered parliament's refusal to draw up a new constitution by dissolving it and the Council of State, and himself taking autocratic power as Lord Protector. The agents of his rule in the country were the major-generals of the army. Martial rule alienated the gentry in the shires, while resentment grew at the strict Puritan morality imposed on the nation in the name of godliness.

Meanwhile Cromwell struggled to find a satisfactory constitutional base for his rule. He refused the crown, but by the Humble Petition and Advice of 1657, which restored a bicameral legislature, he was given the title of "His Highness" and the right to nominate his successor. The monarchy had been brought back in all but name.

1660

Stuart Line Restored to the English Throne

Charles II claims his crown and issues an amnesty

On the death of Oliver Cromwell in 1658, the title of Lord Protector of England passed to his son Richard, a weak ruler under whom the country was in danger of sinking into anarchy. To prevent this, General George Monck used the army to force the Long Parliament to dissolve itself in 1660. A newly elected parliament voted to invite Charles II to return from his European exile as king in return for his promise, made in the Declaration of Breda, of an amnesty to the anti-royalists in the Civil War and of full liberty of religious conscience. The Stuart line was restored, and a brief experiment in republicanism came to an end.

Charles upheld his promise of an amnesty, granted to everyone except the regicides themselves, 11 of whom were executed. After a decade of imposed Puritan morality, theaters reopened and sports returned. The restoration did not, however, turn the clock back to pre-revolutionary times. It was itself a revolution. The legislation of 1641, passed by the Long Parliament, was confirmed by Charles's parliaments. Royal absolutism was checked, and the achievement of the parliamentarians in taking England along the road to limited, constitutional monarchy vindicated.

Cromwell's inability to work with parliament, his costly foreign policy and intolerant, joyless rule alienated the English people. It required only his death in 1658 to open the door to a Stuart restoration.

1667

Louis XIV Invades the Spanish Netherlands

The Sun King goes to war to restore France's "natural frontiers"

Louis XIV delighted in war and for 30 years his ambitions dominated the affairs of Europe. He saw himself as the heir of Charlemagne and coveted the imperial throne and the Spanish empire. When King Philip IV of Spain died in 1665, Louis used a curious law that prevailed in parts of the Spanish Netherlands to press the claim of his wife, Maria Theresa, to inherit the kingdom ahead of Carlos II, her stepbrother. The law was that property devolved upon daughters of a first marriage in preference to sons of a second.

Skillful diplomacy by Hugues de Lionne ensured that no major power was prepared to come to Spain's aid when the War of Devolution, as it came to be called, began with a rapid French advance into the Spanish Netherlands in 1667. The French successes alarmed the Habsburg emperor, Leopold I, who in a secret treaty promised that on Carlos II's death (he was ailing) he would divide the Spanish empire with Louis. Louis would gain the Netherlands, Luxembourg, Franche-Comté, Naples and Milan. In return Louis would content himself for the time being with the towns already taken by his armies.

Since a Triple Alliance between Sweden, the Netherlands and England had just been formed against him, Louis accepted the bargain. Peace was made with Spain by the Treaty of Aix-la-Chapelle in 1668. But Carlos lived on until 1701, and the secret compact never came into effect.

Louis was a great patron of the arts; here, in Lemonnier's painting, he is showing off to the court at Versailles Puget's statue of Milo of Crotona.

1670

Hudson's Bay Company Founded

English merchants seek profits in the fur trade of Canada

The oldest joint-stock merchant company in the English-speaking world, the Hudson's Bay Company, was the creation of the French fur traders and explorers, Médard Chouart and Pierre Radisson.

After an expedition in 1659, during which they discovered a great store of beaver and heard of "the bay of the north sea," they sought, but failed to find, French backers for their enterprise. In England, however, they found investors for their plan to bypass the St. Lawrence (in French control) and gain access to the fur-rich region south of Hudson Bay.

Prince Rupert, Charles II's cousin, and a group of noblemen backed the scheme and, two years after the first expeditions set sail, the king granted them a charter of incorporation. This gave the company exclusive rights to trade in and govern the vast territory—named Rupert's Land—traversed by rivers flowing into Hudson Bay.

DUELING

Dueling grew out of the medieval "wager of battle," a supervised legal proceeding in which the accused sought to prove his innocence by defeating his accuser. It was abolished in France in the mid-16th century, and private dueling arose in its place. In England dueling flourished in the relaxed social atmosphere of the Restoration, and popular places of recreation witnessed almost nightly bloodshed. Among the nobility and army officers, it remained a fashionable method of avenging wounded "honor" throughout the 18th century, and the fashion was transported to America. Most nations abolished dueling in the 19th century.

1672

France Makes War on the Dutch

Louis XIV's aggression provokes the Grand Alliance of the Hague

The War of Devolution showed that Spain was no longer a major power. The great obstacle to Louis XIV's designs on the Spanish Netherlands came from the United Provinces, whose Calvinism and republicanism, in any case, he regarded as a personal affront.

Dutch control of trade in the Baltic and the Levant had already provoked France to use tariffs to drive Dutch shipping from its ports; in 1672 the Dutch retaliated by banning all French imports for a year. Before attacking the Dutch, Louis bought off the German provinces and detached England and Sweden from their alliance with the republic.

In April 1672, the French struck, with such initial success that the Dutch leader, Prince William of Orange, was driven in retreat to Amsterdam. Had the French forces, under the command of Marshal Turenne, followed swiftly, the war might have ended at once. Instead, Louis made slow progress, basking in the glory of receiving the surrender of town after town. William ordered the dikes to be broken, and Holland and Zeeland found temporary security behind the water line. That breathing space changed the course of the war.

Emperor Leopold I entered the lists against Louis in 1673, and in 1674 Spain, Lorraine and the important German provinces also joined in what became the Grand Alliance of the Hague. Stalemate lasted until peace terms were agreed in Nijmegen in 1679. France retained Franche-Comté, Lorraine and the chief Alsatian towns. Despite the heavy cost of the war and Louis's failure to gain any territory from the United Provinces, the French hailed their king as "Louis le Grand."

An outstanding commander, whose abilities later won even Napoleon's admiration, Turenne led Louis's armies to victory for some 30 years.

1672

Royal African Company Founded

England gains the upper hand in the slave trade from West Africa

By 1660, despite the Spanish claim to the whole of the Caribbean, England had firm possession of Barbados, Jamaica and five of the Leeward Islands. The supply of slaves to the region was almost a monopoly of the Dutch. West African trade thus became a chief element in the complicated wars of the 1660s and '70s involving France, England and Holland.

In 1662 the African Company had been established in England to try to wrest the lucrative slave trade from the Dutch. But a decade of struggle on the west coast of Africa brought the company financial ruin and few gains. It relinquished its charter in 1672, and in the same year the more ambitious Royal African Company was founded as its successor.

The efforts of the new company were rewarded. It strengthened the only existing English trading post, at Cape Coast Cattle, built six new forts on the Gold Coast, and established the center of its operations farther east, in Whydah. The coast between the Gold Coast and the Niger River delta became known as the Slave Coast. None of the European nations was interested in penetrating the interior: the sole object was the trade in slaves.

England's chief rival by the end of the century was no longer Holland but France (Portugal continued to supply Brazil from Angola). In the 18th-century wars with France, Great Britian emerged the victor and took control of more than half of the slave trade.

1683

King of Poland Stops the Turks

Islamic advance is halted as the siege of Vienna is lifted

Hungary in the late 17th century was a semi-autonomous Habsburg frontier province, exposing the Habsburg empire to the double threat of Magyar rebellion and invasion by the Ottoman Turks. The two threats merged in 1682, when the Magyars appealed to the Turks to recognize Imre Tokoli as king of Upper Hungary in place of Emperor Leopold I, and the Turks agreed to do so.

The Turkish advance on Vienna in 1683 was thus combined with a Magyar war of independence. Thanks chiefly to a large Polish army of 27,000, whose commander, John Sobieski, King John III of Poland, took charge of the imperial forces, the Turkish siege of Vienna, led by the grand vizier Kara Mustafa, was raised. From that date Ottoman power was on the wane.

The immediate result, effectively sealed by the victory of Charles V of Lorraine over the Turks at Mohács in 1687, was to liberate Hungary from 150 years of Ottoman rule. Since every defeat of the Turks was also a defeat of the Magyars, Habsburg control over Hungary was extended. The monarchy ceased to be elective and became hereditary in the Habsburg line. Hungary was reduced to the status of Bohemia, an administrative province within the Habsburg domain. By the Treaty of Karlowitz (1699) the Turks recognized Habsburg possession of Hungary and Transylvania.

The Ottoman empire lasted until 1918, but never again did it offer a threat to Europe.

1685

Louis XIV Revokes the Edict of Nantes

Huguenots flee as religious tolerance ends in France

Cardinal Richelieu's determination to rid France of the Huguenot threat to royal authority achieved its object in 1629. After a series of revolts, the Huguenots were compelled by the superior strength of the king's army to sign the Grace of Alais. By it they retained liberty of worship but surrendered their separate assemblies, law courts and fortresses. Thereafter they showed exemplary loyalty to the Crown. Their freedom from persecution had helped to win France Protestant allies during the Thirty Years' War, and their contribution to the nation's industry far exceeded what might have been expected from their numbers.

Louis XIV nevertheless conceived their mere existence to be an affront to absolute monarchy in a Roman Catholic nation. The end of the Dutch war in 1679 allowed him to ignore foreign opinion, and after 1680 a series of edicts attacked the Huguenots at every point. The professions were closed to them; Huguenot churches built after the Edict of Nantes in 1598 were destroyed; Huguenot academies were closed; and, by billeting soldiers on them, Louis hoped to harry them into conversion.

Finally, in 1685, the Edict of Nantes itself was revoked. Protestant worship was banned, all children were to be baptized into the Roman faith, and persons attempting to emigrate were to be executed or sent to the galleys. Despite this, a great exodus, from iron and textile towns especially, ruined French industry and profited that of its rivals, Great Britain and Holland above all.

One of the great art collections in London is that of Samuel Courtauld, whose Huguenot forebear, Augustin, an excellent silversmith, made this candlestick in 1711.

1687

Newton Publishes "Principia Mathematica"

The new cosmology receives its definitive expression

Isaac Newton was born in 1642, the year of Galileo's death, and went to Cambridge University in 1661. When the university was closed in 1664-66 because of the plague, he went to his home in Woolsthorpe in Lincolnshire and there, at the age of 23, formed the basic ideas that were his great achievement. They were given to the world, in their refined shape, in the *Principia Mathematica* of 1687.

The starting point of Newton's system was that a body at rest is no more "natural" than a body in motion: force was needed to stop a moving body, not to keep it moving. He accepted the idea of straight-line motion and assumed that interplanetary space was empty. Galileo had assumed circular motion and left force out of his reckonings. The task before Newton was to explain the force that interfered with straight-line motion and gave the planets their closed orbits.

Gravitation was not, in itself, a new concept: men knew that apples fell to the ground. But Newton was able to establish a uniformity of gravitational explanation for both terrestrial and celestial motion. He had no new facts unknown to his contemporaries. The achievement was not based on observational discoveries; it was an achievement of the musing mind. It made good what Copernicus had urged, but not demonstrated: that cosmology, to make sense, must conform to principles of physics, that the universe was to be understood in terms of physics. Just as important, it gave physics a habitation in pure, or abstract, mathematics. Newton's world, for all that has happened since, is still ours.

1688

James II Flees England

The "Glorious Revolution" places William of Orange on the throne

James II became king of England in 1685. He was a staunch Roman Catholic, at odds with the religion of the vast majority of his subjects. He had, however, no intention of returning England to the Roman faith by force, since he expected the crown to be inherited by his Protestant daughter, Mary, wife of William of Orange. But he wished to remove all penal laws against Catholics. To prepare the way, he filled hundreds of offices with Catholics and tampered with the electoral system to produce a favorable parliament.

Already disquieted by such actions, Protestants took alarm at the birth of a Catholic son to James in 1688 and at the prosecution, in the same year, of seven bishops who refused to read from their pulpits a royal declaration of indulgence to Catholics. Leading Whigs therefore invited William of Orange to come to England and take the throne to defend Protestantism.

William invaded with an army much smaller than James's. But no fighting was necessary. James fled to France. Hence the "Glorious Revolution" is also called the "Bloodless Revolution."

William and Mary accepted the throne as joint sovereigns. The Bill of Rights (1689) confirmed the revolution and resolved that no Roman Catholic could wear the crown. The revolution scotched the chance that royal absolutism might flourish in England and, by the parliamentary means that placed William and Mary on the throne, implicitly made England a limited constitutional monarchy.

During William's reign, much of the old Tudor palace at Hampton Court was torn down and rebuilt by Sir Christopher Wren, the architect of St. Paul's Cathedral in the City of London. The Fountain Court is typical of his fine design and masterly combination of brick and stone.

1697

Peace of Ryswick Ends War of the League of Augsburg

Louis's third war makes no headway

The third of Louis XIV's wars began in 1688. The imperial diet and the papacy had both decided against Louis's candidates in arbitration of the disputed succession to two vacancies in the Rhineland, those of the elector Palatine and the archbishop of Cologne. Since 1679 Louis had been acquiring bits of German territory—called *réunions* to signify that historically they were within France's "natural frontiers"—by the mere threat of war.

This policy raised a second grand alliance against him, the League of Augsburg (1686), comprising Brandenburg, Bavaria, Saxony, Spain, Sweden, Savoy, the United Provinces and the Holy Roman Empire. By defeating the Turks at Mohács in 1687 and clearing Transylvania and Hungary of the Ottomans, Emperor Leopold I was freed to direct his attentions to the west. When, therefore, in 1688, Louis installed his own candidate in Cologne by force and invaded the Palatinate, all Europe took up arms against him.

For nine years France held its own; however, no headway could be made. France won victories, but, as Voltaire wrote, "she was perishing to the sound of *Te Deums*." To the heavy cost in money and men was added a succession of bad harvests. An exhausted France made peace in 1697. By the Treaty of Ryswick Louis relinquished every gain he had made since 1679, except Alsace, and restored Luxembourg to Spain and Lorraine to a local ruler.

1701

Jethro Tull's Seed Drill Transforms Agriculture

A technical innovation heralds the agricultural revolution

Jethro Tull's mechanical seed drill was the first of a series of technical innovations which contributed to the agricultural revolution in 18th-century England. It enabled wheat and root vegetables to be sown in straight lines far enough apart for horse-drawn plows to cultivate the rows between them. The drill did not come into general use until the 1730s, when its benefits were enhanced by the Rotherman triangular plow (1730).

Mechanical improvements were not, at any rate, the most important element in the transformation of agricultural production. More important were, first, the enclosure movement and the expansion of farming into large consolidated units, with the attendant decline and disappearance of medieval open-field strip farming; and, second, the extension of arable farming over previously uncultivated land (combined with new crop rotations, famously the Norfolk one, which used fallow land for winter turnip). The third factor was the adoption of intensive livestock husbandry.

The great increase in agricultural production—wheat yields doubled between 1750 and 1850—was of critical importance, not simply to meet the ever-rising demand of an increasing population, but to enable the release of labor into the manufacturing sector. In 1700 two agricultural laborers fed three other people; by 1800 they were feeding five others. Without that improved agricultural productivity, industrialization would have proceeded at a far slower pace than in fact it did.

1689–1701

ENGLAND

● **1689 Bill of Rights**
One of the fundamental instruments of the English constitution. Forbade English monarch to be, or marry, a Roman Catholic; declared illegal prerogative courts, levying taxation or keeping a standing army without parliamentary consent, and prosecutions for petitioning the Crown. Formally declared that James II had abdicated.

● **1689 Toleration Act**
Exempted Protestant Dissenters (except Unitarians) from certain penal laws, guaranteeing them freedom of worship; did not extend toleration to Roman Catholics. Dissenters still subject to civil disabilities, such as ban on holding public office, imposed by Test Acts (1673, 1678).

● **1694 Triennial Act**
Made the maximum life of a parliament and the maximum length of time between dissolutions three years; lasted until Septennial Act (1716).

● **1701 Act of Settlement**
Awarded crown (should Queen Anne die without issue) to Sophia, electress of Hanover (granddaughter of James I), and her heirs; monarch to be a communicant of the Church of England. Also stipulated that judges were to be appointed during good behavior, not the monarch's pleasure.

1703

St. Petersburg Founded as New Russian Capital

Peter the Great turns Russia toward the West

As the 18th century opened Russia faced three choices: to stagnate into the condition of China or Turkey; to submit to conquest by Sweden or Poland and become a west European colony; or to expand and, by modeling itself on the West, become a great power. Peter the Great's decision to build a new capital on the Neva in 1703—in its formal, regular, almost neoclassical appearance entirely unlike Moscow—was a bold symbol, hateful to Muscovites, of his determination to expand and westernize the backward Russian state.

Peter had visited the West in 1697 and 1698. He admired its applied science, its economic institutions, and its navies and shipbuilding. Peter banned beards and Muscovite dress. But his deep internal reforms—extending the nobles' duties of state service, founding a national network of technical schools, creating a standing army, centralizing the state administration—were all intended to speed the expansion of Russia.

His great foreign policy success, victory over Sweden in the Great Northern War (1700-21), ended in the Treaty of Nystad. Russia gained Livonia, Estonia, Ingria (on the swamps of which St. Petersburg arose, at great cost) and Karelia, ending Sweden's might forever and making Russia a Baltic maritime power. Against Turkey Peter was not successful, but his wars in the southwest announced the pan-Slavic theme, the right to protect the Slavic people of the Balkans, that became a permanent element of Russian policy.

1704

Marlborough Wins Battle of Blenheim

Great Britain inflicts a heavy defeat on the French

The War of the Spanish Succession, which began in 1702, pitted Louis XIV and his allies, Spain and Bavaria, against the grand Alliance of England, the United Provinces, Sweden, Denmark and most of the German princes. For the first two years the center of action was the Netherlands. But in 1704 Prince Eugène of Savoy called for aid in the defense of Vienna against France's impending assault.

The most brilliant general of the age, John Churchill, duke of Marlborough, who had revolutionized military tactics by abandoning limited marches and perpetual sieges in favor of aggressive advances and open-field engagements, led a force of 40,000 men on a three-month march to the banks of the Danube. There they joined an army of 10,000 men under Prince Eugène.

Marshal Tallard, the French commander, had encamped with a slightly larger force on the west bank of the Nebel, in Bavaria, believing he was protected from attack by the fortified village of Blenheim. But there, on August 13, in the most important engagement of the war, the French were overwhelmed. Four-fifths of their troops were killed or captured, against one in five of the Allied troops. The battle was a turning point in the war: Vienna was saved, Bavaria occupied, and the legend of French invincibility destroyed.

Marlborough's coolness in battle and his ingenuity as a strategist were matched by Eugène's courage and generalship; together they were invincible. Louis Laguerre's painting shows the victorious leaders at the Battle of Blenheim.

1709

Abraham Darby Smelts Iron with Coke

A Quaker ironmaster introduces a revolution in the iron industry

Industrial revolution in the cotton industry was largely a matter of using machines to cut labor costs. The revolution in the iron industry was accomplished by economizing on raw materials. The crucial change was the switch in fuel from charcoal to coke, made from coal, a switch made necessary by the rapidly diminishing forests of Great Britain.

The beginning of the revolution was Abraham Darby's development of a coke-smelting process in his Coalbrookdale works in Shropshire. He seems to have experimented with the method in 1709 and by 1718 was employing it exclusively. No other manufacturer used it before 1750, chiefly because charcoal furnaces had lower operating costs and the high capital costs of using coke were bearable only if the manufacturer could generate higher revenues.

Darby accomplished this by patenting a method of making thin-walled castings that produced superior, high-priced vessels such as the iron boilers for Thomas Newcomen's steam engine. By this method, which he kept secret, he was able to use only half the amount of metal employed by his competitors.

For the iron industry as a whole, real economies were not attainable until the late 18th century, when the steam engine improved the blast from furnaces and Henry Cort's puddling and rolling process (1783) permitted large-scale production of iron bars using coal. In 1760 Great Britain produced about 30,00 tons of pig iron; by 1800 the figure was nearly 1 million tons.

1713

Treaty of Utrecht Ends War of Spanish Succession

Great Britain gains an advantage in the contest for overseas empire

The War of the Spanish Succession was both the last of Louis XIV's wars fought for political and territorial mastery in Europe and the first of the great colonial trade wars fought for commercial supremacy. In those 18th-century wars Great Britain, rising to trading dominance over its old enemy France and its ally Holland, established the basis of its worldwide empire.

The Treaty of Utrecht, by which France and Spain were the losers, was the starting point. The seal was placed on Spain's long decline: Philip V renounced his claim to the French throne and ceded the Spanish Netherlands, Lombardy, Naples and Sardinia to Habsburg Austria. Louis XIV, for his part, was forced to abandon his conquests in the Rhineland; 40 years of warfare had gained France only Alsace and Franche-Comté.

The victor was Great Britain. The Hanoverian succession was recognized by France. More important, Great Britain gained Newfoundland, St. Kitts and an unchallenged title to the Hudson Bay region of Canada from France. From Spain it acquired Gibraltar, Minorca and the *asiento*, a 33-year monopoly (renewed in 1748, but abandoned in 1750 for a lump payment) of the lucrative sale of African slaves to Spain's New World colonies.

1715

"The Fifteen" Fails to Restore the Stuarts to the English Throne

A Jacobite rebellion collapses for want of French support

Support for the Stuart line and the "Old Pretender," James Stuart (the son of James II), was strongest among the Roman Catholic and Episcopalian minority of Scotland. When Queen Anne died in 1714 and George I came to the throne, James and his followers, led by the earl of Mar, saw their chance to return from exile in France and raise a Jacobite rebellion.

Probably it was doomed to fail whatever the circumstances. The promise of French support died with Louis XIV's death on September 1; and English Tories were restrained from participating by their doctrine of non-resistance to kings. The rising was, however, ill-managed and undertaken without sufficient preparation among its supporters in Great Britain. It began in Braemar on September 6, 1715. By the time that James, a cold and irresolute figure unlikely to inspire valor, had arrived in Scotland in mid-December, Mar's Highland army, three times larger than the royal army under the duke of Argyll, had been halted at Sheriffmuir on November 13. That battle was decisive, but the rising was not quelled until April 1716.

The Pretender and Mar fled to France and lived out their days in Europe.

GIN LANE

The Dutch began to distil gin in the 16th century. Its name comes from the juniper, or genever, whose berries flavored it. Introduced into England in the 1690s, its cheapness gave rise to the squalid "Gin Lane" depicted by Hogarth. By 1737 there were nearly 9,000 gin and brandy shops in London alone. Gin was also sold in prisons, factories, workhouses and barber shops, and the streets of working-class districts, like Seven Dials, were strewn with men, women and children made unconscious by it. In the 1730s one in seven adult deaths in the capital was attributed to gin drinking. The "gin era" came rapidly to an end after a heavy tax of 1751 put the drink beyond the budget of the mass of the population.

1720

South Sea Bubble Ruins English Speculators

A financial collapse opens Walpole's path to power

In 1717 the paymaster general, Robert Walpole, established a sinking fund into which a portion of the revenue raised by taxes was to be placed in order to reduce the national debt. Eager to find other means to liquidate the debt, the government in 1720 accepted an offer from the South Sea Company to assume responsibility for much of the debt. This joint-stock company, floated in 1711, had a trading monopoly with South Sea Islands and South America. The offer was accompanied by the grant of large numbers of shares to politicians and the king's mistresses.

Amid the financial confidence that the establishment of the sinking fund had stimulated, speculation ran riot. Share prices leaped tenfold and then collapsed, ruining thousands of investors. The Bubble Act of 1720, passed as a result, made joint-stock companies illegal save by royal charter, gained by a private act of parliament.

The pace of the Industrial Revolution may have been slightly retarded by the bursting of the bubble. The chief political effect was on Walpole's career. A parliamentary investigation could not be avoided. But Walpole's great skill in stemming discontent and saving the court from scandal raised him to the position of first lord of the treasury. He remained chief minister, or Great Britain's first prime minister, until his resignation in 1742.

1733

Molasses Act Imposed on American Colonies

An imperial statute stirs feelings of independence

The abstention from interference in the domestic affairs of the American colonies practiced by the British government in the first half of the 18th century was accompanied by a rapid rise in colonial prosperity. It also encouraged the colonists' belief that the mother country had no right—contrary to British notions of parliamentary sovereignty—to interfere. The Molasses Act of 1733, therefore, came as a rude shock.

The act was directed at the import of molasses from the French West Indies into the northern colonies. Since the north had no staple products to exchange for British manufactured goods, it had taken to turning West Indian molasses into rum for the purpose. But the British parliament, eager to protect its own West Indian planters from French competition, passed the 1733 act to place heavy duties on imports of foreign molasses or rum into a British colony.

The British maintained that the act merely controlled trade and so did not interfere in the colonies' domestic concerns; the colonists argued that it was really a form of taxation. The British government deferred to colonial protests: the act was scarcely enforced. But 40 years before the final independence crisis arrived, the Americans had raised the cry of "no taxation without representation," and the success of the protest encouraged the colonists to believe that the mother country was happy to respect their legislative freedom.

The collapse of the South Sea Company provided satirists with the opportunity to indulge their barbed wit at the expense of wealthy and greedy speculators.

1733

John Kay Invents the Flying Shuttle

The weaving trade takes its first step toward industrialization

The Industrial Revolution occurred first in cotton manufacturing. In 1800 cotton accounted for about 4 percent of the national income of Great Britian; by 1830 the cotton industry was supplying more than half the value of British exports. The immediate cause of that growth, the steam-powered loom invented by Edmund Cartwright in 1784, was preceded by five crucial inventions.

The first, patented in 1733, was John Kay's flying shuttle, which, by having a cord to pull the shuttle from side to side, enabled a weaver to leave one hand free to press the weft. It was widely adopted in the 1760s. The second, Lewis Paul's carding machine, patented in 1748, came into use around the same time.

Together the two inventions, by greatly increasing the productivity of weavers, created a bottleneck: four spinners were needed to supply one weaver with yarn. Then, in 1764, James Hargreaves invented the labor-saving spinning jenny. His first machine had eight spindles; by 1800 there were more than 100. The shortage of yarn was thus overcome.

The fourth invention was Richard Arkwright's water-frame (patented in 1769), a factory machine, operated first by water, later by steam, which produced cotton strong enough to serve as warp as well as weft and so led to the production of linen-free cotton. Finally, Samuel Crompton's mule (patented in 1779) combined the principles of the jenny and the water-frame to produce a finer cotton to compete with, and soon overtake, cotton from India.

1738

John Wesley Begins Open-Air Preaching

The Church of England is challenged by a revivalist movement

At Oxford University in 1729 a small band of undergraduates, led by John Wesley, who had been ordained an Anglican priest a year before, formed a Holy Club. The members practiced abstinence from food and sleep and visited prisons and hospitals in the search for salvation. For their methodical devotion they were nicknamed "methodists."

In 1735 Wesley and his brother, Charles, went as missionaries to Georgia, where they were impressed by the intensely personal religion of the Moravians. After his return to England John had a mystical experience, in which he felt deeply the presence of Christ as the bearer of his sins. The event took place in May 1738, when he was 35. Thereafter, until his death in 1791, Wesley preached an emotional, revivalist Christianity that rejected predestination and bypassed the episcopacy: each man's salvation was within his own power.

Distrustful of "enthusiasm," the Church of England closed its doors to Wesley, but he simply took the Gospel outdoors, thereby reaching a wider audience. He traveled 224,000 miles and preached more than 40,000 sermons. Other preachers were organized into circuits, and from 1744 there was an annual Methodist conference.

Methodist societies were given legal status in 1784, when there were 356 chapels in England and Wales. Methodism had grown into the most powerful body of opinion in the land. Wesley never broke formally with the Church of England; the schism came only in 1795.

Factory owners quickly took up John Kay's invention, for it meant cloth could be woven twice as fast, but they formed a cartel to avoid paying him royalties, and he died in poverty.

1740

Frederick the Great Invades Silesia

Prussian aggression begins the War of the Austrian Succession

The diplomatic and political history of Germany and Europe in the 18th century was dominated by the rise of Brandenburg-Prussia to the status of a great power. Ever since the reign (1640-88) of the elector Frederick William, the Prussian administration and army had been developing into the most efficient of such machines in Europe.

But Brandenburg was separated from Prussia by Poland and Hanover, and access to the Baltic was partially blocked by Sweden's possession of western Pomerania. Brandenburg-Prussia had either to expand or stagnate, a dilemma resolved by Frederick the Great's invasion of its southern neighbor, Habsburg Silesia, on the western boundary of Poland, in 1740.

The invasion began the War of the Austrian Succession, so named because a series of treaties concluded before the accession of Maria Theresa to the imperial throne in 1740 had guaranteed the integrity of the Habsburg empire. Frederick's bold stroke triggered a conflict between Prussia and the Habsburg empire that was to last for more than a century and to end only in 1871, with a Prussian-dominated German confederation.

The war begun in 1740 lasted until 1748, when the Treaty of Aix-la-Chapelle gave Prussia its first great prize by awarding it Silesia.

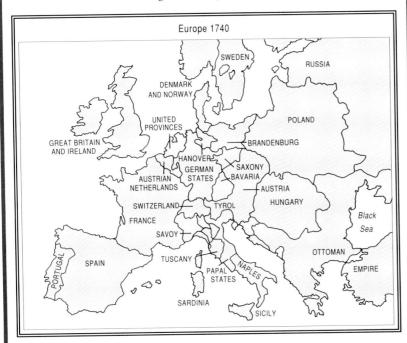

Europe 1740

1746

Jacobite Rebellion Ends at Culloden

Bonnie Prince Charlie abandons his hopes of the throne

The second Jacobite rising to restore the Stuarts to the English throne began in 1745. "Bonnie Prince Charlie," or Charles Edward Stuart, son of the "Old Pretender," landed in the Hebrides from Paris on July 25. On August 19, having gathered a force of Highlanders, he raised his standard in Glenfinnan. He then marched to Edinburgh and defeated George II's army at Prestonpans on September 21. He crossed into England on November 8. A month later, having met little resistance, he had taken Preston, Manchester and Derby.

That was the highwater mark of the uprising. The French had failed to invade in its support, and the anticipated spontaneous rising in the south had not taken place. To proceed beyond Preston was to keep the Jacobite cause alive; it was also to face destruction. Charles followed his military councilors' advice and retreated.

On December 20 his men crossed again into Scotland. The duke of Cumberland's army pursued them to Culloden Moor. There, on April 16, 1746, in a bloody battle, the Highlanders were defeated: they lost 1200 men, the English only 76. Jacobitism, as a factor in British politics, was dead.

This contemporary woodcut shows the English forces at Culloden putting the Jacobites to rout, while the duke of Cumberland looks on.

1763

Treaty of Paris Ends Seven Years' War

France loses its North American possessions to England and Spain

The Seven Years' War, fought between Great Britain and Prussia on the one side and France, Austria, Russia and Sweden on the other, was the first "world war" in history. The fighting took place in Europe, where the issue was the struggle for supremacy between Prussia and the Habsburg empire, and in India and North America, where the issue was the colonial rivalry of France and Great Britain. It ended in unqualified British and Prussian victories.

The decisive victories in Europe were at Rossbach and Leuthen (1757), Minden (1759) and Burkersdorf (1762); in Canada at Fort Louisburg and Quebec (1759); in India at Plassey (1757) and Pondichéry (1761). By the Treaty of Hubertusburg (1763), which made peace between Prussia and the Habsburgs, Prussia gained nothing but retained Silesia, which it had won in 1748.

In the separate Treaty of Paris (1763), France ceded all of Canada and all lands east of the Mississippi to Great Britain. It also gave the vast western territory of Louisiana to Spain in exchange for Florida. France was forbidden to build forts or maintain troops in India, though it retained its trading stations. Great Britain was thus the master of India and Canada, and its status as the world's leading colonial power was unchallenged.

1763

Pontiac's Rebellion Crushed

Great Britain puts down an American Indian rising

The expulsion of France from North America in 1763 dismayed the Indians of the Ohio region. They had been armed by the French against the British and, for decades, better treated by the French. No longer could they try to win their survival by buying off one rival European power against the other. The Treaty of Paris gave Great Britain sovereignty over vast tracts of land defined as French possessions in Canada and Louisiana, which the Indians had never conceded to be French.

In May 1763, the Indians burst into action in what is known as Pontiac's Rebellion. Pontiac was the leader of the Ottawa Indians, but many other tribes also took part in the rising, which began with an attack on Fort Detroit and lasted until 1766. The British suffered heavy losses, especially at the Battle of Bloody Run (1763), and for three years the borders of Maryland, Delaware and Pennsylvania were under attack.

Successes in Pennsylvania by the British, under Colonel Henry Bouquet, in 1764 forced the Delaware and Shawnee tribes to make peace, and Pontiac, promised a pardon, was compelled to follow suit in 1766. Although Indian wars were to continue until the late 19th century, the issue of authority in Indian lands had effectively been settled in the white man's favor.

In April 1763 Pontiac and his braves sought a meeting with Major Gladwin, commander of Fort Detroit, with the idea of mounting a surprise attack, but their plot was discovered. A month later the Indians stormed the fort.

1765

James Watt Improves the Steam Engine

Rotary motion ushers in the age of factory production

In 1765 James Watt, an instrument maker at the university of Glasgow, was asked to make repairs to a steam engine of the type invented by Thomas Newcomen in 1712. This was really an atmospheric engine: using a jet of water which condensed the steam, a vacuum was created into which a piston was driven by the force of the earth's atmospheric pressure.

This single-acting cycle was slow, incapable of rotary motion and, since it required alternate heating and cooling during each cycle of operation, uneconomical. Watt discovered that he could keep the cylinder constantly hot by employing a condenser, a separate vessel in which the steam from the cylinder was turned back into water. He also used steam at low pressure, rather than cold air, to drive the piston. At this point rotary motion was still impossible, but thermal efficiency had been greatly increased.

By the addition of his famous "parallel motion," which made a double-acting engine with rotary action possible, Watt created and patented a steam engine that for the first time offered manufacturers a reliable and economical alternative to the waterwheel for driving machinery of all kinds. Introduced in 1782, it paved the way for the Industrial Revolution.

1770

Cook Sails into Botany Bay

The British flag is hoisted in Australia

Lieutenant James Cook of the Royal Navy had already surveyed the coast of Labrador and Newfoundland when, in August 1768, he set sail from Plymouth in the *Endeavour* to chart the transit of Venus. He took with him instructions from the Admiralty that he was ordered not to open until he reached Tahiti in the Pacific.

When he reached the island a year after his departure, Cook learned that he was to search for the "southern continent" about which geographers had been speculating for a century. Two months later he discovered New Zealand and its Maori people; five months of sailing around the islands and charting their coasts proved that they were not part of the southern continent.

On the way home Cook chanced upon Australia, dropping anchor in a wonderful bay, on the edge of fertile land, in April 1770. The team of scientists, led by the young naturalist, Joseph Banks, who had joined the expedition, was enraptured by the rich botanical and zoological novelty spread before them. Cook named the harbor Botany Bay.

On a small island up the coast (now Possession Island) he planted the British flag and claimed for Great Britain the 2,000 miles of coast which he had charted. By July 1771, Cook was back in England, disappointed not to have solved the mystery of the southern continent. Seventeen years later, the first British colonizing fleet, 11 ships carrying 736 convicts, men and women, arrived in Australia.

James Watt's steam engine marked the beginning of viable steam power and transformed production in paper, steel and textile mills.

The red Australian honeysuckle, "Banksia serrata," brought back on Cook's ship, was the first Australian plant to be grown in Britain.

1772

Poland Partitioned

Russia, Prussia and Austria carve up the Polish kingdom

The kingdom of Poland, which had been an autonomous state since its union with Lithuania in 1569, was of great importance to Russia as a buffer state and a land link with the West. After Peter the Great's victory over Sweden at Poltava, in the Ukraine, in 1709, Russia emerged as a European power, and for the next 50 years the Russian minister in Warsaw had paramount influence on Polish affairs. He insisted, for one thing, on a severely limited Polish army.

The idea of partitioning Poland was frequently aired. The partition did not, however, take place until 1772, largely because Russia's war with the Ottoman Empire, begun in 1768, brought such startling success to Russian arms that Austria leagued itself with Turkey and threatened to drag Prussia into war with Russia. All three countries saw a sharing-out of Poland, accompanied by Russia's renunciation of interest in the Turkish Danubian principalities, as a means to avoid war.

The partition cost Poland one-third of its territory: Belorussia to Russia, Galicia to Austria and Pomerelia and Ermeland to Prussia. Two later partitions (1793 and 1795), which gave the greater part of the kingdom to Russia, removed Poland from the map of Europe.

Catherine II, Joseph II and Frederick II point out the part of Poland each proposes to take. The king of Poland is trying to stop his crown falling off!

1773

Pugachev Leads Cossack Revolt

The downtrodden of Russia raise a rebellion against serfdom

Russia under Catherine the Great, a vast empire beyond central control, was prey to disaffection. The great landowners held stringent powers over the serfs, who worked the land and toiled in mines, and between 1762 and 1769 there were 73 local outbreaks of peasant revolt. By far the greatest uprising was led by a Cossack, Pugachev. Claiming to be Tsar Peter III (whom many peasants believed still to be alive), he gathered around him perhaps 30,000 followers, promised them an end to serfdom, and issued them with arms.

In 1773 that rebel army plundered the middle and lower Volga regions and took control of Kazan, before it was bloodily crushed by imperial troops in 1774. Pugachev was captured and broken on the wheel before being beheaded, dismembered and burned. Countless numbers of his band met similarly savage deaths in a revolt that accomplished nothing other than to increase the powers of the landlords as agents of tsarist autocracy and, in the Charter of Nobility of 1785, to extend and deepen the institutions of serfdom.

1773

Boston Holds a Tea Party

American colonists vent their anger against the mother country

On the night of December 16, 1773, a small band of American colonists, led by Samuel Adams and Paul Revere, dressed themselves as Mohawk Indians, boarded three tea ships of the British East India Company anchored in Boston harbor and threw the cargoes into the sea.

The action was a defiant refusal to accept either the monopoly of the tea trade which the British parliament invested in the company or the colonial import tax on tea entering the American colonies. Behind it lay the mounting colonial opposition, most powerful in Massachusetts, to the right of the British parliament to impose any taxation on the American people, and even to the tie with Great Britain itself.

The British reply was to enact, in 1774, a series of punitive measures known as the "Intolerable Acts." These closed the port of Boston to commerce until reparation was paid to the East India Company; provided for the quartering of imperial troops in Boston; replaced the elected chamber of Massachusetts with one appointed by the Crown; and gave the governor the right to send persons from the colony to Great Britain for trial.

In their severity these acts fulfilled Adams's hopes, for they left the colony with no constitutional rights, save by the grace of Britain, and they thus made more remote than ever the possibility of a compromise between Great Britain's determination to uphold its imperial authority and the colonies' wish for independence.

1776

America Declares its Independence

Continental Congress adopts Declaration of Independence

By 1775 relations between Great Britain and the New England colonies had deteriorated so much that King George III, uninterested in conciliation, declared the colonies to be in a state of rebellion. The British would not lift the coercive acts against Massachusetts; the colonists would not tolerate their continuance.

General Thomas Gage, governor of Massachusetts, was instructed to put down the "rebellion." Arresting the leaders of the independence movement was beyond his resources. Instead he sent troops to seize their main supply of arms at Concord. On the way the troops met a colonial militia at Lexington and shots were fired, by which side first is not known. They were the opening shots of the War of Independence. Three weeks later the Second Continental Congress met in Philadelphia, assumed the role of a revolutionary government and prepared for war.

By March 1776, the rebels had forced a British withdrawal from Boston; in April American ports closed to British ships. On July 4 the Congress issued the bold Declaration of Independence, with its ringing call to world opinion to support a people in their struggle for the "inalienable rights" of "life, liberty, and the pursuit of happiness," to secure which rights "governments are instituted among men, deriving their just powers from the consent of the governed." In the mighty task before them, those signing the Declaration pledged to each other "our lives, our fortunes, and our sacred honor."

During the American revolutionary period, militiamen and armed citizens who agreed to be ready for duty at a minute's notice were designated Minutemen. The first men were enrolled in Massachusetts, and they were put to the test at Concord and Lexington.

1781

Victory at Yorktown Wins the United States its Freedom

A new nation rises as "the world is turned upside down"

The decisive colonial victory in the historic War of Independence came early, in 1777, at Saratoga. The British, striking south from Canada, hoped to occupy Albany and the Hudson Heights in New York in order to cut off New England from the rest of the colonies. But General John Burgoyne's army was roundly defeated and, though Great Britain won control of parts of New Jersey, Delaware and Pennsylvania that year, the die was cast. France entered the war on the colonial side in 1778, followed by Spain a year later.

Lord North's government now offered concessions that, had they been offered three years earlier, might have averted the conflict. The Tea Act was repealed; the Massachusetts Assembly was restored; the right to tax the colonies was renounced; and a peace commission was appointed. All this came too late. With French support, the colonials recovered Philadelphia and Rhode Island and gained control of the seas; and during 1778 and '79 Great Britain was diverted into fighting the French in the Caribbean.

The end came at Yorktown in Virginia, on October 17, 1781, when General George Cornwallis, after an 18-day siege, surrendered to a joint American-French force led by George Washington and Count de Rochambeau. As the imperial redcoats marched into captivity, a British band played the popular air, "The World Turned Upside Down." By the Treaty of Paris (1783) Great Britain formally recognized American independence.

1787

American Constitution Adopted

Nine states join the United States of America

Since 1781 the 13 colonies at war with Great Britain had been joined loosely together by the Articles of Confederation. In May 1787, delegates from each colony met in Philadelphia to draw up the world's first formal, written constitution. Its adoption in September changed an alliance of states into a union and a nation.

By its strict division of powers between the executive, the legislative and the judiciary, the constitution was intended to be a bulwark against tyranny. The president and commander-in-chief was to be elected by popular vote filtered through the electoral college. The legislature was to be bicameral: a Senate with two members from each state and a House of Representatives with representation by population. Despite the avowal in the Declaration of Independence that all men were created equal, a slave was to count as three-fifths of a man for that purpose.

The division of powers between the federal government and the state governments left sufficient authority to the states for the issue of states' rights to bedevil the republic in the future. But the central government emerged as the most powerful instrument in the union. Between 1787 and 1798, when the first president, George Washington, took office, nine amendments—known as the Bill of Rights—were added to the constitution. They guaranteed civil liberties such as freedom of speech and worship, the right to bear arms and the right in law not to testify against oneself.

1763–1774

NORTH AMERICA

● **1763 Proclamation**
Issued by British government eager to cut defense costs by making peace with the Indians; made Appalachian watershed western boundary for white settlement, thus blocking colonial expansion. Along with twin policy, initiated in Sugar Act (1764), of making American colonists pay part of defense costs, stirred colonial resentment of British rule.

● **1765 Stamp Act**
Passed by British parliament, imposing tax on American publications and legal and commercial documents; Stamp Act Congress, New York, united colonies against "taxation without representation"; repealed 1766, but Declaratory Act asserted unqualified competence of British parliament to pass legislation for the colonies.

● **1774 Quebec Act**
Passed by British parliament, associated in colonists' minds with the "Intolerable Acts." Thwarted colonial expansion by making the boundaries of Quebec the Ohio River in the south and the Mississippi in the west; raised suspicions in North America by establishing a nominated, not elected, assembly in Quebec.

● **1774 First Continental Congress**
Convention of delegates from all 13 American colonies to press grievances against Great Britain and devise new imperial relationship; after shots fired at Lexington and Concord, superseded by Second Congress (1775), which raised an army and made Washington commander-in-chief.

1789

Estates-General Summoned by Louis XVI

The Third Estate proclaims itself a national assembly

The French monarchy faced a mounting crisis in the 1780s. To the large debts accumulated during a century of war were added an economic slump and a run of poor harvests. A middle class largely excluded from political influence, and a depressed peasantry and urban working class, were resentful of a privileged aristocracy and restless for change. Before them lay the example of revolutionary America.

To overcome the financial crisis, Louis XVI laid taxes on the nobility. Its protests forced Louis to summon the estates-general to Versailles for the first time since 1614. When it met on May 5 a quarrel broke out over whether the three estates should debate and vote by order (giving the aristocracy and clergy a permanent majority over the *bourgeoisie*) or as a single body.

The matter was settled when the Third Estate, at its separate meeting, declared itself a National Assembly. When it was locked out of its meeting place by the king's order, it adjourned to a nearby real tennis court, and on June 20 took the famous Tennis Court Oath not to disband until it had given France a new constitution.

On June 27, Louis gave in and ordered the other estates to join the National Assembly. Rioting and looting of aristocrats' property began in the provinces and a Paris mob stormed the Bastille on July 14 and released its prisoners. There were only five of them (and two lunatics), but the act, together with the proclaiming of the National Assembly, signified that revolution had begun.

When news of the Tennis Court Oath reached Paris, the people started rioting: the French Revolution had begun. This preliminary sketch for a painting of the scene in the tennis court is by Jacques Louis David (1748-1825).

1791

France Gets a New Constitution

"Liberté, fraternité, égalité" becomes the revolutionary watchword

Within a few days of its founding in July 1789, the revolutionary National Assembly of France directed its attention to its main task—the drafting of a new constitution. In September it endorsed the proposal for a single-chamber legislature and voted to allow the monarch only a suspensive veto to delay legislation for a maximum of four years.

The franchise for elections to the national Legislative Assembly was conferred on every male of at least 25 years of age, resident in one place for a year and not a domestic servant. For local elections the franchise was restricted to "active" citizens who paid taxes equivalent to three days' wages: 6 million adult males were thus deprived of the vote. These decisions were all made before the end of 1789, but the new constitution was not promulgated until 1791. Members of the National Assembly declared themselves ineligible to sit in the new Assembly.

Elected in September 1791, that assembly faced two overriding questions: what to do with the king and his supporters and how to deal with the threat of foreign intervention on their behalf. Gradually two factions emerged: the extreme Jacobins and the moderate Girondins, whose positions on the left and right of the chamber gave rise to the political use of the terms "left" and "right."

1792

France Declares War on Austria and Prussia

The Revolution is carried beyond France's borders

Two factors influenced the decision of the French National Assembly to go to war in 1792. One was that freedom-loving people in foreign countries would welcome French aid in helping them to overthrow oppressive regimes. They could then establish their own republics on the revolutionary model. The other, more directly pressing, was the fear that an international coalition would intervene to restore absolutism and undo the work of the assembly.

Louis XVI's attempt to flee the country in June 1791, though he was captured at Varennes and brought back to Paris, intensified alarms. A month later Austria and Prussia implicitly threatened war by issuing a public statement that they would refrain from it unless they were joined by Great Britain and other powers. In the National Assembly the Girondins led the cry for war, arguing that it would unite the nation.

In February 1792, Austria and Prussia formed a new alliance and declared their intention to see Louis restored in his ancient rights. France declared war on both powers in April and, in so doing, led the nation into a 20-year struggle for mastery in Europe.

1793

Louis XVI Beheaded

The execution of the monarch initiates the "Reign of Terror"

Louis's flight from the Tuileries with his family, in a heavily curtained coach, in June 1791, doomed constitutional monarchy in France even before the new constitution was promulgated in September. Whether Louis merely intended to join a loyal army in Lorraine or to cross into Luxembourg and, therefore, into Habsburg arms is a question never resolved. But news of the flight polarized France.

Over the next year the flow of *emigré* royalists abroad quickened and republicanism grew strident. In September 1792, a mob attacked the royal residence, and a newly elected assembly, the Convention, abolished the monarchy. In January 1793, the Convention found Louis guilty of treason by an overwhelming majority and sentenced him to immediate execution. Soon afterward, defeats by *emigré* armies and a royalist uprising in the Vendée provoked a leftward turn in the revolution.

Maximilien Robespierre came to the fore as the head of the Jacobins, who formed a Committee of Public Safety, with dictatorial powers, to raise a *levée en masse*, or national revolutionary army, and to root out enemies at home. Republicanism passed into the Terror. Between March 1793 and the end of July 1794, when Robespierre himself was overthrown and beheaded, 14,000 "enemies of the republic" were led to the guillotine.

1789–1795

FRANCE

• 1789 Abolition of Feudalism
Resolutions of August 4 in National Assembly (later embodied in acts) abolished legal basis of the seigneurial, or manorial, system and many aristocratic, ecclesiastic and corporate privileges; peasant dues to lord, tax exemptions for nobility, manorial courts, private ownership of public offices, tithes and annates to the Vatican abolished.

• 1789 Declaration of the Rights of Man and of the Citizen
Adopted by National Assembly on August 26; declared the "nation" sovereign and enumerated natural rights: "liberty, property, security and resistance to oppression"; civic rights included freedom of speech and print, freedom from unlawful arrest or detention, consent to taxation; three more similar declarations, 1793-95.

• 1790 Civil Constitution of the Clergy
Enacted by National Assembly after it seized Church lands; selection of priests by district electoral assemblies; payment of bishops and clergy by government; abolition of all papal jurisdiction in France.

• 1793 Committee of Public Safety
Executive arm of the Convention, led by Danton, Robespierre and Carnot; rooted out monarchists, anti-centralists and Girondins during the Terror.

• 1795 Directory
Five-man executive council established by the Convention along with bicameral legislature; granted full executive power, except for control of public finances (given to Treasury Commission).

THE FRENCH REVOLUTION

Elisabeth Vigée-Lebrun's portrait of Marie Antoinette, queen of France, captures her frivolous, pleasure-loving nature. The scandal attached to her name, her extravagance and, after the revolution, her resistance to the National Assembly's attempts to curtail the king's power made her the butt of the political agitators and the main object of the crowd's hatred. Marie Antoinette's schemes to shore up the king's position and to arrange the rescue of the royal family all failed, and she was guillotined in October 1793.

When the Bastille was stormed by the Paris mob on July 14, 1789, the event was greeted by Charles James Fox, leader of the Whig opposition in Great Britain, with exultation. "How much the greatest event it is that ever happened in the world!" he exclaimed, "and how much the best." The euphoria which liberals everywhere felt at the fall of France's *ancien régime* was tempered as the opening triumphs of the French Revolution—the elections to a National Assembly, the promulgating of a new constitution, the abolition of feudalism—gave way to regicide, the Terror and general European war. Yet the revolution in France remains the most resonant event in recent history.

The causes of the revolution were too multifarious and complex for summary. One fact is, however, worth recording. On July 14, 1789, the price of bread in Paris was higher than it was on any other day in the 18th century. The great importance of the revolution in the development of political institutions is that, like the American Revolution a few years earlier, it gave practical expression to a change in men's attitudes that had long been forming. As the mists of kingly rule by divine right slowly dissipated, governments came to justify themselves on two grounds: that they derived their authority from the consent of the governed and that they justified that authority by using

The storming of the Bastille by the Paris mob on July 14, 1789, above, was an event of more psychological than actual significance. At the time it had only seven inmates, none of whom was a political prisoner; but the fortress was a hated symbol of authoritarian rule, and the day of its destruction is still commemorated as a national holiday in France.

In April 1792 Austria and Prussia invaded France and threatened to destroy Paris if the king were harmed. When the revolutionaries discovered that the king had been in touch with the enemy, he was tried and found guilty of treason. On January 21, 1793, Louis XVI, or Citizen Capet, as he was called, was executed in the Place de la Révolution.

it to promote the happiness of the people. "Happiness," said the Jacobin, Louis de Saint-Just, "is a new idea in Europe." The revolutionary age which dawned in Europe in 1789 replaced the subject by the citizen, the monarch by the people and the dynasty by the nation. It threw aside concepts of "liberties" and "privileges" accorded to certain ranks, or "estates," and raised up the idea of the rights of man. "Liberty, equality, fraternity" became the watchword of the new age.

The revolution had many concrete achievements: it established the equality of all men before the law, it freed the peasantry from ancient dues and from the payment of tithes to the Church, it established a unified national market with a common system of coinage and weights and measures. It represented the *embourgeoisement* of France. Yet it was something more than a French affair. By appealing to the "rights of man" the French revolutionaries broadcast a universal message. Every nation could take up the torch of revolution.

Paradoxically, perhaps, this universalist revolution also sounded the tocsin of modern nationalism. Nationalism in the past had almost always attached itself to religion or to a dynasty, usually to both. The French revolutionaries put the secular, democratic nation in arms. The *Grande Armée* was the National Assembly in battledress.

Neither the 17th-century English revolution, nor the American War of Independence, raised up such tribal emotions as the French. Nor did either pursue unlimited objectives. The English roundheads sought to restore the ancient liberties of the English people. The American rebels, though the language of the Declaration of Independence foreshadowed that of the French revolutionaries, fought to cast off the colonial yoke.

The French revolutionaries rose against the whole of the past. They proclaimed the beginning of a new world, the rebirth of history, the institution of justice for all men.

165

1793

Eli Whitney Invents the Cotton Gin

A mechanical sifter of cotton transforms the American economy

Eli Whitney made his first cotton gin in 1793. It was of the type called a "saw" gin, in which a toothed cylinder revolved against a grate enclosing the cotton and separated the seeds from the fibers. Together with the mechanization of the textile industry in Great Britain, it enabled cotton cloth to replace wool as the leading textile on the world market.

By its great saving of labor costs—a slave could clean 50 lb. of greenseed cotton a day instead of 1 lb.—it helped give the Industrial Revolution in Great Britain its breakthrough in the first three decades of the 19th century. In the United States it contributed to the rise of "King Cotton"—the expansion of the cotton plantations beyond South Carolina and Georgia to the whole of the south and southwest as far as Texas and the Indiana Territory west of Kentucky.

From 1815 to 1860 King Cotton ruled the southern economy. By 1820 it was already the leading crop, with 160m lb. produced annually. By 1850 nearly 60 percent of the slaves in the United States were working the cotton fields, and by 1860 the crop, weighing 2,300m lb., accounted for two-thirds of American exports.

Having little need, during the cotton boom, to encourage manufacturing industry, the south grew farther and farther away from the north in its economic needs and its way of life and, eventually, the U.S. was driven to civil war.

1793–1805 REVOLUTIONARY CALENDAR

The French Revolutionaries, believing that they were recasting the world, adopted a new calendar. The birth of the Republic was the first day.

Vendémiaire (Vintage) (Sept. 22-Oct. 21)   *Brumaire* (Mists) (Oct. 22-Nov. 20)
Frimaire (Frost) (Nov. 21-Dec. 20)   *Nivôse* (Snow) (Dec. 21-Jan.19)
Pluviôse (Rain) (Jan. 20-Feb. 18)   *Ventôse* (Wind) (Feb. 19-Mar. 20)
Germinal (Buds) (Mar. 21-Apr. 19)   *Floréal* (Flowers) (Apr. 20-May 19)
Prairial (Meadows) (May 20-June 18)   *Messidor* (Reaping) (June 19-July 18)
Thermidor (Heat) (June 19-Aug. 17)   *Fructidor* (Fruit) (Aug. 18-Sept. 16)

Sans culottides (Sept. 17-21) These five days were feast days, named for Virtue, Genius, Labor, Reason and Rewards.

There was no week; each month was divided into three groups of 10 days, or decades, with each tenth day a day of rest.

1795

Hutton Publishes "The Theory of the Earth"

A Scottish geologist finds "deep time" in the rocks

The science that attracted most public attention in the early 19th century was geology. In the formation of that popular taste, no man played a larger part than the Scottish geologist James Hutton. In a treatise of 1788 he announced his theory of uniformitarianism—that all changes in the history of the earth were explainable by processes still going on—and the consequent notion of "deep time" in history. The treatise ended with Hutton's immortal words that he could find "no vestige of a beginning, no prospect of an end."

Hutton's ideas received their full statement in his *Theory of the Earth*, published in 1795. They flew in the face both of the catastrophists, who explained changes in rock strata and the fossil record by sudden cataclysmic events, such as floods and earthquakes, and of their allies, the biblical literalists, who believed the world had been created about 5,800 years earlier. By Archbishop Ussher's 17th-century calculation, this had occurred on Sunday, October 23, 4004 B.C. precisely.

By giving both water and heat a function in the making of the earth's surface, Hutton also defused the conflict between the Neptunists and the Vulcanists. Uniformitarianism was not widely accepted until Charles Lyell, without discounting catastrophes, stamped his authority on it in *The Principles of Geology* (1830-33). From the discovery of slow evolution in rocks over millions of years it was to be a short step to the theory of evolution in biology.

1796

Jenner Finds Safe Vaccine Against Smallpox

Inoculation with cowpox replaces older methods

Smallpox replaced the plague as the greatest scourge in 18th-century Europe. It caused death in the virulent form of the disease and disfiguring pockmarks in the mild form. Many thousands died from it every year. Since the 11th century the Chinese had inoculated against it, and Lady Mary Wortley Montagu, the wife of the English ambassador to Turkey and herself a victim of the disease, introduced inoculation to Europe in 1718.

Three years later, during an epidemic in Boston, Massachusetts, a physician, Zabdiel Boylston, inoculated 240 persons against the disease: all but six survived. But inoculation was still a matter of giving persons a very mild dose of the disease in order to induce immunity against severe attack. The death rate was about three to every 100 persons inoculated, and survivors could pass the disease on.

It was not until 1796, when the English surgeon Edward Jenner demonstrated that inoculation with cowpox, which was not infectious, was successful at preventing smallpox, that vaccination became generally acceptable. In 1853 vaccination of infants was made compulsory in England.

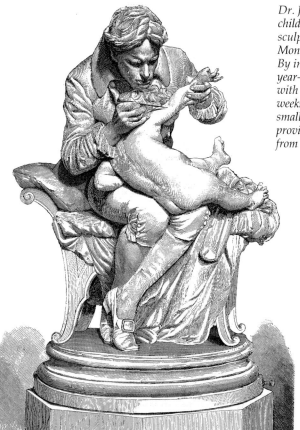

Dr. Jenner inoculates a child; from the sculpture by Professor Monteverde of Rome. By inoculating eight-year-old James Phipps with cowpox, and six weeks later with smallpox, Jenner provided protection from the killer disease.

1798

France Defeated at Battle of the Nile

Nelson's victory stalls Napoleon's campaign against the British empire

France gained the initiative in the early years of the Revolutionary Wars. Prussia withdrew from the war by the Treaty of Basel (1795) and, after Napoleon's lightning successes in Italy in 1797, Austria made peace in Campo-Formio (1797). France was confirmed in its possession of the Netherlands, Belgium, the left-bank Rhineland, Nice and Savoy, Switzerland and most of northern Italy. Those lands were either incorporated within the *grande nation* or else they were ruled by satellite governments effectively subservient to Paris.

Napoleon was now the most powerful man in the country. In 1798 he struck at the British empire, leaving Toulon with 30,000 men to seize Egypt and open the road to India. In July he defeated the Mamluk army at Alexandria and entered Cairo. It was a high point in his military career. But a few days later the French fleet was engaged by Horatio Nelson in Aboukir Bay. Nelson, by trapping the French ships between two lines of British vessels, was able to crush his opponents. Only two of France's 13 ships escaped. The French troops were thus cut off from their base, and the threat to India was ended.

1799

Napoleon Overthrows the Directory

France comes under the personal rule of its rising star

The National Convention, which had given France a republican constitution in 1792, executed the king in 1793 and carried the "Mountain," or radical Jacobins, to power in the state, took a turn to the right after the fall of Robespierre and the "Mountain" in 1794. A new constitution gave France a bicameral legislature and placed executive authority in a Directory consisting of five-members.

During its existence from 1795 to 1799 the Directory, notable for corruption, came to rely more and more on the support of the army—that is, on Napoleon Bonaparte. On 18 *brumaire* in the new Revolutionary calendar (November 10) he joined a conspiracy led by one of the Directors and overthrew the Directory in a *coup d'état*. It was replaced by the Consulate, with Napoleon as first consul.

The Revolution had taken a course that was to become familiar in world history; an initial attempt at moderate constitutional reform was followed by a period of savage radical rule, which, in its turn, gave way to the reinstatement of stable government and the final emergence of a strong man. For the next 15 years Napoleon ruled France as an autocrat. In 1804 he proclaimed himself emperor, was confirmed in the title by a plebiscite, and was crowned by Pope Pius VII in Notre-Dame in Paris.

1800

Great Britain and Ireland United

The legislature in Dublin is abolished

After centuries of subservience to Westminster, the Irish parliament in Dublin was, in 1782, granted full legislative autonomy by the British government. A decade later a republican independence movement, led by the Society of United Irishmen, gained strength in the wake of the revolution in France. A French expeditionary force sailed into Bantry Bay in 1796 (bad weather prevented its landing), and in 1798 the United Irishmen (officially banned in 1794) staged an ill-managed rebellion against the British Crown. The leader of the uprising, Wolfe Tone, was hanged for treason.

But the British government, under William Pitt the Younger, was fearful of a permanent Franco-Irish threat, and resolved to bring Ireland into union with Great Britain. The Act of Union, which came into effect on January 1, 1801, gave Ireland 100 members at Westminster in return for the abolition of the Dublin assembly. It also provided for virtual free trade between Ireland and Great Britain.

From the beginning the union was unpopular with many Roman Catholics, whose opposition grew stronger as years passed without fulfillment of the promise made in 1800 that the law would be altered to enable them to sit in the House of Commons. Throughout the 19th century the "Irish question," which ranged from demands for fair treatment to campaigns for outright independence, was a thorn in the side of the British government. The union lasted until 1920.

At Wolfe Tone's trial in Dublin he declared his desire "in fair and open war to produce the separation of the two countries."

1803

Thomas Jefferson Purchases Louisiana

U.S. territory is doubled in size at a bargain price

By the Treaty of Paris in 1763, all the French lands in North America west of the Mississippi, known as Louisiana, were ceded to Spain. In 1800 Napoleon forced Spain to give the territory back. His ambition was to build a French empire to compensate for the loss of Canada in 1763. An expedition to put down a slave rebellion in Santo Domingo (Haiti) was to advance to New Orleans and enter Louisiana.

President Jefferson, who got news of the plan, was alarmed, especially since Kentucky and Tennessee, which had joined the United States in 1792 and 1796 respectively, were showing signs of separatist yearnings. In 1803, therefore, he sent James Monroe to Paris to negotiate the purchase of New Orleans. To Monroe's surprise, he was offered all of Louisiana for what in the end came to only $27m (about five cents an acre). Monroe concluded the purchase, and American sovereign territory was thus doubled at a stroke.

Why did Napoleon do it? The explanation may be partly that the failure of the Santo Domingo expedition, and the loss of the island, robbed Louisiana of much of its value to him. In addition, Jefferson was threatening to form an Anglo-American alliance against France. Finally, the imminent renewal of war in Europe (suspended since the Peace of Amiens in 1802) was likely to lead to a British attack on New Orleans. Napoleon remarked that "this accession of territory affirms forever the power of the United States and I have just given England a maritime rival that sooner or later will lay low her pride."

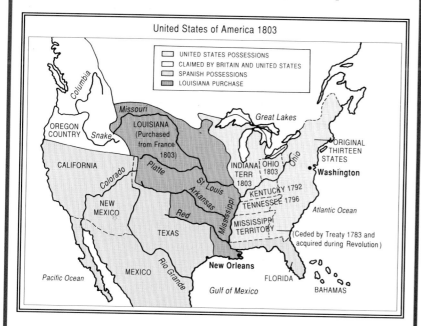

United States of America 1803

UNITED STATES POSSESSIONS
CLAIMED BY BRITAIN AND UNITED STATES
SPANISH POSSESSIONS
LOUISIANA PURCHASE

Columbia — OREGON COUNTRY — Snake — Missouri — LOUISIANA (Purchased from France 1803) — Great Lakes — CALIFORNIA — Colorado — Platte — St. Louis — Arkansas — INDIANA TERR 1803 — OHIO 1803 — Ohio — ORIGINAL THIRTEEN STATES — Washington — KENTUCKY 1792 — TENNESSEE 1796 — Mississippi — Red — NEW MEXICO — TEXAS — MISSISSIPPI TERRITORY — Atlantic Ocean — (Ceded by Treaty 1783 and acquired during Revolution) — Rio Grande — MEXICO — New Orleans — Pacific Ocean — Gulf of Mexico — FLORIDA — BAHAMAS

1804

Haiti Gains its Independence

Toussaint l'Ouverture leads a slave rebellion against European rule

When the French Revolution began in 1789, the Caribbean island of Hispaniola, discovered by Columbus in 1492, was divided into two parts: French St. Domingue (the eastern third) and Spanish Santo Domingo. Worked by black slaves, the sugar and coffee plantations of St. Domingue were the most valuable in the world.

The French Revolution, with its early promise to abolish slavery, carried its message to the New World, and a decade of guerrilla action was led by the freed slave, Toussaint l'Ouverture, an officer in the French army. In 1800 he conquered the Spanish part of the island, freed its 15,000 slaves and proclaimed himself governor of all Hispaniola.

In France the Consulate restored the legality of slavery and the slave trade within the French empire in 1802, and Napoleon sent an expedition of 35,000 men to put down the rebellion. The expedition was a disaster. Sickness (chiefly yellow fever) claimed the lives of 20,000 French soldiers, and another 8,000 died in battle.

During the struggle Toussaint was gulled by a duplicitous truce, captured and imprisoned in a fortress in the Jura Mountains, where he died in 1803. But the republic of Haiti gained its independence in 1804, the first New World nation after the United States to do so. The success of a slave rebellion, unprecedented in history, startled European opinion and gave fresh impetus to the abolitionist campaign in Great Britain.

1804

First Installment of Code Napoleon Promulgated

Legal reform provides a lasting legacy of the Revolution

In 1802 Napoleon appointed a commission to codify French law. Its reports were debated at more than 100 meetings of the Council of State, many presided over by Napoleon himself. The commission's work was issued in four new codes of law: the great civil code (1804), the code of civil procedure (1806), a commercial code (1807) and a criminal code (1810). Together they make up the Code Napoleon, which is still the basis of French law (though revised in the code of 1958).

The code also left a lasting impression on the law of French satellite states into which it was introduced. Roman law of the *ancien régime* was married to more egalitarian revolutionary principles (civil equality, freedom of speech and worship, for example), although the protection of bourgeois property was the code's chief object. Anomalies in the law prevailing in the various regions of France were eliminated in the new nationally uniform system.

Law reform and codification were not peculiarly Revolutionary achievements. In Habsburg Austria, one heritage of the "enlightened despotism" of Emperor Joseph was the issuing of a new criminal code (1803) and civil code (1811). Chiefly the work of Joseph von Sonnonfels, they were in many respects more liberal than the French codes.

In England, Jeremy Bentham's call for codification was delayed by the Napoleonic wars, but liberalization of the criminal law was one of the achievements of Robert Peel and Tory ministries in the 1820s.

1805

Nelson Dies at the Battle of Trafalgar

Great Britain inflicts a crippling defeat on the French navy

When European war was renewed after the temporary Peace of Amiens during 1802-03 Napoleon's *Grande Armée* swept all before it. By 1805 Great Britain, which had entered the war against Revolutionary France in 1793, stood as the lone bulwark against French domination of Europe. In order to make a cross-Channel invasion, Napoleon had to break the British command of the sea.

The decisive naval engagement of the Napoleonic Wars took place on October 21, 1805, off Cape Trafalgar, not far from the Spanish port of Cadiz. The Royal Navy's 27 ships of the line and four frigates, commanded by Horatio Nelson, faced a Franco-Spanish fleet with 33 ships of the line and seven frigates. The French admiral, Pierre de Villeneuve, deployed his fleet in the expectation of a traditional sea battle—the rivals confronting each other in two parallel lines, single ship fighting against single ship. Nelson, however, separated his fleet, using one section to attack the line, another to break up the enemy column from an oblique angle and prevent its retreat.

The tactic succeeded brilliantly. The French lost 20 ships, and Villeneuve was taken prisoner. Nelson himself was killed in the action, his last service to his nation being to render a French invasion impossible and to confirm Great Britain's mastery of the sea.

During the Battle of Trafalgar, a French sniper on the mast of the "Redoutable" fired the shot that cost Nelson his life. This detail is taken from Nelson's Column in Trafalgar Square, London.

1805

French Arms Defeat Russia and Austria at Austerlitz

The victory is followed by a Prussian defeat at Jena

Great Britain entered into an alliance with Russia and Austria in 1805, an alliance that fought the War of the Third Coalition (1805-07) against Napoleon. The first decisive action was at Austerlitz in Moravia, on December 2, 1805.

Six weeks earlier the French had crushed the Austrian army at Ulm and, although Austria was reinforced by Russian troops so that the French were outnumbered by 85,000 men to 70,000, the allied powers were once more routed by a French attack on their weak center. Emperor Francis II sued for peace and by the Treaty of Pressburg ceded Venetia, Istria and Dalmatia to Italy and recognized Napoleon as king of Italy.

In the summer of 1806 Prussia entered the coalition. But defeats at Auerstadt and Jena led to the fall of Berlin and forced it to withdraw from the war. Russia held on until the summer of 1807, when Napoleon and Tsar Alexander I made peace on a raft on the Niemen River.

In the Treaty of Tilsit Alexander accepted the reduction of Prussia to about half its size and recognized two new French satellites, the kingdom of Westphalia and the grand duchy of Warsaw. Russia gained a free hand in Sweden, from whom she exacted Finland in 1809.

1806

Holy Roman Empire Dissolved

A long chapter in European history comes to a formal close

The Holy Roman Empire, a German creation of Otto the Great, was from his coronation in 962 virtually identical with the German kingdom. And after the foundation of Habsburg rule in 1438 the emperor, though theoretically chosen by the German elector-princes, became hereditary in the Habsburg line.

The medieval contest between empire and papacy had given a tinge of reality to the concept of a Holy Roman Empire, but the Protestant Reformation of the 16th and 17th centuries ended even the semblance of meaning attached to it.

The Protestant princes leagued against the Roman Catholic empire, and by the Treaty of Westphalia (1648) the national sovereignty of the states nominally within the empire was recognized. By the 18th century Voltaire could rightly speak of "this body, which called itself and still calls itself the Holy Roman Empire," but which was "neither holy, nor Roman, nor an empire."

Nevertheless, a long chapter in European history came to a close when Emperor Francis II, after Napoleon established the Confederation of the Rhine in 1806, renounced the title. After Napoleon's defeat in 1815 the empire was not resurrected. In its place was formed the confederation of German States.

Throughout his life, Alexander I sought to be a mediator like his grandmother, who had been called the Arbiter of Europe, and to pull Russia out of the darkness of his father's reign. The constant specter of Napoleon drove him to form the coalition that finally defeated the French emperor.

1792–1814

EUROPE

• 1792–97 War of the First Coalition
Alliance against France of Austria and Prussia (1792), joined by Sardinia-Piedmont (1792), Great Britain, Netherlands, Spain, Naples and the Papal States (1793); Prussia and Spain made separate peaces (1795); Treaty of Campo-Formio (1797) with Austria, after Napoleon's victorious Italian campaign, left Great Britain alone against France.

• 1798–1801 War of the Second Coalition
Alliance chiefly formed by Pitt of Great Britain, Russia, Austria, Naples, Portugal and Turkey; Russia withdrew (1799); Napoleon defeated Austrians at Marengo (1800) and forced Peace of Lunéville (1801) on them; Portugal defeated in same year; Great Britain made Peace of Amiens (1802) and no further wars until 1805.

• 1805–07 War of the Third Coalition
Alliance of Great Britain and Russia (April), extended to include Austria (August); Austrians defeated at Austerlitz and made the Treaty of Pressburg (1805); Prussia joined coalition (1806) but defeated at Jena and Auerstadt; Russia made peace in Tilsit (1807); Great Britain remained in the war.

• 1813–14 War of the Fourth Coalition
Alliance of Russia, Prussia and Great Britain; basis was British financial aid to partners; extended to include Sweden, Austria and Bavaria; on March 31, 1814, allies entered Paris and forced Napoleon to abdicate.

1807

Slave Trade Abolished in British Empire

Great Britain takes the lead in ending the traffic

Between 1783 and 1830 the Tories were continually in office in Great Britain except for one interlude. For 18 months in 1806-07 power lay with the Whig-dominated ministry of "all the talents." Its outstanding achievement was the abolition of the slave trade with the British colonies.

Abolition was the culmination of a long humanitarian campaign fought against the trade by the Anti-Slavery Society, founded in 1787, and the Clapham "Saints," led by the Church of England evangelical and Tory member of parliament, William Wilberforce. Its timing owed something to the overproduction of sugar in the Caribbean and a surplus in European markets (made more damaging by Napoleon's attempt to ruin British trade by the Continental System) and to the competition that established British plantations faced from the new sugar economy of Spanish Cuba. Well-stocked British plantations could prosper if the supply of slaves to their rivals was stopped, and British traders controlled the traffic from Africa.

The failure to gain St. Domingue and the destruction of the world's "sugar bowl" in Toussaint l'Overture's successful bid for independence sealed the matter. Had St. Domingue become British, abolition would have been almost unthinkable. Humanitarianism and commerce walked hand in hand. The British lead in abolishing the trade was followed by France (1815) and by Spain and Portugal (1820).

The tireless campaigning of William Wilberforce finally resulted in the Slavery Abolition Act, passed one month after his death in 1833.

1812

The United States Strikes at Canada

The U.S. government fails to conquer British North America

In 1808 the American government replied to the restrictions on U.S. merchant shipping imposed by Great Britain and France in their war with one another by placing an embargo on trade with both the belligerents. For the next four years the interference with trade caused mounting resentment. This culminated in the decision, made by President James Madison and Congress, to declare war on Great Britain and to attack British North America, or Upper and Lower Canada. Mercantile grievances and expansionism—America's self-proclaimed "manifest destiny" to rule the entire continent—were neatly joined.

For the Canadas, which had a population of 500,000 against the United States' 7½ million, the war was a matter of survival. That they did survive owed much to French-Canadian loyalty and to the superior training of the small British regular force (war in Europe made enlarging it impossible). More was owed to the bungling of the war by the American generals. A concerted attack on Montreal at the outset needed to be decisive. Instead, American strength was diluted in a series of isolated assaults.

After two years of inconclusive fighting, the war ended with the Treaty of Ghent. By conventions of 1817 and 1818, warships were banned from the Great Lakes, and the 49th parallel was fixed as the boundary between the two countries from the Great Lakes to the Rockies (leaving Oregon territory disputed). The territorial settlement of 1783 was thus confirmed.

1812

"La Grande Armée" Retreats from Moscow

Napoleon's army is destroyed and his empire begins to crumble

The Treaty of Tilsit (1807) left Russia and France at peace, and Russia joined Napoleon's trade blockade of Great Britain. But the resulting economic hardship made the French alliance unpopular, while Tsar Alexander I fretted at Napoleon's grip on Poland. When Napoleon annexed the duchy of Oldenburg (lower Saxony) the peace ended.

Napoleon decided to attack Russia, to drive the "northern Barbarians" to the Asian steppes and expel a threat to European "civilization." He assembled a huge army, no longer the great national army of the Revolutionary *levée en masse*, but an international force in which French soldiers were outnumbered 2 to 1 by recruits from allied and vassal states. This armed mass of 700,000 men engaged the Russian army at Borodino, 70 miles west of Moscow, on September 7, 1812, and captured the city.

Casualties were heavy on both sides, but Kutuzov's Russian army was not destroyed and was able to regroup. A week later the *Grande Armée* entered Moscow, to find it in flames. Three-fifths of the city was razed in five days. Napoleon occupied Moscow until October 18, vainly waiting for Russia to make peace. When the tsar held firm, Napoleon decided to retreat to his winter quarters.

The severe cold was too much for his ill-clothed and ill-fed men, who made a pathetic rearguard withdrawal from Russia. Harried by Cossack guerrillas, the withdrawal turned into a rout. Only 30,000 imperial soldiers made it back to Paris; of them, only 1,000 were battle-fit. Napoleon's empire faced collapse.

1814

Napoleon's Conquerors Meet in Vienna

The Congress redraws the map of Europe and restores the Bourbons

Germany was freed from French rule in October 1813 by the coalition powers' victory at the Battle of Leipzig. The powers entered Paris on March 31, 1814; Napoleon abdicated on April 1; and a preliminary peace was signed on May 30. At the Congress of Vienna (September 1814–June 1815) the powers fixed the peace settlement.

The Bourbon restoration in France was confirmed in the person of Louis XVIII. The French Revolution had exalted the nation above the Bourbon dynasty and had unleashed modern nationalism; the makers of the peace upheld dynastic rights and ignored national claims.

The dynasties of Spain, Naples, Piedmont and Tuscany were restored. The Swiss Confederation was reinstituted with a guarantee of its permanent neutrality. Three new political entities were created: the United Kingdom of the Netherlands (Holland, Belgium and Luxembourg); the German Confederation (39 states with no central administration); and the free city, or republic, of Cracow.

Austria's chief acquisition was Lombardy-Venetia; Prussia gained Danzig, much of Saxony and Westphalia and Swedish Pomerania. Norway was united to Sweden. Great Britain retained possessions captured during the war: the Cape of Good Hope, Heligoland, Ceylon, Tobago, Santa Lucia, Mauritius. The treaty also called for the abolition of the slave trade by all the signatories, the granting of civil and political rights to Jews, and the free navigation of the Rhine and Meuse.

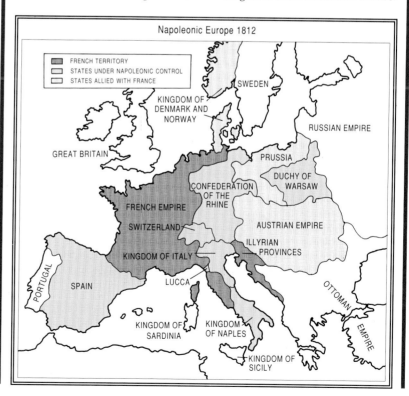

Napoleonic Europe 1812

FRENCH TERRITORY
STATES UNDER NAPOLEONIC CONTROL
STATES ALLIED WITH FRANCE

1815

Napoleon's Comeback Ends at Waterloo

Wellington and Blücher bring down the curtain on the Napoleonic wars

After his abdication as emperor of France, Napoleon was exiled to the island of Elba, off the coast of Tuscany. He escaped in February 1815, and reached Paris on March 20, where he ruled again during the "Hundred Days" until his defeat at Waterloo. On March 25 the governments of Austria, Prussia, Russia and Great Britain agreed to raise one last army to bring him down.

Against the combined armed strength of the rest of Europe, Napoleon's best hope was to deliver a knock-out blow that would split the coalition against him and rally the French nation to his support. On June 12 he left Paris for a showdown against British and Prussian troops in Belgium. Six days later, British troops under Wellington, reinforced by the Prussian troops of Marshal Blücher, destroyed half of Napoleon's army at Waterloo. French losses were more than 30,000; British and Prussian about 23,000. It was, as Wellington remarked, "a damned nice thing—the nearest run thing you ever saw in you life."

Napoleon abdicated for a second time on June 22 and surrendered to the commander of the British warship *Bellerophon* in the Breton port of Rochefort, on July 15. He was exiled to St. Helena in the South Atlantic, where he died in 1821.

1816

Photography Invented

Joseph Niepce's experiments lead to the world's first photographs

The invention of photography was a slow process, involving a number of pioneers, but pride of place goes to the French physicist Joseph Niepce. Ever since the early 18th century it had been known, thanks to Johann Schultze's experiments, that silver nitrate darkened when exposed to light. But it was not until 1816 that Niepce made the first paper negative and not until 1826–27 that he produced his first photograph on metal.

In the meantime John Herschel, the English mathematician and astronomer, had in 1816 discovered the use of sodium thiosulfate as a fixing agent and given it the name "hypo." He also introduced the terms "negative" and "positive."

By 1829 Niepce was working closely with Louis Daguerre, the painter and physicist, who had been experimenting independently to produce photographs on a silver-coated copper plate treated with iodine vapor. That process, which produced images known as daguerreotypes, was perfected by Daguerre after Niepce's death in 1833 and presented to the French Academy of Science, in 1839.

Almost simultaneously the English inventor William Fox Talbot made public his rival calotype (later "talbotype") process, by which a large number of paper positives could be made from a single negative. His *The Pencil of Nature*, published in 1844, was one of the first books to be illustrated with photographs.

On June 18, the Battle of Waterloo brought to an end 23 years of war between France and the other powers in Europe. This detail from a painting of the Battle of Waterloo by Sir William Allen shows Napoleon on his famous white horse, "Marengo."

1817

San Martín and Bolívar Begin Liberation of South America

The Creole rebels force Spain to withdraw from the New World

Between 1817 and 1822 Spanish America experienced a wave of anti-colonial wars unparalleled until the African liberation struggles of the 1960s. They began in Venezuela under Francisco de Miranda in 1809, when the Spanish monarchy was absorbed in war against Napoleon. But the first phase of the wars ended in defeat and Miranda's imprisonment in Cadiz in 1816.

The torch passed to the Creoles (native-born descendants of the Spanish conquerors) José de San Martín and Simón Bolívar. In 1817 San Martín's 5,000-strong "Army of the Andes" made a heroic march with wagons and guns over the mountains from Peru into Chile, where the Spanish were totally overwhelmed at the Battle of Chacabuco. Santiago, the Spanish stronghold, was captured, and Bernardo O'Higgins placed at the head of a revolutionary government. A year later Chile proclaimed its independence.

In 1817 also, Bolívar returned from Jamaica, where he had fled after Miranda's defeat, and began to liberate the northwest of the continent. After defeating the Spanish at Boyaco in 1819, he established the republic of Gran Colombia (comprising modern Venezuela, Colombia, Ecuador and Panama). The federation lasted until 1828, when Bolívar pronounced himself dictator and Venezuela and Ecuador seceded.

By then Peru, liberated by San Martín in 1821, and Bolivia, by Antonio José de Sucre's victory at Ayacucho in 1824, had also won independence. Cuba remained Spanish until it was taken by the United States in 1898.

1820

Electromagnetism Discovered

Hans Oersted sees a compass needle deflected by an electric current

The observation made by the Danish physicist Hans Oersted, in 1820, that a compass needle was deflected by a nearby electric current, marked the beginning of the science of electromagnetism. The needle, in fact, swings back and forth, then settles at right angles to the conductor of the current. The effect was used in the electric telegraph invented by the American Samuel Morse in 1837. Morse placed an electromagnet in the receiver, and it was activated by the making and breaking of an electric circuit.

Oersted's name has been given to the unit of measurement used to quantify the strength of an electromagnetic field, but establishing the full extent of the connection between electricity and magnetism was the work of the Frenchman André Ampère and the Englishman Michael Faraday. Ampère discovered that an electric current exerted force on another current, as on a magnet. The principle allowed the subsequent development of the electric motor.

Faraday's discovery, in 1831, that by stopping or starting a current in a coil a transient current was induced in a neighboring, but unconnected, coil led to the development of the transformer. He also found that moving a magnet in relation to a coil of wire produced a current in the coil, and on the basis of that discovery made the world's first dynamo. On the work of Oersted, Ampère and Faraday, indeed, hangs the whole of modern electrical engineering.

1820

Missouri Compromise Drawn Up to Save the Union

The United States tries a formula to avoid conflict over slavery

In 1819 Missouri, which was part of the Louisiana Territory purchased by President Jefferson in 1803, applied for admission to the Union as a slave state (one in which slavery was lawful). The application raised in a new light the momentous question of slavery and sounded, Jefferson wrote from his retirement, "like a fire-bell in the night...the knell of the Union."

The federal government had not, up to 1819, interfered in Louisiana Territory to disturb the existing slavery inherited from Spanish and French law. Slavery had further entrenched itself after the War of 1812, when slave owners joined the migration westward and took their slaves with them.

In an attempt to satisfy both the slave owners and northern abolitionists, Congress agreed to the so-called Missouri Compromise of 1820. Missouri was admitted to the Union as a slave state (1821), but Maine, in the northeast, was also admitted, as a free state, in which slavery was outlawed. The balance in the Union was thus maintained at 12 slave states and 12 free. It was also enacted that north of latitude 36°30′, slavery was to be prohibited. The compromise lasted until the Kansas-Nebraska Act of 1854.

Differing attitudes to slavery split the North from the South, where scenes such as this were common, eventually bringing about the Civil War.

1821

Greeks Begin War of Independence

A nationalist revolt throws off the Ottoman yoke

After 1815, the greatest threat to the stability of Europe lay in the Balkans, over whose various Christian nationalities the Ottoman Turks held fragile sway. Turkey was the "sick man of Europe," and Austria-Hungary and Russia watched its condition carefully, eyeing each other nervously as they did so. Metternich, the Austrian chancellor, hoped for Turkey's recovery; Russia looked covetously at the prospects that would stem from its demise. So Metternich was disturbed when the first successful nationalist revolt in 19th-century Europe was accomplished in Greece.

It started with a rising of the Greeks, led by Alexander and Demetrios Ypsilanti, in the principalities on the Danube (modern Romania) and Morea in 1821. War in earnest started in 1822, after the rebels proclaimed the country's independence in Epidaurus.

Great Britain, France and Russia rallied to the Greek cause. The failure of their attempt to negotiate a settlement in 1827 was followed by a joint assault on the combined Turkish-Egyptian fleet at Navarino (the last concerted action by the three powers until the Dardanelles campaign of 1915). The Turkish navy was virtually destroyed. Russia then declared war on, and defeated, Turkey.

By the Treaty of Adrianople (1829) Russia gained access to the Danube, the Dardanelles were opened to all commercial shipping, and autonomy was promised to Serbia (under Russian protection) and Greece. In 1832 the independent kingdom of Greece, south of a line drawn from the Gulf of Arta to the Gulf of Volos, came into being.

The destruction of the Muslim fleet at Navarino accelerated Egypt's withdrawal from the war in Greece, exposing Turkey to Russian attack.

Monroe's philosophy was a reaction to concern in America that European powers might try to restore Spain's colonies in Latin America to her.

1823

Monroe Doctrine Announced

The United States asserts its authority in the western hemisphere

Great Britain was the first nation in Europe to recognize the newly independent republics of South America, and in 1823 the British foreign secretary, George Canning, suggested an Anglo-American pact to protect their integrity. Canning's interest was to prosper British commerce with the new republics.

Neither President Monroe nor his secretary of state, John Quincy Adams, was willing, as Adams put it, to be "a cock-boat in the wake of the British man-of-war." Instead, Monroe delivered to Congress, in December 1823, the famous statement that became known as the Monroe Doctrine.

It contained three principal parts. No further European colonization in the western hemisphere would be tolerated; any attempt by a European power to extend its influence there would be interpreted by the United States as an unfriendly act dangerous to its security; and the United States would not interfere in the affairs of Europe. The first two principles have remained a cornerstone of American foreign policy; and isolationism, though breached by the entry into World War I in 1917 and since, has continued to run strongly in American politics.

1825

Stockton-to-Darlington Line Opens in Great Britain

The world's first public railroad begins operations

The opening of the Stockton-to-Darlington railroad in northeast England was a watershed. It marked the end of the pre-locomotive era and heralded the great railroad expansion of the 1830s and '40s that took the Industrial Revolution into its iron phase.

Railroads had appeared in Nottinghamshire and Shropshire in the 1590s—four-wheeled, horse-drawn carts carrying coal on hardwood lines from mines to rivers and roads. By the late 18th century iron tracks were in use, but dramatic expansion awaited the invention of the steam locomotive.

Richard Trevithick invented the first successful railroad locomotive in 1804; in 1814 George Stephenson produced one that ran not on a flanged rail but on an edge; and a new process of the 1820s enabled wrought-iron rails to be rolled cheaply enough to replace the more brittle cast-iron ones. Stephenson constructed the 25-mile line from Stockton to Darlington and opened it in 1825. It was the first public railroad to carry freight (chiefly coal) by locomotive; passenger trains were started in 1833. The Liverpool and Manchester line was opened in 1830, chiefly for the transport of textile goods.

Horse-drawn railroads did not go out of existence until the 1840s, the decade in which Great Britain's comprehensive railroad network was laid down and railroad building began in the United States. By 1834, Belguim had become the first country to establish a state-owned railroad. During the Crimean War (1853-56) the first military railroad made its appearance in Balaklava.

The Liverpool and Manchester line, opened in the presence of the duke of Wellington, covered 40 miles. Revenue from eager passengers was 10 times higher than expected.

1825

Decembrist Uprising Foiled

A rebellion fails to overthrow autocracy in Russia

Tsar Alexander I died in 1825, having expressed the wish that his younger brother Nicholas should succeed him in preference to the elder, Constantine, who had renounced the throne in 1822. Nicholas, in St. Petersburg, proclaimed Constantine tsar; Constantine, in Warsaw, proclaimed Nicholas. For three weeks in December Russia was without a tsar.

This strange circumstance was exploited by a secret society of army officers who had absorbed democratic notions while serving in the West during the Napoleonic wars. They persuaded a number of regiments to join them in a revolt in St. Petersburg, by which they hoped to overthrow tsardom and summon a national assembly. The rebels had, however, neither a clear military strategy nor a coherent political program, and the uprising (betrayed by police spies in the army) was put down by artillery fire in a day.

Although the romantic legend of the "Decembrists" was kept alive by Russian revolutionary secret societies for the rest of the century, the chief consequence of the fiasco was to stiffen the anti-liberalism of Nicholas I (who now took the throne) and to increase the activities of the tsarist terrorist police.

The Decembrists' insurrection made a profound impression on Nicholas I's Russia and, despite his militarist style of government, revolutionary activity in the country increased.

1830

July Revolution Topples Charles X

The restored Bourbons give way to a new "bourgeois monarchy"

Charles X, who succeeded his brother Louis XVIII as king of France in 1824, was a reactionary in politics and a narrow Roman Catholic in religion. His rule was masterminded by the chief of police, Prince Jules de Polignac. When elections to the national assembly in 1830 greatly enlarged the ranks of the liberal opposition, led by Adolphe Thiers and François Guizot, Polignac issued a set of repressive decrees.

Those "Ordinances of St. Cloud," issued on July 25, dissolved the new chamber (before it had met), reduced the electorate from 100,000 to 25,000 and banned publications not authorized by the government. The next day mobs mounted the barricades in Paris and by July 30 the rebel coalition of students, workers and liberal politicians had seized control of the capital. Charles abdicated from the throne and took refuge in Great Britain. Thus the restored Bourbon dynasty passed from history almost without bloodshed.

The Duke of Orléans, Louis-Philippe, accepted the crown and a new constitution, by which the liberals triumphed over the democratic republicans. In the upper chamber, those ennobled for their lifetime only replaced those ennobled by family descent; the electorate was widened by reducing the age qualification from 30 to 25 and the property qualification from 300 francs to 200. Censorship was abolished and the connection between the Roman Catholic Church and the state broken. A "bourgeois monarchy" had replaced the clericalism and absolutism of the Bourbons and stemmed the advance of republican democracy.

1830

Belgians Stage National Revolt

Patriots win their national independence from the Netherlands

The July revolution in France was the inspiration for uprisings in several other parts of Europe, but only Belgium staged a successful revolt. Union with the Calvinist Netherlands had been imposed on the largely Roman Catholic French- and Flemish-speaking population of Belgium by the Treaty of Vienna (1815). The Belgians outnumbered the Dutch by 2 to 1, yet had only equal representation with them in the states-general.

Within a month of Charles X's flight from France, liberal nationalists were on the streets of Brussels to demand Belgian autonomy. Street violence soon led to the withdrawal of Dutch troops and the calling of the states-general, which on September 29 voted for separation. On October 4 a provisional Belgian government proclaimed its independence.

A new constitution, more liberal than any other in Europe, was adopted early in 1831. It provided for a severely limited monarchy, with the king to be chosen by representatives of the people; members of the Dutch house of Orange-Nassau were to be ineligible. The legislature was to be elected on a wide property franchise. Prince Leopold of Saxe-Coburg-Gotha was elected King Leopold I.

Dutch troops which invaded late in the year and bombarded Antwerp in an attempt to regain Belgium were repelled with Anglo-French assistance. A conference at London declared the union between Belgium and the Netherlands ended. But not until the Treaty of London of 1839 did the Dutch formally accept Belgium's independence.

On the streets of Brussels, the Belgian people rose up against their Dutch masters and fought to secure their independence.

1832

Nullification Crisis Tests American Union

South Carolina threatens to bring the United States to its knees

The United States constitution of 1787 assigned specific powers to the federal government. By implication at least, authority in any other sphere devolved upon the states. Hence arose the slogan of "states rights" and the theory of "nullification"—that any federal law not expressly provided for by the constitution could therefore be declared null and void by a state government.

The conflict exploded into the open in 1832 when President Andrew Jackson backed Henry Clay's Tariff Act, and South Carolina, led by the vice-president and ardent spokesman for the southern planters, John Calhoun, invoked the doctrine of nullification against it. Much of the south's economic difficulty stemmed from the wasteful, soil-exhausting domination of cotton growing; but the planters, eager to blame the federal government, viewed protective tariffs as an unfair tax on the south to pay for the manufacturing expansion of the north.

Calhoun called a state convention in South Carolina, which declared the tariff to be null and void and prepared to use arms against any federal customs officials who should attempt to enforce it. Jackson issued a proclamation resisting the nullifiers and denying a state's right to secede, while Congress passed a bill empowering the use of federal troops, if necessary, in South Carolina. A compromise tariff of 1833 ended the crisis. South Carolina backed down. But the president predicted that the "next pretext will be the Negro, or slavery, question."

1832

Whigs Pass the Great Reform Act

The foundation of modern democracy is laid in Great Britain

Lord Grey and the Whigs came into office in Great Britain in 1830 pledging to reform the country's ancient electoral system. That system had three chief defects. The first was the numerous "rotten boroughs" which gave rich landowners seats in parliament for their nominees; second was the gross over-representation of the southern portion of the country and the exclusion of the growing industrial towns of the north. Finally, a narrow franchise made the House of Commons socially exclusive.

The radical Whig bill of 1831 proposed to repair those deficiencies. Every borough with a population under 2,000 was to lose its two members; every borough with a population between 2,000 and 4,000 was to lose one of its two members. The resulting loss of representation was to be made up by giving northern towns and the counties more members. And the vote was to be given to every householder who owned or rented premises of an annual rental value of £10. It required an election in 1831 and a threat to create new peers to swamp the Tory opposition in the House of Lords before the bill, in a somewhat amended form, became law in 1832.

Great Britain was still a long way from democracy. The act doubled the electorate, but the working class remained largely outside the property qualification. Even so, the supposed sanctity of the old system, rendering it free from tampering, had gone forever. The imbalance between north and south was substantially, though not fully, redressed. And for the first time the principle of a uniform franchise throughout the country had been established.

1828–1837

NORTH AMERICA

• **1828 Tariff of Abominations**
Raised tariff on imports to average 50 percent of value of goods, compared to 33⅓ percent in 1824; upheld by President Andrew Jackson after election chiefly by anti-tariff south and west in 1828; protected northern manufacturers and led to southern opposition and nullification crisis.

• **1829–37 Indian Treaties**
Ninety-Four Treaties with Indian tribes forced them to surrender millions of acres of land; many forcibly removed west of the Mississippi, with promises (often broken) of money and new land; those with prosperous farms given option to become U.S. citizens; many lives lost by famine and disease, especially cholera, on the journey west; by 1840 few Indians left east of the chain of garrisons built from Lake Superior to the Red River.

• **1832 Bank Veto**
President Jackson vetoed bill renewing charter (due to expire in 1836) of the Bank of the United States; bank a symbol of corporate privilege, monopoly and the eastern "monied" interest; hated by southern and western debtors; Jackson reelected (1832) on bank issue and removed all U.S. funds from the bank; no substitute found for the U.S. Bank until Federal Reserve established in 1913.

THE INDUSTRIAL REVOLUTION

Increased production of iron, coal and textiles formed the focus of the Industrial Revolution. The world's first iron bridge at Coalbrookdale, Shropshire, above, was built in 1779 by Abraham Darby, whose grandfather had increased iron production by developing a blast furnace that used coke rather than charcoal. The successful construction of the bridge was a breakthrough in the use of cast iron and freed engineers from their dependence on stone, brick or timber.

The unwelcome mechanization of the textile industry took cottage craftsmen, above right, away from their homes and into the factories, where mass production of manufacturered goods became a reality. At first Great Britain was protective of its new methods and forbade the export of machinery and workers, but by 1807 Belgium had its own machine shops and became the first continental country to adapt to the changes.

The Industrial Revolution was the second great discontinuity in human history. The first, the change from nomadic, hunting-gathering to a settled, agricultural way of life, occurred first in Mesopotamia between the 8th and 7th millennia. The Industrial Revolution began in England in the latter part of the 18th century. The ancient agricultural revolution was impelled by the pressure of rising population upon food. The Industrial Revolution was impelled by the pressure of population upon fuel resources. By 1750 England had nearly exhausted its supply of forest land, hence of charcoal. Steam-power filled the want.

The textile industry was the first to be industrialized: at its center was the replacement of the handloom by the power loom. The social upheaval which the change brought produced outbreaks of violence, especially machine-breaking in the Midlands, among the distressed handloom weavers whom the new technology threw out of work. The change from cottage industry (with workers paid piecemeal for work done at home) to factory production was very gradual. By the mid-19th century the second, iron, phase of the revolution was being propelled by railroad expansion; in 1830 Great Britain was mining 75 percent of Europe's coal. Yet large mills and forges belching out smoke were still the exception in most towns, although the 1851 census disclosed that for the first time more than half the population lived in towns. The proportion of the labor force employed in agriculture was 45 percent in 1780, barely 20 percent in 1851.

The new experience of industrial urban life, with people crowded in small back-to-back houses in unsanitary conditions, working long hours for low wages in fetid factories and unsafe mines, focused attention on the evils of early capitalism. Industrialization was widely condemned. Yet those very houses, so necessary to shelter a rapidly increasing population, were built with bricks whose manufacture depended upon coal. Nor should it be forgotten that agricultural laborers lived in far more unhealthy dwellings and worked longer hours for less money than their industrial comrades.

Most historians now agree that a fall in prices after 1815, in conjunction with stable wage levels, produced a rising standard of living in the early 1800s, and that, with fluctuations, the trend continued for the rest of the century. Some individuals, of course, suffered. But without industrialization only a dramatic reversal of the population trend could have prevented even greater hardship: from 1800-50 the British population doubled from 9 to 18 million.

Against the short-term effects of industrialism are to be pitted the long-term benefits. There was a vast increase in, and cheapening of, the production of ordinary consumer goods. Technological innovation gave a spur to science and education. Urban life, by bringing large numbers of working people together proved fertile for the growth of mass movements for political and social reform. On a more mundane level, the change in dress, from heavy woollens to easily washed cottons, meant that the English went about cleaner than ever before.

The belching smoke and dirt produced during this period of intense industrial growth can be seen in "Forging the Anchor," by W.J. Muller, top. The effects on the landscape 100 years later are reflected in the urban desolation shown in this detail from a painting done in 1942 by L.S. Lowry.

1833

Great Britain Abolishes Slavery

Slavery is made illegal throughout the empire

After the ending of the slave trade in the British empire in 1807, Anglican evangelicals and dissenting radicals stepped up the campaign for emancipation, inside and outside Parliament. In the 1830 elections, which finally spelled the downfall of the Tories, many Whigs and Radicals raised the cry for the abolition of slavery itself.

Tories and West Indian planters went down to heavy defeat in 1832 in the first elections held under the terms of the Great Reform Act. The West Indies were far less important to the emerging industrial economy of 19th-century England than they had been to the old mercantilist economy. The new parliament of 1833, which contained 104 members who had pledged themselves to abolition on the hustings, passed an act to abolish slavery throughout the empire.

Radical humanitarians were disappointed that the act delayed emancipation until the slaves had served a period of "apprenticeship" in limited freedom (seven years for slaves who worked on the land, five years for the rest). They also condemned the award of £20m to slave owners in compensation for the loss of their "property." But Great Britain had become the first major power to outlaw slavery.

Feelings ran high at public meetings around Britain, where members of parliament aligned themselves with the movement that, in 1833, put an end to slavery.

1835

Boers Set Out on the Great Trek

Dutch settlers in South Africa make an historic journey to freedom

By the Treaty of Vienna of 1815, Great Britain, which had abolished the slave trade in 1807, gained control of the Cape of Good Hope in South Africa. The slave system of the Dutch Boers in the region thus brought them into conflict with the British. When slavery was abolished (1833) and an area on the colony's east frontier returned to the Bantu (1836), at a time when the Boers were hard-pressed to find sufficient farmland to maintain themselves, life under British rule became intolerable.

To escape British control, the Voortrekkers, led by Piet Retief, set out on a great trek north across the Orange River and into northern Natal. There they organized themselves, under a new leader, Andries Pretorius, into *laagers* (wagon-encircled camps) as a form of protection against attacks by the Zulus who resisted encroachment on their lands.

In 1839 the Boer republic of Natal was proclaimed. So began a long struggle with the British, who annexed the republic in 1845, forcing the Boers to make new homes in the Transvaal and the Orange Free State, which were recognized by Great Britain in 1852 and 1854.

The Voortrekkers, often facing great hardship and danger in difficult terrain, displayed the same qualities of independence and endurance as the Americans who went West.

1836

Mexicans Storm the Alamo

The heroic defense of a Texas fort gives birth to a legend

By the Adams–Onis Treaty of 1819, Spain ceded to the United States the Floridas and all lands north of the 42nd parallel, the present-day northern boundary of California, Nevada and Utah. Texas, south of the Sabine River, was not included. It remained part of the state of Coahuila in what, by 1821, was the independent republic of Mexico.

Texas was at that time sparsely inhabited, but the Mexican government encouraged American immigration and by the early 1830s some 30,000 white Americans had settled there, with slaves to work the cotton fields. Twice—in 1827 and 1830—United States' offers to buy Texas were rejected.

Aggrieved at the imposition of customs duties in 1830, especially on agricultural machinery from Louisiana, the settlers took matters into their own hands. They drew up a state constitution on the American model and demanded separate status from Coahuila. In 1835, after capturing the Mexican garrison at Anahuac, they formed a Committee of Safety and appointed Sam Houston commander of the Texas army.

Sporadic fighting began in late 1835, and in February 1836 the fort at the Alamo in San Antonio found itself under siege. On Sunday, March 6, 2,000 Mexican soldiers attacked the fort and killed all its 188 defenders, including Colonel William B. Travis, James Bowie (who gave his name to the Bowie knife) and Davy Crockett. But six weeks later, at the mouth of the San Jacinto, Texas troops fell upon a Mexican army of 1,200 with the cry, "Remember the Alamo!," slaughtered half of it and put the rest to flight. With that victory Texas became independent in fact, though not yet in name.

1836

People's Charter Drawn up in London

The Chartists issue a six-point program

The Great Reform Act, by which the urban middle class of Great Britain gained the vote, greatly disappointed radicals by its exclusion of the working class from the politics of the nation. In 1836 they gathered at a great convention in London and drew up the famous charter from which the Chartists got their name. It contained six demands: universal manhood suffrage; a secret ballot; no property qualification for members of parliament (MPs); payment for MPs; equal electoral districts by population; and annual parliamentary elections.

Anger at the harsh new Poor Law (1834) and at long working hours for textile millhands helped to swell the Chartist movement, which reached its peak in 1842, a year of deep economic depression and individual suffering. But the movement was bedeviled by a running quarrel between advocates of armed force to secure its aims and upholders of the purely legal methods of petitioning parliament and staging mass protest demonstrations. The Anti-Corn Law League, too, drew off potential support from the middle classes, essential if the Chartist voice was to make itself heard inside the House of Commons.

After 1842 the movement went into sharp decline, the end coming in the fiasco of a meeting in Kennington Common, London, in 1848, the year of revolution throughout Europe. The Great Reform Act and the repeal of the Corn Laws had, perhaps, done their work in detaching the middle classes from their "inferiors" and saving Great Britian from a revolutionary uprising.

INDUSTRIAL LEGISLATION

Industrialization raised problems of capital–labor relations that provoked government intervention. Great Britain, the first industrial nation, led the way. Factory Acts of 1833 and 1847 and the Mines Act of 1842 outlawed child labor and set maximum hours of work for adults (10 hours a day in the 1847 act for textile mills). As Europe industrialized it followed suit. Austria established a national factory inspectorate in 1883 and a national industrial code in 1907 to limit the working day to 11 hours and to enforce sanitary and safety conditions at the workplace. By 1900 France had a 10-hour day and was pioneering pensions and accident insurance. By 1914 every European country except Russia and the Balkan states had a code of labor legislation.

1845

Great Famine Devastates Ireland

A potato failure depopulates the land-hungry peasantry

In the hundred years between 1750 and 1850 Ireland's population grew faster than that of any other European country. At the same time, Ireland remained largely untouched by the early Industrial Revolution that was transforming the British economy. To meet the population crisis, Irish plots were divided and subdivided, over and over, until by the 1840s the average holding of a peasant and his family was less than five acres.

The mass of the Irish people lived on a subsistence diet: one-third of them lived on the potato alone. The poor harvest that was general in Europe in 1845 hit Ireland hard. The potato crop failed. It failed again in 1846, reducing much of the countryside to famine. Ireland continued to export grain—despite a poor harvest in 1847 and another potato failure in 1848—because the Irish themselves could not afford to buy it.

Between 1845 and 1851 the Irish population of more than 10 million fell by between 2 and 2 ½ million, of whom 800,000 died from starvation or diseases brought on by malnutrition. The rest emigrated, chiefly to the United States.

1845

United States Annexes Texas

The U.S. government provokes a war with Mexico

In 1836 the United States Congress passed resolutions recognizing the independence of Texas. They were followed by a debate over whether to annex it. The opponents of slavery, seeing in the annexationists' cause a plot to tip the national balance in favor of the slave states, blocked a proposal for annexation. But James Polk's victory in the presidential election of 1844 was, effectively, a mandate for such action. Congress approved an annexation bill and the retiring president, John Tyler, signed it in March 1845.

Mexico by then was ready to accept Texas independence; it was not prepared to see it annexed by the United States. Polk wanted more than Texas; his eye was on California. He offered Mexico a settlement of American claims against the government plus $25m for Texas to the Rio Grande, New Mexico and California. The offer was turned down and war followed.

In 1846 General Zachary Taylor ("Old Rough and Ready") defeated Antonio Santa Anna's army in the north (and thereby secured the presidency in 1848), while General Winfield Scott landed at Veracruz and drove into Mexico City with his marines. Mexico capitulated, and by the Treaty of Guadalupe Hidalgo (1848) ceded half its territory—Texas, New Mexico and upper California—to the United States for $30m in compensation.

ANESTHETICS

For centuries a surgeon's most important skill was speed, not only because the less pain there is, the less discomfort a patient feels, but because pain can cause shock, and shock can kill. The need for speed limited the type of operations that could be done, mostly amputations and the removal of external tumors. Some ancient cultures may have practiced simple anesthesia (the Incas probably used cocaine), but modern methods date from 1842, when Crawford Long, in the U.S., removed a neck tumor from a patient rendered insensible by ether. At the same time nitrous oxide (laughing gas) was introduced for dental surgery, and in 1847 Sir James Simpson used chloroform—superior to ether because it was not explosive and was effective in much smaller doses—for an obstetrical operation in Edinburgh. Within the space of a decade it was in general use throughout the world.

1846

Corn Laws Repealed in Great Britain

Defeat for the landed class splits the Conservative Party

Since the Corn Law of 1815, foreign grain entering Great Britain had been subject to a prohibitively high tariff. But the growth of industry encouraged the spread of free-trade ideas, and the argument gained ground that, in order to boost the sale of its exports, Great Britain needed to supply foreign markets with money by buying much of its food abroad.

The Irish potato famine of 1845 was the pretext on which Robert Peel, the Conservative prime minister, in 1846 decided to repeal the Corn Laws (already modified in 1828 and 1842). The ground had been prepared by the propaganda of the Anti-Corn Law League, founded in Manchester in 1838 and led by John Bright and Richard Cobden. Free trade was represented as, and in part was, a victory of the urban manufacturers over the landed gentry.

Peel's defense of his action was that he was removing an element of class conflict by making bread cheap. But for a generation and more the Conservative party, whose electoral support was rooted in the shires, had been the party of agricultural protection. It felt betrayed by its leader's espousal of the radical-liberal cause.

Peel's measure passed with the support of the Whig-Radical opposition. Two-thirds of his own party in the House of Commons, led by Lord George Bentinck and Benjamin Disraeli, voted against it and, shortly afterward, threw him out of office. The split in the party became permanent and it was another 28 years—until the elections of 1874—before the Conservatives again formed a majority in the House of Commons.

1848

"Communist Manifesto" Published

Marx and Engels sound a clarion call to the "workers of the world"

"A specter is haunting Europe—the specter of Communism." So begins the Communist Manifesto, written by the German scholars and revolutionaries Karl Marx and Friedrich Engels and published in London in February 1848. The sentence is followed quickly by another: "The history of all hitherto existing society is the history of class struggles."

Revolutionary Communism was launched on the world in the name of "scientific socialism," scientific because it analyzed the processes of history and announced them to be determined by economic forces, above all the control of the means of production. Men's purposes were fulfilled, not in the kingdom of God, but in the earthly utopia that was in the making. Just as aristocratic feudalism had been replaced by bourgeois capitalism, so it, in turn, would be overcome by a dictatorship of the proletariat and the flowering of a classless society. In that utopia men's spiritual alienation, caused by the theft of the fruits of their labor in the form of profits taken by their employers, would disappear.

That this shift was inevitable, determined by the interplay of economic factors, did not prevent Marx and Engels from exhorting men and women to be in the vanguard of the historical process and to make the inevitable happen. Hence the ringing end to the 12,000-word tract. "The proletarians have nothing to lose but their chains. They have a world to win. WORKING MEN OF ALL COUNTRIES, UNITE!"

Gustave Doré's engraving, "Over London by Rail," made in 1870, shows that the living conditions of working-class people had changed little since the "Communist Manifesto" was written.

1848

Year of Revolution Shakes Europe

Liberalism goes down to defeat in uprisings throughout Europe

"When Paris sneezes,"Metternich said, "Europe catches cold." In February 1848, Paris sneezed. A revolution forced Louis-Philippe from the throne and raised the poet Alphonse de Lamartine to the head of a provisional republican government. The contagion spread to the capitals of Europe, failing only to infect Moscow and London (where the Chartists staged an easily dispersed demonstration in April).

Metternich himself, chief minister of the Austrian empire, resigned, and a liberal assembly took charge in Frankfurt. Liberalism—constitutional, parliamentary rule by the middle classes—and nationalism were the watchwords of revolution: liberalism in France and Spain, predominantly national liberation in Habsburg Hungary and Italy. Monarchical Europe seemed to be in collapse. By 1849 it was everywhere restored.

In France Lamartine lost the presidency to Louis Napoleon, who in 1851 declared himself Emperor Napoleon III. Yet the restoration was not complete. Monarchical authority was weakened. Louis Napoleon's plebiscites in the years that followed paid lip service to notions of popular will. Frederick William IV of Prussia retained a partially elected Diet, in which by 1859 the liberals commanded a majority. In Austria Franz Joseph abstained from reimposing feudal ties on an emancipated peasantry.

The idea of national liberation had been given an impetus. And in the short-lived days of apparent revolutionary triumph, the gospel of socialism was loudly sounded for the first time.

Habsburg empire 1848

1849

Prospectors Pan for California Gold

A spur is given to the opening up of the American West

A few months after the United States purchased California from Mexico, gold was discovered, in December 1848, at Sutter's Mill, 30 miles from Sacramento. The next spring thousands of fortune-seekers, "Forty-Niners" as they came to be called, set out in covered wagons for the far west. Most of them traveled for much of the 2,000-mile journey along the established, pioneer Oregon Trail that ran from Missouri through the Midwestern plains and the Nevada Desert, then across the Sierra Nevada Mountains, to the trading-post at San Francisco.

Cholera and starvation claimed many lives; Indian attacks others. Yet the news that fortunes could be made, simply by separating grains of gold from the sand of river beds in a tin plate, attracted prospectors from all over the world. Before the end of the year 80,000 people had made it to the Pacific coast, some of them by routes via Cape Horn and Panama.

Early in the 1850s the westward migration became more dispersed, when gold was also discovered in Colorado and silver in Nevada. By the end of the decade, the "wild frontier" days of shanty towns and vigilantes had passed, as ordered government followed California's admission to the Union as a state and mining engineers moved in with expensive machinery.

1850

Compromise of 1850 Agreed

The United States strives to preserve the Union

Westward migration in the gold rush brought the question of slavery in the United States to a head. In September 1849, a convention in California drafted a state constitution that prohibited slavery, elected a governor and applied for admission to the Union. The southern slave states faced a crisis. In 1789 the populations of the north and south had been about equal; by 1850 the north had an advantage of nearly a million. The slave economy needed either to expand, or to be protected by the secession of the southern states from the Union.

California's climate made it a natural home for slavery to flourish, but northern abolitionists spoke out against introducing the evil into a new territory. President Zachary Taylor favored the admission of California as a free state and the organization of Utah and New Mexico as territories without reference to slavery. He promised armed intervention to save the Union if the south seceded.

But the federal government was not yet prepared for war; nor the slave states, as shown by the collapse of a hastily called Southern Convention, for separation. Senator Henry Clay's mediatory proposal that California be admitted as a free state and Utah and New Mexico be left to decide the issue for themselves, combined with a stringent law to enforce the recovery of fugitive slaves, won the day.

The Compromise of 1850 lasted for 10 years, but it was evident that the north and the south were incapable of agreement on the fundamental principles of nationhood versus states' rights.

1850

Tai P'ing Rebellion Breaks Out

An uprising against the Manchus wreaks devastation on China

For 14 years, from 1850 to 1864, the Manchu dynasty of China was threatened by a widespread rebellion led by Hung Hsiu-ch'uan, a visionary who announced himself as the younger brother of Christ. In 1850 the military-religious group around him controlled Kwangsi in the south, and he proclaimed himself emperor of the Tai P'ing T'ien-kuo ("Heavenly Kingdom of the Great Peace").

The movement drew a wide spectrum of malcontents, especially peasants offered land and low taxes and women offered equality. By 1853 Tai P'ing troops had reached Tientsin, only to be turned back by imperial armies before reaching Peking (Beijing). For three years the Yangtze valley was the theater of fighting, but by 1856 the Tai P'ing advance was beginning to ebb.

European powers were at first attracted by the mix of Westernism and "Christianity" in the movement, but soon became alarmed at Tai P'ing vehemence against the "unequal treaties" for trade with the West (especially the arrangement by which Chinese vessels could carry foreign flags and thus traffic in opium with impunity). A Tai P'ing victory threatened to end European access to China.

In 1860 British and French troops—the Ever-Victorious Army led by General Charles "Chinese" Gordon—fought the Tai P'ing rebels at Shanghai. Two years later the imperial army used Western rifles and cannon for the first time. Superior firepower carried the day. The last Tai P'ing soldiers were annihilated at Nanking, Hung Hsiu-ch'uan's capital, in 1864. By then more than 10 million people had lost their lives.

The Tai P'ing rulers tried to stamp out gambling, footbinding, slavery and opium smoking, but the drug trade still thrived, as this picture of dealers weighing and testing opium makes clear.

1853

Turkey Defies Russia and Begins the Crimean War

The "Eastern Question" brings an end to an era of peace in Europe

In May 1853, in the wake of alleged persecution of Christians in the Ottoman empire, Prince Menshikoff, the Russian ambassador to Turkey, handed the Turkish government an ultimatum demanding that Christian subjects of the Sultan be confirmed in their ancient rights and immunities or Russia would act to protect them. A draft convention was prepared. When, two months later, Turkey had failed to comply, Russia invaded the Ottoman provinces of Wallachia and Moldavia.

Great Britain, fearful of Russian expansionism toward Afghanistan and India, dispatched her Mediterranean fleet to the Dardanelles in support of Turkey. Negotiations continued throughout the summer, but ended with Turkey's rejection of Russia's Olmütz proposals. These assured Turkey that Russia's sole interest in the region was the rights of Christians, while asking that the Straits Convention of 1841 closing the Dardanelles to foreign ships in peacetime be upheld.

In October Turkey declared war on Russia. Great Britain and France entered the fray in March 1854, after the Russians destroyed a Turkish squadron at Sinope. The war, highlighted by the battles of Balaklava (1854) and Inkerman (1854), ended in 1855 with the capture of Sevastopol by the British and the French.

By the Treaty of Paris (1856), Russia accepted the neutralization of the Black Sea, Turkey agreed to protect Christians' rights and to respect the semi-autonomous status of Wallachia and Moldavia, and the powers undertook to guarantee Turkey's integrity. The war cost France and Russia more than 100,000 lives, Turkey about 30,000 and Great Britain about 23,000.

1854

Commodore Perry Forces "Open Door" on Japan

Gunboat diplomacy brings Japan into trading contact with the West

For two centuries Japan had been closed to all foreign intercourse except for a small trade carried on with the Dutch and Chinese at Nagasaki. In an attempt to pry the old empire open, Commodore Matthew Perry, commander of the East India squadron of the U.S. Navy, anchored an armed squadron, including the steam frigates *Mississippi* and *Susquehanna*, in Tokyo Bay on July 8, 1853.

Perry was ordered to remove the squadron to Nagasaki, but refused, and by this display of independence succeeded in gaining permission to deliver a letter from President Millard Fillmore to the emperor. The letter contained a number of demands, chiefly that shipwrecked sailors be given protection by Japan, that ships be allowed to buy coal in Japanese ports, and that one or more ports be opened to trade with the United States.

Perry then withdrew his squadron to Macao to await a reply.

In February 1854, he returned with a larger fleet, and the shaky Tokugawa shogunate, alarmed by the implied threat of attack, succumbed. By the Treaty of Kanagawa, signed in March 1854, the United States gained trading rights at Shamoda and Hakodate. The treaty opened the way for other Western powers to establish Japanese contacts and marked the beginning of an active role for the United States in the Pacific.

By calling himself an admiral, and arriving with an impressive fleet of ships, Commodore Perry made the first Western entry into Japan for 200 years. Perry's resolute approach to the isolationist policy of Japan resulted, among other things, in permission for a U.S. consul to reside at Shimoda.

1856

Henry Bessemer Invents his Steel Converter

The Industrial Revolution takes a leap forward

At the 1856 meeting of the British Association in Cheltenham, England, Henry Bessemer, the son of a French Huguenot refugee, read a report announcing his latest invention. This was a cylindrical vessel in which pig iron could be converted into what he called "steel."

The "Bessemer process" worked by sending a powerful stream of molten metal from a blast furnace through the mouth of the tilted converter and then, with the cylinder in an upright position, blowing air into it through holes in the bottom. As the air was forced upward through the molten metal, impurities such as carbon and silica combined with oxygen in the air to form oxides. Carbon monoxide burned off, while other impurities formed slag. An iron-manganese-carbon alloy was then added to the metal to give it the requisite properties of steel.

The process was patented in 1856 and went into commercial production. It acted as a spur to the rapid expansion of the steel industry in Europe and the United States.

Bessemer was spurred to develop his process for making steel because cast-iron cannon balls were too weak for a cannon he had invented.

1857

U.S. Supreme Court Finds Against Dred Scott

The decision in favor of slavery widens the north-south divide

In 1834 Dred Scott, a slave in the service of the army surgeon Dr. John Emerson, was taken by his owner from the slave state of Missouri to Illinois, a free state, and then to Fort Snelling in Wisconsin Territory, where slavery was banned by the Missouri Compromise. He married there and four years later was taken back to Missouri by Emerson.

In 1846 Scott sued Emerson's widow for freedom for himself and his family—by then he had two children—and a St. Louis court found in his favor. That decision was quashed by the Missouri Supreme Court, whose verdict was upheld on March 6, 1857, by the federal Supreme Court.

The Supreme Court ruled against Scott on three grounds. First, that a black man, having no standing as a citizen, had no right to sue in a federal court; second, that Scott, as a resident of Missouri, could not have his status affected by the laws of Illinois. Third, that even as a resident north of latitude 36° 30′ he could not be freed, since Congress had no authority to deprive any man, including a slave owner, of his property without "due process of law."

The third ground effectively declared the Missouri Compromise to be unconstitutional. The decision inflamed abolitionist sentiment in the north and brought civil war a step nearer.

1850–1859

UNITED STATES

● **1850 Fugitive Slave Act**
Required every citizen to aid federal officials in returning escaped slaves to owners; arrested slave not given right to testify; owner's statement taken as proof; opposed and defied by abolitionists.

● **1854 Kansas-Nebraska Act**
Act to establish territories of Kansas and Nebraska; slave owners wanted no free territory west of the Missouri; act appeased them by making the issue rest with the territories themselves; effectively repealed the Missouri Compromise by which both would have been free territories; ensuing struggle between the two sides led to "Bleeding Kansas."

● **1854 Republican Party**
Founded in opposition to Kansas-Nebraska Act and slavery; gained members from both Whig and Democratic party splits; John Fremont lost 1856 election to Democrat, James Buchanan.

● **1858 Lincoln-Douglas Debates**
Seven debates between candidates for Illinois Senate, Republican Abraham Lincoln and Democrat incumbent, Stephen Douglas, framer of original Kansas-Nebraska Act; Lincoln stoutly defended the Union, equivocated on slavery; lost election, but gained national fame and 1860 presidential nomination.

● **1859 John Brown**
Hanged for leading 13 whites and five blacks in assault on federal armory at Harpers Ferry, Virginia; had vague aim of founding abolitionist republic in the Appalachians.

1857

Indian Mutiny Breaks Out in Bengal

Indians in the East India Company's army ignite the "Sepoy Rebellion"

Smoldering resentment against British expansion in India at the expense of native princes, and deep suspicion among both Hindus and Muslims of the Christianizing motives of the British were brought to the surface in 1856. During the British annexation of Oudh, Bengali soldiers were issued with cartridges coated in grease made from cattle and pig fat. At one stroke, both Hindus, to whom the cow was sacred, and Muslims, to whom the pig was anathema, were offended.

Although the British quickly withdrew the cartridges, Bengali soldiers, or sepoys, mutinied at Meerut in February 1857 and proclaimed Bahadur Shah II as the emperor of all India. Rebellion spread throughout the north of the country: Delhi was taken, Cawnpore also, and Lucknow was laid under siege.

The loyalty of the Sikh province of Punjab helped Great Britain put down the rebellion, which ended with the recapture of Lucknow in March 1858.

Massacres and atrocities on both sides left permanent ill-feeling, even though the mutiny resulted in some reforms. The East India Company was wound up, and British rule in India passed directly to the imperial government, which decreed that the expropriation of land would cease, tolerance of all religious faiths would be enforced, and Indians would be given jobs in the lower reaches of the imperial administration. At the same time, the ratio of imperial to native troops in the army was increased, and native soldiers were excluded from artillery divisions.

One positive outcome of the Indian Mutiny, after 14 months of bitter fighting, was that the civil service was opened up to qualified Indians and a program of public works was undertaken, notably the construction of a wide railroad network.

1859

Darwin Publishes "Origin of Species"

Evolution by "random mutation" and "natural selection" is explained

In 1857 Alfred Russel Wallace sent a paper to Charles Darwin in which he outlined a concept of evolution based on natural selection. Darwin, a cautious experimental biologist, had, ever since he read Charles Lyell's exposition of evolution in rocks, *Principles of Geology* (1832), been formulating the same ideas.

Wallace's paper forced Darwin to take the bold step (for Victorian society was not eager to learn that human beings were descended from the apes) of making his theory known to the world. With Wallace he wrote a joint paper for the Royal Society in 1858.

It provided convincing evidence against the old "cataclysmic theory" that every species of plant and animal life sprang independently into existence after geological upheavals. In its place the two men proposed that random mutations, occurring without design, proved to be permanent or ephemeral according to whether they assisted a species to survive in its environment. Darwin at once set about writing a more detailed paper for the Linnaean Society, which grew into the book published in 1859 as *On the Origin of Species by Means of Natural Selection, or the Preservation of Favoured Races in the Struggle for Life.*

The Church denounced evolution as contrary to the revealed truth of Genesis, but Darwin's ideas gradually took hold, and his masterpiece came to be recognized as the greatest scientific synthesis of the age and the most important book of the century.

1861

The Confederacy Attacks Fort Sumter

Lincoln's relief expedition provokes the Civil War

The election of the Republican candidate, Abraham Lincoln, as president of the United States in 1860 placed the institution of slavery under mortal threat and produced the expected consequence: the secession of the southern slave states from the Union. The lead was taken in South Carolina, followed by Mississippi, Alabama, Florida, Georgia, Louisiana and Texas.They formed the Confederate States of America on February 8, 1861, and elected Jefferson Davis as their provisional president.

Lincoln was inaugurated as the president on March 4, by which time all but two of the forts and naval yards in the secessionist states had fallen without resistance into Confederate hands. One of the two was Fort Sumter in South Carolina. Attempts to prevent war by negotiation came to nothing, and at the end of March Lincoln ordered the preparation of a relief expedition to Fort Sumter, whose supplies were running out.

At 4.30 a.m. on April 12, in order to prevent Union reinforcements from reaching the fort, Confederate General Pierre Beauregard gave the command to open fire on it. On April 14 Major Anderson surrendered. The next day Lincoln called for 75,000 army volunteers to preserve the nation.

Virginia joined the Confederacy at once, followed in the next five weeks by Arkansas, Tennessee and North Carolina. The Confederacy reached its full size of 11 states. By July it had 112,000 soldiers in its ranks, compared to the Union's 187,000, and on July 21, in the first major battle of the war, the Confederate army routed the Union forces at Bull Run in northern Virginia.

1861

Victor Emmanuel Becomes King of United Italy

The Risorgimento celebrates independence from Austria

The post-Napoleonic settlement of 1815 left Italy divided into numerous small states and Austria in possession of Lombardy, Piedmont and Venetia. The war of independence against Austria, the Risorgimento, led by Count Camillo Cavour, the radical politician Giuseppe Mazzini, and Giuseppe Garibaldi, an able soldier, began in the spring of 1859.

In June the combined forces of Piedmont and France met the Austrians in battle at Modena and Solferino and drove them out of Lombardy. Napoleon III, anxious lest Prussia come to Austria's aid, then made an about-face and signed the Treaty of Villafranca with Austria, by which Austria yielded Lombardy. In August constituent assemblies met at several Italian cities and formed a military alliance to win a united Italy, under Victor Emmanuel II of Sardinia.

A series of military successes in 1860 enabled Cavour to add all the remaining central states except Rome to Piedmont, while Garibaldi conquered Naples and Sicily. In 1861 the first parliament of united Italy met in Turin and acclaimed Victor Emmanuel as king.

1861

Tsar Alexander II Abolishes Serfdom

The emancipation decree initiates a social and economic revolution

As part of the program of liberalization which he had pursued since becoming tsar in 1855, on March 17 (April 5, new style), 1861, Alexander II issued a decree abolishing serfdom. Of the Russian population of 52 million, about 43 million were serfs, outside civil society and, by law, in no real relation to the tsar.

These serfs were not simply agricultural workers, for their owners had put numbers of them to work in mines and factories. By the decree they gained legal, but not economic, freedom. They still had to pay redemption money, collected as taxes, for the abandoned feudal dues and services; and they held land only as shares in the collective property of a village, known as a *mir*. The emancipated peasant was not allowed to migrate to a town or to take up an industrial trade without the *mir's* permission.

By-products of the reform were the institution of new courts (with public trials and juries) to replace the old landlords' courts, and the establishment of *zemstvos*, local elected councils.

Garibaldi was an extraordinary man; an adventurer, a rebel and a tireless fighter for the unification of an Italy that alternately rejected and embraced him. President Lincoln offered him a command in the American Civil War after the spectacular success of his battle on the Volturno River north of Naples in 1860. He refused because he was not given supreme command, but also because Lincoln would not make a complete condemnation of slavery.

THE CIVIL WAR

General Robert E. Lee was offered command of the Union forces but, out of loyalty, he returned to his home state, Virginia, to lead the South.

The inauguration of Abraham Lincoln as Republican president in 1860 was seen by the South as a clear indication of the parting of the ways.

The Civil War, which lasted from April 1861 to April 1865, was fought, Abraham Lincoln said, to preserve the Union. Once the southern states seceded from the Union, that did, indeed, become the issue. Lincoln's position was, indirectly, a denial of the high principle laid down in the Declaration of Independence that governments derived "their just powers from the consent of the governed." The North fought the war to deny the states of the South the right to secede. Southern secession marked the last resort of those states which had upheld the doctrine of states' rights against the power of the central government, and the North's victory was effectively to settle that quarrel in Washington's favor.

Behind that narrow purpose lay the larger issue of the South's "special institution": slavery. Outnumbered by the population of the free states, and therefore seeing little prospect of gaining the presidency and the reins of power, the South was driven to secession. Its agrarian way of life lay under threat from the expanding industrial, capitalist economy of the north. Its traditional, somewhat static, paternalist values found themselves in conflict—political, economic and moral— with a progressive, dynamic, individualist ethos.

In an address to Congress shortly after the war began, Lincoln, in the chaste rhetoric which marked his style, described the war as "a struggle for maintaining in the world that form and substance of government whose leading object is to elevate the condition of men—to lift artificial weights from all shoulders, to clear the paths of laudable pursuit for all, to afford all an unfettered start, and a fair chance in the race of life."

Gettysburg, in rural Pennsylvania, was the scene of the bloodiest battle ever fought on American soil. From July 1-3, 1863, General Lee's Army of Northern Virginia pressed in from the west and north against Major General George Meade's Army of the Potomac. The contemporary painting shows soldiers charging through the Peach Orchard and the Wheatfield, names that have become synonymous with violent death to generations of Americans. In the end, Meade's superior skill in moving his troops rapidly from one danger point to another frustrated Confederate attacks and guaranteed a Union victory.

Photography was in its infancy during the Civil War, but some telling images came out of it. By the time of Gettysburg, official Confederate uniforms had almost vanished, and this rough-and-ready group of soldiers wears a combination of uniform and clothes made from homespun cloth dyed gray or blue.

The long war, which was to bequeath bitterness and division to the United States for generations afterward, was won by the north at a heavy cost: 360,000 Union casualties, 260,000 on the side of the southern Confederacy, more of them from malnutrition and disease than on the battlefield. The losses were greater than those suffered by the United States in either of the world wars of the 20th century. Militarily, the war was notable for providing, at the Battle of Spottsylvania, May 8-12, 1864, the first example of modern trench warfare. From that date to the end of the war, trench warfare was fought in Virginia.

The war began with the advantages all lying with the North. It had, in addition to the organized central government, as opposed to the fledgling Confederate government under Jefferson Davis, deeper economic reserves than the South. It had also, by virtue of the navy, command of the sea. Above all, it represented a population of 19-20 million freemen, against the 5-6 million whites and 3½ million black slaves of the South. The Union's armies outnumbered those of the South by about 3 to 1. Yet under the brilliant command of Robert E. Lee and Thomas "Stonewall" Jackson, the South held its own until the North's victory at Vicksburg and Gettysburg in July 1863.

In 1864 the superior strength of the Union armies began to tell. The "wilderness campaign" of May and June, led by Ulysses Grant, pushed the Confederacy's Virginia army back upon Richmond; General Sherman's summer-long Atlanta campaign, ending in the fall of Atlanta and the devastating "march to the sea" through Georgia, effectively settled the issue of the war, although the South refused to surrender until the Union's capture of Richmond in April 1865.

1862

Pasteur Announces the "Germ Theory" of Infection

A French chemist lays the foundations of bacteriology

After many years' experimentation with fermentation in wine and beer, in 1862, Louis Pasteur, a French chemist and microbiologist, was able to disprove conclusively the theory of the spontaneous germination of microorganisms. At the same time, he proved that every "germ" must arise from other "germs." The discovery led to a new era in the treatment and prevention of infections (thus marking the takeoff point in the world's population expansion). It was also helpful in combating phylloxera in French vineyards in the 1860s.

Together with Robert Koch's discovery in Germany, in 1882, of the tubercle bacillus, Pasteur's breakthrough gave rise to the branch of pathology known as bacteriology. The early fruit of this new science was the process of pasteurization—ridding milk of harmful bacteria by heating it to 145° F (63° C) for 30 minutes and then rapidly cooling it.

In 1868 Pasteur isolated the bacteria causing a disease in silkworms which saved the threatened French silk industry from extinction.

1863

Emancipation Proclaimed by President Lincoln

The ending of slavery raises the Civil War to a moral crusade

At the outset of the Civil War Abraham Lincoln vowed that his sole object in making war on the south was to preserve the Union. It could not be so. Merely to return to the state of affairs that had produced war was to achieve nothing. Above all, the slavery issue needed to be resolved.

In 1862 Congress passed a Confiscation Act, stating that all slaves of Union supporters in rebel states should be forever free. The President's Emancipation Proclamation of January 1, 1863, restated that position as a matter of military strategy. Slaves in border states loyal to the Union were excluded from the proclamation.

Thus, no slaves were actually freed, since the federal government was powerless to enforce the terms of the proclamation in the secessionist states. Even so, the statement had profound significance. It gave the war a defined aim beyond the preservation of the Union, and it probably made emancipation inevitable. Lincoln's role had been subtly changed from conservator to liberator.

1864

First International Founded

Karl Marx presides over the inaugural meeting in London

The growth of socialist ideas in the first half of the 19th century led to the foundation of the First International Workingmen's Association at a meeting in London in 1864. The meeting was called by the London Working Men's Association and attended by delegates from all over Europe. The opening address was given by Karl Marx, who became its first president.

The purpose of the International was mainly to unite the activities of working-class radicals across national barriers in the fight against monopoly capitalism. Annual congresses were held until 1872, the year after Eugène Pottier wrote the *Internationale*, the anthem of the movement.

> *Arise, ye prisoners of starvation!*
> *Arise, ye wretched of the earth...*
> *'Tis the final conflict,*
> *Let each stand in his place,*
> *The International Party,*
> *Shall be the human race.*

Almost from the outset the proceedings of the First International were torn by the quarrel between the advocates of revolutionary action, led by Bakunin and the anarchists, and the advocates of parliamentary action, with whom Marx uneasily allied himself. The First International, hopelessly split on the issue, expelled Bakunin and then dissolved in 1876. It had achieved nothing. Nor did its successor, the Second International (formed in Paris in 1889), which disintegrated in the failure to achieve international working-class opposition to war in 1914.

1865

Confederacy Surrenders at Appomattox

Robert E. Lee's surrender brings the Civil War to a close

By February 1865, the Confederacy was facing defeat in the Civil War. It had failed to gain foreign recognition; Lincoln had been reelected president; economic blockade was creating hardship; and the superior weight of the Union armies under Ulysses S. Grant and William Sherman was proving irresistible. So desperate was the south that it was offering the abolition of slavery to foreign powers in exchange for recognition, and Virginia was arming slaves.

The end came early in April, after nine months of trench warfare on the outskirts of Petersburg, Virginia. On April 1 Sheridan's Union army won a victory at Five Forks, forcing Robert E. Lee to abandon Petersburg. Two days later Grant's army entered Richmond, and within a week Philip Sheridan's forces had blocked a Confederate retreat to the south or west. On April 9 Lee raised the white flag and, in the little village courthouse of Appomattox, he surrendered to Grant.

Two day later, in his last public speech, Lincoln called for a speedy peace. He offered to readmit every secessionist state as soon as 10 percent of its white inhabitants who had voted in the presidential election of 1860 swore the oath of allegiance and established a state government.

1865

German Social Democratic Labor Party Founded

The world's first avowedly socialist party is born in Gotha

The German Social Democratic Labor Party, founded in southern Germany by Wilhelm Liebknecht and August Bebel in 1865, adopted a revolutionary Marxist program at Eisenach in 1869. It was the world's first avowedly socialist political party.

The establishment of a united German empire in 1871, with a national legislature, or Reichstag, elected on a wide franchise, led in 1875 to the party's merging with Ferdinand Lassalle's northern German Workingmen's Association (founded in 1863). Together they formed the Socialist Labor Party, later called the Social Democratic Party. In that new party Lassalle's argument that proletarian interests and parliamentary methods were compatible came to the fore.

The "Gotha program" of 1875 upheld Marx's ideas of the class struggle and the materialist interpretation of history, but abandoned revolutionary means of capturing the state in favor of the ballot. The party's progress was thwarted by Otto von Bismarck's antisocialist laws until 1890, when Bismarck was dismissed from the chancellorship. It then rose rapidly to become the largest socialist party in Europe. It won 112 seats in the elections of 1912, making it the largest party in the Reichstag.

The German example was followed throughout Europe. The Belgian Workers' party was formed in 1885; a Czech party in 1887; Austrian and Swiss social democratic parties in 1888; the Independent Labour party of Great Britain in 1893; and the predominantly Marxist Socialist party of France in 1905.

Clockwise from the bottom left are Liebknecht, Bebel, Lassalle and James Keir Hardie, the dedicated socialist and British labor leader who took up the flag for the workers.

1866

Gregor Mendel Discovers Genetics

Experiments with peas give birth to a new science

The Austrian, Gregor Mendel, entered an Augustine monastery in Brno in 1843 and taught at a local school there until 1868. In those years he spent most of his spare time conducting experiments in cross-breeding garden peas and other plants.

The flowers of the pea contain both male and female gametes, or reproductive cells, and are self-fertilizing. Mendel knew little about the structure or behavior of cells when he began to pollinate the flowers of one plant artificially with pollen from those of another, in order to study the inheritance of their contrasting characteristics, tallness and shortness. After many years, however, Mendel was able to show that an inherited characteristic is the result of the combination of two hereditary units—now called genes, a word not used by Mendel—and that a gene could be either, in the terms he invented, dominant or recessive.

If a plant inherited a dominant *T* (tallness) from both parent cells, it would be "pure tall"; if it inherited a recessive *t* from both, it would be "pure short"; if it had *T* from one and *t* from the other, it would be "mixed tall": tall itself because the *T* was dominant, but able to pass on either tallness or shortness to its descendants. There could never be a "mixed short" because the *t* was always recessive.

Published in 1866, Mendel's results were ignored for a generation or more, until they were rediscovered at the turn of the century, when their importance in laying the foundation of genetics was recognized.

1867

Dual Austro-Hungarian Monarchy Established

A compromise shores up the Habsburg and Magyar empires

In the latter part of the 19th century both German-dominated Austria and Magyar-ruled Hungary faced nationalist discontent from Slavic minorities—Czechs, Poles, Serbs, Croats, Slovaks and Romanians—within their boundaries. Hungary, where the ruling Magyars formed only one-third of the population, was especially endangered.

In common defense against the threatened breakdown of their authority, the two states joined together in the *Ausgleich,* or compromise, of 1867 which created the Dual Monarchy of Austria-Hungary. Emperor Franz Joseph became monarch of the two states, which agreed to have a common foreign and military policy and a common ministry of defense. In other matters each retained its independence, with its own legislature and prime minister.

This compromise, which effectively produced a third government in the region—the Dual Monarchy—was intended to raise a barrier against the tide of national unification and independence, which was flowing strongly in Germany and Italy, and to maintain German and Magyar dominance over the region. It was an old-fashioned piece of statecraft that merely postponed the resolution of national questions in eastern Europe. But it was succesful in doing so. The Dual Monarchy lasted until 1918, when the Habsburg and Hungarian empires collapsed in ruin.

NATIONAL EDUCATION

By 1870 France and Prussia had unified systems of public education, from primary schools to technical colleges and universities. The 1870s and '80s were decades of great expansion for compulsory free education. Prussia nationalized its system in 1872 and made education free in 1888; by 1900 its budget had multiplied 30 times in 30 years. In the 1870s Italy, the Netherlands, Switzerland, Belgium and Great Britain made attendance at primary school compulsory. Compulsory free secondary education was introduced in Great Britain after 1918. The United States has never had a national system of public education (although education is free and mandatory), but by 1900 $15\frac{1}{2}$ million children were enrolled in public schools compared to $1\frac{1}{2}$ million in Great Britain.

1867

Great Britain Introduces Manhood Suffrage

The second Reform Act ushers in the age of mass politics

In 1866 the Liberal government of Great Britain introduced a bill to lower the property qualification for the vote. William Gladstone's bill was a cautious measure, aimed at enfranchising a section of the urban working class without giving that class a preponderance in the electorate. It was defeated by an alliance of right-wing Liberals, the "Adullamites" led by Robert Lowe, and the Conservative opposition.

Defeat drove the Liberals from office. The new Conservative government, led by the Earl of Derby, introduced an even more cautious bill, so hedged with special franchises and conditions as to nullify its superficial radicalism—a simple rated household suffrage as the basis for the vote.

But in the House of Commons, the Conservatives were in a minority, and Benjamin Disraeli, who piloted the bill through the House, was so eager to upset the Liberals that he accepted amendment after amendment by the opposition rather than be defeated. Two critical amendments eliminated the requirements that an elector pay his rates personally (most compounded with their landlords to pay them) and that he prove he had been resident at the same address for two years.

The resulting act of 1867 thus provided the country with nearly universal manhood suffrage. Women were still excluded, and agricultural workers had to wait for the vote until 1884. But in the 1868 elections the working class formed a majority of the electorate for the first time, and the major parties began to adapt their machinery to fit the age of mass politics.

1868

Meiji Restoration Ends Shogun Power in Japan

Japan enters an age of industrial progress and Westernization

In November 1867, Keiki, the young shogun at the head of Japan's ruling *bakufu*, abdicated, handing over the administration to the emperor, Meiji. Early in the new year the restoration of full power to the emperor was proclaimed. Three weeks later the revolution was sealed by victory over an army of the ex-shogun at Toba-Fushimi. So ended 250 years of the Tokugawa shogunate.

Keiki had acted on a counselor's advice that an imperial restoration was required to enable Japan to "take her stand as the equal of other countries." The shogunate had paid, above all, for the resentment at the increasing presence of Western merchants in Japan after Perry's epoch-making mission of 1854. The cry had gone up, "Revere the emperor; expel the Barbarians."

In the eyes of the traditional samurai class, the shogunate was thus fatally weakened by its failure to expel the intruders when, in 1866, it faced a military challenge from the pro-imperial Choshu clan of western Honshu (the main Japanese island). The collapse of its foundations was revealed at the battle of Toba-Fushimi, when numbers of Tokugawa warriors defected to the enemy.

Yet the imperial victory did not mark a return to isolationism. The emperor undertook, in the Charter Oath of April 1868, to seek knowledge from all over the world. In the 1870s the wearing of swords and the topknot was abolished, and Japan set out on a course of industrialization and modernization adapted from the European model.

The women's Western dress at this reception reflects the social change in Japan during the Meiji period.

1869

Pius IX Holds First Vatican Council

The doctrine of papal infallibility is promulgated

As the movements for national unification in Germany and Italy gathered pace, the papacy was placed on the defensive. The loss of its territory and temporal power in Italy (the papacy did not recognize the new Italian state created in 1861 until the Lateran Treaty of 1929) was a great blow. The dominance of Protestant Prussia over the Roman Catholic south in the emerging German confederation was another.

In 1864 Pope Pius IX issued a *Syllabus of Errors*, in which the evils of contemporary Europe—liberalism, secular rationalism, scientific advance—were denounced. Five years later, in 1869, he summoned an ecumenical council to the Vatican. It proclaimed the doctrine of papal infallibility, making it heretical to oppose papal pronouncements on any matter of faith or morals. By that unqualified statement, calling for Roman Catholics' loyalty to the papacy above loyalty to the nation-state, the ground was laid for the *Kulturkampf* ("war of culture") waged by Bismarck against the Roman Church in the 1870s and 80s.

The Jesuits were expelled from Germany and the anti-Catholic Falk Laws of 1873 were passed, compelling, for example, the instruction of the clergy under state supervision and making the civil ceremony of marriage compulsory. They remained in force until 1887, when the conflict was resolved.

1869

Suez Canal Opened

Linking the Mediterranean to the Red Sea opens a passage to India

In 1854 Mehemet Said, the khedive, or governor, of Egypt under the sultan, granted a concession to the French engineer Ferdinand de Lesseps to build a canal to link the Mediterranean to the Gulf of Suez. Lesseps persuaded a group of international (chiefly French) financiers to form a canal company in 1858. Under his supervision construction began in 1859. The canal, which runs for slightly more than 100 miles from Port Said to Port Taufig, was officially opened in 1869. The Middle East once again became a focus for trade and a source of European rivalries.

Great Britain had originally opposed the project as a French device to gain control of trade in the Levant. But in 1875, eager for a voice in the operation of the canal, which was of vital interest as a link to India, the "jewel in the crown" of the British empire, Disraeli bought 40 percent of the khedive's shares in the canal company. Great Britain thus became the single largest shareholder.

By an international convention of 1888, all shipping was given free use of the canal in both wartime and time of peace. The convention was breached during the Spanish–American war of 1898, when Spanish ships were barred, and during both World Wars, when the canal was closed to Axis shipping. The canal, which was nationalized by Egypt in 1956, was again closed, by scuttled ships, during the Arab–Israeli war of 1967. It was enlarged and reopened to shipping in 1975.

Mechanical shovels removed over 100 million cubic feet of soil before the canal could be built. Its completion cut the time taken for voyages between Great Britain and India in half.

1870

Prussian Army Overwhelms France

Bismarck seals Prussia's rise to dominance

Otto von Bismarck, the master of *realpolitik*, told the Prussian House of Delegates in 1862 that the great questions of the day would be settled, not by parliaments, but by "iron and blood." His military victories over Austria in 1866 and France in 1870 demonstrated the point. Bismarck had two great objects: to unify Germany under Prussian leadership and to raise Germany above France as the dominant power in Europe.

Prussia had overrun the Danish province of Schleswig-Holstein in 1864 and, two years later, Bismarck used a dispute between Prussia and Austria over their administration as a pretext for war against Austria. In just six weeks of fighting, marked by an outstanding victory at Sadowa, he subdued Austria.

War against France was provoked by the offer of the Spanish throne to Prince Leopold of the Prussian house of Hohenzollern. It was rejected. But Bismarck edited a telegram, reporting talks between Wilhelm I of Prussia and the French ambassador at Bad Ems (in which the French sought assurance that the offer would not be renewed) in a way that was sure to inflame French opinion and then published it. The trick worked. France declared war in July 1870.

Bismarck's immediate gain was that the southern German states, believing France to be the aggressor, joined the North German Confederation (1870). In 1871 Bismarck became chancellor and Wilhelm I emperor of the new German Reich. The other gain was the humiliation of France, overwhelmed at Sedan in September and forced, in the Treaty of Frankfurt (1871), to cede Alsace and most of Lorraine to Germany.

1871

Paris Commune Has Its Hour in the Sun

A revolutionary council takes control of the French capital

Defeat at Prussian hands after a four-month siege of Paris brought Parisians onto the streets in March 1871, in scenes reminiscent of the revolutionary days of 1848. The rioters' object was to prevent the newly elected national assembly at Versailles, and the provisional government headed by Adolphe Thiers, from making peace with Germany. They hoped also to prevent the establishment of a conservative republic to replace the vanished empire of Napoleon III, who had been declared deposed after his capture at Sedan in September 1870.

Led by the socialist, Auguste Blanqui, the revolutionaries, chanting the slogan, "the Commune," and helped by Thiers' withdrawal of all troops from the capital, seized control of the city. A central committee, calling itself the "Commune," was formed on March 18. What its program was no one knew. Marx hailed it as the dawn of direct proletarian revolutionary action, but it had few links with Marxism and none with the First International.

Two months later it was crushed by national troops, after savage fighting and brutal reprisals by both sides. More people died than in the Terror of 1793-94. Some 17,000 *Communards* were executed, including women and children, 7,500 were deported and many more imprisoned. The French left was immobilized for a decade, and the country entered a conservative phase, but with universal male suffrage, under the Third Republic.

Barricades in the streets of Paris were defended by women during "la semaine sanglante" (Bloody Week), when government troops mounted a successful attack on the "Communards."

1876

Custer Makes His Last Stand

The general and all his men fall to the Sioux at Little Bighorn

The greatest obstacle to the westward expansion of North America, following the discovery of gold in 1848, was presented by the more than 300,000 Indians of the interior. A foretaste of their fate was provided in California. In 1850 there were 100,000 Indians there; by 1860 there were 35,000. As migrants spread west, they slaughtered buffalo, the essential provider of food and clothing to the tribes. They brought disease with them—smallpox, cholera, syphilis. And the native horsemen were no match for pioneers armed with the Colt repeating revolver.

Continual fighting on the plains broke out in 1862, when the Sioux began a desperate struggle to retain their lands. Their greatest victory came in 1876 at Little Bighorn, where Sitting Bull and Crazy Horse ambushed General George Custer, killing him and his 246 men.

Retribution was swift: Crazy Horse was captured and murdered and the Sioux dispersed. Elsewhere, the Indians were very nearly wiped out: the Apaches of the southwest, the Crow and the Blackfeet of Montana, the Nez Percé of the west.

The Dawes Act of 1887 provided for the dissolution of the tribes and the division of their lands among individual members. In 1890 the last major tribal resistance ended at Wounded Knee, South Dakota, in the massacre of 350 Sioux. During the following 50 years tribal landholdings fell from 138 million acres to 48 million, and most of the Indians were reduced to a life of dispirited idleness on more than 200 government reservations.

This photograph of Apache prisoners was taken in 1866, during 25 years of war between the U.S. military and the native Americans of the southwest.

1876

The Telephone Invented

Alexander Graham Bell transmits speech by electric waves

Alexander Graham Bell was a Scot who, after developing a method of "visible speech" and teaching it to the deaf in London, immigrated to Canada in 1870 and then to Boston in 1871. During the next 30 years his output of inventions was prodigious: flat and cylindrical wax phonograph recorders, an induction balance to detect metals in the human body, the photophone to transmit speech by light rays.

But before any of these came Bell's most dramatic and enduring invention, the telephone. He had, for 10 years (along with several others), been playing with the idea of the electrical transmission of speech. The principle was widely understood; the difficulty was to find a method of practical application. Then, in 1876, through a primitive apparatus which he had constructed, Bell spoke the words, "Mr Watson, come here; I want you." His assistant heard the message, and the age of the telephone was born.

Bell demonstrated his machine, which was both a transmitter and a receiver, at the American Academy of Arts and Sciences in Boston in May. Later in the year the whole world saw it demonstrated at the Philadelphia Centennial Exposition, where the emperor of Brazil, Dom Pedro, picked up a cone-like device, heard Bell speak through it, and exclaimed, "My God! it talks."

In 1877 the Bell Telephone Company was incorporated, and by 1914 there were more than 10 million telephones in the United States.

1878

Congress of Berlin Resolves Balkan Crisis

Diplomacy averts a European war over the "Eastern Question"

When the Serbs and Bulgars rose against Ottoman rule in 1875-76, the three eastern powers, Germany, Austria-Hungary and Russia, failed to impose a settlement that would have carved up the Balkans among them. Great Britain's refusal to desert Turkey, based on fears of Russian expansionism and the alleged need to protect the overland route to India (rendered inessential by the Suez canal), encouraged Turkish resistance. A new sultan, Abdul Hamid II, installed by a palace revolt, defeated the Serbs and Bulgars, the latter with a ferocity that earned his deeds—12,000 Christians were barbarously murdered—the name, the "Bulgarian atrocities."

War between Turkey and Russia followed in 1877-78, and the victorious Russians imposed on Turkey the Treaty of Stefano. Great Britain and Austria-Hungary were so alarmed by its pan-slavic terms that a European congress was convened in Berlin to revise them. The much modified Treaty of Berlin that emerged defined the map of the Balkans for the next 30 years.

"Big Bulgaria" (created in the earlier treaty to be a client Russian state) was divided, in utter disregard of nationality, into a small, autonomous Bulgaria and Eastern Rumelia, nominally under Turkish sovereignty, but with a Christian governor. The independence of Serbia, Romania and Montenegro was guaranteed. Russia was confirmed in the Caucasus, Austria-Hungary empowered to occupy Bosnia-Hercegovina and Great Britain to occupy Cyprus. The powers, said Disraeli, the British prime minster, had won "a peace ... with honor."

1882

Great Britain Bombards Alexandria

British occupation of Egypt begins the European "scramble for Africa"

The Liberal government formed by William Gladstone in 1880 took office having denounced the imperialist adventures of Disraeli's outgoing administration, especially the war in Afghanistan of 1878-80. Two years later it secured British occupation of Egypt.

After Disraeli's purchase of the controlling shares in the Suez canal, the shaky finances of the khedive of Egypt, Ismail, had been placed under joint Anglo-French administration. Increasing political influence followed, and in 1879 a puppet khedive acceptable to the British and French replaced Ismail. The result was the first Arab rising, led by Colonel Arabi Pasha, against Western domination in history.

Gladstone knew the justice of the Arab cause; but he overcame his scruples and in 1882 sent a naval squadron to Alexandria as a show of strength. That action inflamed Arab opinion and provoked a massacre of Europeans. The squadron then bombarded the port; troops were landed and Pasha's forces overcome during August-September. Sir Evelyn Baring, installed at Cairo in 1883 as a temporary consul general, remained, as it turned out, as virtual governor until 1907, when he was replaced by Lord Cromer.

The anti-imperialist Gladstone had touched off the "scramble for Africa." In the next two decades the entire continent was to be subjected to rule by European powers.

This cartoon from "Punch" illustrates the wooing of the African Venus. Britain, France, Germany, Portugal and Italy all seek to share her favors.

1885

Karl Benz Invents the Automobile

The world's first motor car takes to the road at Mannheim

Karl Benz was a German mechanical engineer who built the world's first successful gas-powered "horseless carriage" with an internal-combustion engine. Steam-powered private carriages had had a brief vogue, especially in England, *c.* 1870 (Richard Trevithick had built the first one as early as 1801), but they had not proved commercially successful. Benz was driven by a desire to find a replacement for horse-drawn carriages.

His first model, a three-wheeled chassis with a two-cylinder engine, was completed in 1885. He drove it four times around a small cinder track adjoining his factory in Mannheim, which had been established in 1883 to make stationary internal-combustion engines. He stalled only twice. In 1886 his automobile was patented. Although his associates remained skeptical of the machine's future, Benz sold his first model to the Frenchman, Emile Rogers, in 1887.

Benz built his first four-wheeled automobile in 1893 and his first racing car in 1899.

Karl Benz's car had a tubular steel chassis, an open wooden body, and could reach a speed of 9 mph.

1885

Nationalist Crisis Erupts in the Balkans

Serbs and Bulgarians quarrel over Eastern Rumelia

At the Congress of Berlin in 1878 the great powers had given hostages to fortune by dividing Bulgaria into two parts, autonomous Bulgaria north of Sofia and the Turkish province of Eastern Rumelia in the southeast. In 1885, led by the Russian-born Bulgarian nationalist Stefan Stambulov, the Bulgarians achieved a *coup* in the Rumelian capital. It was accompanied by a declaration of the reunification of Eastern Rumelia and Bulgaria under the Bulgarian Prince Alexander, replaced in 1886 by Ferdinand of Saxe-Coburg-Gotha.

Jealous of Bulgaria's increasing power, Serbia declared war in November, but was defeated after a three-day battle at Slivnitza. No great power intervened. Russia, having presented itself to the world as Bulgaria's protector, was reluctant to appear coercive. And Turkey was restrained by Great Britain, which, with Gladstone's Liberals in office, was unwilling to frustrate any legitimate nationalist aspirations.

Great Britain, at any rate, was beginning to see a more powerful bulwark against Russian expansionism in a strong Bulgaria than in the tottering Ottoman empire. So Bulgaria secured international recognition as a united, autonomous principality and the greatest Slavic state in the Balkans.

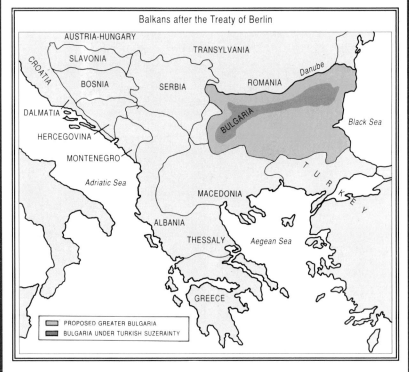

Balkans after the Treaty of Berlin

PROPOSED GREATER BULGARIA
BULGARIA UNDER TURKISH SUZERAINTY

1893

Women Get the Vote in New Zealand

A small nation points the way to full democracy

The suffragette movement began in Great Britain and the United States in the third quarter of the 19th century. And it was in the United States that the first breakthrough was made, when in 1869 women in Wyoming were given the vote in state elections. The first nation to accord women the vote, however, was New Zealand, where women over the age of 21 gained the vote in 1893.

In the United States the National Woman Suffrage Association and the American W.S.A. were founded in 1869, the former by the indefatigable feminist Susan B. Anthony. But the federal vote was not gained until 1920. By then a number of other nations had followed New Zealand's example: Australia (1902), Finland (1907), Norway (1913), Iceland (1914), Denmark (1915), Canada (1917; Quebec 1940), the Netherlands (1917), the Soviet Union (1917) and Germany (1919).

In Great Britain, the National Union of Women's Suffrage Societies was formed, under the presidency of Millicent Fawcett, in 1897. But it required the imprisonment of militant suffragettes, notably Emmeline and Christabel Pankhurst, and women's contribution to the labor force during World War I before the victory was won.

An act of 1918 gave British women over 30 the vote; in 1928 the age was lowered to 21, the same as for men. When the first female member of parliament, Lady Astor, entered the House of Commons after winning the Plymouth Sutton by-election for the Conservatives in 1919, Winston Churchill said that he felt as if he had been surprised in his bath.

The last European nation to give women the vote was Switzerland, in 1971.

1894

Japan Makes War on China

The Land of the Rising Sun signals its imperialist ambitions

Korea had been a vassal state of China for centuries, cut off from the rest of the world, when, in 1876, Japan recognized its sovereign independence and placed a Japanese Resident in Seoul. Then began 20 years of struggle between Japan and China for control of the Korean government. The Korean court itself split into two factions: a conservative, pro-Chinese one, and a modernizing, pro-Japanese one.

By 1894 Japan was ready to assert its supremacy. On August 1 it declared war on China. The Korean government authorized Japan to expel all Chinese forces from its territory and establish an independent Korean government. Against the modern Japanese army and navy, China's ill-led, ill-armed forces made feeble resistance. Japan occupied Manchuria, Formosa and the Liaotung peninsula before China was forced to sue for peace and accept the harsh Treaty of Shimonoseki in 1895.

That treaty gave Japan the Liaotung peninsula, but the so-called "Triple Intervention" of Russia, Germany and France forced Japan to withdraw from all Chinese territory. But Korea was lost and the huge indemnity paid to Japan—nearly £25m—could be paid only by foreign loans. China's revenues came under foreign control. Japan gained "most favored nation" status in Chinese commerce and, with the indemnity, was able to wipe out the national deficit and expand the army and navy. It became an industrial power (with a foothold on the Asian continent), confident of its imperial destiny and with a grievance—the forced return of Liaotung—to avenge.

The Sino-Japanese War (1894-95) gave Japan an opportunity to test her Western-style forces on land and sea. Their decisive victories proved an important incentive in Japan's plans for imperial expansion.

1894

Turks Massacre Armenian Christians

Abdul Hamid launches a campaign of extermination

In the 19th century the ancient Armenian peoples were subject to the rule of Russia (if they lived in the Caucasus) and of Turkey (if they lived in Asia Minor). The Turkish province of Armenia was granted semi-autonomy in 1863, but the Armenians continued to be exposed to repression and abuse by their Ottoman overlords.

The Congress of Berlin of 1878 called upon Turkey to reform its Armenian administration and to protect the Armenians from Kurdish attacks. Instead, in 1886, Sultan Abdul Hamid allowed the Armenian quarter of Constantinople to be burned and looted. In 1894 he launched a campaign of premeditated massacre that amounted to a pogrom. In response to the growth of Armenian nationalism and terrorist attacks on Turkish officials, 200,000 Armenians were slain in 1894-96.

That was only a prelude to the darkest hour in Armenian history. In 1915 the Young Turk government, regarding the Armenians as friends of the Allies (who were then conducting the Gallipoli campaign to gain control of the Dardanelles), decided to deport the whole population—about 1,750,000—to Syria and Mesopotamia. Since there was little chance of their surviving in the desert wastes there, the policy was virtually one of genocide. Estimates of the number who were killed or died in the forced exodus range from 600,000 to more than a million.

The Allied promise to create a sovereign Armenian state after World War I has been unfulfilled.

1894

Dreyfus Affair Splits France

Anti-Semitism in the French army divides the Third Republic

Captain Alfred Dreyfus, a Jewish officer in the French army, was convicted of treason by a secret military court and sentenced to solitary confinement for life on Devil's Island in 1894. The army was a conservative, Roman Catholic stronghold, so when in 1896 Colonel Georges Picquart, the new chief of intelligence, announced that the evidence of Dreyfus' treachery—chiefly a schedule of military information allegedly passed to the Germans—was a forgery, he was silenced and despatched to Tunisia.

Dreyfus had always protested his innocence, and as the scandal unfolded France divided sharply, and acrimoniously, into two camps. The novelist Emile Zola was tried for libel after an attack on the army entitled *J'accuse*, and the affair broadened into a struggle between the crypto-monarchist, anti-Semitic right, backed by the Church, and the republican, anticlerical left, eager to embarrass the government.

In 1898 it was shown that Major Ferdinand Esterhazy and Colonel Henry (Picquart's predecessor) had indeed forged evidence. Esterhazy fled to England, and Henry took his own life. Spasmodic street-fighting between supporters of the two sides occurred throughout 1898 and 1899. In September 1899, Dreyfus was retried, found guilty "with extenuating circumstances" and pardoned. Dreyfusards continued to fight for his name to be cleared, and in 1906 the verdict of the court-martial was overthrown. Dreyfus was readmitted to the army and awarded the Legion of Honor.

Dreyfus' conviction rested largely on a handwriting comparison made by Alphonse Bertillon, a respected criminologist of the time.

1895

The Lumière Brothers Invent Cinematography

A machine to project images onto a screen is patented

The first theater showing of moving pictures took place in Paris in March 1895. The brothers Louis and Auguste Lumière showed a film of workers leaving their factory to members of the *Société d'Encouragement de l'Industrie*.

They were not the sole inventors of cinematography—in the late 1880s several machines (stroboscope, zoetrope, thaumotrope) to show moving images had been invented—but the photographic machine and projector which they patented marked a great advance on Thomas Edison's kinetoscope, or peep show machine, which had been introduced in the United States in the previous year. Only one viewer at a time had been able to watch Edison's moving picture.

The Lumière brothers' film, running at 16 frames per second, was to be the standard for some time. Their first moving picture was followed by one that showed a train arriving at a station. Some of the audience fled in terror. But the age of the movies had been born. In May 1895, the first commercial film show in the United States—a four-minute film of a boxing match—took place on Broadway in New York.

Louis Lumière, with the lightweight camera that could go on location.

1895

Marconi Invents the Wireless

A simple apparatus sends long-wave signals more than a mile

In 1894 Guglielmo Marconi began to experiment with wireless telegraphy at his father's estate near Bologna. By September 1895 he had designed and tested an apparatus that could send and pick up long-wave signals at a range of 1½ miles. He received little encouragement in Italy to continue his experiments, and in 1896 moved to England, where he patented his system.

In 1896-97 he mounted a series of demonstrations of his invention, on Salisbury Plain and along the Bristol Channel. Using kites and balloons to achieve height for the aerials on the receivers, he extended his range of communication to 12 miles. In 1899 he established a station in the south of England and began transmitting to France across the English Channel, more than 30 miles distant.

His invention attracted very little attention, however, until the sensational achievement of trans-Atlantic communication in 1901. In December a receiver in St. John's, Newfoundland, picked up signals sent from Poldhu in Cornwall. The world took notice, and the age of radio communication began.

In 1909 Marconi was awarded the Nobel Prize in Physics.

When Marconi died in 1937, the world observed a two-minute radio silence.

1895

X-Rays Discovered

Wilhelm Röntgen discovers a short-wave ray

In 1895 Wilhelm Röntgen, professor of physics at Würzburg, was working in his laboratory with a cathode-ray vacuum tube (invented by the English physicist William Crookes in 1878), when he observed a strange new phenomenon. When an electric current was passed through the tube, a nearby sheet of paper, coated with barium platinocyanide, gave off a fluorescent glow. The same effect was achieved even if the tube was covered with dense black paper. Röntgen was able to show that it was caused by a ray. Since he did not understand the nature of the radiation—in fact, an electromagnetic radiation with a much shorter wavelength than visible light—he called it an X-ray.

Röntgen's discovery was to have far-reaching effects—on the 20th-century development of X-ray astronomy, for example. Its most immediate application was in medicine, where the ability to photograph inner organs and bones produced a revolution in diagnosis and treatment. The first use of X-rays in medicine took place in Germany in 1903, when Georg Perthes observed their inhibitory effects on cancerous growths.

The first X-ray ever taken shows Bertha Röntgen's ringed hand.

1898

United States of America Goes to War Against Spain

The gain of the Philippines and Cuba marks the rise of a new power

On February 15, 1898, the U.S. battleship *Maine* was blown up and sunk in Havana harbor, killing 260 sailors, and the United States government prepared for war. Early in March the army was mobilized and the Far East squadron sent to Hong Kong, in readiness for an attack on the Spanish fleet in the Philippines. A Spanish inquiry identified the cause of the explosion as an internal flaw; an American investigation reported that it was an attack.

The report was made public and on April 19 Congress recognized Cuban independence and called upon the Spanish administration to withdraw from the island. Three days later Theodore ("Teddy") Roosevelt resigned as secretary of the navy to take command of the volunteer cavalry, the "Rough Riders."

War began on April 22 and lasted more than three months. At the Battle of Manila Bay the U.S. Navy effectively destroyed the Spanish fleet in the Philippines. Victory in the first land battle of the war, at Las Guasimas in Cuba, on June 24, was followed by decisive battles at San Juan Hill (July 2) and Santiago Bay (July 3). By the Treaty of Paris, the United States (which had already annexed Hawaii) gained Puerto Rico, Guam and the Philippines from Spain for a payment of $20m. Cuba was given back its independence.

The war marked the entry of the United States as a major power on the world stage. It also made Teddy Roosevelt a national hero and won him the Republican vice-presidential nomination in 1900.

Roosevelt's Rough Riders were miners, volunteer cowboys, lawmen and college students, famous for their uphill charge at the Battle of Santiago Bay.

1899

Boers and British Go to War in South Africa

Dutch settlers and the British government fight for supremacy

In 1899 the habitual hostility in South Africa between the Dutch Boers, in their independent states of the South African Republic (later Transvaal) and the Orange Free State, and the British Cape Colony and Natal, flared into war. At issue was the claim of "Uitlanders" (foreigners; mostly British), who had been attracted in large numbers to prospect for gold in the Transvaal, to equal rights of citizenship with the Boers.

The Boers, frightened after the brief annexation (1877-81) of the Transvaal by the British and the attempt in the Jameson Raid (1895) to overthrow their government, feared a renewed assault on their independence. In October 1899, after the British had sent troops to the Cape to back the Uitlanders, the Boer republics declared war.

In the first months they won a series of successes and besieged British garrisons at Ladysmith, Mafeking and Kimberley. By August 1900, those garrisons had been relieved and the Boer capital of Pretoria occupied. There followed two years of guerrilla war—marked by Lord Kitchener's notorious rounding up of Boer civilians, including women and children, into concentration camps —before the Boers surrendered.

By the Treaty of Vereeniging (1902), the Transvaal and the Orange Free State were incorporated into the British empire, paid £3m in indemnity and promised future self-government. In 1910 they joined the self-governing dominion, the Union of South Africa.

1900

Boxers Rebel in Peking

Chinese nationalists give vent to anti-Westernism

The European imperialism that carved up Africa in the 1880s and '90s extended itself also to China. There foreign merchants, in what were virtually independent treaty-port settlements, and Christian missionaries established themselves. Germany had commercial control of Shantung province, France a mining monopoly in southern China, and the British a 99-year lease on Hong Kong.

The subsequent wave of anti-foreign sentiment was marked by the revival of the I Ho Chu'an ("Fists of Righteous Harmony"), known to Westerners as the Boxers from their ritual dance reminiscent of boxing. Boxer risings began in 1898 and flowered into full-scale rebellion with an advance on Peking (Beijing) in 1900.

The reactionary court, dominated by the dowager empress Tz'u-hsi, lent government troops to the assault on the foreign legations in the capital. Even so, thousands of Boxers and troops failed in a two-month siege to capture the legation compounds, manned by a mere 533 defenders. In August an international relief expedition began a terrible sacking of Peking and forced Tz'u-hsi to flee to Sian. Although the legations were saved, 231 foreigners, mainly missionaries, lost their lives.

China was forced to pay an indemnity of £67m and to cede the legation quarter to the European powers, together with a military garrison and control of the route from Tientsin to Peking. Opponents of the conservative régime of T'zu-hsi began more and more to pin their hopes on revolution as the only method of restoring China's fortunes.

1900

Max Planck Announces the Quantum Theory

A new description of black-body radiation transforms physics

Classical physics had assumed that bodies emitted and absorbed radiation in continuous flows, or waves. In 1900, however, Max Planck, professor at the University of Berlin, seeking to explain the distribution, or spectrum, of electromagnetic energy, announced a revolutionary theory of black-body radiation. (A black body is an ideal substance in physics, a perfect absorber and emitter of radiant energy.)

Planck proposed that light rays, X-rays and other waves were not emitted at an arbitrary rate. Instead, atoms absorbed and emitted radiation in tiny, discrete bundles, or particles, which he called "quanta." The distinction between particles and waves was largely overthrown: for some purposes it became helpful to think of waves as particles, for others, of particles as waves. For this discovery Planck, awarded the Nobel Prize in 1918, is known as the father of quantum physics.

The break with the classical past was widened in 1926 when Werner Heisenberg announced his uncertainty principle, which stated that a particle did not have a defined position and velocity, only a combination of the two, or a quantum state. The more accurately one was measured, the less accurate the measurement of the other. No particle could be definitely assigned both position and velocity. Determinism, or the prediction of physical events according to unchanging laws—the great ambition of classical physics— became impossible.

Every branch of physics except gravity assimilated the quantum theory and the great task of physics now is to show that the two are irreconcilable or to formulate a new quantum theory of gravity.

1842–1885

CHINA

• **1842 Treaty of Nanking**
Ended Opium War (1839-42) with Great Britain and opened five Chinese ports to foreign trade; Hong Kong ceded to Great Britain; "most favored nation" clause gave every country any concession negotiated by a single nation; followed by China's handing over control of its tariff policy to foreigners in the Treaty of the Bogue (1843); Treaty of Wanghia (1844) gave U.S. most favored nation status.

• **1856 "Arrow" Incident**
Chinese boarding of Hong Kong ship flying British flag; led to Anglo-French war against China (1857-60); Peking savagely looted and 200-building complex of the Summer Palace, an architectural treasure, razed. Tientsin Treaties (1858, 1860) opened 10 more ports to trade, cost China sovereignty over its navigable waters, provided residency rights for foreigners, opened interior to trade, legalized sale of opium, permitted Christian missionaries to travel anywhere in China and set up schools.

• **1885 Tientsin Convention**
China recognized French protectorate over Annam and Tonkin (joined by the French to Cambodia and Cochin-China in 1887, Laos a French protectorate in 1893); at same time China lost buffer state of Burma, annexed to India by Great Britain after three Anglo-Burmese Wars (1824-26, 1852, 1885-86).

1903

Wright Brothers Fly Heavier-Than-Air Plane

North Carolina witnesses the dawn of the age of aviation

The first sustained flight of a plane that was heavier than air and powered by liquid fuel was achieved over the beach at Kitty Hawk, North Carolina, on December 17, 1903. The inventors, the brothers Orville and Wilbur Wright, were bicycle mechanics who used their workshop in Dayton, Ohio, to develop the biplane, which they called *Flyer*. Models were tested in a specially built wind tunnel.

The Wrights' most important change to the gliders of the late 19th century was to introduce movable wing tips, so that the machine could be controlled in flight. The lightweight, 25-horsepower engine also gave the *Flyer* a better power-to-weight ratio than any previous design. On the fourth flight attempted on December 17, the plane, with Orville strapped into a harness attached to the lower wings, stayed in the air for just under a minute and traveled 852 feet. The event was reported by only three newspapers.

Despite a flight at Dayton in 1905, in which a complete circuit of 25 miles was traveled in 38 minutes, it was not until Wilbur had won the Michelin Cup in France in 1908, with a flight of 77 miles in 2 hrs. 20 mins., that the United States Army became interested. In 1909 it awarded the brothers a contract after they demonstrated a machine able to carry two men and reach a speed of 40 mph.

During his historic first flight, Orville Wright, watched from the ground by his brother Wilbur, was in the air for just 12 seconds and traveled a distance of 120 feet.

1904

Japanese Torpedo Russian Fleet at Port Arthur

The surprise attack leads to the Russo–Japanese war

By the terms of an Anglo-Japanese alliance of 1902, Great Britain recognized that Japan had a "peculiar" interest in Korea and guaranteed to remain neutral should Japan and Russia go to war. In 1903 Russia and Japan began negotiations over their rival claims to Korea and Manchuria. The failure of those talks led Japan to launch a surprise attack on the Russian fleet at Port Arthur on February 8, 1904. Two days later the Japanese declared war on Russia.

Hostilities lasted for 18 months. The culminating battle of the land war took place at Mukden, in February and March 1905. Nearly 750,000 soldiers took part, and Japan won a famous victory. In May the Russians were routed at sea, when their Baltic fleet, after a long passage to the Sea of Japan, was destroyed at the Battle of Tsushima. The victory made Admiral Togo a national hero and persuaded Russia to sue for peace. Never before in modern times had an Asian nation defeated a European power in war.

By the Treaty of Portsmouth (negotiated by President Teddy Roosevelt in the United States) Japan gained "predominance" in Korea, the lease of Port Arthur and the Liaotung peninsula, and the southern half of the island of Sakhalin. Both Russia and Japan agreed to evacuate Manchuria and to recognize Chinese sovereignty there. Japan had gained everything that it had been disappointed not to gain after the war with China in 1894-95 and had risen to be indisputably the greatest power in Asia.

1904

France and Great Britain Sign "Entente Cordiale"

The ancient enemies settle their disputes all over the world

Habitual diplomatic tension between Great Britain and France in the imperialist era of the late 19th century was relieved by the signing of the *Entente Cordiale* between the two nations in 1904. The agreement, which owed much to the good offices of King Edward VII, settled all the outstanding colonial disputes between the two nations: in West Africa, Siam, New Hebrides, Newfoundland (fishing rights) and, above all, North Africa. Great Britain was given a free hand in Egypt in return for France's being given the same in Morocco.

The *entente* was not a military alliance. Curiously, at that time— on the eve of the Russo–Japanese War—France was Russia's ally and Great Britain Japan's. But in 1907 Great Britain settled its differences with Russia in an agreement similar to the Anglo-French *entente*. By 1909 the three powers were diplomatically lined up against the Triple Alliance powers of Germany, Austria-Hungary and Italy.

A WOMAN'S PLACE
In Great Britain, a woman was regarded in law as little more than her husband's property until the Marriage and Divorce Acts of the 1850s were passed. A man could still obtain a divorce by evidence of his wife's adultery, while the wife had also to prove cruelty and desertion (the distinction remained until 1923). A wife, unless protected by a marriage settlement, surrendered all her property to her husband until the 1858 act, which gave a woman who left her husband full rights to anything she earned or inherited after their separation. An act of 1870 gave her rights to her earnings while still living with her husband.

1905

"Bloody Sunday" Sparks Revolution in Russia

Nicholas II is compelled to issue a parliamentary constitution

On January 22, 1905, Father Gapon led a march of striking workers to the Winter Palace in St. Petersburg. Their loyal purpose was to petition Tsar Nicholas II for better pay and working conditions. Troops opened fire, and 500 marchers were killed. "Bloody Sunday," coming only three weeks after Russia's defeat by Japan, raised discontent into revolt, not only among ill-paid urban workers, but also among the heavily taxed peasantry.

On February 17 Grand Duke Sergei, the tsar's uncle and advisor, was assassinated by a terrorist bomb. Throughout the countryside peasants seized land and livestock from their landlords. In July the crew of the cruiser *Potemkin* mutinied at Odessa. By October a general strike had been called, and Nicholas was forced to promise concessions: a constitution with guarantees of civil liberties, a democratically elected *duma* (national assembly) and a prime minister.

The tsar's "October Manifesto" satisfied the moderates. But the "Soviet," or workers' committee, (though it did not take action until Lenin's arrival in the country, too late, at the end of November), continued the revolt until it was crushed on January 1, 1906. By April, when the first *duma* was summoned, the countryside was pacified: 15,000 people had lost their lives, and another 70,000 had been arrested.

Order having been restored, Tsar Nicholas betrayed his promises. The *duma* was dismissed after only two months (it met, powerless, three more times before 1914), and Lenin and other Bolshevik leaders sought safety abroad to await the next opportunity.

Grand Duke Vladimir, the chief of Security Police, ordered his troops to open fire on peaceful demonstrators in St. Petersburg, so precipitating the revolution.

1908

Young Turks Take Over in Constantinopole

Abdul Hamid II is ousted by liberal revolutionaries

One effect of the 1905 revolution in Russia was to stimulate liberal aspirations among the younger nobility of Turkey. Their organization, the Committee of Union and Progress, had two avowed objects: to restore the 1876 parliamentary constitution and to westernize Turkish institutions and society.

Their strategy was to detach the army from loyalty to the chief obstacle in their way, Sultan Abdul Hamid II. By intense propaganda they won over the Third Army Corps, stationed at Salonika, and part of the Second Army Corps. In July 1908, the "Young Turks," as they became known, proclaimed the 1876 constitution restored and marched on Constantinopole.

The sultan, helpless in the face of military revolt, called for elections by universal male suffrage to a national parliament and ended press censorship. The Young Turk leader, Enver Bey, assumed *de facto* rule of the country and bent the new assembly to the revolutionaries' will. A counterrevolutionary *coup* by Abdul Hamid in April 1909 was only briefly successful. He was deposed and replaced by a Young Turk puppet, Mohammed V.

Within months it was apparent that hopes of the new régime among the nationalist minorities in the Turkish empire were misplaced. Nor was the promise of a liberal Turkey fulfilled. But internationally the revolution had important consequences: Turkish weakness in 1908 led to the Austro-Hungarian annexation of Bosnia-Hercegovina, and the brutality of Young Turk rule provoked war in the Balkans in 1912.

Despite his educational reforms, the despotic rule of Abdul Hamid II (above) was brought to an end by the Young Turks, organized by the young hero Enver Bey (above right).

1908

Austria-Hungary Annexes Bosnia-Hercegovina

Franz-Joseph overthrows the Treaty of Berlin

The Treaty of Berlin (1878) gave Austria-Hungary the right to occupy the province of Bosnia-Hercegovina, though it remained part of the Turkish empire. Over the next 30 years the Habsburgs ruled the province as though it were a colony, reducing Turkey's role to a merely nominal authority.

Alarm that the Young Turk revolution might lead to a reassertion of Turkish power led Emperor Franz Joseph to seize the opportunity presented by Turkey's internal turmoil and annex the province in October 1908. On the same day, Bulgaria proclaimed its independence of Turkey. Russia, hoping to use those two breaches of the Treaty of Berlin to gain freedom of passage in the Dardanelles in compensation for Austrian gains, called for a European congress.

Neither France, with whom Russia had entered a defensive alliance in 1907, nor Great Britain backed the Russian proposal. Germany, by threatening support for Austria, forced Russia to acquiesce in the annexation. Turkey received financial compensation from Austria-Hungary and from Russia (on behalf of Bulgaria).

The result was to inflame the nationalist Serbs of Bosnia and to draw them, with the Bulgarians, closer to Russia. The friendship between Germany and Austria-Hungary, already members of the Triple Alliance with Italy, was cemented, and the division of Europe into two camps solidified.

1908

King Leopold of Belgium Hands Over the Congo

The Belgian government takes control of Leopold's "free state"

Between 1879 and 1884, under cover of the African International Association, established to found stations in central Africa to help Christian missions and eradicate the slave trade, King Leopold of the Belgians carved out for himself a vast private empire in the Congo basin. Conflict with the French in the region led to an international congress at Berlin in 1884-85, which recognized the Congo Free State as Leopold's personal possession.

For 20 years Leopold ruthlessly exploited its rubber and ivory. His claim to have abolished the export of slaves was justified, but in its place he instituted forced labor, more brutal than the slave system he destroyed, to work the rubber plantations. During the years of his personal rule the native population of the Congo Free State fell by nearly a half.

The Irishman Roger Casement, an official in the British diplomatic service, exposed the atrocities of Leopold's rule in a report of 1904. Four years later the king was forced to hand over the Congo Free State to the Belgian government, which then administered it as a colony.

This advertisement reflects the growth of the ivory trade and exposes the exploitation of the Congo basin by Leopold II, who made the area his personal domain.

VÉRITABLE EXTRAIT DE VIANDE LIEBIG.

1911

Mexican Rebels Overthrow Porfirio Diaz

The end of dictatorship ushers in a decade of turmoil

Porfirio Diaz's Mexican dictatorship, founded by a U.S.-assisted *coup* in 1876, rested on the subjection of the native population to poverty, while foreign capital flowed into the country. By 1900 foreign interests, chiefly American, owned most of the country's mines, oilfields, sugar and coffee plantations, and cattle ranches. The textile industry was in the hands of French businessmen.

In 1911, insurrections all over the country, notably those led by Pancho Villa in Chihuahua and by Emiliano Zapata in Morelos, forced Diaz to resign. He was replaced as president by Francisco Madero, who had been imprisoned when he announced his candidacy in the 1910 election, but freed after Diaz's electoral victory. Ten years of turmoil followed, with one provisional president after another—the revolutionary general Victoriano Huerta in 1913, Venustiano Carranza in 1916—until stability was restored when General Alvaro Obregon became president in 1920.

The outstanding achievement of those years was Carranza's 1917 constitution, the most far-reaching attempt the world had seen to establish a welfare state. All land was declared the inalienable property of the state; and the constitution granted an eight-hour working day, profit-sharing, a minimum wage, compensation for industrial injuries, the right to organize unions and the right to strike. The Church (bribed by Diaz) was barred from owning property.

Although not implemented at once, the constitution was, however, profoundly to influence future political developments throughout Latin America.

1912

Manchus Overthrown in China

China becomes a republic

The financial crisis facing China after the war with Japan, and the punitive measures imposed by the West after the Boxer Rebellion, forced the dowager empress to take up reform. But the parliamentary constitution that emerged in the years 1905-08 was a sham, a front for the perpetuation of the Manchu dynasty and imperial power.

The monarchical reformers were left impotent; reforming momentum passed to the revolutionaries, led by Sun Yat-sen. With other leaders he had formed a revolutionary coalition, the T'ung Meng Hui, in 1905. It called for a republic and a socialist land policy. In 1907–11 it sponsored numerous unsuccessful revolts in southern China.

Revolution finally came in 1911, when the government provoked insurrection in Sichuan by trying to nationalize the railroads without compensation to their owners. Revolt, to which the T'ung Meng Hui attached itself, spread through the provinces of the Yangtze valley. Yuan Shih-k'ai, an officer in the imperial army, demanded full military power, which was granted to him, and legal status for the revolutionary groups. He intended, in this way, to make sure that he was the leader after the revolution, whichever side won.

By December all but four provinces had come out against the Manchu dynasty; a provisional government under Yuan was established in Nanking. In February 1912 the empress abdicated. Though Sun Yat-sen received most of the votes, he yielded to Yuan, who thus became republican China's first president.

1912

Balkan League Attacks Turkey

Ottoman power in Europe is nearly eclipsed

Instransigence on the part of the Young Turks in the face of seething nationalist discontents in the Balkans produced an improbable result: Greeks, Serbs, Montenegrans and Bulgars joined together in the Balkan League. In 1912 they took up arms against Turkey. Although Austria-Hungary trembled at the example of full-scale nationalistic wars, and Russia feared Bulgarian expansion toward the Dardanelles, none of the powers intervened.

Early victories for the League gave way to stalemate when the Bulgarians failed to capture Constantinople, and an armistice was followed by the Treaty of London (1913). Together with the Treaty of Bucharest (agreed after the Balkan countries came to blows among themselves in 1913), it greatly diminished Turkey's European territory, while partly recognizing the claims of nationalism.

European Turkey was cut back to a small area around Constantinople and Adrianople; the new, independent state of Albania was created; Serbia, Montenegro and Greece were all enlarged at Bulgaria's expense. Bulgaria, having entered the League on the agreement that it would divide Macedonia with Serbia, saw it divided, instead, between Greece and Serbia. Greece, given the strategic port of Salonika, emerged as the most powerful state in the region.

Stability in the Balkans was further undermined: Bulgaria sought revenge, Serbia determined to liberate the Serbs of Bosnia, and Russia and Austria eyed each other nervously as Turkey, the "sick man of Europe," took to his deathbed.

The boy Pu-Yi, shown standing, succeeded as emperor in 1908, at the age of three. The Republican Revolution forced him out in 1912.

1914

Panama Canal Opens

The United States links the Pacific Ocean to the Atlantic

The acquisition of a Pacific empire in 1898, as a result of the Spanish–American war, fueled interest in the United States in the building of a canal from the Caribbean to the Pacific. A concession to build a canal through Panama, then part of Colombia, had been held by the French Panama Company since 1878, and Congress, after rejecting an alternative route through Nicaragua (where a volcano erupted in 1902), decided to purchase the concession from the French owners.

An agreement for a lease in perpetuity to America of the 10-mile-wide canal zone was signed by the Colombian attaché at Washington in January 1903. The Colombian government, however, dithered in ratifying the agreement, and President Teddy Roosevelt worked with Panamanian nationalists to provoke an uprising in the isthmus. In November a revolutionary army proclaimed the independence of Panama, while U.S. battleships prevented Colombian forces from landing and putting down the revolt. "I took Panama," Roosevelt later boasted.

The United States, on payment of $10m and an annual ground rent of $250,000 to the new republic, gained exclusive control of the canal zone. Building began in 1904, and the canal was at last opened to commercial shipping in August 1914. In 1977 the United States agreed to hand over the canal to Panama in 1999.

1914

Archduke Franz-Ferdinand Assassinated

A Serbian nationalist lights the fuse that starts World War I

On July 28, 1914, Archduke Franz-Ferdinand, heir to the throne of Austria-Hungary, and his wife, the duchess of Hohenburg, were assassinated while driving in an open car through the streets of Sarajevo, the principal town in Bosnia. The assassin was a young student, Gavrilo Princip, a Serbian nationalist protesting Habsburg rule.

Despite conciliatory messages from Serbia, Austria-Hungary at once declared war on Serbia, the beginning of a chain of events that led to World War I. On July 29 Russia ordered the mobilization of more than a million troops; Germany responded the next day by promising mobilization unless Russia demobilized within 24 hours.

At that point railroad schedules came into play. The war had deep causes, among them imperialist rivalries among the European powers and the instability of the Balkans. But at the last moment it became unstoppable because the troop trains could not be halted.

On August 1 Germany, since its ultimatum had been ignored by Tsar Nicholas II, declared war on Russia; on August 3 the kaiser declared war on France. Germany's invasion of Belgium, in violation of Belgian neutrality, on August 4, brought Great Britain into the war. The two European camps, Triple Alliance and Triple Entente, had at last been brought face to face on the battlefield. "The lamps are going out all over Europe"; said Lord Grey, the British foreign secretary, "we shall not see them lit again in our lifetime."

1882–1907

EUROPE

• **1882 Triple Alliance**
Secret agreement of mutual defense signed between Germany, Austria-Hungary and Italy; Germany and Austria-Hungary to come to Italy's aid if attacked by France; each power to assist the others if any one of them attacked by two powers (Great Britain excepted); renewed every five years until 1913; France knew of its existence by 1883, but precise terms not known until 1918.

• **1905 "Dreadnought" Constructed**
Revolutionary "all-big-gun" battleship launched by Great Britain in 1906; 12-in. guns, speed of 21 knots; beginning of naval race between Great Britain and Germany; first German "dreadnought," the *Nassau*, constructed in 1907. At start of WWI Great Britain had 19 dreadnoughts and 13 under construction, Germany 13 and 7 under constuction, U.S. 8, France 8, Japan 4, Austria-Hungary 2 and Italy 1.

• **1907 Triple Entente**
Name for Anglo-Franco-Russian alliance; Franco-Russian military convention (1893) followed by the Dual Alliance (1894), thus finally ending League of the Three Emperors—Russia, Germany, Austria-Hungary (1872). Great Britain brought into the orbit, though with no specific military commitments, by the *Entente Cordiale* with France and the Anglo-Russian entente of 1907, both to settle colonial disputes and agree spheres of influence.

1914

Russian Army Routed at Tannenberg

The Allies suffer a terrible setback on the eastern front

The first critical engagement of World War I on the eastern front took place in eastern Prussia. Two Russian armies, having advanced into German territory in mid-August and enjoyed initial success, suffered a dreadful defeat. In four days of fierce fighting, on August 27-30, the Russian army commanded by General Alexander Samsonov was encircled by German troops, under Generals Ludendorff and Hindenburg, and utterly defeated at Tannenberg.

The Germans took 100,000 prisoners before moving on to attack General Rennenkampf's army in the nine-day (September 6-15) Battle of the Masurian Lakes. There, another 125,000 Russian soldiers were captured. It was little consolation to the Russians that their southern army routed the Austrians at Lemberg in the three weeks between August 23 and September 12.

Defeat at Tannenberg meant that no Russian army invaded Germany for the remainder of the war. Great Britain and France, however, had reason to be grateful to the Russians, for, at a critical moment in the Battle of the Marne on the western front, two German army corps had been diverted to the east.

1914

Allies Thwart Germany at First Battle of the Marne

The Schlieffen Plan breaks down in northern France

Germany's invasion of Belgium, on August 4, was dictated not by policy, but by military strategy. Germany sought a rapid, total victory over France—occupying Paris, taking France out of the war and blocking the deployment of British troops onto the continent. That objective was to be achieved by the Schlieffen Plan which, since the northern Franco-German boundary was hilly and heavily wooded, called for a sweeping movement through the plains of Belgium and then south to Paris.

Germany put nearly two million troops into that initial campaign, which was intended to be over in six weeks. Brussels fell on August 4; Namur, a vital French point of defense, five days later. The Germans were then delayed by a holding action against the Belgian army at Antwerp and badly weakened by sending two army corps to fight the Russians in eastern Prussia. The decisive action took place from September 5 to 14 on the River Marne, northeast of Paris. There Generals Joffre and Galliéni led the French forces, supported by the British Expeditionary Force, to victory. The Germans were pushed back to the Aisne River in the north, and Paris was saved.

The Schlieffen Plan had failed. Antwerp fell, but the Germans failed to capture the channel ports during the first Battle of Ypres (October 12-November 11). British support could therefore continue to reach the French. Throughout the fall, the two sides dug themselves into trenches, and the war in the west settled into a grim stalemate that was to last until 1918.

Affectionately known in France as "Papa" Joffre, General Joseph Joffre became chief of staff of the French Army in 1911. His impenetrable calm and courage helped to sustain the army's morale in the desperate days of 1914, although his failure to prevent the senseless slaughter at Verdun finally brought his active career to an end.

1915

Germans Use Chlorine Gas at Ypres

An alarming new weapon fails to break the Allied front

Ypres, a small Belgian town on a salient on the French border, was three times the site of a major engagement in World War I. The first battle, in October-November 1914, was the first attempt at trench warfare. It brought down the curtain on the "race for the sea"— the battle for Flanders after deadlock had beeen reached on the Marne. An Allied victory stopped the Germans from gaining control of the Channel ports and allowed the Allies to complete a trench barrier from Switzerland to the coast.

The second battle took place in the spring of 1915, when the Germans again failed to break Allied defenses. For the first time, gas was used in warfare. On the second day of action, April 22, German soldiers wearing helmets fitted with gas masks fell upon mainly French and Canadian troops behind a four-mile-long cloud of greenish-yellow chlorine gas. Though Allied losses were heavy—on the first day the French had 69,000 soldiers killed or captured—the gas attacks proved unreliable, and Germany abandoned the offensive on May 24, with the Allied front unbroken.

This French officer wears a crude, early type of mask against gas attack.

1915

"S.S. Lusitania" Sunk by German Torpedoes

Diplomacy keeps the United States out of the war

American neutrality in World War I was sorely tested from the outset, first by the British naval blockade, which virtually shut off American trade with the European continent, and then by the German response to that blockade. In February 1915 Germany declared that all waters around the British Isles constituted a war zone. It laid mines in those waters and prepared to launch submarine attacks on neutral vessels.

On May 7, 1915, the Cunard liner *Lusitania* was sunk by German torpedoes off the coast of Ireland. Among the 1,195 passengers who were drowned were 128 American citizens. Germany justified the attack on the ground that the *Lusitania* was carrying munitions and that passengers had been warned of the risk of traveling on it. The warning, however, had been posted only on the morning of departure, and in the United States the sinking provoked a cry for war, led by Teddy Roosevelt.

It was silenced by the outcome of negotiations between President Woodrow Wilson and the German government. Germany agreed to pay reparations for the attack and to desist from attacks on passenger ships without adequate warning. Amicable relations between Germany and the United States were restored, and the United States remained out of the war until 1917.

WOMEN AT WAR

The emancipation of women took a step forward during World War I. Military recruitment caused a labor shortage in factories and offices that employers were happy to fill with women. When the war ended women were reluctant to return to servants' jobs, by far the largest sector of female employment before 1914. That change wrought a revolution in the relations between the middle and the working classes. Except for the rich, household servants became a thing of the past. During the years of high unemployment which marked most western European countries after the war, women lost their places on the factory floor. But large numbers remained in white-collar jobs. By and large, the professions—medicine, law, the Church—continued to close their doors to women.

Auxiliary policewomen in the East End of London helped the war effort. By 1916, there were 1.6 million women working in Britain, half of them in the munitions factories, and many millions elsewhere in Europe. "Women Come And Help!" appeared on recruitment posters designed to keep production levels up.

WORLD WAR I

World War I was distinguished from previous wars by the sustained artillery bombardments that preceded every advance. Guns, such as the howitzer depicted in Paul Nash's dramatic painting, would pound enemy lines for days on end, sapping the men's morale and devastating the countryside.

The real drama of the war took place in Europe, where gas was first used in battle, and aircraft and tanks made their debut. The life expectancy of a British pilot in 1917 was 17½ flying hours. Norman Arnold captured the tragic moment, above, when the 20-year-old British ace, Albert Ball, V.C., with 43 enemy planes to his credit, was shot down by German Fokkers.

The first real tank battle in history, the Battle of Cambrai was planned in the utmost secrecy; tanks and men were massed over a period of two weeks before the attack opened. The painting by W. L. Wyllie shows the tanks rolling forward at dawn on November 20, 1917, across open, tussocky grassland: perfect tank country. Initially so successful, the battle did not result in significant gains of territory, but the tank proved its worth as a weapon of war.

World War I, which contemporaries called the Great War, was meant to be over in six weeks. It was meant to be the war to end all wars. It was meant to make the world safe for democracy. Instead it lasted for four years and led directly to the rise of antidemocratic, totalitarian régimes in Europe and to the far more destructive World War II.

That the Allies were fighting to defend democracy—an idea not put forward until Woodrow Wilson attached it to the American entry into the war in 1917—was not a convincing proposition. France and Great Britain were not notably more democratic than Germany or Italy, and their other major ally against the Central Powers was autocratic, tsarist Russia.

The immediate cause of the war was the nationalist ferment in the Balkans, especially in Serbia, where the old empire of Austria-Hungary maintained an enfeebled, but still oppressive, sway. A succession of Balkan crises had been defused in the recent past. In 1914 diplomacy was not given a chance. Great Britain, France and Germany were drawn into the conflict after years of rivalry for overseas empire and trade. Great Britain and Germany had for nearly a decade been competing to establish maritime supremacy in a race of battleship-building; and the series of alliances that had been built up since the 1880s had divided Europe into two camps—the Triple Entente and Triple Alliance nations. Perhaps all that can be said is that in 1914 the great powers of Europe were ready for war.

World War I was the first experience of "total war," war that brought every element of modern industrial and technological states into play. Once the fighting began, so evenly matched were the combatants in manpower, weaponry and industrial resources, that it became difficult to foresee why or how it should ever end. It was essentially a war of attrition, a war of the trenches, of inches painfully gained and painfully lost. The American entry into the war tilted the balance against the Central Powers, but, remarkably, there were no really decisive battles. Russia withdrew in 1917 because of internal turmoil and the hunger and war-weariness of its people. When the armistice was signed on November 11, 1918, German armies were still ranged across the continent, from France to the Black Sea. Germany surrendered, not precisely because it had lost the war, but because it came to believe that it could not win it.

In the end it was not evident to the victors that anything had been won, at least not anything to compensate for the dreadful loss of life and the deep injury caused to the European economy. France, it is true, regained Alsace-Lorraine and thus secured the long-hoped-for revenge against Germany. The Ottoman and Austro-Hungarian empires were no more. But neither France nor Great Britain had entered the conflict with a clear understanding of what their war aims were. The victors, therefore, struggled to discover what kind of peace they should make, and a series of treaties left both Europe and the Middle East nurseries of conflict and future wars.

1915

Allies Retreat from Gallipoli

A mismanaged British offensive ends with nothing gained

On April 26, 1915, British, French and ANZAC (Australia and New Zealand Army Corps) troops established themselves, after a day of heavy fighting, at six positions along the Gallipoli peninsula. The object of the landings was to knock Turkey out of the war, capture Constantinople and so open a route by which assistance could be provided to Russia.

The campaign was undermined from the start by indecision within the British war cabinet, torn between committing itself to action in the Dardanelles and putting all its resources into the war on the western front. Two months elapsed between the Royal Navy's first bombardment of Turkish coastal fortifications and the landings, by which time Turkish defenses were well prepared, and an Allied breakthrough proved elusive.

A second landing in August, at Suvla Bay, was no more successful. Fighting continued until the nights of December 18 and 19. The greater part of the peninsula was abandoned: 90,000 men, along with 4,500 animals and 1,700 vehicles, were evacuated without loss of life. The campaign had cost the Allies 25,000 dead, 13,000 missing, 172,0000 sick and wounded.

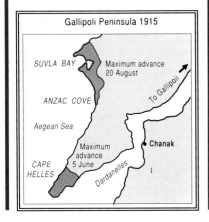

Gallipoli Peninsula 1915

SUVLA BAY — Maximum advance 20 August

ANZAC COVE

Aegean Sea

Maximum advance 5 June

CAPE HELLES

Chanak

To Gallipoli

Dardanelles

1916

Germany Launches Assault on Verdun

A ten-month offensive is thwarted by heroic French resistance

At the start of 1916 four million troops were entrenched on the western front, still locked in stalemate after 18 months of warfare. German successes in 1915 on the eastern front had driven the Russian army out of Poland and cost the lives of two million Russian soldiers. But the Russian army was still in the field, and General Erich von Falkenhayn, the German chief of staff, turned his attention once more to the west.

In February 1916, he launched a massive assault—19 divisions concentrated on a few square miles—on the French fortress at Verdun. Time and again on the western front it had been shown that offense was more costly than defense. But the German strategy was to force France to bring all its resources to the defense of the most critical point guarding Paris from the east and, by a sustained offensive, gradually to bleed the French army, and the French nation, to death. It failed, even though German losses, at 330,000, were in this instance less than the French total of 350,000. The beginning of conscription in Great Britain in January 1916 enabled British reinforcements to mount a challenge to the Germans on the Somme, taking the pressure off the French.

The French defense of Verdun, led by General Henri Pétain, gave birth to the legendary cry, "They shall not pass," and when the campaign ended in December Verdun remained in Allied hands.

1916

Irish Republicans Stage Easter Rising in Dublin

British troops crush the rebellion

In 1911 the British parliament passed an act which deprived the House of Lords of its veto over bills passed by the Commons. Home rule for Ireland at once became a possibility. An act conferring it, while reserving control of strategic and fiscal matters to the imperial government, was introduced by the Liberal government and passed into law in January 1913.

The Protestants of Ulster, in the north, united in opposition to home rule and gained the near-treasonable support of the Conservative opposition for the stance they adopted: "Ulster will fight, and Ulster will be right." War broke out in Europe before the act was to come into force, and republicans in southern Ireland, chiefly members of the old Irish Republican Brotherhood, but also some adherents of the new Sinn Fein ("We ourselves"), staged a rebellion for full independence and a united Ireland on Easter Sunday, 1916.

Led by Patrick Pearse and James Connolly, the rebels captured the Post Office at Dublin and proclaimed the independent republic of Ireland. But they numbered only 1,000 and they were powerless against a large British force, landed to put down the rising. After four days of British bombardment, they surrendered.

Pearse, Connolly and 13 other leaders were summarily executed after convictions by courts-martial. One who escaped the death penalty was Eamon de Valera, the future leader of Sinn Fein and president of Eire (1959-73).

1916

British and German Fleets Clash at Jutland

An indecisive engagement sends the German battleships back to port

For nearly two years after the outbreak of World War I the British and German fleets restricted themselves to occasional skirmishes in the economic war of blockade and counter-blockade. Great Britain was content to maintain its supremacy of the seas and, from its station at Scapa Flow, to watch the German High Seas Fleet, anchored behind mines in North Sea harbors.

On May 31, 1916, the naval peace was broken. Admiral Reinhard Scheer decided to attempt to lure part of the British fleet into action and destroy it. A decoy squadron of cruisers under Vice-Admiral Franz von Hipper's command put into open water, sailing past the Danish province of Jutland. In the afternoon it engaged a British cruiser squadron under Vice-Admiral David Beatty.

Behind the cruisers the battleship flotillas of each side steamed toward each other. They clashed in the evening. The British Grand Fleet, under Admiral John Jellicoe, suffered marginally worse damage — losing three battle-cruisers, three armored cruisers and eight destroyers against the German loss of one battleship, five cruisers and five destroyers. Moreover, the British suffered 6,097 casualties against the Germans' 2,545.

But lasting victory went to the British. By morning the German fleet was back in port, not again to venture forth for the duration of the war. Two years later, after a bloodless surrender at Scapa Flow, it was scuttled by its own crews—a strange end to the naval war that never happened, after the great naval race of the pre-war years that had contributed much to the growth of war fever.

One of the nine British battle-cruisers at Jutland, H.M.S. "Tiger" steams into action. Another separate engagement involved a monstrous clash of British and German dreadnoughts.

1869–1923

IRELAND

● 1869 Irish Church Disestablished
Bill of Gladstone's Liberal government passed by British parliament to end statutory privileges and special status of the "Anglican" Church of Ireland; Irish bishops ceased to sit in House of Lords; Irish Church property sold, with first right of purchase to existing tenants; Church courts abolished.

● 1881 Irish Land Act
Introduced by Gladstone's Liberal government after organized "land war" against landowners by Parnell's Land League (founded 1879); recognized the three "Fs"— fixity of tenure, fair rents and free sale—throughout Ireland; commission established to set fair rents; sale of land at three-quarters of the market price.

● 1886 Home Rule Bill
Introduced by Gladstone's Liberal government in House of Commons with equal Liberal and Conservative strength; 86 Irish Home Rulers held balance; bill to give Ireland own parliament and executive with no representation at Westminster, but no control of "imperial affairs"; defeated by combination of "Liberal imperialists" and Conservatives; permanent split in Liberal party.

● 1922–23 Irish Civil War
Guerrilla fighting by de Valera-led IRA opponents of 1921 treaty; called off by de Valera in May 1923; Irish government executed 77 rebels and imprisoned 12,000.

1916

Sharif Hussein Raises Flag of Arab Revolt

Mecca and Jeddah fall to rebels against Ottoman rule

In 1914 the Ottoman Empire in Asia extended over the Islamic heartland of Palestine, Syria, Mesopotamia and Arabia (except for the southern coast, which was largely under British influence). When the war ended, Arab nationalism and war had combined to crumble that empire, just as it had crumbled in the Balkans in the years before 1914. The leader of Arab nationalism was Hussein ibn Ali, the grand sharif of Mecca.

Great Britain, which in 1915 had landed troops at Basra to protect the Persian oil supply, thus beginning the interplay of oil and Western politics in the region, was eager for Arab allies against Turkey. It was, therefore, equivocal in its attitude to Hussein's demand for the independence of all lands south of Kurdistan. For one thing, French interests in Syria had to be consulted.

But when Hussein's son Feisal led an Arab revolt in June 1916, and Mecca and Jeddah were captured, the British, who had assisted the rising, recognized Hussein as king of the Hejaz (northwestern Saudi Arabia). The British took Jerusalem in 1917 and entered Damascus with Arab soldiers in 1918.

Strategically the Arab Revolt was of great value to the Allies; but the Arabs were deceived by the West. In 1917 a secret agreement was uncovered, by which France and Great Britian planned to award Syria and Iraq to each other after the war. It increased the distrust fostered among Arabs by Lord Balfour's declaration (1917) which proclaimed the right of Jews to a "national home" in Palestine. In the redrawing of the Middle East map after the war the Arabs were to have little say.

Feisal's men were photographed by T. E. Lawrence as they rode into the strategic port of Wejh on the Red Sea.

1916

Somme Campaign Begins

Four and a half months of bloody trench warfare end in stalemate

On July 1, 1916, Great Britain and France launched an attack on German troops dug in along the Somme River in Picardy. The assault was preceded by a 5-day bombardment, the largest artillery barrage yet seen and was one of the costliest campaigns in modern history. More than three million men were engaged. Never before had so large a British army—26 divisions —gone into battle. The French force was 18 divisions, less than half of that originally planned because of losses incurred at Verdun.

On the very first day the British sustained nearly 60,000 casualties: 20,000 killed in action and another 37,000 missing or wounded. Tanks were used for the first time—in a British offensive of September 15. The battle along a 20-mile front lasted until November 15. At no point were the Germans pushed back more than 10 miles.

The final toll of casualties was 794,000 for the Allies, 540,000 for the Central Powers. At the time the carnage seemed futile, since the battle ended in virtual stalemate. But after the war, the Germans attested that the losses had so debilitated their war effort that the Somme was the turning point of the war.

British soldiers struggled out of their trenches and "over the top," often carrying up to 66 lb. of equipment.

1917

United States Enters the War

Unrestricted submarine warfare by Germany ends American neutrality

Although Woodrow Wilson ran for re-election as president in the autumn of 1916 on the slogan, "He kept us out of war," he began to prepare for war. Renewed peace overtures at the end of the year failed, even after the slaughter on the Somme and the loss in Galicia of 1½ million lives. At the same time the Germans began to wage unrestricted submarine warfare against the British naval blockade.

Three events in March 1917 helped to swing American opinion toward war: the famous "Zimmermann note" (a telegram from the German foreign minister to the German ambassador to Mexico, uncovered by British intelligence), which outlined a Mexican-German alliance to win Texas, New Mexico and Arizona for Mexico; the overthrow of the tsar in Russia; and, above all, the destruction of five U.S. merchant vessels by German U-boats. On April 2 Wilson asked Congress to declare war. Both honor and peace, he said, could no longer be preserved. Congress voted its approval on April 6.

1917

Passchendaele Offensive Gets Bogged Down in Mud

The dismal war of attrition continues on the western front

From June to November 1917, British forces, in an effort to relieve the heavily besieged French army (which had just lost 100,000 soldiers in a prolonged battle in Champagne) carried out a great offensive in Flanders. For the third time Ypres bore the brunt of some of the heaviest fighting of the war.

The campaign had two phases: the first on the Messines Ridge; the second, beginning in August, on the fields around Passchendaele. The battle was the occasion of the first use of sustained air cover for land fighting (German bombers had blitzed London in June). It was also the occasion of the heaviest artillery fire in the war, heavier even than that on the Somme. The bombardment destroyed many of the irrigation dikes in the area, aggravating the effects of an unusually rainy late summer and turning the low-lying battlefields near Passchendaele into a treacherous bog. In four months of desperate action the Allies gained a mere five miles of ground. No other engagement of the war left such bitter memories.

A recruiting poster, left, heralds America's entry into the war. Some 300,000 British and Commonwealth soldiers lost their lives at Passchendaele, above, many drowning in the mud.

1917

Bolsheviks Seize Power in Russia

Kerensky's liberal-democratic government is overthrown

The toll of Russian lives by 1917—more than 8 million had been killed, wounded and captured—and food shortages at home doomed the Romanov dynasty. Strikes at Petrograd (modern Leningrad) were followed by a mutiny of the troops on March 10, 1917. Five days later Tsar Nicholas II abdicated. A provisional government was headed by Prince Lvov until July, when he was replaced by the lawyer Alexander Kerensky.

Kerensky aimed to continue the war and to establish a liberal constitutional government. But in April the German high command, hoping that revolution would force Russia out of the war, had given the Bolshevik leader, Vladimir Lenin, safe passage back to Russia from Switzerland. Lenin allied himself with the Petrograd Soviet of Workers' and Soldiers' Deputies against Lvov and Kerensky. A July revolt by the soviet failed and Lenin fled to Finland.

Another disastrous Russian offensive in Galicia produced widespread desertions in the army. Peasant recruits, hearing of plans for the redistribution of land by the revolutionary left, returned home. Lenin's program was peace with Germany, land redistribution and power to the soviets.

Kerensky's plan to summon a constituent assembly turned to dust when, on the night of October 24 (new style: November 6), Lenin staged a *coup*. Blank shots were fired from the *Aurora*, anchored in the Neva River, and soldiers, sailors and factory Red Guards seized control of the government. Kerensky resigned, and Lenin was proclaimed leader of the Council of People's Commissars, with Leon Trotsky as commissar for foreign affairs and Joseph Stalin as commissar for national minorities.

1918

Woodrow Wilson Announces His "Fourteen Points"

The American president presents his vision of the postwar world

The war aims of the European Allied partners in World War I were never clearly stated. In his speech asking for American entry into the war in 1917 Woodrow Wilson had said that the war was to make the world "safe for democracy." On January 8, 1918, after an Allied conference had failed to agree on war aims, he listed for Congress his famous "Fourteen Points"—less a definition of war aims than an outline for a just and durable peace.

The points were these: (1) open covenants of peace (i.e., no secret treaties); (2) freedom of navigation everywhere in peace and war; (3) removal of barriers to free trade; (4) arms reduction; (5) impartial adjustment of colonial claims; (6) evacuation by Central Powers of all Russian territory; (7) evacuation of Belgium; (8) evacuation of France and return of Alsace-Lorraine to France; (9) readjustment of Italy's frontiers in line with nationality; (10) autonomous development of the peoples of Austria-Hungary; (11) evacuation of Romania, Serbia and Montenegro; (12) sovereignty to Turkish portions of the Ottoman empire; (13) an independent Poland with access to the Baltic; (14) an association of nations to preserve nations' independence.

Wilson's immediate objective, to drive a wedge between the German people and their government, achieved some success (the speech was widely circulated in Germany and Austria-Hungary). His wider aim, a new world society based on national self-determination, was defeated in the peace treaties drawn up after the war.

1918

Bolsheviks Sign Treaty of Brest-Litovsk

Exhausted Russia accepts humiliating peace terms

On November 8, 1917, one day after the Bolshevik *coup* in Russia, Leon Trotsky announced publicly that Russia would consider any peace terms. He meant to appeal to the peoples of all countries over the heads of governments and force a general peace conference. He failed. Russia alone sat down with Germany at Brest-Litovsk to make a separate peace on December 3.

Trotsky hoped that by stalling for nine weeks, revolution would spread to Germany and Austria-Hungary before the peace terms were signed. It did not. And a German advance deep into Russian territory in mid-February forced the Bolsheviks to accept humiliating terms in the Treaty of Brest-Litovsk, which was signed on February 28.

Russia ceded Poland, Lithuania, and part of Belorussia to Germany; it accepted the independence of the Baltic states and of the Ukraine; and it surrendered the Caucasus to Turkey. The treaty was a great blow to Russia's partners. It robbed Russia of one-quarter of its European land, two-fifths of its population and three-quarters of its iron and coal. It released German troops from the east, and it compelled Romania's surrender to the Central Powers.

The West intervened to try to dislodge the Bolsheviks; Germany's interest was to keep them in power. But in the end the treaty was nullified by the defeat of the Central Powers and the postwar peace settlements.

The leaders of the Big Four (from left to right) Orlando Vittorio, Italy; David Lloyd George, Great Britain; Georges Clemençeau, France; and Woodrow Wilson, U.S., met at Versailles.

1918

Allies Win Second Battle of the Marne

Germany's final push on the western front is repulsed

On March 21, 1918, General Erich Ludendorff launched what turned out to be the final German offensive of World War I. He began to advance once more toward the Marne. The Allied powers, for the first time, established a unified command under Marshal Ferdinand Foch to meet the spring offensive. By then abundant supplies and troops were reaching Europe from the United States and Foch's strategy was to delay a major counterattack until the Germans were stretched along the front to their utmost.

In July the second Battle of the Marne began in earnest, with a series of attacks on the bulge in the center of the German line. In August the British took 20,000 prisoners at Amiens; in September French troops took another 30,000 just below Soissons and forced the Germans to retreat. Blow after blow followed, delivered with such rapidity that the Germans could not recover before the next one fell.

By November the British had broken into open country, the Americans had reached Sedan and the French were closing in on Lorraine. Hindenburg and Ludendorff sued for peace. At the Allies' insistence, Kaiser Wilhelm abdicated on November 9. Two days later, at 11:00 a.m., Germany signed an armistice in Marshal Foch's railroad car in the forest of Compiègne. The war was over. Germany had admitted defeat. But Germany at least had the satisfaction of knowing that there were no Allied troops on German soil.

1919

Victors Impose "Diktat" of Versailles

The seeds of future conflict are sown in Germany

The Allied countries that met in Paris to work out the terms of a peace treaty with Germany acted in the same manner as Germany had acted toward Russia at Brest-Litovsk. The Treaty of Versailles that Germany was forced to sign included a clause which laid the whole guilt for the war upon the German people.

It then proceeded to lay heavy obligations upon Germany: disarmament (its army was never to have more than 100,000 men nor its navy more than six warships above 10,000 tons); a huge reparations payment (fixed in 1921 at $40,000 m); the return to France of Alsace-Lorraine (German since 1871) and parts of Prussia to a re-created Poland (extinct since 1795); the dismemberment of the German overseas empire and its distribution among the Allied powers; a ban on union with Austria. In addition, the Rhineland was to be occupied by the Allies and the Saarland governed by the League of Nations, with French control of its rich coalfields. Germany lost 13 percent of its pre-war land, 10 percent of its population, 75 percent of its iron ore and 25 percent of its best coal.

The victors' biggest mistake was, perhaps, to exclude Germany from the conference table. Nothing was to be of more capital use to Hitler and the German right than the opportunity given to them to denounce the "diktat" of 1919. It was an imposed peace, not a negotiated one, and one, therefore, to which the German people had never been a party.

1919–1923

PEACE TREATIES

● **1919 Brest-Litovsk Rescinded**
Baltic states of Finland, Lithuania, Estonia and Latvia freed to become independent states; Poland reconstituted; Danzig made a free city with a "corridor" to Poland, giving Poland access to the Baltic.

● **1919 Treaty of Saint-Germain** (with Austria)
Austria ceded land to Italy (Trieste, Istria and the Tyrol), to the new state of Czechoslovakia (Bohemia, Moravia, Austrian Silesia), to Romania (Bukovina) and to the new state of Yugoslavia (Bosnia-Hercegovina, Dalmatia and the new, enlarged Serbia); Austria reduced to one-quarter its former size and one-fifth its former population.

● **1919 Treaty of Neuilly** (with Bulgaria)
Bulgaria cut back to 1914 borders, thus confirming losses of 1913.

● **1920 Treaty of Trianon** (with Hungary)
Hungary ceded more than half its territory, including Transylvania, to Romania; three million Magyars placed under foreign rule.

● **1923 Treaty of Lausanne** (with Turkey, to replace rejected 1920 Treaty of Sèvres)
Turkey surrendered all non-Turkish parts of the Ottoman Empire. As a result of the end of the Ottoman Empire, modern Syria and Lebanon (French mandates) and Iraq, Transjordan and Palestine (British mandates) created.

1919

British Troops Crush Amritsar Rising

Indian nationalism is given a spur

After the mutiny of 1857, Great Britain tightened its grip on India and extended the territory under its control. At the same time it continued with reforms, increasing education among the Indians and bringing them more into administration. With education came the demand for independence.

The Indian National Congress, founded in 1885, made little headway in persuading the British to provide self-government until World War I. The Morley-Minto reforms of 1909, which brought a few Indians into ruling councils, left full power in the hands of the viceroy and the India Office in London. But Indian troops played so large a part in the war that the nationalist issue could no longer be shelved. The hardships of war and a great influenza epidemic fueled discontent and a revolutionary agitation led by Mahatma Gandhi.

An act of 1919, granting partial self-government to the provincial assemblies, was well received by Indian moderates; but whatever good the act achieved was destroyed in April of that year, when Brigadier-General Reginald Dyer ordered Indian troops in the imperial army to fire on a mob at Amritsar. In the masssacre 379 Indians were killed and more than 1,000 wounded.

That bloodshed—the worst since the mutiny—permanently alienated the Indian population from British rule. The initiative passed from the Raj to Gandhi and his civil disobedience campaign, though it took 25 years to bear fruit.

PROHIBITION IN THE U.S.

For 13 years, from 1920 to 1933, the manufacture and sale of alcoholic beverages was forbidden by the 18th Amendment to the Constitution. Prohibition, which had first appeared at state level in Maine in 1851, had its roots in rural, evangelical America. It did not stop people from drinking. In large cities the police connived at breaches of the law. The "roaring twenties," the era of the Charleston and the "flapper," was also the decade of bootleggers and home brewers. The public saloon was converted into the "speakeasy." Disrespect for the rule of law increased, as gangsters—Al Capone was a bootlegger—made huge profits from the black-market trade, frequently in corrupt alliance with agents of the Prohibition Bureau.

1919

League of Nations Established

The United States votes against joining

Into each of the treaties worked out in Paris after World War I, the covenant of the new League of Nations was inserted. Its purpose was to provide an international forum to help secure international peace. Its headquarters were in Geneva in Switzerland.

In both the assembly and council (whose original members were Great Britain, France, Italy and Japan) all decisions were required to be unanimous. The League had no armed force with which to uphold its authority: it was to rely on sanctions against aggressor states. It also formed the Court of International Justice for the arbitration of disputes. One of the first tasks completed by the League was to assign certain parts of the world—chiefly the new states of the Middle East and former German colonies—to the European powers to be ruled as mandates and protectorates.

It was weakened from the start by the refusal of the United States to ratify the Treaty of Versailles and hence to join the League of Nations, so that the world's greatest power, as the United States had become by 1918, remained aloof from its proceedings. Germany was excluded from membership, but was admitted in 1926. The Soviet Union joined in 1934.

The League had a number of successes in settling disputes between small states, and in such matters as bringing aid to refugees and poor nations, but it was impotent in preventing the aggressive actions of Germany, Italy and Japan in the 1930s. It was dissolved in 1946, after World War II, when the United Nations Organization was established.

1922

Irish Free State Established

The dáil votes to accept partition

World War I ended with Home Rule for Ireland on the statute books. It could not, however, be implemented. Nations were being created in eastern Europe, and the Sinn Fein movement for complete independence now commanded southern Irish opinion. In January 1919, Sinn Fein established its own national assembly, the Dáil Eireann, and proclaimed the independent "Free State" of Ireland.

In 1920 the British parliament passed an amending act for Ireland, granting home rule to a Dublin parliament, from which the six Protestant counties of the north were to be excluded. The act was rejected by Sinn Fein, led by Eamon de Valera (representing the military wing) as president and Arthur Griffith (from the civil wing) as vice-president. But in the north a self-governing province, generally called Ulster, with an assembly and government of its own in Stormont, came into existence. Thus came to pass what no Irish leader had ever envisaged: the partition of the country. Two years of war between the republicans in the south and the British troops, known as the "Black and Tans," followed.

In October 1921, Lloyd George called a conference in London, where, on December 6, a treaty making the Irish Free State a self-governing dominion within the British Comonwealth, still owing allegiance to the Crown, was agreed. Although de Valera resigned from the dáil rather than accept non-republican status for the new nation, the dáil ratified the treaty on January 7, 1922. Thus Irish self-government was restored.

1922

Mussolini Marches on Rome

The Fascists seize power in Italy

In the industrial and political unrest of Italy after the war there grew up workers' soviets in factories on the left and, on the right, armed bands of anti-Communist war veterans. Of the latter the most important was the *Fasci di combattimento*, founded in 1919 in Milan by Benito Mussolini, "Il Duce," a former socialist.

Mussolini was elected to parliament in 1921 and made his maiden speech, "antisocialist and antidemocratic" as he said, from "the benches of the extreme right, where formerly no one dared to sit." For two years his black-shirted followers with their symbol derived from the *fasces* of ancient Rome—a bundle of rods enclosing an axe—waged a war of terror on the streets. On October 28, 1922, Mussolini addressed a rally in Naples and declared that he would lead them in a "march on Rome."

In strict formation, 30,000 Fascists marched to the capital (Mussolini himself arrived by train, wearing a bowler hat) and the threat of revolution was enough to win over 400 non-Fascist deputies in parliament. King Victor Emmanuel III invited Mussolini to form a government, and parliament voted him dictatorial powers for a year, enough time for him to remake the state as a totalitarian instrument of the Fascist party.

Fearing a Communist takeover, the capitalists encouraged the Fascists to make their bid for power. Here Mussolini (center), in Naples in 1922, prepares to march on Rome.

1923

Nazis Stage "Putsch" at Munich

Adolf Hitler is arrested and charged with treason

In 1923, when rampant inflation and the French occupation of the Ruhr were rocking the Berlin government, Adolf Hitler saw an opportunity to strike. He had by then forced himself to the leadership of Anton Drexler's German Workers' party, added "National Socialist" to its name, adopted the swastika and styled himself "Führer." On November 8-9 he and General Ludendorff attempted to overthrow the Bavarian state government in the famous Munich *putsch,* intended to be the prelude to an assault on Berlin.

With 3,000 *Sturmabteilung* ("stormtroopers") Hitler marched on the center of Munich. A whiff of grapeshot from the police was sufficient to end the rising in fiasco. Hitler was arrested two days later. At his trial for treason he put on a magnificent show of bombast and right-wing nationalist rhetoric, exploiting the sentiment in Germany that the army had been "stabbed in the back" in 1918 by the "criminal" politicians of the Weimar Republic, who had overthrown the monarchy and accepted humiliation at Versailles. "If today I stand here as a revolutionary," he said, "it is as a revolutionary against the revolution. There is no such thing as high treason against the traitors of 1918."

Hitler was sentenced to a mere five years in Landsberg Prison (Ludendorff was acquitted). There he dictated *Mein Kampf* to Rudolf Hess, a fellow-conspirator, and was released after less than a year. The episode had raised him to national status in German politics.

1926

General Strike Fails in Great Britain

The largest strike in British history collapses after 10 days

Despite the recovery of postwar production in Great Britain, more than a million people were unemployed in 1925, mostly in the old staple industries, above all coal-mining, the largest employer in the country. British mines were running at a loss, and the view of management and the Conservative government, led by Stanley Baldwin, was that exports required lower prices and therefore wage reductions. The Samuel commission of inquiry into the coal industry recommended, in March 1926, a reorganization of the industry and a reduction of wages.

The mine owners rejected these suggestions and demanded lower wages and longer hours. "Not a penny off the pay; not a minute on the day," replied the miners. When the miners refused to accept local wage settlements and reduced pay, they were locked out. That was on May 1. On the same day a trade union conference called for a general strike on May 3, to begin at midnight. Miners, transportation and rail workers, printers, builders, gas and electricity workers and many others came out. Almost none returned until the strike was called off on May 12.

Little violence marked the strike; volunteers kept essential services running. The miners, by refusing to accept Baldwin's offer to implement the Samuel report, returned to work having gained nothing. They were compelled to accept longer hours, lower wages and district agreements. No reorganization of the industry took place. And no general strike has since been called in Great Britain.

During the 10-day strike, armored cars were used to protect food supplies brought from the docks.

1926

John Logie Baird Makes First Television Transmission

Moving pictures are transmitted by radio in London

In 1926, at a laboratory in Soho, London, John Logie Baird, a Scottish inventor, demonstrated television for the first time. Dim, flickering images of faces were seen on a screen, projected by Baird's "televisor," which was unlike later instruments in being partly mechanical. The scanning of objects to be televised was mechanical: light passed through holes on a rotating disk and fell on a photoelectric cell, which converted the light waves into electrical signals. The electric waves were then projected through a second rotating disk, which reconstructed the image on a screen.

In 1927 the American engineer, Philo Farnsworth, used his own invention, the image dissector tube, to devise a completely electronic television transmission. It was publicly demonstrated that year with pictures of Herbert Hoover in his office in Washington. In 1929 the first color transmission (bands of the primary colors on three separate channels) was beamed between New York and Washington using Bell Telephone Laboratories' 50-line system. The first television broadcast of synchronized sound and vision—a variety show from the Coliseum Theatre in London—was made by the British Broadcasting Corporation in 1930.

1927

Chinese Nationalists Take Shanghai and Nanking

Chiang Kai-shek leads the Kuomintang to victory

After the death of Yuan Shih-k'ai in 1915 no national government was able to establish its authority over the clash of rival warlords in the new republic of China. The activities of the Nationalist Party, or Kuomintang, founded by Sun Yat-sen in 1891, were initially restricted to southern China (where it set up a government at Canton). Then, in 1926, Chiang Kai-shek, Sun's successor as leader of the Nationalists, began to advance northward with his "Red Army."

With Russian aid, by September the Nationalists gained control of Hankow, an important treaty port, and Hangyang, the largest military arsenal in the country. In March 1927, they captured Shanghai. Nanking fell in the same month. The revolutionary government had already moved from Canton to Hankow, in central China, and by the autumn of 1928 the Kuomintang had established an effective government.

Chiang had earlier announced that his aim was "a revolution for all the people," not "a dictatorship of the proletariat." He abandoned Sun Yat-sen's policy of alliance with the Communists, whom he resolved to expel from the Kuomintang and to bar from office in his government. So began a struggle for power between Nationalists and Communists which continued until the Communists' victory in 1949.

The Nationalists' struggle caused great confusion in China, with soldiers and refugees crowding together in any available transportation.

1928

Alexander Fleming Discovers Penicillin

A Scottish biologist observes the effect of mold on bacteria

The discovery of penicillin by Alexander Fleming, at Queen Mary's Hospital in London, was an accident. By chance, Fleming left a quantity of staphylococcus bacteria exposed for a few days in his laboratory. He then observed a mold growth on the bacteria and noticed that around the mold patches were areas free from the bacteria.

Fleming was able to identify the mold as *Penicillium notatum*—the sort that often grows on stale bread—and to demonstrate that it could be effective against disease in human beings. However, research to isolate the chemical in the mold that killed the bacteria delayed publication of the results achieved by a group of biologists, notably H. W. Florey and E. B. Chain, until 1941.

The finding marked a dramatic breakthrough in chemotherapy, the branch of therapeutics that began with the discovery in 1911, by the German bacteriologist Paul Ehrlich, of salvarsan, effective against syphilis. Penicillin was the first antibiotic: a drug that not only prevents the growth of a bacterium within the body, but destroys it.

In 1945 Fleming shared the Nobel Prize in Physiology and Medicine with Chain and Florey.

1928

Kellogg-Briand Pact Brings Hope of Lasting Peace

Sixty-five nations sign an agreement renouncing war

In the pursuit of international security after World War I two agreements stand out. The first was the Locarno Treaty of 1925, by which France, Germany and Belgium, with Great Britain and Italy as guarantors, agreed to respect existing Franco-German and Belgo-German borders and the demilitarization of the Rhineland. The treaty failed to prevent the Nazis from sending troops into the Rhineland in 1936.

The second major agreement, the Kellogg-Briand Pact of 1928, was less specific and no more successful. In 1927 the French foreign minister, Aristide Briand, proposed to his American counterpart, Frank Kellogg, a pact to declare that the two countries renounced war as an instrument of national policy. Kellogg succeeded in widening the scope of the agreement by calling a nine-power conference in Paris in 1928. There the Kellogg-Briand pact was signed by the participants at the conference, including Germany (represented at the conference by Gustav Stresemann) and the Soviet Union (still not a member of the League of Nations).

The pact, which was eventually signed by 65 nations, reserved to each nation the right to defend its legitimate interests (i.e., colonies) and made no provision for collective action against aggressors. It thus proved to be impotent against outbreaks of aggression in the 1930s, such as the Italian invasion of Ethiopia in 1935.

1929

"Black Thursday" Hits Wall Street

The collapse of the New York stock market leads to a world depression

Despite worrying signs in the American economy—the high level of public and private debt and a worsening agrarian recession—Herbert Hoover's election as Republican president in 1928 was greeted with enthusiasm by financiers. The *laissez-faire* policies of the "roaring twenties" were to continue. Between December 1928 and September 1929, common stocks in the United States rose in value from 117 to 225; stockbrokers increased their bank borrowings from $3.5 billion in 1927 to $8.5 billion in 1929.

Despite the speculative boom the Federal Reserve Board did nothing to temper its easy credit policy. Yet the economy was heading for recession. By October 1929, steel production was in decline, freight haulage was rapidly falling off, and house-building was nearing a standstill. The financial crash came on October 24—"Black Thursday." In a single day's trading 12,894,650 shares changed hands, at constantly falling prices. Fortunes were ruined overnight.

In the wake of financial collapse came unemployment throughout the industrialized world, though the full effects were delayed for two years. In Great Britain the crisis led to a split in the Labour pary when, in 1931, the prime minister, Ramsay MacDonald, formed a coalition national government with the Conservatives and Liberals. In Germany, where to the burden of reparations payments was added a rise in unemployment, from 1.3 million in September 1929 to 6 million by 1933, the Nazis reaped the whirlwind.

1929

Leon Trotsky Expelled from the Soviet Union

Stalin begins the ruthless elimination of rivals in the Communist Party

From the power struggle in the Soviet Union that followed the death of Lenin in 1924, Joseph Stalin emerged the victor. His chief rival was Leon Trotsky. On the surface the men stood for different approaches to the future of the Marxist revolution—Stalin for "socialism in one country," concentrating on the transformation of the Soviet Union, and Trotsky for the export of the revolution abroad.

By 1925 Trotsky had been removed as the people's commissar for war (in which post he had created the Red Army) and edged out of any policy-making role in the party. In an attempt to block Stalin's rise to dictatorial power, Gregori Zinoviev and Lev Kamenev, originally Stalin's allies in the triumvirate that emerged in 1924, sided with Trotsky. In 1927, as famine produced a crisis in the Soviet Union, Stalin expelled all three from the party as "counter-revolutionaries."

With 30 other anti-Stalinists, Trotsky was sent into internal exile at Alma-Ata on the Chinese border. Two years later he was deported to Turkey. Stalin's power was now virtually unlimited, as was shown a few years later by the famous "show trials" of 1936.

When Trotsky was banished from Soviet territory, he went to the island of Prinkipo, where he completed his history of the Russian Revolution.

1921–1938

SOVIET UNION

• 1921 New Economic Policy
Lenin's relaxation of strict central controls of the socialist economy, after food shortages had provoked peasant riots and economic production had fallen to half of 1913 level; small industry and land restored to private owners; allowed limited freedom of internal trade; heavy industry, transport, banking remained under central control; production back to 1914 level by 1928.

• 1928 First Five-Year Plan
Stalin's reversal of the NEP to achieve "socialism in one country"; priority to heavy industries (industrial output doubled by 1932); enforced collectivization of farms killed some 5 million peasants; burning of crops and slaughter of livestock by resisting peasants caused famine (1932-34); 10–15 million died of starvation. Second Five-Year Plan (1933) concentrated on production of consumer goods; Third Five-Year Plan (1938) cut consumer production to concentrate on armaments.

• 1935–38 Great Purge
Show trials held to rid party of alleged anti-Stalinists; most famous victims were Stalin's early allies Kamenev and Zinoviev; defendants forced to confess to treasonable crimes (plotting to assassinate Stalin, spying for the Nazis); purge extended to army in 1937 and thousands of officers executed or placed in prison camps; perhaps 1 million people executed during the terror and another 12 million allowed to die in prison camps.

1930

Gandhi Marches to the Sea

The Indian nationalist leader is arrested and imprisoned

The campaign for self-government in India after World War I—the British government had promised it in 1917—was led by Mahatma Gandhi. Gandhi had three major aims: self-government, the revival of village industry (especially spinning and weaving) and the abolition of the caste system, with its "untouchables." His method was to organize mass demonstrations of non-violent civil disobedience. His watchword was *satyagraha*, which he defined as "holding onto truth, hence truth-force."

Twice in the 1920s Gandhi was imprisoned by the British authorities; but the election of a Labour government in 1929 heralded a change in imperial policy. In October 1929, the viceroy, Lord Irwin, publicly promised India dominion status. To Great Britain's surprise the reply of the Indian National Congress was to declare independence and begin a fresh wave of civil disobedience.

In 1930 Gandhi, together with 80 supporters, followed by a truck full of hand-woven cotton, marched 320 miles from Ahmedebad to the Gulf of Cambay. There he defied the imperial monopoly of salt manufacture by extracting and tasting some sea salt. He was again imprisoned, and the British began a new, severe policy of repressing nationalist demonstrations.

Gandhi was released from prison in 1931 to attend a Round Table Conference in London. In 1934, having failed to win support for the Congress position, he withdrew from the discussions.

Gandhi arrives at Number 10 Downing Street to meet Ramsay MacDonald and Stanley Baldwin during his 1931 visit to London as sole representative of the Indian National Congress.

1931

Japan Seizes Manchuria

The "Mukden Incident" begins Japan's assault on China

In 1915 Japan presented China with the famous "Twenty-one Demands" that would have reduced China to a Japanese vassal state. They were rejected, but the Japanese intention to exercise imperial sway in Asia was made manifest.

Japan was by far the greatest military and industrial power in the Orient. The Great Depression hit its economy badly, especially the silk industry, for whose products American demand almost vanished. Depression coincided with poor rice harvests and a rapidly rising population.

In those circumstances the vast open spaces of Manchuria looked attractive. Japanese army officers were stationed in Manchuria, where Japan had the South Manchurian railroad and certain iron and coal rights. In September 1931, a group of them, without authorization from the government in Tokyo, exploded a bomb on the railroad near Mukden and blamed it on Chinese saboteurs.

The commander of the Japanese Army in Korea at once ordered his troops to advance on the town, which was captured in 24 hours. The "Mukden Incident" embarrassed the Tokyo government. It accepted a League of Nations resolution calling upon the army to withdraw to the railroad zone. The army ignored the government. By 1932 it had control of the whole of Manchuria and part of Mongolia.

When the League of Nations again called upon Japan to withdraw, Japan simply left the League. Manchuria remained Japanese. Democratic government in Japan was revealed as subservient to the army, and the country entered a decade which its historians call the "Dark Valley."

1932

Cockcroft and Walton Split the Atom

Two Cambridge physicists usher in the nuclear age

At the Cavendish Laboratory in Cambridge in 1932 two physicists, the Irishman Ernest Walton and the Englishman John Cockcroft, carried out an experiment in particle physics that was to change the world. Using a linear accelerator—the world's first atom-smashing machine—they bombarded an isotope of the element lithium with artificially accelerated protons taken from hydrogen.

The result was to transmute the lithium nucleus into a pair of helium nuclei. For the first time nuclear fission (the term was not yet in use) had been achieved by controlled means. (In 1919 Ernest Rutherford had split nitrogen nuclei by firing at them the fast alpha particles that radium emits naturally).

Experimental proof was thus given to Einstein's famous mass–energy equation, $E = mc^2$. Walton and Cockcroft found that the energy of the pair of helium atoms was greater than that of the bombarding protons—a phenomenon explainable only if energy were created by a loss of mass in the interacting nuclei. This mass defect, as it is called, was found to be exactly equivalent to the energy gained, as Einstein's equation predicted.

By 1939 the work of many scientists, especially Lise Meitner, her nephew Otto Frisch, and Hans Bohr, demonstrated that a chain reaction of nuclear fission, without constant artificial bombardment by protons, could occur in uranium-235. The manufacture of atomic weapons became possible.

Walton and Cockcroft received the Nobel Prize for Physics in 1951.

1933

Franklin Roosevelt Introduces the "New Deal"

The president begins a program to fight the Depression

In the speech in which he accepted the Democratic nomination for president in July 1932, Franklin Roosevelt pledged himself to "a new deal for the American people." Overcoming unemployment and the business recession was the great task of his first two administrations (1933-41). The measures he adopted became known as the "New Deal."

The "first" New Deal, of 1933-34, was meant chiefly to stimulate financial recovery and reduce unemployment. At its core were the National Recovery Administration (NRA), the Agricultural Adjustment Administration (AAA) and the Public Works Administration (PWA). Together they helped to restore and stabilize prices, especially in agriculture, and they laid the foundation for the recovery in employment which later took place.

The political significance of the New Deal, after 12 years of *laissez-faire* Republican administration, lay in the central government's intervention in the national economy on an unprecedented scale. The Supreme Court threw out the NRA in 1935 and the AAA in 1936.

The "second" New Deal (1935-40) emphasized welfare legislation and a continued war against unemployment. The foundations of the social security system were laid in 1935, along with the Works Progress Administration and the National Youth Administration. The Wages and Hours Act (1937) established a national minimum wage in certain industries for the first time in American history.

Despite the New Deal, the Depression is real for this Oklahoma family as they trudge in search of employment.

1933

Hitler Sworn in as German Chancellor

The Weimar Republic takes a gamble with the Nazi leader

At the elections to the German Reichstag in 1930 the Nazis took a leap forward. Their vote jumped from 810,000 in 1938 to 6.5 million and the number of their deputies from 12 to 107. At the elections of July 1932, they won 37 percent of the vote and 230 seats, making them the largest party in the country. On the streets, violence mounted. From 6,000 members in 1930, the brownshirted S.A., the *Sturmabteilung*, or stormtroopers, swelled to a formidable private army of 500,000 by the end of 1932.

Ever since the failure of the Munich *putsch*, Hitler had followed a constitutional path to power. He made no secret of his motive. He repeatedly said that his party used parliamentary means to overthrow parliamentary democracy. Yet in the autumn of 1932 negotiations to find a stable government ended with his being given the chancellorship in January 1933.

Conservatives hoped to tame him. Hitler was the head of a coalition government in which Nazis were a minority. "We've hired him for our act," said the ex-chancellor, Franz von Papen. On January 30, 1933, Hitler was sworn in as chancellor, and hour after hour that night a torchlight procession of swastika-brandishing Nazis filed past the chancellery saluting him with shouts of "Heil, Hitler."

1934

Hitler Purges the S.A.

The "Night of the Long Knives" causes little outcry in Germany

By 1934 the Nazi stormtroopers, the S.A., were becoming powerful enough to threaten Hitler's domination of the National Socialist party. Hitler, perhaps genuinely believing fabricated reports of the S.S., the security branch, and the Gestapo, or secret police, that its leaders were plotting against him, decided to destroy the S.A.'s pretensions. In the early hours of June 30, 1934, S.S. officers burst in upon the leader of the S.A., Ernst Röhm, in a hotel just outside Munich. Röhm was taken to a prison and shot the next day.

The purge of the S.A. leaders occurred throughout the country. The S.S. also settled a few old scores that had nothing to do with Hitler's quarrel with the S.A.: Gustav Kahr, who had testified against Hitler at the Munich trial in 1923; Erich Klausener, the leader of Catholic Action; and Kurt von Schleicher, the ex-chancellor, were murdered. In all, 83 summary executions were carried out.

Hitler used Röhm's homosexuality as a justification for his action. Its real purpose was to reassure the army and the Nazi party that the S.A. was no threat to them. Neither the army, nor the party, nor the Church raised a murmur of protest. "You have saved the German people from a great peril," the dying president, Paul von Hindenburg, telegraphed. "He who wishes to make history must also be able to shed blood."

1935

Italy Invades Abyssinia

The League of Nations fails to stop Fascist aggression

The European scramble for Africa in the late 19th century left one country independent: the ancient kingdom of Ethiopia, or Abyssinia as the Italians called it. An Italian attempt to conquer it ended in defeat at Adowa in 1896. Thereafter friction with Italians on the Eritrean and Somali frontiers was never absent, and it continued after 1928, despite that year's pact of friendship between the two nations.

In December 1934, Ethiopian and Italian troops clashed at the oasis of Walwal. Whether it belonged to Ethiopia or Italian Somaliland was disputed; Italy occupied the oasis and demanded compensation for the death of 30 soldiers. Ethiopia appealed to the League of Nations, but in October 1935, without declaring war, Mussolini ordered the occupation of Abyssinia. With the help of fighter planes and poison gas, the Italian army overran the country and proclaimed King Victor Emmanuel emperor. Haile Selassie, emperor since 1930, fled the country.

The League of Nations branded Italy an aggressor and called for economic sanctions against it. Oil, however, was left off the list of sanctioned items, and only an oil embargo might have forced Mussolini to withdraw. Italy retained control of Abyssinia until Egyptian and British forces liberated the country in 1941.

1935

Mao's Long March Ends at Yen-an

A new Chinese "soviet" takes root in the north

After being crushed by Nationalist forces in 1927, the Chinese Communists dispersed and retreated to places of safety. The most important "soviet" was established in the southern mountains of Kiangsi Province. There, a peasant from Hunan, Mao Tse-tung, built up a following among the peasantry, breaking with the official party line that revolution must come from the urban proletariat. In 1935 he became chairman of the party.

His first task as leader was to break out of Kiangsi, where his rebel army of about 100,000 was encircled by 750,000 soldiers of the Nationalist government. In October 1934, Mao and his soldiers began the "Long March" to Yen-an, 6,000 miles to the north in the province of Shensi. The journey, by a circuitous 8,000-mile route along the edges of Tibet's snowy peaks and through the steppes of central Asia, took a year. When Mao reached Yen-an in October 1935, he had lost more than three-quarters of his followers: 70,000 were killed by Nationalists and warlords or by starvation and disease.

In the arid hill-caves of Shensi, Mao began to build another Chinese soviet. For the immediate future the Communists posed no threat to the Kuomintang. But Mao had established himself as the undisputed leader of Chinese Communism and a revolutionary of great strength of will.

Mao's long march

COMMUNIST STRONGHOLDS

CHINGHAI
SHENSI
Wuchu
Yenan
Paban
KANSU
SHANTUNG
Yellow Sea
CHINA
HONAN
ANHWEI
KIANGSU
Nanking
SINKIANG
Chadhua
SICHUAN
HUPEH
Shanghai
Moukung
Luting Bridge
Wuhan
CHEKIANG
Chunking
Ipin
Tayung
Sichang
Tungste
Techang
Tsunyi
KIANGSI
FUKIEN
INDIA
HUNAN
Ningyuan
Yutu
Juichin
Kunming
KWANGSI
KWANTUNG
YUNNAN
Canton
BURMA
TAIWAN
(FORMOSA)
FRENCH-INDOCHINA

1933–1934

GERMANY

● **1933 Reichstag Fire**
German parliament building razed to the ground on February 27; Nazis blamed it on the Communists, though probably the act of a lone young Dutch anti-Nazi, Marinus van der Lubbe; used by Hitler to justify presidential decree of February 28 giving him near-dictatorial powers.

● **1933 Enabling Law**
"Law for Removing the Distress of People and Reich," passed by the Reichstag (minus the 81 Communist deputies) on March 23; gave the government authority to make laws and conclude treaties with foreign states without the consent of the Reichstag for four years; thus overthrew the democratic Weimar Constitution.

● **1933 Concordat**
Nazi agreement with the Vatican to protect Roman Catholic property in return for clerical non-interference in politics.

● **1934 Law for the Reconstruction of the Reich**
State diets abolished and sovereign powers of the states transferred to the Reich; states themselves not abolished, but federalism ended.

● **1934 Abolition of Parties**
Law of July declared the National Socialists the only legal party in Germany; the Catholic Center party, the Democrats and the People's Party had already dissolved themselves, and the Communist Party had had its assets and property confiscated; the Social Democrats and Nationalists were, therefore, the chief victims of the law.

1936

Germany Reoccupies the Rhineland

Hitler breaks the Treaty of Versailles with impunity

By the peace treaty of 1919 the Rhineland—the area of northwest Germany along the Rhine—was made a permanently demilitarized zone. It was also to be occupied and governed by the Allies for 15 years. After demilitarization was confirmed by the Locarno pact of 1925, Germany, through the efforts of Gustav Stresemann, secured the withdrawal of British troops in 1926 and French troops in 1930. The Allied occupation was over.

Hitler's rise to power brought a new element into international relations. In 1934 he took Germany out of the League of Nations. On March 7, 1936, encouraged by the League's failure to stop Mussolini from taking Abyssinia, he sent two divisions of the *Wehrmacht* into the Rhineland. Great Britain, France and the League did nothing more than protest. "I go the way that Providence dictates," Hitler told a cheering crowd in Munich a few days later, "with the assurance of a sleepwalker."

Europe's future was transformed at a stroke. Germany could proceed to build its "Siegfried Line" as a shield for aggressive action in the east. France was exposed to attack. And Hitler was encouraged to believe that the democracies lacked the will to resist him.

1936

Civil War Breaks Out in Spain

General Franco takes charge as Spain falls under dictatorship

The civil war in Spain, which began in July 1936, lasted for 32 months, largely because the two sides were equally balanced in resources. On the one side were the republicans, socialists and Communists, supported by volunteers from the Western democracies; on the other, the monarchists and the Falangists, backed by the Church and assisted by Nazi Germany and Fascist Italy.

In the first six months of the war the rebels, led by General Franco, gained control of the south and west; the republican government of Largo Caballero held on in the north and east, including Madrid. At the end of 1936 the League of Nations obliged foreign states not to intervene in the conflict. The democracies sent no supplies to the republicans; the rebels continued to gain aid from Germany, Italy and Portugal. On April 26, 1937, the undefended Basque town of Guernica was bombed by German planes and Almeria bombarded by German warships.

That aid proved decisive in 1938. In the late spring Franco's forces, swollen by 100,000 Italian troops and outfitted with German equipment, began a thrust eastward to the sea. Barcelona, to which the republican government had removed in 1937, fell in January 1939, Valencia and Madrid in March. On April 7 Spain announced its adherence to the German–Italian–Japanese anti-Communist league.

A million lives had been lost. Franco was installed as dictator and proceeded to build a one-party state on the Italian model. The war showed that the dictatorships would unite to defeat democratic governments. Mussolini named the Italian-German alliance of 1936 the "Rome–Berlin axis"—"around which can revolve those European states with a will to collaboration and peace."

Passions aroused by the war in Spain led to thousands of volunteers from Europe and the U.S., the International Brigades, joining the fight. Massive loss of both Republican and Nationalist life was exacted before the war ended.

1936

Edward VIII of England Abdicates

The king chooses Wallis Simpson over the throne

After a reign of 325 days, King Edward VIII of England, on December 10, 1936, relinquished his crown to marry the American divorcée, Mrs. Wallis Simpson. The king announced his decision in a famous radio broadcast to the nation: "At long last I am able to say a few words of my own...I have found it impossible to carry the heavy burden of responsibility and to discharge my duties as king as I would wish to do without the help and support of the woman I love."

King Edward had informed the Conservative prime minister, Stanley Baldwin, of his intention to marry on November 16. Baldwin took the side of the Church and replied that its "supreme governor" could not marry a divorcée. He was supported by both the Liberal and Labour parties. Nor, after consulting the leaders of Commonwealth countries, did Baldwin find that a morganatic marriage (a private act denying the bride the rank and title of queen) would be acceptable.

Public opinion supported the king, but it was of no account against parliament and the Church. On December 5 Edward agreed to abdicate. Two days after making his announcement he retired with Mrs. Simpson to France, where they lived out their lives as the Duke and Duchess of Windsor.

On New Year's Day, 1939, the Duke and Duchess of Windsor were in the south of France. During the war he was governor-general of the Bahamas.

1937

Nanking Falls to the Japanese

The "Marco Polo Bridge Incident" leads to fresh Japanese aggression

As the 1930s progressed, Japan's government fell more and more under military influence. In 1934 Japan renounced the Washington and London agreements (1922 and 1930) that limited its navy and began a massive ship-building program. By 1935 its army controlled China from the Great Wall south to within 15 miles of Peking (Beijing). The Anti-Comintern pact with Germany in 1936 gave Japan protection against the U.S.S.R. on its northwestern Chinese flank. Japan was ready to bid for empire in the East and the raw materials that the East Indies, the Philippines, Indochina and Malaya could supply to its industry.

From Japan's perspective, World War II began in 1937. On July 7 Japanese and Chinese troops exchanged fire at the Marco Polo Bridge just outside Peking. That began the Sino-Japanese War, which broadened later into the Pacific War. A full-scale invasion of Nationalist China began in August. Peking was stormed, then Tientsin, then Shanghai. In December Japanese forces took Nanking, the capital of Chiang Kai-shek's government, and subjected it to an orgy of murder and destruction. About 200,000 Chinese civilians were slaughtered.

Chiang was forced to move his government to Chungking in the province of Sichuan. The year 1938 opened with Japan in control of China's major cities, its ports and railroads. The United States began to strengthen its Pacific defenses, and President Roosevelt extended a loan to the Nationalists.

THE RISE OF EUROPEAN DICTATORSHIPS

Hindenburg's status as twice-elected German president, World War I hero and champion of traditional right-wing values lent a respectability to his appointment of Hitler, head of the Nazi Party, as chancellor in 1933. The appointment was justified with the slogan, "Never…will the Reich be destroyed if it is united and true."

In Spain, on April 28, 1937, German planes in the service of Franco took the opportunity to flex their muscle by bombing the town of Guernica. Aroused by the horror of so many civilian deaths, Picasso embarked on his famous "Guernica," above right, now recognized as one of the greatest paintings of human suffering. Although it contains no representation of the specific event, it is a powerful warning against the dark forces of barbarian aggression.

When World War I ended in 1918 one singular fact stood out. The democracies had carried the day. The dynastic states had either, like Romanov Russia, collapsed or, like Germany, Austria-Hungary and Turkey, been defeated. The victors were France, Great Britain and its overseas dominions, Belgium, Italy and the United States. The moral seemed to be inescapable, and, except for Russia, where the Bolsheviks had instituted one-party control in 1917, the defeated European nations embarked on democratic experiments as they approached the difficult task of postwar reconstruction.

Yet the interwar years were remarkable, above all, for the emergence of dictatorial, and to varying degrees, totalitarian, régimes in three western European countries. In Italy, united in the 19th century by the liberal patriots of the Risorgimento, Mussolini's Fascists seized power in 1922. In Germany, whose education system was the envy of its neighbors, the fragile Weimar Republic succumbed to Hitler's National Socialists in 1933. And in Spain, whose *cortés* was one of the oldest representative assemblies in Europe, civil war ended in 1939 in the victory of General Franco and the Falangists. It is impossible to say what course Soviet history might have taken had Lenin not died in 1924, except that it would scarcely have been democratic.

The factors that aided the rise of dictatorship varied from country to country. But authoritarian parties everywhere profited

from the instability and unemployment which followed the coming of peace and recruited with great success among dislocated veterans of the war. Without the Great Depression Hitler may never have gained office. It was after 1929 that the Nazis' fortunes took a leap forward. They were also able to exploit the widespread fear of Bolshevism. And all the dictators used language that glorified war and made military greatness the test of a nation's strength.

Totalitarian dictatorship, with its intolerance of any form of dissent, was the logical offspring of 19th-century nationalism, just as authoritarian Soviet Communism had its roots in 19th-century socialism. It was racist and anticlerical because it demanded unadulterated loyalty to the tribe and to the hero-leader at its head. Although political parties, trade unions, a free press, and all the other hallmarks of liberal democratic society were necessarily dictatorship's victims, true totalitarian success was achieved only when the very minds of its citizens were rendered incapable of dissent.

In difficult times democratic societies reveal their strength by resisting the call for a strong leader who can relieve citizens of the burden of choice. Italy, Spain and Germany failed that test. So did Japan. Authority was preferred to freedom, childlike obedience to responsible maturity. Fascism, the pediatrician, Donald Winnicott, wrote in 1940, is a "permanent alternative to puberty."

Popular support for Nazism was helped by the dramatization of the leader cult, and similar methods were applied to promote Joseph Stalin, shown in the Kremlin. His popular image relied heavily on his peasant background and allowed him to be presented as a "father" of the people. However, between 1935 and 1939 he was responsible for the deaths of more than six million Russians, either by execution or in the camps of Siberia. After this ruthless purging of Party followers, the armed forces, government and industry, Stalin exercised complete power over a demoralized Russia. This action fatally weakened Russia against the growing powers of Germany and Japan.

1938

"Anschluss" Unites Germany and Austria

The German people rejoice at the creation of "Greater Germany"

Adolf Hitler's last revision of the Treaty of Versailles—and last achievement without bloodshed—was the *Anschluss*, or union, of Germany and Austria. The way was prepared by an underground Nazi movement, funded from Berlin, which brought terror to Austria's streets and nurtured the virulent strain of Viennese anti-Semitism.

In February 1938, Hitler summoned the Austrian chancellor, Kurt von Schussnigg, to his Alpine residence, the Berghof, and told him of his resolve to absorb Austria into the German empire. Von Schussnigg, who had earlier appealed in vain to the democracies to guarantee Austrian integrity, was forced to sign the "Berghof Agreement." It gave Austrian Nazis freedom to agitate, made Austrian foreign and economic policy subservient to the Reich, and installed Hitler's puppet, Arthur Seyss-Inquart, as Austria's security minister.

On March 8 von Schussnigg announced a plebiscite, to be held five days later, to test Hitler's assertion that the Austrian people wished to unite with Germany. It was never held. On March 11 Nazi troops poured over the border, and Hitler demanded von Schussnigg's resignation.

The next day Hitler entered Vienna to the cheers of vast crowds and signed a law proclaiming the "reunion" of Austria and Germany. At home his popularity reached a new high, once it was realized that mobilization had not brought foreign intervention and that the Führer had again demonstrated his ability to achieve whatever he set out to achieve.

1938

Chamberlain Brings Home "Peace with Honor"

The Munich Agreement dismembers Czechoslovakia

Two weeks after the *Anschluss* with Austria, Hitler told Konrad Heinlein, the leader of the large German population in the Sudeten region of western Czechoslovakia, that the "Czechoslovakian question" would soon be settled. Hitler planned to conquer eastern Europe and build a slave empire ruled by the Aryan master-race. Czechoslovakia and Poland were his first targets.

But in the autumn of 1938 war was averted by a conference in Munich attended by Hitler and the heads of government of Great Britain, France and Italy (Neville Chamberlain, Edouard Daladier and Benito Mussolini). Czechoslovakia was not represented. Chamberlain's purpose was not to protect Czechoslovakia, but to avert war. "How horrible, fantastic, incredible it is," he said in a radio broadcast of September 27, "that we should be digging trenches and trying on gasmasks here because of a quarrel in a faraway country between people of whom we know nothing."

Two days later he and Daladier agreed to transfer the 13,000 square miles of the Sudetenland—almost one-third of Czechoslovakia—to Germany by October 1 and promised a settlement of Hungarian and Polish claims on that country. Eduard Beneš, Czech president, resigned in protest. Hitler declared that the Sudetenland was "the last territorial claim which I have to make in Europe."

Chamberlain brought back to London "peace with honor...peace for our time." "England," Winston Churchill told the House of Commons, "has been offered a choice between war and shame. She has chosen shame—and will get war."

Nazis sticker a Jewish shop during the 24-hour terror of "Kristallnacht."

1938

Anti-Jewish Violence Unleashed in "Kristallnacht"

The German people withhold their approval

Official Nazi policy toward the Jews after Hitler took office as chancellor in 1933 was to encourage their emigration from Germany. Despite persecution and legal disabilities, only one-third of the nation's half-million Jews had left by November 1938, the month in which the first organized mass violence against them broke out.

The murder of Ernst von Rath, a German official at the Paris embassy, by a 17-year-old Polish Jew was the signal for the pogrom. Rath died on November 9. The next night Joseph Goebbels, the Nazi propaganda minister, gave orders to S.S. and S.A. members throughout the Reich to begin "spontaneous" acts of violence against the Jews. During the next 24 hours 100 Jews were killed, hundreds severely wounded and more than 30,000 arrested and sent to concentration camps; 7,500 Jewish shops and businesses were destroyed and 250 synagogues were set on fire.

The result was not what the Nazis intended. *Kristallnacht,* the "Night of Broken Glass," was met by silent disapproval in Germany. Thereafter the Nazis shrouded their plans for the enslavement and murder of European Jewry in secrecy.

1939

Nazi Armored Divisions Invade Poland

Great Britain and France declare war on Germany

World War II in Europe began on Friday, September 1, 1939, when the German *Luftwaffe* bombed Polish airfields and comunications centers, and an army of more than one million—including six armored divisions and eight motorized divisions—poured across Poland's border from every direction. Hitler's aim was to cut off Danzig (modern Gdansk) and the Polish corridor (thus ending East Prussia's separation from Germany) and, by a blitzkrieg, or "lightning war," to conquer Poland before France and Great Britain could mount an offensive in the west.

Poland had received an Anglo-French pledge of support in April. At 9 a.m. on September 3 Great Britain delivered an ultimatum to the German government, giving it two hours to begin a withdrawal from Poland. The ultimatum expired, unanswered, at 11 a.m. and Great Britain declared war. The French declaration followed at 5 p.m. that afternoon.

The Allies, having failed to gain the support of the Soviet Union, could do nothing to save Poland. The German fear of a war on two fronts was removed when Stalin signed a mutual nonaggression pact with Hitler on August 23. Its secret clauses included the sharing out of Poland.

On September 16 Nazi panzer divisions reached Warsaw. Soviet troops entered the country from the east the next day. By the beginning of October, Polish resistance had collapsed. Bliztkrieg—made possible by the strafing power of Hitler's Ju87 Stuka dive-bombers—had notched up its first success that afternoon.

1940

Allies Retreat from Dunkirk

"Operation Dynamo" saves British and French forces from annihilation

In the spring of 1940, after six months of "phoney war," the German blitzkrieg carried all before it. Denmark and Norway fell in April, Belgium and the Netherlands in May, France in June. In an unsuccessful attempt to save Belgium, the British Expeditionary Force (B.E.F.) had advanced into the Low Countries with the French First Army. At first they held their own. But the Germans broke through the Maginot Line of French fortifications at Sedan on May 13. One week later Germany captured Amiens and reached the sea near Abbeville. The Allied forces were cut off.

Forseeing such a disaster, the British had drawn up "Operation Dynamo," a plan for the evacuation of the Allied forces from Dunkirk and its surrounding beaches. The "retreat to the sea" began on May 27 and was completed by June 4.

The plan succeeded beyond the highest Allied expectations. On the first day, only 7,669 troops were evacuated from Dunkirk harbor, which was under constant air attack. The rest of the evacuation was from the beaches north of the town. Every type of vessel was used in the operation. By the end 338,226 officers and men, 139,911 of them French, made it to England. Almost the entire B.E.F. was saved.

Dunkirk was a great triumph, of incalculable benefit to British morale. It was also a great setback. The B.E.F. left behind its artillery, tanks and other equipment. Six destroyers were sunk and 19 damaged; and the Royal Air Force lost 177 airplanes.

Survivors from Dunkirk climb aboard the "Branlebas." The men were ferried out to larger ships lying offshore by some 300 "little ships," such as cabin cruisers and yachts, whose owners answered the call to help evacuate the trapped troops. The operation was a resounding success.

1940

France Falls Under the Swastika

Marshal Pétain heads a government in Vichy

The Dunkirk evacuation succeeded in its defensive purpose, but it left France at Germany's mercy. On May 20 Maxime Weygand was appointed the French Supreme Commander. He established a French line along the Somme in a desperate attempt to defend Paris. The task was hopeless. By June 10 the Germans had captured Rouen. The French government abandoned Paris without a fight and moved to Tours in the southwest. The German army entered the French capital, unchallenged, on June 14 and hoisted the swastika on top of the Eiffel Tower. Weygand advised the government to sue for peace.

Once again British troops were evacuated, 136,000 of them under "Operation Ariel." The French government, led by Paul Reynaud, resigned. Reynaud was replaced by the "hero of Verdun," the 83-year-old Marshal Henri Pétain, who announced France's surrender on June 17. Four days later humiliating peace negotiations took place—at Hitler's insistence in the very railroad car at Compiègne in which the German High Command had surrendered to Marshal Foch in 1918. There were, in fact, no negotiations. Hitler gave the French one hour to accept his terms before the German army would resume the war.

Pétain was made the French prime minister and sent to the spa of Vichy to run a government of the unoccupied southeastern part of France. By 1942, when the Germans occupied Vichy France, he was a puppet dictator of the Nazis.

After the surrender of the French government, the northern half of the country, including Paris, was occupied by Germany. The rest of the country was ruled from Vichy by right-wingers, many of whom had been ousted from office by the Popular Front in 1936.

1940

Germany Thwarted in the Battle of Britain

The "Luftwaffe" fails to clear the skies for "Operation Sealion"

After the brilliant success of blitzkrieg in the spring of 1940, Great Britain stood alone against Germany. Hitler, who had hoped that Great Britain would remain out of the war, leaving him to have his way in eastern Europe, was forced into a battle that his army and navy viewed with foreboding. But Hermann Goering, the chief of the *Luftwaffe*, believed that Great Britain could be knocked out by a massive air strike.

The German invasion of Britain, codenamed "Operation Sealion," called for transporting 260,000 troops, 62,000 horses and 34,000 vehicles across the English Channel. That exercise could be undertaken only if Germany's 1,400 bombers and 1,000 fighters gained supremacy in the air. Against them, Great Britain pitted, at the outset, 591 Hurricane and Spitfire fighters. The air battle, known as the Battle of Britain, began on July 10, 1940. The Germans bombed airfields and shipping, then, from September 7, towns and cities, above all London.

The decisive action of the battle took place on September 15, when 57 German aircraft were shot down against only 26 British losses. Although the air war continued until October 31, invasion was postponed, never to be revived. But the blitz on London—night raids with incendiary bombs, chiefly—now began in earnest: "total war" meant the bombing of civilians to depress morale. It continued well into 1941. Indeed, the worst night of the blitz was the last, May 10, 1941, when in 540 sorties the Germans killed 1,400 civilians. Sporadic attacks on British cities continued until the end of the war.

1941

President Roosevelt Signs Lend-Lease Act

The American economy is placed in the service of the Allies

On December 29, 1940, in one of his radio "fireside chats," Franklin Roosevelt told the American people that the United States "must be the great arsenal of democracy." Six months earlier, against much opposition, Roosevelt had begun to sell navy planes and munitions to the Allies. By the end of 1940 Great Britain needed more help. Its financial reserves were nearly gone, and its foreign trade was very rapidly diminishing.

The United States was still officially neutral. But in January 1941, Roosevelt asked Congress to support those nations fighting in the defense of "Four Freedoms": freedom of speech, freedom of religion, freedom from want and freedom from fear. Congress responded by passing the Lend-Lease Act in March 1941.

The president was empowered to "sell, transfer, exchange, lease, lend" any military equipment to any country whose defense was a matter of vital interest to the United States. Within two weeks Congress had voted supplies to the value of $7 billion. By the end of the war the total had risen to $50 billion. Without that aid Great Britain and the Soviet Union would have struggled to remain in the war after 1941. And the act had the unforeseen benefit of gearing the American economy to war production eight months before the Japanese attack on Pearl Harbor brought the United States into the war.

1941

Nazis Invade the U.S.S.R.

Blitzkrieg receives a setback

Despite the nonaggression pact of 1939 with Stalin, Hitler told his generals in July 1940 that the Soviet Union could be defeated in a six-week campaign. He was obsessed with building an eastern slave empire and exterminating the Jews, and after the failure to invade Great Britain, he turned his attention once more to the east. In doing so, he let slip the opportunity to attack the British empire at its vulnerable points in the Mediterranean and North Africa.

"Operation Barbarossa," to which 148 German divisions—80 percent of the *Wehrmacht*—were committed, began on June 22, 1941. It was to be a three-pronged attack: on Leningrad through the Baltic republics, on Moscow, and on Kiev and the southwest. Romanian and Finnish troops took part. For a few weeks, as Nazi troops advanced deep into Soviet territory, events seemed to bear out Hitler's optimism. The Kiev offensive was a spectacular success and the Ukraine, the Crimea and the Donetz industrial basin fell into Nazi hands.

But the Soviet Union was a vast country with a huge armed strength. It was soon clear that the era of blitzkrieg was over. And by the early winter, when a frontal assault was launched on Moscow, the German troops were short of equipment and winter clothing.

In mid-December Hitler ordered the German lines bogged down on the approach to Moscow to stand fast. He dreaded a Napoleonic retreat, and he was probably right to do so. But the pause in the fighting until spring 1942, by which time the U.S. had entered the war, was to prove disastrous.

The Muscovites dogged defense of their city—here the Bolshoi Theater—and the bitter winter signaled the later defeat of Hitler's armies in Russia and marked a turning point in Germany's fortunes.

1941

Japan Bombs Pearl Harbor

The United States enters the war

By the autumn of 1941 Japan was well forward with its plan to establish an empire, or a "Great East Asia Co-Prosperity Sphere," in the Far East. China lay virtually under its control, and in July it had announced a protectorate over Indochina. There remained Malaya, the East Indies and the Philippines. Negotiations between the United States and Japan to bring a halt to Japanese expansion broke down in the autumn Japan never meant for them to succeed.

On November 26, 1941, a fleet of six aircraft carriers (with 360 bombers and covering fighters), two battleships, two heavy cruisers and 11 destroyers set out from the Kuril Islands north of Japan. On November 27, President Roosevelt warned the navy in Manila and Pearl Harbor on Oahu Island, Hawaii, to expect an attack on the Philippines, Thailand or Malaya. It came on Pearl Harbor in the early morning of December 7.

On that day 2,403 American sailors, soldiers, marines and civilians were killed. Five battleships and 200 airplanes were put out of action. The Japanese returned home having lost 29 aircraft and about 30 men. The next day the United States Air Force in Manila was almost completely destroyed; Guam was bombarded and Japanese troops landed on the Malay peninsula. The United States and Great Britain declared war on Japan on December 8. On December 11 Germany and Italy declared war on the United States.

In the attack, more than 90 ships, including the "West Virginia" and "Tennessee" were badly damaged; the battleship "Arizona" blew up.

1942

The Gestapo Plans the "Final Solution" at Wannsee

Jewish extermination camps are built in Poland

Between 1939 and 1941 the Nazi "euthanasia program" for the mentally ill claimed the lives of 90,000 men and women, most of them killed in purpose-built gas chambers. In those years official Nazi policy toward the Jews was to encourage their emigration. Genocide had to be conducted secretly. In Nazi-occupied Poland, special commando groups, the *Einsatzgruppen*, were liquidating the Polish ruling and educated classes and shooting Jews in the countryside.

By the autumn of 1941 so many Jews had come under Nazi occupation that shooting them could not accomplish their extermination in the time available nor with the essential secrecy. There were 3 million Polish, and nearly 2 million Soviet, Jews alone. The decision was taken to build death camps in Poland; and by an order of October 23 the emigration of Jews from occupied Europe was forbidden.

In January 1942, at a conference in Wannsee, Germany, Heinrich Himmler, head of the S.S., Reinhard Heydrich, deputy chief of the Gestapo in charge of the extermination program, and Adolf Eichmann, who organized the transportation of Jews across Europe, unveiled the details of the "Final Solution." All Jews were to be "evacuated" to the east. "Zyklon-B" cyanide gas was chosen as the murder agent.

As the war turned against him, Hitler became obsessed with leaving behind one great achievement: ridding Europe of Jewry. The final toll of deaths—at Auschwitz, Buchenwald, Belsen, Chelmno, Dachau, Salaspils, Treblinka, the list went on and on—was at least 5 million and probably nearer 6.

1942

Malaya and Singapore Fall to Japan

Great Britain suffers one of its worst military defeats

On December 8, 1941, Vice-Admiral Tom Phillips, commander of the British fleet in Singapore, learned of an imminent Japanese landing on the Malayan coast. He had few planes and no aircraft carriers. He nevertheless put out to sea with the battleship *Prince of Wales* and the heavy cruiser *Repulse*.

On December 10 the vessels were attacked by Japanese bombers and sunk in the Gulf of Siam. Some 3,000 men, including Phillips, died. It was the worst British naval disaster of the war—the first time in history that aircraft alone had sunk such large ships at sea.

Worse, however, followed. The loss of two capital ships was a blow to British pride more than to British strategy. The real deficiency in the Far East was in fighter aircraft. The admiralty had insisted that only the navy should defend Singapore, and as Japanese troops advanced southward down the Malayan peninsula, the lack of aircraft proved critical. The fortress guns protecting Singapore were also ineffective: their armor-piercing shells, powerful against ships, made little impact on the Japanese infantry.

On February 15 General Arthur Percival, commander of the British forces in Malaya, surrendered in Singapore with 130,000 British and empire troops—the largest capitulation in British history. British prestige in the Far East, never before really tested, was shattered. By May Japan had captured Java, the Dutch East Indies, the northern part of New Guinea, the Solomon Islands and Burma.

Prior to the Battle of Midway, the Americans broke the Japanese codes and were able to move a task force into position. Here, Japanese planes try to escape U.S. dive-bombers.

1942

United States Navy Wins Battle of Midway Island

Japanese expansion into the mid-Pacific is halted

A Japanese attack on Midway Island, some 1,150 miles northwest of Honolulu at the western tip of the Hawaiian archipelago, was intended to lure the U.S. Pacific fleet into the open, where it could be destroyed by the larger Japanese fleet. Japan also hoped to capture two American air bases on islands adjacent to Midway.

The battle took place on June 4, 1942. Like the Battle of the Coral Sea in May, it was fought by naval aircraft without the opposing fleets catching sight of one another. Owing to superior American intelligence operations, the Japanese admiral, Isoroku Yamamoto, was outwitted by Admiral Nimitz. The Japanese lost four aircraft carriers to the United States' one in the first Japanese naval defeat of the 20th century.

American forces poured into Australia, New Zealand and Samoa over the next two months. In August they and the Australians gained a beachhead at Guadalcanal in the Solomon Islands. The perimeter of Japanese expansion in the Pacific had been established.

1942

Allies Suffer Heavy Losses at Dieppe

Canadians bear the brunt of a costly rehearsal for D-Day

Churchill and the senior Allied commanders planned, in January 1942, to make an amphibious raid on Nazi-occupied Europe. The purpose was not so much to attempt to open up a second front against the Germans' "Atlantic Wall" as to test German preparedness for an Allied invasion. However by the time the raid took place, on August 19, it was hoped to relieve some of the pressure on the Soviet Union.

In the event, the raid provided no test. When one sector of the operation ran into a German merchant convoy and its armed escort, the landings lost the essential element of surprise. Moreover, neither sufficient air cover nor battleship support was provided for the small landing craft. Of the 6,000 troops who were employed in the raid—5,000 of them Canadians—more than 4,000 were killed or captured.

If any good came of the fiasco, it was to teach the lesson that a repeat invasion needed better planning and more powerful weapons. In the words of Lord Mountbatten, director of the commando raids on Norway and France, "for every soldier who died at Dieppe, ten were saved on D-Day."

1942

Montgomery Leads Allied Victory at El Alamein

The tide turns against the Axis powers in North Africa

The war in North Africa opened well for the Axis powers. After early Italian defeats in Libya, General Rommel—dubbed the "Desert Fox" by Allied soldiers—was made commander of the Afrika Corps in February 1941. By the summer of 1942 he had retaken Tobruk (June 20) and pushed the Allies back 600 miles, almost to Alexandria. He was promoted to field marshal and declared to be "unbeatable."

To stop the Axis advance, the Allied commander, General Claude Auchinlek, chose to make a stand at El Alamein, a small coastal town 70 miles west of Alexandria. The first Battle of El Alamein, which lasted throughout July, was a stalemate. At its end, the Eighth Army had lost 13,000 men and was exhausted, but the Afrika Corps, which had run out of artillery ammunition, had been checked. Auchinlek had prevented an Axis breakthrough to Cairo and the Nile. Even so, disappointed by Auchinlek's failure to continue the fighting, Churchill replaced him with General Bernard Montgomery.

The decisive second Battle of El Alamein was fought in October. In an action reminiscent of World War I, it began with an intense bombardment from 1,000 massed guns. Then British armored tanks advanced and in two weeks routed the Italian and German forces, harassing them with heavy bombing as they streamed back along the coast road to Libya.

Axis losses were 60,000 men, 450 tanks and 1,000 guns. As Winston Churchill, Great Britain's prime minister since May 1940, said, "Before Alamein we never had a victory. After Alamein we never had a defeat."

Believing that the morale of the troops was "the greatest single factor in war," Montgomery took every opportunity to meet his men and boost their confidence.

1943

Germans Surrender at Stalingrad

Nazi Germany faces its blackest day of the war

At a huge Nazi rally at the Berlin Sports Palace in October 1941, Hitler claimed that the back of the Soviet Union had been broken. Russia would never rise again. Then, in December, came the startling news that the attack on Moscow had been halted. With the spring thaw, the attack was renewed.

The offensive of 1942 was based on a fatal miscalculation: to open up a two-pronged attack and attempt to take the Caucasus and Stalingrad simultaneously. Had the Germans gained control of the vital oilfields of the Caucasus before advancing on Stalingrad, the course of the war might have been altered. As it was, the German army was overstretched and vulnerable to counterattack. Hitler refused to believe reports of Soviet armed strength that reached him at his "Wolf's Lair" in eastern Prussia.

By November, 20 divisions of the Nazi Sixth Army, commanded by General Paulus, had made it to Stalingrad, only to find themselves encircled. The German chiefs of staff argued for withdrawal. Hitler, assured by Goering that supplies could be dropped from the air, would not hear of it. "We are not budging from the Volga." The besiegers became the besieged.

Paulus held out until he and his staff were captured on January 31, 1943. The surrender delivered 90,000 German soldiers into Soviet captivity. The battle on the eastern front had been lost, and it was impossible to believe that the German war effort could renew itself. Hitler's last, desperate hope was that the alliance between the Christian, democratic West and the atheist, totalitarian Soviet Union would fall apart.

1943

Warsaw Ghetto Uprising Suppressed

Polish Jews offer heroic resistance to the Nazis

The operation of the Final Solution was so sophisticated that few Jews had the time or opportunity to mount violent opposition. But resistance did occur, most famously in the spring of 1943 in the Warsaw ghetto, where half a million Jews had been walled in since 1940. About 80 percent of the ghetto's inhabitants had disappeared in the previous summer, and news of their fate at Treblinka had reached the remaining 40,000. Jewish rebels decided to fight back.

Their organization, the Z.O.B., had about 500 members, armed with molotov cocktails, grenades, pistols, a handful of rifles and one or two submachine guns. Against them the German commander, Major-General Jurgen Stroop, had a daily muster of 2,000 well-armed men. On April 19, when troops marched in for the final destruction of the ghetto, the Z.O.B. opened fire.

More and more of the ghetto population joined the resistance, and kept fighting. Not until May 16 were they silenced, by which time the ghetto had been reduced to rubble by bombing and arson. Perhaps 70 Jews escaped. The rest died in the fighting or in Treblinka. German losses were 16 killed and 85 wounded, according to Stroop.

The uprising was the first significant urban revolt against the Nazis in occupied Europe. The rebels did not expect to survive. They fought for Jewish honor. Their heroism inspired Jewish resistance elsewhere, and they forced the Nazis to invest a large number of men and weapons in their struggle against the Jews.

The Warsaw ghetto's heroic uprising encouraged and consolidated the resistance movement in other ghettos and in concentration camps.

1944

Normandy Landings Breach the Axis "Atlantic Wall"

The Allies open up a second front in the west

From 1942 Soviet leaders urged the Allies to open up a second front in the west to relieve the pressure on the Soviet Union. In 1942-43, however, they concentrated on North Africa. Apart from the disastrous Dieppe raid in August 1942, there was no cross-Channel invasion of Europe until the landings on the coast of Normandy in 1944.

Stalin was informed of the plan, codenamed "Operation Overlord," at his meeting with Churchill and Roosevelt in Teheran in November 1943. The American general Dwight Eisenhower was appointed the Supreme Commander of the Allied Expeditionary Force, and half a million Americans were transported to Great Britain to take part in the D-Day landings.

On June 6, 4,000 ships, preceded by minesweepers, converged on Normandy. The German chiefs of staff, expecting landings in the Pas-de-Calais and fooled by a feint attack in Flanders, were taken by surprise. Previous air bombing had wrought heavy damage on German coastal defenses, airfields and radar communications.

On the first day 130,000 men were landed (U.S. troops on the western beaches, British and Canadian in the east); by the end of the week, 326,000, on a 50-mile-wide bridgehead; after a month, nearly a million, with only 9,000 killed. On June 7, the day after D-Day, two huge artificial harbors were floated into position, and although only one functioned fully, tanks and heavy equipment and guns could be brought ashore from them with relative ease.

The Allies encountered fierce resistance around Caen, but the Germans were held there while American troops advanced through Brittany and Maine toward the Seine. The liberation of Paris from the enemy was at hand.

1944

Paris Liberated

The "tricolore" flies again on the Eiffel Tower

The D-Day landings of June 1944, by forcing Germany to wage war on two fronts, enabled the Soviet armies to forge ahead in eastern Europe. (Indeed the Germans were fighting on three fronts, since by then they were virtually alone in defending Italy, where Rome fell to the Allies on June 4.) By the end of July all Soviet territory had been liberated, the Nazis had been pushed out of the Baltic states, and Soviet armies stood on the border of eastern Prussia and the outskirts of Warsaw.

On August 15, a new American army, commanded by General Alexander Patch, had landed in southern France. With French reinforcements it advanced up the Rhône valley. General George Patton's Third Army at the same time swept through Orléans and Chartres to meet British troops closing in on Rouen. The Allies now had 2 million soldiers in France.

As the Germans retreated across the Seine, the first of the Allied forces to enter Paris, on August 25, was the French Second Armored Division, commanded by General Jacques Leclerc. Despite pockets of German resistance, the French capital was liberated almost without a struggle. Nearly 20,000 German prisoners were taken.

On August 26 Charles de Gaulle, the leader of "Free France" since 1940, led a victory parade down the Champs Elysées, and his provisional government was recognized by the Allies. The Vichy government retreated before the Allied advance to Sigmaringen in Germany, where it collapsed with the German surrender in April 1945.

Protected by naval gunfire, the U.S. First Army landed on "Utah" and "Omaha" beaches, despite rough weather and strong German opposition.

1945

Berlin Falls to the Allies

Hitler commits suicide in his bunker

In the late summer and autumn of 1944 Soviet troops advanced relentlessly westward through eastern Europe, conquering the Balkan states or leaving Communist partisans to do the work for them. In April they occupied Vienna, and by the middle of the month Marshal Georgi Zhukov's army was in the suburbs of Berlin. Elsewhere throughout the Reich the western Allies were taking 5,000 prisoners a day. Germany was near collapse.

In Berlin, in his bunker under the chancellery, Hitler refused to surrender. In two savage edicts on March 18 and 19 he ordered a general evacuation of western Germany (tantamount to sending hundreds of thousands of civilians to their deaths) and the destruction of every military, communications and industrial installation in the Reich (the so-called "Nero Order"). He intended his conquerors to inherit a wasteland. Two things spared Germany. Albert Speer, who was in charge of armaments and the war economy, went behind Hitler's back and countermanded the sabotage order. And the Allied advance was too swift for evacuation to be carried out.

As bombs fell on Berlin in late April, Hitler prepared his suicide. He would neither be captured nor suffer the fate of Mussolini, who on April 28 was shot and hung up for public display by Italian anti-Fascists. On April 30 he shot himself.

Field Marshal Wilhelm Keitel formally surrendered to the Allies on May 8. Prague was the last city to be liberated, on May 10. The war in Europe was over.

In 1942 Churchill and Roosevelt sanctioned secret work on a nuclear bomb. In August 1945, President Truman unleashed its power on Japan.

1945

A-Bombs Dropped on Hiroshima and Nagasaki

Warfare enters a terrifying new age

President Truman greeted the news that the first atomic bomb had been dropped with the words: "This is the greatest thing in history." The date was August 6, 1945. The target was the Japanese city of Hiroshima. The bomb, made from uranium-235 and called "Little Boy," was carried by a B-29 Superfortress bomber, named *Enola Gay*. It weighed four tons, it had the power of 13,000 tons of high explosive. Dropped from a height of 31,000 feet, it exploded at 1,900 feet. Between 75,000 and 100,000 people died in the fireball and blast wave.

On August 9 a second, plutonium, A-bomb was dropped on Nagasaki. It killed over 80,000 people. The city was flattened. Within five years nearly half a million people died of radiation effects from the two bombs. The bombings had their intended effect. Emperor Hirohito announced Japan's surrender on August 10. The formal surrender took place on September 2 on board the U.S.S. *Missouri*. In 1959 Truman said, at Columbia University, that dropping the atom bomb was no "great decision. It was merely another powerful weapon in the arsenal of righteousness."

1941–1945

ALLIED CONFERENCES

● **1941 Atlantic Charter**
Statement of war aims after meeting of Churchill and Roosevelt in Newfoundland in August: national self-determination, collective security, disarmament of aggressors, economic cooperation; chiefly propaganda exercise.

● **1943 Casablanca Conference**
Meeting of Churchill and Roosevelt in January; Charles de Gaulle attended; planned invasion of Sicily; issued demand for "unconditional surrender" of Axis powers.

● **1943 Teheran Conference**
Meeting of Stalin, Churchill and Roosevelt in November; discussed coordination of D-Day landings and Soviet offensive in the east.

● **1945 Yalta Conference**
Second meeting of Stalin, Churchill and Roosevelt, in the Crimea, in February; Stalin agreed to enter war against Japan and to support United Nations; French, British, American and Soviet occupation zones of postwar Germany agreed; Curzon line and Oder–Niesse line accepted as Poland's borders.

● **1945 Postdam Conference**
Last Allied wartime meeting, July 16–August 2, of Truman, Stalin and Churchill; Churchill replaced by Attlee after July 24, when British election results declared; Allied control of Germany and reparations discussed; Stalin informed that U.S. had A-bomb.

WORLD WAR II

One of the chief causes of World War II was the legacy of resentment left in Germany by defeat in 1918 and by the punitive peace terms forced upon the German nation at Versailles. In the Far East, too, 1918 left business unfinished. Japan's sights remained fixed on the building of an Asian empire, and the progressive militarization of Japanese government in the 1920s and '30s matched Germany's descent into Nazi totalitarianism.

It is not altogether surprising, therefore, that the 1939-45 war should bear striking similarities to its predecessor. Both wars began because a central European power looked aggressively toward eastern Europe (Austria-Hungary in 1914, Germany in 1939), and both were set in motion because France and Great Britain fulfilled treaty obligations to smaller powers (Belgium in 1914, Poland in 1939). In each war Germany faced two Allied European fronts. In each the western democracies leagued themselves with autocratic Russia, and in each the United States came late, but decisively, into the fray.

The second war was, however, more truly a world war than the first. Fighting in the Pacific, Asia and Africa was more extensive and more critical in determining the outcome. It was also far more destructive. Perhaps 10 million recruits died in action on both sides in World War I; the World War II figure was about 24 million. By far the heaviest losses were on the European eastern front: in 1945 the figure for armed forces of the Soviet Union killed or missing was 13.6 million. Sickness and disease added to the toll in 1914-18—a million people died of typhus in the Balkans alone—but the devastation was small compared to the 40 million civilians who in 1939-45 lost their lives from disease, enemy fire, or murder in extermination and labor camps. Japanese and German cities after the war bore somber witness to the destruction wrought by aerial bombardment.

The two wars were similar, too, in the unforeseen consequences of their outcome. War spawned the Bolshevik revolution of 1917 in Russia; 20 years later it provided conditions that helped the Communists to push to victory in China's long civil war. Austria-Hungary was dismembered in 1918; Germany was partitioned after 1945. Europe itself emerged from the war a far weaker element in international affairs than it had been for centuries, and the postwar years brought not only the rise of the United States and the Soviet Union to "superpower" status, but the slow, painful withdrawal of the European nations from their colonial empires.

The great difference between the two wars lay in men's and women's perception of what it was that they were fighting for and what it was they achieved. Whatever they felt at the outset in 1939, by 1945 the West knew that it had defeated two great challenges, from Japan and Germany, to freedom and national independence. The feeling was that moral victory had been won and that human decency had triumphed over barbarism. The feeling of moral uplift gained international expression, when, at Nuremberg, military and political leaders were tried and convicted of "war crimes."

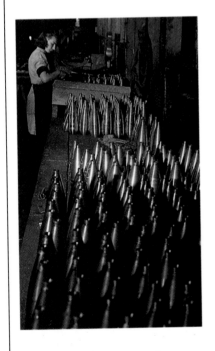

As fighting took its heavy toll, and more and more men enlisted, middle-class women increasingly did their bit for the war effort, working in the fields on farms or even in munitions factories.

A U.S. Marine, his face smeared with protective cream, operates a flame-thrower during the bitter fighting for Japanese-held Guadalcanal.

Against a stark backdrop of devastation and destruction, two German women, with what few belongings they can carry, flee from Berlin as the Russian onslaught intensifies. The Soviet attack on the city was launched from all sides on the morning of April 26, 1945. Although German resistance was ferocious, Soviet superiority in numbers guaranteed the ultimate collapse of German resistance with the taking of the Reichstag on April 30. A Russian soldier triumphantly hoists the Red Flag above the ruined city, probably innocent of the fact that Hitler, sensing impending doom, had taken his life that very day.

1945

War Crimes Trials Begin in Nuremberg

The Allied victors put Nazi "war criminals" on trial

The decision by the victors in World War II—Great Britain, France, the United States and the Soviet Union—to try Nazis for "war crimes" was unprecedented. The court, or tribunal, in Nuremberg had no basis in any sovereign authority. But whatever its status, it acted with full authority to judge and sentence.

The trials lasted from November 1945 to August 1946. In all, 127 German and Austrian political and military leaders were charged, but the principal trial was of 22 leading Nazis. Ten were sentenced to death and executed: Wilhelm Frick (interior minister), Alfred Jodl (army chief of staff), Ernst Kaltenbrünner (head of security), Wilhelm Keitel (head of the chiefs of staff), Joachim von Ribbentrop (foreign minister), Alfred Rosenberg (minister for occupied eastern Europe), Fritz Sauckel (minister for slave labor), Arthur Seyss-Inquart (governor of the Netherlands), Hans Frank (governor of Poland), and Julius Streicher (publisher of the Nazi organ, *Der Stürmer*). Hermann Goering was sentenced to death, but committed suicide on the eve of his execution. Martin Bormann escaped arrest and was sentenced to death *in absentia*. Heinrich Himmler comitted suicide when arrested by the Allies in May 1945.

Seven defendants were given life imprisonment, among them Karl Dönitz, Rudolf Hess and Albert Speer. Three were acquitted: Hanz Fritzsche (head of radio propaganda), Hjalmar Schacht (economics minister), and Franz von Papen (vice-chancellor in Hitler's first government).

1947

Marshall Plan Outlined

The United States promises financial aid to war-torn Europe

World War II was fought at great cost by the nations of Europe. When it ended, many people, their farmland ravaged, faced severe food rationing, even famine. Industrial production was about half what it had been in 1939, and the economies needed to be restored to peacetime production. The loss of so many young men's lives also produced labor shortages. Lend-lease expired in 1945, leaving Great Britain, for example, with foreign debts, mostly to the United States, of $14,000 million.

The United States, untouched by fighting on its soil, emerged from the war as the world's economic superpower. On June 5, 1947, the secretary of state, General George Marshall, suggested an aid package for Europe. France and Great Britain immediately accepted the idea. The Soviet foreign minister, Molotov, after lengthy negotiations, rejected it. Neither the Soviet Union, nor the eastern European countries behind the new "Iron Curtain," therefore, received help under the European Recovery Program, which was popularly known as the Marshall Plan. (Finland and Spain also decided to reject the proffered American aid.)

The aid was offered on condition that the European nations take steps toward closer economic cooperation. In April 1948, the Organization for European Economic Cooperation was formed by 18 countries. By 1952, when some $17,000 million had been sent to Europe as grants—Great Britain received the most, followed by France, West Germany and Italy—plus additional sums in loans, industrial and agricultural output had recovered to pre-war levels.

WORLD HEALTH

Medical advances in the industrial world were extended to the Third World after 1945 with mixed results. In Europe the conquest of disease was spread over time, and the birth rate accommodated itself to a falling death rate. In the Third World the story has been different. In Sri Lanka (Ceylon) DDT virtually extinguished the malarial mosquito between 1945 and 1952: the death rate fell from 22 to 14 per 1,000 in the year 1946-47, and the annual rate of population growth soared to 4.5 percent. The death rate in Mauritius, over a seven-year period, fell from 27 to 15 per 1,000; the growth rate rose to 5 percent. Such abrupt increases in population, caused by the failure of birth rates to match the much lower death rates, puts great strain on the resources of Third World countries and increases poverty among their people.

1947

The Sun Sets on the Raj

India and Pakistan celebrate national independence

In order to win cooperation from India during World War II, Sir Stafford Cripps was sent there in 1942 to offer it self-government, the road to which had been opened by the 1935 India Act. Gandhi rejected the plan. Both he and the Indian National Congress held out for full independence.

After the war the new Labour government, led by Clement Attlee, honored its long commitment to independence. Lord Mountbatten, the last viceroy of India, presided over the twilight of the Raj and smoothed the path to independence by his diplomacy. The chief difficulty was the opposition of the Muslims of northern India, represented by Muhammed Jinnah and the Moslem League, to absorption into a primarily Hindu dominion. In elections immediately after the war the League had won overwhelming victories in Muslim areas, giving substance to Jinnah's demand for a separate Pakistan, including the Punjab and five other provinces.

Great Britain set a deadline of mid-May 1948 for its withdrawal from the subcontinent, and the Congress Party, led by Jawaharlal Nehru, reluctantly agreed to partition. On August 15, 1947, independent India and Pakistan (much smaller than Jinnah had fought for) came into existence within the Commonwealth. Fierce fighting, costing 200,000 lives, followed, chiefly in the Punjab; and 2 million refugees were exchanged by the two sides. Nehru became the first prime minister of India, Jinnah the first president of Pakistan's constituent assembly.

1948

South Africa Chooses "Apartheid"

The Nationalists win an election on a full segregationist platform

The victory of the predominantly Afrikaner Nationalist party, under Dr. Daniel Malan, in the 1948 elections in South Africa did not mark a sharp discontinuity in the country's racial history. Pass laws to restrict the movements of blacks had been introduced into the Cape as early as 1760, and legislation to deprive blacks of the franchise was passed in the British Cape Colony in the 1890s. But the victory, which threw out of office the more liberal government of Jan Smuts, was won on a frank promise to secure the safety of the white population (about 20 percent of the total) by complete racial *apartheid*, or separation.

The promise was kept. The Population Registration Act of 1950 required that every inhabitant be classified as white, colored (of mixed descent) or black. It was the basis on which other legislation—for example, the prohibition of mixed marriages (1949) and acts of the 1950s to segregate education—could be enforced. At the same time, the pass laws were coordinated and strengthened for their more efficient enforcement, and the Group Areas Act (1950) laid down rules for strict segregation in property ownership, residential areas, employment and trade.

Because of its racial policy South Africa was virtually forced to withdraw from the Commonwealth in 1961. Banned from the 1964 and all subsequent Olympic Games, it has now (1991) been readmitted.

Black sitters looking after white children were exempt from the color bar in this Johannesburg playground.

1948

Communists Seize Power in Czechoslovakia

All of eastern Europe is brought within the Soviet bloc

By the end of World War II the Soviet Union had occupied the Baltic states, part of eastern Finland, much of eastern Prussia and eastern Poland, the Ruthenian region of Czechoslovakia, and the Bessarabian part of Romania. Those regions were, as it turned out, simply absorbed into the Soviet Union. Soviet predominance in the rest of eastern Europe (except Greece) was recognized by the West at Yalta in 1945. That predominance was, however, meant to be temporary: it was agreed that, throughout Europe, national self-determination, expressed at free elections, should be upheld.

Most eastern European states formed "popular-front" governments with Communists at the forefront. Their refusal to accept Marshall Aid in 1947, and the founding of the Cominform (Communist Information Bureau), a kind of resurrected International of the east, revealed Stalin's resolve to form a united Communist bloc against the West. Opposition parties were suppressed. Except in Czechoslovakia, elections returned Communist majorities.

In 1946 the Communists gained only 38 percent of the vote in Czechoslovakia. To prevent further losses at elections scheduled for 1948, the party staged a *coup* in February. Communist control of the police and paramilitary party "action committees" forced the center and right-wing members of President Eduard Beneš' government to resign. Armed demonstrations and industrial strikes secured the formation of a Communist-dominated government. The Soviet bloc was now fully in place.

1948

State of Israel Founded in Palestine

The first Arab–Israeli war continues into 1949

In 1897 Theodor Herzl presided over the first Zionist Congress in Basel, Switzerland and from that date it was the object of Zionists to found a Jewish state in Palestine. For nearly 2,000 years there had been few Jews living there. When World War I began (and Palestine was part of the Ottoman Empire), the number was 85,000, compared to 535,000 Arabs. In 1917 the British foreign secretary, Arthur Balfour, promised that Great Britain would use its "best endeavors" to secure for the Jewish people a "national home" in Palestine.

In 1918 Great Britain was given a mandate over Palestine, and in the interwar years Jewish immigration continued. By 1939 the number of Jews was more than one-third that of the Arab population. Though Arabs sold land to Jews, and the British authorities tried to maintain amicable relations between the two groups, terrorism and rioting approached open warfare by 1938.

After World War II the West felt obliged to assist the survivors of the holocaust. An Anglo-American inquiry recommended the immediate intake by Palestine of 100,000 Jews. Great Britain still hoped to erect a bipartisan Palestinian state. The American government bowed to domestic pressure from the Jewish lobby. The outcome was the United Nations' partition of Palestine in 1948, and the creation of an independent Israel and an enlarged Jordan to include eastern Palestine. War between Israel and Arab states opposed to its creation lasted until March 1949.

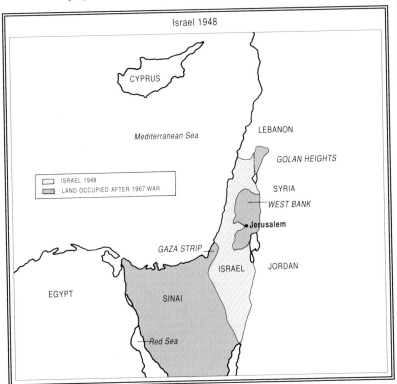

1948

Soviet Union Blockades West Berlin

The Western powers mount a round-the-clock airlift

By an agreement reached at Yalta, Berlin, like Germany itself, was divided into four zones to be administered by the Soviet Union, the United States, Great Britain and France. From their zones in West Germany the Western powers were granted corridors of access to the city through the Soviet zone (east Prussia). Disputes arose early over elections in the city and over the introduction in 1947 of a new West German currency, which the Soviet authorities rejected for Berlin.

On March 20, 1948, the Soviet delegates walked out of a meeting of the Allied Control Council that governed Germany and claimed that it no longer functioned. Ten days later restrictions were placed on rail traffic to Berlin. By May the Soviet army was effectively blockading Berlin by stopping all road traffic from the west as well. Great Britain and the United States responded by organizing a round-the-clock airlift of food, fuel and other essentials to the western sector of Berlin. Fear of potential war brought the Soviet Union to negotiations in February 1949. In May the blockade was lifted and, after 200,000 flights, the airlift ended.

The West had successfully stood up to Soviet pressure. The episode contributed to the formation in 1949 of the North Atlantic Treaty Organization (NATO) to provide for the collective self-defense of western Europe. Its direct consequence was to divide Berlin into two distinct sections and Germany itself into the Soviet-dominated German Democratic Republic (East Germany) and the Federal Republic of Germany in the west.

With immaculate organization, planes flew in supplies to Templehof Airport at the rate of one every four minutes.

1949

People's Republic of China Founded

The civil war ends in victory for Mao and the Communists

Japan's defeat in 1945, and its withdrawal from Manchuria and northern China, brought the struggle for ascendancy between the Chinese Communists, led by Mao Tse-tung, and the Kuomintang, or Nationalist, government of Chiang Kai-shek to a head.

Communist guerrillas established themselves in Manchuria, while the Kuomintang, aided by American air and naval supplies, moved thousands of troops into the cities of northern and eastern China. The attempt of the American general, George Marshall, to negotiate a coalition government failed, but in December 1945 a truce was declared officially between the two factions.

The truce ended in July 1946, and civil war began in earnest. After initial Kuomintang successes, the Communists slowly gained the initiative; and by 1948, when they established control of Manchuria and pushed decisively into northern China, the government forces were near collapse. Famine and high inflation combined to weaken the Nationalists' hold on their territory. In January 1949, Tientsin and Peking (Beijing) fell to the Communists, followed quickly by Nanking, Shanghai and Canton.

By the late summer the war was over. On October 1, 1949, the People's Republic of China was proclaimed. A number of non-Communist political groups were invited to work with the Communists; in fact, a single-party dictatorship was established by Chairman Mao. Chiang fled to the island of Taiwan (Formosa) and established a Nationalist government there.

1950

North Korea Invades to its South

The United States and United Nations defeat Communist aggression

At the end of World War II Korea was divided along the 38th parallel into two occupation zones, Soviet in the north, and American in the south. By 1948 these had become the People's Democratic Republic and the Republic of Korea, popularly called North and South Korea.

In a surprise attack on June 25, 1950, Communist troops from North Korea invaded the south. The United States at once lent South Korea military, naval and air support, and the United Nations supplied troops from 15 other nations to serve under the command of the U.S. general, Douglas MacArthur. By October MacArthur had driven the Communists back across the 38th parallel and captured the capital of Pyongyang; by November they had been forced to retreat to the Yalu River (the border with China). China then entered the war on behalf of North Korea, whose troops again invaded the south and took Seoul, the capital, in January 1951.

MacArthur called for an all-out war against Communism in the Far East; President Truman restricted his ambition to a war of "containment" to restore the *status quo ante bellum*. MacArthur was relieved of his command for publicly quarreling with the president and replaced by General Matthew Ridgway. Negotiations for a truce began in July 1951, but a ceasefire was not secured until July 1953. The subsequent peace settlement confirmed the 38th parallel as the border between the two countries. The war cost about 3 million lives in all.

U.N. chaplains read the funeral service at a mass burial of men killed in action on the Korean front line.

1952

Mau Mau Violence Breaks Out in Kenya

The Kikuyu tribe seeks to drive white farmers off their land

One of the earliest manifestations of the post-1945 upsurge of anti-colonial nationalist movements in Africa was the creation in 1948 of a secret society, the Mau Mau, by the Kikuyu tribe of Kenya. The society, which was infused with a strong religious reaction against the Christian Church established by missionaries, did not avow political independence as its object. It sought to drive colonial settlers off land taken from the Kikuyu people.

Under the leadership of Jomo Kenyatta, the Mau Mau began a terrorist campaign in October 1952. Kenyatta was arrested within a few days and kept in prison until 1959. The Mau Mau lost support among the Kikuyu people by murdering those who held aloof from the struggle, especially by the massacre of 80 Africans in Lari in March 1953. The rebellion was not finally ended until 1956, when the Mau Mau were driven into the highlands and the Kikuyu restricted to a heavily guarded area.

In the war 11,000 or more Mau Mau rebels were killed along with nearly 2,000 other Africans. The imperial troops and white settlers suffered fewer than 250 casualties. The state of emergency, proclaimed by the British government in October 1952, was not lifted until 1960, when Great Britain began the transformation to Kenyan independence, which was achieved in 1963. In 1964 Kenyatta became the new republic's first president.

1953

Structure of DNA discovered

Francis Crick and James Watson unravel life's basic genetic matter

DNA, or deoxyribonucleic acid, is the genetic substance of all living cells. It is the programer of life, the means by which information, encoded in the structure of DNA molecules, is passed on from generation to generation. It was discovered by the German biochemist Friedrich Miescher in 1869. But nearly a century passed before its structure was determined.

In 1951 James Watson, a young American biochemistry student, saw X-ray diffraction studies of DNA by the English biophysicist Maurice Wilkins at a scientific meeting in Naples. The pictures aroused his interest in the search for the molecular structure of DNA, and he went to Cambridge University to work with the molecular biologist Francis Crick. Two years later he and Crick produced their model of DNA.

Previous research had shown that DNA consisted of alternating phosphate and sugar groups, along with nitrogenous bases attached to the sugars. The Watson-Crick model showed DNA as a double helix, somewhat like a spiral staircase: two intertwined sugar-phosphate chains with two sets of flat-lying base pairs (adenine linked to thymine and guanine to cytosine) forming steps between them. Because the two chains were complementary, each would serve as the pattern for the formation of the other if they were separated. It was thus discovered how genes and chromosomes duplicate themselves. Crick, Watson and Wilkins shared the 1962 Nobel Prize in Medicine and Physiology.

From top to bottom: Watson, Crick and Wilkins, who published their paper in the journal "Nature" and, in fewer than 1,000 words, opened the door to modern molecular genetics.

1954

Algerian Nationalists Rise Against French Rule

Independence is gained after an eight-year war

Algeria was colonized by France in the 1830s and retained until 1962. For most of that period the Muslim population was given no political rights, though in 1919 a few Arabs who took French citizenship and renounced Islam were given the vote, and in 1947 a restricted citizenship was granted to them.

Throughout the 20th century the standard of living of Algerians declined, partly because French merchants expropriated grain-growing land and turned it over to vineyards. In 1947 France promised to introduce self-government, but no steps were taken to implement that promise. The result was a guerrilla war waged by the Algerian National Liberation Front, known as the (FLN).

The FLN, led by Ahmed Ben Bella, began the liberation struggle in the Aures Massif on November 1, 1954. Throughout the war the French imperial forces remained in control; in 1962 the armed struggle was still at a stalemate. But the loss of a million lives and the repression of the Algerian population weakened the resolve of Paris to maintain the colony.

In Evian in March 1962, Georges Pompidou, the prime minister of France, and Ben Bella agreed to an immediate ceasefire, to the withdrawal of French troops from Algeria by the end of the year, and independence for Algeria. In a plebiscite on July 1, offering a choice of integration with France, self-government with association with France, or independence, 91 percent of Algerians voted for the country's independence.

1954

Dien Bien Phu Falls to the Viet Cong

The knell is rung on the French presence in Indochina

The defeat of Japan in 1945 left a vacuum in Indochina (Cochin China, Tonkin, Annam, later united to form Vietnam, Laos and Cambodia). Power was exercised in the north by nationalist forces led by the Communist, Ho Chi Minh. In September 1945, Ho proclaimed the Democratic Republic of Vietnam. France, however, was eager to restore its colonial authority in the area (abandoned to the Japanese in 1941), and war broke out in 1946.

It continued until 1954, when the nationalist guerrillas won a decisive battle at Dien Bien Phu, a village in northern Vietnam. The French commander, General Henri Navarre, captured the village in November 1953, and turned it into a French fort. Viet Minh forces, under General Giap, positioned heavy artillery in the surrounding hills and prevented supplies from reaching the villlage. After eight weeks of siege and heavy bombardment, the French surrendered on May 7, 1954. Of the 16,500 troops garrisoned at Dien Bien Phu only 9,000 survived, and many of them died in prison camps.

An armistice was signed in July, and by the Geneva Agreements Laos and Cambodia gained their independence. Vietnam was partitioned, and Ho Chi Minh was tacitly recognized as the president of North Vietnam. South Vietnam was ruled by an American-backed anti-Communist government. In 1954 the United States, France, Great Britain, New Zealand, Thailand, Pakistan and the Philippines formed SEATO (Southeast Asian Treaty Organization) to defend Asia against communism.

1956

Nasser Nationalizes the Suez Canal

The United States refuses to back Anglo-French military action

In June 1956, the last British troops protecting the international status of the Suez Canal left the region in accordance with a 1954 agreement with Egypt. A month later, on July 26, the president of Egypt, Gamal Nasser, having failed to get international financial backing for the proposed Aswan Dam on the Nile, nationalized the Suez Canal Company, in which the British government and French investors were the chief shareholders.

In October, a surprise Israeli attack on Sinai was followed by an Anglo-French invasion. When their demands for an Israeli–Egyptian ceasefire were rejected by Nasser, the British and French governments attacked Egyptian military bases from the air and landed troops at Port Said. But they had failed to secure the backing of either the Soviet Union or the United States, and American pressure and the willingness of the United Nations to send a peacekeeping force to the area stopped the invasion. Israel withdrew from Sinai.

The consequences of the Anglo-French adventure, which made manifest Great Britain's lost status as a great power, were varied and widespread. Anthony Eden, the British prime minster, lost esteem both in the Commonwealth and at home and resigned in January 1957. Nasser, having successfully stood up to the West, assumed leadership of the Arab World and in 1958 formed the United Arab Republic with Syria.

Indian paratroopers from the United Nations peacekeeping force start a tour of duty in the Suez buffer zone.

1956

Soviet Troops Crush Hungarian Reform Movement

Imre Nagy is replaced as premier by Janos Kadar

The death of Joseph Stalin in 1953 was followed by a softening of the Soviet Union's attitude toward its satellite Warsaw-Pact states. At the 20th party congress in February 1956, the Soviet leader, Nikita Khrushchev, denounced Stalin in a speech that encouraged liberal elements throughout the Soviet bloc. In Hungary it coincided with a food and fuel shortage and the resignation in July (with Soviet encouragement) of the hard-line party leader Matyas Rakoski.

The new prime minister, Imre Nagy, reduced the power of the secret police, released political prisoners, announced a return to multiparty politics and free elections, and, with the Kremlin's approval, the withdrawal of Soviet troops from the country. Finally, Nagy announced that Hungary would withdraw from the Warsaw Pact.

Neither the Kremlin nor the Hungarian party secretary, Janos Kadar, was ready to accept such a sweeping and rapid change in Hungary's international status. On November 4, Soviet tanks re-entered Hungary in support of Kadar, who had established a rival government to Nagy's in eastern Hungary. Supporters of the "counterrevolutionary" Nagy and their buildings in Budapest were fired upon. Refugees numbering more than 200,000 escaped to the West. Nagy himself was arrested and executed, and Kadar installed as prime minister. One-party rule was thus maintained, and Hungary was kept within the Warsaw Pact.

1957

President Eisenhower Sends Federal Troops to Little Rock

Washington forces Arkansas to desegregate its schools

In a unanimous 1954 judgment on racial segregation in schools, in the case of *Brown v. the Board of Education, Topeka, Kansas,* the United States Supreme Court ruled that segregated education contravened the 14th amendment to the constitution. This guaranteed every citizen the "equal protection of the laws." The court thus overthrew the 1896 ruling that public institutions could be racially "separate," as long as they were "equal." In May 1955, the court required that school districts carry out desegregation "with all deliberate speed."

At the beginning of 1957 no school in the south had been desegregated. A federal court ordered that a start be made in Little Rock, Arkansas, that autumn. In reply, the governor of Arkansas, Orville Faubus, called out the National Guard, or state militia, to prevent black students from enrolling at Central High School. President Eisenhower sent federal troops to Little Rock to uphold the rule of law. On September 25, protected by 1,000 paratroopers, nine black children entered the school.

Legal quarrels followed, and in June 1958, the school board of Little Rock won an order from a district judge permitting it to delay integration for two years. By 1960 there was still no integrated school in Alabama, Georgia, Louisiana, Mississippi or South Carolina.

1955–1965

UNITED STATES: CIVIL RIGHTS

● **1955 Alabama Bus Boycott**
Rosa Parks arrested for refusing to give up seat to a white man in Montgomery; Martin Luther King organized blacks to boycott the buses; King emerged as national leader and in 1957 formed the Southern Christian Leadership Conference for nonviolent civil rights agitation.

● **1962 University of Mississippi Desegregated**
James Meredith refused admission; Supreme Court ruled that he must be admitted; state governor Ross Barnett used police to prevent Meredith from enrolling; President Kennedy upheld court decision by sending federal troops to the campus at Oxford; Meredith then registered.

● **1964 Civil Rights Act**
Made racial discrimination in places of public accommodation illegal; strengthened statutes for black voter registration; established Equal Opportunity Commission to fight discrimination in employment; empowered federal agencies to withold funds from state projects that discriminated against blacks.

● **1965 Voting Rights Act**
Replaced existing method of individual lawsuits to gain registration to vote; empowered federal agents to enroll voters in any district where less than 50 percent of the adult population was unregistered; great increase in black registration in the Deep South in next three years.

1957

The Soviet Union Launches Sputnik

A small satellite orbits the earth as the Space Age begins

The Soviet Union became the first country to explore space with a man-made satellite when *Sputnik I* was launched into orbit on October 4, 1957. It weighed 184 lb. and was 23 inches in diameter. It traveled 500 miles above the earth's surface at a speed of 18,000 mph, or 95 minutes per orbit. From two radio transmitters it emitted signals which were clearly picked up by receivers throughout the world.

One month later the Soviet Union launched *Sputnik II* with a live animal, a dog named Laika in order to study the effect of weightlessness on a living being. She survived without any difficulties until the oxygen ran out. On January 4, 1958, after 1,367 orbits, *Sputnik I* disintegrated on re-entering the earth's atmosphere. *Sputnik II* also failed to return.

On January 31, 1958, the United States launched its first satellite, the 30-lb., grapefruit-sized *Explorer I*. It orbited the earth at altitudes of between 230 and 2,000 miles and was responsible for the discovery of the Van Allen radiation belts.

The first man in space was the Soviet astronaut Yuri Gagarin, who was launched, on April 12, 1961, in the *Vostok I* spacecraft, weighing almost 5 tons. He reached a maximum altitude of 188 miles and returned safely after completing one orbit in just under 90 minutes.

The world's first traveler in space, Laika, in Sputnik II; three other dogs preceded Gagarin into space.

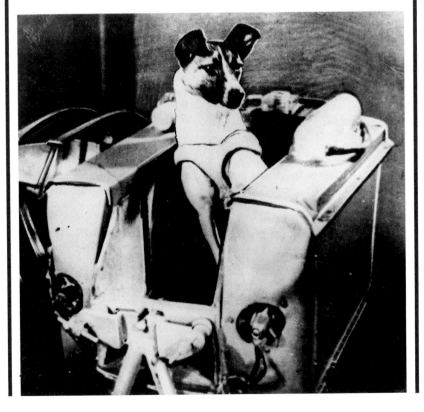

1957

European Economic Community Established at Rome

Six nations sign a treaty to bind themselves to economic cooperation

By the Treaty of Rome, concluded in 1957, six European countries—Belgium, France, Italy, Luxembourg, the Netherlands and West Germany—formed the European Economic Community, popularly known as the Common Market. It came into existence on January 1, 1958. On the same day the six countries also came together in Euratom (the Atomic Energy Commission) to develop the peaceful uses of atomic energy.

The EEC was formed to establish a common market with free movement of people, goods and capital within its borders. It was also to develop a common external tariff policy and a common agricultural policy. Its institutions were, and have remained, the Council of Ministers and the Commission, the joint executive arm of the community, and an Assembly, with a debating function. The European Court of Justice was established to settle any legal disputes arising from EEC matters.

In 1959 a ring of seven outer European states—Austria, Denmark, Great Britain, Norway, Portugal, Sweden and Switzerland—formed the European Free Trade Association (EFTA), a much looser alliance with the sole important objective of working toward free trade among the countries within it.

The EEC became the European Community (EC) in 1967, when the executives of the EEC, Euratom, and the European Coal and Steel Community merged. The EC gradually acquired new members: Denmark, Ireland, Great Britain (all 1973), Greece (1981), Spain and Portugal (both 1986).

1958

China Takes a "Great Leap Forward"

A radical economic program ends in failure

In May 1956, Chairman Mao launched a campaign of liberalization in China. Criticism and open debate were to be let loose. To Mao's displeasure, the Communist party and its chairman themselves came under attack. At the same time unemployment remained high and industrialization proceeded slowly. The result was a return to hard-line, Marxist-Leninist orthodoxy and the implementation of a radical economic program, called the "Great Leap Forward."

At its heart was the establishment of large farming communes—the precursors, Mao promised, of a truly Communist society. Increased agricultural output was to finance the development of light and heavy industry. Coal mining and steel production were to be attached to the communes. This transformation of the economy was to be accompanied by communal regimentation, reduced consumption, and the abolition of material incentives to the workers. It was to be achieved by enthusiasm for the Communist millenium. About 24,000 communes were organized, each with a population of about 30,000. But by 1961 the economy was near ruin. It had been hit by three successive years of natural disasters and, in the wake of the Sino-Soviet split after Khrushchev's anti-Stalinist speech of 1956, by the withdrawal of Soviet technical aid. The Great Leap Forward was abandoned.

This Chinese poster promises a bright new future with the collectivization of agriculture: a smiling and newly clothed community, supplied with modern farm equipment, looks forward to years of security. In actuality, more than 50 million people died in the course of the Great Leap Forward, which was marked by tyranny, inefficiency and isolation.

1959

Fidel Castro Overthrows Batista in Cuba

The United States backs the successful resistance movement

Except for the years 1944-52 Cuba was ruled from 1932 to 1959 by the dictator, General Fugencio Batista, either directly or indirectly through puppet presidents. Against his repressive régime, in 1956 the young revolutionary lawyer Fidel Castro organized a guerrilla force (which included Ché Guevara) in the Sierra Maestra mountains.

The United States, alarmed by the suspension of Cuba's democratic constitution in 1952 and the increasingly tyrannical rule of Batista, ended the supply of arms to Cuba. Instead they lent aid and encouragement to Castro, who promised a return to democracy and the restoration of civil liberties.

On January 1, 1959, after 25 months of guerrilla warfare, in which Castro's propaganda campaign brought more and more Cubans to his side, the rebel forces entered Camp Colombia, the headquarters of Batista's army. The army, thoroughly disaffected, offered no resistance. Batista himself had fled to the Dominican Republic the day before.

The victory of the revolution was proclaimed and a new government installed under President Manuel Urrutia in the provisional capital of Santiago de Cuba, Castro's headquarters throughout the guerrilla war. Castro became prime minister and minister of the armed forces. Elections were promised within 18 months. None has yet taken place.

1960

Sharpeville Killings Stun Blacks of South Africa

Police open fire on pass-law protesters

On March 21, 1960, 20,000 black men and women besieged the police station in the black township of Sharpeville, near Vereeniging, in the southern Transvaal. They were demanding an end to the pass laws requiring black and colored people to carry identification pass-books at all times and severely restricting their freedom of movement.

The police fired on the unarmed demonstrators, killing 67 of them and wounding another 186. It was the worst incident of racial strife since the formal introduction of *apartheid* in 1948. The South African government, led by Hendrik Verwoerd, declared a state of emergency. On March 30, 30,000 blacks marched to the center of Cape Town to demand the release from prison of their leaders.

The killings and the march drew unprecedented world attention to the state of South Africa. Condemnation of the government by the Commonwealth led to South Africa's withdrawal from the organization in 1961. The United Nations, its African membership increased by newly independent nations, condemned *apartheid*; and in 1962 the general assembly passed a resolution calling for economic and diplomatic sanctions by 67 votes to 16. Great Britain and the United States voted in the minority. The resolution was not binding on U.N. member states.

1961

Bay of Pigs Invasion Fails to Overthrow Castro

A CIA-backed invasion turns into a fiasco

After the overthrow of General Batista by Fidel Castro in January 1959, Cuban–American relations turned sour. The United States disliked Castro's program of nationalization (which included American firms) and land reform (which put large plantations under state control). It viewed with alarm growing economic and diplomatic ties between Havana and Moscow. Early in 1961 the United States broke off diplomatic and trading relations with Cuba.

Castro had not fulfilled his promise to restore Cuban democracy; he had courted the Cuban Communists (who had not taken part in the revolution). As a result many Cubans had taken refuge in the United States. In March 1961, the Cuban revolutionary council, set up by exiles in New York and led by the former Cuban premier José Cardona, called for a revolt against Castro.

On April 15 two American aircraft, manned by Cubans, attacked military bases near Havana. On April 17 Cardona led 1,600 Cuban exiles, trained by the CIA, in a landing near Bahia de los Cochinos, the Bay of Pigs. By April 20 they had been repelled. A rising of the Cuban people, which exiles had told the CIA would take place, did not materialize.

During the crisis the Soviet Union promised aid to Castro. In December Castro announced his conversion to Marxist-Leninism. He amalgamated his movement with the Socialist People's, or Communist, Party. Early in 1962 he named it the United Party of the Socialist Revolution and declared it the only legal party in Cuba.

The CIA miscalculated Cuban national support for the new régime and lost 400 men and 1,100 prisoners in their attempt to topple Castro.

1961

Berlin Wall Goes Up Overnight

East Germany acts to stop emigration to the West

Berlin remained in the control of the four occupying powers after the creation of the two independent, sovereign nations of West and East Germany in 1955. In 1958 the suggestion of the Soviet premier Nikita Khrushchev that Berlin be made a demilitarized, free city was rejected by the other three powers.

The West suspected that the ultimate Soviet objective was the absorption of the whole of the city within East Germany. The great difficulty for the Soviet Union and East Germany was the flow of skilled workers from the Soviet sector of the city to West Berlin (where the standard of living was much higher) at mounting cost to the East German economy.

A Soviet "free-city" proposal was again rejected in 1961. The Soviet response was to erect the Berlin Wall, a barrier of concrete slabs and barbed wire put up along the line dividing the eastern from the western sector. The building was begun at night on Sunday, August 13; within 24 hours it was substantially in place.

The West declared the wall to be illegal, but though Soviet and American tanks faced each other across the dividing line, there were no hostilities. Armed East German guards lined the wall and turned back 50,000 East Berliners who tried to make the journey to their work in West Berlin on that Monday morning. The wall remained a source of East–West friction until its destruction in 1989.

1962

Cuban Missile Crisis Brings Superpowers to Brink of War

An American blockade of Cuba forces Khrushchev to back down

On October 14, 1962, a United States U-2 aircraft took photographs of Soviet missile bases in Cuba, 90 miles off the coast of Florida. The Soviet Union claimed that it was supplying Cuba with defensive weapons only. President John Kennedy countered that the missile bases were for offensive purposes. He demanded their removal and, on October 22, established an air and sea blockade to prevent Soviet shipments of arms from reaching Cuban ports.

For six days the world waited to see whether the two great nuclear powers would go to war. Nikita Khrushchev, the Soviet premier, asked the United States to withdraw its missiles from Turkey in return for a Soviet withdrawal from Cuba. The United States rejected the proposal. The crisis ended on October 28 when, without any public agreement about Turkish bases, Khrushchev announced that the Cuban bases would be dismantled under the United Nations' supervision if the United States agreed to lift the blockade and gave a pledge not to invade Cuba.

On November 2 Kennedy pronounced himself satisfied that the bases were being dismantled. The blockade ended on November 20. The United States later quietly removed its nuclear missile bases from Turkey.

THE·PILL

In 1955 a team of American biologists, led by Gregory Pincus, discovered that the hormones estrogen and progesterone, when taken orally, were highly effective in preventing ovulation. The next year Pincus began mass trials of the pill in Puerto Rico. In 1960 the first oral contraceptive, Enovid-10, was marketed in the United States. Great Britain got the pill a year later. Its widespread use (by the mid-1970s it was estimated that 40 million women were taking it) contributed to the so-called sexual permissiveness of the 1960s and '70s. Depression is a common side-effect, and by the 1980s concern was growing (the debate is unresolved) that taking the pill might increase women's risk of developing cervical cancer.

1963

Test Ban Treaty Signed by Soviet Union and the United States

De Gaulle keeps France out of the agreement

In 1963 there were four nuclear powers in the world: the United States (1945), the Soviet Union (1949), Great Britain (1952) and France (1960). In August that year three of them (excluding France) concluded the first agreement to limit the testing of nuclear armaments. The Moscow Agreement was signed after five years of negotiation and a voluntary suspension of testing by the three powers in 1958-61.

The signatories to the treaty—by 1965 the number had risen to almost 100 nations—agreed not to test any nuclear explosive above ground (in the atmosphere or outer space) or underwater. Underground testing was not banned. China, which became a nuclear power in 1964, did not sign the treaty and continued, with France, to conduct nuclear tests in the atmosphere. The treaty included no provisions for limiting the production of nuclear arms.

Nikita Khrushchev addresses guests at a reception after the signing of the test ban treaty by Lord Home, Dean Rusk and Andrei Gromyko.

1963

President Kennedy Assassinated in Dallas

Lyndon Johnson is sworn in as the new president

On Friday, November 22, 1963, John Kennedy and his wife Jacqueline, made a trip to Dallas, Texas. Its purpose was chiefly to rally support for the Democrats in a state that was going to be difficult to carry in the next autumn's presidential election. As they were traveling in a motorcade through the center of the city with the governor of Texas, John Connally, and his wife, shots were fired at the open car. The president was hit and died less than half an hour later in a hospital. Lyndon Johnson, the vice president, took the oath of office aboard the presidential plane as it returned to Washington.

A few hours later Lee Harvey Oswald was arrested in a nearby cinema and charged with the murder. On Sunday morning he was shot and killed by Jack Ruby, a local nightclub operator, while he was being transferred from the Dallas police headquarters to the county jail.

Despite many people's doubts, Oswald, a supporter of Castro and the son-in-law of a KGB colonel, was found by the 1964 commission headed by the chief justice, Earl Warren, to have been the sole assassin. Ruby, convicted of murder, died in prison in 1967.

Kennedy was the fourth president of the United States to be assassinated. The others were Abraham Lincoln (1865), James Garfield (1881) and William McKinley (1901). Kennedy's shooting was followed by that of his brother Robert in 1968, the same year in which the black civil rights leader Martin Luther King was murdered.

A bodyguard leaps onto the car in a vain attempt to help the fatally wounded president, assassinated after only 34 months in office.

1964

United States Sends Troops to Vietnam

Congress passes the Gulf of Tonkin Resolution

France's withdrawal from Indochina in 1954 set the stage for a long civil war between the Communists of North Vietnam, led by Ho Chi Minh, and the republic of South Vietnam, under its president, Ngo Dinh Diem. The United States came to the aid of South Vietnam, which it saw as a bulwark against the spread of Communism throughout Southeast Asia. According to the "domino theory," if South Vietnam fell, other states would fold under the impact in a chain reaction.

From 1961 to 1964 the American involvement was officially stated to be restricted to the sending of technical aid and advice, but in 1964 movements of American warships in the Gulf of Tonkin, off North Vietnam, provoked the Viet Cong into offensive action. Torpedo attacks on the destroyer, U.S.S. *Maddox*, on August 2 led the United States to bomb North Vietnamese naval bases and an oil installation.

On August 7 Congress voted almost unanimously to support the Gulf of Tonkin Resolution, which gave President Johnson full executive authority to take "all necessary steps" against North Vietnam in the defense of the freedom of SEATO nations. So began the Vietnam War.

Full-scale American fighting started with heavy bombing of North Vietnam in March 1965. By the end of the year the American forces in Indochina had risen to nearly 150,000; by the end of 1966 to 400,000. The United States was spending more on the Vietnam War than on its entire welfare program, and President Johnson's "Great Society" reforms were brought to a standstill.

1965

Ian Smith Declares Rhodesian Independence

White Rhodesia throws off the British colonial yoke

Southern Rhodesia was a British colony which, in 1923, was given limited self-government, Great Britain retaining a veto over legislation affecting black Africans. Although whites accounted for only 10 percent of the population, the colonial government was entirely white. After the demise of the Federation of Rhodesia and Nyasaland (1953-63), it sought independence for Rhodesia.

In October 1965, the Rhodesian prime minister, Ian Smith, met the British prime minister, Harold Wilson, in London. Smith's demand for independence was refused, and no agreement was reached on progress toward majority rule. On November 11 Smith made a unilateral declaration of independence. The British government declared his government illegal and, backed by the United Nations, imposed economic sanctions against it. Great Britain declined the advice of the Organization of African Unity that military force be used.

Talks in 1966 between Smith and Wilson on H.M.S. *Tiger* and, later, on H.M.S. *Fearless*, failed to shift the Rhodesian government from its opposition to black participation in government. There followed 14 years of guerrilla action against the white population. Led by Joshua Nkomo and Robert Mugabe, it was in the end successful. At a London conference in 1979 a settlement was reached, and in 1980 Southern Rhodesia became the independent republic, within the Commonwealth, of Zimbabwe, with a constitution that guaranteed one man, one vote.

1958–1982

NUCLEAR ARMS CONTROL

• **1958 Campaign for Nuclear Disarmament**
Founded in London, with Bertrand Russell as its first president, for the elimination of nuclear weapons; staged annual marches from the nuclear warhead factory at Aldermaston, Berkshire, to London; similar organizations subsequently founded throughout the West.

• **1968 Non-Proliferation Treaty**
Agreement between U.S.S.R., U.S. and Great Britain not to sell nuclear arms or give information about their manufacture to non-nuclear nations; other nations joined the treaty and non-nuclear ones agreed not to become nuclear powers; a number of nuclear (or nuclear-capable) nations— Argentina, Brazil, India, Israel, Pakistan, South Africa—have remained outside the treaty.

• **1972 SALT I**
Strategic Arms Limitation Talks treaty signed, after talks that began in 1969, by U.S.S.R. and U.S.; each power agreed to limit its stock of offensive nuclear weapons and of antiballistic missiles; SALT II talks broke down when tentative agreement not ratified by the U.S., following the Soviet invasion of Afghanistan in 1979.

• **1982 START**
Strategic Arms Reduction Talks begun by U.S.S.R. and U.S.; resulted in 1987 agreement by each power to destroy all its intermediate-range nuclear warheads (those deployed by NATO and the Warsaw Pact in Europe).

RETREAT FROM EMPIRE

The home rule movement in India under Mahatma Gandhi, advocate of passive resistance, finally achieved its aim in 1947, when independence was gained after some 200 years of British rule. Standing next to Lord Mountbatten, viceroy of India, as he takes the final salute, top, is Muhammed Jinnah, who became the first president of independent Pakistan.

Two suspected Mau Mau are taken for questioning by a sergeant in the Kenya Regiment and a Kenya police constable. After much bloodshed, the Mau Mau rebellion of the Kikuyu people against British domination resulted in independence in 1963.

Europe's retreat from world leadership in the years after 1945 was marked above all by the success of anticolonial movements throughout Asia and Africa in throwing off the imperialist yoke. In South America (excluding the Caribbean) the battle had largely been won in the first half of the 19th century, when the white man's takeover of Asia and Africa had hardly been put in motion.

In a few places national independence in the 20th century was won without an armed struggle. The United States withdrew peacefully from the Philippines in 1947 and Great Britain from Burma in 1948, after each power had cooperated with the nationalists in expelling the Japanese. India, which gained its independence in 1947, offers the only instance of national freedoms being won by a long campaign of nonviolent protest and civil disobedience.

Almost everywhere else freedom was gained only after prolonged and bloody guerrilla warfare. Harold Macmillan, the British prime minister, in an address to the South African parliament in 1960, spoke of a "wind of change" that was blowing through the African continent; the change was effected by the rifle. The list of places where guerrilla action eventually won the day is a long one. It includes Kenya (the land of the Mau Mau), Algeria, Cyprus, Aden, Oman, Guinea-Bissau, Mozambique, Angola and Rhodesia. By the early 1980s only a few small European dependencies remained.

The classic instance of a long guerrilla struggle was that which took place in Indochina. There the Viet Cong military leader, General Giap, finally expelled the French in 1954 by employing the strategy Mao Tse-tung had used successfully in China. That strategy involved winning the confidence of the people, persuading them of the justice of the cause, and then engaging the enemy in a battle that might take years, never meeting him in open combat, but absorbing his assaults and attacking him obliquely from elusive positions. Having defeated the French in North Vietnam, the Viet Cong had to take on the United States in the south. The longer the war continued, and the American objective of a speedy resolution to it was thwarted, the more the imperialist power was led to question its presence there. In the end the Viet Cong won because the United States lost heart for the fight.

The desire for national freedom can be put in chains; it cannot be extinguished. That has been the lesson of every successful liberation struggle of the 1950s and '60s. The freedom fighter was working for national survival; the imperialist had somewhere else to go. The European powers eventually decided that the price of maintaining colonies whose value to them was debatable was too great. They went home.

Where the imperialist power has made the colony its home, where its agents have become a settled, and for all practical purposes indigenous, people, the experience has been different. The IRA in Ireland have, so far, had little evident success. And in Africa the last great struggles have occurred where the white man has most made himself at home—in Rhodesia, which became independent Zimbabwe in 1980, and in South Africa, where the issue is unresolved.

Braving storms, shipwreck and pirates in search of refuge from the Communists, about 425,000 people fled Vietnam in open boats between 1975 and 1979. International reaction was sympathetic and many Western nations took in the boat people. However, as the exodus continued in the 1980s sympathy waned, particularly when it became clear that most were economic migrants searching for a better life, rather than refugees escaping political persecution. The problem persists today.

The "imperialist occupation" in Ireland is of such ancient lineage that the description of the IRA as anticolonial freedom fighters makes sense only to its keenest supporters. The struggle now manifests itself in a state of near civil war and age is no barrier to involvement.

1966

Mao Tse-tung Proclaims "Cultural Revolution" in China

Thousands of students are organized into the Red Guards

The failure of the Great Leap Forward—marked by industrial inefficiency in the thousands of small factories and a slump in food production—led to Mao Tse-tung's resignation as head of state in late 1958 and his replacement by Liu Shao-ch'i. In 1962 Mao emerged from retirement to head the Socialist Education Movement, a campaign to lead the Chinese on the true path to Communism. The "bible" of the movement was Mao's *Little Red Book*; the instrument of the campaign was the army.

By 1965 Mao had gathered enough support to launch the "Cultural Revolution" against the enemies of socialism (whom Marshal Lin Piao identified as liberal "Khrushchevians") and against Liu and other of his adversaries in the government. In June 1966, schools and universities were closed in the state of emergency created by the Red Guards, the army cadets who formed the vanguard of Maoism. Thousands of students enlisted in the Red Guards. Mass rallies were held. The cult of Mao grew. Opponents were tortured and murdered. Red Guards fought with industrial workers and peasants.

In 1968, with China on the verge of civil war, the schools were reopened and the Red Guards disbanded. Anti-Maoists in the government were removed, including Liu. Millions of students were sent to work in the countryside, and revolutionary committees of the army were established to run the country. The Cultural Revolution was declared over in 1969. In 1970 Mao was named supreme commander of the army and the nation.

1967

Israel Defeats Egypt in the "Six-Day War"

Sinai and the West Bank come under Israeli occupation

Israel felt threatened by its Arab neighbors (who had never officially recognized the new state). In May 1967, the Egyptian president, Gamal Nasser, had ordered the United Nations peacekeeping force, sent in 1956 to police the Israeli-Egyptian border, out of Sinai; and a renewed Egyptian naval blockade closed the Gulf of Aqaba to Israeli shipping. Then on June 5, after months of conflict, during which Israeli tanks had crossed into Syria and Mirage fighters had shot down six Syrian aircraft, Israel launched an attack against Syria, Jordan and Egypt.

In just one day Israel had virtually destroyed the air forces of Syria, Jordan, Egypt and Iraq. That initial success, which prevented an Arab invasion of Israel, was followed by the occupation of Arab Jerusalem on June 7. On the same day Egyptian troops were overrun in Sinai, and the Suez Canal was reached. Israeli forces also occupied all of the west bank of the River Jordan and the Golan Heights in Syria.

The war was over by June 10. Israel retained all its gains. Arab Jerusalem was incorporated into the state of Israel; Sinai, the Golan Heights and the West Bank were declared "occupied zones." The West Bank contained much of Jordan's economic resources and half of its population: 600,000 Palestinians came under Israeli control. The U.N. resolutions of 1967, requiring Israel to retreat to its pre-war borders and calling for a settlement of the Palestine refugee question, have never been enforced.

Israeli soldiers pray at the Wailing Wall in East Jerusalem, reunited with the west of the city after 20 years.

1968

Tet Offensive Strikes at Saigon

Antiwar sentiment grows in the United States

On January 30, 1968, the forces of North Vietnam launched an attack on 90 South Vietnamese towns and cities, including Saigon, in an attempt to topple the régime of Generals Nguyen Cao Ky and Nguyen Van Thieu. It was the beginning of the "Tet Offensive," named after the New Year celebrations during which it was launched. The losses on both sides were high and, though neither side could claim victory, the offensive was the great turning point of the Vietnam War. The United States began to doubt the wisdom of remaining in Indochina.

On March 31 President Johnson announced a cessation of bombing north of the 20th parallel. For the next 12 months the antiwar campaign in the United States grew rapidly and in June 1969, when there were 541,000 American troops in the region, Johnson's successor, Richard Nixon, announced the beginning of the American withdrawal. As the Paris peace talks made no headway, American domestic opinion, shocked by mounting casualties, turned decisively against the war, especially after Nixon extended it to Laos and Cambodia by bombing the Vietnamese Communist (Viet Cong) command centers there.

A ceasefire was finally agreed on January 28, 1973, and the last American troops left Vietnam on March 29. The American death toll stood at 45,600. The United States had achieved nothing. Saigon fell to the Viet Cong in April 1975, and the city was renamed Ho Chi Minh City. An all-Vietnam assembly established the united Socialist Republic of Vietnam in 1976.

1968

"May Days" Bring Barricades to the Streets of Paris

Students and workers unite in antigovernment demonstrations

Demonstrations by students at the University of Nanterre on May 2, 1968, which spread to other campuses, including the Sorbonne in Paris, forced the closure of French universities and led to a general outbreak of antigovernment protests and activities. The students' demands, inspired by the similar movement on American campuses (where "student power" and antiwar sentiment vied for supremacy), were for higher government spending on education, the modernization of curricula and reduced spending on nuclear arms.

Widespread street fighting between protestors and the police was accompanied by industrial action which, at its peak, approached a general strike. The crisis, which brought a virtual halt to the French economy, lasted until mid-June. The French president, Charles de Gaulle, promised university reform and a rise of 33⅓ percent in the national minimum wage. The elections to the national assembly that month returned the Gaullists to power with a healthy majority and cost the Radicals a drop in their representation.

The crisis may, nevertheless, have had a delayed effect on the president's popularity. In a referendum of April 1969, the French electorate rejected his proposals for constitutional reform, and he resigned and retired to his country seat at Colombey-les-deux-Eglises.

Police used water cannon to try to force rioting students hurling cobblestones into the side streets during a series of pitched battles on the Boulevard St. Germain in Paris.

1968

Soviet Tanks Crush the "Prague Spring"

Armored divisions scotch "socialism with a human face"

On August 20, 1968, 200,000 Soviet troops, including a token number from its satellites in the Warsaw Pact, entered Prague to crush the movement for the liberalization of the Communist régime known as the "Prague Spring." "Socialism with a human face," the Czechoslovakian leader, Alexander Dubcek, called it.

The details of Dubcek's reform program remain unclear, but they included the introduction of some market elements into the economy and a reduction in the totalitarian monopoly of the Communist Party in politics. At a meeting with Soviet leaders at the end of July, he sought to reassure them that his policy was neither to abandon socialism nor to weaken Czechoslovakia's commitment to the Warsaw Pact. His protestations availed him nothing.

On August 20 he was arrested and taken away to Moscow. Despite Czech protests, the Soviet army of occupation was increased to 650,000 troops and a return to orthodoxy—including strict censorship and the banning of political clubs—enforced. At the price of renouncing economic reforms, Dubcek was allowed to return to Czechoslovakia. In April 1969 (a few days after Czechs had poured into the streets to celebrate a victory over the Soviet Union in the world ice hockey championships), he was removed as party first secretary. Thousands of "anti-Communists" were arrested, and Dubcek was replaced by a Soviet *apparatchik*, Gustav Husak.

1969

Neil Armstrong Sets Foot on the Moon

The American astronaut takes a "giant leap for mankind"

At 10:56 a.m., United States eastern time, on July 21, 1969, Neil Armstrong, the commander of the American spacecraft, *Apollo 11*, disembarked from his lunar module and became the first man to set foot on the moon. Hundreds of millions of television viewers around the world then heard him speak words that have become unforgettable: "That's one small step for a man, one giant leap for mankind." He added that he found himself in a landscape of "soft powder" with "a beauty all of its own, like some desert of the United States."

Armstrong was then joined by his fellow astronaut, Edwin (Buzz) Aldrin. They collected rock samples and moon dust, took photographs and planted the American flag before returning to the module. The third crew member, Michael Collins, remained in the spacecraft.

The moon landing followed the orbiting of the earth by the three-man *Apollo 7* in 1968. It was the high point of the Apollo project, begun in 1961 when President Kennedy set the American space establishment the goal of landing a man on the moon and returning him safely to earth before 1970.

The Apollo project was brought to an end in 1975, after a successful docking in space between *Apollo 16* and the Soviet spacecraft, *Soyuz 19*.

Buzz Aldrin was photographed on the moon by fellow astronaut Neil Armstrong; the photographer and lunar module are reflected in Aldrin's helmet. The two men then set up the American flag, which had to be specially wired so it would "fly" in a world that has no wind. When they departed they left behind, among other things, a gold olive branch as a traditional symbol of peace.

1969

British Troops Sent to Northern Ireland

Roman Catholics appeal to Westminster as violence mounts

In 1968 the "Troubles" returned to Northern Ireland after a decade relatively free from sectarian violence. A march by the Roman Catholic Civil Rights Association, to protest against anti-Catholic discrimination in housing and employment, took place on October 5 in Londonderry (Derry to the Catholics) despite a ban placed on it by the government of Northern Ireland. In clashes with the police five Catholics were killed and more than 100 injured.

An intensification of marching by both Catholic and Protestant organizations and an acceleration of violence between the two groups followed. By the summer of 1969 Catholic strongholds in Belfast and Londonderry—especially the Bogside area of Londonderry—were "no-go" areas to the Royal Ulster Constabulary. In July and August riots cost the lives of eight Catholics and two Protestants. British troops were sent to Northern Ireland, at the request of the provincial government, to maintain order. Catholics cheered them on their arrival in the Bogside on August 15: they were, they believed, all that stood between them and a pogrom.

The British troops have not since been withdrawn. After "Bloody Sunday," January 13, 1972, in Londonderry, when troops killed 13 marchers for a united Ireland, Great Britain suspended the Northern Ireland Assembly at Stormont and imposed direct rule from the British Parliament. With one brief interlude (June 1973 - May 1974) direct rule has been retained.

1971

Idi Amin Seizes Power in Uganda

An army takeover ousts Milton Obote from the presidency

On January 25, 1971, the army and police of Uganda took advantage of the absence of the president, Milton Obote, and overthrew his government. The leader of the *coup* was Idi Amin, a major general in the army. Obote, who was flying back to Kampala from a Commonwealth conference in Singapore, had himself become president in 1966 in a *coup* which ousted King Museta.

Idi Amin established a military dictatorship. In 1969, after an attempt on his life, Obote had banned all opposition parties and ended the federal constitution which, in deference to Uganda's tribal divisions, had been promulgated when Uganda achieved independence from Great Britain in 1962. But Amin introduced a reign of terror, torturing and murdering thousands of Obote's supporters. His chief opponents, the Asian middle class, dominant in the country's commercial life, were expelled from the country in 1972.

In 1976 Amin declared himself president for life. Three years later forces from Tanzania (where Obote had taken refuge in 1971) invaded Uganda and overthrew him. Obote returned from exile and was president from 1980 until 1985, when he was again deposed from office in a bloodless *coup*.

1957–1989

EXPLORATION OF SPACE

1957 U.S.S.R. launched *Sputnik 1*

1958 U.S.A. launched *Explorer 1*

1959 *Luna 2* (U.S.S.R.) made first hard landing on the moon

1961 Yuri Gagarin (U.S.S.R.) first man in space

1965 Alexei Leonov (U.S.S.R.) first astronaut to leave spacecraft (*Voshkod 2*) and float in space

1966 *Luna 9* (U.S.S.R.) made first soft landing on the moon; sent TV pictures back to earth

1967 U.S.S.R. achieved automatic link-up between two unmanned orbiting satellites

1969 U.S. astronauts set foot on the moon; manned Soviet spacecraft linked up in orbit; two astronauts transferred from *Soyuz 5* to *Soyuz 4*

1971 *Apollo 15* (U.S.) astronauts traveled in a vehicle on the moon's surface; *Mariner 9* (U.S.) the first spacecraft to orbit another planet (Mars)

1973 *Skylab* (U.S.), a satellite research station, put into orbit

1975 *Apollo 18* (U.S.) and *Soyuz 19* (U.S.S.R.) docked in space

1976 *Viking 1* (U.S.) made soft landing on Mars; sent back pictures of its surface

1977 *Voyager 1* and 2 (U.S.) launched; passed Jupiter and Saturn, 1979-81

1978 *Pioneer Venus 1* and 2 (U.S.) reached Venus

1986 *Voyager 2* reached Uranus; discovered 10 new moons

1989 *Voyager 2* reached Neptune

1972

Palestinian Terrorists Storm the Munich Olympics

Ten Israeli athletes die in the attack

Of all the acts of Middle Eastern terrorism that took place in the early 1970s, none seized the world's attention more dramatically than the attack on the Israeli compound at the Munich Olympic Games in 1972. Eight members of the Palestinian organization, Black September, were spotted climbing a high fence surrounding the Olympic Village at 4:30 a.m. on September 5, but they were assumed to be athletes returning late. They entered the Israeli living quarters, killed one athlete and took nine hostages.

The terrorists demanded the freeing of 200 Palestinians held in Israeli prisons in return for the release of the hostages. The Israeli government refused to negotiate. Eventually the terrorists agreed to leave the compound when the West German government promised them safe passage to Cairo. The West German offer was a ruse that backfired. In a shoot-out at the airport five of the Palestinians, one German police officer and all nine hostages were killed.

The chief objective of terrorism, publicity for the terrorists' cause—in this instance the plight of the homeless Palestinians—was brilliantly achieved. The Olympic Games and, therefore, the crisis were carried by television all over the world. "It was," a Palestinian spokesman said, "like painting the name of Palestine on the top of a mountain that can be seen from the four corners of the earth."

The horror of the Munich episode sparked worldwide indignation and renewed demands for an end to Arab terrorism.

1973

President Allende of Chile Ousted by Military Coup

An experiment in Marxist reform is nipped in the bud

When Salvador Allende, after three unsuccessful attempts, was elected president of Chile in September 1970, he became the first declared Marxist to be freely elected as a head of state anywhere in the world. Allende was the leader of the Socialist Party which he had founded in 1933; his 1970 campaign was mounted on behalf of Popular Unity, a coalition of Communists, socialists and radicals.

Allende set out to dismantle the capitalist and imperialist structure of the Chilean economy and to improve the workers' standard of living. He nationalized the banks and the copper-mining industry and began a program of land redistribution. More than 95 percent of the land was owned by three percent of the population in 1970; the vast majority of the peasantry was landless. Progress was impeded by high inflation (above 300 percent in 1971) and by the hostility of the Chilean middle class and powerful American corporations with large investments in Chile.

The Central Intelligence Agency of the United States encouraged opposition to Allende and, in September 1973, commanders of the army, supported by the paramilitary police and the air force, stormed the presidential palace. In a bombing raid which set the palace on fire, Allende was killed. His government was replaced by a military junta headed by General Pinochet, who declared an "indefinite recess" of politics. Thousands of Allende's supporters were arrested and executed. In 1974 Pinochet assumed dictatorial powers as head of state.

1973

Israel Wins "Yom Kippur War"

*The territorial gains of 1967
are confirmed*

The fourth and fiercest Arab–Israeli war began on October 6, 1973, when Egypt and Syria launched surprise attacks on Sinai and the Golan Heights, territory taken from them by Israel in the 1967 war. The date was the Jewish Day of Atonement, Yom Kippur, the most sacred day in the Jewish calendar. But since Israel had shot down 13 Syrian fighter jets in September, each side branded the other as the aggressor.

Egyptian forces crossed the Suez Canal within two days and advanced some miles beyond Israeli frontline positions; Syrian troops, reinforced by Iraqi units, advanced into the Golan Heights. By October 12, however, the Syrians were pushed back to the 1967 ceasefire line, and the Israeli army made progress toward Damascus. With Jordan's help and military aid from the Soviet Union (the United States was giving aid to Israel), the capital was defended. On the Suez front a massive tank battle began on October 17. Egypt held onto its position on the east bank of the Suez Canal, the first military gain ever achieved against Israel.

A ceasefire was established by the United Nations on October 24. The 1967 boundaries were confirmed, and a UN peacekeeping force was sent to the Golan Heights in 1974. The war cost the lives of 2,800 Israeli, 15,000 Egyptian and 7,000 Syrian soldiers.

1974

Turkey Invades Cyprus

*The island is partitioned into Greek
and Turkish sections*

In March 1959, after four years of guerrilla warfare, Greek Cypriots celebrated their island's independence from Great Britain. The leaders in the independence struggle, Archbishop Makarios and Colonel George Grivas, the head of the terrorist organization EOKA, were hailed as national heroes. The London agreement that gave Cyprus its independence ruled out both union with Greece (*enosis*) and the partition of the island into Greek and Turkish sections.

Independence was the prelude to rising tension between the Greek population of the island and the Turkish minority. Recurring violence and the threat of war between Greece and Turkey led the United Nations to send a peacekeeping force to Cyprus in 1964. An uneasy peace was rendered more fragile by the dispute within the Greek community between supporters of *enosis* among EOKA veterans and the supporters of Makarios, who was elected president. Relations between Greeks and Turks worsened in 1970 when the Turkish community in the north withdrew from the national assembly at Nicosia and established its own unofficial government at Famagusta.

When an EOKA-led *coup* deposed Makarios in 1974, Turkey seized the opportunity to land troops in the north and proclaim an independent "Turkish Federated State." Greek Cypriots fled to the south. The island was, however illegally, effectively partitioned. It has stayed so, and Turkish troops have remained in the northern half of the island. In 1983 the Turkish Republic of Northern Cyprus was proclaimed. Greek Cypriots have never recognized its legitimacy.

House-to-house fighting during the violence of 1964 took its toll of citizens from both communities.

1974

Yassir Arafat Addresses the United Nations

International recognition is given to the Palestine liberation leader

Although Israel achieved a military victory in the Yom Kippur War, it sustained a diplomatic setback. The Arab countries' agreement to cut oil production and Saudi Arabia's embargo on oil exports to the Netherlands and the United States revealed their ability to act together to damage the economies of industrial nations, whose governments made a notable shift toward the Arab position in the Middle East. In the Third World, too, Israel lost friends: 23 African nations severed relations with Israel.

One result was to focus attention on the plight of Palestinians in Israeli-occupied territory. The Palestine Liberation Organization was led by Yassir Arafat, the founder of the guerrilla movement, Al Fatah. To exploit the changed mood, Arafat scaled down the PLO's demand for the whole of Palestine to be made a democratic, nonsectarian state. He announced that he would be prepared to accept a small Palestine including Gaza and the West Bank.

In September 1974, the United Nations for the first time included the Palestine question as a separate item on its agenda. On November 13 Arafat, with a pistol in his hip pocket, addressed the general assembly: "I have come bearing an olive branch and a freedom fighter's gun. Do not let the olive branch fall from my hand." The U.N. recognized the PLO as the "sole legitimate representative of the Palestinian people." Israel has still refused to grant it recognition.

1974

Watergate Scandal Forces Richard Nixon Out of the White House

An American president resigns for the first time in history

At 2 a.m. on June 17, 1972, five men with surveillance equipment were found inside the Democratic Party campaign headquarters at the Watergate Building in Washington, DC, and arrested. On the following day, Richard Nixon's campaign manager, John Mitchell, told the American people that the men were not there on behalf of the president or the Republican Party. The Democratic candidate for president, George McGovern, tried in vain to make the break-in an election issue. In November Nixon won a landslide victory.

Nixon's repeated assertion that he knew nothing of the affair and that he was not mounting a "cover-up" to protect himself and his advisors was gradually undermined. The resignations of senior aides, beginning with John Erlichmann and Bob Haldeman in April 1973, were followed by the dismissal of John Dean, who had been appointed to conduct an in-house inquiry into the break-in.

In testimony to a senate committee Dean implicated Nixon. Nixon's refusal to hand over tapes of his White House conversations to the special Watergate prosecutor, Archibald Cox, deepened suspicions. In October the Supreme Court ordered the surrender of the tapes. They had been tampered with (itself damning evidence), but even so clearly demonstrated Nixon's guilt.

In the summer of 1974 the Senate set impeachment proceedings in motion. To avoid impeachment Nixon resigned on August 9. His successor, Gerald Ford, awarded him a pardon, but a number of Nixon's aides were imprisoned.

1975

Portugal Concedes Independence to Mozambique and Angola

White South Africa is left nearly isolated on the continent

By 1970 most of Africa except for the "white south"—South Africa itself and Rhodesia—had thrown off the European colonial yoke. The most important exceptions were Mozambique and Angola, which remained possessions of the first European colonial power, Portugal. Together with Rhodesia, they formed a buffer between South Africa and independent black Africa to the north.

Angola and Mozambique were both overseas provinces with a degree of local autonomy, but they were considered integral parts of Portugal, for which, President Antonio Salazar repeatedly stated, independence was not a possibility. In the 1960s two opposing trends became clearly visible: an expansion of the provinces' economies, marked by a rapid increase in white settlement (in Angola from 170,000 in 1960 to more than 500,000 in 1970), and a rising tide of African nationalism.

After 15 years of guerrilla warfare, and ruthless suppression of the independence movements by the Lisbon authorities, the MPLA (Popular Movement for Angolan Liberation; founded 1956) and FRELIMO (Mozambique Liberation Front; founded 1962) forced Portugal to grant both provinces full independence in 1975. Angola then suffered a long war against invading forces from Zaire and South Africa, a second "war of liberation."

Portugal's overthrow radically altered the political balance in Africa south of the Zambezi River, giving renewed purpose to the ZANU movement in Rhodesia (which won Zimbabwe its independence in 1980) and leaving South Africa an embattled outsider.

1975

Khmer Rouge Captures Phnom Penh

Pol Pot takes power and initiates a campaign of genocide

In 1970–75 a civil war raged in Cambodia between the government forces of Lon Nol, backed by the United States, and the Communist Khmer Rouge ("Red Cambodia") party. The Communists gradually won control and in April 1975 took the capital, Phnom Penh. Prince Sihanouk returned as head of state (he had been overthrown by Lon Nol in 1970) and appointed Pol Pot prime minister.

Sihanouk resigned seven months later, and Pol Pot became premier. In January 1979 he was overthrown by a Vietnamese army which invaded Cambodia on behalf of the Kampuchean (Cambodian) National Front. Political purges, pogroms and executions, enforced starvation and disease, together with the year-long fight against the Vietnamese and the National Front in 1979, claimed the lives of 1½ million people, a quarter of the country's population. Pol Pot conducted a campaign of genocide, against anyone not of pure Khmer stock—Chinese, Vietnamese, Laotian, Thai, Indian and Pakistani. He also resolved to rid the country of religion: there were 60,000 Buddhist monks in 1975, fewer than 30,000 by 1979. In 1989, a United Nations report stated that Pol Pot's violations of human rights were "the worst to have occurred anywhere in the world since Nazism."

The skulls and skeletons of Kampucheans—the legacy of Pol Pot— provide a grim reminder of this recent holocaust. Although Cambodia tried to remain neutral during the Vietnam War, routes through the jungle, used by Communists to infiltrate the South, were bombed by U.S. planes, and the disruption that followed led to the formation of the Khmer Rouge and the subsequent massive loss of life.

1978

Israel and Egypt Make Peace at Camp David

Sadat and Begin sign the first Arab-Israeli peace treaty

The visit to Israel in November 1977, of Anwar Sadat, the Egyptian president, and his address to the Israeli parliament, the Knesset, marked the first tacit recognition by an Arab head of state of Israel's sovereignty. It was followed a year later by the peace accord worked out at Camp David, Maryland. Sadat and the Israeli prime minster, Menachem Begin, were invited to meet there by President Jimmy Carter. The meeting lasted from September 5 to 17; its fruit was the Camp David Accords.

That historic agreement, the first peace accord of any kind between Israel and an Arab state, had three main components: first, the gradual withdrawal of Israeli troops from Sinai; second, the gradual demilitarization of a security zone along the Israeli-Egyptian border; and third, a statement of intent to find a solution to the question of an autonomous Palestinian state in the West Bank.

The Palestine Liberation Organization denounced the accord; and, although a formal peace treaty between Israel and Egypt was signed in March 1979, and Sinai was returned to Egypt in 1982, no progress has been made toward a settlement of the Palestinian issue.

Sadat and Begin shared the 1978 Nobel Peace Prize.

1979

Muslim Revolution Overthrows Shah of Iran

The Ayatollah Khomeini returns from exile to lead the revolution

Opposition to the rule of the Shah, Muhammed Reza Pahlavi, had grown to such an extent by the mid-1970s that the experiment in party democracy, begun in 1964, was abandoned. In 1975 the Shah formed a new political movement, the National Resurrection Party, and banned opposition parties.

The chief opposition came from *shi'a* Muslims who disliked the liberal secularism of the Shah's rule and scorned his dependence upon the United States. It was heightened by the poverty of the mass of the people in an age when oil exports were bringing great wealth into the country. Rioting against the government became a recurrent event in Iran's major cities.

The opposition was led by the religious leader, the Ayatollah Khomeini. He was exiled in 1963 and for 15 years had cultivated a following among the *shi'a* Muslims of Iraq, when, in 1978, he was again banished and made Paris his headquarters. From there, in the same year, he called upon the army to overthrow the Shah and establish an Islamic Republic in Iran. Support for the Shah seeped away and on January 16, 1979, he fled the country. Three weeks later Khomeini returned in triumph.

For the next 10 years, until his death in 1989, he presided over an Islamic theocracy in Iran, although constitutionally the head of state was the president, the first being Abal Hassan Bani-Sadr, elected in 1980. Bani-Sadr was arrested for alleged pro-Western sympathies in 1981. He escaped abroad, but hundreds of other "counterrevolutionaries" were executed.

This greeting card, celebrating the Iranian New Year, depicts the Ayatollah Khomeini exacting his revenge on the exiled Shah of Iran. The overthrow of the Shah meant, in reality, a return to fundamentalism and a violent wave of anti-Western sentiment.

1979

Soviet Troops Occupy Afghanistan

Islamic nationalists refuse to yield to foreign aggression

The monarchy was abolished in Afghanistan in 1973 and a republic established under the presidency of General Mohammed Daoud. Five years later he was himself ousted in a *coup* by the Armed Forces Revolutionary Council, a Marxist organization backed by the Kremlin. Nationalist and Muslim opposition to the new régime posed the threat of civil war.

To avert this, Soviet troops, some of whom were already present in Afghanistan as "advisors," invaded the country in the last week of December 1979. President Hafizulla Amin was murdered and his government replaced by a puppet Soviet régime, led by Babrak Karmal. By January 1980, there were nearly 100,000 Soviet soldiers in Afghanistan.

Millions of Afghans fled to Iran and Pakistan. The West denounced the invasion, but limited its opposition to a partial boycott of the 1980 Moscow Olympics. Resistance to the Soviet occupation was mounted by the Mujaheddin ("holy warriors"), a movement of Muslim nationalist guerrillas led by Ahmed Shah Massoud. It had its external bases in Pakistan and was supplied with arms by the United States. By 1983 every province of Afghanistan was the scene of guerrilla warfare. The center of Mujaheddin operations was the Panjshir valley, north of Kabul, which remained in its control despite annual assaults by Soviet troops.

In 1987, apparently with Soviet approval, Karmal was replaced by General Mohammed Najibullah, who offered the Mujaheddin a ceasefire in 1987. By 1989 the last Soviet units had been withdrawn from Afghanistan.

1979

Sandinistas Take Control in Nicaragua

The United States assists the overthrow of the Somoza family

From 1936 to 1979 Nicaragua was ruled by the Somoza family, which made a vast fortune from coffee planting and cultivated close ties with American business interests. Its demise came in July 1979, when General Anastasio Somoza Debayle was overthrown by the Sandinista National Liberation Front. He resigned the presidency and fled the country.

The Sandinista movement had a strong Marxist flavor, but Somoza was not brought down by a simple Communist *coup*. His violations of human rights and his heavy bombing of Sandinista areas in the spring and early summer of 1979 lost him support among the middle classes, the trade unions and the Church. Critically, he lost the backing of the American president, Jimmy Carter, whose administration took part in the negotiations that installed in power a five-man junta, representing the military, business interests and the Sandinistas.

The civil war continued, and the Sandinistas, led by Daniel Ortega, gained control of the government and began to implement a program of nationalization and massive land reform. Carter's successor, Ronald Reagan, accused the Sandinistas of establishing a Marxist dictatorship and assisting guerrilla rebels in El Salvador. He failed, however, to win public support at home for his policy of giving aid to the opponents of the Sandinistas, the Contras. In 1984 Ortega was elected as president of Nicaragua.

1980

Iraq Invades Iran

Saddam Hussein bids to take control of the Shatt al-Arab waterway

Saddam Hussein became president of Iraq, at the head of the ruling Ba'ath Party, in 1979. Ba'ath means "Arab renaissance" and the party is nonsectarian. Although the majority of Iraq's population is *shi'a* Muslim, a Ba'athist régime has been in power since 1963. Within a few months of Saddam's assumption of office, Ayatollah Khomeini was calling, from Teheran, for the *shi'a* Muslims of Iraq to overthrow Saddam's godless rule.

On September 17, 1980, Saddam denounced the 1975 Algiers agreement between Iran and Iraq (by which they had agreed to settle differences peaceably) and launched an invasion of Iran. His object was to seize control of the 120-mile Shatt al-Arab waterway at the head of the Persian Gulf, which formed a border between the two nations. By the 1975 agreement it was to be shared between them.

Iraq had greater military strength than Iran and the support of most Arab states (the West also preferred Iraq to revolutionary Islamic Iran); Iran had three times Iraq's population and the support of Syria (which effectively blocked Iraq's oil exports). Neither side was able to gain a decisive military advantage on the ground or in the air (Iraq's use of chemical weapons was condemned by the United Nations in 1984 and 1986). In August 1988, after dreadful casualties on both sides, a ceasefire was agreed.

THE MICROCHIP

The first microprocessor, or "computer on a chip," was developed by Intel of California in 1971. The basis for the technological revolution it heralded was laid in 1915, when an American physicist, Manson Benedicks, discovered that a germanium crystal could be used to convert an alternating current to a direct current and thus produce an integrated circuit. The same crystal was used to produce the silicon chip, or microprocessor. Intel's chip was a few millimeters square, with hundreds of thousands of magnetic "bubbles" that stored information and allowed it to be retrieved within 100 microseconds. The advent of the microprocessor affected every aspect of life, from video games to medical diagnosis and telecommunications.

1980

"Solidarity" Trade Union Movement Launched in Poland

Lech Walesa leads the Polish "opposition"

After three decades of Communist rule, Poland began the 1980s in economic crisis: food and housing shortages, rationing of electric power, and public transportation in disarray. The party first secretary, Edward Gierek, warned of declining trade and higher prices. The response was a series of strikes.

On August 14 the workforce at Gdansk's Lenin Shipyards laid down tools. An Interfactory Strike Committee was formed under Lech Walesa. On August 18 Gierek promised to accept "sensible" demands by the strikers. The ISC renamed itself "Solidarity" and demanded the right of Poles to form free trade unions. Agreements between Walesa and the government provided for independent trade unions, the reduction of working hours and greater freedom for newspapers and television.

When, in the autumn of 1981, Solidarity called for free unions in other Communist countries, and clashes between police and trade unionists intensified, the Kremlin asked the Polish authorities to clamp down. In December, 14,000 trade unionists were arrested; Walesa was imprisoned and martial law imposed by the new party leader, General Jaruzelski.

Solidarity was forced to operate in a semi-underground manner until 1989, when the ban on it was lifted. In the 1989 elections, the first in Poland since before World War II, Solidarity's candidates won impressive victories and its nominee, Tadeusz Mazowiecki, was made prime minister in a coalition government with the Communists.

Lech Walesa, the leader of the striking workers in the Gdansk shipyards, became the new Polish hero. After years of struggle, Poland regained its independence, and Walesa is now the country's president.

1982

Argentina Invades the Falklands

Great Britain regains possession of the South Atlantic islands

On April 2, 1982, 2,000 Argentinian troops landed at Port Stanley and overcame the small garrison of Royal Marines stationed there. Seventeen years of talks between Great Britain and Argentina had failed to resolve the issue of the possession of the Falkland Islands, or the Malvinas, peacefully. Argentina decided to take them by force.

Great Britain broke off relations with Argentina. On April 3 the United Nations called upon Argentina to withdraw. Instead the Argentinian presence in the islands was increased to 20,000 soldiers. On April 5 a British naval task force, headed by H.M.S. *Hermes* and H.M.S. *Invincible*, was sent to the South Atlantic. In the three weeks that it took for that force to make its way to the Falklands, United Nations and American representatives tried, but failed, to negotiate a settlement.

The first British success in the conflict came on April 25, when troops retook the island of South Georgia. By June 14, when the Argentinians surrendered at Port Stanley, the fighting was over. The Falklands remained British. Three days later General Galtieri, Argentina's president, and also her military commander, resigned.

The war cost 225 British and 725 Argentinian lives (368 of them when the cruiser *General Belgrano* was sunk by a British submarine on May 2).

1982

Israel Attacks PLO Headquarters in Lebanon

Yassir Arafat is forced to leave Beirut

Lebanon has a unique place in the Arab world: half its people are Christian. And to the persistent tension—and recurrent outbreaks of civil war—between Christians and Muslims has been added the disruptive presence of Palestinians. In 1982 there were about 400,000 of them in Lebanon, where the Palestine Liberation Organization made its headquarters. After Jordan's suppression of PLO guerrilla activities in 1970-71, Lebanon remained the only PLO base. It was, therefore, a prime target for Israeli attack. Israel's first invasion of Lebanon, in 1978, was dwarfed by the 1982 invasion.

On June 6, one day after the Israeli ambassador to London had been shot by PLO gunmen, Israel launched a major assault against the PLO. An army of 20,000 advanced to the Lebanese capital, Beirut. It lay under siege for two months. Syria joined in the land and air battle against Israel.

Thousands of people died during the bombardment and tens of thousands were made homeless, chiefly Palestinians and *shi'a* Muslims. Superior American technology gave Israel ascendancy over the Soviet-supplied Syrians. On August 21 Yassir Arafat, the PLO leader, agreed to leave Beirut with his guerrillas. Israel's other aim, to drive Syria from its military positions in Lebanon, was not achieved.

A postscript was the massacre, at Israel's invitation, of 2,000 encamped Palestinians by Christian Phalangists on September 15-16. Israeli troops prevented residents from escaping and lit the night sky with flares to assist the Phalangists.

The first group of PLO guerrillas from Beirut waits in Cyprus for their transfer to Iraq or Jordan.

1983

United States Marines Invade Grenada

Socialism is quashed in the Caribbean island

Grenada's four-year experiment in socialism ended dramatically in October 1983, when a military *coup*, backed by an invasion by the American marines, overthrew the Revolutionary Military Council. Although Grenada was a member of the Commonwealth, the British government was not informed of the invasion by President Ronald Reagan.

In mid-October the prime minister of Grenada, Maurice Bishop, was deposed by colleagues in his "New Jewel Movement" who considered him insufficiently radical. (Bishop had himself gained power in a bloodless *coup* against the prime minister, Eric Gairy, in 1976, two years after Grenada had won its independence.) Bishop was placed under house arrest and, after a brief escape, executed. General Hudson Austin assumed supreme power in the state at the head of a Revolutionary Military Council.

On October 25—in a direct application of Reagan's doctrine that the United States had a vital interest in the political activities in its "own backyard"—6,000 American marines and commandos, with token troop support from some Caribbean countries, invaded. In two days resistance to the Americans collapsed. The Marxists were hunted down, General Austin was arrested, and the RMC disbanded. The governor-general, Sir Paul Scoon, assumed the authority of government, assisted by an advisory council. He at once promised to restore the 1974 constitution and to hold elections. In 1984 the conservative New National Party won a majority at the polls.

1986

President Marcos Driven from Philippines

Cory Aquino takes power in Manila

The Philippines, which became an American possession after the Spanish–American war of 1898, gained their full independence in 1946. From 1965 the republic was ruled by the right-wing Ferdinand Marcos. Mounting opposition to his rule led him to suspend the constitution in 1972 and to assume near-dictatorial powers. Martial law was imposed.

In 1983 the leader of the main opposition movement, Benigno Aquino, was assassinated at Manila Airport on his return from a three-year exile in the United States. His place at the head of the People's Power Movement was taken by his widow, Corazon (Cory) Aquino. Her popularity increased as the economy declined and Marcos's political and financial corruption drew increasing criticism, not least from the United States.

To give his régime respectability Marcos called a presidential election for July 1986. Cory Aquino stood against him. Marcos officially won the election, but only by extensive bribery, the intimidation of Aquino supporters and a fraudulent recount of the ballot papers. Aquino claimed the victory and held a rival inaugural ceremony as president. Marcos bowed to international pressure, resigned as president and took refuge in the United States. Cory Aquino then formed a new government.

A helicopter carrying scientists flies over the Chernobyl plant to assess the radiation levels from the damaged Number 4 reactor. Eight tons of radioactive material had escaped into the atmosphere.

1986

Nuclear Reactor Explodes at Chernobyl

An explosion in the Soviet Union spreads radioactivity across Europe

On April 26, 1986, for the first time, an "accident" at an operating nuclear power station released a substantial quantity of radioactive material into the earth's atmosphere. The explosion occurred at the Chernobyl station at Pripyat, in the Soviet Union, about 65 miles north of Kiev.

When Swedish scientists, who had detected high levels of radioactivity in the atmosphere, asked whether there had been an accident, the Soviet Union at first denied it. The evidence mounted, however, as radioactive particles were carried by winds into all of Scandinavia and central Europe. Meat and dairy products from affected countries were embargoed, and some livestock—most prominently the reindeer of Lapland—were destroyed. American satellite photographs showed that the top of the reactor had been blown off by an explosion and that the graphite moderator was ablaze.

At an international conference in August the Soviet authorities gave details of the disaster. At least 30 persons had died in the immediate explosion and many others were being treated for radiation sickness; 135,000 people had been evacuated from an area of 300 square miles around the reactor. It was also disclosed that the explosion had been caused by unauthorized experiments with safety procedures. In 1987, senior officials at the plant were convicted of negligence and imprisoned.

Thousands more persons are expected to die over the next few years from cancers caused by the release of radioactive material.

1989

Berlin Wall Torn Down

The Iron Curtain disintegrates, and Germany is reunited

By far the most dramatic event in the collapse of Communist authority in eastern Europe in 1989-90 was the dismantling of the Berlin Wall. For more than a generation it had been the most poignant symbol of the Cold War and of the Soviet Union's hegemony over the Iron Curtain countries.

In September Hungary opened its borders for East Germans to flee to the West; in October mass protest rallies in the cities of East Germany forced the resignation of the East German president, Erich Honecker; early in November Czechoslovakia opened its borders. Then, on November 9, came the dramatic news that the East German authorities had decided to open its barrier.

Guards on the Berlin Wall were instructed to let anyone who wished to pass through the military checkpoints. Bulldozers made additional gaps in the wall, and joyful East Germans used pickaxes to destroy it. East German citizens streamed into West Germany in the hundreds of thousands over the next few weeks.

The Kremlin, which had stood aside as Hungary and Poland had declared for free elections, did nothing to prevent the collapse of the central arch in its European policy. In 1990 East Germany was reunited with West Germany and in 1991 both the Warsaw Pact (the Communist counterpart to NATO) and COMECON (the organization that linked the economies of the Iron Curtain countries to Soviet economic planning) were dissolved.

1990

Iraq Occupies Kuwait

United Nations sanctions use of force against Saddam Hussein

The army of Saddam Hussein, the president of Iraq, occupied Kuwait on August 2, 1990. Four days later the security council of the United Nations imposed a mandatory embargo on trade with Iraq. On November 29 the council approved a resolution empowering member states to use "all necessary" means to expel Iraqi forces from Kuwait if they were not withdrawn by January 15, 1991. By the time that resolution was passed, a heavy buildup of American forces, backed by Great Britain and 27 other countries, including Arab states, had been preparing for attack for more than three months.

The January deadline passed with no movement from Baghdad to begin, or undertake to begin, a withdrawal. The anti-Iraqi coalition, commanded by the American general, Norman Schwarzkopf, began to bombard Baghdad and other areas of Iraq on January 16. Minor Iraqi missile attacks on Israel over the next few weeks failed to draw her into the war and thus failed to detach the Arab states from the coalition. Iraq was subjected to the fiercest, most unrelenting campaign of air bombardment in history.

On February 23 the war on the ground began. On the first day, thousands of Iraqi soldiers surrendered almost without a fight. The numbers of Iraqi prisoners of war grew daily, and on February 26, Kuwait City was recaptured. The next day, the cream of the Iraqi forces, the Republican Guard, was encircled. On the 28th Saddam Hussein agreed to a ceasefire, and the war came to an end.

1989

EASTERN EUROPE

April 16 Ban on Solidarity lifted in Poland.

June 5 Solidarity won crushing victory in elections to 35 percent of the Polish assembly.

August 24 Tadeusz Mazowiecki, the Solidarity nominee, appointed Polish prime minister, the first non-Communist prime minister in the Eastern bloc.

September 11 Hungary opened borders with Austria to allow 60,000 East Germans access to the West.

October 10 Hungarian Communist party dissolved itself and renounced Marxist-Leninism in favor of social democracy.

October 18 East German leader, Erich Honecker, resigned in wake of huge protest rallies; replaced by hardliner, Egon Krenz.

November 7 East German cabinet resigned; new politburo appointed, headed by liberal reformer, Hans Modrow.

November 10 Bulgarian leader, Todor Zhivkov, resigned; replaced by Petar Mladenov.

November 24 Milos Jakes and the entire Czechoslovakian politburo resigned; Alexander Dubcek returned to Prague to address cheering thousands.

December 10 First non-Communist government in Czechoslovakia sworn in.

December 22 Nicolae Ceausescu, the Romanian president, overthrown by the army; executed on Christmas Day, December 25.

A DICTIONARY OF PEOPLE

A

Abdul Hamid II (1842-1915) Turkish sultan (1876-1909); rescinded the parliamentary constitution and ruled as a despot until deposed by the Young Turks.

Abdullah ibn Husein (1882-1951) King of Jordan (1946-51); prominent in the Arab Revolt against the Ottoman empire during WWI; assassinated at Jerusalem.

Abelard, Peter (1079-1142) French philosopher, theologian and monk; founder of the University of Paris; condemned as a heretic by the Council of Sens (1140).

Aberdeen, George Hamilton-Gordon, 4th earl of (1784-1860) British Conservative politician, foreign secretary (1828-30, 1841-46) and prime minister (1852-55); forced out of office by mismanagement of Crimean War.

Acheson, Dean (1893-1971) U.S. secretary of state (1949-53); a developer of the Marshall Plan and NATO.

Adams, John (1735-1826) U.S. diplomat and Federalist politician, vice-president (1789-97) and president (1797-1801); a leading agitator for separation from Great Britain and signatory of the Declaration of Independence (1776); negotiator of the Peace of Paris (1783); first president to occupy the White House.

Adams, John Quincy (1767-1843) U.S. Republican secretary of state and president (1825-29); son of President Adams; firm opponent of extension of slavery and chief architect of the Monroe Doctrine (1823).

Adenauer, Konrad (1876-1967) German co-founder of the Christian Democratic Party (1945) and its president (1946-66); chancellor of West Germany (1949-63) and foreign minister (1951-55).

Addington, Henry, 1st viscount Sidmouth (1757-1844) Tory prime minister of England (1801-04), responsible for the Peace of Amiens (1802); as home secretary (1812-22) introduced the repressive Six Acts after the Peterloo Massacre (1819).

Adrian IV (c. 1100-59) English abbot, born Nicholas Breakspear; the only English pope (1154-59); his "donation" of Ireland as a papal fief to Henry II of England is disputed.

Aethelbald see **Ethelbald**
Aethelbert see **Ethelbert**
Aethelred see **Ethelred**

Aetius (c. 396-454) Roman general, commander in Gaul who defeated Attila at Mauriac Plain (451); murdered by Emperor Valentinian III, who was jealous of his success.

Alanbrooke, Alan, 1st viscount (1883-1963) British chief of staff (1941-46); distinguished himself during the evacuation of Dunkirk.

Alaric I (c. 370-410) Visigoth chief who overran the Balkans and led the "Barbarian" sack of Rome (410).

Alba [or Alva], Fernando Alvarez de Toledo, duke of (1507-82) Spanish general; led the campaign to suppress the revolt of the Netherlands (1572), but failed to bring order and was recalled (1573).

Albert, Prince (1819-61) German prince, of Saxe-Coburg-Gotha, consort of Queen Victoria (1840-61); patron of arts and sciences and promoter of the Great Exhibition (1851).

Alcuin [or Albinus] (c. 735-804) English scholar and cleric, chief intellectual presence at Charlemagne's court at Aachen from c. 781: founded the medieval curriculum of the seven liberal arts.

Alexander I (1777-1825) Tsar of Russia (1801-25); with Metternich the chief architect of the post-Napoleonic, reactionary Holy Alliance.

Alexander II (1818-81) Tsar of Russia (1855-81); emancipated the serfs (1861) and introduced the *zemstvo* for local self-government; suppressed the Polish uprising (1863).

Alexander III (1845-94) Tsar of Russia (1881-94); reactionary who increased police oppression, especially of Jews and non-Russians.

Alexander VI (c. 1421-1503) Spanish pope (1492-1503), born Rodrigo de Borja (*It* Borgia); defined the line of demarcation between Spanish and Portuguese New World possessions (1494).

Alexis [Aleksei Mikhailovich] (1629-76) Tsar of Russia (1645-76); his codification of law (1648) remained in force until the early 19th century.

Alfred the Great (848-99) King of Wessex (871-99), recognized as king of all England; bought peace with the Danish invaders by establishing the Danelaw; built a strong central monarchy and created a navy.

Allenby, Edmund, 1st viscount (1861-1936) British general; commanded the 3rd Army in France (1915-17); captured Jerusalem (1917); high commissioner of Egypt (1919-25).

Allende Gossens, Salvador (1908-73) President of Chile (1970-73); founder of the Chilean Socialist Party; his radical social and economic program led to an army *coup* against him, during which he died (perhaps by suicide).

Amin, Idi (c. 1925-) Ugandan dictator; ousted Obote in military *coup* (1971) and declared himself president for life (1976); fled to Libya after being overthrown (1979).

Anderson, Elizabeth Garrett (1836-1917) English physician; the first woman to qualify as a doctor in Great Britain (1865).

Andrassy, Gyula, count (1823-90) Hungarian nationalist and first premier (1867-71); as Austro-Hungarian foreign minister (1871-79), presided over worsening relations with the Balkan provinces.

Andropov, Yuri (1914-84) U.S.S.R. premier (1982-84); chief of the KGB (1967-82).

Anna (Ivanovna) (1693-1740) Empress of Russia (1730-40), during whose reign Russia was ruled by her favorite, Biron; gained Poland in the War of the Polish Succession (1733-35).

Anne (1665-1714) Queen of England (1702-14), daughter of James II; a staunch Protestant; last of the Stuart line and last British sovereign to exercise the royal veto (1707).

Anne of Cleves (1515-47) German sister of William, duke of Cleves, and fourth queen of Henry VIII of England; the diplomatic marriage (1540) ended in divorce after six months.

Anselm, St. (c. 1033-1109) Italian prelate, archbishop of Canterbury (1093-1109); banished by William II for opposing lay investiture, but recalled by Henry I; a Doctor of the Church and founder of scholasticism.

Anthony, Susan B. (1820-1906) American suffragette and feminist; with Elizabeth Stanton gained women's rights over children and property in New York law and organized the Woman Suffrage Association (1869).

Antonescu, Ion (1882-1946) Romanian general and dictator (1940-44); allied Romania with the Axis powers in WWII; executed for war crimes.

Aquino, Corazon (1933-) President of the Philippines, installed after officially losing 1986 election to Ferdinand Marcos, who was forced to flee the country; member of the rich land-owning class.

Arafat, Yassir (1929-) Palestinian nationalist, founder of the guerrilla movement, Al Fatah, later absorbed in the Palestinian Liberation Front, of which he became chairman (1969); gained U.N. recognition of the PLO as the sole legitimate representative of the Palestinian people (1974).

Armstrong, Neil (1930-) American astronaut, the first man to set foot on the moon, during the *Apollo 11* mission of July 1969.

Arnold, Benedict (1741-1801) American general, infamous for treachery after plotting (1780) to deliver the rebel post under his command at West Point to the British during the American War of Independence; he escaped capture and fought for the British.

Arthur, Chester (1883-86) U.S. Republican president (1881-85); elected vice-president in 1880, he gained the White House on the assassination of James Garfield.

Asquith, Herbert, 1st earl of Asquith and Oxford (1852-1928) British Liberal prime minister (1908-16); introduced old-age pensions and unemployment insurance; successfully led campaign to deprive House of Lords of its legislative veto; resigned in the face of criticism of his war leadership.

Astor, Nancy, viscountess (1879-1964) British Conservative politician, the first woman to sit in the House of Commons (1919-45); hostess of the appeasement circle, the Cliveden Set, in the 1930s.

Atatürk, Kemal (1881-1938) Turkish nationalist, first president (1923-38) of modern Turkey; co-founded Young Turk movement (1908); reforms made Turkey a more Western and secular state.

Athanasius, St. (c. 297-373) Doctor of the Church and patriarch of Alexandria (328-73); chief architect of Nicene orthodoxy against heretical Arianism; the Athanasian creed is no longer ascribed to him.

Attila (d. 453) Sole king of the Huns (445-53) after murdering his co-ruler or brother; by military campaigns extorted tribute from the Eastern and Western empires, but his invasion of Gaul was checked by the Romans (451) and his advance into Italy (452) was abandoned before reaching Rome.

Attlee, Clement, 1st earl (1883-1967) British Labour prime minister (1945-51); led first Labour government with a majority in the House of Commons and by nationalization and social reforms, especially the National Health Service (1946), vastly extended the welfare state.

Auchinlek, Sir Claude (1884-1981) British commander-in-chief in the Middle East (1941-42), where he defeated Axis forces under Rommel in Libya before being forced to retreat to Egypt; commander-in-chief in India (1943-47).

Augustine, St. (384-430) Doctor of the Church and bishop of Hippo (396-430); considered the father of Christian theology for his attacks on Manichaeism and Pelagianism; laid the foundations of Christian anti-feminism; wrote the *Confessions*, a classic of Christian mysticism.

Augustus, Caesar (63 B.C.-A.D. 14.) First Roman emperor (29 B.C.-A.D. 14); gained control of all Roman territories by his naval victory over Antony and Cleopatra at Actium (31B.C.); returned Rome from military dictatorship to constitutional rule; patron of Vergil, Livy, Ovid and Horace.

Aurangzeb [*or* **Aurangzib]** (1618-1707) Mogul emperor of India (1658-1707); the Mogul Islamic empire reached its greatest extent under his rule, but his persecution of Hindus and Sikhs provoked uprisings that fatally weakened it.

B

Babur (1483-1530) Sultan of Delhi and founder of the Indian Mogul dynasty.

Bacon, Francis (1561-1626) English philosopher-writer and statesman, lord chancellor (1618-21) until found guilty of accepting bribes; one of the great scientific investigators of his age and a fierce apologist for the inductive method of reasoning; works include *Novum Organum* (1620) and *De Augmentis Scientiarum* (1623).

Bacon, Roger (*c*. 1214-*c*. 1294) English scholastic theologian and natural philosopher, a teacher at Oxford; an Aristotelian, he preached and practiced close observation and experimentation in science.

Bakunin, Mikhail (1814-76) Russian revolutionary anarchist; exiled to Siberia after joining in 1848 revolutions in France and Germany; escaped to London (1861) and worked with the First International, where his

individualist creed clashed with Marxism; expelled in 1872.

Balboa, Vasco de (*c*. 1475-1519) Spanish explorer, discoverer of the Pacific Ocean after seizing command of an expedition from Martin de Enciso and crossing by land the isthmus of Panama (1513); executed for treason.

Baldwin, Stanley, 1st earl (1867-1947) British Conservative prime minister (1923-24, 1924-29 and, as leader of the National government, 1935-37); presided over defeat of the General Strike (1926); instrumental in forcing Edward VIII's abdication (1936).

Balfour, Arthur, 1st earl (1848-1930) British Conservative prime minister (1902-05) and foreign secretary (1916-19); resigned premiership in 1905 in defense of free trade against the imperial protectionists; issued "Balfour Declaration" (1917) promising Jews a "national homeland" in Palestine.

Banda, Hastings (*c*. 1902-) Nationalist leader of Malawi, who led the independence struggle and proclaimed Malawi as an independent state with himself as chief executive (1966); made president for life of the one-party state in 1971.

Bandaranaike, Sirimavo (1916-) Sri Lankan politician, wife of the prime minister, Solomon Bandaranaike (assassinated in 1959), and herself prime minister 1959-80, when she was expelled from parliament for corruption of power; the world's first woman prime minister.

Banting, Sir Frederick (1891-1941) Canadian physician, awarded Nobel Prize in 1923 for his isolation of the hormone insulin (1921).

Barbarossa, Frederick *see* **Frederick I**

Barnard, Christiaan (1922-) South African physician who introduced open-heart surgery and in 1967 performed the world's first heart transplant, on Louis Washkansky, in Cape Town.

Bede, St. (*c*. 673-735) English Benedictine monk, the "Venerable Bede"; passed his life at the monasteries of Wearmouth and Jarrow and wrote on all aspects of learning; most famous for *Ecclesiastical History of the English Nation*; the only English Doctor of the Church.

Begin, Menachem (1913-) Polish-born Israeli politician, leader (1943-48) of the underground organization, Irgun Zvai Leumi, during the fight for Israeli nationhood, founder of the Herut party (1948) and prime minister at

the head of the Likud party (1977-83); signed the 1979 peace treaty with Egypt and won the 1978 Nobel Peace Prize.

Bell, Alexander (1847-1922) U.S. inventor of the telephone, first demonstrated by the transmission of a sentence to his assistant in 1876; devised teaching methods improved education for the deaf.

Benedict, St. (*c*. 480-*c*. 547) Italian monk, founder of the Benedictine order.

Benes, Eduard (1884-1948) Czech prime minister 1935-38; resigned after the Munich pact; during WWII president of the provisional government in London; president again from 1945 until the Communist *coup* of 1948, when he refused to sign the new constitution.

Ben-Gurion, David (1886-1973) Polish-born Israeli politician, a Zionist from 1914 and leader in the struggle for nationhood after WWII; first prime minister (1948-53, 1955-63) of the new state of Israel.

Bentham, Jeremy (1748-1832) British political philosopher, founder of Utilitarianism, the concept that actions are to be judged on a calculus of the pleasure they bring against the pain; had signal influence on the early 19th-century reform of English law; his most famous work, the *Introduction to the Principles of Morals and Legislation* (1789), argued that legislation should advance the "greatest happiness of the greatest number."

Bernard of Clairvaux, St. (*c*. 1090-1153) French churchman, abbot from 1115 until his death in the Cistercian abbey which he founded at Clairvaux; his profound spirituality and veneration of the Virgin Mary inspired the reform movement known as the *devotio moderna*; chief mover in the condemnation of Peter Abelard (1140).

Besant, Annie (1847-1933) British feminist and reformer; deprived of her children after divorce (1879) because of her avowed atheism; persistent advocate of birth control, charged with Charles Bradlaugh on that account with immorality (1877), but acquitted; after 1889 a leading international theosophist.

Bethmann-Hollweg, Theobald von (1856-1921) German chancellor (1909-17); opposed to war, but drifted into it and dismissed treaty guaranteeing Belgian neutrality as "a scrap of paper"; delayed submarine warfare and was pushed from office by the military.

Bevan, Aneurin (1897-1960) British Labour minister of health (1945-51), responsible for introducing the National Health Service (1946); led left wing of the Labour party in the 1950s, especially as a unilateralist nuclear disarmer.

Bhutto, Benazir (*b*. 1953-) Pakistani prime minister (1988-89), daughter of Zulfikar Bhutto, prime minister 1973-77; first female head of an Islamic state; ousted from office by the military.

Biko, Steve (1946-77) South African black political leader, luminary of the "black consciousness" movement of the 1960s and '70s; arrested for subversion in 1977, he died in police custody, almost certainly murdered.

Bismarck, Prince Otto von (1815-98) Prussian statesman, chief minister of Prussia (1862-71) and chancellor of Germany (1871-90); in three armed victories over Schleswig-Holstein (1864), Austria (1866) and France (1870) established German hegemony in Europe and did much to bring about the unification of Germany; chief architect of the "alliance system" in late 19th-century European diplomacy; dismissed by Wilhelm II over disagreements in domestic and foreign affairs.

Black Prince *see* **Edward, the Black Prince**

Blériot, Louis (1872-1936) French aviator, the first (1909) to fly across the English Channel in a heavier-than-air machine (a monoplane of his own design); crossed from Calais to Dover in 37 min.

Bodin, Jean (*c*. 1530-96) French political theorist, whose *Six Books of the Commonwealth* (1576) argued for the unqualified sovereignty of a single ruler, thus pointing the way to the absolute monarchies of the European nation-states.

Bolívar, Simón (1783-1830) Venezuelan soldier and statesman, the "Liberator" of South America.

Bonaparte, Napoleon *see* **Napoleon**

Booth, William (1829-1912) British philanthropist and Methodist, founder of the Salvation Army (1878), which grew out of his Christian Mission (1865) in Whitechapel, London; the Army, which combined Christian mission with material help for the outcast, spread throughout the British empire and the U.S.

Borgia, Cesare (1476-1507) Italian soldier and politician, son of Pope Alexander VI; subdued cities of the Romagna and became its duke (1501); ultimately failed to carve out an empire in central Italy, but by his methods—implication in the murder of his brother, the duke of Gandia, in 1498 and of a brother-in-law in 1500—compelled the admiration of Machiavelli.

Boyle, Robert (1627-91) Irish physicist and chemist, called the "father of chemistry" for separating it from alchemy; famous for law (1662) that the pressure and volume of a gas are in inverse proportion to each other.

Brandt, Willy (1913-) German SPD chancellor (1969-74); resigned because of spy scandal in his administration; awarded Nobel Peace Prize (1971) for efforts to reduce East–West tensions.

Brezhnev, Leonid (1906-82) U.S.S.R. first secretary of the Communist party (1964-82), the longest-serving after Stalin; after constitutional revision in 1977, first to head both the party and, as president of the presidium, the state; justified invasion of Czechoslovakia (1968) by the "Brezhnev doctrine" of the duty to protect socialism.

Brunel, Isambard (1806-59) British engineer, designer of the *Great Western* (1838), the first transatlantic steamship, the *Great Britain* (1845), the first iron ocean-going steamship with screw propellers, and the *Great Eastern* (1858).

Bruning, Heinrich (1885-1970) German chancellor (1930-32) and leader of the largely Roman Catholic Center party; governed by decree, but failed to stem Depression by severe deflationary policy.

Buchanan, James (1791-1868) U.S. Democratic secretary of state (1845-49) and president (1857-61); attempt to balance moral opposition to slavery with defense of existing slave states split his party and helped Lincoln win the 1860 election.

Buckingham, George Villiers, 1st duke of (1592-1628) English royal favorite and lord high admiral (1619-28); disgraced by granting monopolies to relatives and weakened by negotiating (1624) Charles I's marriage to the Roman Catholic Henrietta of France, also by the failed Cadiz expedition of 1625; impeached (1626) but not tried, because Charles dissolved parliament; murdered by a naval officer.

Bulganin, Nikolai (1895-1975) U.S.S.R. marshal and politician, first secretary of the Communist party (1955-58); ousted by Khrushchev and expelled from the party's central committee.

Bülow, Bernhard von (1849-1929) German chancellor (1900-09), whose aggressive foreign policy helped to harden antipathies between the Triple Entente and Triple Alliance; announced (1897) Germany's bid for her "place in the sun."

Burghley [*or* Burleigh], William Cecil, 1st baron (1520-98) English statesman, chief minister of Elizabeth I as secretary (1558-72) and lord treasurer (1572-98); strongest advocate of the execution (1587) of Mary, Queen of Scots.

Burke, Edmund (1727-92) Irish politician and man of letters; Westminster member of parliament (1765-92), as a Whig supporter of Irish and American grievances against the imperial government and opponent of the Crown; chief instigator of the impeachment of Warren Hastings (1787); turned Tory after the outbreak of revolution in Paris and wrote his most famous book, *Reflections on the Revolution in France* (1790).

Bush, George (1924-) U.S. Republican vice-president (1981-89) and president (1989-); an oil millionaire; head of the Central Intelligence Agency (1976-77).

Bute, John Stuart, 3rd earl of (1713-92) English prime minister (1761-63), the representative of the "new Whigs," chosen by George III allegedly to be the tool of royal ambition to recapture effective political power; resigned for want of parliamentary support.

C

Cabot, John (*fl.* 1460-98) Italian-born English navigator.

Calhoun, John (1782-1850) U.S. Republican secretary of war (1817-25), vice-president (1825-32) and senator for South Carolina (1832-43, 1845-50); leading spokesman for states' rights against the central government and staunch defender of slavery.

Caligula [Caius Caesar Germanicus] (A.D. 12-41) Roman emperor (A.D. 37-41), called Caligula (*Lat* "little boots") from his boyhood military boots; noted for cruelty, especially against the Jews; by legend made his horse a consul.

Callaghan, James, baron (1912-) British Labour chancellor of the exchequer (1964-67), home secretary (1967-70), foreign secretary (1974-76) and prime minister (1976-79); his government was the first to be defeated on a vote of no confidence since 1841.

Calvin, John (1509-64) French Protestant theologian and reformer.

Campbell-Bannerman, Sir Henry (1836-1908) British Liberal prime minister (1905-07); opposed British policy in the Boer War and during premiership granted self-government to Transvaal and Orange Free State.

Canning, George (1770-1827) British Tory foreign secretary (1807-09, 1822-27) and prime minister (1827); his appointment as prime minister split the Tory party; first European foreign minister to recognize the independence of the South American republics.

Canute *see* **Cnut**

Carter, James (1924-) U.S. Democratic president (1977-81), defeated in bid for re-election, partly because of failure to bring American hostages back from Iran.

Cartier, Jacques (1491-1557) French explorer who made three expeditions to North America between 1534 and 1541; discovered the St. Lawrence River and founded transient settlements at Hochelega (Montreal) and Stadacona (Quebec City).

Castlereagh, Robert Stewart, 2nd viscount (1769-1822) British Tory foreign secretary (1812-22), a leading figure at Vienna peace talks (1815) and supporter of the conservative Holy Alliance; committed suicide by slitting his throat.

Castro, Fidel (1926-) Cuban revolutionary and president (1959-); with American backing overthrew the Batista dictatorship; thereafter, as a strict Marxist-Leninist, forfeited American support and took Cuba into the Soviet orbit.

Catherine II (1729-96) Empress of Russia (1762-96), called Catherine the Great; came to power when her lover, Grigori Orlov, and other rebels overthrew her husband Peter III (and later murdered him); gained much territory, including the Crimea, at the expense of Ottoman Turkey; after suppressing Pugachev's revolt (1773), greatly increased power of aristocracy over the peasantry.

Cavour, Camillo di, count (1810-61) Italian nationalist; introduced liberal constitution and reforms as premier of Sardinia (1852-59, 1860-61); chief mover in the unification of Italy (1861).

Ceausescu, Nicolae (1918-89) Romanian Communist president (1974-89) and dictator; overthrown and executed in the collapse of East European Communist governments in 1989.

Cetswayo [*or* Cetewayo] (*c.* 1825-84) Zulu chief or king (1856-84); engaged by the British in a series of wars and decisively defeated at Ulundi (1879) and robbed of most of his kingdom; died discredited in exile.

Chamberlain, Neville (1869-1940) British Conservative politician, prime minister of National government (1937-40); made famous "appeasement" deal with Hitler at Munich (1938); forced from office after disastrous Norwegian campaign in WWII.

Charlemagne [Charles the Great] (*c.* 742-814) King of the Franks (768-814) and Roman Emperor in the West (800-814).

Charles I (1600-49) King of England (1625-49); by ruling without parliament (1629-40) and by following a High Anglican policy in religion, alienated parliamentarians and Puritans; defeated in the English Civil War and executed.

Charles II (1630-85) King of England (1660-85), restored to the throne after the Cromwellian interregnum; forced by his ministers to forgo religious tolerance of Roman Catholics and Protestant dissenters in the Clarendon Code (1661) and Test Act (1673).

Charles V (1500-58) King of Spain (1516-56) and Holy Roman Emperor (1519-58), ruler of the vast Habsburg empire in Europe and the New World (Mexico and Peru were conquered early in his reign); vainly opposed the Protestant Reformation in northern Europe, but played key role in the Counter-Reformation; was recurrently, and largely successfully, at war with France for supremacy in Italy.

Charlie, Bonnie Prince *see* **Stuart, Charles**

Chatham, earl of *see* **Pitt, William**

Chernenko, Konstantin (1911-85) General secretary of the Communist party and president of the U.S.S.R. (1984-85).

Chiang Kai-shek (1887-1975) Chinese Nationalist leader, successor (1925) to Sun Yat-sen as leader of the Kuomintang; head of the Nationalist government (1928-37) and of the Nationalist-Communist anti-Japanese front (1937-45); driven by the Communists to Taiwan, where he was president of "Nationalist China" (1950-75).

Chou En-lai [*or* Zhou Enlai] (1889-1976) Chinese Communist leader; early ally of Mao in the building of the Red Army and the "Long March" in the 1930s; foreign minister (1949-76), who established diplomatic ties with Japan and the U.S. in the 1970s.

Christina (1626-89) Queen of Sweden (1632-54), who made her court a magnet for artists and scholars; converted to Roman Catholicism and abdicated; tried unsuccessfully to regain the throne on the death of Charles X in 1660.

Churchill, Sir Winston (1874-1965) British Conservative prime minster (1940-45; 1951-55); a Liberal until 1924 and minister in Liberal and coalition governments (1908-15, 1917-22); reputation scarred, as lord high admiral, by the disastrous Gallipoli campaign (1915); chancellor of the exchequer(1924-29); prominent "anti-appeaser" in the 1930s; famous for eloquent, morale-lifting speeches during WWII.

Cid, El (1043-99) Spanish soldier and national hero.

Claudius I (10 B.C.-A.D. 54) Roman emperor (A.D. 42-54); landed in Britain (A.D. 43) and made it a province of the empire; also added Macedonia to the empire.

Clay, Henry (1777-1852) U.S. Republican, then Whig, statesman, senator for Kentucky and secretary of state (1825-29); leading spokesman for the agrarian West and chief architect of the Missouri Compromise (1820) and the Compromise of 1850; three times (1824, 1832, 1844) failed to win the presidency.

Clemenceau, Georges (1841-1929) French prime minister (1906-09, 1917-20), known as "the Tiger"; outspoken defender of Dreyfus; chief architect of the severe peace terms imposed on Germany at Versailles (1919).

Cleveland, Grover (1837-1908) U.S. Democratic president (1885-89, 1893-97); his nomination in 1884 was a victory over the machine politicians of "Tammany hall"; an anti-imperialist, he resisted a forward policy in Hawaii; by his opposition to "free silver" lost 1896 nomination to William Jennings Bryan.

Clive, Robert, baron Clive of Plassey (1725-74) British soldier, after his victory at Plassey (1857) the first British governor of Bengal (1757-59, 1765-67); made Great Britain the dominant European power in India.

Cnut [or **Canute**] (c. 994-1035) Danish invader of England (1013), who divided the kingdom with Edmund Ironside after victory at the Battle of Assandun (1016) and remained king until his death; King of Denmark from 1019.

Colbert, Jean (1619-83) French director of finances (1665-83) under Louis XIV; greatly expanded French industry and trade under a mercantilist policy; chief founder of the modern French navy.

Columbus, Christopher (1451-1506) Italian navigator in service of Spain, discoverer of America (1492).

Constantine I (c. 288-337) Roman emperor (306-37), known as Constantine the Great; born in present-day Yugoslavia; proclaimed emperor at York in 306 by his soldiers, but not secure until victory over rival claimant Maxentius at Milvian Bridge (312); first Christian emperor.

Cook, James (1728-79) British naval captain and explorer of Australia and New Zealand; killed by Hawaiian natives.

Coolidge, Calvin (1872-1933) U.S. Republican president (1923-29); staunch believer in small government and *laissez-faire* economics; encouraged frenzy of stock-market speculation that led to the Great Crash of 1929.

Copernicus, Nicholas (1473-1543) Polish astronomer; propounder of heliocentric theory of planetary motion.

Cortes, Hernan [or **Hernando Cortez**] (1485-1547) Spanish explorer and conqueror of Mexico.

Cranmer, Thomas (1489-1566) English prelate, archbishop of Canterbury (1533-56); chief author of the Book of Common Prayer (1549) and sole author of the revision (1552); his Forty-two Articles of the Church of England (1553), never accepted, were the basis of the Thirty-nine Articles.

Cromwell, Oliver (1599-1658) English soldier and Puritan statesman; lord protector of England (1653-58).

Cromwell, Thomas, earl of Essex (c. 1485-1540) English merchant and politician, chief minister to Henry VIII after 1530; chief mover behind Henry's divorce from Catherine of Aragon and maker of the legislation separating the English Church from Rome; fell from favor and was executed.

Custer, George (1839-76) U.S. army general, the youngest ever on his promotion in 1763.

Cuvier, Georges (1769-1832) French naturalist, by his classification of four phylla in the animal kingdom, a father of modern zoology; one of the early pioneers of paleontology, he deduced and reconstructed soft parts of fossils.

D

Daguerre, Louis (1789-1851) French painter and physicist, inventor (1829) of the daguerreotype photograph; developed with Niepce and first publicly displayed in 1839, it was made on a silver-coated copper plate treated with iodine gas.

Daladier, Edouard (1884-1970) French Radical prime minister

(1933, 1934, 1938-40); signed Munich Pact (1938); interned by the Vichy government (1942-45) after attempting to run an anti-Nazi government of France from north Africa.

Dalton, John (1766-1844) British physicist, father of modern atomic theory; drew up table of atomic weights (1803); propounded "Dalton's Law," that the total pressure exerted by a homogeneous mixture of gases is equal to the sum of the pressures exerted by the individual gases.

Danton, Georges (1759-94) French Revolutionary leader; prime mover in carrying the Revolution by war beyond France's borders; leader of the Committee of Public Safety in its first months; opposed the Terror and was executed as a moderate.

Darnley, Henry Stuart, Lord (1545-67) Scottish courtier, second husband of Mary, Queen of Scots, and father of James I of England; conspired in murder of Mary's secretary, David Rizzio, and was himself murdered, probably at Bothwell's instigation.

Darwin, Charles (1809-82) British naturalist, co-founder with Alfred Wallace of the theory of the evolution of species.

Davis, Jefferson (1808-89) U.S. statesman, president (1862-65) of the secessionist Confederate states during the Civil War; captured in 1865, but released in 1867 without being prosecuted.

Dayan, Moshe (1915-1981) Israeli soldier and politician; chief of staff during the 1956 Sinai campaign, minister of defense (1967-74) and foreign minister (1977-79); chiefly responsible for negotiating Camp David accord (1978) with Egypt.

de Gaulle, Charles *see* **Gaulle, Charles de**

Deng Xiaoping (1904-) Chinese political leader; active in the "Long March" (1934-35) and the Communist victory in the civil war after WWII; after Mao's death (1976), the leader (despite holding no high office) in the government's effort to make links with the West and to introduce free-market ideas into the economy.

Derby, Edward Stanley, 14th earl of (1799-1869) British Conservative prime minster (1852, 1858-59, 1866-68); the longest-serving Conservative leader, from 1846, when he led the protectionists against Peel's repeal of the Corn Laws, to 1868.

De Valera, Eamon (1882-1975) U.S.-born Irish politician; life sentence for part in Easter Rising (1916)

commuted to one year; elected president of Sinn Fein (1917) and the revolutionary assembly, Dáil Eireann (1919); founded the Fianna Fáil party, was prime minister (1932-48, 1951-54, 1957-59) and introduced constitution making Eire an independent state (1937).

Diaz, Porfirio (1830-1915) President of Mexico (1876-1911); an autocrat, whose sale of natural resources to foreign companies, expropriation of peasant land, and failure to usher in democracy led to his overthrow in the 1911 revolution.

Disraeli, Benjamin, 1st earl of Beaconsfield (1804-81) British Conservative prime minister (1868, 1874-80); led Tory revolt against Peel and the repeal of the Corn Laws (1846); introduced the 1867 Reform Act giving urban working men the vote; only novelist to be British prime minister.

Dollfuss, Engelbert (1892-1934) Austrian chancellor (1932-34); assassinated during abortive Nazi *putsch*.

Dominic, St. (c. 1170-1221) Spanish founder of the Dominican order (1216); chief preacher of Roman orthodoxy among the Albigensian heretics of southern France.

Douglas-Home, Sir Alec, baron Home of the Hirsel (1903-) British Conservative prime minister (1963-64) and foreign secretary (1970-74); renounced hereditary earldom to become prime minister on Macmillan's resignation (1963); made life peer (1974).

Drake, Sir Francis (c. 1543-96) English navigator and admiral, first Englishman to circumnavigate the globe (1577-80); inflicted heavy defeat on Spanish fleet at Cadiz (1587) and was vice-admiral of the fleet that defeated the Armada (1588).

Dreyfus, Alfred (1859-1935) French army officer, center of the Dreyfus affair.

Dubcek, Alexander (1921-) Communist president of Czechoslovakia (1968-69), driven out by Soviet tanks for attempting, during the "Prague Spring," to liberalize the politics and economics of the country and to give "socialism a human face."

Dulles, John (1888-1959) U.S. Republican secretary of state (1953-59), resolute Cold Warrior, who moved from "containment" of Communism to "brinkmanship"; led buildup of nuclear capacity for "massive retaliation."

Durham, John Lambton, 1st earl of (1792-1840) British Whig/Radical politician; one of committee of four that drew up the 1832 Reform Bill;

his 1839 Report was the basis of responsible self-government for Canada within the British empire.

Duvalier, François (1907-71), President and dictator of Haiti (1957-71), known as "Papa Doc"; ruled by terror and corruption, and kept the country in a constant state of economic stagnation and illiteracy.

E

Ebert, Friedrich (1871-1925) SPD president of the German republic (1919-25); accepted Versailles treaty and presided over introduction of the democratic Weimar constitution.

Eck, Johann von (1486-1543) German theologian; denounced Luther's reforming theses and, after returning to Germany with the papal bull condemning Lutheranism (1520), led the Roman opposition to Protestantism.

Eden, Sir Anthony, 1st earl of Avon (1897-1977) British Conservative prime minister (1955-57); resigned as foreign secretary (1938) in opposition to Chamberlain's appeasement of Hitler; led Great Britain into the disaster of the Suez conflict with Nasser (1956), which forced his resignation.

Edison, Thomas (1847-1931) U.S. inventor, especially of the phonograph (1873) and the electric light bulb (1879).

Edward I (1239-1307) King of England (1272-1307), sometimes called the "English Justinian" for his law reforms; gave parliament a permanent status and brought Wales under English rule.

Edward II (1284-1327) King of England (1307-27); in 1301 made first prince of Wales; continual disputes with his great barons ended in his deposition and murder.

Edward III (1312-77) King of England (1327-77); reign dominated by the Hundred Years' War with France; founded Order of the Garter (1348), the oldest order of knighthood in Europe.

Edward IV (1442-83) Yorkist king of England (1461-70, 1471-83); deposed Henry VI after victory over the Lancastrians at Towton (1461); briefly deposed by Warwick the Kingmaker in 1470-71.

Edward V (1470-83) Yorkist king of England (1483), but deposed by his uncle, the duke of Gloucester, Richard III; imprisoned with his brother, Richard, in the Tower of London, where they died, almost certainly murdered by Richard III.

Edward VI (1537-53) King of England (1547-53) under protectorates of Somerset and then Northumberland; a firm Protestant, required use of the Book of Common Prayer in all churches and attempted to leave throne to Lady Jane Grey, rather than Mary I; died from tuberculosis.

Edward VII (1841-1910) King of England (1901-10); immensely popular as prince of Wales and king; concluded the *Entente Cordiale* (1904) with France.

Edward VIII (1894-1972) King of England (1935-36); abdicated in order to marry the divorced American, Mrs. Wallis Simpson; thereafter lived in France as the duke of Windsor.

Edward, the Black Prince (1330-76) Son of Edward III, distinguished soldier at the battles of Crécy (1346) and Poitiers (1356); named after the color of his armor; harsh ruler of Aquitaine (1362-72).

Edward the Confessor (c. 1003-66) King of England (1042-66); reared at the Norman court and gained some disfavor by use of Norman advisors; founded Westminster Abbey.

Eichmann, Adolf (1906-62) German Nazi official in charge, after 1941, of the deportation of Jews to extermination camps; arrested by Allies in 1945, but escaped to Argentina; captured in 1960, tried in an Israeli court (1961) and executed for crimes against humanity.

Einstein, Albert (1879-1955) German physicist, propounder of the Theory of Relativity; awarded Nobel Prize (1922); fled Nazi Germany in 1933 and lived thereafter in the U.S.A.

Eisenhower, Dwight D. (1890-1969) U.S. general and Republican president (1953-61); supreme commander of Allied forces in Europe (1944-45); supervised D-Day landings (1944); never denounced Senator McCarthy; sent federal troops to Little Rock, Arkansas (1957) to enforce desegregation in schools.

Eleanor of Aquitaine (1122-1204) Queen consort of Louis VII of France (1137-52) and Henry II of England (1154-89); estranged from Henry after 1170, established her own court at Poitiers; aided her sons in failed revolt against Henry (1173).

Elizabeth I (1533-1603) Queen of England (1558-1603); remained unmarried, using prospects of marriage in international diplomacy; achieved Protestant settlement of the religious question

(1559); retained throne against several rebellions and plots; by pageantry and portraiture made herself a cult figure, greatly enhancing prestige of the monarchy.

Elizabeth (1709-62) Empress of Russia (1741-62); usurped throne by overthrowing Ivan VI; took sides against Frederick II of Prussia in the Seven Years' War.

Erasmus, Desiderius (c. 1466-1536) Dutch humanist, commanding intellectual figure of the northern Renaissance and the Reformation; attacked Roman abuses, e.g. in *In Praise of Folly* (1509), but quarreled with Luther and remained loyal to Rome.

Erhard, Ludwig (1897-1977) West German chancellor (1963-66); as minister of economic affairs (1949-63) presided over West Germany's "miracle" of economic recovery; resigned when his cabinet would not support tax increases to ward off recession.

Eric the Red (fl. 10th century) Norse navigator; banished from Iceland (where he had settled) after a feud, he set sail and discovered Greenland (c. 983), where he established (c. 986) the colony of Brattahlid.

Essex, Robert Devereux, 2nd earl of (1567-1601) English courtier and military commander, successor to his stepfather, Leicester, as favorite of Elizabeth I; captured Cadiz (1596), but led failed expedition to the Azores (1597); executed for treason after abortive rebellion against the Cecil court faction.

Ethelbald (d. 757) King of Mercia (716-57); made his kingdom the greatest in England, extending it to the Humber River; murdered by his bodyguards.

Ethelbert (c. 552-616) King of Kent (c. 560-616); most powerful English ruler of his age; first Christian English king and first to leave surviving records of a law code.

Ethelred (the Unready) (c. 965-1016) Anglo-Saxon king of England (978-1016); made the tribute money called the Danegeld a regular payment, but was unable to resist Danish plunder and invasion.

F

Faraday, Michael (1791-1867) British scientist; built the first dynamo and discovered electromagnetic induction (1831); formulated (1834) Faraday's Law, which describes the process of electrolysis.

Farnese, Alessandro (1545-92) Italian soldier and diplomat, the

duke of Parma; made his reputation as a soldier at the Battle of Lepanto (1571) and, as governor of the Netherlands (1578-92), nearly succeeded, by his diplomacy and military successes, in retaining the Netherlands for Philip II and the Spanish Crown.

Ferdinand I (1503-64) Habsburg king of Hungary and Bohemia (1526-64) and Holy Roman Emperor (1558-64); established Habsburg absolutism in Bohemia and returned the kingdom to Roman Catholicism; negotiated the Peace of Augsburg (1555).

Ferdinand II (1578-1637) Habsburg king of Bohemia (1617-37) and Hungary (1618-37) and Holy Roman Emperor (1619-37); defeated the Bohemian nobles' choice of king, the Protestant Frederick (the "Winter King"), in 1620, thus starting the Thirty Years' War; instigated assassination (1634) of his great military commander, Wallenstein.

Ferdinand III Habsburg king of Hungary (1626-57) and Bohemia (1627-57) and Holy Roman Emperor (1637-57); leader of the imperial forces in the Thirty Years' War after 1634; last emperor to wield power beyond the family lands of the Habsburgs.

Ferdinand II (1452-1516) Spanish king of Aragon (1479-1516) and, after marriage to Isabella of Castile (1469), Ferdinand IV of Castile (1474-1504); also king of Sicily (1468-1516) and Naples (1504-16); with Isabella took Granada and expelled the Moors from Spain (1492); sponsored Christopher Columbus's Atlantic voyage (1492).

Ferdinand VII (1784-1833) King of Spain (1808-33); imprisoned in France (1808-14) during Peninsular War; on return to Spain revoked liberal constitution (1812) framed by nationalist opponents of Napoleon and ruled as absolute monarch.

Fillmore, Millard (1800-74) U.S. Whig president (1850-53), succeeding on the death of Zachary Taylor; his compromise policy on slavery (he tried to enforce the Fugitive Slave Act) cost him his party's nomination for the presidency in 1852.

Fleming, Sir Alexander (1881-1955) Scottish bacteriologist; discovered penicillin (1928) and lysozyme (1922); awarded Nobel Prize (1945).

Foch, Ferdinand (1851-1929) French marshal; with Joffre and Galliéni stopped the Germans at the Marne (1914); commander of British, French and American forces in Europe (1918).

Ford, Gerald (1913-)
U.S. Republican president (1974-77), succeeding on resignation of Richard Nixon; issued pardon to Nixon for Watergate; defeated by James (Jimmy) Carter in 1976 election.

Fox, Charles (1749-1806) British Whig politician, leading orator and liberal of his day; formed coalition government, as foreign secretary, with Lord North (1783); opponent of British military intervention against Napoleon; foreign secretary in "ministry of all the talents" (1806-07) and introduced bill to outlaw slave trade, passed (1807) after his death.

Francis of Assisi, St. (*c.* 1182-1226) Italian friar, founder of the Franciscan order (1209).

Francis I (1494-1547) King of France (1515-47); after a brilliant beginning at the Battle of Marignano (1515) failed, over his reign, to gain Italian territory for France in the Valois–Habsburg Wars; lost election to imperial title in 1519 to Charles V; backed French exploration of Canada.

Franco (Bahamonde), Francisco (1892-1975) Spanish general and *caudillo*, or ruler, (1939-75); head of the rebel Nationalist government that fought the republic in the Civil War (1936-39); thereafter a repressive dictator, despite declaring (1947) Spain a kingdom with himself as regent pending nomination of a king; kept Spain a non-belligerent during WWII.

Franklin, Benjamin (1706-90) Colonial American writer, statesman and scientist; published *Poor Richard's Almanack* (1732-57); proved existence of electricity in lightning with kite experiment and invented the lightning rod; leading advocate at the Albany Congress (1754) of abortive plan for union of the colonies; helped to draft the Declaration of Independence (1776).

Franz Joseph (1830-1916) Last effective Habsburg emperor of Austria (1848-1916); subdued Hungary and ruled autocratically (1867-1916) over the Dual Monarchy of Austro-Hungary.

Frederick I (*c.* 1125-90) Hohenstaufen king of Germany (1152-90) and Holy Roman Emperor (1155-90), known from his red beard as Frederick Barbarossa; failed to impose imperial power on Italy and recognized Lombard League, which defeated his forces decisively at Legnano (1176); drowned on the Third Crusade.

Frederick II (1194-1250) Hohenstaufen king of Germany (1212-20) and Holy Roman Emperor (1220-50); also king of Sicily (1197-1250) and Jerusalem (1229-50); long struggle with the papacy permanently weakened the house of Hohenstaufen and signaled the decline of German, or imperial, authority in Italy.

Frederick III (1415-93) Habsburg king of Germany (1440-93) and Holy Roman Emperor (1452-93); reunited many Habsburg lands and gained Burgundy by marriage of his son Maximilian to Mary, daughter of Charles the Bold; the last emperor to be crowned at Rome.

Frederick II (1712-86) Hohenzollern king of Prussia (1740-86), known as Frederick the Great; friend of Voltaire and leading exemplar of an "enlightened despot"; gained Upper and Lower Silesia for Prussia (1742, 1745), and by victories in the Seven Years' War (1756-63) and the partition of Poland (1772) made Prussia the greatest continental power; reformed Prussian legal and educational system and by transport works stimulated industry.

Frederick William (1620-88) Hohenzollern elector of Brandenburg (1640-88), known as the Great Elector; gained Prussian sovereignty from Poland (1657) and greatly strengthened centralized Prussian state; laid the foundations of its great army.

Frederick William I (1688-1740) Hohenzollern king of Prussia (1713-40); during peaceful reign built up economic surplus and expanded the Prussian army.

Frederick William IV (1795-1861) Hohenzollern king of Prussia (1804-61); after early setbacks, crushed liberal revolution of 1848-49 and framed conservative constitution of 1850 that remained in force in Germany until 1918.

G

Gadaffi [*or* Qadhafi], Muammar (1942-) Libyan chief of state (1969-); a pan-Arab and Islamic revolutionary socialist; overthrew King Idris I in 1969; supporter of the Palestine Liberation Organization.

Gagarin, Yuri (1934-68) U.S.S.R. cosmonaut; made the first manned space flight (1961), orbiting the earth in *Vostok I* in 1 hr. 48 min.; died on an aircraft training flight.

Galileo [Galileo Galilei] (1564-1642) Italian cosmologist and mathematician; by his development of the telescope and his investigation of planetary laws advanced astronomy; discovered that projectiles follow a parabola in flight and that the acceleration of falling bodies is independent of mass and density and proportional to time; recanted heliocentric opinion at Pisa before the Inquisition (1633).

Gama, Vasco da *see* **Vasco da Gama**

Gambetta, Léon (1838-82) French republican politician; a leader of the opposition to the Second Empire; organized resistance to the German forces (1870) and helped establish the Commune; premier (1881-82) of the Third Republic.

Gandhi, Indira (1917-84) Prime minister of India (1966-77, 1979-84) as head of the Congress party; defeated at 1977 elections after proclaiming a state of emergency and ruling by decree (1975); assassinated by Sikh nationalist members of her bodyguard.

Gandhi, Mohandas (1869-1948) Indian nationalist leader, known as Mahatma ("great soul"); worked for racial equality in South Africa (1893-1914); as president (1924-34) of the National Congress party, turned it into a mass movement for independence from Great Britain by campaigns of non-violent civil disobedience; repeatedly imprisoned; helped to negotiate independence (1947); assassinated by a Hindu fanatic.

Garfield, James (1831-81) U.S. Republican president (1881); Union soldier in the Civil War and a Radical Reconstructionist in Congress after 1863; shot (July 2) after barely three months in office and died on September 19.

Garibaldi, Giuseppe (1807-82) Italian nationalist leader during the Risorgimento; his "1,000 red-shirts" took Sicily and Naples (1860) on behalf of Victor Emmanuel, thus ensuring a united kingdom of Italy.

Garrison, William (1805-79) U.S. antislavery campaigner; born in Massachusetts; published the abolitionist newspaper, *The Liberator* (1831-65); sought immediate and total emancipation by non-violent means.

Garvey, Marcus (1887-1940) U.S. black nationalist leader; founded (1914) the Universal Negro Improvement Association, to promote pan-African awareness, advocated non-integration and a "back to Africa" movement; jailed (1925) and deported to Jamaica (1927) for fraud in connection with his steamship company, the Black Star Line.

Genghis [*or* Jenghiz] (*c.* 1167-1277) Khan of the confederacy of Mongols (1206-27).

George I (1660-1727) Elector of Hanover (1698-1727) and king of Great Britain (1714-27); the first of the Hanoverian rulers of Great Britain; by his prolonged absences in Hanover contributed to growth of parliamentary power and cabinet government in England.

George II (1683-1760) King of Great Britain and elector of Hanover (1727-60); last English monarch, at Dettingen (1743), to lead troops into battle.

George III (1738-1820) King of Great Britain (1760-1820); reasserted royal authority after cabinet advance under his predecessors; staunch opponent of American independence; dismissed (1801) his long-serving minister, Pitt the Younger, rather than concede Catholic emancipation; afflicted by mental illness, and last 10 years of his reign under the regency of the prince of Wales.

George IV (1762-1830) Deeply unpopular prince-regent (1810-20) and king of Great Britain (1820-30); gambler and philanderer; secretly (and illegally) married the Catholic Mrs. Fitzherbert in 1785; married Caroline of Brunswick (1795) and sought to divorce her (1820); implacable opponent of Catholic emancipation.

George V (1865-1936) King of Great Britain (1910-36); immensely popular as prince of Wales; in 1917 changed the name of the royal house from Saxe-Coburg-Gotha to Windsor.

George VI (1895-1952) King of Great Britain (1936-52); second son of George V, he succeeded on the abdication of his elder brother, Edward VIII.

Giolitti, Giovanni (1842-1928) Italian prime minister five times between 1892 and 1921; without solid party backing, relied on shifting coalitions, and his combination of corruption and intimidation was known as *giolittismo*.

Giscard d'Estaing, Valéry (1926-) French president (1974-81) and finance minister (1962-66, 1969-74) under Charles de Gaulle and Pompidou; defeated in 1981 presidential election.

Gladstone, William (1809-98) British Liberal prime minister (1868-74, 1880-85, 1886, 1892-94); originally a Tory, sided with Peel on Corn Law repeal (1846) and gradually moved to the Liberals; notable reforms included Irish disestablishment (1869) and land reform (1870), national education (1870), secret ballot (1872) and enfranchisement of rural workers (1884); split Liberal party on Irish home rule issue in 1886.

Glyndwr, Owen *see* **Owain Glyndwr**

Goderich, Henry Robinson, 1st viscount and 1st earl of Ripon (1782-1859) British Tory prime minister (1827-28), successor to Canning and leader of the Whig-Canningite coalition; weak and tearful, he resigned after barely four months, without ever facing parliament.

Godolphin Sidney, 1st earl of (1645-1712) English Crown servant and political manager, financial adviser to Charles II, James II and Anne; first lord of the treasury (1690-97, 1700, 1702-10); financed Marlborough's wars; promoted union with Scotland (1707).

Goebbels, Paul Joseph (1897-1945) German Nazi minister of propaganda (1933-45); PhD in literature; arranged mass meetings and torchlight parades; committed suicide shortly after Hitler.

Goering, Hermann (1893-1946) German Nazi leader; made commander of the *Stürmabteilung* (SA) in 1922; as minister of the interior in Prussia after 1933, created the Gestapo; as aviation minister built up the *Luftwaffe*; sentenced to death at Nuremberg trials, committed suicide on eve of his intended execution.

Gomulka, Wladyslaw (1905-82) Polish head of state, first secretary of the Communist party (1956-70); ousted after outbreaks of unrest and replaced by Edward Gierek.

Gorbachev, Mikhail (1931-) U.S.S.R. head of state, general secretary of the Communist party and president (1985-); introduced concepts of *glasnost* ("open government") and *perestroika* ("restructuring") to Soviet government; proposed limited exercise of free-market economics and profit-incentives at 1986 party conference; remained passive in face of crumbling Communist régimes in eastern Europe in 1989-90.

Gordon, Charles (1833-85) British general and colonial administrator, known as "Chinese Gordon" after defending Shanghai (1863-64) during the Tai P'ing Rebellion; killed by forces of the Mahdi after disobeying orders to evacuate Khartoum, two days before relief expedition reached the besieged British garrison there.

Göring, Hermann *see* **Goering, Hermann**

Grafton, Henry Fitzroy, 3rd duke of (1735-1811) British Whig prime minister (1768-70); pressures from the "Wilkes and liberty" affair and from the mounting colonial crisis in America forced his resignation.

Grant, Ulysses S. (1822-85) U.S. general and Republican president (1869-77); commander of the Union forces in the Civil War; victorious Vicksburg campaign (1862-63) ended Confederate control of the Mississippi; made a general in 1866, the first U.S. citizen to be given the rank since Washington; presidency marked by Radical Reconstruction policies and widespread financial corruption and bribery.

Gregory I, St. (*c.* 540-604) Italian pope (590-604) and Doctor of the Church; a Benedictine monk and abbot; appointed Augustine (596) to lead Christian mission to Britain.

Gregory VII, St. (*c.* 1020-85) Italian pope (1073-85), called Hildebrand; one of the great reforming popes; period of office dominated by the "investiture contest."

Gregory IX (*c.* 1143-1241) Italian pope (1227-41); excommunicated Holy Roman Emperor Frederick II in 1227 for delaying a crusade, and forced by imperial party into exile (1228-30); again excommunicated Frederick (1239) in struggle over Italian liberties and the authority of the papacy.

Gregory XIII (1502-85) Italian pope (1572-85); devised the reformed Gregorian calendar, named after him; leading figure at the Council of Trent (1545) and, by his encouragement of the Jesuits, in the Counter-Reformation.

Grenville, George (1712-70) British Whig prime minister (1763-65); prosecution of John Wilkes initiated the "Wilkes and liberty" movement; his Stamp Act (1765), imposing direct taxation on American colonists, raised the imperial crisis in America to a new pitch.

Grey, Charles, 2nd earl (1764-1845) British Whig prime minister (1830-34); unofficial leader of the Whig opposition (1806-30); head of illustrious reforming government which introduced the Great Reform Act (1832), the abolition of slavery (1833) and the new Poor Law (1834).

Grey, Lady Jane (1537-54) Queen of England for nine days; named, at protector Northumberland's bidding, successor by Edward VI; proclaimed queen on his death on July 10, 1553, but unseated by supporters of the rightful successor, Mary Tudor; imprisoned and beheaded after her father joined Wyatt's rebellion.

Gromyko, Andrei (1909-89) U.S.S.R. politician; foreign minister (1957-85), the longest-serving in European history; an architect of *détente* in the 1970s.

Guevara, "Che" [Ernesto Guevara de la Serna] (1928-67) Argentinian revolutionary; leader in Castro's guerrilla war in Cuba (1956-59) against Batista; advocate of the "permanent revolution" throughout South America; executed by the Bolivian army while trying to found a guerrilla movement there.

Guizot, François (1787-1874) French statesman and historian; leader in the July revolution (1830) and supporter of the bourgeois monarchy (1830-48) of Louis Philippe; effective head of the government after 1840 and prime minister (1847-48); a conservative, he was overthrown by the revolution of 1848.

Gustavus I [or Gustav I] (1496-1560) King of Sweden (1523-60), founder of the Vasa line; elected king (thus ending Kalmar union of Sweden, Denmark and Norway) after leading peasants of Dalarna in their defeat of the Danes (1521); established national Protestant Church (1527) and laid the foundations of the modern Swedish state and its army; made monarchy hereditary (1544).

Gustavus II [or Gustav II] (1594-1632) King of Sweden, known as Gustavus Adolphus; played prominent role on Protestant side in the Thirty Years' War (1618-48); gained Ingermanland from Russia (1617) and Livonia and important Baltic ports from Poland (1629); stunning sweep of his army through Germany in 1631-32 ended in his death at the Battle of Lützen.

H

Hadrian [or Adrian] (A.D. 76-138) Spanish Roman emperor (117-38); distinguished himself in military command in Dacia; ruled harshly in Palestine and ruthlessly suppressed Bar Kokba's revolt; visited Britain *c.* 121 and initiated the building of Hadrian's Wall.

Haig, Douglas, 1st earl (1861-1928) British field marshal; commander-in-chief (1915-18) of the British army; largely responsible for the war of attrition on the western front, especially the Somme (1916) and Passchendaele (1917) campaigns, which took a heavy toll in lives.

Haile Selassie (1891-1975) Emperor of Ethiopia (1930-74); fought in the field against Italy (1935-36) and fled to England when Ethiopia annexed; returned in 1941; reforms included establishing a national assembly (1955); ousted by military; died in captivity.

Hamilton, Alexander (1755-1804) U.S. Federalist politician; Washington's aide-de-camp in the War of Independence; leading influence on the framing of the constitution; as secretary of the treasury (1789-95) the most powerful member of Washington's administration; his "American system," including a tariff on industrial imports and a central bank, favored the central government against the states; pro-British and anti-French; killed in a duel with Aaron Burr.

Hammarskjøld, Dag (1905-61) Swedish secretary-general of the U.N. (1953-61); created first U.N. emergency force to help resolve Suez crisis (1956); died in airplane crash en route to war-torn Congo.

Hampden, John (1594-1643) English member of parliament (1621-43); consistent and prominent opponent of arbitrary government; famous for stiffening opposition to Charles I's rule without parliament by refusing to pay "ship money," a tax on coastal towns which Charles levied inland (1637).

Hardie, Keir (1856-1915) British politician and trade unionist; secretary of the Scottish Miners' Federation from 1886; founded Scottish Labour party (1888); first member of parliament (MP) (1892-95) to sit as the workers' representative; a founder of the Independent Labour party (1893) and its president until 1900; a founder of the Labour Representation Committee; Labour MP (1900-15).

Harding, Warren (1865-1923) U.S. Republican president (1921-23); his administration was infamous for financial corruption, especially the "Teapot Dome" scandal; died suddenly before its exposure could ruin him.

Harley, Robert, 1st earl of Oxford (1661-1724) British member of parliament, Revolution Whig who introduced the Triennial Act (1694) limiting parliaments to three years; turned Tory and was ousted from office as secretary for the north (1704-08) by Marlborough; returned to office with the Tory, Henry St. John (Bolingbroke), in 1710; negotiated Treaty of Utrecht (1713) and impeached, but acquitted, on that account.

Harold II (*c.* 1020-66) Last Saxon King of England, elected on death of Edward the Confessor (1066); killed at the Battle of Hastings.

Harrison, Benjamin (1833-1901) U.S. Republican president (1889-93); defeated Grover Cleveland in the 1888 elections on electoral college vote, though with smaller popular vote; lost 1892 election to Cleveland.

Harrison, William (1773-1841) U.S. Whig president (1841); as governor of Indiana Territory (1800-12), defeated brother of the Indian leader Tecumseh at Tippecanoe (1811), hence his nickname and the 1840 campaign slogan, "Tippecanoe and Tyler (running mate) too"; died after only one month in office.

Harun ar-Rashid (*c.* 764-809) Abbasid caliph of the Islamic empire (786-809); ruled, while Baghdad at its height, over most of southwest Asia and, until near the end of his reign, north Africa; eliminated the powerful Barmecide family of Persia (798), which had helped him gain the caliphate; lavish patron of the arts.

Harvey, William (1578-1657) English physician, the "father of modern medicine"; first to demonstrate the function of the heart and the circulation of the blood.

Hastings, Warren (1732-1818) First British governor-general of India (1774-84); implemented far-reaching financial, legal and administrative reforms; resigned office after being criticized for interfering in provincial affairs; impeached (1787) for alleged corruption, but acquitted after seven-year trial.

Havel, Vaclav (1936-) Czech dramatist, the first president of Czechoslovakia (1990-) after the overthrow of the post-WWII Communist régime; a founder (1977) and leading member of the Charter 77 reform movement; imprisoned (1979-84) for subversion.

Hayes, Rutherford (1822-93) U.S. Republican president (1877-81); elected controversially by the electoral college, which gave him a majority of one vote over Tilden by awarding him all the disputed votes from Florida, Louisiana, South Carolina and Oregon; by withdrawing federal troops from Louisiana and South Carolina ended the era of Reconstruction.

Heath, Edward (1916-) British Conservative prime minster (1970-74); first elected leader of his party (1965); introduced decimal currency (1971); took Great Britain into the European Economic Community (1973); led Conservatives to defeat (1974) after a long struggle, with a miners' strike and the imposition of a three-day working week to conserve energy.

Henry I (1068-1135) King of England (1100-35); by marrying Matilda, niece of Edgar the Etheling, united English and Norman royal lines; took Normandy (1106) from brother, Robert; healed split with Church over lay investiture.

Henry II (1133-89) King of England (1154-89); greatly extended royal authority in judicial system; exacted homage from Malcolm III of Scotland; quarreled with Thomas à Becket.

Henry III (1207-72) King of England (1216-72); during his minority, until 1227, England ruled by the justiciar, Hubert de Burgh; reign dominated by expensive and fruitless wars with France and by struggle with the great barons, led by Simon de Montfort.

Henry IV (1367-1413) First Lancastrian king of England (1399-1413), nicknamed "Bolingbroke" after his birthplace; joined the "Appellants" in opposition to Richard II and exiled to France (1398); invaded England and seized throne from deposed Richard; defeated Welsh rebellion of Owain Glyndwr.

Henry V (1387-1422) King of England (1413-22); as prince of Wales led campaigns against Owain Glyndwr; defeated the French at Agincourt (1415) and won inheritance (but died before it was his) of the French crown in the Treaty of Troyes (1420); suppressed Lollardy in England.

Henry VI (1421-71) Last Lancastrian king of England (1422-61, 1470-71); reign dominated by factious maneuverings between Lancastrians and Yorkists; insane after 1453; deposed by Edward of York (1461) and briefly restored to the throne by Warwick the Kingmaker; founded Eton College (1440) and King's College, Cambridge (1441).

Henry VII (1457-1509) First Tudor king of England (1485-1509); won crown at Bosworth Field (1485), ending the Wars of the Roses; by marrying Elizabeth of York united the Lancastrian and Yorkist factions; greatly increased royal power through institutions such as the Court of Star Chamber.

Henry VIII (1491-1547) King of England (1509-47) and of Ireland (1540-47); separated the English Church from Rome and dissolved the monasteries; greatly extended the role of parliament and the central bureaucracy; married to Catherine of Aragon (1509-33; mother of Mary I; divorced), Anne Boleyn (1533-36; mother of Elizabeth I; beheaded), Jane Seymour (1536-37; mother of Edward VI; died), Anne of Cleves (1540; annulled), Catherine Howard (1540-42; beheaded) and Catherine Parr (1543-47; widowed).

Henry IV (1553-1610) First Bourbon king of France (1589-1610), known as Henry of Navarre, of which he

was also king (1572-1610); abjured his Protestantism (1593) to secure the throne, reputedly saying "Paris is well worth a mass"; granted toleration to Huguenots in Edict of Nantes (1598); assassinated by a disaffected Roman Catholic, François Ravaillac.

Henry the Navigator (1394-1460) Portuguese prince, son of John I; patron of maritime exploration whose school for geographers and navigators at Sagres (established 1416) laid the basis for Portugal's great age of overseas exploration.

Herzl, Theodor (1860-1904) Hungarian Jew, the founder of modern Zionism; organized the first Zionist World Congress (1897) and devoted his life to preaching the necessity of a Jewish national state.

Hess, Rudolf (1894-1987) German Nazi leader; took part in the Munich *putsch* (1923), and in prison Hitler dictated *Mein Kampf* to him; deputy leader of the Nazi party (1933-45); made sensational unauthorized flight to Scotland (1941), apparently to negotiate peace with Great Britain; sentenced at Nuremberg to life imprisonment at Spandau prison, where he died.

Heydrich, Reinhard (1904-42) German Nazi official, deputy chief of the Gestapo (1934-39) and chief planner of the "final solution"; assassinated by Czech patriots.

Himmler, Heinrich (1900-45) German Nazi leader; took part in Munich *putsch* (1923); head of the S.S. blackshirts (from 1919) and, after 1936, of the Gestapo; with Heydrich masterminded the "final solution"; arrested by British troops in May 1945, he committed suicide by taking poison.

Hindenburg, Paul von (1847-1934) German field marshal and president (1925-34); commander-in-chief of German forces in the east during WWI; won famous victory at Tannenberg (1914); a figurehead president, of deep conservative and *junker* sympathies, he appointed Hitler chancellor in 1933.

Hirohito (1901-89) Emperor of Japan (1926-89); renounced divine status in 1946; first emperor in 2,000 years to travel extensively abroad.

Hitler, Adolf (1889-1945) Austrian-born German Nazi Führer, chancellor of Germany (1933-45); became chairman of the tiny National Socialist German Workers' party in 1921; imprisoned (1923-24) after abortive Munich *putsch*; wrote *Mein Kampf* in prison; ruled as totalitarian dictator; anti-Semitic policies ended in the "final solution," the mass extermination of nearly 6 million European Jews after 1941; invasion of Poland

began WWII; committed suicide in his Berlin bunker as Allied troops liberated the city.

Ho Chi Minh (1890-1969) Vietnamese Communist leader; founded the Indochinese Communist party in 1930; organized independence movement during WWII and proclaimed the Democratic Republic of Vietnam in 1945; after final defeat of the French, was president of North Vietnam (1954-69).

Honorius (384-423) Roman emperor in the West (395-423); assumed personal rule in 408, when he murdered his guardian, the general Stilicho; remained at Ravenna during the sack of Rome by the Visigoth Alaric (410).

Hoover, Herbert (1874-1964) U.S. Republican president (1929-33); secretary of commerce (1921-28); created the Reconstruction Finance Corporation (1932) to stimulate industry, but the Depression caused him a landslide defeat by Franklin Roosevelt in the 1932 presidential election.

Hubble, Edwin (1889-1953) U.S. astronomer; chief propounder of the theory of the constantly expanding universe containing galaxies distributed almost uniformly in all directions; theory based on the observation, known as Hubble's Law or Hubble's Constant (1929), that the more distant a galaxy from ours, the faster it is moving away.

Hus, John (*c.* 1372-1415) Bohemian religious reformer; rector of the university of Prague (1409-11), excommunicated (1411) for anti-Roman opinions, including exalting Scripture as the sole source of Christian doctrine; condemned as a heretic by the Council of Constance and burned at the stake.

I

Ibn Saud (*c.* 1888-1953) Founder and first king (1932-53) of Saudi Arabia; exiled in Kuwait, led force that recaptured ancient family seat, Ar Riyad, in the Najd (1912); by 1925 controlled most of Arabian peninsula; proclaimed the kingdom of Saudi Arabia in 1932; first oil multimillionaire Arab ruler.

Ignatius of Loyola, St. (1491-1556) Spanish founder of the Jesuit order.

Innocent III (*c.* 1160-1216) Italian pope (1198-1216); formulated doctrine of supremacy of Church over secular rulers; reign dominated by struggle between European monarchs and papacy; promoted the Fourth Crusade (1199) and the Albigensian Crusade (1208).

Isabella I (1451-1504) Queen of Castile and León (1474-1504) and of Aragon (1479-1504); by marrying Ferdinand of Aragon (1469) united the Spanish crowns; with Ferdinand, a prime mover in the expulsion of the Moors from Spain (1492) and the explorations of Columbus.

Ito, Hirobumi (1841-1909) Japanese politician; the most important figure in the modernization of Japan after the Meiji restoration (1868); introduced Western ideas, including cabinet government and a civil service (1885); three times prime minister between 1892 and 1901; assassination by a Korean led to Japanese annexation of Korea (1910).

Ivan III (1440-1505) Grand duke of Moscow (1462-1505), known as Ivan the Great; first to call himself "tsar."

Ivan IV (1503-84) Grand duke of Moscow (1533-84), first to be officially crowned (1547) tsar of Russia; known as Ivan the Terrible for capricious tyranny in his later years, including the murder of several wives and his son, Ivan (1581); greatly reduced power of local boyars and established autocratic central authority; called first general council of the realm (*zemsky sobor*) in Russian history (1556); greatly expanded Russia eastward, taking Kazan (1552) and Astrakhan (1556).

J

Jackson, Andrew (1767-1845) U.S. Democratic president (1829-37), nicknamed "Old Hickory"; led the victory over the British at the Battle of New Orleans (1815); rallied the west and south against the financial interests of the east in the cause of "Jacksonian democracy"; upheld central power against the states in the nullification crisis of 1831-32; supported local banks against the central bank.

Jackson, Thomas (1824-63) U.S. Confederate general in the Civil War, known as "Stonewall" Jackson after determined resistance at first Battle of Bull Run (1861); killed at the Battle of Chancellorsville.

James I (1566-1625) King of England (1603-25) and James VI of Scotland (1567-1625); first of the Stuart line in England; announced anti-Puritan religious position at Hampton Court Conference (1604); upheld doctrine of the divine right of kings and his reign was disfigured by constant quarreling with parliament.

James II (1633-1701) King of England (1685-88); lord high admiral (1660-73); became a Roman Catholic and resigned after Test Act passed (1673); crushed Monmouth's rebellion (1685), but Catholic appointments and policies led to his overthrow in the "Glorious Revolution."

Jay, John (1745-1829) U.S. statesman and diplomat; president of the Continental Congress (1778-79); negotiated peace with Great Britain to end War of Independence and "Jay's Treaty" (1794) regulating commercial and other relations between the U.S. and Great Britain; first chief justice of the Supreme Court (1789-95).

Jefferson, Thomas (1743-1826) U.S. Republican president (1801-09); Virginia slave owner and leader of the movement for independence; chief drafter of Declaration of Independence (1776); secretary of state (1790-93) in Washington's first administration; fought against Hamilton in defense of agrarian interest and states' rights; as president made the Louisiana Purchase (1803) and sponsored the Lewis and Clark expedition to the Pacific (1803-06).

Jerome, St. (*c.* 347-420) Dalmatian theologian, Father of the Church; experienced a vision (375) at Antioch and forswore pagan studies for Christian scholarship; his translations of the Scriptures were the basis of the Latin Vulgate.

Jesus Christ (*d.c.* 30) Palestinian preacher, born, according to the Gospels, at Bethlehem, probably between 8 B.C. and 4 B.C.; in Christianity, the son of God, the fulfilment of the Old Testament prophecy of the Messiah; in Islam, a prophet; ministry largely confined to his last three years, after his baptism by John the Baptist; famous for miracles, especially of healing, and parables; core of his teaching found in the Sermon on the Mount; *c.* 30 entered Jerusalem for the Passover, drove the money-changers from the Temple, was arrested, convicted of blasphemy for allegedly claiming to be the Messiah, and crucified.

Jiménez [*or* Ximénez] de Cisneros, Francisco (1436-1517) Spanish prelate and royal servant; a Franciscan; archbishop of Toledo (1495-1507) and inquisitor general (1507-17); financed and led expedition that captured Oran (1509).

Jinnah, Muhammed (1876-1948) Pakistani national leader; left Hindu-dominated Indian National Congress in 1934 to organize the Muslim League, the organ of the campaign for the partition of India; first president (1947-48) of independent Pakistan.

Joan of Arc (*c.* 1412-31) French national heroine, the "Maid of Orleans."

Joffre, Joseph (1852-1931) French marshal, commander-in-chief (1911-16); won praise for his part in Allied victory on the Marne (1914), but replaced after German near-success at Verdun (1916).

John (1167-1216) King of England (1199-1216); lost most of the Angevin empire in France; excommunicated (1209-13) for refusing to accept papal nominee, Stephen Langton, as archbishop of Canterbury; signed Magna Carta (1215).

John of Austria (1545-78) Spanish admiral and general; won famous naval victory at Lepanto (1571); governor-general of the Spanish Netherlands (1576-78).

John of Gaunt (1340-99) Duke of Lancaster, most powerful of the feudal "over-mighty subjects"; virtually ruled England in old age of his father, Edward III; led opposition that eventually overthrew Richard II (1398).

Johnson, Andrew (1808-75) U.S. Republican president (1865-59); succeeded on assassination of Lincoln, having been chosen as his running mate as a southern Union Democrat in the Civil War; only president to be impeached (1868), but survived by one vote in the Senate.

Johnson, Lyndon (1908-73) U.S. Democratic president (1963-69); succeeded on assassination of Kennedy; "Great Society" program included Civil Rights Act (1964); took the U.S. into war against North Vietnam; won 1964 election with largest share of the popular vote (61.1%) in U.S. history.

Joseph II (1741-90) Habsburg Holy Roman Emperor (1765-90) and king of Hungary and Bohemia (1780-90); "enlightened despot" whose "bourgeois" legal, social and economic reforms included the abolition of serfdom (1781).

Justinian I (483-565) Roman, or Byzantine, emperor (518-27); reign dominated by struggle with the Monophysites; enduring legacies are his great law code and the Hagia Sophia.

K

Kádár, Janos (1912-) Hungarian Communist premier (1956-58, 1961-65); purged, when minister of the interior, and imprisoned (1950-54) for pro-Tito views; a reforming premier who made Hungary the least repressive of Iron Bloc countries.

Kaunda, Kenneth (1924-) Zambian independence leader and first president (1964-); formed Nationalist party (1958) and negotiated independence from Great Britain (1964); instituted one-party state (1972).

Kennedy, John (1917-63) U.S. Democratic president (1961-63); first Roman Catholic president; authorized abortive "Bay of Pigs" invasion of Cuba (1961); signed nuclear test ban treaty (1963); assassinated at Dallas.

Kenyatta, Jomo (*c.* 1891-1978) First president of independent Kenya (1964-78); formed the nationalist organization, the Kenyan African Union (1946), but spent the Mau Mau years in prison (1952-61).

Kepler, Johannes (1571-1630) German astronomer and mathematician; famous for three laws of planetary motion.

Kerensky, Alexander (1881-1970) Russian revolutionary; prime minister (1917) of the provisional government; leader of the Mensheviks, overthrown by the Bolsheviks after the October Revolution.

Kitchener, Horatio, 1st earl (1850-1916) British field marshal; reconquered the Sudan (1896-98) and crushed Boer guerrilla resistance in the South African War (1899-1902), using concentration camps to intern civilians; secretary of war (1914-16); drowned on mission to Russia, when his cruiser was mined off the Orkneys.

Knox, John (*c.* 1514-72) Scottish theologian, founder of Scottish Presbyterianism; ordained a Roman Catholic priest (1540); a Protestant by 1545; helped to prepare the second Book of Common Prayer; met Calvin in exile from Mary Tudor's England and returned to play leading part in establishing the Scottish Kirk (1560); officially accepted after abdication (1567) of Mary, Queen of Scots.

Kohl, Helmut (1930-) West German Christian Democrat chancellor (1982-); forced the pace of German reunification (1990) and was re-elected as first chancellor of reunited Germany.

Kossuth, Lajos [Louis] (1802-94) Hungarian revolutionary leader; prime actor in the liberal, nationalist revolution of 1848; president of Hungarian republic (1849) until overthrown by Russian troops supporting the Austro-Hungarian monarchy.

Kruger, Paul (1825-1904) Afrikaans South African statesman, a founder of the Transvaal (1852); leader of independence campaign after the Transvaal annexed (1877) by Great Britain; led rebellion that regained independence (1881) and served as president of the Transvaal (1893-98); colonized Rhodesian gold-mining lands and maintained anti-British policy, refusing to grant citizenship to "Uitlander" settlers in the Transvaal.

Kublai (*c.* 1215-94) Khan of the Mongolian confederacy and founder of the Yuan dynasty of China.

L

Lafayette [*or* La Fayette], Marie Joseph du Motier, marquis de (1757-1834) French general; went to America (1777) to support the revolution and was made a major general by the Continental Congress; appointed commander of the militia (later National Guard) in France (1789), but moderate position cost him much influence in the French Revolution.

Lanfranc (*c.* 1005-89) Italian churchman, archbishop of Canterbury (1070-89); replaced English clergy with Normans and subjected York to Canterbury; brought Hildebrandine reforms to the English Church.

Laud, William (1573-1645) English archbishop of Canterbury (1633-45); carried out Charles I's policy of "Thorough" in the Church, upholding Anglo-Catholic ritual and persecuting Puritans in church courts and Star Chamber; condemned to death by a bill of attainder in the House of Commons and executed.

Laurier, Sir Wilfrid (1841-1919) Canadian Liberal prime minister (1896-1911); the first French Canadian to be prime minister; resigned when defeated on a reciprocity trade treaty with the U.S.

Laval, Pierre (1833-1945) French prime minister and foreign minister (1931-32, 1935-36); with Samuel Hoare of Great Britain devised plan (1935) to give Italy most of Ethiopia; held near-dictatorial power (1942-44) under the Vichy government and instituted a fascist terror; executed for treason.

Lavoisier, Antoine (1743-94) French chemist and physicist, considered the father of modern chemistry; pioneer in quantification of chemical reactions; established basis of modern classification of chemical elements and compounds.

Law, Bonar (1858-1923) Canadian-born British Conservative prime minister (1922-23), the "unknown prime minister"; as leader of Conservative party (1911-23) led Ulster's opposition to Irish home rule; led Conservative withdrawal from Lloyd George's coalition (1922).

Lawrence, Thomas (1888-1935) British adventurer and soldier, known as "Lawrence of Arabia"; joined Arab revolt (1916) against Turkey; delegate to the Paris Peace Conference (1919).

Lee, Robert E. (1807-70) U.S. Confederate general; declined offer to command Union forces (1861) and resigned from the army; commanded southern army at defeat of the Union at Second Battle of Bull Run (1861); twice had invasions of the north halted, the second at Gettysburg (1863); surrendered to Grant at Appomattox (1865).

Leibnitz, Gottfried, baron von (1646-1716) German mathematician and philosopher; invented the calculus (results published 1684) concurrently with, but independently of, Newton.

Leicester, Robert Dudley, earl of (1532-88) English courtier, favorite of Elizabeth I; leader of the party for war with Spain, commanded expedition to the Netherlands (1585) and was made governor of the Netherlands (1586-87).

Leif Ericsson (*fl.* 1000) Norse explorer, probably born in Iceland; on return to Greenland after visit to Norway (*c.* 999), blown off course and landed in a country of wheat and grapes, probably the Atlantic coast of America; thus probably the first European discoverer of the New World.

Lenin, Vladimir (1870-1924) Russian revolutionary and Marxist theorist; led Bolshevik overthrow of Kerensky in the October Revolution of 1917 and established a Soviet government; made peace with Germany (March 1918) and presided over the "dictatorship of the proletariat," in reality of the Communist party; massive nationalization only slightly deflected by the New Economic Policy (1924).

Leo I, St. (*c.* 400-61) Italian pope (440-61), a Doctor of the Church; reign dominated by struggle against Manichaeism and Monophysitism; negotiated Attila's retreat from Italy (452).

Leo III, St. (*d.* 816) Italian pope (795-816); crowned Charlemagne emperor in the West (800); strove to preserve East–West unity in the Church by refusing to include the *filioque* clause (affirming belief in the Holy Ghost, as proceeding from the Father and the Son).

Leo IX (1002-54) German pope (1049-54); zealous reformer, especially of the abuses of simony and worldly living; excommunication of Michael, patriarch of Constantinople (1054),

announced formal schism between the Eastern and Western Churches.

Leo XIII (1810-93) Italian pope (1878-93); brought the war between Church and state in Germany, the *Kulturkampf*, to an end (1887); by his encyclicals, *Immortale Dei* (1885) and *Rerum novarum*, distanced the Church from antimodern reaction by embracing democratic ideals and criticizing capitalism.

Leopold I (1640-1705) Habsburg king of Hungary (1655-1705) and Bohemia (1656-1705) and Holy Roman Emperor (1658-1705); with Polish aid resisted Turkish siege of Vienna (1683); recurrently at war with France, rarely with success.

Leopold II (1835-1909) King of the Belgians (1865-1909); gained personal rule of the Congo (1885) and milked its rubber resources, by barbarous use of forced labor, to his own profit; forced by scandalous revelations to relinquish rule of the Congo to the Belgian government (1905).

Lincoln, Abraham (1809-65) U.S. Republican president (1861-65); made name as opponent of Stephen Douglas in 1858 senatorial campaign, in which he opposed extension of slavery; led Union cause to victory in the Civil War; proclaimed emancipation of the slaves (1863); assassinated at Ford's Theater by John Booth.

Lindbergh, Charles (1902-74) U.S. aviator; made first nonstop solo flight (1927) across the Atlantic (from New York to Paris) in the *Spirit of St. Louis*; flight lasted 33 hrs. 30 min.

Liverpool, Robert Jenkinson, 2nd earl of (1770-1828) British Tory prime minister (1812-27); severely repressed popular movements after Waterloo (1815), but began liberalization of trade and the criminal law in the 1820s.

Llewellyn ap Gruffydd (*d.* 1282) Welsh overlord; adopted title "prince of Wales" (1258); last ruler of independent Wales.

Lloyd George, David, 1st earl Lloyd-George of Dwyfor (1863-1945) British Liberal prime minister at head of coalition government (1916-22); 1909 "people's budget," as chancellor of the exchequer (1908-15) introduced social insurance; took bold lead in reorganizing government and the military in latter stages of WWI; Chanak crisis (1922) and establishment of Irish Free State (1922) brought about Conservative withdrawal of support, causing the fall of his government.

Louis VI (*c.* 1081-1137) Capetian king of France (1108-37), known as Louis the Fat; in almost

continual war against England in Normandy, checked English advance; greatly extended royal power.

Louis IX (1214-70) Capetian king of France (1226-70), known as St. Louis; went to Egypt on Seventh Crusade (1248), was captured at Al Mansurah (1250) and held for ransom until 1254; by Treaty of Paris (1259) gained renunciation of Normandy, Anjou and other lands from Henry III of England; ascetic and pious model of an able medieval monarch; died on the Eighth Crusade at Tunis.

Louis XIII (1601-43) Bourbon king of France (1610-43); a weak ruler, whose administration was in the hands of Richelieu (1624-30) and Mazarin (1630-43).

Louis XIV (1638-1715) Bourbon king of France (1643-1715), known as the "Sun King"; ruled in person after death of Mazarin (1661) and raised central, absolute monarchy, marked by lavish formal ceremony, to a new height; revoked (1685) the Edict of Nantes, causing Huguenots to flee France; greatly expanded trade and industry under Colbert's mercantilist policy; established France's military might in series of wars, but the last, the War of the Spanish Succession (1701-14), greatly weakened France financially and militarily; built royal palace at Versailles.

Louis XV (1710-74) Bourbon king of France (1715-74); obtained Lorraine in the War of the Polish Succession (1733-35), but lost most of France's overseas possessions in the Seven Years' War (1756-63); expensive wars left monarchy near bankruptcy.

Louis XVI (1754-93) Bourbon king of France (1774-93); attempts at reform, under his minister Turgot, blocked by party attached to his wife Marie Antoinette and the *parlements*; Necker's financial reforms undermined by expense of intervening on American side in the War of Independence (1776-83); recalled estates-general (1789), but failed to stave off revolution; executed.

Louis Philippe (1773-1850) Orléanist king of France (1830-48); lived in exile 1793-1814; supported liberal opposition to Louis XVIII and Charles X; chosen king after July Revolution of 1830 and his reign known as the July Monarchy; abdicated on outbreak of 1848 revolution and took refuge in England, where he died.

Ludendorff, Erich (1865-1937) German general, chief of staff and prime strategist during WWI; sued for armistice; took part in Kapp *putsch* (1920) and Nazi Munich *putsch* (1923) against the Weimar Republic; leading anti-Semite.

Lumumba, Patrice (1925-61) First prime minister (1960-61) of independent Congo; killed during the civil war provoked by declaration of independence by Katanga province.

Luther, Martin (1483-1546) German friar, prime mover of the Protestant Reformation.

M

MacArthur, Douglas (1880-1964) U.S. general; Allied supreme commander in the southwest Pacific during WWII; virtually ruled Japan as commander of occupying forces (1945-51) and gave it a democratic constitution; commander-in-chief of U.N. forces in Korean War (1950-51), but relieved of command for publicly disputing President Truman's refusal to carry the war into China.

McCarthy, Joseph (1908-57) U.S. Republican senator (1947-57); infamous for smear tactics in accusing public officials of allegiance to Communism; whipped up "reds under the bed" frenzy; reached height of publicity in the army hearings of 1954, but entirely discredited by attacking even President Eisenhower.

Macdonald, Sir John (1815-91); Conservative; born in Scotland; took over Northwest Territories from Hudson's Bay Company (1869); built the trans-Canada railroad (completed 1885).

MacDonald, Ramsay (1866-1937) First Labour prime minister of Great Britain (1924, 1929-31); split Labour party by adopting tight-money policy to counter the Depression and heading (1931-35) the coalition National government with the Conservatives and Liberals.

McKinley, William (1843-1901) U.S. Republican president (1897-1901); won 1896 election on platform of a protective tariff and adherence to the gold standard; annexed Hawaii (1900), initiated "open door" policy in China, and gained the Philippines in the Spanish–American War (1898); assassinated at Buffalo by the anarchist, Leon Czolgosz.

Macmillan, Harold, 1st earl of Stockton (1894-1986) British Conservative prime minister (1957-63); presided over economic boom; introduced life peerages; resigned because of ill health after his government shaken by the Profumo sex scandal (1963).

Madison, James (1751-1836) U.S. Republican president (1809-17); leading figure at the Constitutional Convention (1787) and nicknamed "master builder of the Constitution"; led U.S. into the inconsequential War of 1812 with Great Britain.

Magellan, Ferdinand (*c.* 1480-1521) Spanish navigator.

Mahomet *see* **Mohammed**

Makarios III (1913-77) President of Cyprus (1960-77) and archbishop; led movement that gained Cyprus its independence (1960); opposed union with Greece; forced to accept partition of the island after Turkish occupation (1974).

Malenkov, Georgi (1902-88) U.S.S.R. prime minister (1953-55); organized the collectivization of farms in the 1930s; denounced for "antiparty" activities in 1957 and expelled.

Mandela, Nelson (1918-) South African black nationalist leader; leading figure for racial equality; imprisoned for life (1964) on conviction of subversion; released in 1990.

Mao Tse-tung [*or* Zedung] (1893-1976) Chairman of the People's Republic of China (1949-76); led 20-year revolutionary struggle that ended in Communist overthrow of Chiang Kai-shek (1949).

Marat, Jean (1743-93) French revolutionary leader; a Jacobin; publisher of the journal *L'ami du peuple*; while treating his severe skin condition in a bath, murdered by the Girondin, Charlotte Corday.

Marconi, Guglielmo (1874-1937) Italian inventor of the wireless (1896).

Maria Theresa (1717-80) Austrian archduchess, queen of Bohemia and Hungary (1740-80); succeeded to Habsburg lands (1740) by virtue of the Pragmatic Sanction of 1713, causing the War of the Austrian Succession to begin; lost Silesia to Prussia in the war, but in return gained election of her husband, Francis I, as emperor (1745); ruled jointly with her son, Joseph II, after 1765.

Marie Antoinette (1755-93) Consort (1774-93) of Louis XVI of France; daughter of emperor Francis I and Maria Theresa; unpopular, both for her Austrian nationality and her extravagant living; executed during the Terror.

Marlborough, John Churchill, 1st duke of (1650-1722) British general; crushed Monmouth's rebellion (1685); supported William and Mary and the Whigs; won a series of brilliant victories in the War of the Spanish Succession, including Blenheim (1704), Ramillies (1706) and Oudenarde (1708); dismissed as commander-in-chief (1711) when the Whigs fell from office.

Marx, Karl (1818-83) German historian and economist; prophet of the "dictatorship of the proletariat" and analyst of the economic determination of historical change; published, with Engels, the *Communist Manifesto* (1848); exiled to England after revolutions of 1848 and lived there until his death; published *Das Kapital* (1867-94).

Mary I (1516-58) Tudor queen of England (1553-58), known as "Bloody Mary"; married Philip of Spain and restored papal authority in England; persecuted Protestants; lost Calais (1558).

Mary II (1662-94) Queen of England, wife of William III, daughter of James II; ruled with William as joint sovereign after the "Glorious Revolution" put him on the throne (1689).

Mary, Queen of Scots [Mary Stuart] (1542-87) Queen of Scotland (1542-67); ruled personally from 1561 until, implicated in murder of her second husband, Lord Darnley, she abdicated in 1567 and fled to England; executed by Elizabeth I.

Masaryk, Tomáš (1850-1937) Czech nationalist leader; chief founder and first president (1918-35) of independent Czechoslovakia.

Matilda [*or* Maud] (1102-67) Queen of England (1141-42).

Maurice of Nassau (1567-1625) Prince of Orange (1618-25) and stadtholder of Holland and Zeeland (1584-1625) and Utrecht (1589-1625); as captain-general and admiral of the United Netherlands distinguished himself in the fight for independence from Spain; virtually won Netherlands independence by forcing Spain to a truce (1609); established supremacy of the house of Orange in the Netherlands.

Maximilian I (1459-1519) Habsburg Holy Roman Emperor (1493-1519); by war, but also by marriages, especially that of his son Philip (later Philip I of Castile) into the Spanish royal house, greatly expanded the Habsburg empire inherited by Charles V.

Mazarin, Jules (1602-61) Italian-born French cardinal and royal servant; after deaths of his mentor, Richelieu (1642), and Louis XIII (1643), virtually ruled France; firm use of central authority helped to provoke the Fronde (1648-53).

Mazzini, Giuseppe (1805-72) Italian nationalist; founded revolutionary society, Young Italy (1831); in 1848 revolutions liberated Milan and headed triumvirate in control of the Roman republic; a republican, he refused to support, from exile, the movement that led to the independent kingdom of Italy.

Medici, Cosimo de' (1389-1464) Italian merchant banker, first Medici ruler of Florence (1434-64); abandoned traditional alliance of Florence with Venice against Milan and assisted Sforza family to power in Milan; patron of Brunelleschi, Donatello and Ghiberti.

Medici, Lorenzo de' (1449-92) Italian merchant prince, ruler of Florence (1469-92), known as Lorenzo the Magnificent; survived the papal Pazzi plot against him (1478); used public funds to cover his own debts; great patron of the arts and learning, who bought vast numbers of classical manuscripts and had them translated, thus performing great service to the Renaissance.

Meir, Golda (1898-1978) Israeli prime minister (1969-74); leader of the Mapai socialist party, but headed coalition governments.

Melbourne, William Lamb, 2nd viscount (1779-1848) British Whig prime minister (1835-41); as home secretary (1830-34) prosecuted the Tolpuddle Martyrs; acted as father figure to the young Queen Victoria after 1837; separated from his wife, the notorious Lady Caroline Lamb, in 1825.

Mendel, Gregor (1822-84) Austrian monk, the founder of genetics.

Menzies, Sir Robert (1894-1978) Australian prime minister (1939-41, 1949-66), first as head of the United Australia party, after WWII as leader of the party he reconstructed, the Liberal party; deposed by his own cabinet in 1941; longest continual period in office of any Australian prime minister.

Metternich, Clemens, Fürst von (1773-1859) Austrian foreign minister (1809-48), so dominant in European affairs that post-Napoleonic Europe is often called the "age of Metternich"; pursued repressive policy at home and, as guiding spirit of the Holy Alliance, sought to suppress liberal revolutions abroad; prop of the balance of power; turned Austrian attention away from Germany to its Italian possessions; driven into exile by 1848 revolutions.

Michael (1596-1645) Tsar of Russia (1613-45); founder of the Romanov dynasty; his election as tsar ended the "Time of Troubles"; greatly extended serfdom.

Mirabeau, Honoré Riqueti, comte de (1749-91) French revolutionary figure, chief spokesman of the Third Estate in 1789; sought to create a constitutional monarchy, after 1790 in the pay of Louis XVI; buried in the Panthéon, but remains removed when his secret dealings with the royal court were uncovered.

Mitterand, François (1916-) French Socialist president (1981-); active in the Resistance during WWII; lost 1974 presidential election, but won in 1981 and 1988.

Mohammed [or Mahomet, Muhammad] (c. 570-632) Arabian founder of Islam.

Molotov, Vyacheslav (1890-1986) U.S.S.R. prime minister (1930-41) and foreign minister (1939-49, 1953-56); a member of the military committee that planned the October Revolution (1917); youngest member of the politburo (1921); built up the network of treaties tying eastern Europe to the U.S.S.R. after WWII; a staunch Cold Warrior who refused Marshall Aid.

Moltke, Helmut, graf von (1800-91) Prussian field marshal and chief of staff (1858-88); architect of victories over Denmark (1864), Austria (1866) and France (1870-71) that gave Prussia and Bismarck ascendancy in the new German empire formed in 1871.

Monroe, James (1758-1831) U.S. Republican president (1817-25) during the "era of good feeling"; acquired Florida (1819); signed Missouri Compromise (1820); issued Monroe Doctrine (1823); won 1820 election with the loss of only one electoral college vote.

Montfort, Simon de, earl of Leicester (c. 1208-65) English leader of the baronial opposition to his father-in-law, Henry III.

Montgomery, Bernard, 1st viscount Montgomery of Alamein (1887-1976) British field marshal; distinguished victor at the Battle of El Alamein (1942); commander of field forces during the Normandy landings (1944).

More, Sir Thomas (1478-1535) English humanist scholar and royal servant, chancellor (1529-32); resigned in opposition to Henry VIII's divorce from Catherine of Aragon; published *Utopia* (1516); convicted of treason on perjured evidence and executed.

Mussolini, Benito (1833-1945) Fascist dictator of Italy (1922-43), known as "Il Duce"; seized power after the march on Rome; ruled one-party corporate state after 1928; annexed Ethiopia (1936); allied Italy to Germany in WWII; forced to resign because of imminent Allied invasion of Italy and imprisoned; liberated by Nazis, acted as puppet ruler in north Italy until captured and shot by Italian partisans.

Nagy, Imre (1896-1958) Communist prime minister of Hungary (1953-55, 1956); liberal

policies brought his dismissal and expulsion from the party in 1955; restored briefly at beginning of the abortive Hungarian uprising of 1956; secretly tried and executed for treason.

N

Napoleon I [Napoleon Bonaparte] French Revolutionary general and emperor (1804-14), born in Corsica; associated with the Jacobins in the Revolution; won victory over the British at Toulon (1793), and campaign as commander in Italy ended with favorable Treaty of Campo Formio (1798); became first consul after *coup* that overthrew the Directory (1799); proclaimed himself emperor in 1804; after naval defeat at Trafalgar (1805) implemented Continental System against Great Britain; won great victories at Austerlitz (1805) and Jena (1806); *Grande Armée* forced to retreat from Moscow (1812); finally defeated in attempt to conquer all of Europe, abdicated (1814) and exiled to Elba; escaped, returned, ruled for 100 days until defeated at Waterloo (1815); exiled to St. Helena, where he died; transformed French administration and law, especially by the Code Napoleon; abolished Holy Roman Empire (1806).

Napoleon III (1808-73) French emperor (1852-70), nephew of Napoleon I; elected president of the Second Empire (1848), made himself emperor by a *coup* and ruled thereafter as a dictator; ambitious, but unsuccessful, foreign policy ended in defeat and his overthrow in the Franco–Prussian war (1870-71).

Nasser, Gamal (1918-70) Egyptian president (1954-70); nationalized the Suez Canal (1956); established United Arab Republic with Syria (1958-61)

Necker, Jacques (1732-1804) French director of finance (1777-81, 1788-89); reforms came too late to restore national finances and save the *ancien régime*.

Nehru, Jawaharlal (1889-1964) First prime minister of independent India (1947-64) as head of the Congress party; associate of Gandhi in the long campaign for independence and imprisoned several times; initiated India's non-aligned foreign policy and mixed economy.

Nelson, Horatio, 1st viscount (1758-1805) British admiral; crippled French navy at Aboukir (1798) and finally vanquished it at Trafalgar (1805) in which action he was mortally wounded.

Nero (54-68 A.D.); began persecution of Christians after accusing them of

starting the fire that nearly destroyed Rome (A.D. 64); committed suicide during revolts.

Newcastle, Thomas Pelham-Holles, 1st duke of (1693-1768) English secretary of state (1724-54) and Whig prime minister (1754-56, 1757-62); master of using patronage and electoral machinery to secure parliamentary majorities for Walpole and himself.

Newton, Sir Isaac (1642-1727) English mathematician and natural philosopher; in a burst of activity in the mid-1660s, discovered the calculus (independently of Leibnitz), propounded the theory of universal gravitation, and, in optics, discovered that white light consists of all the colors of the spectrum; also constructed (1668) the first reflecting telescope.

Ney, Michel (1769-1815) French marshal, outstanding commander in the Revolutionary and Napoleonic wars; his greatest achievement was the command of the rear of the *Grande Armée* on its retreat from Moscow (1812); commanded the French army at Waterloo (1815).

Nicholas I (1796-1855) Tsar of Russia (1825-55); crushed Decembrist uprising on the first day of his reign; codified Russian law (1832-33); gained lands in the southwest in wars with Persia (1826-28) and Turkey (1828-29).

Nicholas II (1868-1918) Last tsar of Russia (1894-1917); after defeat by Japan (1904-05) led to 1905 Revolution, promised liberal constitution, but reneged on the promise; forced to abdicate in 1917.

Nightingale, Florence (1820-1910) English nurse, known as the "Lady with the Lamp"; organized unit of women nurses that served at Scutari in the Crimean War (1854-56); founded training school for nurses (1860) at St. Thomas's hospital, London; first woman to be awarded the Order of Merit (1907).

Nixon, Richard (1913-) U.S. Republican president (1969-74); narrowly lost 1960 election to Kennedy; ordered invasions of Kampuchea (1970) and Laos (1971) and saturation bombing of North Vietnam before bringing Vietnam War to a close (1972); first president to visit Communist China (1972); forced to resign after cover-up of Republican burglary (1972) of the Democratic party's headquarters at the Watergate Hotel.

Nkrumah, Kwame (1909-72) First president (1960-66) of independent Ghana; founded Convention People's party (1949) to campaign for independence; dictatorial methods and economic collapse led to his overthrow by the army.

North, Frederick, 2nd earl of Guildford (1732-92) British Tory prime minister (1770-82); retained favor of George III partly by unyielding resistance to American rebels; resigned after news of British surrender at Yorktown reached London.

Nyerere, Julius (1922-) First president (1962-85) of independent Tanganyika; ruled a one-party state and sought to make Tanganyika's economy an autarchy; negotiated union of Tanganyika and Zanzibar (1964) to form state of Tanzania; dramatically increased national literacy rate to highest in Africa.

O

O'Connell, Daniel (1775-1847) Roman Catholic Irish nationalist leader, known as "the Liberator"; founded Catholic Association (1823), which largely forced Westminster to accept Catholic members of parliament (1829); led movement for repeal of the Union with Great Britain in the 1830s and '40s.

Offa (c. 796) King of Mercia (757-96); claimed (774) to be king of all England and at some time between 784 and 796 built dike from the Dee Estuary to the Wye Estuary as a barrier between the English and Welsh tribes.

Oleg (d.c. 912) Varangian (Viking) founder of Kievan Rus; successor to Rurik at Novgorod, he took Kiev c. 879 and made it his capital; established trading links with Byzantium.

Otto I (912-73) Holy Roman Emperor (962-73) and German king (936-73); often considered the first Holy Roman Emperor and known as Otto the Great; established central authority over German duchies and brought Italy, Burgundy and Lotharingia under his sway; defeated Magyars at Lech (955); crowned emperor by Pope John XII.

Owain Glyndwr (c. 1359-c. 1416) Welsh nationalist; led last great revolt against English rule.

P

Pahlavi, Mohammed (1919-80) Shah of Iran (1941-79); attempted to make Iran a liberalized, westernized society, which, together with aloofness from the Arab cause, provoked the Islamic opposition which overthrew him; died in exile in Egypt.

Palmerston, Henry Temple, 3rd viscount (1784-1865) British Whig prime minister (1855-58, 1859-65); pursued aggressive "gunboat diplomacy" in long stints as foreign secretary (1830-34, 1835-42, 1846-51);

called to prime ministership to prosecute the Crimean War; conservative in domestic policy.

Pankhurst, Emmeline (1858-1928) British suffragette, mother of another prominent suffragette, Sylvia; founded the Women's Social and Political Union, which followed militant policy in pursuit of equality and the vote for women; imprisoned several times in 1912-13.

Parnell, Charles (1846-91) Protestant Irish nationalist leader; organized National Land League (1879) and its anti-landlord campaign; worked with Gladstone on abortive home rule bill of 1886; career ruined when cited as co-respondent in a divorce case (1889).

Pasteur, Louis (1822-95) French biochemist, founder of the science of bacteriology.

Patrick, St. (c. 385-461) Romano-British founder of Irish Christianity.

Patton, George (1885-1945) U.S. general; in WWII commanded a north African corps (1942-43); commanded the 3rd Army (1944-45) which swept through northern France, winning the Battle of the Bulge and liberating France.

Paul, St. (dc. 67) Roman citizen, born Saul in Tarsus, Asia Minor; chief apostle of the Christian Gospels to the gentiles; probably a Pharisee; after missionary work from the time of his conversion in c. 32, was arrested at Jerusalem (c. 59) for causing a riot, imprisoned for two years, then sent to Rome, where he was also imprisoned; the circumstances of his death are unknown.

Paul I (1754-1801) Tsar of Russia (1796-1801); reversed policy of his mother Catherine the Great by curtailing expansionism and banning foreign works of literature in Russia; murdered by a military conspiracy.

Peel, Sir Robert (1788-1850) British Conservative prime minister (1834-35, 1841-46); laid foundations of modern Conservative party by accepting 1832 Reform Act as a *fait accompli*; split party by carrying the repeal of the Corn Laws (1846); founded the metropolitan police (1829); died after falling from his horse.

Pelham, Henry (c. 1696-1754) British Whig prime minister (1743-1754); brother of duke of Newcastle, the real power in his administration.

Penn, William (1644-1718) English Quaker, founder of Pennsylvania (1681); colony became a refuge for Quakers; notable for establishing amicable relations with native Indians.

Pepin III (c. 714-68) King of the Franks (751-68), known as Pepin

the Short; overthrew the Merovingians and established the Carolingian line; dubious "donation" of lands to the pope (754) is traditionally accounted the origin of the Papal States.

Perceval, Spencer (1762-1812) British Tory prime minister (1809-12); assassinated in the House of Commons by Henry Bellingham.

Péron, Juan (1895-74) President of Argentina (1946-55, 1973-74); elected by huge majority in 1946, established a dictatorship and began a program of nationalization with a view to self-sufficiency; overthrown by military *coup* in 1955; re-elected in 1973.

Pétain, Henri (1856-1951) French marshal, hero of WWI; head of the Nazi-collaborationist Vichy government (1940-44); convicted of treason (1945); death sentence commuted to life imprisonment by Charles de Gaulle.

Peter I (1672-1725) Tsar of Russia (1682-1725), known as Peter the Great; pursued ruthless program of Westernization (including debearding the nobility) and industrialization (including state mines and factories); reign dominated by long Northern War with Sweden (1700-21), during which foundations of modern army were laid; built St. Petersburg and moved capital there from Moscow.

Philip II (1125-1223) King of France (1180-1223), known as Philip Augustus; doubled royal domains and consolidated Capetian monarchy; gained Normandy, Brittany, Anjou, Maine and Touraine (1204) from John of England.

Philip IV (1268-1314) King of France (1285-1314), known as Philip the Fair; by securing election of Clement V as pope, began the Great Schism in the papacy.

Philip VI (1293-1350) King of France (1328-50), founder of the Valois royal line; reign dominated by the early years of the Hundred Years' War.

Philip II (1527-98) King of Spain (1556-98), of Naples and Sicily (1554-98) and, as Philip I, of Portugal (1580-98); built up absolute monarchy in alliance with the Inquisition; extended Spanish colonial empire to the southern part of the present U.S. and the Philippines; extensive wars and the cost of containing the revolt in the Netherlands left the monarchy financially weak by the end of his reign.

Pierce, Franklin (1804-69) U.S. Democratic president (1853-57); forfeited renomination by supporting the compromise

Kansas-Nebraska Act (1854) and outraging slavery abolitionists.

Pitt, William, 1st earl of Chatham (1708-78) British Whig prime minister (1766-68); leading member of the opposition "Patriots" in the 1740s and '50s and real power in Newcastle's ministry of 1757-62; chiefly responsible for victory over French in Canada during Seven Years' War (1756-63); sought in vain to persuade parliament to adopt a conciliatory policy toward America.

Pitt, William (1759-1806) British Tory prime minister (1783-1802, 1804-06); at 24 the youngest prime minister in British history; after initial liberal period, backing freer trade and parliamentary reform (never instituted) turned increasingly Tory and repressed reformist organizations during the French Revolution; introduced sinking fund (1786) and first income tax (1798) in British history; negotiated union with Ireland (1800).

Pius IX (1792-1878) Italian pope (1846-78); issued doctrine of papal infallibility at the first Vatican Council (1869).

Pius XII (1876-1958) Italian pope (1939-58); during WWII maintained relations with all belligerents and was criticized for not speaking out against Nazi persecution; in 1949 excommunicated Italian Roman Catholics who joined the Communist party.

Pizarro, Francisco (c. 1476-1541) Spanish conquistador, conqueror of Peru.

Poincaré, Raymond (1860-1934) French president (1913-20) and prime minister (1912-13, 1922-23, 1926-29); worked for a severe Versailles Treaty (1919); and disliked its leniency; as prime minister headed a bloc of conservative parties; occupied the Ruhr (1923-25) in attempt to force German payment of reparations.

Pol Pot (c. 1928-) Kampuchean (Cambodian) leader of the Khmer Rouge and premier (1976-79).

Polk, James (1795-1849) U.S. Democratic president (1845-49); fought 1844 election on slogan, "54° 40′ or fight," but settled Oregon dispute with British North America by accepting the 49th parallel as the boundary; acquired California after war with Mexico (1846-48).

Polo, Marco (c. 1254-c. 1324) Venetian merchant and traveler to the Far East.

Pombal, Sebastiano, marqués de (1699-1782) Portuguese chief minister (1756-77) to king Joseph; ruled by terror until banished upon

Joseph's death; suppressed the Inquisition and expelled Jesuits from Portugal.

Pompidou, Georges (1911-74) President of France (1969-74); elected by the National Assembly after Charles de Gaulle's resignation; prime minister (1962-68) under de Gaulle, who dismissed him after the student demonstrations of 1968.

Portland, William Bentinck, 3rd duke of (1738-1809) British Tory prime minister (1807-09); as a Whig, nominal head of Fox-North ministry (17830; led conservative Whigs in transfer of support to Pitt in reaction to French Revolution.

Ptolemy (fl. 2nd century) Greco-Egyptian mathematician and cosmologist.

Pym, John (c. 1583-1643) English parliamentarian, leading opponent of Stuart rule; organized impeachment of Buckingham (1626); leading force behind reforms of the Long Parliament; managed Roundhead finances in early part of the Civil War.

R

Raleigh [or Ralegh], Sir Walter (c. 1554-1618) English soldier, explorer and royal favorite; led expedition to plant first (ill-fated) English colony in America at Roanoke Island (1585); traveled up the Orinoco in search of El Dorado (1596); convicted of plotting with Spanish to overthrow James I and imprisoned in the Tower of London (1603-16); released to head second El Dorado expedition; executed on his return.

Reagan, Ronald (1911-) U.S. Republican president (1981-89); Hollywood actor (1937-64); governor of California (1967-74); oldest man to enter the White House for the first time.

Rhodes, Cecil (1853-1902) British imperialist; made fortune in diamonds and gold in South Africa and founded (1887) the British South Africa Company that developed what became Rhodesia; prime minister of Cape Colony (1890-96); dismissed for implication in Jameson Raid (1895) to overthrow Boer republic in the Transvaal.

Richard I (1157-99) King of England (1189-99); known, after defeat of Saladin at Arsuf on the Third Crusade (1190-92), as *"Coeur de Lion"* (Lion-Heart); captured on return by Leopold V of Austria and released (1194) on payment of large ransom; last years (1194-99) spent in France in war against Philip Augustus; killed in action.

Richard II (1367-1400) King of England (1377-99); deceitfully placated rebels at personal meeting with them in London during Peasants' Revolt (1381); absolute rule without the advice of his great barons led to his deposition.

Richard III (1452-85) Yorkist king of England (1483-85); seized throne by imprisoning (and almost certainly murdering) the young Edward V; overthrown by Henry Tudor at Bosworth Field.

Richelieu, Armand du Plessis, duc de (1585-1642) French cardinal, chief minister (1624-42) to Louis III and the young Louis XIV; assisted growth of absolute monarchy by reducing power of the great nobles; defeated Huguenots at La Rochelle (1628) and ended their privileges.

Robert I [Robert the Bruce] (1274-1329) Scottish king (1306-29); hero of the Battle of Bannockburn (1314).

Robespierre, Maximilien (1758-94) French Revolutionary leader, nicknamed the "Incorruptible," head of the Jacobin faction in the Convention; dominated the Committee of Public Safety and organized the Terror (1793); moderate reaction resulted in his arrest and execution.

Rockingham, Charles Watson-Wentworth, 2nd marquis of (1730-82) British Whig prime minister (1765-66, 1782); attempted to conciliate America by repealing (1766) the Stamp Act; early proponent of the idea of government by party united by principles and acting together in pursuit of office.

Röhm, Ernst (1887-1934) German Nazi leader; organized the *Sturmabteilung* (S.A.); imprisoned for part in the Munich *putsch* (1923); murdered on the "Night of the Long Knives" (1934).

Rommel, Erwin (1891-1944) German field marshal; known after his successful command of the Afrika Corps in Libya (1941) as the "Desert Fox"; recalled just before final defeat at El Alamein (1942); committed suicide after taking part in failed July plot (1944) against Hitler.

Roosevelt, Franklin D. (1882-1945) U.S. Democratic president (1933-45); only president to run for a third term of office; won four consecutive elections; introduced massive program of state aid, the New Deal, to combat the Great Depression; agreed Lend-Lease deal with Great Britain (1941); arranged postwar Europe with Stalin and Churchill at Yalta (1945).

Roosevelt, Theodore (1858-1919) U.S. Republican president (1901-09); took office after assassination of McKinley; gained hero status as leader of the "Rough Riders" in the

Spanish-American War (1898); presidency marked by frequent "trust-busting" under the Sherman Anti-trust Act; awarded the Nobel Peace Prize (1906) for negotiating end of Russo–Japanese War, split Republican party and ran as Progressive ("Bull Moose") candidate in 1912 presidential election.

Rosebery, Archibald Primrose, 5th earl of (1847-1929) British Liberal prime minister (1894-95); leader of the imperialist wing of the party.

Rudolf I (1218-91) German king (1273-91), founder of the Habsburg ruling house; brought much of Bohemia within Habsburg lands.

Rupert, Prince (1619-82) Bohemian-born count palatine of the Rhine; son of Frederick, the "Winter King," and nephew of Charles I of England; outstanding Royalist general in the English Civil War.

Russell, John 1st earl (1792-1878) British Whig prime minister (1846-52, 1865-66); helped to draft and introduced Great Reform Act (1832); dismissed Palmerston as foreign secretary (1851) for unauthorized recognition of Napoleon III *coup*; carried out important social reforms, including Ten Hours Act (1847) and Public Health Act (1848); foreign secretary (1859-65).

Rutherford, Ernest, 1st baron (1871-1937) British physicist, born in New Zealand; awarded Nobel Prize (1908) for discovery of alpha and beta radiation and theory of radioactive transformation of atoms; published results (1919) of first splitting of the atom.

S

Sadat, Anwar al- (1918-81) President of Egypt (1970-81); made dramatic visit to Israeli knesset (1970), an initiative which led to the Camp David talks and the Israeli–Egypt peace treaty (1979); awarded Nobel Peace Prize (1978).

St John, Henry, 1st viscount Bolingbroke (1678-1751) British Tory statesman; favorite of Marlborough, was secretary for war (1704-08); secretary of state (1710-14); impeached for attempting to subvert Hanoverian succession (1714); he fled to France and helped to plan the Jacobite rising of 1715; pardoned in 1723, he returned to England.

Saladin (*c.* 1137-93) Muslim warrior-hero, sultan of Egypt (1169-93).

Salazar, Antonio (1889-1970) Portuguese prime minister (1932-68); ruled with dictatorial powers and erected a corporatist state; resisted independence movements in Portugal's African colonies.

Salisbury, Robert Cecil, 3rd marquis of (1830-1903) British Conservative prime minister (1885-86, 1886-92, 1895-1902); long tenure of office dependent on support of Liberal Unionists who left Liberal party in split over Irish home rule (1886); imperialist policy exhibited in war against the Boers of South Africa (1899-1902); cautious in domestic policy.

Salk, Jonas (1914-) U.S. microbiologist, discoverer of vaccine aginst poliomyelitis (1954).

San Martín, José de (1778-1850) Argentinian revolutionary; invaded Chile (1817) and defeated the Spanish at Chacabuco, the decisive victory leading to Chile's independence (1818); took Lima (1821) and became protector of Peru; resigned to make way for Bolívar (1822).

Savonarola, Girolamo (1452-98) Italian Dominican monk; reformer and scourge of the papacy under the corrupt Alexander VI; ruled Florence after expulsion of the Medici (1494) and supported the invasion by Charles VIII of France; excommunicated (1497) after disobeying papal order to stop preaching; declared Alexander "no pope"; hanged for schism and heresy.

Scharnhorst, Gerhard von (1785-1813) Prussian general; reorganized army after 1807, turning a mercenary force into a people's army; paved the way for introduction of conscription (1814).

Schlieffen, Alfred, graf von (1833-1913) German field marshal; as chief of staff (1891-1905) formulated the Schlieffen Plan for rapid German victory in western Europe, partially implemented in 1914.

Schmidt, Helmut (1918-) West German SPD chancellor (1974-82); forced to leave office when, in economic difficulties, the Free Democrats withdrew their support.

Shelburne, William, 2nd earl of (1737-1805) British Whig prime minister (1782-83); negotiated Treaty of Paris (1783) that gave America independence; overthrown by Fox-North coalition.

Sherman, William (1820-91) U.S. Civil War general; distinguished himself on the Union side in the Vicksburg campaign (1863); after burning Atlanta (1864) commanded famous "march to the sea," laying waste the countryside; swept north through South Carolina and received surrender of General Johnston (1865).

Sigismund (1368-1437) Holy Roman Emperor (1433-37) and king of Hungary (1387-1437), Germany (1411-37) and Bohemia (1419-37); led

persecution of Hussites in Bohemia, secured death of John Hus (1415).

Smuts, Jan (1870-1950) South African Unionist prime minister (1919-24, 1939-48); of Boer descent, fought against Great Britain in the Boer War (1899-1902); helped to create Union of South Africa (1910); made a field marshal during WWII and held high place in British war councils.

Somerset, Edward Seymour, duke of (*c.* 1506-62) English protector of the realm (1547-49) in Edward VI's boyhood; ruled virtually independently of the Council of Regency and with Cranmer enforced use of Book of Common Prayer in the Act of Uniformity (1549); overthrown by the earl of Warwick, imprisoned and beheaded for felony.

Stalin, Joseph (1879-1953) U.S.S.R. Communist first secretary (1922-53); ruled progressively dictatorially after Lenin's death (1924); exiled Trotsky (1929); mass industrialization and farm collectivization accompanied by massive terror, costing millions of lives, in the 1930s; show trials used to purge party of enemies; signed nonaggression pact with Hitler (1939); drew up plans for postwar Europe with Churchill and Roosevelt at Yalta (1945).

Stephen (*c.* 1097-1154) King of England (1135-41, 1142-54).

Stephenson, George (1781-1848) British engineer, inventor of the first locomotive to use the steam blast (1815).

Stolypin, Piotr (1862-1911) Prime minister of Russia (1906-11) during "constitutional" period after the 1905 revolution; used secret police to murder thousands of opponents; connived at anti-Semitic outrages; assassinated by revolutionary police agent.

Strafford, Thomas Wentworth, 1st earl of (1593-1641) English royal servant, lord deputy of Ireland (1632-39); implemented Charles I's policy of "Thorough" during the years of rule without parliament (1629-40); impeached and executed.

Stresemann, Gustav (1878-1929) German chancellor (1923) and foreign secretary (1923-29); accepted Versailles treaty and worked for Germany's reintegration in the international order; won Nobel Peace Prize (1926) for part in drawing up the Locarno Treaty (1925).

Strijdom, Johannes (1893-1958) South African Nationalist prime minister (1954-58); greatly extended racial *apartheid* and deprived blacks of the vote; initiated the great "treason trial" of 156 signatories of the "Freedom Charter" (1956).

Sukarno, Achmed (1901-70) First president of independent Indonesia (1949-68); jailed for most of the 1930s as leader of anti-Dutch nationalists; dispensed with parliamentary democracy after 1956; murdered 300,000 supposed leftists after surviving attempted army *coup* (1965).

Suleiman I (1494-1566) Sultan of the Ottoman empire (1520-66), known as Suleiman the Magnificent; extended empire into Hungary, but failed to take Vienna (1529); undertook extensive reform of the army and the law.

Sully, Maximilien de Béthune, duc de (1560-1614) French superintendent of finances (1598-1611); after Henry III's extravagance and the costly Wars of Religion, rescued French monarchy from bankruptcy by a series of tax measures and retrenchments; left large financial surplus by end of Henry IV's reign.

Sumner, Charles (1811-74) U.S. senator (1831-74); leading abolitionist and active in formation of the Republican party (1856); led the Radical Reconstructionists after the Civil War; took leading part in impeachment of Andrew Johnson.

Sun Yat-sen (1866-1925) Chinese revolutionary; founded the revolutionary league, T'ung Meng Hui (1905), for nationalism, democracy and socialism; provisional president of the Chinese Kuomintang (1912) and united it with the Communist party (1924); president of national government of south China, proclaimed at Canton (1921).

Suzman, Helen (1917-) South African politician; co-founder of the liberal Progressive party (1959) and the party's only member of parliament from 1961 to 1974; waged one-woman struggle for universal suffrage and the end of *apartheid*.

T

Taft, William (1857-1930) U.S. Republican president (1909-13) conservative domestic policy split party; lost 1912 election to Woodrow Wilson when Teddy Roosevelt stood as third candidate; forged "dollar diplomacy" in Latin America; chief justice of the Supreme Court (1912-30).

Talleyrand, Charles de (1754-1838) French Revolutionary statesman; foreign minister (1797-99, 1799-1807); assisted Napoleon to overthrow the Directory (1799); chief architect of the Confederation of the Rhine (1806); chief French delegate at Congress of Vienna (1815).

Tamerlane *see* **Timur**

Tasman, Abel (*c.* 1603-59) Dutch explorer, discoverer (1642) of New Zealand and Tasmania; first man to circumnavigate Australia.

Taylor, Zachary (1784-1850) U.S. Whig president (1849-50); gained nickname "Rough and Ready" as army major and colonel; chief commander in the Mexican War (1846-48); died of cholera.

Tecumseh (*c.* 1768-1813) Chief of the Shawnee Indians of North America; led confederacy of south and northwest tribes to resist American expansion; confederacy collapsed after defeat of his brother at Tippecanoe (1811); died in action on the British side in the War of 1812.

Thatcher, Margaret (1925-) British Conservative prime minister (1979-90); first woman prime minister in British history; first to lead a party to three consecutive election victories; longest consecutive tenure of 10 Downing Street since Lord Liverpool (1812-27); resigned after failing to win outright on first ballot of leadership vote by Conservative members of parliament.

Theodoric (*c.* 425-526) Ostrogothic king; conquered Italy, overthrowing Odoacer.

Theodosius I (*c.* 346-95) Roman emperor in the East (379-95) and the West (392-95); known as Theodosius the Great; issued edict (380) condemning Arianism and upholding the Trinity; virtually rid the empire of Arianism and paganism; by dividing imperial rule between his sons, made the split between East and West permanent.

Theresa, St. (1515-82) Spanish Carmelite nun, Doctor of the Church; one of the principal saints of the Roman Church; her great spirituality and practical energy in founding convents contributed greatly to the Counter-Reformation in Spain.

Thiers, Adolphe (1797-1877) French prime minister (1836, 1840, 1848) and president (1871-73); helped to gain Louis Philippe the throne in the July Revolution (1830); liberal who opposed the socialists and the rule of Napoleon III, crushed the Commune (1871) and became first president of the Third Republic.

Thomas à Becket, St. (1118-70) English archbishop of Canterbury (1162-70); chancellor (1154-62) to Henry II; resisted Henry's efforts to bring clergy under secular jurisdiction; exiled in France (1164-70); murdered in Canterbury Cathedral.

Timur [*or* **Tamerlane]** (*c.* 1336-1405) Last great Mongol conqueror.

Tirpitz, Alfred von (1849-1930) German admiral, secretary of state for the navy (1897-1916); fostered escalating naval race with Great Britain before WWI; at outbreak of war began construction of submarines and resigned when Bethmann-Hollweg refused to sanction unrestricted submarine warfare.

Tito, Josip [Josip Broz] (1892-1980) Yugoslavian Communist president (1945-80); became head of Yugoslav Communist party (1937); built up support as leader of 300,000 partisans in WWII; broke with the U.S.S.R. (1948) and presided over liberal régime that allowed play of market forces.

Togo, Heihachiro (1846-1934) Japanese admiral; national hero for his victories over the Russian navy at Port Arthur (1904) and Tsushima (1905).

Togo, Hideki (1884-1948) Japanese general and prime minister (1941-44); dictatorial premiership marked triumph of the military over civilian politicians and led to the attack on Pearl Harbor (1941); resigned after U.S. successes in the Marianas; executed by Allied occupying forces for war crimes.

Torquemada, Tomás de (1420-98) Spanish inquisitor; a Dominican; made confessor to Ferdinand and Isabella (1483) and charged with organizing the Spanish Inquisition; supervised the expulsion of the Moors from Granada (1492).

Toussaint l'Ouverture, François (*c.* 1744-1803) Haitian leader of first successful slave rebellion against white rule in the New World.

Trajan (*c.* A.D. 53-117) Roman emperor (A.D. 98-117); conquered Dacia and most of Parthia.

Trotsky, Leon (1879-1940) Russian Revolutionary leader, prominent in the October Revolution (1917); resigned as people's commissar for foreign affairs in Lenin's government (1918) in protest against Treaty of Brest-Litovsk; lost leadership struggle after Lenin's death (1924) to Stalin; stood for world revolution against Stalin's "socialism in one country"; exiled by Stalin (1929); assassinated in Mexico by Soviet agent.

Truman, Harry (1884-1972) U.S. Democratic president (1945-53); succeeded on Roosevelt's death; won upset victory (1948) over Thomas Dewey; took decision to use atomic bombs against Japan (1945); presidency saw adoption of Marshall Plan (1947) and formation of NATO (1949); second term dominated by Korean War.

Turenne, Henri de la Tour d'Auvergne, vicomte de (1611-75) French marshal; outstanding commander during last part of the Thirty Years' War (1618-48); won famous victories in the War of Devolution (1667-68) and the third Dutch War (1672-78); killed in action during the latter.

Tyler, John (1790-1862) U.S. Whig president (1841-45); first to succeed to White House from the vice-presidency (on death of Harrison); concluded Webster-Ashburton treaty with Great Britain (1843), settling boundary disputes in the northeast and Great Lakes region; annexed Texas (1845).

U

Ulbricht, Walter (1893-1973) East German head of state and secretary-general of the German Communist party (1950-71); the most Stalinist of all east European leaders; carried out enforced collectivization of agriculture, built the Berlin Wall (1961).

V

Van Buren, Martin (1782-1862) U.S. Democratic president (1837-41), protégé of Andrew Jackson; presidency marred by economic recession, lost 1840 election.

Vasco da Gama (*c.* 1460-1524) Portuguese navigator, the first European to reach India by sea.

Vesalius, Andreas (1514-64) Flemish anatomist, the "father of medicine."

Vespucci, Amerigo (1454-1512) Italian navigator, after whom America was named; sailed for the West Indies and discovered the mouth of the Amazon (1499); explored the north coast of South America, which he established as a continent (1501).

Victor Emmanuel II (1820-78) King of Sardinia-Piedmont (1849-78) and Italy (1861-78); firm supporter of Cavour and the Risorgimento, became the first king of unified Italy.

Victoria (1819-1901) Queen of England (1837-1901), the longest-reigning monarch in British history; spent middle years of her reign, after death (1861) of her husband Albert, in virtual seclusion; re-emerged and gained great popularity, especially at the Diamond Jubilee (1897).

Villa, Francisco (*c.* 1877-1923) Mexican revolutionary bandit, known as "Pancho"; took part in revolution (1910) that overthrew Porfirio Diaz; with Emiliano Zapata, occupied Mexico City (1914-15), before being defeated by forces of President Carranza;

pursued by U.S. army for a year (1916-17) without being captured; assassinated.

Vladimir I (*d.* 1015) First Christian grand duke of Kiev (980-1015).

W

Walesa, Lech (1943-) Polish president (1990-); founder of the free trade union "Solidarity" (1979), and leader of the anti-Communist movement in Poland in the 1980s.

Wallace, George (1919-) U.S. Democratic politician, governor of Alabama (1963-67, 1971-79, 1983-87); diehard racial segregationist and white supremicist; won nearly 10 million votes as third candidate in 1968 presidential election.

Wallenstein [*or* Waldstein] Albrecht von (1583-1634) Bohemian general; chief imperial commander to Ferdinand II in the Thirty Years' War; conducted secret peace negotiations (1632) and was executed for treason.

Walpole, Robert, 1st earl of Orford (1676-1745) British Whig first lord of the treasury (1721-42), usually considered the first prime minister; ruled by patronage and support of the Crown; period of office saw advance of cabinet government; resigned during military setbacks in the war with Spain.

Warwick, Richard Neville, 1st earl of (1428-71) English nobleman and vast landowner, known as "the Kingmaker"; supported Yorkist cause in the Wars of the Roses; established Edward IV on the throne; intrigued against Edward with the duke of Clarence and was killed in action against Edward at the Battle of Barnet.

Washington, George (1732-99) First U.S. president (1789-97); commander (1775-83) of the continental army in the War of Independence; president of the federal convention which adopted the constitution (1787) and chosen unanimously as president in the new federal government; gradually assumed lead of the Federalists against the Jeffersonians; farewell address warned Americans against "permanent alliances" with European powers.

Webster, Daniel (1782-1852) U.S. senator (1827-41, 1845-50); outstanding orator and defender of the powers of central government against the states; after 1836 a leading figure in the Whig party; as secretary of state (1841-43) negotiated the Webster-Ashburton treaty (1843) settling northeast boundary disputes with Great Britain; incurred enmity of anti-slavery movement for powerful backing of the Compromise of 1850.

Weizmann, Chaim (1874-1952) Russian-born Zionist leader, first president (1948-52) of Israel; as a British subject after 1910, worked behind the scenes to secure the Balfour Declaration (1917) in favor of a national homeland for the Jewish people.

Wellington, Arthur Wellesley, 1st duke of (1769-1852) British general and Tory prime minister (1828-30), known as the "Iron Duke"; hero of the Peninsular War (1809-13) that drove Napoleon's army from Spain and Portugal; victor, with Blücher, at Waterloo (1815); as prime minister secured Catholic emancipation (1829), splitting the Tory party; fell from office when refused to consider parliamentary reform; first non-royal person to receive a state funeral.

Wesley, John (1703-91) British preacher, founder of Methodism; ordained in Church of England (1728); led group of outdoor preachers, including brother Charles and George Whitefield, in evangelical movement to revivify the Church; emphasized individual salvation through personal communion with God; never broke with the Church of England, but established legal status of Methodist societies (1784).

Whitney, Eli (1765-1825) U.S. inventor of the cotton gin (1793); his firearms factory, founded in 1798, mass produced the first muskets to have standard, interchangeable parts.

Wilberforce, William (1759-1833) British Tory member of parliament (1780-1824) and social reformer; leading member of the "Clapham Saints" who campaigned for abolition of the slave trade (1807) and of slavery (1833); as a leading Evangelical in the Church of England, established the Society for the Suppression of Vice (1802).

Wilhelm I (1797-1888) King of Prussia (1861-88) and emperor of Germany (1871-88); appointed Bismarck prime minister (1762) and thereafter relied entirely upon him.

Wilhelm II (1859-1941) German emperor (1888-1918); dismissed Bismarck as chancellor (1890) and thereafter exercised dominant power in German politics; abdicated at the dictation of the Allies and lived in exile in the Netherlands.

Wilkes, John (1727-97) British Radical, expelled from parliament (1763) for seditious libel against George III in the *North Briton*; later three times elected and refused permission to sit by the House of Commons; finally successful (1774); "Wilkes and liberty" movement formed around him fought for franchise reform; Wilkes forced

Crown to cease the issue of "general warrants" (not specifying person to be arrested) and asserted rights of the electorate over parliament.

William I (*c.* 1027-87) Duke of Normandy (1035-87) and king of England (1066-87), known as William the Conqueror; defeated Harold at Hastings to take English throne; filled offices in Church and state with Normans; introduced feudalism to England.

William II [William Rufus] (*c.* 1060-1100) King of England (1087-1100); suppressed revolt of his brother, Robert (1088); gained Cumbria from the Scots (1092).

William III (1650-1702) Prince of Orange; stadtholder of the Netherlands (1672-1702) and king of England (1689-1702); ruled jointly with Mary until her death (1694); placed on throne by "Glorious Revolution" that overthrew James II; secured Protestantism in Ireland at the Battle of the Boyne (1690) and in Scotland at the Battle of Killiecrankie (1689); ruled through Whig ministers.

William IV (1765-1837) King of England (1830-37); by agreeing to a creation of peers, if necessary, contributed signally to the passing of the Great Reform Act (1832).

William of Orange (1533-84) Dutch statesman, also known as William the Silent; hero of the Dutch War of Independence against Spain; united the Dutch provinces in the Pacification of Ghent (1576) with the aim of expelling the Spanish; assassinated before his great object was gained.

Williams, Roger (*c.* 1603-83) English Puritan clergyman, founder of Rhode Island colony (1636); expelled from Massachusetts Bay colony (1635) for challenging the oligarchy; powerful advocate of democracy in state affairs and entire liberty of conscience in religion; befriended the Indians.

Wilson, Harold, baron Wilson of Rievaulx (1916-) British Labour prime minister (1964-70, 1974-76); led party to four election victories (1964, 1966, 1974 twice); founded Open University (1969); held referendum (1975) to gain popular approval of British membership of the EEC.

Wilson, Woodrow (1856-1924) U.S. Democratic president (1913-21); fought to keep U.S. out of WWI, but entered the war (1917) when Germany renewed unrestricted submarine warfare; "14 Points" laid down basis for a postwar world "safe for democracy," but was disappointed by harsh Treaty of Versailles (1919); failed to persuade

Senate to ratify U.S. membership of the League of Nations; awarded Nobel Peace Prize (1919).

Witt, Jan de (1625-72) Dutch statesman, leader of the Republican party and opponent of the house of Orange; as grand pensionary (1653-72) negotiated end to the first and second Dutch Wars (1652-67) and the War of Devolution (1667-68); resigned when William of Orange made stadtholder (1672); killed by mob when visiting brother in prison.

Wolsey, Thomas (*c.* 1473-1530) English prelate and royal servant; archbishop of York (1514-30); cardinal (1515); chancellor (1515-29) to Henry VIII; fell from office for failing to secure immediate papal approval of Henry's divorce; arrested for treason, but died before trial.

Wright, Orville (1871-1948) **and Wilbur** (1867-1912) U.S. inventors of the first successful heavier-than-air airplane (1903).

Wycliffe [*or* Wyclif], John (*c.* 1328-84) English theologian and Oxford don; condemned as heretic (1380, 1382) for denying transubstantiation and challenging papal authority; gave rise to reform movement known as Lollardy.

X

Ximénez de Cisneros, Francisco *see* **Jiménez de Cisneros, Francisco.**

Z

Zapata, Emiliano (*c.* 1879-1919) Mexican revolutionary; an Indian, he led Indian band during the revolution (1910-19) in attempt to regain expropriated lands; assassinated by agents of President Carranza.

Zhukov, Georgi (1896-1974) Soviet military commander, known in WWII as the "undefeatable general," took part in defense of Leningrad (1941) and commanded the Moscow front (1941), the relief of Stalingrad (1942), and the final assault on Berlin (1945).

Zwingli, Huldreich (1484-1531) Swiss Protestant reformer; renounced Rome (1518) and founded Swiss Protestant Church on the basis of the sole authority of the Scriptures.

A DICTIONARY OF PLACES

A

Aachen [Aix-la-Chapelle] Town in western Germany, probable birthplace of Charlemagne and his northern capital, a place of great learning; site of the signing of the Treaty of Aix-la-Chapelle (1748), which ended the War of the Austrian Succession.

Abraham, Plains of Field outside Quebec, where in 1759 the British under General Wolfe defeated the French under General Montcalm, establishing British supremacy in North America.

Alamein, El Town on the Egyptian Mediterranean coast, site of two major engagements of WWII; at the first (July 1942) General Auchinlek checked an Italian-German advance under Rommel toward Cairo; General Montgomery led a successful Allied counteroffensive (October-November 1942) which led to the expulsion of the Axis powers from north Africa by the spring of 1943.

Alsace-Lorraine Coal-rich industrial provinces of northern France, annexed by Germany in the Franco-Prussian War (1870-71); the object of French revanchism until restored to France by the Treaty of Versailles (1919).

Amritsar Town in the Punjab, India, home of the sacred Sikh shrine, the Golden Temple; site of a massacre of Indian nationalists by the British army under General Dyer, in which 393 Indians were killed and 1,200 wounded.

Anjou Former region of France, part of the English Crown lands 1154-1204, roughly corresponding with, but slightly larger than, the modern region of Maine-et-Loire.

Antioch [Antakya] City in south Turkey, near the Mediterranean coast, a great commercial and military center of the Roman Empire; captured by Persia in 637, by Byzantium in 969 and by the Seljuk Turks in 1085; one of the Christian states won in the First Crusade, it was sacked by the Mamluks in 1268 and fell into decline.

Agadir Atlantic port of Morocco, center of the second Moroccan crisis (1911), when the German gunboat *Panther* arrived, allegedly to protect German commercial interests; fears of a German annexation of Morocco nearly provoked a war of Great Britain and France against Germany.

Aquitaine Former duchy and kingdom of southwest France, a powerful medieval state; held as a vassal state of the French Crown by Henry II of England, but recovered by the French monarchy during the Hundred Years' War.

Ardennes High wooded plain in southeast Belgium, north Luxembourg and north France; site of a German counterattack (December 1944) which began the Battle of the Bulge, won by the Allies at a cost of 77,000 casualties.

Augsburg City in Bavaria, a great financial and commercial center in the 15th and 16th centuries; home of the Fugger banking family; site of the temporary truce gained in the 16th-century wars of religion by the Peace of Augsburg (1555) and of the German defensive alliance, the League of Augsburg (1686), against France.

Austerlitz Town in south Czechoslovakia, site of Napoleon's great victory over Russia and Austria (1805) at the so-called Battle of the Three Emperors.

Avignon Ancient ramparted city of southeast France, on the Rhône, the papal residence during the "Babylonian Captivity" (1309-78) and home to antipopes during the Great Schism (1309-78).

B

Balaklava Town in the Crimea, now part of Sebastopol; site of the famous Charge of the Light Brigade in the battle (October 1854) of the Crimean War in which the British forces repulsed a Russian assault on the military base there.

Balkans Name for the southeast peninsula of Europe, comprising Greece, Albania, Bulgaria, most of Yugoslavia, southeastern Romania and, under the Ottomans, Turkey-in-Europe; continual source of national and international tensions in the 50 years before WWI.

Barbary States Name for four north African provinces of the Ottoman empire; Tripolitania, Tunisia, Algeria and Morocco; famous for Turkish piracy in the 17th and 18th centuries.

Bay of Pigs [Sp Bahia de Cochinos] Bay on the south coast of Cuba where Cuban exiles, supported by the U.S., landed in an abortive attempt (1961) to overthrow Fidel Castro.

Berchtesgarten Alpine town in Bavaria, outside which, at Obersalzberg, Adolf Hitler had his residence, called the Berghof.

Bethlehem Town in Israeli-occupied West Bank, previously part of Jordan; considered to be the birthplace of Jesus and one of the great centers of religious pilgrimage.

Biafra Southeast region of Nigeria, whose dominant people, the Ibo, staged an unsuccessful independence struggle in 1967-70.

Bighorn River rising in Wyoming and flowing into Montana, at the mouth of which a federal trading post was established in 1807; site, at the junction of the Bighorn and the Little Bighorn, of the battle (1876) between Sioux Indians and federal forces led by General Custer.

Blenheim Village in Bavaria, just outside which Anglo-Austrian forces under the duke of Marlborough and Prince Eugène of Savoy defeated (1704) a Franco-Bavarian army in the War of the Spanish Succession; Blenheim Palace, a gift from the British nation to Marlborough, is in Woodstock, Oxfordshire.

Bohemia Medieval kingdom in the western part of modern Czechoslovakia of a largely Czech population; from the late 15th century dominated by the Habsburgs and in 1627 robbed of its status as an independent kingdom and demoted to an imperial Crown land of the Austro-Hungarian empire.

Borodino Village in the central European U.S.S.R., site of Napoleon's indecisive victory (1812) over the Russian army under General Kutuzov in a battle which resulted in more than 100,000 casualties.

Bosnia-Hercegovina Provinces of present-day Yugoslavia, where a peasant rebellion against Ottoman rule in 1875 led to the Russo-Turkish war of 1877-78 and the administration of the provinces by the Austro-Hungarian empire, under nominal Turkish sovereignty; annexed by Austria-Hungary in 1908, they were the site of fierce Serbian nationalism, leading to the assassination (1914) of Archduke Ferdinand at Sarajevo.

Bosporus [or Bosphorus] Narrow strait separating Asia Minor from Europe, joining the Black Sea to the Sea of Marmara; Istanbul (formerly Constantinople) stands on the north shore.

Boston City in Massachusetts, on the northeast coast, founded in 1630 as the center of the Puritan Massachusetts Bay Company; site

of the Boston Tea Party (1773) and of the Battle of Bunker Hill (1775), both seminal events in the American colonies' struggle for independence from Great Britain.

Botany Bay Inlet on the east coast of Australia, just south of Sydney, claimed for Great Britain by Captain James Cook in 1770; not the site of the first British penal colony, which was at Port Jackson, Sydney.

Boyne River in northern Ireland which has given its name to the battle of 1690, fought near Drogheda, at which the Protestant army of William III defeated the deposed Stuart king, the Roman Catholic James II, and so secured the British throne for William.

Breda Town in the southern Netherlands, where, in 1660, before being restored to the English throne, Charles II issued the Declaration of Breda, in which he promised amnesty to former enemies of the Stuart line and religious toleration.

Bull Run Small stream in northeast Virginia, site of two Civil War battles, the first (July 1861) being the opening engagement of the war, in which General "Stonewall" Jackson resisted the Union advance, and the second (July 1862) also being a Confederate victory; also called the first and second battles of Manassas.

Burgundy Region of east France, a powerful duchy and kingdom in the Middle Ages, emerging in the 5th century and thereafter waxing and waning with constantly shifting boundaries; at its peak, in the late 14th and 15th centuries, it covered most of modern Belgium and the Netherlands and east-central France.

C

Calcutta City in west Bengal, India, founded *c.* 1690 by the British East India Company; in 1856 captured by the nawab of Bengal, who killed most of the Company's garrison by imprisoning it in a small, airless chamber known as the "black hole of Calcutta."

Calvary Hill outside Jerusalem where Jesus was crucified, of uncertain location, but traditionally placed inside the present Church of the Holy Sepulcher; also called Golgotha (Hebrew for "skull").

Camp David Presidential retreat in Maryland, where in 1978 Jimmy Carter met Menachem Begin of

Israel and Anwar al-Sadat of Egypt and achieved an historic agreement for the return of Sinai to Egypt and future talks on Palestinian autonomy.

Camulodunum Capital of Roman Britain, erected in A.D. 49 on the site of the central settlement of the indigenous tribe of Trinovantes; later called Colchester.

Canossa Village in north Italy where in 1077 Henry IV of France did penance to escape excommunication by Pope Gregory VII; hence Bismarck's statement, during the *Kulturkampf* with the papacy, that he would not "go to Canossa."

Canterbury City in Kent, England, the spiritual center of English Christianity since St. Augustine founded an abbey there (597) and became the first archbishop of Canterbury; Thomas à Becket murdered in the cathedral (1170).

Cape Canaveral Cape on the east coast of Florida, since 1947 the chief launching base for American missile tests and space missions; called Cape Kennedy from 1953 to 1973.

Casablanca Town in Morocco, site of the Allied conference (January 1943) at which Churchill and Roosevelt agreed to demand the "unconditional surrender" of the Axis powers.

Castile Ancient kingdom of north-central Spain, united (1469) with the kingdom of Aragon under the strong central monarchy of Isabella (of Castile) and her husband, Ferdinand (of Aragon).

Charlottetown City in Prince Edward Island, Canada, site of the conference in 1864 between British and colonial officials that led to Canadian confederation (1867).

Chernobyl Town in the Ukraine, 24 miles from the Soviet nuclear power station, which exploded in April 1986, releasing vast amounts of radioactive material and forcing the evacuation of 135,000 residents of the area.

Cluny Former abbey in eastern France, founded in 910 by the monk, St. Bernard; the Cluniac order became a leading Christian order and the abbey a center of faith and learning.

Cochin China Historic region of Vietnam, a French colony from 1862 to 1954, when, after a successful liberation struggle, it became part of South Vietnam.

Concord Town in Massachusetts, site of the first battle of the American War of Independence; colonial militia fired the opening shots across the Concord River at

British soldiers arriving to seize the colonial arsenal.

Copenhagen Danish capital, site of the famous battle of 1801 during the Napoleonic wars, in which the British navy commanded by Sir Hyde Parker and Horatio Nelson destroyed the Danish fleet; site also of British bombardment (1807).

Coral Sea Stretch of ocean in the southwest Pacific, where on May 4-8, 1942, in the first of a series of aircraft-carrier engagements, the U.S. successfully blocked Japan's intended advance toward Australia.

Corunna [*or* **La Coruña**] Port of northwest Spain, site of the famous battle (1809), in the Peninsular War against Napoleon, in which the British general Sir John Moore was killed, but the town successfully defended.

Crimea Peninsula of the Ukraine on the north coast of the Black Sea; taken from the Tatars by the Ottoman Turks in the late 15th century and annexed by Catherine the Great of Russia in 1783; site of the Crimean War (1853-56) between Russia and the allied powers of Turkey, France, Great Britain and Sardinia.

Culloden Moor in northeast Scotland, site in 1745 of the final battle which ended the Jacobite rising under Bonnie Prince Charlie; 1,000 Highlanders lost their lives and 1,000 were taken prisoner by the victorious army of George II.

Curragh Town near Dublin, Ireland, site of a British military camp, where in March 1914, in the "Curragh incident," 57 officers announced that they would prefer dismissal to taking action against Ulstermen who refused to accept Irish home rule.

D

Dachau Town in Bavaria, site of the first concentration camp established by the Nazis in 1933 and the model for the rest.

Damascus Syrian city, reputed to be the oldest permanent settlement in the world (since *c.* 2000 B.C.); on the road to Damascus Saint Paul (A.D. 67) was miraculously converted to Christianity; he later escaped persecution by being lowered outside the city walls in a basket.

Danelaw Area of England, including Northumbria, much of the east Midlands, and East Anglia, controlled by the Danes from the late 9th to the early 11th centuries; originally the word applied simply to the Danish body of law that prevailed there after the agreement between King Alfred and the Danes (886).

Danzig [**Gdansk**] Baltic port at the mouth of the Vistula, Prussian from 1793 to 1919, Polish since 1945; made a "free city" under League of Nations administration by the Treaty of Versailles (1919) and connected by a short corridor to Poland in order to give Poland an outlet to the sea; the "Solidarity" movement began in the shipyards there in 1980.

Dardanelles Strait linking the Aegean to the Sea of Marmara and separating Asian from European Turkey; of great strategic importance as Russia's water gateway to Asia and the Middle East; scene of two failed Allied campaigns of 1915 to take Constantinople and gain control of the Black Sea.

Dettingen Town in central Germany on the River Main, site of the battle in 1743, during the War of the Austrian Succession (1740-48), in which George II was the last English king to lead his troops into battle.

Devil's Island Small Caribbean island off French Guiana, site of an infamous French penal colony (1852-1951), chiefly for political prisoners; its most famous inmate was Alfred Dreyfus.

Dien Bien Phu Former French army base in North Vietnam, on the Laos border; site of the battle of 1954 in which, after a 56-day siege, the French succumbed to the Viet Minh forces of Ho Chi Minh, thus ending the French presence in Indochina.

Dieppe French port on the Normandy coast, site of unsuccessful Allied raid on German occupied France, August 19, 1942; 6,000 men took part, 5,000 of them Canadians, only 1,600 returned.

Dogger Bank Area of the North Sea in which on October 21, 1904, during the Russo-Japanese war, the Russian Baltic fleet mistook Hull fishing trawlers for Japanese torpedo boats and opened fire, sinking one trawler and taking two lives; the "Dogger Bank" incident almost led to an international crisis.

Drogheda Town in east central Eire on the River Boyne, site of Cromwell's massacre of the inhabitants (1649) and of the Battle of the Boyne (1690) which, by William III's victory over James II, sealed Protestant ascendancy in Ireland; the Drogheda statutes (1494), known after their author as Poynings' Laws, gave England legislative authority over Ireland.

Dumbarton Oaks Village near Washington, DC, where a series of meetings (August-October 1944), attended by Great Britain, the U.S.,

China and the U.S.S.R., laid down the basis for the United Nations.

Dunkirk [*Fr* **Dunkerque**] French North Sea port, site of the epic naval evacuation (May 26-June 4, 1940) of 300,000 Allied troops cut off from a land retreat by German divisions; more than 850 boats, many of them very small craft, took part.

E

East Indies Popular name for parts of the Far East, originating because Columbus's search for the Indies took him to the West Indies; applied first to India (the British East Indies), then to all southeast Asia and, finally, to Indonesia (the Dutch East Indies).

Edgehill [*or* **Edge Hill**] Ridge on the Warwickshire/Oxfordshire border in central England, where in 1643 the first great battle of the English Civil War ended indecisively.

Elba Island off Tuscany, in the Tyrrhenian Sea, where Napoleon was exiled from May 1814 to February 1815, before escaping and returning to France.

Ems [*or* **Bad Ems**] Spa in western Germany where, in 1870, Bismarck drew up and dispatched the "Ems telegram," deliberately misreporting an interview between the French ambassador and Kaiser Wilhelm to provoke war between France and Germany.

F

Falkland Islands [*Sp.* **Islas Malvinas**] Island group in the south Atlantic, off Argentina; a British Crown colony, claimed by Argentina and successfully defended against Argentina in the Falklands War of 1981.

Fashoda Town in Sudan, on the upper Nile, site of a crisis in 1898, when both Great Britain and France laid claim to the region; Great Britain, advancing up the Nile after the victory over the Dervishes at Omdurman, met a French contingent; the crisis was resolved diplomatically when France abandoned its claim to the upper Nile in return for part of the Sahara.

Field of the Cloth of Gold Plain near Calais in northwest France, where in 1520 Henry VIII of England and Francis I of France met for a fortnight of banquets and chivalric tournaments; its purpose was to forge Anglo-French amity, but a year later England entered into an anti-French alliance with the Habsburg emperor Charles V.

Flanders Region of northwest Europe, chiefly in Belgium, but extending into the Netherlands and

France, enriched in the Middle Ages by the cloth industry; a major battleground throughout WWI; the Battle of Flanders in WWII lasted from the German invasion of the Low Countries on May 10, 1940, until the British evacuation from Dunkirk three weeks later.

Flodden Field in northern Northumberland, near the Scottish border, where in 1513 James IV of Scotland was killed by English troops resisting a Scottish invasion.

Forbidden City Fortress area of Peking (Beijing); enclosing imperial palaces, built between 1421 and 1911, entry to which was granted only to the highest ranks of Chinese society.

Fosse Way Roman road of ancient Britain, built to link forts along the frontier of the province, and extending from Exeter to Lincoln.

G

Gallipoli Narrow peninsula at the eastern end of the Dardanelles in European Turkey; scene of a WWI campaign (1915) in which, after heavy casualties, the Allied forces failed to gain control of the Dardanelles and Bosporus and so failed to open a Black Sea route to Russia.

Gaul Name for the northern territory of the Roman empire, including all the land north of the Pyrenees and south and west of the Rhine.

Gaza Strip Coastal strip of land, covering about 58 square miles, in the southwest part of former Palestine; inhabited chiefly by Palestinian refugees, it was administered by Egypt from 1949 to 1967, since when it has been occupied by Israel.

Gettysburg Town in Pennsylvania; Abraham Lincoln made an historic address at the dedication of the national cemetery there in 1863; site of the greatest battle of the Civil War (1863), at which the Confederate advance under Robert Lee was turned back by Union forces under George Meade.

Gibraltar High rock and peninsula in the south of Spain, jutting into the Mediterranean; with Mount Acha at Ceuta in Africa one of the "Pillars of Hercules"; a British Crown colony since the Treaty of Utrecht (1713).

Golan Heights Uplands running from south Lebanon to south Syria, occupying some 500 square miles; taken by Israel during the 1967 war and formally annexed in 1981.

Good Hope, Cape of Southern tip of Cape Province, South Africa; rounded by Bartholomew Diaz in

1488; first settled from Europe by the Dutch, later known as the Afrikaners, or Boers, in 1652.

H

Hague, The City in the Netherlands, site of two international peace conferences (1899, 1907), which failed to achieve arms reduction, but the first of which established the Permanent Court of Arbitration, later (1945) known as the International Court of Justice.

Hanover Former electorate in the duchy of Brunswick and (1815-71) independent kingdom of northwest Germany, bordering on the Netherlands and the North Sea; the elector George Louis became George I of England in 1714 by virtue of his marriage to Sophia, granddaughter of James I; the Hanoverians remained on the English throne until the death of William IV (1837).

Heligoland German island in the North Sea, ceded to Germany by Great Britain in 1890 in exchange for colonial concessions in east Africa; a German naval base during WWI and WWII; fortifications destroyed after WWI, rebuilt in 1936, and again demolished in 1947.

Helsinki Capital city of Finland, site of a European Security Conference (1975), attended by delegates of 35 nations; agreed resolutions to prevent accidental confrontations between East and West, to provide for social and economic cooperation, and to secure basic human rights.

Helvetic Republic French revolutionary state established in Switzerland by the Directory at the invitation of exiled Swiss reformers in 1798, merged the cantons in a central state; lasted until 1803.

I

Indochina Name for the French empire in southeast Asia, comprising Cochin China, Tonkin, Annam, Cambodia and Laos; the first four came under French rule between 1862 and 1884 and were merged in the union of Indochina in 1887; Laos was added in 1893; after a long post-WWII war of liberation, independence was gained and three states—Vietnam, Cambodia and Laos—were established by the Geneva Agreements of 1954.

Inkerman Town on the outskirts of Sebastopol in the Ukraine, site of a Russian defeat (1854) by Great Britain and its allies in the Crimean War.

J

Jamestown First permanent English settlement (1607) in the

present-day U.S., founded by the London Company on a peninsula of the James River, Virginia; tobacco first cultivated there in 1612; fell into decay by the end of the 17th century.

Jena City on the Saale River in southeast Germany, site of a decisive victory (1806) by Napoleon against the Prussian army commanded by General Hohenlohe (1806); together with the simultaneous French victory at Auerstadt it led to the fall of Berlin to France.

Jerusalem, Latin Kingdom of Christian state established in 1099 by the First Crusade in lands taken from the Muslims in Palestine and Syria; the first ruler, Godfrey of Bouillon, took the title "Defender of the Holy Sepulcher," the second, Baldwin I, the title of king; included Jerusalem and its environs, Antioch, Edessa and Tripoli; Edessa was recaptured by the Seljuk Turks in 1144, Jerusalem in 1187 and the kingdom was virtually destroyed at the Battle of Gaza (1244).

Jutland North European peninsula, comprising continental Denmark and the German province of Schleswig-Holstein; the Battle of Jutland (known in German history as the Battle of Skagerrak), 60 miles off the coast, was the only major, but indecisive, naval engagement (1916) of WWI; Great Britain, under Vice-Admiral Beatty and Admiral Jellicoe, suffered greater losses than the German fleet, under Admiral Scheer and Rear-Admiral von Hipper, which escaped back to port where it remained for the rest of the war.

K

Kalmar Town in Sweden, which gave its name to the union of the crowns of Sweden, Denmark and Norway under Margaret I of Denmark, effected there in 1397; Sweden left the Kalmar Union in 1523 and the union of Denmark and Norway was dissolved in 1814.

Katyn Village in west-central U.S.S.R., near Smolensk, where, in 1943, occupying German forces discovered the mass grave of more than 4,000 Polish officers; evidence suggests that they were murdered by Soviet agents, though the U.S.S.R. maintains they were the victims of a Nazi massacre of 1941.

Kiev City in the Ukraine, center of the first Russian state, known as Kiev (or Kievan) Rus, comprised chiefly of the modern Ukraine and Belorussia; founded by the Viking (or Varangian) Oleg *c*. 879, Kievan Rus expanded to the lower Volga and the Caucasus in the 10th

century, but was already weakened by civil strife by the time it was overrun by the Mongols in 1237.

L

Ladysmith Town in Natal, South Africa, site of a famous siege by Boer forces under Piet Joubert of a British garrison, lasting from November 1899 to February 1900, during the Boer War; Ladysmith was relieved by a force under the command of Lord Roberts.

Leningrad City in the U.S.S.R., on the Gulf of Finland, founded in 1703 and originally called St. Petersburg, then Petrograd; capital of Russia 1721-1918; besieged by German and Finnish forces for more than two years (September 1941-January 1944) and heavily bombed by the *Luftwaffe*, though the greater part of the casualties, totaling perhaps 1½ million, were from famine and cold.

Lewes Town in east Sussex, England, site of a victory (1264) by the baronial opposition, led by Simon de Montfort, over King Henry III; Henry was captured and forced to summon what is considered the first English parliament.

Little Rock Capital city of Arkansas, where in 1957 the modern civil rights movement in the U.S. began, when President Eisenhower sent in federal troops to prevent Governor Faubus from using the Arkansas National Guard to block the desegregation of the Central High School.

Locarno Swiss town, on Lake Maggiore, where in 1925 the Locarno Pact was concluded between the major European states, including Germany; guaranteed Germany's existing borders with Belgium and France and agreed that her eastern borders could be altered only by arbitration; affirmed demilitarization of the Rhineland; promised Germany admission to the League of Nations.

Lombardy Region of north Italy, bordering on Switzerland, having Milan as its center; kingdom of the Barbarian Lombards after 569, absorbed by Charlemagne in 774; divided among city-states until it fell under Spanish control in 1535, maintained until 1713, when it passed to Austria; liberated during the Risorgimento in 1859.

M

Manchukuo Japanese puppet-state, founded in 1932 after the Japanese invasion of Manchuria (1931), including Manchuria and the Chinese province of Jehol; ruled by the last Manchu emperor Henry Pu-Yi; returned to China after WWII.

Marengo Village in north Italy, site of a major engagement (1800) of the Napoleonic Wars, in which, after an initial surprise attack gave Austria the upper hand, a French counter-attack won victory.

Marne River in northeast France, flowing into the Seine 5 miles southeast of Paris, which gave its name to two WWI battles (1914, 1918); in the first the opening German offensive of the war was halted at the Marne, causing the Germans to abandon the Schlieffen Plan; in the second the last great German advance of the war was turned back.

Mason-Dixon Line Boundary between Maryland and Pennsylvania, named after two English surveyors who drew the line in the 1760s; popularly considered the pre-Civil War line dividing free states from slave states.

Midway Island group in the central Pacific, unpopulated save for a U.S. navy base; near it occurred the Battle of Midway (1942) in WWII, a decisive Allied victory over Japan, in which air destruction of four Japanese aircraft carriers (the U.S. lost one) dealt a crippling blow to the Japanese navy.

Mukden City of northeast China, on the Hun River (now called Shen-yang); site of the Mukden, or Manchurian, incident (1931), when a bomb exploded on a Japanese railway near the city and the Japanese military seized the explosion as a pretext for occupying the city and, eventually, conquering Manchuria.

My Lai Village in South Vietnam, supposedly a Viet Cong hideout, whose civilian inhabitants (about 350) were massacred by a U.S. army division under Lt. William Calley in 1968 (convicted of murder by a court-martial in 1971); fueled the antiwar movement in the U.S. when details of the massacre were disclosed in 1969.

N

Navarino Town on the Greek coast; its harbor was the site of the destruction of the Egyptian-Turkish navy (1827) by a British, French and Russian squadron during the Greek war of independence from the Ottoman empire; shortly thereafter Egypt withdrew from the war.

Navarre Province of northern Spain, an independent kingdom in the early Middle Ages, when in addition to the present province it included the Basque provinces and a small part of southern France; ruled by the French Crown 1305-1479, when all but the French region passed to the Spanish Crown.

Northeast Passage Name for the water route between the Pacific and the Atlantic, along the north coast of Europe and Asia; explored from the 16th century, it was first successfully navigated by the Swedish explorer Nils Nordenskjold in 1878-79.

Northwest Passage Name for the Arctic water route between the Atlantic and the Pacific along the coast of Canada and Alaska; first explored (1576-78) by the English navigator Martin Frobisher, its existence was proved in 1854 when Robert McClure, traveling eastward, arrived at Viscount Melville Sound, which William Parry had reached from the east.

Novgorod City in northwest U.S.S.R., on the Volkhov River, the central city of the first Russian state, founded c. 862 when the inhabitants of Novgorod asked the Viking, Rurik, to be their ruler; occupied by the Germans in WWII (1941-44).

O

Oder-Niesse Line Poland's western frontier with Germany, running along the Oder and Niesse rivers; established at the Yalta Conference (1945), confirmed at Potsdam later that year.

Old Sarum Most notorious rotten borough of the pre-1832 electoral system in Great Britain, north of Salisbury in Wiltshire; though uninhabited by the start of the 19th century, it sent two members of parliament to Westminster.

Omdurman City in central Sudan, on the White Nile, across from Khartoum; near it, at Karari, occurred the Battle of Omdurman (1898), in which an Anglo-Egyptian force under Lord Kitchener defeated the Mahdi, bringing Sudan under Anglo-Egyptian control.

Oregon Trail Pioneer route, first traveled in the 1840s, in the westward expansion of the U.S., from Independence or Westport (part of present-day Kansas City) on the Missouri River to the Willamette Valley of the Columbia River.

P

Palatinate Name of two historic regions of medieval Germany, the Rhineland (or Rhenish) Palatinate (also known as the Lower Palatinate), west of the Rhine and bordering on France and Luxembourg, and the Upper Palatinate, in northeast Bavaria; each ruled by a count palatine.

Panama Canal Man-made waterway, 40 miles long, across the center of the isthmus of Panama in Central America, linking the Pacific and Atlantic; built between 1908 and 1914; leased, together with land 5 miles wide on either side, to the U.S. in 1903; by a 1978 treaty to be returned to Panama in 1999.

Papal States Region of central Italy under the temporal rule of the pope, "donated" by the Frankish king, Pepin the Short, in 754 and confirmed by Charlemagne in 774; originally a large area centered on Ravenna, but since the unification of Italy (1861), only the Vatican City in Rome, confirmed by the Lateran Treaty of 1929.

Plate [*Sp* **Rio de la Plata**] Estuary of the Parena and Uruguay rivers, site of the first major naval engagement (December 13, 1939) of WWII, where major damage was inflicted on the German pocket battleship *Graf Spee*, which was scuttled four days later.

Polish Corridor Narrow strip of land in northern Germany, running along either side of the Vistula River from Poland to the Baltic, granted to Poland by the Treaty of Versailles (1919) to give Poland access to the sea; Danzig (Gdansk), at the mouth of the Vistula, was made a free city under the League of Nations; incorporated within Poland after WWII.

Pompeii Coastal city of ancient Italy, near Naples, at the foot of Mount Vesuvius; destroyed by a volcano in A.D. 79; rediscovered in 1748 and since then extensively excavated.

Potsdam Town in Germany, near Berlin, site of the Potsdam Conference (1945), at which Truman, Stalin and Churchill drew up an agreement for the four-power occupation and administration of Germany after WWII and the redrawing of Germany's borders (chiefly with Poland at the Oder-Niesse line), pending a final peace treaty.

R

Rapallo Town on the Italian riviera, where in 1922 Germany and the U.S.S.R. signed the Treaty of Rapallo, by which Germany recognized the Soviet government (the first power to do so) and the two nations renounced all war debts to, and war claims on, each other.

Rhineland Unofficial region of northeast Germany, chiefly Prussia, but also including the Rhenish Palatinate and other lands; permanently demilitarized and handed over to the Allied powers for 15 years by the Treaty of Versailles (1919); remilitarized by Hitler in 1936.

Roanoke Island Atlantic island, off North Carolina, site of the first English colony in the New World, established by Walter Raleigh in 1585; all the colonists were dead or departed when John White led an expedition there in 1591 and the settlement was abandoned.

S

Saarland Coal-rich region of Germany, west of the Rhine, in the Saar valley, administered by the League of Nations (1919-35), with the product of its mines given to France; restored to Germany after a plebiscite (1935).

Sadowa Town in Bohemia (modern Czechoslovakia), 60 miles east of Prague, where the Prussian army, under the command of General von Moltke, won the decisive battle in the Austro-Prussian War (1866).

St. Helena Island in the South Atlantic, 1,200 miles off the African coast, one of a group with Ascension Island and Tristan da Cunha; Napoleon was exiled there (1815) and died there (1821).

Schleswig-Holstein Duchies in present-day north Germany, bordering on the North Sea and the Baltic, and comprising the south part of the Jutland peninsula; for centuries in dispute between Denmark (whose king ruled them from the Middle Ages) and Germany; Bismarck gained them by a brief war in 1864 and Schleswig passed under Prussian administration, Holstein under Austrian.

Schmalkalden Town in northeast Germany, where in 1531 the Schmalkaldic League, an alliance of Protestant princes, was formed to defend Lutheranism against the Holy Roman Emperor.

Sedan Town in northeast France, on the River Meuse, site of the decisive battle (1870) of the Franco–Prussian war, in which Napoleon III's surrender led to the downfall of the Second Empire and the establishment of the Third Rebublic.

Sharpeville Black township in South Africa, near Vereeniging, site of anti-*apartheid* demonstration in 1960 in which 67 blacks were killed and nearly 200 wounded; international condemnation instrumental in South Africa's withdrawal from the Commonwealth (1961).

Sinai Triangular peninsula in northeast Egypt , between the Gulf of Aquaba and the Suez Canal, occupied by Israel 1956 and 1967-82, when Israeli troops withdrew in accordance with the Camp David peace agreement between Israel and Egypt (1979).

Soweto Black township in South Africa, near Johannesburg, where in 1976 riots against the government's plan to enforce Afrikaans as the language in all schools ended with 236 blacks killed (government figure; blacks claim more than 600) and more than 1,000 injured.

Spanish Main Spain's mainland colonies in the New World, but especially the coastal area from Panama to the Orinoco River; famous for English piracy of Spanish cargo ships in the 17th and 18th centuries.

Spice Islands Popular European name in the early modern period for the Molucca Islands group of present-day Indonesia, famous for nutmeg and cloves; explored by Magellan (1511-12) and colonized by the Dutch East India Company in the 17th century.

Spithead East part of the channel between England and the Isle of Wight, site of a naval mutiny (1797) which gained ordinary sailors better pay and conditions.

Stalingrad City in the U.S.S.R. (since 1961 Volgograd), on the lower Volga, site of a heavy German defeat at the hands of the Soviet army, commanded by General Zhukov, in a prolonged WWII battle (September 1942-January 1943); the defeat marked the turning of the tide in the Allies' favor on the eastern front.

Sudetenland Unoffical name for region of eastern Czechoslovakia, formerly largely German-speaking, bordering on Germany; annexed by Nazi Germany after the Munich agreement between Germany and Great Britain (1938); returned after WWII to Czechoslovakia, who drove out 3 million German-speaking people and resettled the area with Czechs.

Swabia Historic region of southwest Germany, which gave its name to the commercial alliance of towns in the later Middle Ages, called Swabian League; the League was prominent in helping Luther and the German princes to suppress the Peasants' War (1524-25).

T

Tannenberg Town in Prussia (now part of Poland), site of two historic battles: at the first, in 1410, combined forces of Lithuanians and Poles defeated the Teutonic Knights and halted their progress eastward; at the second, in August 1914, the first decisive WWI battle on the eastern front, German forces under Ludendorff and Hindenburg defeated two Soviet armies and took more than 100,000 prisoners.

Tolpuddle Town in Dorset, England, home of the "Tolpuddle Martyrs," six agricultural laborers, who in 1834 were sentenced to seven years transportation to Australia (sentence remitted in 1836 after public outcry) for allegedly administering secret oaths as members of the Friendly Society of Agricultural Laborers.

Tonkin Gulf Arm of the South China Sea, between North Vietnam and China, site of Viet Cong torpedo attack on U.S. destroyers in August 1964; U.S. Congress response, the Tonkin Gulf Resolution, was taken as authorization for U.S. war in Vietnam.

Tsushima Straits lying between Korea and Japan, the site of the virtual destruction of the Russian Baltic fleet by the Japanese navy, commanded by Admiral Togo, in the decisive battle (1905) of the Russo-Japanese war.

U

Ulster In the High Middle Ages an earldom in the extreme northeast of Ireland; name later popularly used to mean the nine northern counties and, after the creation of the essentially Roman Catholic Irish Free State (1922), the six counties of the Protestant-dominated province of Northern Ireland which remained within the United Kingdom.

United Arab Republic Brief union of Egypt and Syria with Abdul Nasser as president, intended as a steppingstone to a greater Arab union; established in 1958 and dissolved in 1961 when Syria withdrew (though Egypt retained the name until 1971).

V

Van Dieman's Land Name originally given to Tasmania, the island state of Australia, discovered by the Dutch explorer Abel Tasman in 1642.

Vendée Region (now department) of west France, on the Bay of Biscay, the center of the peasant resistance to the French Revolution, beginning with a royalist insurrection in 1793, savagely repressed, and continuing until 1796, when a royalist, *emigré*, landing from Great Britain at Quiberon was defeated.

Verdun Town in northeast France, on the River Meuse, the center of the longest WWI battle (February-December 1916); ended indecisively, with Germany suffering about 330,000 casualties, France about 350,000.

Vichy City in central France, on the Allier River, home of the Nazi-collaborationist government of occupied France led by Marshal Pétain from July 1940 to the end of WWII.

Vicksburg Town in west Mississippi, the major target of General Grant's Vicksburg campaign in the Civil War; fell to the Unionists (July 1863) after withstanding land and naval assault for 14 months, thus placing the Mississippi River in Unionist control.

Vinland Name given to part of North America probably discovered by the Norse seaman, Leif Ericsson, *c.* 1000; he found an uncharted land, with wheat and grapes, that was probably south New England, the northeast coast of present-day U.S.

W

Weimar City in southeast Germany, on the Ilm River, site of the national constituent assembly which, after the abdication of Kaiser Wilhelm II, established the German Federal Republic, or "Weimar Republic," in 1919; the democratic Weimar constitution was overthrown by Hitler in 1933.

Worcester City in central England, on the Severn River, the site of Oliver Cromwell's final, decisive victory (1651) over Charles II and the Scots in the English Civil War.

HISTORICAL CHARTS

ROMAN EMPERORS
From the birth of Christ to the last emperor in the West

27 BC-AD 14	Augustus	218-222	Heliogabalus	284-305	Diocletian	**EMPERORS IN THE WEST**	
14-37	Tiberius	222-235	Alexander Severus	286-305	Maximian	395-423	Honorius
37-41	Caligula	235-238	Maximin	305-306	Constantius I	409-411	Maximus
41-54	Claudius I	238	Gordian I	305-310	Galerius		*(usurper in Spain)*
54-68	Nero	238	Gordian II	306-312	Maxentius	421	Constantius III
68-69	Galba	238	Balbinus	306-337	Constantine I	425-455	Valentinian III
69	Vitellius	238	Pupienus Maximus	308-313	Maximin	455	Petronius Maximus
69-79	Vespasian	238-244	Gordian III	308-324	Licinius	455-456	Avitus
79-81	Titus	244-249	Philip	337-340	Constantine II	457-461	Majorian
81-96	Domitian	249-251	Decius	337-350	Constans	461-465	Libius Severus
96-98	Nerva	251	Hostilianus	337-361	Constantius II	467-472	Anthemius
98-117	Trajan	251-253	Gallus	350-353	Magnetius	472-473	Olybius
117-138	Hadrian	253	Aemilianus	361-363	Julian	473-474	Glycerius
138-161	Antoninus Pius	253-260	Valerian	363-364	Jovian	474-475	Julius Nepos
161-169	Lucius Verus	253-268	Gallienus	364-375	Valentinian I	475-476	Romulus Augustulus
161-180	Marcus Aurelius	268-270	Claudius II	364-378	Valens		
180-192	Commodus	270-275	Aurelian	375-383	Gratian	**EMPERORS IN THE EAST**	
193	Pertinax	275-276	Tacitus	379-395	Theodosius I	395-408	Arcadius
193	Didius Julianus	276	Florianus	375-392	Valentinian II	408-450	Theodosius II
193-211	Severus	276-282	Probus	383-388	Maximus	450-457	Marcian
211-212	Geta	282-283	Carus	392-394	Eugenius	457-474	Leo I
211-217	Caracalla	283-284	Numerianus			474	Leo II
217-218	Macrinus	283-285	Carinus				

HOLY ROMAN EMPERORS

SAXON DYNASTY		1250-1273	*Interregnum*	1612-1619	Matthias
962-973	Otto I (the Great)			1619-1637	Ferdinand II
973-983	Otto II	1273-1291	Rudolf I (Rudolf of Habsburg)	1637-1657	Ferdinand III
983-1002	Otto III	1292-1298	Adolf of Nassau [Luxembourg]	1658-1705	Leopold I
1002-1024	Henry II	1298-1308	Albert I [Habsburg]	1705-1711	Joseph I
		1308-1313	Henry VII [Luxembourg]	1711-1740	Charles VI
SALIAN (FRANCONIAN) DYNASTY		1314-1346	Louis IV [Wittelsbach]		
1024-1039	Conrad II	1346-1378	Charles IV [Luxembourg]	1740-1742	*Interregnum*
1039-1056	Henry III	1379-1400	Wenceslaus [Luxembourg]		
1056-1105	Henry IV	1400-1410	Rupert [Wittelsbach]	1742-1745	Charles VII
1105-1125	Henry V	1410-1437	Sigismund [Luxembourg]		[Wittelsbach/Habsburg]
1125-1137	Lothair II (or III)				
		HABSBURG DYNASTY		**HABSBURG / LORRAINE DYNASTY**	
HOHENSTAUFEN DYNASTY		1438-1439	Albert II	1745-1765	Francis I
1138-1152	Conrad III	1440-1493	Frederick III	1765-1790	Joseph II
1155-1190	Frederick I (Barbarossa)	1493-1519	Maximilian I	1790-1792	Leopold II
1190-1197	Henry VI	1519-1558	Charles V	1792-1806	Francis II
1198-1208	Philip of Swabia	1558-1564	Ferdinand I		
1209-1215	Otto IV	1564-1576	Maximilian II		
1220-1250	Frederick II	1576-1612	Rudolf II		

KINGS AND QUEENS OF FRANCE

CAPETIAN DYNASTY

987-996	Hugh Capet
996-1031	Robert II (the Pious)
1031-1060	Henry I
1060-1108	Philip I
1108-1137	Louis VI
1137-1180	Louis VII
1180-1223	Philip II (Augustus)
1223-1226	Louis VIII
1226-1270	Louis IX (St Louis)
1270-1285	Philip III
1285-1314	Philip IV (the Fair)
1314-1316	Louis X (the Quarrelsome)
1316	John I (the Posthumous)
1316-1322	Philip V (the Tall)
1322-1328	Charles IV (the Fair)

VALOIS DYNASTY

1328-1350	Philip VI
1350-1364	John II (the Good)
1364-1380	Charles V
1380-1422	Charles VI
1422-1461	Charles VII (the Well Served)
1461-1483	Louis XI
1483-1498	Charles VIII
1498-1515	Louis XII [Valois-Orléans]
1515-1547	Francis I [Valois-Angoulême]
1547-1559	Henry II [Valois-Angoulême]
1559-1560	Francis II [Valois-Angoulême]
1560-1574	Charles IX [Valois-Angoulême]
1574-1589	Henry III [Valois-Angoulême]

BOURBON DYNASTY

1589-1610	Henry IV (of Navarre)
1610-1643	Louis XIII
1643-1715	Louis XIV (the Sun King)
1715-1774	Louis XV
1774-1793	Louis XVI
1793-1814	*Interregnum*
1814-1824	Louis XVII
1824-1830	Charles X
1830-1848	Louis-Philippe [Orléans]

PRESIDENTS OF THE FRENCH REPUBLIC

1870-1873	Adolphe Thiers
1873-1879	Patrice MacMahon
1879-1887	Jules Grévy
1887-1894	Sadi Carnot
1894-1895	Jean Périer
1895-1899	Felix Faure
1899-1906	Emile Lonset
1906-1913	Armand Fallières
1913-1920	Raymond Poincaré
1920	Paul Deschanel
1920-1924	Alexandre Millerand
1924-1931	Gaston Doumergue
1931-1932	Paul Doumer
1932-1940	Albert Lebrun
1947-1959	René Coty
1959-1969	Charles de Gaulle
1969-1974	Georges Pompidou
1974-1981	Valéry Giscard d'Estaing
1981-	François Mitterand

KINGS AND QUEENS OF ENGLAND

NORMAN DYNASTY

1066-1087	William I (the Conqueror)
1087-1100	William II (Rufus)
1100-1135	Henry I
1135-1154	Stephen (of Blois)
[1141-1142	Matilda]

ANGEVIN (PLANTAGENET) DYNASTY

1154-1189	Henry II
1189-1199	Richard I (Lion-Heart)
1199-1216	John
1216-1272	Henry III
1272-1307	Edward I
1307-1327	Edward II
1327-1377	Edward III
1377-1399	Richard II

LANCASTRIAN DYNASTY

1399-1413	Henry IV (Bolingbroke)
1413-1422	Henry V
1422-1461	Henry VI
1461-1470	Edward IV [Yorkist]
1470-1471	Henry VI [Lancastrian]

YORKIST DYNASTY

1471-1483	Edward IV
1483	Edward V
1483-1485	Richard III

TUDOR DYNASTY

1485-1509	Henry VII
1509-1547	Henry VIII
1547-1553	Edward VI
1553-1558	Mary I
1558-1603	Elizabeth I

STUART DYNASTY

1603-1625	James I
1625-1649	Charles I
1649-1660	*Interregnum*
1660-1685	Charles II
1685-1688	James II
1689-1694	William III (of Orange) and Mary II
1694-1702	William III
1702-1714	Anne

HANOVERIAN DYNASTY

1714-1727	George I
1727-1760	George II
1760-1820	George III
1820-1830	George IV
1830-1837	William IV
1837-1901	Victoria
1901-1910	Edward VII [Wettin]

WINDSOR DYNASTY

The name of the royal line was changed from Wettin to Windsor in 1917. In 1952, Elizabeth II, wife of Philip Mountbatten, decreed that the name of Windsor should be retained.

1910-1935	George V
1935-1936	Edward VIII
1936-1952	George VI
1952-	Elizabeth II

CHANCELLORS OF GERMANY 1871-1990

1871-1890	Otto von Bismarck (non-party)		1928-1930	Hermann Müller (Social Democrat)
1890-1894	Leo von Caprivi (non-party)		1930-1932	Heinrich Brüning (Center)
1894-1900	Chlodwig zu Höhenloe-Schillingsfurst (non-party)		1932	Franz von Papen (Center)
1900-1909	Bernhard von Bülow (non-party)		1932-1933	Kurt von Schleicher (non-party)
1909-1917	Theobald von Bethmann-Hollweg (non-party)		1933-1945	Adolf Hitler (National Socialist)
1917	Georg Michaelis (non-party)		1945	Karl Dönitz (National Socialist)
1917-1918	Georg Hertling (non-party)			
1918	Prince Maximilien of Baden (non-party)		**WEST GERMANY**	
1918-1919	Friedrich Ebert (Social Democrat)		1949-1963	Konrad Adenauer (Christian Democrat)
1919	Philipp Scheidemann (Social Democrat)		1963-1966	Ludwig Erhard (Christian Democrat)
1919-1920	Gustav Bauer (Social Democrat)		1966-1969	Kurt Kiesinger (Christian Democrat)
1920	Hermann Müller (Social Democrat)		1969-1974	Willy Brandt (Social Democrat)
1920-1921	Konstantin Fehrenbach (Center)		1974-1982	Helmut Schmidt (Social Democrat)
1921-1922	Joseph Wirth (Center)		1982-1990	Helmut Kohl (Christian Democrat)
1923	Gustav Stresemann (People's)			
1923-1924	Wilhelm Marx (Center)		**GERMANY**	
1925-1926	Hans Luther (non-party)		1990-	Helmut Kohl (Christian Democrat)
1926-1928	Wilhelm Marx (Center)			

TSARS OF RUSSIA

RURIK DYNASTY

1462-1505	Ivan III (the Great)
1505-1533	Vasily III
1533-1584	Ivan IV (the Terrible)
1584-1598	Fydor I

GODUNOV DYNASTY

1598-1605	Boris Godunov
1605	Fydor II

USURPERS

1605-1606	Dimitri
1606-1610	Vasily IV
1610-1613	*Interregnum*

ROMANOV DYNASTY

1613-1645	Michael
1645-1676	Alexis

1676-1682	Fydor III
1682-1696	Ivan V and Peter I (the Great)
1696-1725	Peter I (the Great)
1725-1727	Catherine I
1727-1730	Peter II
1730-1740	Anna
1740-1741	Ivan VI
1741-1762	Elizabeth
1762	Peter III
1762-1796	Catherine II (the Great)
1796-1801	Paul I
1801-1825	Alexander I
1855-1881	Nicholas I
1855-1881	Alexander II
1881-1894	Alexander III
1894-1917	Nicholas II

USSR: GENERAL SECRETARIES OF THE COMMUNIST PARTY 1922-1985

1922-1953	Joseph Stalin
1953	Georgi Malenkov
1953-1964	Nikita Khrushchev
1964-1982	Leonid Brezhnev
1982-1984	Yuri Andropov
1984-1985	Konstantin Chernenko
1985-	Mikhail Gorbachev

UNITED STATES ELECTIONS

KEY D=Democratic F=Federalist P=Progressive R=Republican W=Whig

		Popular Vote	Electoral College
1788	G WASHINGTON (F)		
	Unanimously elected		
	Vice-President	J Adams	
	Senate F	House of Representatives F	
1792	G WASHINGTON (F)		
	Unanimously elected		
	Vice-President	J Adams	
	Senate F	House of Representatives R	
1796	J ADAMS (F)		71
	T Jefferson (R)		68
	Vice-President	T Jefferson	
	Senate F	House of Representatives F	
1800	T JEFFERSON (R)		73
	A Burr (R)		73
	J Adams (F)		65
	G C Pinckney		64
	Vice-President	A Burr	
	Senate R	House of Representatives R	
1804	T JEFFERSON (R)		162
	G C Pinckney (F)		14
	Vice-President	G Clinton	
	Senate R	House of Representatives R	
1808	J MADISON (R)		122
	G C Pinckney (F)		47
	Vice-President	G Clinton	
	Senate R	House of Representatives R	
1812	J MADISON (R)		129
	G Clinton (F)		89
	Vice-President	E Gerry (1813-14)	
	Senate R	House of Representatives R	
1816	J MONROE (R)		
	Virtually unopposed		
	Vice-President	D D Tompkins	
	Senate R	House of Representatives R	
1820	J MONROE (R)		
	Virtually unopposed		
	Vice-President	D D Tompkins	
	Senate R	House of Representatives R	
1824	J Q ADAMS (R)		84
	A Jackson (R)		49
	W H Crawford (R)		41
	H Clay (R)		37
	Vice-President	J C Calhoun	
	Senate R	House of Representatives R	
1828	A JACKSON (D)	642,553	178
	J Q Adams (W)	500,897	83
	Vice-President	J C Calhoun	
	Senate D	House of Representatives D	
1832	A JACKSON (D)	701,780	219
	H Clay (W)	484,205	49
	Vice-President	M Van Buren	
	Senate D/W	House of Representatives D	
1836	M VAN BUREN (D)	764,176	170
	W H Harrison (W)	550,816	73
	Vice-President	R M Johnson	
	Senate D	House of Representatives D	
1840	W H HARRISON (W)	1,275,390	234
	M Van Buren (D)	1,128,854	60
	Vice-President	J Tyler	
	Senate W	House of Representatives W	
1844	J R POLK (D)	1,339,494	170
	H Clay (W)	1,300,004	l05
	Vice-President	G M Dallas	
	Senate D	House of Representatives D	
1848	Z TAYLOR (W)	1,361,393	163
	L Cass (D)	1, 223,460	l27
	Vice-President	M Fillmore	
	Senate D	House of Representatives D	
1852	F PIERCE (D)	1,607,510	254
	W Scott (W)	1,386,942	42
	Vice-President	W R King (1853)	
	Senate D	House of Representatives D	
1856	J P BUCHANAN (D)	1,836,072	174
	J C Fremont (R)	1,342,345	114
	Vice-President	J C Breckinridge	
	Senate D	House of Representatives D	
1860	A J LINCOLN (R)	1,865,908	180
	S A Douglas (D)	1,380,202	12
	Vice-President	H Hamlin	
	Senate R	House of Representatives R	
1864	A J LINCOLN (R)	2,218,388	212
	G B McClellan (D)	1,812,807	21
	Vice-President	A Johnson	
	Senate R	House of Representatives R	
1868	U S GRANT (R)	3,013,650	214
	H Seymour (D)	2,708,744	80
	Vice-President	S Colfax	
	Senate R	House of Representatives R	
1872	U S GRANT(R)	3,598,235	286
	H Greeley (D)	2,834,761	63
	Vice-President	H Wilson (1873-75)	
	Senate R	House of Representatives R	
1876	R R HAYES (R)	4,034,311	185
	S J Tilden (D)	4,288,546	184
	Vice-President	W A Wheeler	
	Senate R	House of Representatives D	
1880	J A GARFIELD (R)	4,446,158	214
	W S Hancock (D)	4, 444,260	155
	Vice-President	C A Arthur	
	Senate R/D	House of Representatives R	
1884	S G CLEVELAND (D)	4,874,621	219
	J G Blaine (R)	4,484,936	182
	Vice-President	T A Hendricks (1885)	
	Senate R	House of Representatives D	

Year	Candidate	Popular Vote	Electoral College
1888	R HARRISON (R)	5,443,892	233
	S G Cleveland (D)	5,534,488	168
	Vice-President	L P Morton	
	Senate R	House of Representatives R	
1892	S G CLEVELAND (D)	5,551,883	277
	B Harrison (R)	5,179,244	145
	Vice-President	A F Stevenson	
	Senate D	House of Representatives D	
1896	W McKINLEY (R)	7,108,840	271
	W J Bryan (D)	6,511,499	176
	Vice-President	G A Hobart (1897-99)	
	Senate R	House of Representatives R	
1900	W McKINLEY (R)	7,218,039	292
	W J Bryan (D)	6,358,345	155
	Vice-President	T Roosevelt	
	Senate R	House of Representatives R	
1904	T ROOSEVELT (R)	7,626,593	336
	A B Parker (D)	5,082,898	140
	Vice-President	C W Fairbanks	
	Senate R	House of Representatives R	
1908	W H TAFT (R)	7,676,258	321
	W J Bryan (D)	6,293,152	162
	Vice-President	J S Sherman (1909-12)	
	Senate R	House of Representatives D	
1912	W WILSON (D)	6,293,152	435
	T Roosevelt (P)	4,119,207	88
	W H Taft (R)	3,486,333	8
	Vice-President	T R Marshall	
	Senate D	House of Representatives D	
1916	W WILSON (D)	9,126,300	777
	C F Hughes (R)	8,546,789	254
	Vice-President	T R Marshall	
	Senate R	House of Representatives R	
1920	W G HARDING (R)	16,133,314	404
	J Cox (D)	9,140,884	27
	Vice-President	C Coolidge	
	Senate R	House of Representatives R	
1924	C COOLIDGE (R)	15,717,553	382
	J W Davis (D)	8,386,169	136
	R La Follette (P)	4,814,050	13
	Vice-President	C G Dawes	
	Senate R	House of Representatives R	
1928	H C HOOVER (R)	21,411,991	444
	A Smith(D)	15,000,185	87
	Vice-President	C Curtis	
	Senate R	House of Representatives R	
1932	F D ROOSEVELT (D)	22,825,016	472
	H C Hoover (R)	15,758,397	59
	Vice-President	J N Garner	
	Senate D	House of Representatives D	
1936	F D ROOSEVELT (D)	27,747,636	523
	A Landon (R)	16,679,543	8
	Vice-President	J N Garner	
	Senate D	House of Representatives D	
1940	F D ROOSEVELT (D)	27,263,448	449
	W Wilkie (R)	22,336,260	82
	Vice-President	H A Wallace	
	Senate D	House of Representatives D	
1944	F D ROOSEVELT (D)	25,611,936	432
	T E Dewey (R)	22,013,372	99
	Vice-President	H S Truman	
	Senate D	House of Representatives D	
1948	H S TRUMAN (D)	24,105,587	303
	T E Dewey (R)	21,970,017	189
	Vice-President	A W Barkley	
	Senate D	House of Representatives D	
1952	D D EISENHOWER (R)	33,936,234	442
	A Stevenson (D)	27,314,992	89
	Vice-President	R M Nixon	
	Senate R/D	House of Representatives R	
1956	D D EISENHOWER (R)	35,590,472	457
	A Stevenson (D)	26,022,752	73
	Vice-President	R M Nixon	
	Senate D	House of Representatives D	
1960	J F KENNEDY (D)	34,226,731	303
	R M Nixon (R)	34,108,157	219
	Vice-President	L B Johnson	
	Senate D	House of Representatives D	
1964	L B JOHNSON (D)	43,129,566	486
	B Goldwater (R)	27,178,188	52
	Vice-President	H H Humphrey	
	Senate D	House of Representatives D	
1968	R M NIXON (R)	31,785,480	301
	H H Humphrey (D)	31,275,166	191
	Vice-President	S T Agnew	
	Senate D	House of Representatives D	
1972	R M NIXON (R)	47,169,911	520
	G McGovern (D)	29,170,383	17
	Vice-President	S T Agnew (1973)	
		G R Ford (1973-74)	
	Senate D	House of Representatives D	
1976	J E CARTER (D)	40,830,763	297
	G R Ford (R)	39,147,793	240
	Vice-President	W F Mondale	
	Senate D	House of Representatives D	
1980	R W REAGAN (R)	43,904,153	489
	J E Carter (D)	35,483,883	49
	Vice-President	G H H Bush	
	Senate R	House of Representatives D	
1984	R W REAGAN (R)	54,445,075	525
	W F Mondale (D)	37,577,185	13
	Vice-President	G H H Bush	
	Senate R	House of Representatives D	
1988	G H H BUSH (R)	47,662,777	426
	M Dukakis (D)	40,817,438	112
	Vice-President	T D Quayle	
	Senate D	House of Representatives D	

Unelected Presidents M FILLMORE (W) *(on death of Zachary Taylor)* 1850-53
A JOHNSON (D) *(on death of Abraham Lincoln)* 1865-69
C A ARTHUR (R) *(on death of James Garfield)* 1881-85
G R FORD (R) *(on resignation of Richard Nixon)* 1974-77

ADMISSION OF STATES TO THE UNITED STATES

1787	Delaware	1812	Louisiana	1863	West Virginia
	New Jersey	1816	Indiana	1864	Nevada
	Pennsylvania	1817	Mississippi	1867	Nebraska
1788	Connecticut	1818	Illinois	1876	Colorado
	Georgia	1819	Alabama		Montana
	Maryland	1820	Maine		North Dakota
	Massachusetts	1821	Missouri		South Dakota
	New Hampshire	1836	Arkansas		Washington
	New York	1837	Michigan	1890	Idaho
	South Carolina	1845	Florida		Wyoming
	Virginia		Texas	1896	Utah
1789	North Carolina	1846	Iowa	1907	Oklahoma
1790	Rhode Island	1848	Wisconsin		Arizona
1791	Vermont	1850	California		New Mexico
1792	Kentucky	1858	Minnesota	1959	Alaska
1796	Tennessee	1859	Oregon		Hawaii
1803	Ohio	1861	Kansas		

CHIEF JUSTICES OF THE UNITED STATES SUPREME COURT

1789-1795	John Jay
1795	John Rutledge
1796-1800	Oliver Ellsworth
1801-1835	John Marshall
1836-1864	Roger Taney
1864-1873	Salmon Chase
1874-1888	Morrison Waite
1888-1910	Melville Fuller
1910-1921	Edward White
1921-1930	William Taft
1930-1941	Charles Hughes
1941-1946	Harlan Stone
1946-1953	Fred Vinson
1953-1969	Earl Warren
1969-1986	Warren Burger
1986-	William Renquist

GERMAN LEGISLATIVE ELECTIONS SINCE 1871
Leading Parties

	Seats held
1871 NATIONAL LIBERAL	125
Reich	67
Center	65
Conservative	57
Progressive	47
Social Democrat	2
1874 NATIONAL LIBERAL	155
Center	91
Progressive	50
Reich	36
Conservative	22
Social Democrat	9
1877 NATIONAL LIBERAL	128
Center	93
Progressive	52
Conservative	40
Reich	38
Social Democrat	12
1878 NATIONAL LIBERAL	99
Center	94
Conservative	59
Reich	57
Progressive	39
Social Democrat	9
1881 PROGRESSIVE	115
Center	100
Conservative	50
National Liberal	47

Reich	28
Social Democrat	12
1884 CENTER	99
Conservative	78
Progressive	74
National Liberal	51
Reich	28
Social Democrat	24
1887 NATIONAL LIBERAL	99
Center	98
Conservative	80
Reich	41
Progressive	32
Social Democrat	11
1890 CENTER	106
Progressive	76
Conservative	73
National Liberal	42
Social Democrat	35
Reich	20
1893 CENTER	96
Conservative	72
National Liberal	53
Progressive	48
Social Democrat	44
Reich	28
1898 CENTER	102
Social Democrat	56
Conservative	56

Progressive	49
National Liberal	46
Reich	23
1903 CENTER	100
Social Democrat	81
Conservative	54
National Liberal	51
Progressive	36
Reich	21
1907 CENTER	105
Conservative	60
National Liberal	54
Progressive	49
Social Democrat	43
Reich	24
1912 SOCIAL DEMOCRAT	110
Center	91
National Liberal	45
Conservative	43
Progressive	42
Reich	14
1920 SOCIAL DEMOCRAT	102
Independent Socialist	84
Nationalist	71
People's	65
Center	64
Democrat	39
Bavarian People's	21
Communist	4

	Seats held
1924 SOCIAL DEMOCRAT	100
(May) Nationalist	95
Center	65
Communist	62
People's	45
National Socialist	32
Democrat	28
Bavarian People's	16

1924 SOCIAL DEMOCRAT	131
(Dec) Nationalist	103
Center	69
People's	51
Communist	45
Democrat	32
Bavarian People's	19
National Socialist	14

1928 SOCIAL DEMOCRAT	153
Nationalist	73
Center	62
Communist	54
People's Democrat	25
Bavarian People's	16
National Socialist	12

1930 SOCIAL DEMOCRAT	143
National Socialist	130
Communist	77
Center	68
Nationalist	41
People's	30
Democrat	20
Bavarian People's	19

1932 NATIONAL SOCIALIST	230
(Jul) Social Democrat	133
Communist	89
Center	75
Nationalist	37
Bavarian People's	22
People's	7
Democrat	4

1932 NATIONAL SOCIALIST	196
(Nov) Social Democrat	121
Communist	100
Center	70
Nationalist	52
Bavarian People's	20
People's	11
Democrat	2

1933 NATIONAL SOCIALIST	288
(Mar) Social Democrat	120
Communist	81
Center	74
Nationalist	52

Bavarian People's	18
Democrat	5
People's	2

1933 NATIONAL SOCIALIST	661
(Sep)	

WEST GERMANY

1949 CHRISTIAN DEMOCRAT*	139
Social Democrat	131
Free Democrat	52

1953 CHRISTIAN DEMOCRAT	244
Social Democrat	151
Free Democrat	48

1957 CHRISTIAN DEMOCRAT	270
Social Democrat	169
Free Democrat	41

1961 CHRISTIAN DEMOCRAT	242
Social Democrat	190
Free Democrat	67

1965 CHRISTIAN DEMOCRAT	245
Social Democrat	202
Free Democrat	49

1969 CHRISTIAN DEMOCRAT	242
Social Democrat	224
Free Democrat	30

1972 SOCIAL DEMOCRAT	230
Christian Democrat	225
Free Democrat	41

1976 CHRISTIAN DEMOCRAT	243
Social Democrat	214
Free Democrat	39

1980 CHRISTIAN DEMOCRAT	226
Social Democrat	218
Free Democrat	53

1983 CHRISTIAN DEMOCRAT	244
Social Democrat	193
Free Democrat	34
Green	27

1987 CHRISTIAN DEMOCRAT	223
Social Democrat	186
Free Democrat	46
Green	42

GERMANY

1990 CHRISTIAN DEMOCRAT*	268
Social Democrat	239
Free Democrat	79
Green	0

*Figures for the Christian Democrats include seats
won in Bavaria by the Christian Social Union.

NOTE It is commonplace to say that the Social Democrats became the largest party in the state in 1912 when for the first time they were the largest party in the Reichstag. The popular vote from 1890 tells a different story.

	Seats held	Votes
1890		
CENTER	106	1,342,100
Progressive	76	1,307,500
Conservative	73	895,100
National Liberal	42	1,177,900
Social Democrat	35	1,427,300
Reich	20	482,300
1893		
CENTER	96	1,468,500
Conservative	72	1,038,400
National Liberal	53	997,000
Progressive	48	1,091,700
Social Democrat	44	1,786,700
Reich	28	438,400
1898		
CENTER	102	1,445,100
Social Democrat	56	2,107,100
Conservative	56	859,200
Progressive	49	862,500
National Liberal	46	971,300
Reich	23	343,600
1903		
CENTER	100	1,875,300
Social Democrat	81	3,010,800
Conservative	54	948,400
National Liberal	51	1,317,400
Progressive	36	872,700
Reich	21	333,400
1907		
CENTER	105	2,179,700
Conservative	60	1,060,200
National Liberal	54	1,637,600
Progressive	49	1,234,000
Social Democrat	43	3,529,000
Reich	24	471,900
1912		
SOCIAL DEMOCRAT	110	4,250,400
Center	91	1,996,800
National Liberal	45	1,662,700
Conservative	43	1,126,300
Progressive	42	1,497,000
Reich	14	367,100

BRITISH ELECTIONS SINCE 1885

		Seats held
1885	LIBERAL	321
	Conservative	250
	Irish Home Rule	86
	Labour	5
	Other	8

W E Gladstone formed a Liberal government

1886	CONSERVATIVE	316
	Liberal	190
	Liberal Unionist	79
	Irish Home Rule	85

Lord Salisbury formed a Conservative government

1892	LIBERAL	270
	Conservative	268
	Liberal Unionist	47
	Irish Home Rule	81
	Labour	4

W E Gladstone formed a Liberal government

1895	CONSERVATIVE	341
	Liberal	177
	Liberal Unionist	70
	Irish Home Rule	82

Lord Salisbury formed a Conservative government

1900	CONSERVATIVE	334
	Liberal	184
	Liberal Unionist	68
	Irish Home Rule	82
	Lib-Lab	2

Lord Salisbury formed a Conservative government

1906	LIBERAL	375
	Conservative	134
	Labour	29
	Lib-Lab	25
	Liberal Unionist	24
	Irish Nationalist	83

H Campbell-Bannerman formed a Liberal government

1910	LIBERAL	275
(Jan)	Conservative	242
	Liberal Unionist	31
	Irish Nationalist	82
	Labour	40

H H Asquith formed a Liberal government

1910	LIBERAL	270
(Dec)	Conservative	240
	Liberal Unionist	34
	Irish Nationalist	84
	Labour	42

H H Asquith formed a Liberal government

1918	COALITION	
	(Lloyd George	
	Libs & Cons)	481
	Conservative	50
	Labour	60
	Liberal	29
	Sinn Fein	73
	Other	14

D Lloyd-George formed a Coalition government

1922	CONSERVATIVE	343
	Liberal	116
	Labour	142
	Other	14

A Bonar Law formed a Conservative government

1923	CONSERVATIVE	258
	Labour	191
	Liberal	159
	Other	7

S Baldwin formed a Conservative government

1924	CONSERVATIVE	419
	Labour	151
	Liberal	40
	Other	5

S Baldwin formed a Conservative government

1929	LABOUR	287
	Conservative	260
	Liberal	59
	Other	5

R MacDonald formed a Labour government

1931	NATIONAL	
	GOVERNMENT	521
	Labour	52
	Liberal	37
	Other	5

R MacDonald formed a National government

1935	NATIONAL	
	GOVERNMENT	431
	Labour	158
	Liberal	21
	Other	5

S Baldwin formed a National government

1945	LABOUR	398
	Conservative	209
	Liberal	12
	Other	21

C R Attlee formed a Labour government

1950	LABOUR	315
	Conservative	299
	Liberal	90
	Other	2

C R Attlee formed a Labour government

1951	CONSERVATIVE	321
	Labour	295
	Liberal	6
	Other	3

W S Churchill formed a Conservative government

1955	CONSERVATIVE	344
	Labour	277
	Liberal	6
	Other	3

R A Eden formed a Conservative government

1959	CONSERVATIVE	365
	Labour	258
	Liberal	6
	Other	1

M H Macmillan formed a Conservative government

1964	LABOUR	318
	Conservative	303
	Liberal	9

J H Wilson formed a Labour government

1966	LABOUR	363
	Conservative	253
	Liberal	12
	Other	2

J H Wilson formed a Labour government

1970	CONSERVATIVE	330
	Labour	287
	Liberal	6
	Other	7

E R Heath formed a Conservative government

1974	LABOUR	301
(Feb)	Conservative	297
	Liberal	14
	Other	23

J H Wilson formed a Labour government

1974	LABOUR	319
(Oct)	Conservative	276
	Liberal	13
	Other	27

J H Wilson formed a Labour government

1979	CONSERVATIVE	339
	Labour	269
	Liberal	11
	Other	16

M Thatcher formed a Conservative government

1983	CONSERVATIVE	397
	Labour	209
	Alliance	23
	Other	21

M Thatcher formed a Conservative government

1987	CONSERVATIVE	375
	Labour	229
	Alliance	22
	Other	24

M Thatcher formed a Conservative government

INDEPENDENT MEMBER NATIONS OF THE COMMONWEALTH
WITH DATES OF ADMISSION

1931	Australia			Western Samoa		Tonga
	Antarctic Territory		1963	Kenya	1972	Bangladesh
	Christmas Island			Malaysia	1973	Bahamas
	Cocos Islands		1964	Malawi	1974	Grenada
	Norfolk Island			Malta		St. Vincent and the Grenadines
	Canada			Tanzania	1975	Papua New Guinea
	New Zealand			Zambia	1976	Seychelles
	United Kingdom		1965	Gambia	1978	Dominica
1947	India			Singapore		Solomon Islands
1948	Sri Lanka (Ceylon)		1966	Barbados		Tuvalu
1957	Ghana			Botswana	1979	Kiribati
1960	Nigeria			Guyana		St. Lucia
1961	Cyprus			Lesotho	1980	Vanuatu
	Sierra Leone		1968	Mauritius	1981	Antigua and Barbuda
1962	Jamaica			Nauru		Belize
	Trinidad and Tobago			Swaziland	1983	St. Christopher-Nevis
	Uganda		1970	Fiji		

FRENCH LEGISLATIVE ELECTIONS SINCE 1945

		Seats held				Seats held
1945	COMMUNIST	148		1967	GAULLIST	232
	Popular Republican	141			Socialist	117
	Socialist	134			Communist	72
	Conservative/Moderate	62			Democratic Center	45
	Radical Socialist	35		1968	GAULLIST	349
1946	POPULAR REPUBLICAN	160			Socialist	57
(Jun)	Communist	146			Communist	33
	Socialist	115			Democratic Center	31
	Conservative/Moderate	62		1973*	UDR	183
	Radical Socialist	39			Socialist	102
1946	COMMUNIST	166			Communist	73
(Nov)	Popular Republican	158			Independent Republican	55
	Socialist	90			Reformist	34
	Conservative/Moderate	70			Center Democrat	30
	Radical Socialist	55		1973*	RPR	154
1951	GAULLIST	107			UDF	124
	Communist	97			Socialist	103
	Socialist	94			Communist	86
	Conservative/Moderate	87		1981	SOCIALIST	285
	Popular Republican	82			RPR	85
	Radical Socialist	77			UDF	65
	Poujadist	51			Communist	44
1956	COMMUNIST	147		1986	SOCIALIST	206
	Conservative/Moderate	95			RPR/UDF	147
	Socialist	88			RPR	76
	Radical Socialist	73			UDF	53
	Popular Republican	71			Communist	35
	Gaullist	16			National Front	35
1958	GAULLIST	198		1988	RPR/UDF	271
	Conservative/Moderate	133			Socialist	206
	Popular Republican	57			Communist	27
	Socialist	44				
	Radical Socialist	44				
	Communist	10				

There were two elections in 1973, both in March.

1962	GAULLIST	229
	Radical Socialist	208
	Conservative/Moderate	84
	Communist	41

KEY   RPR = Assembly for the Republic
UDF = Union for French Democracy
UDR = Union of Democrats for the Republic

WORLD WAR I: MANPOWER
Approximate figures

Allies	Total Mobilized	Killed or Died	Wounded	Prisoners & Missing
Russia	12,000,000	1,700,000	4,950,000	2,500,000
France	8,410,000	1,358,000	4,266,000	537,000
British Empire	8,905,000	908,000	2,096,000	192,000
Italy	5,615,000	650,000	947,000	600,000
US	4,355,000	126,000	234,000	4,500
Japan	800,000	300	907	3
Romania	750,000	336,000	120,000	80,000
Serbia	707,000	45,000	133,000	153,000
Belgium	267,000	14,000	45,000	35,000
Greece	230,000	5,000	21,000	1,000
Portugal	100,000	7,000	14,000	12,000
Montenegro	50,000	3,000	10,000	7,000
	42,189,000	5,152,300	12,836,907	4,121,503

Central Powers				
Germany	11,000,000	1,776,000	4,216,000	1,153,000
Aust/Hungary	7,800,000	1,200,000	3,620,000	2,200,000
Turkey	2,850,000	325,000	400,000	250,000
Bulgaria	1,200,000	88,000	152,000	27,000
	2,850,000	3,389,000	8,388,000	3,630,000

GRAND TOTAL	65,039,000	8,541,300	21,224,907	7,751,503

WORLD WAR II: MANPOWER
Approximate figures

Country	Wartime Population (Approx)	Armed Forces (Peak)	AF Killed or Missing	Civilians Killed or Missing
Australia	7m	680,000	34,000	100
Belgium	8m	800,000	10,000	90,000
Brazil	41m	200,000	1,000	0
Bulgaria	48m	450,000	19,000	NR
Canada	11m	780,000	43,000	0
China	541m	5m	1.5m	20m*
Czechoslovakia	15m	180,000	7,000	310,000
Denmark	4m	15,000	4,000	3,000
Finland	4m	250,000	79,000	11,000
France	42m	5m	245,000	173,000
Germany*	79m	10m	3.5m	2m
Great Britain*	48m	4.7m	420,000	70,000
Greece	7m	150,000	17,000	391,000
Hungary	14m	350,000	147,000	280,000
India	389m	2.4m	48,000	0
Italy*	45m	4.5m	380,000	180,000
Japan*	73m	6m	2.6m	953,000
Luxembourg	297,000	12,000	2,000	5,000
Netherlands	9m	500,000	14,000	242,000
New Zealand	2m	157,000	17,000	0
Norway	3m	25,000	5,000	8,000
Poland	35m	1m	600,000	6m
Romania	20m	600,000	73,000	465,000
South Africa	11m	140,000	9,000	0
United States	132m	16.4m	292,000	10
USSR	193m	20m	13.6m	7.7m
Yugoslavia	16m	3.7m	305,000	1.4m

* There are no official figures for China's civilian casualties. Germany's figures include Austria and colonial and annexed countries. The figures for Great Britain include 22,000 colonial AF casualties (excluding India). The figures for Italy, Japan and the USSR include colonial or annexed countries.

ADMISSION OF NATIONS TO THE UNITED NATIONS

1945	Argentina	France	Poland	1950	Indonesia		Tunisia
	Australia	Greece	Saudi Arabia	1955	Albania	1957	Ghana
	Belguim	Guatemala	South Africa		Austria		Malaysia
	Bolivia	Haiti	Syria		Bulgaria	1958	Guinea
	Brazill	Honduras	Turkey		Cambodia	1960	Benin
	Belorussia	India	Ukraine		Finland		Burkina Faso
	Canada	Iran	USSR		Hungary		Cameroon
	Chile	Iraq	United Kingdom		Ireland		Central African
	China*	Lebanon	United States		Italy		Republic
	Colombia	Liberia	Uruguay		Jordan		Chad
	Costa Rica	Luxembourg	Venezuela		Laos		Congo
	Cuba	Mexico	Yugoslavia		Libya		Cyprus
	Czechoslovakia	Netherlands	1946 Afghanistan		Nepal		Gabon
	Denmark	New Zealand	Iceland		Portugal		Ivory Coast
	Dominican	Nicaragua	Sweden		Romania		Madagascar
	Republic	Norway	Thailand		Spain		Mali
	Ecuador	Panama	1947 Pakistan		Sri Lanka		Niger
	Egypt	Paraguay	Yemen, North	1956	Japan		Nigeria
	El Salvador	Peru	1948 Burma		Morocco		Senegal
	Ethiopia	Philippines	1949 Israel		Sudan		Somalia

	Togo		Maldives	
	Zaire		Singapore	
1961	Mauritania	1966	Barbados	
	Mongolia		Botswana	
	Sierra Leone		Guyana	
	Tanzania		Lesotho	
	(Tanganyika)	1967	Yemen, South	
1962	Algeria	1968	Equatorial Guinea	
	Burundi		Mauritius	
	Jamaica		Swaziland	
	Rwanda	1970	Fiji	
	Trinidad and	1971	Bahrain	
	Tobago		Bhutan	
	Uganda		Oman	
1963	Kenya		Qatar	
	Kuwait		United Arab	
1964	Malawi		Emirates	
	Malta	1973	Bahamas	
	Zambia		Germany (East)	
1965	Gambia		Germany (West)	

1974	Bangladesh
	Grenada
	Guinea-Bissau
1975	Cape Verde
	Comoros
	Mozambique
	Papua New
	Guinea
	São Tomé and
	Principe
	Suriname
1976	Angola
	Seychelles
	Western Samoa
1977	Djibouti
	Vietnam
1978	Dominica
	Solomon Islands
1979	St. Lucia
1980	Zimbabwe

	St. Vincent and
	the Grenadines
1981	Antigua and
	Barbuda
	Belize
	Vanuatu
1983	St. Christopher-
	Nevis
1984	Brunei

*Nationalist China, or Formosa (Taiwan) after the Communist revolution of 1949, was a member of the UN from 1945 to 1971, when its seat was given to the Peoples' Republic of China.

NOTE The following independent states are not members of the UN: Andorra, Kiribati, North Korea, South Korea, Liechtenstein, Monaco, Nauru, San Marino, Switzerland, Taiwan, Tonga, Tuvalu, Vatican City.

SECRETARIES-GENERAL OF THE UNITED NATIONS

1946-1953	Trigve Lie (Norway)
1953-1961	Dag Hammarskjøld (Sweden)
1962-1971	U Thant (Burma)
1972-1981	Kurt Waldheim (Austria)
1982-	Javier Perez de Cuellar (Peru)

POPULATION TABLES
Figures in thousands

WORLD Estimated totals

1750	750,000
1850	1,200,000
1950	2,500,000
1970	3,700,000
1980	4,400,000
1990	5,300,000

UNITED STATES e=estimate

1790	3,929	1890	62,947
1800	5,308	1900	75,995
1810	7,240	1910	92,228
1820	9,638	1920	106,022
1830	12,866	1930	123,203
1840	17,069	1940	132,165
1850	23,192	1950	151,326
1860	31,443	1960	179,323
1870	38,558	1970	203,236
1880	50,156	1980	226,546
		1990	247,000e

GREAT BRITAIN AND IRELAND e=estimate

1700	8,500e	1891	37,734
1750	10,500e	1901	41,459
1800	15,000e	1911	45,221
1810	18,000e	1921	43,750e
1821	20,894	1931	46,000e
1831	24,028	1941	48,216e
1841	26,709	1951	50,225
1851	27,369	1961	52,673
1861	28,927	1971	55,347
1871	31,484	1981	55,678
1881	34,885	1991	57,100e

NOTE After 1931 the population of Eire is excluded from the total.

LIFE EXPECTANCY AT BIRTH

		1875	1905	1925	1950	1965	1990
England	M	41	51	56	66	68	72
	F	45	55	59	71	74	78
France	M		45	52	64	68	72
	F		49	56	69	75	80
Germany*	M	36	45	56	65	68	72
	F	38	48	59	68	73	78
Russia	M		31	42	61	66	64
(USSR)	F		33	47	67	74	73
US	M		47	58	66	67	71
	F		50	61	71	74	78
Japan	M		44	42	56	68	75
	F		45	43	60	73	81
India	M	25	23	27	32	42	53
	F	25	23	27	32	40	52
Egypt/	M			36	41	52	59
UAR	F			41	47	54	62
Chile	M			40	50		68
	F			41	54		75

*After 1945 West Germany

CRUDE DEATH RATES
per 1,000 total population e=estimate

	1750–1780	1840–1850	1890–1900	1920–1930	1940–1950	1960–1965	1985–1990
England	30.4	22.4	18.2	12.2	11.9	11.8	11.3
France		23.2	21.5	17.3	15.8	11.2	9.7
Germany*		26.8	22.2	12.9	11.2	11.1	11.2
Russia/USSR			34.1	22.6	18.0	7.2	9.8
US	23e		19.0	11.9	10.3	9.5	8.8
Japan			20.9	17.7	8.6	7.3	6.2
India			44e	36e	23e	12.9	10.8
Egypt/UAR			27e	26.1	24.9	16.5	9.1
Chile			33e	27.8	18.5	11.8	5.8

* After 1945 West Germany

NATIONS GAINING INDEPENDENCE SINCE 1945

1946	Jordan (GB)
	Syria (FRA)
1947	India (GB)
	Pakistan (GB)
	Philippines (US)
1948	Burma (GB)
1949	Indonesia (NETH)
	Vietnam (FRA)
1951	Oman (GB)
1953	Cambodia (FRA)
1954	Laos (FRA)
1956	Morocco (FRA)
	Sudan (GB)
	Tunisia (FRA)
1957	Ghana (GB)
	Malaya (GB)
1958	Guinea (FRA)
1959	Singapore (GB)
1960	Benin (FRA)
	Burkina Faso (FRA)
	Cameroon, Rep. of (FRA)
	Central African Republic (FRA)
	Chad (FRA)
	Cyprus (GB)
	Gabon (FRA)
	Ivory Coast (FRA)
	Madagascar (FRA)
	Mali (FRA)
	Mauritania (FRA)
	Niger (FRA)
	Nigeria (GB)
	Senegal (FRA)
	Somalia (GB, IT)
	Togo (FRA)
1961	Cameroon, Federal Republic of (GB)
	Kuwait (GB)
	Sierra Leone (GB)
	Tanganyika (GB)
1962	Algeria (FRA)
	Burundi (FRA)
	Jamaica (GB)
	Rwanda (BEL)
	Western Samoa (GB)
	San Marino (IT)
	Trinidad & Tobago (GB)
	Uganda (GB)
1963	Kenya (GB)
1964	Malawi (GB)
	Malta (GB)
	Zambia (GB)
1965	Gambia (GB)
	Maldives (GB)
1966	Barbados (GB)
	Botswana (GB)
	Guyana (GB)
	Lesotho (GB)
1968	Equatorial Guinea (SP)
	Mauritius (GB)
	Nauru (GB, AUS, NZ)
	Swaziland (GB)
1970	Fiji (GB)
	Tonga (GB)
1971	Bahrain (GB)
	Bangladesh (PAK)
	Qatar (GB)
1973	Bahamas (GB)
1974	Grenada (GB))
	Guinea-Bissau (PORT)
	St. Vincent and the Grenadines (GB)
1975	Angola (PORT)
	Comoros (FRA)
	Papua New Guinea (AUS)
	São Tomé e Principe (PORT)
	Suriname (NETH)
1976	Seychelles (GB)
1977	Djibouti (FRA)
1978	Dominica (GB)
	Solomon Islands (GB)
	Tuvalu (GB)
1979	Kiribati (GB)
	St. Lucia (GB)
1980	Vanuatu (GB, FRA)
	Zimbabwe (GB)
1981	Antigua & Barbuda (GB)
	Belize (GB)
1983	St. Christopher-Nevis (GB)
1984	Brunei (GB)

WINNERS OF THE NOBEL PEACE PRIZE

1901	Jean Dunant (SWI)
	Frederic Passy (FRA)
1902	Elie Ducommon (SWI)
	Charles Gobat (SWI)
1903	William Cremer (GB)
1904	Institute of International Law (BEL)
1905	Bertha von Suttner (AUSTRIA)
1906	Theodore Roosevelt (US)
1907	Ernesto Moneta (IT)
	Louis Renault (FRA))
1908	Klas Arnoldson (SWE)
	Fredrik Bajer (DEN)
1909	Auguste Beernaert (BEL)
	Paul Estournelles de Constant (FRA)
1910	International Peace Bureau (SWI)
1911	Tobias Asser (NETH)
	Alfred Fried (AUSTRIA)
1912	Elihu Root (US)
1913	Henri Lafontaine (BEL)
1914	Not awarded
1915	Not awarded
1916	Not awarded
1917	International Red Cross Committee
1918	Not awarded
1919	Woodrow Wilson (US)
1920	Léon Bourgeois (FRA)
1921	Hjalmar Branting (SWE)
	Christian Lange (NOR)
1922	Fridtjof Nansen (NOR)
1923	Not awarded
1924	Not awarded
1925	Austen Chamberlain (GB)
	Charles Dawes (US)
1926	Aristide Briand (FRA)
	Gustav Stresemann (GER)
1927	Ferdinand Buisson (FRA)
	Ludwig Quidde (GER)
1928	Not awarded
1929	Frank Kellogg (US)
1930	Lars Soderblom (SWE)
1931	Jane Addams (US)
	Nicholas Butler (US)
1932	Not awarded
1933	Norman Angell (GB)
1934	Arthur Henderson (GB)
1935	Carl von Ossietzky (GER)
1936	Carlos Lamas (ARG)
1937	Edgar Cecil (GB)
1938	Nansen International Office for Refugees (NOR)
1939	Not awarded
1940	Not awarded
1941	Not awarded
1942	Not awarded
1943	Not awarded
1944	International Red Cross Committee
1945	Cordell Hull (US)
1946	Emily Balch (US)
	John Mott (US)
1947	American Friends Service Comm. (US)
	Friends Service Council (GB)
1948	Not awarded
1949	John Boyd Orr (GB)
1950	Ralphe Bunche (US)
1951	Léon Jouhaux (FRA)
1952	Albert Schweitzer (FRA)
1953	George Marshall (US)
1954	UN High Commission for Refugees
1955	Not awarded
1956	Not awarded
1957	Lester Pearson (CAN)
1958	Georges Pire (BEL)
1959	Philip Noel-Baker (GB)
1960	Albert Luthuli (SA)
1961	Dag Hammarskjøld (SWE)
1962	Linus Pauling (US)
1963	International Red Cross Committee
1964	Martin Luther King (US)
1965	UNICEF
1966	Not awarded
1967	Not awarded
1968	René Caggin (FRA)
1969	International Labor Organization
1970	Norman Borlaug (US)
1971	Willy Brandt (W GER)
1972	Not awarded
1973	Henry Kissinger (US)
	Le Duc Tho (VIET) (declined)
1974	Sean McBride (IRE)
	Eisaku Sato (JAP)
1975	Andrei Sakharov (USSR)
1976	Mairead Corrigan (GB)
	Betty Williams (GB)
1977	Amnesty International
1978	Menachem Begin (ISR)
	Anwar Sadat (EGYPT)
1979	Mother Theresa (INDIA)
1980	Adolfo Esquivel (ARG)
1981	UN High Commission for Refugees
1982	Alva Myrdal (SWE)
	Alfonso Robles (MEX)
1983	Lech Walesa (POL)
1984	Desmond Tutu (SA)
1985	International Physicians for the Prevention of Nuclear War (USSR; US)
1986	Elie Wiesel (US)
1987	Oscar Sanchez (COSTA RICA)
1988	UN Peacekeeping Force
1989	Dalai Lama (TIBET)
1990	Mikhail Gorbachev (USSR)

MAJOR INVENTIONS

Date	Invention	Inventor
c105	Paper	Ts'ai Lun (CH)
c250	Gunpowder	(China)
c800	Printing	(China)
c1045	Movable type	Pi-sheng (CH)
1086	Magnetic compass	Shen-kua (CH)
1267	Camera obscura	Roger Bacon (GB)
c1590	Microscope	Z Janssen (NETH)
1604	Thermometer	G Galilei (IT)
c1608	Telescope	H Lippershey (NETH)
1622	Slide rule	W Oughtred (GB)
1642	Adding machine	B Pascal (FRA)
1643	Mercury barometer	E Torricelli (IT)
c1656	Pendulum clock	C Huygens (NETH)
1679	Pressure cooker	D Papin (FRA)
1701	Seed drill	J Tull (GB)
c1705	Atmospheric steam engine	T Newcomen (GB)
c1714	Mercury thermometer	G Fahrenheit (GER)
1733	Flying shuttle	J Kay (GB)
1736	Ship's chronometer	J Harrison (GB)
1745	Leyden jar	P van Musschenbroek (NETH)
1758	Sextant	J Bird (GB)
1764	Spinning jenny	J Hargreaves (GB)
1769	Water frame	R Arkwright (GB)
1775	Flush toilet	A Cummings (GB)
1776	Submarine	D Bushnell (US)
1779	Spinning mule	S Crompton (GB)
1783	Hot-air balloon	J and J Montgolfier (FRA)
	Electric cell	L Galvani (IT)
1785	Power loom	E Cartwright (GB)
1786	Threshing machine	A Meikle (GB)
1787	Steamboat	J Fitch (US)
1793	Cotton gin	E Whitney (US)
1798	Lithography	A Senefelder (GER)
1800	Electric battery	A Volta (IT)
1801	Punch cards	J Jacquard (FRA)
	Gas lamp	P Lebon (FRA)
1804	Glider	G Cayley (GB)
	Steam locomotive	R Trevithick (GB)
1815	Safety lamp	H Davy (GB)
1816	Photography	J Niepce (FRA)
1829	Sewing machine	B Thimonnier (FRA)
1831	Mechanical reaper	C McCormick (US)
1833	Digital computer	C Babbage (GB)
1834	Mechanical refrigerator	J Perkins (US)
	Braille writing	L Braille (FRA)
1835	Repeating revolver	S Colt (US)
1837	Electric telegraph	W Cooke/C Wheatstone (GB)
c1839	Bicycle	K MacMillan (GB)
1850	Bunsen burner	R Bunsen (GER)

Date	Invention	Inventor
1852	Airship	H Giffard (FRA)
1856	Steel converter	H Bessemer (GB)
1861	Gatling gun	R Gatling (US)
1866	Dynamite	A Nobel (SWE)
1867	Typewriter	C Sholes (US)
1875	Dental drill	G Green (US)
1876	Telephone	A Bell (US)
1877	Phonograph	T Edison (US)
1878	Filament light bulb	J Swan (GB)
	Cathode-ray tube	W Crookes (GB)
1879	Electric train	W von Siemens (GER)
	Incandescent light bulb	T Edison (US)
1884	Machine gun	H Maxim (GB)
	Steam turbine	C Parsons (GB)
	Fountain pen	L Waterman (US)
1885	Motor car	K Benz (GER)
	Motor bicycle	G Daimler (GER)
1887	Motion-picture camera	E Marey (FRA)
1888	Pneumatic tire	J Dunlop (GB)
1892	Diesel engine	R Diesel (GER)
1895	Wireless radio	G Marconi (IT)
c1900	Cloud chamber	C Wilson (US)
1901	Vacuum cleaner	H Booth (GB)
1903	Biplane	O and W Wright (US)
	Electrocardiograph	W Einthoven (NETH)
1907	Washing machine	Hurley Machine Co (US)
	Teleprinter	C Krumm (US)
1909	Bakelite plastic	L Bakeland (US)
c1914	Tank	E Swinton (GB)
1926	Television	E Logie Baird (GB)
	Liquid-fuel rocket	R Goddard (US)
1927	Iron lung	P Drinker (US)
1932	Cycloctron	E Lawrence (US)
1935	Radar	R Watson-Scott (GB)
1938	Binary calculator	K Zuse (GER)
1939	Jet airplane	E Heinkel (GER)
	DDT	P Muller (SWI)
1940	Electron microscope	RCA Ltd (US)
1944	Digital computer	H Aiken (US)
	Kidney machine	W.Kolff (NETH)
1948	Transistor radio	J Bardeen/W Brattain/ W Shockley (US)
1951	Nuclear reactor	US Atomic Energy Commission
1954	Contraceptive pill	G Pincus/H Hoagland (US)
1955	Hovercraft	C Cockerell (GB)
1956	Videotape recorder	Ampex Corporation (US)
1957	Space satellite	(USSR)
1959	Silicon chip	Hoeni (US)
1960	Laser	T Maiman (US)
1971	Microprocessor	Intel Ltd (US)
1975	Prestel	Post Office (GB)

INDEX

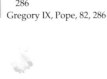